Warriner's English Grammar and Composition

LIBERTY EDITION

Fourth Course

Warriner's English Grammar and Composition

LIBERTY EDITION

John E. Warriner

Fourth Course

Harcourt Brace Jovanovich, Publishers

Orlando   San Diego   Chicago   Dallas

THE SERIES:

English Grammar and Composition: First Course
English Grammar and Composition: Second Course
English Grammar and Composition: Third Course
English Grammar and Composition: Fourth Course
English Grammar and Composition: Fifth Course
English Grammar and Composition: Complete Course
Annotated Teacher's Edition, Part I; Teacher's Edition, Part II

CORRELATED SERIES:

English Workshop: First Course
English Workshop: Second Course
English Workshop: Third Course
English Workshop: Fourth Course
English Workshop: Fifth Course
English Workshop: Review Course

Composition: Models and Exercises, First Course
Composition: Models and Exercises, Second Course
Composition: Models and Exercises, Third Course
Composition: Models and Exercises, Fourth Course
Composition: Models and Exercises, Fifth Course
Advanced Composition: A Book of Models for Writing, Complete Course

Vocabulary Workshop: First Course
Vocabulary Workshop: Second Course
Vocabulary Workshop: Third Course
Vocabulary Workshop: Fourth Course
Vocabulary Workshop: Fifth Course
Vocabulary Workshop: Complete Course

John E. Warriner taught English for thirty-two years in junior and senior high schools and in college. He is chief author of the *English Grammar and Composition* series, coauthor of the *English Workshop* series, general editor of the *Composition: Models and Exercises* series, and editor of *Short Stories: Characters in Conflict.* His coauthors have all been active in English education.

To the Student

The reason English is a required subject in almost all schools is that nothing in your education is more important than learning how to express yourself well. You may know a vast amount about a subject, but if you are unable to communicate what you know, you are severely limited. No matter how valuable your ideas may be, they will not be very useful if you cannot express them clearly and convincingly. Language is the means by which people communicate. In your part of the world, it is English, a remarkably rich and flexible language. By learning how your language functions and by practicing language skills, you can acquire the competence necessary to express adequately what you know and what you think.

You have two guides to help you in your study of English. One is your teacher; the other is your textbook. This textbook is designed to help you improve your ability to use English. It will show you how the English sentence works, how words are combined in sentences, and how the parts of sentences may best be arranged for clear communication. You will learn the difference between sentences which are strong and clear and smooth, and sentences which are weak and confusing and awkward. You will learn to plan and organize units of writing much larger than the sentence. You will learn to use standard English, the kind of English that is most widely considered acceptable. The more you put to use the things you learn from this book—in other words, the more you practice the skills explained here—the greater will be your command of English.

Do not limit your use of this book to the times when you are given an assignment in the book. Learn to use the book as a reference book in which you can look up answers to questions that arise when you are writing something for an assignment in any of your courses. As you become familiar with the contents and arrangement of the book, you will know where to look for specific kinds of information. By using the index, you can quickly find answers to questions about grammar and standard usage, punctuation, capital letters, sentence structure, spelling, outlining, letter writing, and many other matters. By using the book in this way, you are actually teaching yourself, which is a very good way to learn.

J.W.

CONTENTS

3. The Phrase 67

PREPOSITIONAL, VERBAL, APPOSITIVE
PHRASES

4. The Clause 94

INDEPENDENT AND SUBORDINATE CLAUSES

Part Two: USAGE

5. The English Language   125
HISTORY AND USAGE

6. Agreement   141
SUBJECT AND VERB, PRONOUN AND ANTECEDENT

7. Using Pronouns Correctly   168
NOMINATIVE AND OBJECTIVE CASE

8. Using Verbs Correctly   192
PRINCIPAL PARTS, TENSE, VOICE

Part Four: COMPOSITION: The Writing Process

14. Writing Paragraphs 342

STRUCTURE OF PARAGRAPHS

15. Writing Paragraphs 383

DEVELOPMENT OF PARAGRAPHS

17. Writing Expository Compositions

SPECIFIC EXPOSITORY WRITING
ASSIGNMENTS

18. Writing Persuasive Compositions 496

BUILDING AN ARGUMENT

19. Writing Narration and Description   531

STORIES; CHARACTER AND BIOGRAPHICAL SKETCHES

21. Writing Business Letters   614
FORM AND CONTENT OF BUSINESS
CORRESPONDENCE

Part Five: MECHANICS

Part Six: AIDS TO GOOD ENGLISH

30. The Dictionary   780
ARRANGEMENT AND CONTENT OF
DICTIONARIES

31. Vocabulary   798
LEARNING AND USING NEW WORDS

32. Spelling 821

IMPROVING YOUR SPELLING

33. Studying and Test Taking 844

SKILLS AND STRATEGIES

Part Seven: SPEAKING AND LISTENING

34. Public Speaking   871
GIVING A TALK AND LISTENING

35. Group Discussion 889

DISCUSSION, PARLIAMENTARY PROCEDURE,
INTERVIEWS

Warriner's English Grammar and Composition

LIBERTY EDITION

Fourth Course

PART ONE

GRAMMAR

The Parts of Speech

THEIR IDENTIFICATION AND FUNCTION

Words are classified according to the jobs they perform in sentences. Some name or otherwise identify people and objects; others express action, connect other words, or do still other kinds of work. There are eight main ways in which words are used in sentences; the eight kinds of words that perform these jobs are called *parts of speech*. They are *noun, pronoun, adjective, verb, adverb, preposition, conjunction*, and *interjection*.

DIAGNOSTIC TEST

Identifying the Parts of Speech. Number your paper 1–20. After the proper number, write each italicized word in the following sentences and indicate what part of speech it is. Use the abbreviations *n.* (noun), *pron.* (pronoun), *adj.* (adjective), *v.* (verb), *adv.* (adverb), *prep.* (preposition), *conj.* (conjunction), and *interj.* (interjection).

1. In the *thirty* years following the Civil War, millions of longhorn cattle were driven *over* long trails from ranches in Texas to railroads in Kansas.
2. When the drive was *over,* the cattle *were shipped* to northern cities to meet the need for hides, meat, and tallow. [*were shipped* = single part of speech]

3. During this *period,* the cowboy *became* an American hero.
4. Novels *and magazine* articles glorified life on the range.
5. Cowboys *who* rode the range, however, endured *many* hardships.
6. Even on *unusually* long drives, the cowboy spent *most* of his time in the saddle.
7. There *were few* comforts on the trail.
8. In fact, on early drives *each* cowboy cooked for *himself.*
9. Some *improvement* came after *Charles Goodnight* put together the first chuck wagon.
10. A hinged lid swung *down* to form a simple *but* complete kitchen.
11. The *first* chuck wagons were pulled *by* oxen.
12. *These* were later replaced by mules *or* horses.
13. The cook *not only* prepared meals *but also* served as a barber, a doctor, and a dentist.
14. Details of life on the trail are shown in the paintings of Charles M. Russell, which became *quite popular.*
15. His paintings show that cowboys worked *unbelievably* hard but that *they* also enjoyed many light moments.
16. *Most* of the cowhands who took part in the historic cattle drives remain *nameless.*
17. *In spite of* their anonymity, cowboys have added color to *our* history.
18. Moreover, they were *instrumental* in opening trails used by the men and women who *settled* the frontiers.
19. *Railroads soon* began to crisscross the country; the cowboy was no longer needed to drive cattle.
20. *Oh,* how the bravery and independence of the cowboy continue to stir the *imagination*!

THE NOUN

1a. A *noun* is a word used to name a person, place, thing, or idea.

A noun names something. Your own name is a noun. The name of your state is a noun. *Tree* is a noun. The names of things that you cannot see or touch are nouns: for example, *sympathy, fairness, width, generosity, magic, truth.* These words do not name tangible things, but they do name qualities or ideas. The name of a quality or an idea is just as much a noun as the name of anything that has size or shape.

A noun names the thing we are talking about.

EXERCISE 1. Identifying Nouns in Sentences. There are twenty-five nouns in the following paragraph. Write them in order, and place before each the number of the sentence. If a noun is used more than once, write it each time it appears.

1. Women now compete in sports that were once limited to men. 2. Many teen-age girls in this country play soccer. 3. For years, the game had been played almost exclusively by males. 4. Girls now also play baseball on teams in organized leagues. 5. For the first time in history, female crews participate in international rowing events. 6. Female runners are a familiar sight to spectators at marathons. 7. Driving cars at high speeds, women race for the checkered flag.

EXERCISE 2. Identifying Nouns in Sentences. Number your paper 1–10. After the proper number, write the nouns that appear in each of the following sentences. Treat as single nouns all capitalized names of more than one word. Do not include years (for example, 1820).

1. Elizabeth Cady Stanton, an outspoken leader in the suffragist movement, was born in Johnstown, New York, in 1815. 2. She received a superior education in the classics and in mathematics both at home and at the Troy Female Seminary, from which she graduated in 1832. 3. From an early age she watched as her father practiced law; she was struck by the injustices suffered by women, especially in education and politics. 4. She became interested in the antislavery cause and in 1840 married Henry Stanton, a prominent abolitionist. 5. At an antislavery convention in London, Mrs. Stanton was outraged at the denial of recognition to the female delegates, among them Lucretia Mott. 6. She and Mrs. Mott later organized the first meeting addressed to the rights of women. 7. At this convention, held in Seneca Falls, New York, Mrs. Stanton read her "Declaration of Sentiments," outlining the inferior status of women and calling for reforms. 8. Later she joined forces with Susan B. Anthony, and for fifty years both women planned campaigns and spoke in statehouses and before congressional committees. 9. Mrs. Stanton, an accomplished writer and orator, was complemented by Miss Anthony, a superb organizer and tactician. 10. Both women also worked tirelessly for the abolition of slavery.

The Proper Noun and the Common Noun

Nouns may be divided into two classes: *proper nouns* and *common nouns*. A proper noun names a *particular* person, place, or thing; a common noun names a *class* of things.

PROPER NOUNS	COMMON NOUNS
Atlanta, Nantucket, Mount McKinley	city, island, mountain
Louisa May Alcott, General Patton	novelist, general
Museum of Fine Arts, the World Trade Center	museum, building
Queen Elizabeth 2	ship

☞ **NOTE** Compound nouns are made up of two or more words put together to form a single noun. Some compound nouns are written as one word (*basketball*), some as two or more words (*car pool, Arts and Crafts Club*), and some with hyphens (*passer-by, sister-in-law*). Notice that in the following example, the compound nouns are in boldfaced type.

XAMPLE   His **mother-in-law** is a member of the **Tennis Club,** which holds its tournaments at the **Greenvale Courts.**

EXERCISE 3. Writing Proper Nouns.   For each of the following common nouns, write a proper noun after the corresponding number.

EXAMPLE   1. river
              1. *Mississippi River*

1. play
2. valley
3. bicycle
4. song
5. ocean
6. pond
7. church
8. composer
9. newspaper
10. county
11. president
12. writer
13. street
14. short story
15. desert
16. poem
17. car
18. ship
19. lake
20. state

WRITING APPLICATION A:
Using Nouns to Make Your Writing Specific

Nouns that name a quality or an idea are called *abstract nouns*. For example, *freedom* is an abstract noun. A good way to make abstract nouns clear is to give examples using nouns that a person can clearly picture in his mind.

EXAMPLE kindness: 1. my *mother* washing my PE clothes   2. my *friend* listening to my problems   3. a *person* helping someone with heavy packages   4. a *driver* who helps someone with a dead battery   5. a *friend* who loans you some money when you forget yours

Writing Assignment

Select one of the following abstract nouns. Beside it, jot down six specific nouns that come to your mind as you think about your subject. Underline these nouns.

CHOICES fear compassion liberty
happiness success beauty

THE PRONOUN

1b. A *pronoun* is a word used in place of a noun or of more than one noun.

EXAMPLE Susan watched the monkey make faces at her little sister and brother. **She** laughed at **it** more than **they** did. [*She* is used in place of *Susan, it* in place of *monkey, they* in place of *sister and brother.*]

Personal Pronouns

The pronouns that have appeared in the preceding example are called *personal* pronouns. In this use, *personal* refers to one of the three possible ways of making statements: The person speaking can talk about himself or herself (first person) or about the person being spoken to (second person) or about anyone or anything else (third person). The few pronouns in English that have different forms to show person are called *personal pronouns*.

	Singular	*Plural*
FIRST PERSON	I, my, mine, me	we, our, ours, us
SECOND PERSON	you, your, yours	you, your, yours
THIRD PERSON	he, his, him she, her, hers it, its	they, their, theirs, them

Here are some other kinds of pronouns that you will encounter as you study this textbook.

RELATIVE PRONOUNS (used to introduce adjective and noun clauses; see pages 99–100, 105–106)

> who   whom   whose   which   that

INTERROGATIVE PRONOUNS (used in questions)

> Who . . .?   Whose . . .?   What . . .?
> Whom . . .?   Which . . .?

DEMONSTRATIVE PRONOUNS (used to point out a specific person or thing)

> this   that   these   those

INDEFINITE PRONOUNS (not referring to a definite person or thing)

all	each	more	one
another	either	most	other
any	everybody	much	several
anybody	everyone	neither	some
anyone	everything	nobody	somebody
anything	few	none	someone
both	many	no one	such

REFLEXIVE PRONOUNS (the *–self, –selves* forms of the personal pronouns)

> myself   ourselves
> yourself   yourselves
> himself, herself, itself   themselves

☞ **NOTE**   Never write or say *hisself* or *theirselves.*

EXERCISE 4. Identifying Pronouns in Sentences.   Number your paper 1–7. Referring if necessary to the preceding lists of pronouns, write after the proper number the pronouns in each of the following sentences. You should find at least twenty-five pronouns.[1] If a pronoun is used more than once, write it each time it appears.

---

[1] When words in the list on page 7 immediately precede a noun (*my* friend, *your* brother, etc.), they are considered possessive *pronouns* in this book, rather than *adjectives.*

1. Everybody in my family likes to go camping, but few of us enjoy the experience more than I do.   2. Last summer several of my cousins and I stayed at a rustic camp in the mountains, which are not far from our hometown.   3. At camp we all learned how to build a campfire and how to keep it going.   4. A group of us even went beyond that— we learned to cook meals over the open fire.   5. One of our counselors showed those who were interested how to cook simple meals. 6. Each of his recipes was easy to follow, and everyone ate everything in sight.   7. Anything cooked over an open fire tastes good, don't you agree?

THE ADJECTIVE

1c. **An** *adjective* **is a word used to modify a noun or a pronoun.**

Adjectives are words used to make the meaning of a noun or a pronoun more definite. Words used in this way are called *modifiers*.

An adjective may modify a noun or a pronoun by telling *what kind* it is.

blue ink   **old** friends   **strong** winds

An adjective may indicate *which one*.

this park   **these** papers   **that** house

An adjective may tell *how many*.

twenty-five kilometers   **two** men   **several** apples

An adjective is not always placed next to the word it modifies. It may be separated from the word it modifies by other words.

The sky was **cloudy.** [cloudy sky]

That joke is **clever.** [clever joke]

☞ **NOTE**   An adjective modifying a pronoun is almost always separated from the pronoun.

They look **happy.**   She is **strong.**

Articles

The most frequently used adjectives are *a, an,* and *the.* These little words are usually called *articles.*

A and *an* are *indefinite* articles; they refer to one of a general group.

EXAMPLES   **A** ranger helped us.
We kept watch for **an** hour.
They planted **an** acre with corn.

A is used before words beginning with a consonant sound; *an* is used before words beginning with a vowel sound. Notice in the second example above that *an* is used before a noun beginning with the consonant *h* because the *h* in *hour* is not pronounced. *Hour* is pronounced as if it began with a vowel (like *our*). Remember that the *sound* of the noun, not the spelling, determines which indefinite article will be used.

The is the *definite* article. It indicates that a noun refers to someone or something in particular.

EXAMPLES   **The** ranger helped us.
The hour dragged by.
They planted **the** acre with corn.

EXERCISE 5. Identifying the Words that Adjectives Modify.

Number your paper 1–10. In the following paragraph the adjectives (except *a, an,* and *the*) are printed in italics. Write the adjectives after the appropriate number, and after each adjective, write the word it modifies.

1. By the 1890's, an *extraordinary* craze for bicycling had swept the United States.   2. Though bicycles had been *available* for years, the *early* versions made for an *awkward* ride.   3. These *ungainly* cycles featured a very *tall* wheel in the front and a *small* wheel in the back.   4. In 1885, however, a more *sensible* bicycle was introduced, one that resembled the *modern* vehicle.   5. *Energetic* people everywhere suddenly took to *this* bicycle.   6. Bicycling soon became a *national* sport.   7. Cyclists joined *special* clubs that planned *vigorous* tours through the countryside.   8. A *typical* ride might cover *twenty* miles, with a *welcome* stop for refreshments.   9. Races were also *popular* with *enthusiastic* spectators, who often outnumbered those at

ball games. 10. The fans enjoyed watching *these* tests of endurance, which sometimes lasted *six* days.

EXERCISE 6. Supplying Interesting Adjectives to Complete Sentences.
Write the following sentences, supplying adjectives in the blank spaces. Use meaningful, interesting adjectives. Read the paragraph through before you start to write.

1. Hillcrest Gardens offers the visitor a —— oasis within the —— , —— jungle of city life. 2. It is especially —— in the springtime. 3. Everywhere you will discover the —— sights and —— scents of plants blooming after a —— winter. 4. You can take a —— walk along the —— paths or simply relax on one of the many —— benches in this —— garden. 5. As you meander along, feast your eyes on the —— beds of —— and —— tulips and on the —— clusters of daffodils. 6. Your visit will not be complete until you stroll under the —— canopy of —— flowering fruit trees. 7. Nearby are —— , —— bushes of —— lilacs. 8. They fill the air with a —— fragrance. 9. However, the most —— spot for visitors is the goldfish pond. 10. Here rays of —— sunlight cause the —— fish to gleam like —— jewels.

WRITING APPLICATION B:
Using Adjectives to Describe an Imagined Self

Have you ever imagined what it would be like to be an object or an animal? Some outstanding writers have done just that. In one of his stories, Franz Kafka writes about a man who awakens to discover that he is changed into a cockroach! One characteristic of a creative writer is a fruitful imagination.

EXAMPLE   The speaker in a poem by Sylvia Plath is a mirror:

> I am silver and exact . . .
> I am not cruel, only truthful —

Writing Assignment

Imagine that you are changed into an animal or an object. Using at least ten carefully chosen adjectives, describe yourself. Underline these adjectives. Do not count articles as adjectives.

Pronoun or Adjective?

Some words may be used either as adjectives or as pronouns (*this, which, each,* etc.). To tell them apart, keep in mind what they do.[1]

Adjectives *modify* nouns, while pronouns *take the place of* nouns. In the first sentence in each of the following pairs, the boldfaced word is used as a pronoun. In the second sentence of each pair, the word is used as an adjective.

PRONOUN   **Those** are excited fans.
ADJECTIVE   **Those** fans are excited.

PRONOUN   **Many** cheered the famous athlete.
ADJECTIVE   **Many** fans cheered the famous athlete.

PRONOUN   Did **some** wave banners?
ADJECTIVE   Did **some** fans wave banners?

Notice that a noun must follow immediately if the word is used as an adjective.

EXERCISE 7. Identifying Words as Adjectives or Pronouns. Write the numbered, italicized words in a column on your paper. After each word, tell whether it is used as a pronoun or an adjective, using the abbreviations *pron.* or *adj.* For each adjective, write the word it modifies.

a. Ants, (1) *which* are related to wasps, are significantly unlike (2) *those* insects.
b. (3) *All* ants are social; (4) *most* wasps are solitary.
c. (5) *Most* of the solitary wasps are hunting wasps.
d. (6) *These* make (7) *many* nests in soil or in decaying wood.
e. (8) *These* wasps congregate to form a permanent colony of adults and young.
f. There are 35,000 species of ant; (9) *each* contains three castes: males, queen, and workers.
g. (10) *Some* colonies include half a million ants; (11) *others* may be much smaller.

---

[1] Pronouns used before nouns (*my* friend, *your* brother) are sometimes called adjectives because they modify a noun. In this book such pronouns are called *possessive pronouns*. Follow your teacher's wishes in referring to such words.

h. (12) *Many* species form nests with only a (13) *few* individuals.

i. (14) *Some,* like the army ants, do not build nests.

j. Instead they travel in large armies (15) *that* sometimes number 150,000.

k. (16) *Several* species build mounds; (17) *these* mounds are often a foot high and five or six feet in diameter.

l. With (18) *which* kinds of ants are you familiar?

m. A species of interest is the harvester ant, (19) *which* gathers and stores seeds for food.

n. It was once thought that the ants planted the seeds, but (20) *this* is now believed to be untrue.

EXERCISE 8. Writing Sentences with Words Used as Pronouns or Adjectives. The following words may be used as either pronouns or adjectives. Write a pair of sentences for each word. In the first sentence of each pair, use the word as a pronoun; in the second, use it as an adjective.

1. more	5. these	8. many
2. both	6. all	9. few
3. each	7. neither	10. which
4. another		

Nouns Used as Adjectives

Sometimes nouns are used as adjectives.

salad bowl	**grocery** store
chicken dinner	**gold** chain

When you are identifying parts of speech and find a noun used as an adjective, call it an adjective.

REVIEW EXERCISE A. Identifying Nouns, Pronouns, and Adjectives. Number your paper 1–10. Next to the proper number write and label the nouns (*n.*), pronouns (*pron.*), and adjectives (*adj.*) used in the following sentences. After each adjective, write the word that it modifies. (Do not include the articles *a, an,* and *the.*)

1. Our teacher, Mr. Lopez, identified the various trees along the nature trail.

2. The bird feeder in the elm tree in my yard attracts cardinals and chickadees.

3. The flag over the hotel was a welcome sight to the two travelers.
4. The antique doll was dressed in a sailor hat and a blue suit.
5. Autumn leaves colored the highway along the Hudson River with bright splashes of red and orange.
6. A large cake sat in the center of the kitchen table.
7. Someone has filled the fruit bowl with dates and walnuts.
8. As a child Susan B. Anthony was taught the religious tenets of the Quakers, which include the belief in the equality of women.
9. Because many of our streams are impure, fish cannot survive in them.
10. The book cover on that anthology has seen better days.

THE VERB

1d. A *verb* is a word that expresses action or otherwise helps to make a statement.

All verbs help to make statements. Some do it by expressing action, others by telling something about the subject.

Action Verbs

Words such as *bring, say, shout,* and *jump* are action verbs. Some action verbs express an action that cannot be seen—for example, *ponder, trust, evaluate,* and *review.*

EXERCISE 9. Writing a List of Action Verbs. Make a list of twenty action verbs not including those just listed. Include and underline at least five verbs that express an action that cannot be seen.

There are two general classes of action verbs—*transitive* and *intransitive.* A verb is *transitive* when the action it expresses is directed toward a person or thing named in the sentence.

EXAMPLES   She **flew** the airplane. [The action of the verb *flew* is directed toward *airplane*. The verb is transitive.]
Zora Neale Hurston **wrote** novels.

In these examples the action passes from the doer—the subject—to the receiver of the action. Words that receive the action of a transitive verb are called *objects*.

A verb is *intransitive* when it expresses action (or helps to make a statement) without reference to an object. The following sentences contain intransitive verbs.

EXAMPLES The birches **swayed.**
The train **stops.**

The same verb may be transitive in one sentence and intransitive in another. A verb that can take an object is often used intransitively when the emphasis is on the action rather than on the person or thing affected by it.

EXAMPLES Miss Castillo **weeds** the garden every day. [transitive]
Miss Castillo **weeds** every day. [intransitive]

Elsa **swam** the channel. [transitive]
Elsa **swam** for many hours. [intransitive]

EXERCISE 10. Identifying Verbs as Transitive or Intransitive.
Some of the action verbs in the following sentences are transitive and some are intransitive. Write the verb of each sentence after the proper number on your paper, and label it as a dictionary would—*v.t.* for transitive, *v.i.* for intransitive.

1. The strong winds died down.
2. We quickly packed lunch for a trip to the seashore.
3. The whitecaps on the ocean had disappeared.
4. The sun sparkled on the gently splashing surf.
5. At low tide, Rosita suddenly spotted a starfish.
6. She noticed its five purplish arms.
7. She touched a soft, brown sponge floating nearby.
8. She added it to her collection of shells and dried seaweed.
9. Her collection includes several conch shells.
10. Three horseshoe crabs swam in the tidal pool.

WRITING APPLICATION C:
Using Verbs to Enliven Your Writing

Have you noticed the many ways sports writers avoid the monotony of saying that one team *defeated* another?

EXAMPLES Johnson High *Rocks* Jefferson
Wakulla *Smashes* Blountstown
Hamilton *Blasts* Eastern

Writing Assignment

Revise each of the following sentences by thinking of new, lively verbs to substitute for the underlined words.

1. Cham opened the door and told Tom to hurry up.
2. Mother suddenly stepped on the brakes and the car stopped.
3. He frowned as I sang loudly the words to our alma mater.
4. She lay down on her bed and began to cry.

Linking Verbs

Linking verbs help to make a statement not by expressing an action but by serving as a link between two words.

The most commonly used linking verbs are forms of the verb *be*. You should become thoroughly familiar with these.

be	were	shall have been	should have been
being	shall be	will have been	would have been
am	will be	should be	could have been
is	has been	would be	
are	have been	can be	
was	had been	could be	

Any verb ending in *be* or *been* is a form of the verb *be*. In addition to *be*, the following verbs are often used as linking verbs.

Other Common Linking Verbs

appear	grow	seem	stay
become	look	smell	taste
feel	remain	sound	

Notice in the following sentences that each verb is a link between the words on either side of it. The word that follows the linking verb fills out or completes the meaning of the verb and refers to the subject of the verb.

Kelp **is** the scientific name for seaweed. [*Kelp* = name]
Kelp **tastes** good in a salad. [good kelp]
Most seaweed **becomes** brown as it ages. [brown seaweed]
Kelp **can be** a basic source of iodine. [Kelp = source]

☞ **NOTE** Many of the linking verbs listed above can be used as action (nonlinking) verbs as well.

Emilia **felt** calm at the seashore. [linking verb: calm Emilia]
Emilia **felt** the rubbery strands of the ribbon kelp. [action verb]
Some kelps **grow** long. [linking verb: long kelps]
Some kelps **grow** large bulbs. [action verb]

Even *be* is not always a linking verb. It may be followed by only an adverb: *They are here.* To be a linking verb, the verb must be followed by a word that refers to (names or describes) the subject.

EXERCISE 11. Writing Sentences Using Verbs as Both Linking and Action Verbs. For each of the following verbs, write two sentences. In the first sentence, use the verb as a linking verb; in the second sentence, use it as an action verb.

1. appear   2. sound   3. smell   4. grow   5. look

The Verb Phrase

A verb frequently has one or more *helping verbs*. The verb and the helping verbs make up a unit that is called the *verb phrase*.

Commonly used helping verbs are *will, shall, have, has, had, can, may, might, do, does, did, must, ought, should, would,* and the forms of the verb *be* (see page 16).

EXAMPLES   This year's budget **has been approved.**
We **are leaving** tomorrow.
Sally **will launch** the canoe.
Did she **paint** the house?
You **might have helped** with the trim.
You **can clean** the brushes now.

EXERCISE 12. Identifying Verbs as Action Verbs or Linking Verbs. Study each italicized verb in the following sentences. Tell whether it is an action verb or a linking verb.

1. Situated on the banks of the Nile in Egypt, the ruins at Karnak *are* some of the most impressive sights in the world.
2. The largest ruin *is* the Great Temple of Amon.
3. Its immense size is astonishing to people who *know* little about the scale of Egyptian architecture.
4. If you *should follow* the avenue of sphinxes which leads to the main entrance, you *would be amazed* at the 42-meter-high gateway.

5. The ceiling of the temple *is* extremely high—more than 23 meters above the floor.
6. The central columns that *support* the stone roof *are* enormous.
7. The surfaces of the columns *are decorated* with low relief carvings.
8. Even an amateur engineer *can appreciate* the tremendous efforts which *must have gone* into the completion of this temple.
9. We now *know* that inclined planes, combined with levers and blocking, *enabled* the ancient Egyptians to raise the large stones.
10. Nevertheless, the temple *seems* an incredible undertaking.

EXERCISE 13. Identifying Verbs and Verb Phrases. Number your paper 1–10. Write the verbs in each of the following sentences. Be sure to include all the helping verbs, especially when the parts of the verb are separated by other words.

☞ **NOTE** The word *not* in a phrase such as *could not go* is not a verb. *Not* is an adverb.

---

1. The first performance of the marching band would occur tonight on the football field. 2. Marcia and the other flute players were clapping their hands vigorously, because their fingers had already become numb in the raw, chilly air. 3. It would not be funny if their fingers froze to the keys of their flutes. 4. Music would stream out in a shrill blast, and the spectators would be startled. 5. The other band members would no doubt skip a beat, and chaos might spread across the field. 6. With all the musicians out of step, the flute players might stumble into the clarinet players, who would certainly collide with the trombone players, who just might trip over the drummers. 7. As the time for their performance drew near, Marcia and her friends rolled their eyes and laughed about the dreadful scene they had just imagined. 8. Surely such a disaster could not possibly happen. 9. "Oh, no!" Marcia exclaimed as the band marched onto the field. "It is snowing!" 10. People were already leaving the stands when the principal announced over the loudspeaker: "Ladies and gentlemen, please remain in your seats; the band will now play 'Jingle Bells.'"

EXERCISE 14. Identifying Verbs and Verb Phrases. After the proper number, list all twenty-five verbs in the following sentences. Include all the parts of every verb.

1. After the United States purchased the Louisiana Territory from the French government, President Jefferson chose Meriwether Lewis as leader of a scouting expedition.   2. Lewis selected William Clark, an experienced guide and soldier, as his partner.   3. Lewis and Clark hoped that they would discover an overland route to the Pacific Ocean.   4. In the spring of 1804, the forty-five member expedition started up the Missouri River from St. Louis.   5. By fall they had traveled 1,600 miles.   6. In what is now the state of North Dakota, a Shoshoni Indian woman, Sacajawea, joined the party as an interpreter.   7. The expedition proceeded northwest by boat until the rivers became too shallow.   8. They outfitted horses and rode north through Lolo Pass. 9. With the help of local residents, they constructed canoes and paddled down the Snake River to the Columbia River, which they followed until it flowed into the Pacific.   10. The next year they returned to St. Louis by approximately the same route.   11. Because of the great care with which plans had been made, the expedition was remarkably successful.   12. Lewis and Clark had lost only one man, who had probably been a victim of appendicitis.   13. They had found a land route to the Pacific and improved the nation's access to the Oregon Territory, which was rich in resources.

THE ADVERB

1e. An *adverb* is a word used to modify a verb, an adjective, or another adverb.

Adverbs qualify the meaning of the words they modify by telling *how, when, where,* or *to what extent.*

Adverbs Modifying Verbs

Just as there are words (adjectives) that modify nouns and pronouns, there are words that modify verbs. For example, the verb *sing* may be modified by such words as *loudly, softly, haltingly,* or *cheerfully.* The verb *dive* may be modified by *smoothly, quickly, gracefully,* etc. A word that modifies a verb is an *adverb.* An adverb qualifies the meaning of the verb.

EXAMPLES   The bird was chirping **downstairs.** [*where*]
The bird chirped **today.** [*when*]
The bird chirped **loudly.** [*how*]
Our bird chirped **constantly.** [to *what* extent]

EXERCISE 15. Identifying Adverbs and the Verbs They Modify.
There are ten adverbs in the following sentences. Write them after the proper number. After each adverb, write the verb that it modifies.

1. The first balloonists floated gently above Paris in a hot-air balloon that had been cleverly designed by the Montgolfier brothers.
2. Although their earlier attempts had failed, the Montgolfiers never stopped trying and finally settled on a balloon made of paper and linen.
3. These early balloons differed significantly from modern balloons, which are sturdily constructed of coated nylon.   4. Despite their ingenuity, the Montgolfiers first thought that smoke would effectively push a balloon skyward.   5. In their first experiments, they bravely prepared fuel from rotten meat and old shoes.

Adverbs Modifying Adjectives

Sometimes an adverb modifies an adjective.

EXAMPLES   It was a **fiercely** competitive game. [The adverb *fiercely* tells *how* and modifies the adjective *competitive.*]
The police officer was **exceptionally** brave. [The adverb *exceptionally* modifies the adjective *brave.*]

☞ **NOTE**   Probably the most frequently used adverb is *very*. It is so overworked that you should avoid it whenever you can and try to find a more exact word to take its place.

EXERCISE 16. Identifying Adverbs and the Adjectives They Modify.
Number your paper 1–10. In each of the following sentences, there is an adverb modifying an adjective. After the proper number, write these adverbs. After each adverb, write the adjective it modifies.

1. An immensely long wagon train started out from Denver.
2. Both oxen and mules were used to pull unusually large wagons.
3. The trail through the mountains was fairly hazardous.

4. A moderately hard rain could turn the trail into a swamp.
5. When the trail was too muddy, the heavier wagons became mired.
6. Wagons that were extremely heavy then had to be unloaded before they could be moved.
7. Stopping for the night along the trail was a consistently welcome experience.
8. It offered relief to thoroughly tired bones and muscles.
9. Nights in the mountains could be quite cold.
10. On terribly cold nights, the travelers would roll themselves in blankets and sleep close to their campfires.

Adverbs Modifying Other Adverbs

You have learned that an adverb may modify a verb or an adjective. An adverb may also modify another adverb.

EXAMPLE   The guide spoke **too** slowly.

You can recognize *slowly* as an adverb modifying the verb *spoke*. It tells *how* the guide spoke. You can also see that *too* modifies the adverb *slowly*. It tells *how* slowly.

☛ **NOTE**   Many adverbs end in *–ly*. Do not make the mistake, however, of thinking that all words ending in *–ly* are adverbs. For instance, the following words are adjectives: *homely, kindly, lovely, deadly*. Moreover, some common adverbs do not end in *–ly:* for example, *always, never, very, soon, not, too.*

EXAMPLE   The U.S. hockey team did **not** win an Olympic gold medal between 1960 and 1980. [The adverb *not* comes between the parts of the verb phrase *did win*.]

EXERCISE 17. Writing Sentences Using Adverbs.   Use each of the following adverbs in a sentence. Draw an arrow from the adverb to the word it modifies.

1. happily	5. forward	8. early
2. quickly	6. backward	9. late
3. sometimes	7. soon	10. quite
4. yesterday		

EXERCISE 18. Identifying Adverbs and the Words They Modify.
There are twenty-five adverbs in the following paragraphs. Write them
after the proper numbers on your paper. After each, write the word
that the adverb modifies and tell whether this word is a verb, an
adjective, or another adverb.

1. Yesterday my sister June and I shopped for houseplants.
2. The large ones were too expensive for us.   3. We also knew that
large plants are almost always raised in hothouses.   4. They do not
adjust easily to homes in extremely cold climates.   5. Suddenly June
had a brainstorm.   6. "Let's buy some seeds and grow them indoors.
7. That way we can choose a rare species, and the seedlings will
automatically adapt themselves to the climate in our house."   8. At
the seed store the owner, Mrs. Miller, greeted us cheerfully.   9. We
told her we wanted seeds for a plant seldom sold in local shops.
10. We mentioned that our room hardly ever gets bright sunlight and
that during the winter it is especially dark.   11. "I know what you
need," Mrs. Miller promptly replied.   12. "These are seeds of
the bo tree, an unusually hardy member of the fig family native to
India.   13. There it is sacred to Buddhists, for it is said that the
Buddha received enlightenment under a bo tree."   14. At home we
carefully planted the seeds in a container filled with moist dirt and a
layer of damp peat moss.   15. We then covered the container with a
sheet of transparent plastic film.   16. Eventually the seeds sprouted
and our trees grew.   17. To our surprise, we discovered that each
leaf of the bo tree ends in a delicately tapered tip.   18. The leaves
were the most unusual ones we had ever seen!

EXERCISE 19. Using Words as Adjectives or Adverbs.   The following words may be used as either adjectives or adverbs. Write a
pair of sentences for each word. In the first sentence, use the word as
an adjective; in the second, use it as an adverb.

EXAMPLE   1. kindly
          1. *She had a kindly manner.* [adjective]
             She spoke kindly. [adverb]

1. daily   2. fast   3. late   4. more   5. far

REVIEW EXERCISE B. Identifying the Parts of Speech of Words.
Number your paper 1–50. After the proper number, write on your
paper the italicized words in the following paragraphs. After each

word, tell what part of speech it is. In a third column, write the word
modified by each italicized adjective and adverb.

With a (1) *thunderous* roar an avalanche (2) *slides* (3) *swiftly* down
a mountainside. (4) *It* sometimes travels at speeds of more than 200
miles an hour and poses a (5) *deadly* threat to skiers, mountain climbers, and the people (6) *who* live and work in the mountains.

The (7) *best* way to survive an avalanche is to make swimming
motions in order to remain on top of the snow. People who are caught
in an avalanche, however, (8) *rarely* survive. They are (9) *usually*
completely immobilized, and the slide (10) *itself* forces snow into the
victim's nose and mouth.

Avalanche workers both in the (11) *United States* and abroad have
(12) *long* realized the (13) *potential* (14) *destructiveness* of selected
slide paths. They (15) *have concluded* that an avalanche can be (16)
substantially reduced if explosives (17) *are used* to trigger a (18) *series*
of (19) *smaller* slides before (20) *one* large mass of snow can build up.
(21) *Today* the detonation of explosives has become a standard (22)
practice for controlling avalanches in (23) *this* country.

Parts of the (24) *Wasatch Range* near Salt Lake City are strafed
by (25) *more* avalanches than any (26) *other* populated area on (27)
our continent. (28) *This* is therefore the (29) *best* place to learn how
an avalanche threat (30) *is controlled*.

Avalanche (31) *forecasters* study the snowpack on the Wasatch
slopes from the (32) *first* snowfall in (33) *autumn*. Ski patrollers observe the snowpack for (34) *unstable* pockets of snow. (35) *Such*
pockets are (36) *generally* (37) *capable* of triggering an avalanche.
Patrollers (38) *always* carry hand charges under (39) *their* parkas, for
(40) *easy* (41) *access*. (42) *These* charges (43) *are thrown* only from
islands of (44) *safety* such as (45) *thick* groves of trees. (46) *Nobody*
in (47) *avalanche* control believes that avalanches can be controlled
(48) *completely*. From time to time, (49) *nature* continues to gain the
(50) *upper hand*.

WRITING APPLICATION D:
Using Adverbs to Express Intense Feeling

Perhaps you have strong opinions and feelings about such issues as environmental pollution, inadequate facilities for the handicapped, and so forth. The careful use of adverbs helps you express intense feelings and opinions.

EXAMPLE I am *ardently* concerned about world hunger.

Writing Assignment

Select an issue that affects many people. Write a paragraph in which you express your opinions and feelings about this topic. Use at least three adverbs. Underline them. Try to avoid *very, extremely,* or *quite.*

THE PREPOSITION

1f. A *preposition* **is a word that shows the relationship of a noun or a pronoun to some other word in the sentence.**

Prepositions are important because they point out different relationships. Notice in the following examples how the prepositions in boldfaced type show three different relationships between *village* and *rode* and between *river* and *park.*

> I rode **past** the village   The park **near** the river is quiet.
> I rode **through** the village.   The park **beside** the river is quiet.
> I rode **beyond** the village.   The park **across** the river is quiet.

A preposition always introduces a phrase (see page 69). The noun or pronoun that ends a prepositional phrase is the *object* of the preposition which introduces the phrase. In the previous examples the objects of the prepositions are *village* and *river.*

Commonly Used Prepositions

aboard	amid	beneath	by
about	among	beside	concerning
above	around	besides	down
across	at	between	during
after	before	beyond	except
against	behind	but (meaning	for
along	below	"except")	from

in	off	since	until
inside	on	through	up
into	onto	to	upon
like	outside	toward	with
near	over	under	within
of	past	underneath	without

Compound prepositions consist of more than one word.

according to	in addition to	instead of
because of	in front of	on account of
by means of	in spite of	prior to

☞ **NOTE** The same word may be either an adverb or a preposition, depending on its use in a sentence.

EXAMPLES   Marge climbed **down.** [adverb]
Marge climbed **down** the ladder. [preposition]

EXERCISE 20. Writing Sentences Using Words as Prepositions.
Use the following words as prepositions in sentences. Underline the phrase that each preposition introduces. Be able to tell between which words the preposition shows a relationship.

1. during   3. through   5. beyond   7. into   9. aboard
2. beneath   4. with   6. between   8. toward   10. among

EXERCISE 21. Writing Sentences Using Words as Adverbs.
Use the following words as adverbs in sentences.

1. up   3. on   5. besides   7. along   9. by
2. near   4. across   6. past   8. around   10. over

THE CONJUNCTION

1g. A *conjunction* joins words or groups of words.

Conjunctions are used to join parts of a sentence that function in the same way or in a closely related way. The parts joined may be words, phrases, or clauses. In the following examples the conjunctions are in boldfaced type, and the words they join are underscored.

EXAMPLES   The orchestra played one waltz **and** two polkas.
We can walk to the shopping mall **or** take a bus.
I looked for Hal, **but** he had already left.

There are three kinds of conjunctions: *coordinating, correlative,* and *subordinating.*

Coordinating conjunctions.   Conjunctions that join equal parts of a sentence are called *coordinating conjunctions.* They are *and, but, or, nor, for, so,* and *yet.*[1]

Correlative conjunctions.   Some conjunctions are used in pairs. Examples of these are *either . . . or, neither . . . nor, both . . . and, not only . . . but also.* Study the pairs of conjunctions in the following sentences. Conjunctions of this kind, used in pairs, are *correlative conjunctions.*

Either the head coach **or** the assistant coach will time your sprint.
Neither the baseball team **nor** the football team has practice today.
Both the track team **and** the volleyball team enjoyed a winning season.
Their victories sparked the enthusiasm **not only** of students **but also** of teachers and townspeople.

Subordinating conjunctions will be discussed later in connection with subordinate clauses (page 102).

EXERCISE 22. Identifying Coordinating and Correlative Conjunctions.   Write the coordinating and correlative conjunctions in the following sentences.

1. Once Nantucket and New Bedford were home ports of great whaling fleets.   2. Whaling channeled tremendous profits into these ports, but the golden days of whaling ended about the time of the War Between the States.   3. A whaling trip was no pleasure cruise for either the captain or the crew, for they worked long hours during a day on the sea.   4. Maintaining order was no easy task on a long

---

[1] The conjunctions *and, but, or,* and *nor* can join words, phrases, and clauses. *For, so,* and *yet* usually join clauses. For this reason some grammarians consider these last three words subordinating conjunctions, not true coordinating conjunctions. Follow your teacher's wishes in classifying these last three conjunctions.

voyage, because the food and living conditions gave rise to discontent. 5. Inevitably the sailors had time on their hands, for they didn't encounter a whale every day. 6. To relieve the dullness and boredom on long voyages, whaling ships often would exchange visits. 7. Not only the captain but also the whole crew looked forward to such visits. 8. All enjoyed the chance to chat and exchange news. 9. The decline of whaling and of the whaling industry began about 1860. 10. Our country no longer needed large quantities of whale oil; for kerosene, a cheaper and better fuel, had replaced it.

THE INTERJECTION

1h. An *interjection* is a word that expresses emotion and has no grammatical relation to other words in the sentence.

There are a few words that can be used to show sudden or strong feeling, such as fright, anger, excitement, or joy.

EXAMPLES **Ouch!** **Ugh!** **Wow!** **Oops!** **Oh!**

These words are usually followed by an exclamation mark. An interjection that shows only mild emotion is followed by a comma.

Well, I'm just not sure.

EXERCISE 23. Writing a List of Interjections. Make a list of ten interjections other than those given above. Be sure to include an exclamation point after each interjection.

DETERMINING PARTS OF SPEECH

1i. What part of speech a word is depends on how the word is used.

In the following sentences you will see that one word is used as three different parts of speech. What part of speech is *light* in each sentence?

Rich heard the **light** patter of raindrops.
The room was filled with **light.**
Let's **light** some candles this evening.

EXERCISE 24. Determining the Parts of Speech of Words.
Number your paper 1–20. Study the use of each of the italicized words in the following sentences. On your paper, write the part of speech of the word after the proper number. Be prepared to explain to the class why the word is that part of speech.

1. They decided that the hedge needed a *trim*.
2. Their hedges always look *trim* and neat.
3. We usually *trim* the tree with homemade ornaments.
4. Mother always *shears* a couple of inches off the top of the tree.
5. Later she uses garden *shears* to cut straggling branches.
6. My brother *spices* fruit pies with nutmeg and allspice.
7. These *spices* are available in most stores.
8. Sage adds a tangy *flavor* to stew.
9. Many chefs also *flavor* stew with basil.
10. In their family, a *cross* word is rarely spoken.
11. You will find their house where Pine Avenue and Hazelnut Street *cross*.
12. We looked for a constellation of stars shaped like a *cross*.
13. After sundown, the two counselors *spin* tales for their eager audience.
14. In the evening, we sometimes go for a *spin* in the car.
15. One night we spotted wild horses near a *turn* in the road.
16. "*Turn* off the headlights!" we cried.
17. We were all *safe* and sound after our adventure.
18. Her mother keeps her important papers in a *safe*.
19. To get back home, we must make the next *right* turn.
20. Turn *right* when you see the old barn.

REVIEW EXERCISE C. Writing Sentences Using Words as Different Parts of Speech.
Write three sentences for each of the following words, using the word as a different part of speech in each sentence. At the end of the sentence, write the part of speech.

1. long   2. cut   3. back   4. fast   5. iron

REVIEW EXERCISE D. Determining the Parts of Speech of Words.
Now that you have reviewed the eight parts of speech, you should be able to classify each italicized word. Number your paper

1–10. After the appropriate number, list the italicized words, and after each, write what part of speech it is.

1. Some of the strangest living creatures *are* freshwater tropical fish.
2. The pacú, for example, *lives* in streams overhung with grapevines.
3. *Often,* overripe grapes fall *into* the water, *and* hungry pacús eat them.
4. The pacú is *probably* the only grape-eating fish in the world.
5. The leaf fish is also very *strange*.
6. *It* is thin, with a jagged *outline*.
7. It *remains* motionless *near* the *surface* of the water.
8. *Its* blotchy gold and brown coloring makes it look like *either* a *dead* leaf *or* a piece of bark.
9. Another *oddity* that amazes *anyone* who sees it is the archerfish.
10. This *small* striped fish *can shoot* a stream of water *at* an insect a few feet away and bring it *down*.

REVIEW EXERCISE E. Determining the Parts of Speech of Words. Number your paper 1–25. After the proper number, write the part of speech of each italicized word or expression.

(1) *Early* farmers on the (2) *Great Plains* eked out a rough existence, (3) *for* there were few towns, stores, (4) *or* other hallmarks of civilization. Their first homes were constructed with sod bricks, (5) *which* were cut out of the prairie. Trees were in short supply on these vacant lands, (6) *but* the resourceful settler might find a few (7) *cottonwoods* growing (8) *along* a stream. (9) *These* (10) *could be used* to build a frame for the roof, which was then covered (11) *lightly* with grassy earth. Grass (12) *both* on the roof (13) *and* in the sod cemented the structure together. The door to (14) *this* primitive house might be constructed from timber, (15) *but* usually a cowhide (16) *was draped* across the entrance. Inside was a dirt floor that was covered with (17) *either* a bearskin (18) *or* a buffalo robe.

Furnishings were (19) *always* (20) *homemade*. Farmers usually slept in (21) *rustic* beds made with rawhide strips that were pulled (22) *tautly* (23) *across* a wooden frame. (24) *Their* mattresses were often straw-filled ticks, somewhat lumpy but sweet-smelling. With a few crude benches, a wooden table, and cooking utensils, the house of the early settler was (25) *complete*.

CHAPTER 1 REVIEW: POSTTEST 1

Determining the Parts of Speech of Words. Number your paper 1–25. After the proper number, write each italicized word in the following sentences and indicate what part of speech it is. Use the abbreviations *n.* (noun), *pron.* (pronoun), *adj.* (adjective), *v.* (verb), *adv.* (adverb), *prep.* (preposition), *conj.* (conjunction), and *interj.* (interjection).

1. *Pioneer* aviator Amelia Earhart was born in *Kansas* in 1897.
2. As a child she lived in many different states, *for* the Earharts moved *often*.
3. Amelia *graduated* from *high school* in Chicago in 1916.
4. She *became* an army nurse in Canada during World War I and later *briefly* attended Columbia University and the University of Southern California.
5. She learned to fly *and* worked *remarkably* hard to support her flying.
6. In 1928 she *was chosen* by publisher G. P. Putnam to take part in a transatlantic flight *as* passenger and standby pilot; she thus became the first woman to fly the Atlantic.
7. In 1931 *she* married Putnam but *continued* to use her own name.
8. Determined to fly the Atlantic by *herself,* Amelia Earhart took off in a single-engine plane *that* now hangs in the Smithsonian Air and Space Museum.
9. She flew *out* over the Atlantic, where she *almost* immediately experienced bad weather.
10. Ice on the wings forced *her* to fly at *extremely* low altitudes.
11. Fifteen hours *after* takeoff, she landed in a pasture in Ireland and became *famous* overnight.
12. *This* accomplishment earned her the *Distinguished Flying Cross*.
13. She was widely acclaimed *not only* as an aviator *but also* as an inspiring example of courage.
14. In 1935 she became the first person to fly from Hawaii to California; *this* was a less *eventful* crossing than the Atlantic trip.

15. She flew steadily at *comfortable* altitudes and maintained *reasonably* good radio contact.
16. For a time, Amelia Earhart *was* a *career* counselor to women at Purdue University.
17. In 1937 she *undertook* a round-the-world *flight* in an airplane purchased by trustees of Purdue.
18. *Because of* an accident at takeoff, she and her copilot were forced to set out *once* again.
19. At first the flight was *relatively smooth*.
20. On an *overcast* morning in July, she and her copilot left New Guinea for Howland Island; they *never* arrived.
21. Radio contact was broken, and *neither* Amelia *nor* her copilot was ever heard from again.
22. Decades later rumors *still* circulate about Amelia Earhart's *fate*.
23. *Some* believe that she was on a secret mission and *was taken* prisoner as a spy.
24. *Others* maintain that she is *alive* and living somewhere in seclusion.
25. *Well,* what do *you* think?

CHAPTER 1 REVIEW: POSTTEST 2

Determining the Parts of Speech of Words. The italicized words in the following paragraphs have been numbered. After the proper number, write each italicized word and indicate what part of speech it is. Use the abbreviations for the parts of speech that you used in Chapter 1 Review: Posttest 1.

Since the (1) *condition* of the roads prevented (2) *extensive* use of wheeled vehicles, the most reliable means of transportation in colonial times was the (3) *saddle horse*. Some (4) *exceptionally* wealthy people kept carriages, but (5) *these* were usually heavy vehicles (6) *that* were pulled by two or more horses. The carriages were (7) *satisfactory* for short trips, (8) *but* they were not practical for long journeys.

Stagecoaches were introduced in (9) *America* about 1750. By this time roads ran (10) *between* such major cities as New York and Boston. Although these roads (11) *were* little more than muddy tracks, (12) *most* were wide enough for a four-wheeled coach. Three (13) *or* four pairs of horses (14) *were harnessed* to a coach. The vehicles were so heavy, however, that (15) *coach* horses tired (16) *quite* (17) *rapidly* and (18) *either* had to be rested frequently (19) *or* changed at post houses along the route.

On the (20) *frontier* there were no roads at all. The (21) *Conestoga wagon* was developed for long trips. It had huge wheels that were sometimes (22) *six* feet in diameter, and (23) *its* body was built like a barge. When a Conestoga wagon (24) *approached* a river that was too deep to be forded, the wagon was floated (25) *across*.

CHAPTER 1 REVIEW: POSTTEST 3

Writing Sentences with Words Used as Different Parts of Speech.
Number your paper 1–20. Use each of the following words in a sentence. Then write the part of speech of the word in the sentence.

EXAMPLES 1. gold
1. *Maria bought a gold bracelet.* adjective
2. that
2. *That is a very funny story!* pronoun

1. novel	8. are laughing	15. or
2. Park Avenue	9. yesterday	16. but
3. this	10. tomorrow	17. both . . . and
4. silver	11. quietly	18. oh
5. hiked	12. often	19. whew
6. appeared	13. inside	20. in
7. tasted	14. underneath	

SUMMARY OF PARTS OF SPEECH

Rule	Part of Speech	Use	Examples
1a	noun	names	**Larry** picks **grapefruit**.
1b	pronoun	takes the place of a noun	**You** and **he** sing well. Do not let **anyone** guess.

Rule	Part of Speech	Use	Examples
1c	adjective	modifies a noun or a pronoun	That was a **happy** sight. They were very **noisy.**
1d	verb	shows action or helps to make a statement	He **jumps** and **spins.** She **might take** the prize.
1e	adverb	modifies a verb, an adjective, or another adverb	He learns **quickly.** She is **always** right. It flies **quite** high.
1f	preposition	relates a noun or a pronoun to another word	The cats are **in** the shade **under** the oak tree **near** the garage.
1g	conjunction	joins words	Nancy **and** Sheila passed the test.
1h	interjection	expresses strong emotion	**My goodness!** **Hey,** stop that!

CHAPTER 2

The Sentence

SUBJECTS, PREDICATES, COMPLEMENTS

DIAGNOSTIC TEST

A. Identifying Subjects, Verbs, and Complements. Number your paper 1–10. After the proper number, write the italicized word or word group in the following sentences. Correctly identify each, using these abbreviations: *s.* (subject); *v.* (verb); *p.a.* (predicate adjective); *p.n.* (predicate nominative); *d.o.* (direct object); *i.o.* (indirect object).

1. Native *cactuses* in the Southwest are in trouble.
2. Some species are already *vulnerable* to eventual extinction.
3. Cactuses *are being threatened* by landscapers, collectors, and tourists.
4. Many people illegally harvest these wild *plants*.
5. There are many unique and unusual *species* in Arizona.
6. Arizona is therefore an active *battlefield* in the war against the removal of endangered cactuses.
7. "Cactus cops" *patrol* the streets of Phoenix on the lookout for places with illegally acquired cactuses.
8. Authorized dealers must give *purchasers* permit tags as proof of legal sale.
9. First violations are *punishable* by a minimum fine of five hundred dollars.
10. Illegally owned cactuses *are impounded.*

B. Classifying Sentences as Declarative, Interrogative, Imperative, or Exclamatory. Number your paper 11–20. After the proper number, classify each of the following sentences as declarative, interrogative, imperative, or exclamatory. After each classification write the proper end punctuation in parentheses.

11. What a thorny problem cactus rustling has become
12. Why are illegal harvesters so hard to keep track of
13. Many work at night and sometimes use permit tags over and over again
14. Go to the library and read about imperiled cactuses in the December 1980 issue of *Smithsonian*
15. The author describes a trip into the desert with a legal hauler
16. Can you imagine a saguaro worth three hundred dollars
17. A crested saguaro is even rarer and can sell for thousands of dollars
18. No wonder illegal harvesting is booming
19. Always examine a large cactus for bruises
20. Legally harvested plants should not show any damage

In speech, we often leave out parts of our sentences. For example, we often answer a certain kind of question in a few words, not bothering to speak in sentences.

"What happened to Laura?"
"Sprained wrist."
"Too bad."
"Sure is."

When we write, however, our words have to convey the whole message. Our readers cannot hear us, and if they do not understand, they cannot ask for a repetition. Therefore, when we put our thoughts on paper, we are expected to express them in complete sentences. Before we discuss all that can go into a complete sentence, we must review the definition of a sentence.

2a. A *sentence* is a group of words containing a subject and a verb and expressing a complete thought.

The two parts of this definition are closely related. To express a complete thought, a sentence must refer to someone or something (the subject), and it must tell us something about that person or thing. This job of telling about something is done by the predicate, which always contains a verb.

SUBJECT AND PREDICATE

2b. **A sentence consists of two parts: the** *subject* **and the** *predicate*. **The** *subject* **of the sentence is the part about which something is being said. The** *predicate* **is the part that says something about the subject.**

subject	*predicate*
Some residents of the desert	have ingenious ways of evading the life-threatening effects of a drought.

predicate	*subject*
Bizarre and unbelievable is	the method of the Australian frog.

subject	*predicate*
These water-holding frogs	can lie in a trance for as long as three years between rainfalls.

EXERCISE 1. Identifying Subjects and Predicates.

Find the subject and predicate of each of the following sentences. If your teacher directs you to write the sentence on your paper, draw *one* line under the complete subject and *two* lines under the complete predicate. Keep in mind that the subject may come after the predicate.

1. The discovery of platinum has been credited to a variety of countries.
2. Spanish explorers in search of gold supposedly found the metal in the rivers of South America.
3. They considered it a worthless, inferior form of silver.
4. Their name for platinum was *platina,* or "little silver."
5. Back into the river went the little balls of platinum!
6. The platinum might then become gold, according to one theory.
7. Europeans later mixed platinum with gold.
8. This mixture encouraged the production of counterfeit gold bars and coins.
9. Platinum commands a high price today because of its resistance to corrosion.
10. Such diverse products as jet planes and jewelry require platinum in some form.

The Simple Predicate and the Complete Predicate

The predicate of a sentence is the part that says something about the subject. This part is properly called the *complete predicate*. Within the complete predicate, there is always a word or word group that is the "heart" of the predicate. It is essential because it is the key word in completing the statement about the subject. This word or word group is called the *simple predicate,* or *verb*.

2c. The principal word or group of words in the complete predicate is called the *simple predicate,* or the *verb*.

EXAMPLE   Spiders **snare** their prey in an intricate web. [complete predicate: *snare their prey in an intricate web;* verb: *snare*]

The Verb Phrase

Often the simple predicate, or verb, will consist of more than one word. It will be a verb phrase like the following: *are walking, will walk, has walked, might have walked,* etc. When this is so, do not forget to include all parts of a verb phrase when you are asked to pick out the simple predicate of any sentence.

EXAMPLES   **Has** Sally **helped** you? [simple predicate: *has helped*]
The new theater **will** not **have** permanent seats. [simple predicate: *will have*]

In the following sentences, the verb is underscored; the complete predicate is in boldfaced type. Study the sentences carefully so that you will be able to pick out the verb in the sentences in the next exercise.

The fishermen **steered their boat toward the middle of the lake.**
They **had heard about this popular spot.**
They **switched off the motor.**
Paul **is using his best lures.**
Everyone **is optimistically looking forward to a winning season.**

Throughout the rest of this book, the simple predicate is referred to as the verb.

EXERCISE 2. Identifying Verbs or Verb Phrases in Sentences.
Number your paper 1–10. Find the verb in each of the following sentences, and write it after the proper number. Be sure to include all parts of a verb phrase.

1. Scientists throughout the world have expressed concern about the fate of the giant panda of China.
2. The animal's natural habitat has slowly become smaller.
3. Many forests of bamboo have died.
4. Every day, a panda may devour as much as forty pounds of bamboo.
5. Each tender, green shoot of bamboo contains only a small amount of nutrients.
6. The large but sluggish panda is not known as a successful hunter of small animals.
7. In their concern for the panda's survival, scientists are now studying the daytime and nighttime habits of this animal.
8. They hold a captured panda in a log trap for several hours.
9. During this time, the scientists attach a radio to the panda's neck.
10. The radio sends the scientists valuable information about the released animal's behavior.

The Simple Subject and the Complete Subject

The subject of a sentence is the part about which something is being said. This part is properly called the *complete subject*. Within the complete subject there is always a word (or group of words) that is the "heart" of the subject, and this principal word within the complete subject is called the *simple subject*.

2d. The *simple subject* is the main word or group of words in the complete subject.

EXAMPLE   A **dog** with this pedigree is usually nervous. [complete subject: *A dog with this pedigree;* simple subject: *dog*]

In naming the simple subject, consider compound nouns as one word.

EXAMPLE   The **Taj Mahal** in India is one of the most beautiful buildings in the world. [complete subject: *The Taj Mahal in India;* simple subject: *Taj Mahal*]

Throughout the rest of this book, unless otherwise indicated, the word *subject* will refer to the simple subject.

Caution: Remember that *noun* and *subject* do not mean the same thing. A *noun* is the name of a person, place, thing, or idea. A *subject* is the name of a part of a sentence; it is usually a noun or pronoun.

How to Find the Subject of a Sentence

Because the subject may appear at almost any point in the sentence, you will find it easier to locate the subject if you pick out the verb first. For example:

> The shutters on that house are always closed.

The verb is *are closed*. Now ask yourself: Who or what are closed? The answer is *shutters,* so *shutters* is the subject. In the sentence *Beyond the brook stands a cabin,* the verb is *stands.* Ask yourself: Who or what stands? The answer is *cabin,* so *cabin* is the subject.

EXERCISE 3. Identifying Subjects and Verbs. Number your paper 1–10. Find the subject and verb of each sentence, and write them—subject first, then verb—after the proper number. Underline the subject once and the verb twice.

1. Despite their fragile appearance, butterflies often fly over a thousand miles during migration.
2. The painted lady, for example, has been seen in the middle of the Atlantic Ocean.
3. In northern Europe, this species was once spotted over the Arctic Circle.
4. During the spring, millions of painted ladies flutter across North America.
5. This huge flock of colorful butterflies leaves its warm winter home in New Mexico.
6. These butterflies' impressive journey sometimes takes them as far north as Newfoundland, Canada.
7. In September, the brilliant orange-and-black monarch flies south from Canada toward Florida, Texas, and California.
8. The migratory flight of the monarch may cover a distance of close to two thousand miles.
9. Every winter for the past sixty years, monarchs have gathered in a small forest not far from San Francisco.
10. The thick clusters of their blazing orange wings make this forest very popular with tourists.

2e. The subject is never in a prepositional phrase.

A prepositional phrase is a group of words that begins with a preposition and ends with a noun or pronoun: *through the yard, of mine.*

Finding the subject when it is followed by a phrase may be difficult.

EXAMPLE One of my relatives has taken a trip to Europe.

You see at once that the verb is *has taken*. When you ask "Who has taken?" you may be tempted to answer *relatives*. However, that is not what the sentence says. The sentence says, "*One* of my relatives has taken a trip to Europe." The subject is *One*. Notice that *relatives* is part of the phrase *of my relatives*. In many sentences you can easily isolate the subject and verb simply by crossing out all prepositional phrases.

EXAMPLE The team ~~with the best record~~ will play ~~in the state tournament~~.
[verb: *will play;* subject: *team*]

EXERCISE 4. Identifying Subjects and Verbs. Write the following sentences on your paper. Cross out each of the prepositional phrases. Underline each verb twice and its subject once.

1. A book about the Chinese experience in America has been written by Victor G. Nee and Brett de Bary Nee.
2. The title of the book is *Longtime Californ': A Documentary Study of an American Chinatown.*
3. The book traces the history of Chinese immigration and the development of the Chinese-American community.
4. The first immigrants came for the jobs in the gold mines and on the railroads in the 1850's.
5. In the beginning only men could immigrate.
6. In time the early immigrants sent to China for their wives.
7. During the 1920's the cohesive family society of Chinatown developed.
8. Interviews of old and young residents of Chinatown give the book its authentic character.
9. A good example of this technique is the interview with Lisa Mah about her return to Chinatown after her family's departure.
10. The spirit of the Chinatown community is subtly captured.

EXERCISE 5. Completing Sentences by Supplying Predicates; Identifying Subjects and Verbs. Complete each of the following sentences by adding predicates to the complete subject. After you have done so, underline the subject once and the verb twice.

1. Last month —— .
2. A white fence —— .
3. My favorite uncle —— .
4. Most gardeners in my neighborhood —— .
5. The students in our school —— .
6. The surf —— .
7. A cottage near the lake —— .

8. The plastic cup —— .
9. The road by my house —— .
10. My warmest memories —— .

REVIEW EXERCISE Ⓐ Identifying Complete Subjects and Predicates and Identifying Subjects and Verbs. Write the following sentences on your paper. Insert a vertical line (I) between the last word in the complete subject and the first word in the complete predicate. Then underline the subject once and the verb twice.

1. Benjamin Banneker was born in Maryland of a free mother and a slave father.
2. Banneker himself was considered free.
3. As a result, he attended an integrated private school.
4. With the equivalent of an eighth-grade education, this young man became a noteworthy American astronomer and mathematician.
5. His knowledge of astronomy led to his acclaimed prediction of the solar eclipse of 1789.
6. The first of his almanacs was published a few years later.
7. These almanacs contained tide tables and data on future eclipses.
8. A number of useful medicinal products were also listed.
9. Banneker's almanac appeared annually for more than a decade.
10. Banneker is best known, however, for his contribution as a surveyor during the planning of Washington, D.C.

The Subject in an Unusual Position

Two kinds of sentences may confuse you when you wish to find the verb and its subject. These are (1) sentences that begin with the words *there* or *here* and (2) sentences that ask a question.

Sentences Beginning with *There* or *Here*

When the word *there* or *here* comes at the beginning of a sentence, it may appear to be the subject, but it is not. Use the "*who* or *what*" formula to find the subject.

EXAMPLE   There are two apples in the refrigerator. [What are? *Apples.*]

Sentences That Ask Questions

Questions usually begin with a verb or a verb helper. Also, they frequently begin with words like *what, when, where, how,* and *why.* Either way, the subject usually follows the verb or verb helper.

EXAMPLES Why is **he** running?
How do **you** feel?

In questions that begin with a helping verb, the subject always comes between the helping verb and the main verb. Another way to find the subject is to turn the question into a statement, find the verb, and ask "Who?" or "What?" in front of it.

EXAMPLES *Question:* Were your friends early?
Statement: Your friends were early.
[Who were early? *Friends. Subject:* **Friends**]

Question: Has Mrs. Williams read our compositions?
Statement: Mrs. Williams has read our compositions.
[Who has read the compositions? *Mrs. Williams. Subject:* **Mrs. Williams**]

EXERCISE 6. Identifying Subjects and Verbs. Number your paper 1–10. Select the verb and the subject in each of the following sentences, and write them after the proper number. Select the verb first. Be sure to write all parts of a verb phrase.

1. There were three questions on the final exam.
2. Here is my topic for the term paper.
3. What did you choose for a topic?
4. Will everyone be ready on time?
5. There will be no excuse for lateness.
6. When should we go to the library?
7. There were very few books on the subject.
8. Are there any magazine articles about the bald eagle?
9. Where will our conference be held?
10. Have you begun the next chapter?

Sentences in Which the Subject Is Understood

In requests and commands, the subject is usually left out of the sentence. The subject of a command or request is *you* (understood but not expressed).

EXAMPLES   Rake the yard.
Pick up the fallen branches.

In these sentences the verbs are *rake* and *pick*. In both sentences the subject is the same. Who must *rake* and *pick*? The subject is *you*, even though the word does not appear in either of the sentences. A subject of this kind is said to be *understood*.

Compound Subjects and Verbs

2f. Two or more subjects connected by *and* or *or* and having the same verb are called a *compound subject*.

EXAMPLE   **Mr. Oliver** and his **daughter** planted a vegetable garden. [verb: *planted;* compound subject: *Mr. Oliver* (and) *daughter*]

2g. Two or more verbs joined by a connecting word and having the same subject are called a *compound verb*.

EXAMPLES   At the street festival, we **danced** the rumba and **sampled** the meat pies. [compound verb: *danced* (and) *sampled;* subject: *we*]
I **have written** these letters and **addressed** the envelopes. [The subject is *I;* the compound verb is *have written* (and) *have addressed*. Notice that the helping verb *have* goes with both *written* and *addressed*.]

EXERCISE 7. Writing Sentences.   Write two sentences containing an understood subject, two containing a compound subject, two containing a compound verb, two in which the subject follows the verb, and two in which the subject is followed by a prepositional phrase.

EXERCISE 8. Identifying Subject and Verbs.   Number your paper 1–10. After the proper numbers, write the subject and the verb of each sentence. If the subject of the sentence is understood, write *you* as the subject, placing parentheses around it.

EXAMPLES   1. Usually, there are three jays in that oak tree.
1. *jays are*

2. My grandmother and aunt will drive to New Mexico and visit Santa Fe.
2. *grandmother, aunt will drive,* [*will*] *visit*

    3. Show me the map.
    3. (*you*) *show*

1. Jackets and ties are required in the dining room.
2. Are there bears living in these woods?
3. There are five new students in our class this semester.
4. Bring both a pencil and a pen to the exam on Thursday.
5. Frank neither sings nor plays an instrument.
6. Where do you and Liz buy your cassettes?
7. Both of the math problems were difficult.
8. Play ball!
9. There is much wisdom in folk sayings and proverbs.
10. Is one of the kittens sick?

REVIEW EXERCISE B. **Identifying Subjects and Verbs.** Number your paper 1–10. After the proper number, write the subject and verb of each sentence. If the subject is understood, write (*you*). Remember to write all the parts of a compound subject or compound verb. Underline the subject once and the verb twice.

1. Only birds, bats, and insects can fly.
2. Other animals can move through the air without flying.
3. The flying fish swims fast and then leaps out of the water.
4. How does the flying squirrel glide from tree to tree?
5. There are flaps of skin between its legs.
6. Why can birds fly?
7. Their wings lift and push them through the air.
8. Look carefully at an insect's wings.
9. Most have two sets of wings.
10. The pair in front covers the pair in back.

WRITING APPLICATION A:
Adding New Interest to Your Writing by Placing Subjects in Different Positions

Have you ever had a chore that was really boring? Perhaps you feel that way about cleaning your room or taking out the trash or even doing homework. One of the ways people sometimes approach tedious tasks is by doing them in a different way. Variety can add new interest.

Listening to music while you clean up your room can make the task seem more pleasant. Similarly, you can make your writing less tedious and more interesting by selecting different positions for the subjects of your sentences.

EXAMPLES   1. Awakened by a strange noise, *I* was instantly alert.
2. Waking up in the night, *I* heard an unfamiliar noise.
3. From far down the hall came a strange, unfamiliar *noise*.
4. Suddenly, *I* heard a strange noise.
5. Although soft and low, the strange *noise* was frightening.

Writing Assignment

Think back to an incident in your life that taught you something important. It may have been a time when you learned the value of friendship, when you realized the importance of honesty, when you recognized that you are responsible for the consequences of your actions, or when you suddenly understood how much a relative meant to you. Write a paragraph describing that incident in detail. Read what you have written; see if you can make it less tedious and more interesting. In at least three sentences, try to place the subject somewhere other than first. Underline the subject each time you do this.

FRAGMENTS

You have learned that a sentence contains a verb and its subject. However, not all groups of words containing a subject and a verb are sentences. Some do not express a complete thought. For example, *Because she concentrates* contains a verb and its subject—the verb is *concentrates,* and the subject is *she.* Yet the group of words is not a sentence because it does not express a complete thought. It suggests that more is to be said. It is a fragment, a part of a longer sentence.

She does well in tennis because she concentrates.

Now you have a sentence. The thought has been completed.

EXERCISE 9. Identifying Sentences and Fragments.   Number your paper 1–20. If a word group is a sentence, write an *S* beside the proper number on your paper. If it is not a sentence, write an *F* for fragment. Ask yourself whether the group of words has a verb and a subject and whether it expresses a complete thought.

1. Willa Cather was born in Back Creek Valley, in northern Virginia
2. In 1883, when she was ten years old
3. Her family moved to the treeless prairie of Nebraska
4. Fascinated by the wild and rolling plains
5. She tracked buffalo and collected prairie flowers
6. Listened to the stories of neighboring settlers
7. They told memorable tales about the harsh struggles of the homesteaders
8. In her first novel, *O Pioneers!*
9. She describes how farmers turned the unruly plains into neat fields of wheat and corn
10. After high school in the village of Red Cloud, Nebraska
11. She attended the recently established University of Nebraska in Lincoln
12. Although she was first interested in science
13. She discovered her talent for writing
14. Stories and reviews by Willa Cather soon appeared in the local newspapers of Lincoln
15. At first, her writing was relatively unnoticed
16. She worked for several years as a schoolteacher and then as a magazine editor in New York City
17. Although she relished the glamour of New York
18. She never lost touch with the sights and sounds of her childhood in the Midwest
19. *My Ántonia* describes Nebraska's open spaces as well as its grueling challenges
20. In this novel a boy grows up and leaves the Midwest yet holds a deep reverence for his past

THE SENTENCE BASE

Every sentence has a base. It is the part upon which all other parts rest. The sentence base is usually composed of two parts, the subject and the verb.

EXAMPLES A gaggle of geese flew overhead. [base: *gaggle flew*]
The animals in the barnyard have been fed. [base: *animals have been fed*]

In these examples, the sentence base consists of only a subject and a verb. In many sentences, however, something else is required in the predicate to complete the meaning of the subject and verb. This third element is a *complement* (a "completer").

COMPLEMENTS

2h. A *complement* is a word or group of words that completes the meaning begun by the subject and verb.

The following example will show you how the complement does this.

```
  S      V           C
Snow covered the hillside.
```

"Snow covered" would not be a complete statement by itself, even though it contains a subject and a verb. "Snow covered *what?*" a reader would ask. The word *hillside* completes the meaning of the sentence by telling *what* the snow covered. Study the following sentences, in which subjects, verbs, and complements are labeled. Name the part of speech of each complement.

```
         S      V           C   PN
Mrs. Smith is our new mayor.
     S    V.         C
She seems quite effective.
         S                     V          C
The student in the front row asked a tough question.
      S   V      C    PN
That book is an autobiography.
        S      V    C   DO
Mark Twain wrote novels about his boyhood.
         S      S  V          C   A
Both Eric and Bob felt rather gloomy.
```

EXERCISE 10. Writing Sentences with Subjects, Verbs, and Complements.
Construct sentences from the following sentence bases. Do not be satisfied with adding only one or two words. Make interesting sentences.

SUBJECT	VERB	COMPLEMENT
1. cyclists	planned	trip
2. musicians	performed	duet
3. speaker	looked	enthusiastic
4. problem	was identified	

5. infants	seemed	content
6. novel	is	suspenseful
7. engine	sputtered	
8. coats	were	heavy
9. celebrities	donated	money
10. town	is sponsoring	carnival

> ☞ **NOTE** Like the subject of a sentence, a complement is never part of a prepositional phrase.

I intercepted **one** of the passes. [The complement is *one*, not *passes; passes* is part of a prepositional phrase.]

An adverb modifying a verb is not a complement. Complements may be nouns, pronouns, or adjectives.

Lucy plays **hard**. [*Hard,* an adverb, is not a complement.]
These pears are **hard**. [*Hard,* an adjective, is a complement.]

EXERCISE 11. Identifying Subjects, Verbs, and Complements.

Number your paper 1–20. For each of the following sentences, write the subject and the verb. If there is a complement, write it after the verb. Arrange your answer in the labeled columns: *Subject, Verb, Complement.*

1. A hurricane is actually a tropical cyclone.
2. These large, revolving storms are accompanied by destructive winds.
3. The rains of a hurricane are almost always heavy.
4. A hurricane has no fronts but has a strange central area.
5. This area is the eye of the hurricane.
6. Here there is neither wind nor rain.
7. Around the eye, however, the winds whirl violently.
8. All hurricanes originate on the western sides of the ocean, in the doldrums.
9. A hurricane moves slowly through the tropics and speeds up only in the middle latitudes.
10. The tracks of most hurricanes are shaped like parabolas.
11. Most hurricanes blow themselves out to sea and vanish.
12. Some, however, leave the normal hurricane path and continue toward the coast.

13. Such storms usually lose some of their intensity but may still be violent and destructive.
14. Most hurricane damage is the result of gigantic waves.
15. These waves are generated along coastal areas and are sometimes accompanied by high tides.
16. The famous Galveston hurricane in 1900 took the lives of thousands of people.
17. Many of them were drowned by giant waves.
18. In 1960 a hurricane struck the Atlantic Coast and destroyed property worth billions of dollars.
19. Fierce winds and flooding caused devastation.
20. Today satellites discover hurricanes and other storms and provide weather forecasters with advance information about the severity of an approaching storm.

The Subject Complement

2i. A *subject complement* is a noun, pronoun, or adjective that follows a linking verb. It identifies, describes, or explains the subject.

EXAMPLES Jerry is a soccer **player.**
Susan seems **confident.**

In the first example, *player* identifies the subject, *Jerry.* In the second, *confident* describes the subject, *Susan.*

There are two kinds of subject complements. If the subject complement is a noun or a pronoun, it is a *predicate nominative.* If it is an adjective, it is a *predicate adjective.*

—Predicate nominatives (nouns and pronouns) explain the subject or give another name for the subject. Predicate adjectives describe the subject. Both predicate nominatives and predicate adjectives are linked to the subject by linking verbs. The common linking verbs are *be, become, feel, smell, taste, look, grow, seem, appear, remain, sound, stay.*[1]

EXAMPLES The caterpillar becomes a **butterfly.** [predicate nominative]
The rug looks **green**, but it is actually **blue.** [predicate adjectives]

[1] The forms of *be* are *am, is, are, was, were,* and verb phrases ending in *be* or *been,* such as *can be* and *has been.*

EXERCISE 12. Identifying Subject Complements as Predicate Nominatives or Predicate Adjectives.   Number your paper 1–10. Select the subject complement from each of the following sentences, and write it after the corresponding number on your paper. (First find the verb and its subject, then the complement.) After each complement, write what kind it is: predicate nominative or predicate adjective.

1. The last scene of the play is very tense.
2. The two small birds are finches.
3. The music sounded lively.
4. This costume looks elegant.
5. My goldfish is growing larger every day.
6. Andrea's report on digital recording is a detailed one.
7. The setting of the story is an old castle.
8. Your solution to this algebra problem is clever.
9. We felt full after our huge dinner.
10. His entire story seems almost unbelievable.

Distinguishing Between Subject and Complement

When the subject is not in the normal position before the verb, it is sometimes hard to tell the subject from the complement. When the word order is normal, there is no problem—the subject comes before the verb and the subject complement comes after:

     S   V   C
Martin Luther King, Jr., is a national hero.

When the word order is reversed, as in questions, the subject still comes before the subject complement in most cases:

V   S   C
Was he a recipient of the Nobel Peace Prize?

Sometimes, however, a writer or speaker may put the subject complement first for emphasis.

      C   V   S
How elusive is victory!
         C   S   V
What a fine speaker Rev. King was!

When this happens, you must consider which word is more likely to be the subject of the sentence. Usually the subject will be the word that specifically identifies the person or thing that the sentence is about. The first example above presents little difficulty because *elusive* is an adjective and cannot be the subject. In the second example, however, both the subject complement (*speaker*) and the subject (*Rev. King*) are nouns. In this case you must ask yourself which noun more specifically identifies the subject. *Rev. King* has a more specific meaning than *speaker;* consequently, it is a more likely subject for the sentence.

EXERCISE 13. Identifying Subjects, Verbs, and Subject Complements. Write the following sentences, and pick out the subject, the verb, and the subject complement. Label the subject of the sentence *S,* the verb *V,* and the subject complement *C.*

1. Are those girls your cousins?
2. How friendly everyone seems!
3. Ginger is a superb athlete.
4. "A Rose for Emily" is a haunting story.
5. How bright the stars seem tonight.
6. What a fine cook your father is!
7. When does a house become a home?
8. Our dog is usually friendly.
9. Clara Maass was a nurse of extraordinary dedication.
10. Life is a precious gift.

Direct Objects and Indirect Objects

There is another kind of complement that does not refer to the subject. Instead, it receives the action of the verb or shows the result of the action.

EXAMPLE The receptionist answered the **phone.** [base: *receptionist answered phone*]

In sentences of this kind, the complement is called the *direct object.*

2j. The *direct object* is a word or group of words that directly receives the action expressed by the verb or shows the result of the action. It answers the question *What?* or *Whom?* after an action verb.

$$\overset{\text{S}}{}\quad\overset{\text{V}}{}\quad\overset{\text{DO}}{}$$

EXAMPLES The mechanic fixed our car.

$$\overset{\text{S}}{}\quad\overset{\text{V}}{}\quad\overset{\text{DO}}{}$$

She replaced the broken muffler.

In the first example, *car* is the direct object. It directly receives the action expressed by the verb. It answers the question *What?* after the verb. Fixed what? Fixed *car*. In the second sentence, *muffler* is the direct object. Replaced what? Replaced *muffler*.

Objects are used after action verbs only. Verbs like *study, dream, understand,* which express mental action, are just as much action verbs as are verbs that express physical action: *push, leap, stumble*.

EXERCISE 14. Identifying Verbs and Their Direct Objects.

Number your paper 1–10. After the proper number, write the direct objects in the following sentences. Be able to name the verb whose action the object receives. *Caution:* Like all complements, the object of a verb is never part of a prepositional phrase.

1. I borrowed my parents' new camera recently.
2. First I loaded the film into the camera.
3. Then I set the opening of the shutter.
4. I focused the camera on a distant object.
5. I could read the shutter speed in the viewfinder.
6. A flashing red light means an incorrect setting.
7. Slowly and carefully I pressed the button.
8. I then moved the film forward for the next shot.
9. By the end of the day, I had snapped thirty-six pictures.
10. Unfortunately, the film processor lost my roll of film.

2k. An *indirect object* is a noun or pronoun in the predicate that precedes the direct object. It tells *to whom* or *for whom* the action of the verb is done.

EXAMPLES The teacher read the assignment.
The teacher read **us** the assignment.

In both examples you should recognize *assignment* as the direct object. Read what? Read *assignment*. In the second example, however, another word also receives the action of the verb *read*. The word *us*, which comes before the direct object, tells *to whom* the assignment was read. It is an indirect object.

What is the indirect object in this sentence?

The chef showed the diners the new kitchen.

Kitchen is the direct object. *Diners* is the indirect object. It is the diners *to whom* the kitchen was shown.

If the words *to* or *for* are used in the sentence itself, the word following them is part of a prepositional phrase and not an indirect object. Compare the following pairs.

Jeff served me fresh vegetables. [indirect object: *me*]
Jeff served fresh vegetables to me. [no indirect object]
We bought my family several souvenirs. [indirect object: *family*]
We bought several souvenirs for my family. [no indirect object]

Caution: When identifying complements, do not be confused by adverbs in the predicate.

They turned **right.** [*Right* is an adverb telling *where*.]
You have the **right** to remain silent. [*Right* is a noun used as a direct object.]

Compound Complements

Complements may be compound.

EXAMPLES   The names of our cats are **Jezebel** and **Koomba.** [compound predicate nominative]
The alley is **long** and **narrow.** [compound predicate adjective]
We used paper **plates** and **napkins.** [compound direct object]
The trip had given my **sister** and **me** the best vacation ever. [compound indirect object]

EXERCISE 15. Identifying Direct and Indirect Objects. Number your paper 1–10. After the proper number, write the objects in each sentence. Write *i.o.* after an indirect object and *d.o.* after a direct object. Not all sentences contain both kinds of objects.

1. Last spring Steve told us his plans for the Olympics.
2. He wants a place on the swim team.
3. This goal demands hours of hard practice.
4. We all gave Steve encouragement and support.
5. Steve showed us the practice pool in the college gym.
6. Every day Steve swims a hundred laps in the pool.
7. His coach teaches him the fine points of swimming.
8. Such intense training has cost Steve a social life.
9. A rigorous schedule leaves an athlete little time to spend with friends.
10. Nevertheless, Steve wants that gold medal.

EXERCISE 16. Writing Sentences. Write one sentence containing a compound subject, one containing a compound verb, two containing a compound predicate nominative, two containing a compound predicate adjective, two containing a compound direct object, and two containing a compound indirect object.

REVIEW EXERCISE C. Identifying Sentences and Fragments; Identifying Complements. Number your paper 1–10. If one of the following word groups is not a complete sentence, write *F* (for *fragment*) after the proper number. If a word group is a complete sentence, write it after the proper number and underline the subject once and the verb twice. If a sentence has a complement, identify the complement, using these abbreviations: *p.a.* (predicate adjective), *p.n.* (predicate nominative), *d.o.* (direct object), *i.o.* (indirect object). If a sentence has compound parts, label all the words that belong to each part. Remember to insert correct end punctuation.

1. Has the committee announced the date of the school carnival
2. Perhaps next week
3. Linda gave us a summary of her science project
4. It was long and interesting
5. Although it was well written
6. Books and papers covered the desk and spilled onto the floor
7. One of those dogs is obedience-trained
8. Helen gave the children a box of oatmeal cookies
9. Kim, Juan, and Tracey were winners at the track meet
10. How happy they were

SENTENCES CLASSIFIED BY PURPOSE

2l. Sentences may be classified according to their purpose.

There are four kinds of sentences: (1) declarative, (2) imperative, (3) interrogative, and (4) exclamatory.

(1) A sentence that makes a statement is a *declarative* sentence.

Its purpose is to declare something. Most of the sentences you use are declarative.

EXAMPLES As a matter of fact, this yard needs more shade trees.
An oak would thrive in the west corner.

(2) A sentence that gives a command or makes a request is an *imperative* **sentence.**

EXAMPLES   Pass the salt, please.
Speak softly.

(3) A sentence that asks a question is an *interrogative* **sentence.**

An interrogative sentence is followed by a question mark.

EXAMPLES   Can you speak Spanish?
What did you say?

(4) A sentence that expresses strong feeling is an *exclamatory* **sentence.**

An exclamatory sentence is followed by an exclamation point.

EXAMPLES   What a beautiful day this is!
How we love cool, sunny weather!

Caution: A declarative, an imperative, or an interrogative sentence may be spoken in such a way that it is exclamatory. In this case it should be followed by an exclamation point.

EXAMPLE   This is inexcusable! [Declarative becomes exclamatory.]
Stop the car! [Imperative becomes exclamatory.]
How could you say that! [Interrogative becomes exclamatory.]

EXERCISE 17. Classifying Sentences as Declarative, Imperative, Interrogative, or Exclamatory.   Classify the sentences below according to whether they are declarative, imperative, interrogative, or exclamatory. Write the proper classification after the number of each sentence.

1. The loudspeakers in our living room are small yet powerful.
2. Turn down the sound!
3. Is that music or noise, Shirley?
4. Listening to loud music every day can damage one's hearing.
5. How many watts does your amplifier produce?
6. Sound levels are measured in units called decibels.
7. Do you know that an increase of ten decibels represents a doubling in the sound level?
8. Do not blast your sound system.
9. Keep it quiet!
10. Music played softly is relaxing.

WRITING APPLICATION B:
Catching a Reader's Interest with Appropriately Varied Sentences

When a fisherman sees another boat full of fish, one of the first questions he wants to ask is, "What are you using for bait?" In order to catch your reader's interest, you should also use the right bait. Your opening sentence contains this bait. Select the most appropriate opening sentence.

EXAMPLES   1. I don't need eight hours' sleep every night (declarative)
2. Be sure to get eight hours' sleep every night. (imperative)
3. Do all people need eight hours' sleep every night? (interrogative)
4. How silly to think that all people need the same amount of sleep! (exclamatory)

Writing Assignment

Sometimes it is fun to disagree with something that other people have always seemed to accept without question. Select one of the following topics or think of one of your own. Write four different opening sentences for your topic, one of each classification (declarative, imperative, interrogative, and exclamatory). Then select the one that is the best "bait" for your ideas. Write the paragraph.

Ideas: 1. Don't walk in the rain.
2. Don't talk back.
3. Keep your elbows off the table.

DIAGRAMING SENTENCES

The first thing to do in making a diagram is to draw a horizontal line on your paper. On this horizontal line you will write the sentence base. In approximately the center of the line you will draw a short vertical line cutting the horizontal one. This vertical line is the dividing point between the complete subject and the complete predicate. The subject and all words relating to it (complete subject) go to the *left* of this vertical line; the verb and all words relating to it (the complete predicate) go to the *right*.

Diagraming the Subject and Verb

The subject of the sentence is written on the horizontal line to the left of the vertical line. The verb is written to the right of the vertical line.

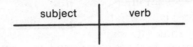

For an understood subject, write the word *you* in parentheses as the subject in your diagram.

EXAMPLE Answer the phone.

Diagraming Modifiers

Modifiers of the subject and verb (adjectives and adverbs) are written on slanting lines beneath the subject or the verb.

EXAMPLE **The blue** car **quickly** swerved **left.**

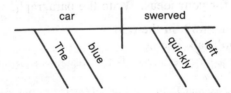

Diagraming Compound Subjects and Compound Verbs

If the subject is compound, diagram it as in the following example. Notice the position of the coordinating conjunction on the broken line.

EXAMPLE **Maria** and **Patsy** are hiking.

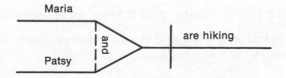

If the verb is compound, diagram it this way:

EXAMPLE   Roger **swims** and **dives.**

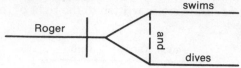

If the sentence has both a compound subject and a compound predicate, diagram it this way:

EXAMPLE   **She** and **I dance** and **sing.**

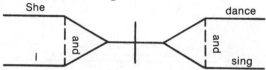

Notice how a compound verb is diagramed when the helping verb is not repeated.

EXAMPLE   Sally **was reading** and **studying.**

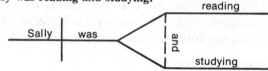

Since *was* is the helping verb for both *reading* and *studying*, it is placed on the horizontal line, and the conjunction *and* joins the main verbs *reading* and *studying*.

When the parts of a compound subject or a compound predicate are joined by correlative conjunctions, diagram the sentence this way:

EXAMPLE   **Both** Nancy **and** Beth will **not only** perform **but also** teach.

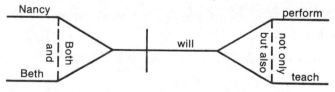

Diagraming *Here, There,* and *Where* as Modifiers

When the words *here, there,* and *where* are modifiers of the verb, diagram them in the following way:

EXAMPLE **Here** come the astronauts!

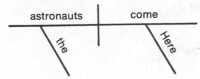

EXAMPLE **There** goes the shuttle!

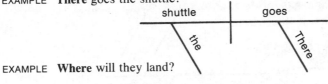

EXAMPLE **Where** will they land?

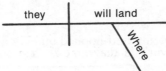

Diagraming *There* When It Is Not a Modifier

When *there* begins a sentence but does not modify either the verb or the subject, it is diagramed on a line by itself, as in the following example. When used in this way, *there* is called an *expletive*.

EXAMPLE **There** are seven astronauts.

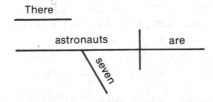

Diagraming a Modifier of a Modifier

A word that modifies another modifier is diagramed like this:

EXAMPLE They performed **exceptionally** well.

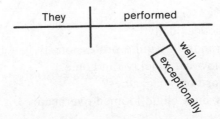

EXERCISE 18. Diagraming Sentences. Diagram the following sentences. Diagrams of the first five are provided for you to copy and fill in.

1. Clouds move very swiftly.

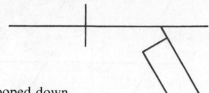

2. A hawk swooped down.

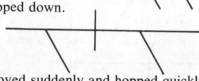

3. The rabbit moved suddenly and hopped quickly away.

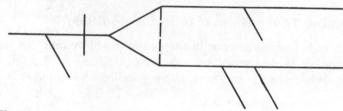

4. There was a sudden noise.

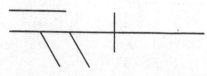

5. Never drive too fast.

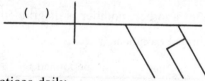

6. The choir practices daily.
7. The new sopranos sing quite professionally.
8. The large yellow cat quickly ran home.
9. Where are those old magazines?
10. An ominously dark cloud loomed overhead.

11. Jack usually sits there.
12. The winner jogged along easily.
13. There were no floods here.
14. Our elm tree was blown down.
15. He leaned forward and looked sideways.
16. Where will they play tomorrow?
17. Does the express train still stop here?
18. Run ahead!
19. Karen not only sings well but also dances beautifully.
20. This car and that truck were designed and built here.

Diagraming the Predicate Nominative and the Predicate Adjective

A subject complement (predicate nominative or predicate adjective) should be placed on the same horizontal line with the simple subject and the verb. It comes after the verb, and a line drawn upward from the horizontal line and slanting toward the subject separates it from the verb. The line slants toward the subject to show that the subject complement is closely related to the subject.

PREDICATE NOMINATIVE Some dogs are good **companions**.

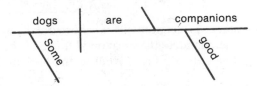

PREDICATE ADJECTIVE That dog is **friendly**.

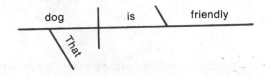

EXERCISE 19. Diagraming Sentences with Predicate Nominatives and Predicate Adjectives. Diagram the following sentences.

1. Some old books are very valuable.
2. Does the recording sound scratchy?
3. That might have been her fastest race.

4. Hockey is my favorite sport.
5. Most cats are seldom affectionate.
6. Are you our new teacher?
7. Drivers should be more careful.
8. Charles has grown careless lately.
9. This sweater is too large.
10. Beggars can not be choosers.

Diagraming the Direct Object and the Indirect Object

The direct object is diagramed in almost the same way as the predicate nominative. The only difference is that the line separating the object from the verb is vertical (not slanting).

EXAMPLE Cathy led the **band.**

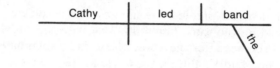

EXAMPLE We heard **boos** and **hisses.**

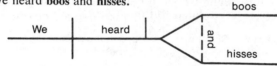

The indirect object is diagramed on a horizontal line beneath the verb. A slanting line connects the horizontal line and the verb. Notice how the slanting line extends slightly below the horizontal line.

EXAMPLE They gave **her** a present.

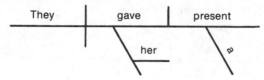

EXERCISE 20. Diagraming Sentences with Complements. Diagram the following sentences.

1. The sky was blue and cloudless.
2. The sunlight seemed unusually harsh.
3. The intense heat wilted the roses.
4. My neighbors and I always plant a vegetable garden.
5. My coach patiently taught me a new stunt.

REVIEW EXERCISE D. Understanding the Parts of a Sentence.
Number your paper 1–10. In your own words, give a definition of each
of the following, and make up an example to illustrate it.

1. A sentence
2. A complete subject
3. A complete predicate
4. A subject (simple)
5. A subject complement

6. A verb (simple predicate)
7. A verb phrase
8. A direct object
9. An understood subject
10. An indirect object

REVIEW EXERCISE E. Identifying Subjects and Verbs. Number
your paper 1–10. Select from each of the following sentences the
subject and the verb, and write them after the proper number on your
paper. Be especially careful to include all parts of a verb phrase.

1. How would you like this canoe?
2. There will be a few rapids along the way.
3. Each rapid has been mapped and measured by the guides.
4. Are there many of these trips each year?
5. We have often seen dozens of canoes at this campsite.
6. A friendly guide smiled at us and then pointed out an easy stretch
   of the river.
7. Every successful trip is accomplished by a team effort.
8. Never stand up in a canoe or turn suddenly.
9. With one sweep of the paddle, you can easily turn the canoe left
   or right.
10. Where can we rent a lightweight aluminum canoe?

**REVIEW EXERCISE F. Identifying Subjects, Verbs, and Comple-
ments.** Number your paper 1–25. After the proper number, write the
italicized word or word group in the following paragraphs. Correctly
identify each, using these abbreviations: *s.* (subject); *v.* (verb); *p.a.*
(predicate adjective); *p.n.* (predicate nominative); *d.o.* (direct object);
i.o. (indirect object).

The (1) *pyramids* of Egypt certainly are a wonder. How could an
ancient (2) *race,* even with 100,000 workers, build such enormous
(3) *monuments*? Almost every visitor (4) *makes* a trip out into the
desert to see the massive tombs. They appear (5) *majestic* from a
distance. The Great Pyramid of Khufu is (6) *one* of the wonders of
the ancient world. (7) *It* was once encased with blocks of polished
limestone. However, weather and thievery (8) *have combined* to de-

stroy its original casing. The pyramids (9) *look* (10) *weather-beaten*. Still, they are impressive (11) *sights*.

Invading Arabs about A.D. 650 needed (12) *stone* for the palaces and mosques in Cairo. Naturally it was (13) *easier* for them to obtain blocks of stone from the pyramids than to cut new ones from the quarries. They removed the outer limestone blocks. Unfortunately, the two-ton (14) *blocks* at the bases of the pyramids were too (15) *heavy*. The task became (16) *impossible*. There was no way of leveling the pyramids to the ground.

One Arab ruler decided to rob the tomb of Khufu. With hundreds of workers at his disposal, he gave the (17) *men* his (18) *instructions*. The workers hacked through the solid blocks of granite. The stone was (19) *hard*. By accident, they suddenly broke into a tunnel. Imagine the (20) *excitement*! All too soon they (21) *discovered* an enormous (22) *plug* of granite blocking their way. They cut around the passage plug and soon reached the inner (23) *chamber*.

Strangely enough, there was no (24) *gold*. No vast treasures (25) *sparkled* under the light of the torches. The tomb had probably been robbed many centuries earlier by Egyptians familiar with its secret entrances.

CHAPTER 2 REVIEW: POSTTEST 1

A. Identifying Subjects, Verbs, and Complements. Number your paper 1–15. After the proper number, write the italicized word or word group in the following sentences. Correctly identify each, using these abbreviations: *s.* (subject); *v.* (verb); *p.a.* (predicate adjective); *p.n.* (predicate nominative); *d.o.* (direct object); *i.o.* (indirect object).

1. Have *you* ever met a robot?
2. In the field of robotics, scientists have built vastly improved *robots*.
3. Today these machines *have been put* to work in factories, laboratories, and outer space.
4. How were these complex *machines* first used?
5. There are a *number* of interesting early examples of robots at work.
6. One of the first robots was a mechanical *figure* in a clock tower.

7. It raised a hammer and struck a *bell* every hour.
8. At the 1939 New York World's Fair, Sparko and Elektro were popular *attractions*.
9. Elektro was *tall,* more than seven feet high.
10. Electric motors gave *Elektro* power for a variety of amazing tricks.
11. Sparko was Elektro's *dog*.
12. Sparko *could bark* and even *wag* his tail.
13. Today *some* of the simplest robots are drones in research laboratories.
14. Basically, they are *extensions* of the human arm.
15. They can be *useful* in many different ways.

B. Classifying Sentences as Declarative, Interrogative, Imperative, or Exclamatory. Number your paper 16–25. After the proper number, classify each of the following sentences as declarative, interrogative, imperative, or exclamatory. After each classification, write the proper end punctuation in parentheses.

16. Can you picture a robot twenty-five feet tall
17. Step up and say hello to Beetle
18. CAM is another, even more advanced robot
19. Perhaps you have already heard of CAM
20. It can travel on long legs across rough terrain as rapidly as thirty-five miles an hour
21. How like a science-fiction creature it looks
22. Has CAM ever walked on the moon
23. A smaller version of this vehicle is used as a walking wheelchair for the physically disabled
24. Who are the most famous robots
25. R2-D2 and C-3PO are known to *Star Wars* buffs around the world

---

CHAPTER 2 REVIEW: POSTTEST 2

Identifying Subjects, Verbs, and Complements. Number your paper 1–25. After the proper number, write the italicized word or word group in the following paragraphs. Correctly identify each, using these abbreviations: *s.* (subject); *v.* (verb); *p.a.* (predicate adjective); *p.n.* (predicate nominative); *d.o.* (direct object); *i.o.* (indirect object).

Since 1960 the Special Olympics Games (1) *have been held* the same year as the Olympic Games. From all over the world (2) *athletes* come to compete in these Special Olympics. Are (3) *you* (4) *aware* of the history of these games? Games for the disabled (5) *began* after World War II. Their (6) *purpose* was the (7) *rehabilitation* of soldiers with war injuries. They demonstrated the (8) *abilities* of disabled athletes. Now disabled men, women, and children (9) *can participate* in almost every sport. (10) *One* of the requirements for participation (11) *is* previous (12) *competition*. An athlete (13) *must win* at city, state, and national levels.

(14) *Scott Roveson* and (15) *Nina Bey* are Special Olympics (16) *swimmers.* (17) *Both* have won gold medals. Bob Tusa has set a world discus (18) *record*. He developed a (19) *technique* for throwing from a sitting position. With only one leg, (20) *Mike Maker* won a gold medal in gymnastics.

(21) *Competition* in the Special Olympics demands skill and drive. Athletes (22) *must be* at the top of their form. People in the sports world give (23) *them* great (24) *respect* and serious (25) *attention*.

CHAPTER 2 REVIEW: POSTTEST 3

Writing Sentences. Write sentences according to the following guidelines. Underline the subject once and verb twice in each sentence. If the subject is understood write (*You*).

1. a declarative sentence with a verb phrase
2. a sentence beginning with *There*
3. an interrogative sentence
4. an exclamatory sentence
5. an imperative sentence
6. a sentence with a compound subject
7. a sentence with a predicate nominative
8. a sentence with a compound direct object and an indirect object
9. a sentence with a predicate adjective
10. a sentence with a compound verb

CHAPTER 3

The Phrase

PREPOSITIONAL, VERBAL, APPOSITIVE PHRASES

DIAGNOSTIC TEST

Classifying Phrases.   Number your paper 1–20. After the proper number, write each italicized phrase in the following sentences and indicate what kind of phrase it is. Use the abbreviations *prep.* (prepositional phrase), *part.* (participial phrase), *ger.* (gerund phrase), *inf.* (infinitive phrase), and *app.* (appositive phrase). Do not identify a prepositional phrase that is part of a larger phrase.

EXAMPLE   1. The sundial was one of the first instruments for *telling time*.
      1. *telling time, ger.*

1. *Regarded chiefly as garden ornaments,* sundials are still used in many areas *to tell time*.
2. The shadow-casting object *on a sundial* is called a gnomon.
3. Forerunners of the sundial include poles or upright stones *used as gnomons by early humans*.
4. *Setting the gnomon directly parallel to the earth's areas of rotation* greatly improved the accuracy of the sundial.
5. The development of trigonometry permitted more precise calculations for *constructing sundials*.
6. A sundial is not difficult *to make with simple materials*.
7. First find a stick *to use as a gnomon*.
8. *At high noon,* put the stick *in the ground*.

9. It is important *to tilt the stick slightly northward.*
10. *To mark the first hour,* place a pebble at the tip of the shadow made by the stick.
11. An hour later put another pebble at the tip *of the shadow.*
12. Continue this process *throughout the afternoon.*
13. *Starting the next morning,* repeat the hourly process.
14. Be sure *to place the last pebble at high noon.*
15. *Observing the completed sundial,* you will note that the pebbles are not equidistant.
16. The unevenly spaced markers, *a characteristic of the sundial,* demonstrate that shadows move faster in the morning and the evening than at noon.
17. For everyday use, *owning a watch* has obvious advantages over *using a sundial.*
18. However, sundials were long employed for *setting and checking watches.*
19. The heliochronometer, *a sundial of great accuracy,* was used until 1900 *to set the watches of French railway workers.*
20. The difference *between solar time and clock time* is correlated by the use of tables *showing daily variations in sun time.*

You already know that a group of words used as a verb is a verb phrase. In a verb phrase, one or more helping verbs and a verb are used together as one verb: *have been writing, is writing, will be writing.* Similarly, other groups of related words are sometimes used as a single part of speech. Such phrases may be used as adjectives, as adverbs, or as nouns.

3a. A *phrase* is a group of related words that is used as a single part of speech and does not contain a verb and its subject.

In the first of each of the following pairs of examples, a single word is boldfaced. In the second part of each pair, a group of words that performs exactly the same function in the sentence appears in boldfaced type. These word groups are *phrases.*

> Carbon monoxide is an **odorless,** very toxic gas. [adjective]
> Carbon monoxide is a very toxic gas **without an odor.** [adjective phrase]
>
> Why not plant the rosebushes **here**? [adverb]
> Why not plant the rosebushes **near the fence**? [adverb phrase]

The phrases in the examples above are *prepositional phrases*. You have already learned something about this kind of phrase. In this chapter you will study prepositional phrases in greater detail, and you will also explore verbal phrases and appositive phrases.

PREPOSITIONAL PHRASES

3b. A *prepositional phrase* is a group of words beginning with a preposition and usually ending with a noun or pronoun.

The prepositional phrases are boldfaced in the following examples:

They were standing **near the door.**
The woman **with the helmet** is a motorcyclist.
The cashier gave the change **to me.**

The preposition in the last example is *to*. Do not confuse this common preposition with the *to* that is the sign of the infinitive form of a verb: *to watch, to learn, to drive.*

3c. The noun or pronoun that ends the prepositional phrase is the *object* of the preposition that begins the phrase.

PHRASE	PREPOSITION	OBJECT
beyond the steep hill	beyond	hill
before the second stoplight	before	stoplight
along the highway	along	highway
in the garage	in	garage
from him	from	him

A preposition may, of course, have a compound object:

near **forests** and **rivers**
despite the **rain, snow,** and **ice**

Prepositional phrases usually do the work of adjectives and adverbs in sentences.

Adjective Phrases

Prepositional phrases may be used to modify nouns or pronouns in much the same way as single-word adjectives.

EXAMPLES a **hopeful** sign   a sign **of hope**
          Israeli cousins   cousins **from Israel**

3d. A prepositional phrase that modifies a noun or pronoun is an *adjective phrase.*

The cottages **by the lake** are quite picturesque.

The families **on my block** are very friendly.

Two or more adjective phrases often modify the same noun:

The picture **of the candidate in today's paper** is not flattering.

An adjective phrase may also modify the object of another prepositional phrase:

The coconut palms in the park **near the bay** were planted a long time ago. [*Near the bay* modifies *park,* the object of the preposition *in.*]

EXERCISE 1. Identifying Adjective Phrases and the Words They Modify. Each of the following sentences contains two adjective phrases. Write them in order on your paper. After each phrase, write the noun it modifies.

EXAMPLE 1. Julius Caesar was one of the most popular generals in ancient Rome.
  1. *of the most popular generals—one; in ancient Rome—generals*

1. The roads of ancient Rome linked the far corners of the empire.
2. Large blocks of the hardest stone paved the surface of the major routes.
3. Close communication between provinces strengthened the position of the Roman rulers.
4. Caesar's interest in military roads showed his concern with communication.
5. Roman roads were one reason for the success of Caesar's military operations.

Adverb Phrases

3e. A prepositional phrase that modifies a verb, an adjective, or another adverb is an *adverb phrase.*

EXAMPLES The mole burrowed **under the lawn.** [The phrase modifies the verb *burrowed.*]

Althea Gibson was graceful **on the tennis court.** [The phrase modifies the adjective *graceful.*]

The party lasted long **into the evening.** [The phrase modifies the adverb *long.*]

Adverb phrases tell *when, where, why, how,* or *to what extent.*

EXAMPLES The town grew quiet **after the storm.** [*when*]
They peered **through the window.** [*where*]
Most street musicians play **for tips.** [*why*]
This summer we're going **by car.** [*how*]
She won the game **by two points.** [*to what extent*]

Unlike adjective phrases, which always follow the words they modify, adverb phrases can appear at various places in the sentence. More than one adverb phrase can modify the same word.

EXAMPLE **In the first inning** she pitched **with great control.** [The adverb phrases *In the first inning* and *with great control* both modify the verb *pitched.* The first adverb phrase tells *when,* and the second adverb phrase tells *how.*]

EXERCISE 2. Identifying Adverb Phrases and the Words They Modify.

Number your paper 1–10, and write the adverb phrases in the following sentences. After each phrase, write the word it modifies and the part of speech of that word.

1. Eerie sounds came from the abandoned house.
2. Are some old houses haunted by ghosts?
3. On a moonlit night, my parents and I searched throughout the unused house.
4. We weren't afraid of any ghosts.
5. In the cellar we found two alley cats.
6. The strange noises were made by these animals.
7. We carefully placed the cats in a box.
8. They both seemed happy with their temporary home.
9. We walked up the steps, out the door, and across the lawn.
10. At a leisurely pace, we returned to our own house.

Diagraming Prepositional Phrases

The preposition that begins the prepositional phrase is placed on a slanting line leading down from the word the phrase modifies. The object of the preposition is placed on a horizontal line drawn from the slanting line. As with the indirect object, the slanting line extends slightly below the horizontal line.

EXAMPLE   The steep slopes **of the mountains** are covered **with forests.**

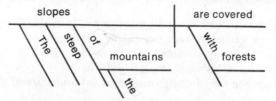

EXAMPLE   They sailed late **in the fall.** [adverb phrase modifying the adverb *late*]

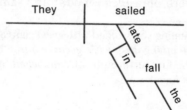

EXAMPLE   They were imprisoned **without food and water.**

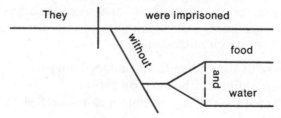

EXAMPLE   **Down the valley** and **over the plain** wanders the river.

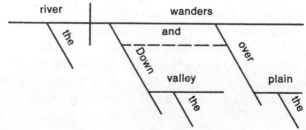

EXAMPLE The princess lived **in a castle on the mountain.**

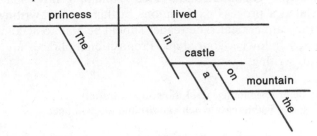

EXERCISE 3. Diagraming Sentences with Adjective and Adverb Phrases. Diagram the following sentences:

1. She paints portraits of young children.
2. The sailor steered through the channel and toward the ocean.
3. They waved to each passer-by on the road.
4. In Illinois during the fall, maple trees turn brilliant red.
5. The dunes on the coast of Australia are unbelievably high.

REVIEW EXERCISE A. Completing Sentences by Inserting Prepositional Phrases. Complete each sentence by inserting an appropriate prepositional phrase in each blank. Be able to tell whether it is an adjective or an adverb phrase.

EXAMPLE 1. —— Mrs. Bowen reads the newspaper.
      1. *In the evening Mrs. Bowen reads the newspaper.*

1. —— the children played hopscotch.
2. I saw a spider —— .
3. We planned a drive —— .
4. Her team played —— .
5. The sky divers jumped fearlessly —— .
6. Hundreds —— stared.
7. —— the cyclists unpacked their lunch.
8. There —— winds a narrow road.
9. This movie runs —— .
10. —— the dancers swayed with the music.

WRITING APPLICATION A:
Using Prepositional Phrases to Clarify Your Directions

Being able to explain something so that another person can understand is an important communication skill. Explaining how something is done is called a *process explanation.* In this kind of writing, details and accuracy are critical. The reader should be able to accomplish the same task by following your steps. Prepositional phrases are useful in this kind of writing.

EXAMPLES **Before beginning,** read the recipe carefully.
     Place **within easy reach** everything you will need.

Writing Assignment

Think of something you know how to do—how to change a tire, how to overcome stage fright—that might be a help to someone else. Write a paragraph explaining exactly how to accomplish this task. Use at least five prepositional phrases; underline these phrases.

REVIEW EXERCISE B. Completing Sentences by Inserting Adverb Phrases. Complete the following five sentences, adding adverb phrases according to the directions.

1. The sound engineer repaired the microphone ———. (Tell *how.*)
2. The microphone was needed ———. (Tell *why.*)
3. The task was completed ———. (Tell *when.*)
4. The repaired microphone was placed ———. (Tell *where.*)
5. The microphone worked ———. (Tell *how.*)

VERBALS AND VERBAL PHRASES[1]

Verbals are forms of a verb that are used not as verbs but as other parts of speech. Verbals act very much like verbs. They may be modified by adverbs and may have complements. Their chief function, however, is to act as other parts of speech: adjectives, nouns, adverbs.

There are three kinds of verbals: *participles, gerunds,* and *infinitives.*

---

[1] For work on verbal phrases as sentence fragments, see page 270. For verbals as dangling modifiers, see page 232.

The Participle

3f. A *participle* **is a verb form that can be used as an adjective. Since the participle can function as a verb or an adjective, it might be called a "verbal adjective."**

EXAMPLES   The **simmering** soup smelled delicious.
A **chipped** fingernail can be annoying.

In the first example, *simmering* is part verb because it carries the action of the verb *simmer*. It is part adjective because it modifies the noun *soup: simmering soup*. In the second example, *chipped* is part verb because it carries the action of the verb *chip*. It is part adjective because it modifies the noun *fingernail: chipped fingernail*. Because *simmering* and *chipped* are formed from verbs and used as adjectives, they are both participles.

There are two kinds of participles: *present* and *past*.

(1) *Present participles* **consist of the plain form of the verb plus** *–ing.*

EXAMPLES   The **smiling** graduates posed for the photographer.
Checking the weather forecast, the captain changed course.

In the first example, *smiling* (formed by adding *–ing* to the plain form of the verb *smile*) is a present participle modifying the noun *graduates*. In the second example, *checking* (formed by adding *–ing* to the plain form of the verb *check*) is a present participle modifying the noun *captain: checking captain*. In both examples, the present participles are verbals.

In addition to its use as a verbal, the present participle can be part of a verb phrase.

EXAMPLES   The graduates **were smiling.**
The captain **is checking** the weather forecast.

A present participle alone cannot be a verb. It can, however, be part of a verb phrase if it is preceded by a helping verb: *were smiling*. A participle in a verb phrase is part of the verb; it is not considered a separate adjective.

(2) *Past participles* **consist of the plain form of the verb plus** *-d* **or** *-ed.* **A few are formed irregularly.**[1]

[1] See the discussion of irregular verbs on pages 195–96.

EXAMPLES **Discovered** by the guard, the **startled** burglar was led away. [The past participles *discovered* and *startled* modify the noun *burglar*.]
Pleased by the capture, the guard continued her rounds. [The past participle *pleased* modifies the noun *guard*.]

Like a present participle, a past participle can also be part of a verb phrase.

EXAMPLES The burglar **was startled** when he **was discovered** by the guard.
The guard **was pleased** by the capture.

EXERCISE 4. Identifying Participles and the Words They Modify.
Number your paper 1–10. Write the participles used as adjectives in the following sentences. After each participle, write the noun or pronoun it modifies.

1. The potato, first cultivated in South America, is both nutritious and versatile.
2. The edible part of the potato, known as "a tuber," is the fleshy tip of its underground stem.
3. Discovered by the Spanish in Peru, the potato was introduced to Europe in the late 1550's.
4. Once worshipped by the Incas, this vegetable was initially scorned by Europeans.
5. Spreading rapidly, rumors about potatoes suggested that this new food could cause leprosy and rickets.
6. Confusing the potato with a plant called "deadly nightshade," many believed that potatoes were poisonous.
7. Potatoes, though, like many other vegetables belonging to the nightshade family, are not poisonous.
8. Providing an adult with half the daily requirement for vitamin C, the potato can be a significant source of nutrition.
9. Scientists, always searching for new sources of energy, report that we may soon be able to make fuel from potatoes.
10. Potatoes have become a more esteemed resource than the Spanish ever imagined.

EXERCISE 5. Revising Sentences by Using Participles.
Each of the following sentences is followed by a participle inside parentheses. Revise each sentence by inserting the participle next to the noun it modifies.

EXAMPLES 1. The candidate thanked each of her supporters. (*winning*)
          1. *The winning candidate thanked each of her supporters.*

          2. We collected funds for the restoration of the building. (*damaged*)
          2. *We collected funds for the restoration of the damaged building.*

1. The train was greeted loudly this afternoon. (*arriving*)
2. The committee selected three television shows for their educational value. (*nominating*)
3. My sister in the living room did not hear the doorbell. (*ringing*)
4. The carpenter was supposed to teach us how to fix this chair. (*broken*)
5. The Tasmanian wolf is a species seen rarely since 1930. (*endangered*)
6. The stream crosses the farmer's land at three places. (*winding*)
7. A message on the back of an envelope was handed to me. (*crumpled*)
8. The book included three interesting facts about dinosaurs. (*illustrated*)
9. A Douglas fir had become the haven for several small creatures. (*fallen*)
10. The plane narrowly missed a tall radio antenna. (*circling*)

EXERCISE 6. Identifying Participles and the Words They Modify.

Identify all the participles, both present and past, in the following sentences. Write them on your paper, and after each one, write the word that the participle modifies. Be careful not to confuse participles with the main verbs of the sentences.

1. Killer whales, long known as "wolves of the sea," have suffered from an undeserved notoriety.
2. Seeking to test the supposedly ferocious nature of the killer whale, scientists have studied its behavior.
3. After extensive study, scientists discovered that there is no documented case of an attack on a human by a killer whale.
4. Trainers, teaching killer whales to perform at amusement parks, learned that their charges were intelligent and gentle.
5. Congregating in Johnstone Strait, a narrow channel between Vancouver Island and mainland British Columbia in Canada, killer whales swim and mate all year round.

6. Choosing this spot to observe the mammals, researchers were able to identify over one hundred individual whales.
7. Noting the unique shape of each whale's dorsal fin, this team of scientists named each whale to keep more accurate records.
8. Impressed by the long life span of killer whales, scientists have estimated that males may live fifty years and females may survive a century.
9. Cruising in groups called pods, killer whales are highly social animals.
10. During the summer and fall in Johnstone Strait, many pods gather, splashing and playing in "superpods."

The Participial Phrase

A participle may be modified by an adverb or by a prepositional phrase used as an adverb, and it may have a complement. These related words combine with the participle to make a participial phrase.

3g. A *participial phrase* **consists of a participle and its related words, such as modifiers and complements, all of which act together as an adjective.**

The participial phrase in each of the following sentences is in boldfaced type. An arrow points to the noun or pronoun that the phrase modifies.

☞ **NOTE** Some participial phrases contain one or more prepositional phrases.

EXAMPLES **Climbing the tree,** the monkey soon disappeared into the topmost branches.

I heard him **whispering to his friend.**

We watched the storm **blowing eastward.**

Nominated unanimously by the delegates, the candidate thanked her supporters.

The concert **scheduled for tomorrow** has been postponed until next week.

EXERCISE 7. Identifying Participial Phrases and the Words They Modify. Each of the following sentences contains one or more participial phrases. Write each participial phrase, and after it write the noun or pronoun it modifies.

EXAMPLE 1. Hindered by bad weather, the British expedition lost the race to the South Pole, arriving a month after the Norwegians.
    1. *Hindered by bad weather—expedition*
    arriving a month after the Norwegians—expedition

1. Hoping to be the first to reach the South Pole, the British explorer Robert Scott, taking four men with him, began his final dash to the pole on January 4, 1912.
2. Leading Scott by sixty miles, however, a Norwegian expedition, commanded by Roald Amundsen, was moving swiftly.
3. Having learned about Amundsen, Scott realized a race was on.
4. Plagued by bad weather and bad luck, Scott fell farther behind.
5. Reaching the pole on January 17, the British found the Norwegians had already been there.
6. Weakened by scurvy, frostbite, and exhaustion, the five explorers, knowing they had little hope of survival, set out on the eight-hundred-mile journey to their base ship.
7. One member of the party, overcome by exhaustion and injuries, died before half the journey had been completed.
8. On March 15, another member, leaving the camp at night, walked deliberately to his death in a violent blizzard.
9. Eight months later, a rescue mission, sent to find out what had happened, found the bodies of Scott and his companions.
10. Today the ill-fated Scott expedition, acclaimed for its heroism, is better known than the successful Amundsen expedition.

WRITING APPLICATION B:
Using Participial Phrases for Clear, Vivid Writing

Participial phrases can make your writing more vivid. However, be sure to place the participial phrase close to the noun or pronoun it modifies. Otherwise the phrase might create confusion or, as in the following example, some unexpected amusement.

CONFUSING Waddling by the lake, we saw two ducks.

CLEAR We saw two ducks waddling by the lake.

Writing Assignment

Write two sentences for each of the following participial phrases. In the first sentence, place the participial phrase in a position that creates an amusing meaning. In the second sentence, place each participial phrase near the noun or pronoun it modifies.

1. sheltered from the tornado
2. filmed in Mexico
3. screaming in terror
4. clustered in groups
5. written last week
6. scrawled illegibly
7. breaking all the rules
8. keeping a tight grip

The Gerund

Gerunds and present participles are formed exactly alike. Both are formed by adding –*ing* to the plain form of the verb. The difference between them is in their use. Present participles are used as *adjectives;* gerunds are used as *nouns.*

3h. A *gerund* is a verb form ending in *-ing* that is used as a noun.

Study the boldfaced words in the following sentences. They are gerunds. Note that each word is part verb and part noun. For instance, *reading* in the first sentence is formed from the verb *read;* it names an action. Yet it also names something; therefore, it is used as a noun. Further indication that *reading* is used as a noun is its use as the subject of a sentence.

EXAMPLES **Reading** will increase your vocabulary.
Tobogganing is a winter sport.
I enjoyed **seeing** you again.
Peppering the soup improved its flavor.
She cleared a path by **shoveling** the snow.

You can see that each of the boldfaced words is used as a noun. In some sentences it is used as the subject; in one it is used as the object of the verb; in the last sentence it is used as the object of a preposition. Note that gerunds always end in –*ing.*

EXERCISE 8. Identifying Gerunds and Participles. Number your paper 1–10. In each of the following sentences, you will find verbals ending in *–ing*. Some will be gerunds and some will be present participles. After the proper number, write each verbal and label it either *ger.* for gerund or *part.* for participle. If the verbal is a gerund, tell how it is used (subject, object, predicate nominative, object of a preposition). If the verbal is a participle, tell what word it modifies.

EXAMPLES 1. Sleeping on the job is foolish.
            1. *Sleeping—ger.—subject*

           2. Let sleeping dogs lie.
            2. *sleeping—part.—dogs*

1. Their giggling annoyed the other viewers.
2. Virginia looks forward to fishing.
3. After studying, how do you relax?
4. A fascinating mystery is my favorite kind of book.
5. Making new friends in a large school can be difficult.
6. The highlight of the season was watching our team win the regional tournament.
7. Spinning around three times, she performed a pirouette.
8. Cindy makes money by walking dogs.
9. My grandmother and I enjoy digging for clams.
10. Sensing the danger nearby, he began to shout for help.

EXERCISE 9. Forming Gerunds and Using Them in Sentences.
From each of the following verbs, make a gerund and use it in a sentence. Tell how each gerund is used. Write at least one sentence for each of the following uses: subject of verb, object of verb, predicate nominative, object of a preposition.

1. bounce   4. shop   7. skate   9. climbing
2. stroll   5. scout   8. whisper   10. turn
3. wither   6. wander

The Gerund Phrase

3i. A *gerund phrase* consists of a gerund together with its complements and modifiers, all of which act together as a noun.

EXAMPLES **Jaywalking in heavy traffic** is especially risky. [The gerund phrase is the subject of the sentence. The gerund *Jaywalking* is modified by the prepositional phrase *in heavy traffic*.]
           She enjoys **hiking in the mountains.** [The gerund phrase is the direct object of the verb *enjoys*. The gerund *hiking* is modified by the

prepositional phrase *in the mountains.*]

He improved his appearance by.**losing weight.** [The gerund phrase is the object of the preposition *by.* The gerund *losing* has a direct object, *weight.*]

EXERCISE 10. Writing Sentences with Gerund Phrases. Write five sentences, each containing one or more gerund phrases. Underline each phrase, and write above it how it is used. Use the following abbreviations: *subj.* (subject); *obj.* (object); *p.n.* (predicate nominative); *o.p.* (object of a preposition). Include an example of each use.

The Infinitive

3j. An *infinitive* is a verb form, usually preceded by *to*, that can be used as a noun, an adjective, or an adverb.

An infinitive consists of the plain form of the verb, usually preceded by *to.* It can be used as a noun, an adjective, or an adverb. Study the following examples carefully.

Infinitives used as nouns

> **To err** is human. [The infinitive *to err* is the subject.]
> Betty wants **to act.** [The infinitive *to act* is the direct object of the verb *wants.*]

Infinitives used as adjectives

> The candidate **to believe** is Villeges. [The infinitive *to believe* modifies the noun *candidate.*]
> They are the easiest dogs **to train.** [The infinitive *to train* modifies the noun *dogs.*]

Infinitives used as adverbs

> The favored team was slow **to score.** [The infinitive *to score* modifies the adjective *slow.*]
> Grandmother has come **to stay.** [The infinitive *to stay* modifies the verb *has come.*]

☞ **NOTE** *To* plus a noun or a pronoun (*to bed, to the movies, to her*) is a prepositional phrase. *To* is the sign of the infinitive only when it is followed by a verb (*to go, to see, to have finished*).

EXERCISE 11. Identifying Infinitives and Their Uses in Sentences. Write on your paper the infinitives in the following sentences. After each infinitive, tell how it is used—as subject, object, predicate nominative, adjective, or adverb. You may use abbreviations.

1. Do you want to meet at the corner?
2. We are eager to go.
3. One way to relax is to listen to classical music.
4. I am easy to please.
5. We are waiting to talk with the principal.
6. The soup is still too hot to eat.
7. To excel, one must practice.
8. This summer she hopes to travel in the West.
9. To hike through the woods is fun.
10. To forgive is sometimes difficult.

The Infinitive Phrase

3k. An *infinitive phrase* consists of an infinitive together with its complements and modifiers.[1]

Like infinitives alone, infinitive phrases can be used as adjectives, adverbs, and nouns.

EXAMPLES **To hit a curve ball solidly** is very difficult. [The infinitive phrase is used as a noun and is the subject of the sentence. The infinitive has an object, *ball,* and is modified by the adverb *solidly.*]
It is sometimes difficult **to listen attentively.** [The infinitive phrase is used as an adverb and modifies the adjective *difficult.* The adverb *attentively* modifies the infinitive.]
She wants **to be a lawyer.** [The infinitive phrase is the direct object of the verb *wants.* The infinitive is followed by the predicate nominative *lawyer.*]

The Infinitive Without *to*

Occasionally, the *to* that is the sign of the infinitive is omitted in a sentence. This happens frequently after such verbs as *see, hear, feel, watch, help, know, dare, need, make, let,* and *please.*

[1] Unlike the other verbals, an infinitive may have a subject: *I asked him to come to my party.* (*Him* is the subject of the infinitive *to come.*) An infinitive phrase that includes a subject may sometimes be called an *infinitive clause.*

EXAMPLES Did you watch her [to] play volleyball?
He will help us [to] paddle the canoe.
We don't dare [to] go outside during the storm.

EXERCISE 12. Identifying and Classifying Infinitive Phrases.

Write on your paper the infinitive phrases in the following sentences. After each phrase, tell how it is used—as subject, object, predicate nominative, adjective, or adverb.

1. Our assignment was to read *I Know Why the Caged Bird Sings*.
2. We were asked to examine Maya Angelou's descriptions of her childhood.
3. To grow up in Stamps, Alabama, was to know hardship.
4. Maya Angelou tried to show the everyday lives of black families during the Great Depression.
5. To accomplish this purpose meant including many descriptions; one passage told about the process for curing pork sausage.
6. Angelou has the ability to capture vivid details.
7. She helps us see her grandmother's store through the eyes of a fascinated child.
8. However, Angelou was eager to experience life beyond Stamps, Alabama.
9. Her ambitions enabled her to gain success as a writer, a dancer, and an actress.
10. To dramatize her Afro-American heritage was a dream she realized by writing a television series.

Diagraming Verbals and Verbal Phrases

Participles and participial phrases are diagramed as follows:

EXAMPLE **Walking to school,** Ted saw the first spring robin.

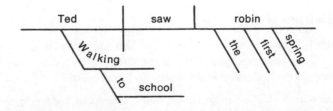

EXAMPLE **Waving her hat,** Sara flagged the train **speeding down the track.**

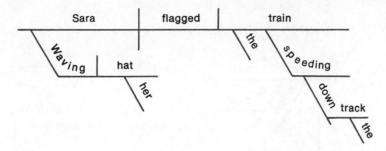

Gerunds and gerund phrases are diagramed differently.

EXAMPLE **Waiting patiently for hours** is usually a sure means of **observing wild animals.** [The gerund phrase *Waiting patiently for hours* is the subject of the verb *is;* the gerund phrase *observing wild animals* is the object of the preposition *of.* The first gerund phrase is modified by the adverb *patiently* and the prepositional phrase *for hours.* In the second gerund phrase, the gerund has a direct object, *animals.*]

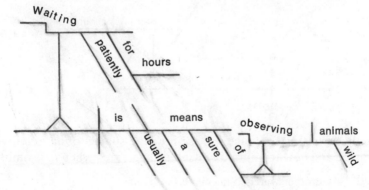

Infinitives and infinitive phrases used as modifiers are diagramed like prepositional phrases.

EXAMPLE He plays **to win.**

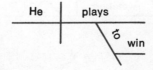

Infinitives and infinitive phrases used as nouns are diagramed as follows:

EXAMPLE **To always be on time** is often difficult.

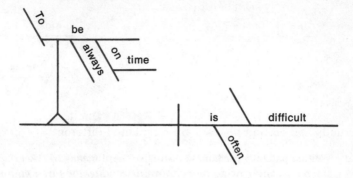

EXAMPLE She is hoping **to see him again.**

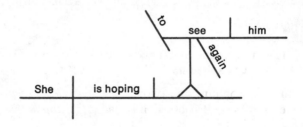

In the following sentence, notice how the subject of an infinitive is diagramed and how the infinitive itself is diagramed when *to* is omitted.

EXAMPLE My brother watched **me climb the tree.**

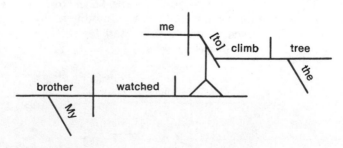

EXERCISE 13. Diagraming Sentences with Verbal Phrases.
Diagram the following sentences.

1. Slowing down, the driver changed gears.
2. We always enjoy picnicking in the park.
3. Jean dreams of traveling to Africa.
4. To join clubs is often a good way to make friends.
5. Joe watched me groom the horses.

APPOSITIVES AND APPOSITIVE PHRASES

Nouns and pronouns, as you know, are modified by adjectives and adjective phrases. Occasionally a noun or pronoun will be followed immediately by another noun or pronoun that identifies or explains it.

EXAMPLE   My cousin **Bryan** is a philatelist.

In this sentence the noun *Bryan* tells which cousin. The noun *Bryan* is said to be in apposition with the noun *cousin*. In this sentence *Bryan* is called an *appositive*.

3l. An *appositive* is a noun or pronoun that follows another noun or pronoun to identify or explain it.

Like any noun or pronoun, an appositive may have adjective or adjective phrase modifiers. If it does, it is called an *appositive phrase*.

3m. An *appositive phrase* is made up of an appositive and its modifiers.

Examine the appositives and the appositive phrases in the following examples. They are in boldfaced type.

EXAMPLES   His grandparents, **the Vescuzos,** live on Miller Road, **a wide street lined with beech trees.**
A diligent and quick-witted student, Mark is studying hard to reach his goal, **becoming a veterinarian.**

☞ **NOTE**   Occasionally (as in the first appositive in the second example above) an appositive phrase precedes the noun or pronoun explained.

Appositives and appositive phrases are set off by commas, unless the appositive is a single word closely related to the preceding word. The comma is always used when the word to which the appositive refers is a proper noun.

EXAMPLES   Dr. Rosen, **our family dentist,** is a cheerful woman.
Her daughter **Karen** is a tennis player.
Jeff, **her youngest son,** is a tennis coach.

In diagraming, place the appositive in parentheses after the word with which it is in apposition.

EXAMPLE   Ed Robbins, **our newest classmate,** comes from Goshen, **a town near Middletown.**

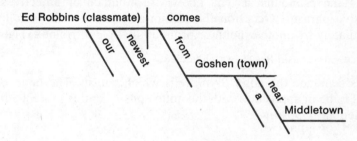

EXERCISE 14. Identifying Appositive Phrases and the Words They Modify.
Write on your paper the appositive phrases in each of the following sentences. Underline the appositive in each phrase. Then write the word each appositive modifies.

1. Soccer, my favorite sport, is more popular in South America than in the United States.
2. Pelé, an internationally famous soccer player, helped Brazil win the world championship.
3. Hausa, a language of the Sudan, is widely used in commerce throughout western Africa.
4. An old friend of the family's, Mr. Zolo will stay with us for several weeks before returning to his home in Puerto Rico.
5. Have you read this article about McMurdo Station, the United States base on Ross Island in Antarctica?

WRITING APPLICATION C:
Writing Sentences with Appositive Phrases

Use appositive phrases to make your writing more specific for your readers. In the following pair of sentences, for example, notice how much more specific the second sentence is than the first.

EXAMPLE   Mr. Jones will be taking our class to see *Macbeth.*

Mr. Jones, *our English teacher,* will be taking our class to see *Macbeth.*

Writing Assignment

Think of ten people you admire. They might be athletes, rock stars, or writers. Write a sentence about each person, with an appositive phrase describing this person.

EXAMPLES   Will Simon Le Bon, the lead singer of Duran Duran, appear on *Saturday Night Live?*
Bernard King, the forward for the New York Knicks, scored two points off a jump shot.

REVIEW EXERCISE C. Identifying Verbal Phrases.   There are twenty verbal phrases in the following sentences. Write them in order on your paper. After each phrase, tell what kind it is: participial, gerund, or infinitive.

Finding a summer job can be a difficult task. The first step is to scan the classified ads listed in your local newspaper. After discovering available opportunities, you can embark on the second step, matching your skills with the varied requirements of a specific job. In most cases you can then get in touch with a prospective employer by phoning the office or by writing a letter. If you are asked to interview for a job, preparing for the interview will be an important step in landing a summer job. To make a good impression, be sure to arrive on time, to dress neatly, and to speak courteously. To appear relaxed at an interview, avoid constantly checking your watch or shuffling your feet. Within a day or two after an interview, it is permissible to call the interviewer. By presenting yourself as calm, confident, and courteous, you may hear the magic words, "We'd like you to work for us."

REVIEW EXERCISE D. Identifying Prepositional, Verbal, and Appositive Phrases.   Number your paper 1–10. After the proper number, write the words and phrases in italics in the following sentences, and identify them by writing *part.* for participle, *ger.* for gerund, *inf.* for infinitive, and *app.* for appositive.

1. Margot had always liked *to sing before an audience.*
2. She took the part of Eliza, *the leading role in the school musical.*

WILLIAMSTON HIGH SCHOOL

3. Eliza Doolittle, *a native of London's East End,* sells flowers on the streets.
4. After *learning the cockney dialect,* Margot sounded just like an East Ender.
5. *Singing with an accent* was a new challenge for Margot.
6. *To gain a better job,* Eliza Doolittle takes speech lessons.
7. Margot then had *to sing with a more proper British accent.*
8. *Practicing daily,* she became more confident.
9. *Enunciating each syllable* made her voice exceptionally clear.
10. Margot later earned a *coveted* role with a local summer theater.

REVIEW EXERCISE E. Identifying Prepositional, Verbal, and Appositive Phrases.

The following sentences contain verbal and appositive phrases. Write the ten phrases on your paper. After each, tell what kind it is: participial, gerund, infinitive, or appositive. Use the abbreviations in Review Exercise D. Modifiers and complements of a verbal are considered part of the phrase.

EXAMPLE 1. To win a marathon, an athlete trained for this race must concentrate on developing stamina.
1. *to win a marathon—inf.*
trained for this race—part.
developing stamina—ger.

1. The Brooklyn Bridge, a remarkable feat of design, spans the East River in New York City.
2. Linking the boroughs of Brooklyn and Manhattan, it was once the longest suspension bridge in the world.
3. Hart Crane, an American poet, immortalized the bridge.
4. Pedestrians walking across the bridge are struck by the grandeur of its graceful cables.
5. Despite its beauty, the bridge is remembered for having cost the lives of many of its builders.
6. To support the twin towers on the bridge, the brilliant John A. Roebling, its engineer, designed airtight caissons filled with concrete.
7. Working underwater on the caissons was painstakingly slow and extremely dangerous.
8. Another perilous job was spinning the cables from one side of the river to the other.

CHAPTER 3 REVIEW: POSTTEST 1

Identifying Prepositional, Verbal, and Appositive Phrases. Number your paper 1–25. After the proper number, write each italicized phrase in the following sentences, and indicate what kind of phrase it is. Use the abbreviations *prep.* (prepositional phrase), *part.* (participial phrase), *ger.* (gerund phrase), *inf.* (infinitive phrase), and *app.* (appositive phrase). Do not identify a prepositional phrase that is part of a larger phrase.

EXAMPLE 1. *Requiring a sense of humor after a saddle-weary day,* the pack trip can nevertheless be a rich experience.
   1. *Requiring a sense of humor after a saddle-weary day—part.*

1. A pack trip *on horseback* is one way *to explore the wilderness.*
2. *Riding with a professional outfitter* can be a safe and rewarding camping experience.
3. Campers are fed and cared for *throughout the trip* by an experienced outfitter.
4. The outfitter's staff is responsible for *setting up and taking down camp.*
5. The outfitter, *known as the lead guide,* supervises the care of the pack animals as well as that of the individual mounts.
6. Previous experience *riding a trail on horseback* is not necessary.
7. Beginners should, however, pay close attention *to the guide's instructions and signals.*
8. A full day's ride, *averaging seven hours,* may cover fifteen miles.
9. Stops *for lunch* give everyone a chance *to rest from the rigors of the trail.*
10. Campers spend their evenings around the campfire *telling stories.*
11. At nightfall, tents are set up for *sleeping in comfort.*
12. For the more hardy rider, trips *into the high mountains* can be arranged.
13. Here campers will find lakes *teeming with fish.*
14. They can observe wild animals *living in their natural habitats.*
15. Meadows *blooming with wildflowers* offer the photographer an opportunity *to take unusual pictures.*
16. A trip can be arranged *to include a variety of activities.*

17. An exciting way *to spend a day* is *rafting through a canyon.*
18. *Climbing rocks and mountains* is another possibility.
19. An added benefit of such trips is *making friends with other camp-ers.*
20. *Traveling the trail together* can lead to lifelong friendships.
21. Most of the trail rides, *sponsored by a number of associations,* are in national parks and national forests in the West.
22. One ride, *a popular trip in the East,* runs from North Carolina into the Great Smoky Mountains.
23. *To demonstrate the pleasure of wilderness recreation,* both The Wilderness Society and the American Forestry Association offer summer trail rides.
24. One goal of The Wilderness Society is *to preserve the wilderness areas.*
25. *An unusual form of outdoor recreation,* the trail ride is presently suffering from a shortage of qualified outfitters.

CHAPTER 3 REVIEW: POSTTEST 2

Identifying Prepositional, Verbal, and Appositive Phrases. Number your paper 1–25. After the proper number, write each italicized phrase in the following paragraphs, and indicate what kind of phrase it is. Use the abbreviations that you used in Posttest 1.

EXAMPLE 1. An interesting career (1) *to consider* is (2) *practicing law.*
    1. *to consider—inf.*
       practicing law—ger.

(1) *To become a lawyer,* one must first earn a degree (2) *from a four-year college.* Then the undergraduate must take the Law School Admissions Test (3) *to gain acceptance at an approved law school.* After (4) *completing three full years of law school,* the graduate is awarded an L.L.B. degree or a J.D. degree. Before (5) *practicing law,* however, the graduate must take an exam (6) *given by the state board of bar examiners.* Only after (7) *passing this exam* is a lawyer ready (8) *to be admitted to the bar* and (9) *to practice law.*

The duty of a lawyer, (10) *also called an attorney or a counselor at law,* is (11) *to provide service and advice* (12) *relating to legal rights.* (13) *Representing a client in court* is only part (14) *of a lawyer's job.* Lawyers must spend hours at (15) *gathering enough evidence* (16) *to defend a client.* Lawyers also devote time (17) *to research* and are required (18) *to write numerous reports.*

Some lawyers spend most of their time in (19) *trying cases in court.* Others work hard (20) *to keep cases* from (21) *ever reaching court.* A lawyer may decide (22) *to take only certain cases.* Criminal lawyers, (23) *the kind glamorized in books and on TV,* handle cases (24) *involving crimes against society or government.* Civil lawyers, on the other hand, handle cases (25) *ranging from labor relations to personal injury.*

CHAPTER 3 REVIEW: POSTTEST 3

Writing Sentences with Prepositional, Verbal, and Appositive Phrases. Write ten sentences using the following phrases. Follow the directions in the parentheses.

1. in the cottage (use as an adjective phrase)
2. for our English class (use as an adverb phrase)
3. in *Nineteen Eighty-Four* (use as an adverb phrase)
4. by the train (use as an adverb phrase)
5. walking by the lake (use as a participial phrase)
6. playing the piano (use as a gerund phrase that is the subject of the sentence)
7. to get a home run (use as an infinitive phrase that is the direct object of the sentence)
8. the new student in our class (use as an appositive phrase)
9. the President of France (use as an appositive phrase)
10. my favorite actress (or actor) (use as an appositive phrase)

CHAPTER 4

The Clause

INDEPENDENT AND SUBORDINATE CLAUSES

A clause, like a phrase, is a group of related words used together as part of a sentence. Clauses, however, contain a subject and verb, whereas phrases do not.

PHRASE We had our midterms **before spring.** [The prepositional phrase *before spring* contains neither a subject nor a verb.]

CLAUSE We had our midterms **before spring began.** [*Spring* is the subject of the clause and *began* is the verb.]

DIAGNOSTIC TEST

A. Identifying Independent and Subordinate Clauses; Classifying Subordinate Clauses. Number your paper 1–10. After the proper number, identify each of the italicized clauses in the following sentences as an independent clause or a subordinate clause. Tell how each italicized subordinate clause functions in the sentence, using the following abbreviations: *adj. cl.* (adjective clause), *adv. cl.* (adverb clause), *n. cl.* (noun clause).

EXAMPLES 1. A soccer field measures 115 yards by 75 yards, and *the netted goals are 8 yards wide by 8 feet high.*
1. *independent clause*

2. Soccer, *which is the national sport of many European and Latin American countries,* has enjoyed only limited success in the United States.

94

2. *subordinate clause, adj. cl.*

1. During a career *that spanned twenty years,* Pelé was probably the most popular athlete in the world.
2. He was named Edson Arantes do Nascimento, but *hardly anyone recognizes that name.*
3. Soccer fans the world over, however, knew Pelé, *who was considered the world's best soccer player.*
4. *While he was still a teen-ager,* he led his Brazilian teammates to the first of their three World Cup titles.
5. *Whenever he played,* fans went wild over the way he moved the ball.
6. Once, he juggled the ball on his foot for fifty yards, eluding four opponents *who were trying to take the ball away from him.*
7. *That he soon became a superstar* is not surprising.
8. *Even though soccer never became a major sport in the United States,* Pelé managed to spark considerable interest in the game.
9. After he signed with the New York Cosmos, *people flocked to the stands to watch him play.*
10. They soon saw *that Pelé was an entertainer as well as an athlete.*

B. Classifying Sentences as Simple, Compound, Complex, or Compound-Complex.

Number your paper 11–20. After the proper number, identify each of the following sentences as simple, compound, complex, or compound-complex.

EXAMPLE   1. Tennis originated in France in the fifteenth century as indoor court tennis, but it did not take its present form as lawn tennis until 1870.
   1. *compound*

11. As the youngest member of a tennis-playing family, Tracy Austin appeared on the cover of *Tennis World* when she was only four years old.
12. At fourteen she had run out of opponents her own age; therefore, she began to look for older competitors.
13. In 1977 she became the youngest player to compete at Wimbledon, but she did not win any major tournaments that year.
14. At age sixteen, she decided to turn professional.
15. She proved equal to the challenge when she defeated a number of more experienced players.

16. By 1979 she had defeated the top women players and eventually won her first major tournament.
17. She defeated Billie Jean King and then went on to break Martina Navratilova's winning streak.
18. When she defeated Chris Evert Lloyd, she became the youngest player to win the U.S. Women's Open.
19. She traveled extensively on the tournament circuit, but she attended school, where she regularly earned good grades.
20. The determination that enabled her to win at tennis also made her an A student.

4a. A *clause* **is a group of words that contains a verb and its subject and is used as part of a sentence.**

KINDS OF CLAUSES

All clauses have a subject and verb, but not all of them express a complete thought. Those that do are called *independent clauses*. Such clauses could be written as separate sentences. We think of them as clauses when they are joined with one or more additional clauses in a single larger sentence. Clauses that do not make complete sense by themselves are called *subordinate clauses*. Subordinate clauses function as nouns, adjectives, or adverbs, just as phrases do.

Independent Clauses

4b. An *independent* **(or** *main***)** *clause* **expresses a complete thought and can stand by itself.**

Each of the following sentences is the same as an independent clause:

> The outfielders were missing easy fly balls.
> The infielders were throwing wildly.

To show the relationship between these two ideas, we can combine them as independent clauses in a single sentence:

> The outfielders were missing easy fly balls, **and** the infielders were throwing wildly.

Independent clauses may also be joined by the conjunctions *but, or, nor, for,* and *yet.*

> Should we go for a walk, **or** is it too hot outside?
> Gladys was not tired, **but** her tennis partner was.

Subordinate Clauses

4c. A *subordinate* **(or** *dependent***)** *clause* **does not express a complete thought and cannot stand by itself.**

Subordinate means "lesser in rank or importance." Subordinate clauses are so called because they need an independent clause to complete their meaning.

SUBORDINATE CLAUSES who spoke to our class yesterday
                     that many students are eligible for scholarships
                     because no students have applied for them

Notice that each of these subordinate clauses has an incomplete sound when read by itself. Each one leaves you expecting more to be said. Words like *if, when, although, since,* and *because* always make the clause they introduce sound unfinished. These words signal that what follows is only part of a sentence: **although** *the store was closed;* **since** *you are leaving.* The subordinate clauses given as examples above fit into sentences as follows:

> The woman **who spoke to our class yesterday** informed us of financial aid for college applicants.
> She said **that many students are eligible for scholarships.**
> Some scholarships are still available **because no students have applied for them.**

EXERCISE 1. Identifying Independent and Subordinate Clauses. Number your paper 1–10. After the proper number, identify each italicized clause as *independent* or *subordinate.*

1. Anne, *who enjoys watching baseball,* is a loyal fan of the Chicago Cubs.
2. *The burglar easily picked the lock;* next, he carefully cut the wires to the alarm system.

3. Mr. Wilson always waves to us *whenever we drive past his house.*
4. *As soon as the movie begins,* you should stop talking.
5. *We played croquet in the back yard* until the mosquitoes began to attack us.
6. The cat *that jumped through my bedroom window* is a stray.
7. Since the tropical storm is gathering force, *it may become a hurricane.*
8. *Donna sang ten songs,* but the audience wanted more.
9. He assumed *that we had already met.*
10. People *who belong to tenants' organizations* usually get better service from their landlords.

Complements and Modifiers in Subordinate Clauses

A subordinate clause, like an independent clause or a simple sentence, may contain complements and modifiers.

EXAMPLES Here is the portrait **that** he painted. [*That* is the direct object of *painted.*]
We couldn't tell **who** they were. [*Who* is a predicate nominative: They were *who.*]
Since she told **us** the **truth** . . . [*Us* is the indirect object of *told; truth* is the direct object of *told.*]
When I am **busy** . . . [*Busy* is a predicate adjective.]
After he had cooked **for us** . . . [*For us* is an adverb phrase modifying *had cooked.*]

EXERCISE 2. Identifying Subjects, Verbs, and Complements in Subordinate Clauses. Write on your paper the italicized subordinate clauses in the following sentences. In each clause, underline the subject once and the verb twice, and identify any complements, using the abbreviations *d.o.* (direct object), *p.n.* (predicate nominative), *i.o.* (indirect object). If the verb has more than one word, underline each word.

EXAMPLE 1. *After he shows us his new boat,* we will go swimming.

              i.o.   d.o.
      1. *After he shows us his new boat*

1. We couldn't see *who had won the race.*
2. They could see *who the winner was,* but they couldn't tell *which country she was from.*

3. She is the celebrity *whom we saw at the restaurant.*
4. Look for the mouse *that you heard last night.*
5. He spotted a horse *that galloped away.*
6. *After we passed the test,* we celebrated.
7. I wake up *whenever I hear a strange noise.*
8. *Because you had not given us the right address,* we missed the party.
9. The package will arrive on time *if you ship it today.*
10. *Until Mike loaned me this book,* I had never heard of John Steinbeck.

THE USES OF SUBORDINATE CLAUSES

Subordinate clauses fulfill the same function in sentences as adjectives, adverbs, and nouns. Subordinate clauses are named according to the job they do in sentences.

The Adjective Clause

4d. An *adjective clause* is a subordinate clause used as an adjective to modify a noun or pronoun.

EXAMPLES The novel **that I borrowed from the library** is about the Irish revolt of 1798.
Our town's civic center, **which was renovated last year,** has just been declared a landmark.

An adjective clause always follows the noun or pronoun it modifies. It is sometimes set off by commas and sometimes not. If the clause is *needed* to identify the word modified, no commas are used. Thus in the first example, the adjective clause is not set off because it is needed to identify *which* novel the sentence is about. If the clause merely adds information that is *not essential,* as in the second example, commas are used. (See pages 686–88.)

Relative Pronouns

Adjective clauses are usually introduced by the pronouns *who, whom, whose, which,* and *that.* These pronouns are called *relative pronouns* because they relate the adjective clause to the word the clause modifies (the antecedent of the relative pronoun). In addition to referring to the word the clause modifies, the relative pronoun has a job to do within the adjective clause.

EXAMPLES   Isabella Baumfree was an abolitionist **who was popularly known as Sojourner Truth.** [The relative pronoun *who* relates the adjective clause to *abolitionist*. *Who* also functions as the subject of the adjective clause.]
She is the person **whom I trust most.** [*Whom* relates the adjective clause to *person*. *Whom* also functions in the adjective clause as the direct object: *I trust whom*.]
The topic about **which he is writing** is controversial. [**Which** relates the clause to *topic*. *Which* also functions in the adjective clause as the object of the preposition *about*.]
Do you know the name of the group **whose recording is number one on the charts?** [*Whose* relates the clause to *group*. *Whose* also functions in the clause as a modifier of *recording*.]

In some cases the relative pronoun is omitted. The pronoun is understood and is thought of as having a function in the clause.

EXAMPLES   Ms. Chung is the legislator [**that**] **we met.** [The relative pronoun—*that* or *whom*—is understood. The pronoun relates the adjective clause to *legislator* and functions in the adjective clause as the direct object.]
Are these the books [**that**] **you read?** [The relative pronoun—*that* or *which*—is understood.]

In addition to relative pronouns, adverbs are sometimes used to introduce adjective clauses.

EXAMPLES   This is the season **when it rains almost every day.**
Here is the spot **where we will have lunch.**

EXERCISE 3. Identifying Adjective Clauses and the Words They Modify.

Each of the following sentences contains at least one adjective clause. Write the adjective clauses. Underline the subject of each clause once and the verb twice, and circle the relative pronoun that introduces the clause. After the clause, write the word it modifies.

EXAMPLE   1. The topic that Melissa chose for her paper was a difficult one.
1. (that) Melissa chose for her paper—topic

1. A speech community is a group of people who speak the same language.
2. There are speech communities that consist of millions of people and some that contain only a few hundred.

3. The language that we use during our childhood is called our native language.
4. A person who has mastered a second language is bilingual.
5. People who conduct business internationally should know more than one language.
6. English, French, and Spanish, which many diplomats can speak, are among the six official languages of the United Nations.
7. Russian, Chinese, and Arabic are the other three languages that are used officially at the U.N.
8. People for whom language study is important include telephone operators, hotel managers, and police officers.
9. Tourists who travel to other countries need to know a language that is understood in different parts of the world.
10. French, for example, is a language which is spoken in Europe, Africa, and Southeast Asia.

Diagraming Adjective Clauses

An adjective clause beginning with a relative pronoun is joined to the noun it modifies by a broken line. This line runs from the modified word to the relative pronoun.

EXAMPLE The coat **that I wanted** was too expensive.

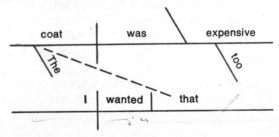

EXAMPLE The box **that contained the treasure** was missing.

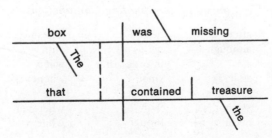

EXAMPLE She is the woman **from whom we bought the used car.**

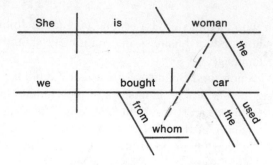

The Adverb Clause

4e. An *adverb clause* **is a subordinate clause that modifies a verb, an adjective, or an adverb.**

Like adverbs, adverbial clauses modify words by telling *how, when, where,* or *under what condition.*

EXAMPLES Donna sounds **as if she has caught a cold.** [*As if she has caught a cold* tells *how* Donna sounds.]
Before we left, we turned off the lights. [*Before we left* tells *when* we turned off the lights.]
You will see our house **where the road turns right.** [*Where the road turns right* tells *where* you will see our house.]
As long as he starts early, he will arrive on time. [*As long as he starts early* tells *under what condition* he will arrive on time.]

The Subordinating Conjunction

Adverb clauses are introduced by subordinating conjunctions. As its name suggests, a subordinating conjunction makes its clause a subordinate part of the sentence—a part that cannot stand alone. Unlike relative pronouns, which introduce adjective clauses, subordinating conjunctions do not serve a function within the clause they introduce.

Common Subordinating Conjunctions

after	before	unless
although	if	until
as	in order that	when
as if	since	whenever
as long as	so that	where
as soon as	than	wherever
because	though	while

whether

☞ **NOTE**   Many of the words in this list can be used as other parts of speech. For instance *after, as, before, since,* and *until* can also be used as prepositions.

Diagraming Adverb Clauses

An adverb clause is written on a horizontal line below the independent clause and is joined to it by a broken line connecting the verb of the adverb clause to the word in the independent clause (usually the verb) that the clause modifies. On the broken line, write the subordinating conjunction that introduces the subordinate clause.

EXAMPLE   **Before a hurricane strikes,** ample warning is given.

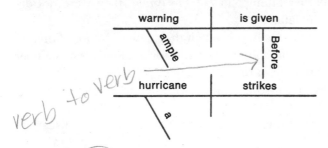

verb to verb

EXERCISE 4. Identifying Adverb Clauses and Subordinating Conjunctions.   Write the adverb clause in each of the following sentences. Circle the subordinating conjunction in each clause.

1. Ruth mowed the lawn while we weeded the flower beds.
2. The grass looked as if it had not been cut in months.
3. Because the house had been empty for so long, the lawn and gardens were choked with weeds.
4. We borrowed tools so that we could weed more efficiently.
5. Until we had pulled out the weeds, we could not see the roses.
6. When we cut through the heavy undergrowth, we used a scythe.
7. In one corner we stacked a mound of debris so that it could be hauled away.
8. After Ruth had mowed about half the lawn, she was exhausted.
9. When we stopped for a rest, we stretched out in the shade.
10. Long hours in the hot sun had made us feel as though the day would never end.

EXERCISE 5. Writing Sentences with Adverb Clauses. Write ten sentences, using in each a different one of the subordinating conjunctions in the list given on page 102. After each, state whether the clause tells *how, when, where, why,* or *under what condition.*

REVIEW EXERCISE A. Distinguishing Between Adjective and Adverb Clauses. Write on your paper the subordinate clauses in the following sentences. After each clause, state whether it is an adjective clause or an adverb clause.

1. In 1978, aeronauts Ben Abruzzo, Max Anderson, and Larry Newman, whose home was Albuquerque, New Mexico, became the first people to pilot a balloon across the Atlantic Ocean.
2. Although Abruzzo and Anderson had been forced to land in the ocean in an earlier attempt in *Double Eagle,* they were not discouraged by this failure.
3. They acquired a new balloon, which they named *Double Eagle II.*
4. Since experience had shown the need for another crew member, they took Newman with them.
5. A balloon rises because it is filled with helium, which is a lightweight gas.
6. If a balloon loses altitude, the crew moves it upward by discarding ballast.
7. When it gains too much altitude, the crew lowers it by releasing some of the gas.
8. Aeronauts must know meteorology so that they can take advantage of favorable winds.
9. As the aeronauts were eager to point out, *Double Eagle II* was flown across the Atlantic; it did not just drift across.
10. On its journey from Maine to France, *Double Eagle II* was airborne for 137 hours, which is a little less than six days.

WRITING APPLICATION A:
Using Subordination to Create a Mature Style

Mature writers generally avoid a long series of short, choppy sentences. One way to express your thoughts in a mature way is to use subordination. Some of the thoughts in the example with short, choppy sentences were combined by using a subordinate clause. The clause is in boldface.

EXAMPLE   I like impressionism. Mary Cassatt is an American artist. I enjoy her painting. She is an impressionist.
I enjoy the works of Mary Cassatt, **who is an American impressionist painter.**

Writing Assignment

Is there a certain artist, musician, or author who particularly appeals to you? In a paragraph of 100 to 150 words, discuss this person. Use specific details and include at least five subordinate clauses. Underline these clauses.

The Noun Clause

4f. A *noun clause* **is a subordinate clause used as a noun.**

Compare the two sentences in each of the following pairs. Notice that in the second sentence in each pair, a *subordinate clause takes the place of a noun in the first sentence.* Tell whether the clause in each sentence is used as a subject, a direct object, an indirect object, a predicate nominative, or an object of a preposition.

She believes that **saying.**
She believes **that lost time is never found again.**

The municipal **garage** is the main item on tonight's agenda.
Where to build the municipal garage is the main item on tonight's agenda.

She has written an article about her **election.**
She has written an article about **how she was elected to the Senate.**

The store owner will give the **winner** a substantial prize.
The store owner will give **whoever wins the contest** a substantial prize.

The happiest time in my life was our **summer** in Columbia.
The happiest time in my life was **when we went to Columbia for the summer.**

Noun clauses are usually introduced by such connectives as *that*, *whether*, *what*, *who*, *whoever*, *whose*, *where*, and *why*. Sometimes the introductory word does not have any function in the clause.

                                    S   V
EXAMPLE   I know **that she is worried.** [The connective *that* has no function in the clause.]

At other times, the introductory word does have a function in the clause.

                        PN   S   V
EXAMPLE   Do you know **what the problem is?** [The connective *what* functions in the clause as the predicate nominative.]

Like adjective clauses, noun clauses are sometimes used without the usual introductory word. Compare the noun clauses in the following paired sentences.

He told us **that attendance is improving.**
He told us **attendance is improving.** [The connective *that* is understood.]

EXERCISE 6. Identifying and Classifying Noun Clauses. There are ten noun clauses in the following sentences. Write them on your paper. Label the subject and the verb of each noun clause. After each clause, identify the clause by means of the following abbreviations: *s.* (subject of the sentence), *d.o.* (direct object), *i.o.* (indirect object), *p.n.* (predicate nominative), or *o. prep.* (object of a preposition).

1. Mr. Perkins told us what we would play at half time.
2. We can never predict what he will choose.
3. We never know whether he will choose a march by Sousa or a show tune.
4. The drummer told Mr. Perkins she did not like Sousa.
5. How she could say that was a mystery to me.
6. Mr. Perkins told us we would play a medley of marches.
7. Whoever did not like this choice could leave the band.
8. His reason is that the band director must have the final say.
9. Whoever shows the most talent will play the solos.
10. The crowd always applauds enthusiastically for whoever plays a solo.

Diagraming Noun Clauses

A clause used as subject, object, predicate nominative, or object of a preposition is supported by an upright line resting on the line of the subject, object, predicate nominative, or object of a preposition.

NOUN CLAUSE AS SUBJECT **What she said** convinced me. [*What* functions in the clause as the direct object.]

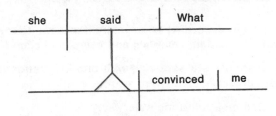

NOUN CLAUSE AS OBJECT We know **that you won the prize.** [*That* has no function in the clause.]

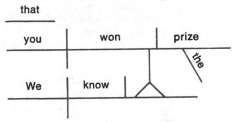

EXERCISE 7. Diagraming Sentences with Noun Clauses. Diagram the sentences in Exercise 6.

REVIEW EXERCISE B. Identifying Adjective, Adverb, and Noun Clauses. The following sentences contain all three kinds of subordinate clauses: adjective, adverb, and noun. Write each clause on your paper. Label the verb and the subject in the clause, and name the kind of clause.

1. When the circus is in town, be sure to go.
2. Jack and Joan, who were in town last week, visited me.
3. After we went to the museum, we strolled through the park.
4. This is what I would call an excellent meal.
5. Camping out was difficult for those who had never done it before.
6. While we ate breakfast, the kitten played with the ball of yarn.

7. One of Marge's complaints was that the weather had been bad.
8. This is the hat that I want for my birthday.
9. We visited Jerusalem before we left Israel.
10. Here is the clothing store that sells leather jackets.

SENTENCES CLASSIFIED BY STRUCTURE

4g. When classified according to structure, there are four kinds of sentences: *simple, compound, complex,* **and** *compound-complex.*

(1) A *simple sentence* **is a sentence with one independent clause and no subordinate clause.**

EXAMPLE   The Hudson is a historic waterway.

Although we often think of simple sentences as short, this is not necessarily so.

EXAMPLE   In the stands at half time, we bragged to friends from another school about our team's prospects for the season. [Notice that there are several phrases but only one subject and one verb.]

The subject and verb are marked with S and V above "we" and "bragged."

(2) A *compound sentence* **is a sentence composed of two or more independent clauses but no subordinate clauses.**

EXAMPLES   A strange dog chased us, but the owner came to our rescue. [two independent clauses]

The film is long, but it is suspenseful, and the time passes quickly. [three independent clauses]

A coordinating conjunction or a semicolon is generally used to connect the independent clauses in a compound sentence. Other words used to join the clauses of a compound sentence are *consequently, therefore, nevertheless, however, moreover,* and *otherwise.* These are called *conjunctive adverbs.* When a word of this kind is used between two independent clauses, it is preceded by a semicolon and followed by a comma.

Each independent clause in a compound sentence is diagramed like a separate sentence. A broken line is drawn between the verbs of the two clauses, and the conjunction is written on a solid horizontal line connecting the two parts of the broken line.

EXAMPLE I bought the blouse, but the brooch was given to me.

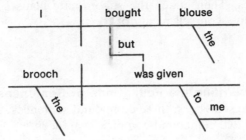

Caution: Do not confuse the compound predicate of a simple sentence with the two subjects and two predicates of a compound sentence.

EXAMPLES   She played basketball and won a sports scholarship. [simple sentence with compound predicate]

She played basketball, and she won a sports scholarship. [compound sentence with two independent clauses]

(3) A *complex sentence* is a sentence containing one independent clause and at least one subordinate clause.

EXAMPLE   As night fell, the storm reached its climax.

Since you have already learned how to diagram a sentence containing a subordinate clause (adjective, adverb, and noun clause), you know how to diagram a complex sentence.

(4) A *compound-complex sentence* contains two or more independent clauses and at least one subordinate clause.

EXAMPLE   The room that Carrie painted had been white, but she changed the color. [two independent clauses and one subordinate clause]

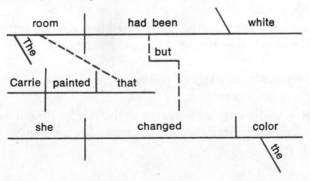

In diagraming a compound-complex sentence, first diagram the independent clauses. Then attach the subordinate clauses to the words they modify. Give yourself plenty of room.

EXERCISE 8. Writing the Four Kinds of Sentences. Write and label two simple sentences, three compound sentences, three complex sentences, and two compound-complex sentences.

EXERCISE 9. Identifying Sentences as Simple, Compound, Complex, or Compound-Complex. Number your paper 1–10. After the proper number, write the kind of sentence each of the following is: simple, compound, complex, compound-complex.

1. Americans, who are familiar with natural disasters like hurricanes, tornadoes, and floods, learned about a less common kind when a volcano in southwest Washington erupted.
2. On May 18, 1980, Mount St. Helens, a volcanic mountain in the Cascade Range, literally blew its top.
3. When the volcano could no longer contain the enormous pressure of molten rock, steam, and gas that had been building inside it, the top blew off in a great explosion.
4. The explosion was equivalent to the force of five hundred atomic bombs of the type that was dropped on Hiroshima.
5. The explosion removed fifteen hundred feet of rock from the top of the ten-thousand-foot mountain, and it left a crater two and one-half miles in diameter and one mile deep.
6. The outflow of superheated mud melted two glaciers and produced a wall of debris that roared down the mountain at thirty miles an hour.
7. The temperature of water in nearby rivers rose from fifty to nearly ninety degrees Fahrenheit.
8. The most costly damage occurred in the region around the mountain, but cities in three states to the east were covered by a fallout of gray ash.

9. For two months before exploding, the mountain had been rumbling ominously, and scientists, who had placed instruments on its slopes to monitor the activity inside, knew the eruption was coming.
10. The area around the volcano, which had been popular for fishing and recreation, was officially closed to the public weeks before the eruption, and many of its permanent residents were evacuated.

EXERCISE 10. Identifying Sentences as Simple, Compound, Complex, or Compound-Complex.   What kind of sentence is each of the following? Be prepared to explain your answer.

1. We will set up the rummage tables after we price each item.
2. The Key Club is sponsoring the rummage sale and will accept donations from everyone.
3. We use whatever is donated, but we especially welcome housewares.
4. Although most items are usually less exotic, someone once donated a stuffed owl.
5. Move that wicker rocking chair here, and pile those pillows on the seat.
6. Have you put price tags on those glasses?
7. The principal donated a bird cage and made lemonade for the volunteers.
8. Since the sale is held outdoors in mid-June, we always have cold drinks on hand.
9. One customer bought a set of encyclopedias, and her husband later purchased an antique bookcase.
10. The Key Club gives the profits from the sale to a local charity.

EXERCISE 11. Diagraming the Four Kinds of Sentences.   Diagram the sentences in Exercise 10.

REVIEW EXERCISE C. Identifying Phrases and Clauses; Classifying Phrases and Clauses.   Number your paper 1–20. After the proper number, identify each of the italicized word groups by means of the following abbreviations: *prep. ph.* (prepositional phrase); *part. ph.* (participial phrase); *ger. ph.* (gerund phrase); *inf. ph.* (infinitive phrase); *adj. cl.* (adjective clause); *adv. cl.* (adverb clause); *n. cl.* (noun clause). Do not identify a prepositional phrase that is part of a longer phrase or a clause.

(1) *Striving to make their mark* in jobs once held only by men, women have recently crossed the gender barrier in space travel. (2) *That women had long been poorly represented in space* is an unfortunate fact. (3) *To change this state of affairs,* NASA began training women astronauts in 1978. (4) *Arriving at Johnson Space Center in Houston,* six women, chosen from hundreds of applicants, made history. (5) *When the first grueling year in Houston was over,* they had earned the title of mission specialist, or astronaut. Then in June 1983, Sally K. Ride became the first American woman who could say (6) *she had orbited the earth.*

As a member (7) *of the crew* of the space shuttle *Challenger,* Ride operated a sixty-foot-long remote manipulator arm. The arm, (8) *which was used in the deployment and retrieval of scientific experiments,* was the focus of Ride's training with NASA. For two years prior to the flight, she had worked with engineers (9) *to design an efficient arm.* Later responsibilities included (10) *serving as "capcom" during shuttle flights.* Capcom, (11) *which is a NASA blend for "capsule communicator,"* is one example of the language designed for space travel. (12) *As the capcom speaks to the orbiting astronauts,* he or she relays instructions given by the flight planners at the Johnson Space Center. Future shuttle crews are often drawn (13) *from the ranks of capcoms.*

(14) *While she was making her historic orbits around the earth,* Ride used the remote manipulator arm to accomplish an important and practical task. This task involved grasping a 3,960-pound satellite, (15) *which was drifting outside the shuttle.* The next step was (16) *to place the satellite securely in the cargo bay,* (17) *where it could be repaired or tested.*

(18) *Growing up in the Los Angeles suburb of Encino,* Ride appeared to be on her way to becoming a tennis star, not an astronaut. She was in high school (19) *when she began competing in local tennis tournaments.* Ride, (20) *who became a nationally ranked amateur,* evidently found astrophysics and space travel more compelling than tennis.

WRITING APPLICATION B:
Using Variety in Sentence Structure to Enliven Your Writing

Would you enjoy eating exactly the same kinds of food for supper every night? Probably not. Looking forward to something different increases interest as well as appetite. This is somewhat the way your reader feels. You should serve different kinds of sentences to maintain interest. Keep in mind that you have four kinds of sentences to choose from: simple, compound, complex, and compound-complex.

EXAMPLE   This morning I looked at the kitchen. (simple) The dirty dishes were piled high on the cabinet, and the trash was overflowing the container. (compound) When I looked in a skillet on the stove, I saw leftover grease. (complex) I knew that I had to clean it all up, but I hated to get started. (compound-complex) Never will I leave the kitchen dirty again! (simple)

Writing Assignment

One type of description presents a view as your eye sees things. For example, you might stand in the doorway of your room and look from one side to the other. Write a description of one of the following areas. Include at least one of each kind of sentence. Write the kind of sentence in parentheses after the sentence, as the writer did in the example above.

AREAS   1. your room   3. a game room
         2. skating rink   4. school cafeteria

CHAPTER 4 REVIEW: POSTTEST 1

A. Identifying Independent and Subordinate Clauses; Classifying Subordinate Clauses.

Number your paper 1–10. After the proper number, identify each of the italicized clauses in the following sentences as an independent clause or a subordinate clause. Tell how each italicized subordinate clause functions in the sentence, using the abbreviations *adj. cl.* (adjective clause), *adv. cl.* (adverb clause), and *n. cl* (noun clause).

EXAMPLE   1. The Brooklyn Bridge, *which was built in the latter half of the nineteenth century,* is still considered one of the world's foremost suspension bridges.
           1. *subordinate clause—adj. cl.*

1. The Brooklyn Bridge, *which spans the strong tides of the East River between Brooklyn and Manhattan,* is one of the engineering wonders of the world.
2. Massive granite towers *that are supported by pneumatic caissons* are its most remarkable feature.
3. *The bridge was designed and built by John and Washington Roebling, a father-and-son engineering team* who were pioneers in the use of steel-wire cables.
4. Because of the steel-wire cables used in its construction, the bridge is a graceful structure *that resembles a spider's web.*
5. *That the bridge combines strength with beauty* remains a tribute to the Roebling family.
6. The Roeblings discovered *that construction work could be both slow and dangerous.*
7. *Although she was not an engineer,* Nora Roebling assisted in the efforts to complete the bridge.
8. *Because at times they were required to work underwater in airtight chambers,* many workers, including Washington Roebling, suffered from caisson disease.
9. Sailors, *who were used to working at great heights,* were hired to string the miles of cable.
10. *John Roebling's foot was injured in an accident,* and he died before the bridge's completion.

B. Classifying Sentences as Simple, Compound, Complex, or Compound-Complex. Number your paper 11–25. After the proper number, identify each of the following sentences as simple, compound, complex, or compound-complex.

EXAMPLE 1. John Augustus Roebling was the German-born engineer who designed and built the Brooklyn Bridge.
      1. *complex*

11. As an aftermath of caisson disease, Washington Roebling, who succeeded his father, was confined to bed.
12. The Roeblings lived in a house that was in the vicinity of the construction site, and Washington supervised by observing progress through a telescope.
13. He dictated instructions to Nora, who was his energetic go-between.

14. No one can say whether the work on the bridge could have continued without her assistance.
15. When the bridge was finally completed, President Chester A. Arthur attended the dedication ceremonies.
16. Because of his illness, Washington was unable to attend.
17. The President, however, came to the Roebling home to honor the man who had struggled so valiantly to complete the bridge.
18. The bridge had taken fourteen years to build and was hailed by some as the eighth wonder of the world.
19. Records show that twenty men lost their lives during its construction.
20. The bridge stands as a monument to the artistry, sacrifice, and determination of the people who had planned and built it.
21. The Roeblings had envisioned cable cars to carry people across the bridge, but today only motorized vehicles pass along the six-lane thoroughfare.
22. Pedestrians stroll or jog along the elevated walkway, another of John Roebling's innovations.
23. The Roeblings built the bridge high enough for all but the tallest ships; therefore, ocean liners can glide beneath its span.
24. Artists, poets, and songwriters have been inspired by the majestic bridge and have contributed to its fame.
25. The bridge that opened as a local wonder has become a national landmark.

CHAPTER 4 REVIEW: POSTTEST 2

Identifying Independent and Subordinate Clauses; Classifying Subordinate Clauses. Number your paper 1–25. After the proper number, identify each of the italicized clauses in the following paragraphs as an independent clause or a subordinate clause. Tell how each italicized subordinate clause functions in the sentence, using the abbreviations *adj. cl.* (adjective clause), *adv. cl.* (adverb clause), and *n. cl.* (noun clause).

EXAMPLE 1. Lichens are plants (1) *that grow on a solid surface, such as a rock.*
   1. *subordinate clause—adj. cl.*

No one observing a lichen would suspect (1) *that it is a complex plant.* The lichen is composed of a fungus and a colony of algae, (2) *which some scientists now classify as bacteria.* (3) *The fungus depends on the algae for food,* but lichenologists can only guess (4) *how this interaction takes place.* Simon Schwendener, a Swiss botanist, maintained (5) *that lichens are a connecting link between fungi and algae.* Schwendener thought of the fungus as a parasite (6) *that surrounded the algae with a net of narrow meshes.* (7) *Although Beatrix Potter supported Schwendener's unpopular theory,* she argued (8) *that the fungus was a contributing partner, not a parasite.* This point of view, (9) *which held favor for years,* was based on speculation; moreover, (10) *it is still not supported by scientific evidence.*

(11) *Even though lichens are not mosses,* many of their common names go back to the time (12) *when they were mistakenly classified as oak moss and reindeer moss.* (13) *Like the mosses, lichens grow on trees and rocks;* however, they also thrive in places (14) *where mosses cannot grow.* They grow in every natural habitat (15) *that one can imagine,* from deserts to rain forests. (16) *Lichens even grow on the backs of certain beetles in New Guinea,* and they thrive in the barren valleys of the Antarctic.

Lichens (17) *that form on rocks* are often colorful. Rocks along a coastline are frequently covered with shrublike lichens (18) *that thrive on the ocean fog.* (19) *When trees lose their leaves in the fall,* their branches sometimes display a thick growth of lichens. On evergreen trees, some lichens grow as strands (20) *that hang like tangled hair.*

(21) *Although many species of lichen can survive extreme heat or cold,* they cannot survive severe air pollution. The disappearance of lichens from an area often warns botanists (22) *that the environment is being threatened.* (23) *Because lichens are so sensitive to air pollution,* they are used as monitors by environmentalists. (24) *Since lichens help to create soil,* they are sometimes called "plant pioneers." (25) *If we lose the lichens to pollution,* we lose with them their enrichment of the soil and their beautification of the landscape.

CHAPTER 4 REVIEW: POSTTEST 3

Writing a Variety of Sentence Structures.   Write your own sentences according to the following guidelines:

1. A simple sentence with a compound verb

2. A compound sentence with two independent clauses joined by the conjunction *but*
3. A compound sentence with two independent clauses joined with the conjunction *and*
4. A complex sentence with an adjective clause
5. A complex sentence with the adverb clause placed at the beginning of the sentence
6. A complex sentence with an adverb clause placed at the end of the sentence
7. A complex sentence with a noun clause used as the direct object of the verb
8. A complex sentence with a noun clause used as the subject of the sentence
9. A complex sentence with a noun clause used as the object of a preposition
10. A compound-complex sentence

GRAMMAR
MASTERY REVIEW: Cumulative Test

A. PARTS OF SPEECH. Number your paper 1–10. After the proper number, write each italicized word in the following passage, and indicate what part of speech it is. Use the abbreviations *n.* (noun), *pron.* (pronoun), *adj.* (adjective), *v.* (verb), *adv.* (adverb), *prep.* (preposition), *conj.* (conjunction), and *interj.* (interjection).

Sojourner Truth (1) *became* (2) *popular* in her lifetime (3) *as* a preacher and an abolitionist. She is believed to have been freed from (4) *slavery* by the New York State Emancipation Act of 1827 and to have lived for a while in (5) *New York City.* Before the Civil War, (6) *she* had (7) *already* become friendly with such abolitionists as the Motts (8) *and* Harriet Beecher Stowe. It is not surprising, therefore, that she addressed (9) *countless* meetings in the abolitionist cause. When criticized at one meeting for not reading the Bible, she replied, "(10) *Oh,* the Lord speaks to me directly."

B. SUBJECTS AND VERBS. Number your paper 11–15. After the proper number, write the subject and the verb in each of the following sentences. Underline each subject once and each verb twice. Be sure to include any understood subjects as well as all the words in a verb phrase and all the parts of a compound subject or verb.

11. Flying elaborate kites is gaining popularity among adults as well as children.
12. Have you ever flown a kite in a park or a grassy meadow on a clear, windy day?
13. My favorite, a black and yellow Indian fighter, darts and maneuvers at the slightest pull of the string.
14. For moderate winds, try an easy-to-launch snowflake kite made of nylon.
15. Kameko and Aki were given a nine-foot Sanjo warrior kite, unquestionably a work of art.

C. COMPLEMENTS. Number your paper 16–20. After the proper number, write the complement or complements in each of the following sentences. Identify each complement, using the abbreviations *p.a.* (predicate adjective), *p.n.* (predicate nominative), *d.o.* (direct object), and *i.o.* (indirect object).

16. The *Andrea Doria* was an elegant passenger liner.
17. Off Nantucket Island, a dense fog enveloped the ship.
18. In the fog, the bow of another liner sliced the starboard hull of the *Andrea Doria* like a butter knife.
19. The captain sent nearby ships an SOS.
20. The rescue at sea was dramatic and inspiring.

D. PHRASES. Number your paper 21–30. After the proper number, write each italicized phrase in the following sentences and indicate what kind of phrase it is. Use the abbreviations *prep.* (prepositional phrase), *part.* (participial phrase), *ger.* (gerund phrase), *inf.* (infinitive phrase), and *app.* (appositive phrase).

21. In 1874 the invention of barbed wire by Joseph Glidden, *an Illinois farmer,* changed the face of the Western plains.
22. *At the end of the Civil War,* this vast area remained largely unsettled land open to herds of wild cattle and buffalo.
23. *To keep these herds off farmland* was almost impossible because there was no available timber for fencing.
24. *With the invention of barbed wire,* unlimited open range became secured private land.
25. Thousands of miles of prickly wire soon divided the land *into pastures and farms.*
26. *Changing an entire way of life so quickly* proved unsettling to many Westerners.
27. Cattle owners who had *to drive their herds to market* viewed fences around water holes and trails as unnecessary restrictions.
28. Fence-cutting wars, *ugly confrontations of violence and injustice,* broke out between various groups.
29. Despite *having once been enemies,* cowhands and sheepherders joined forces against the farmers.
30. Inevitably, however, strands of gleaming wire soon crossed the land, *taming the Wild West forever.*

E. CLAUSES. Number your paper 31–40. After the proper number, identify each of the italicized clauses in the following sentences as an independent clause or a subordinate clause. Tell how each italicized subordinate clause functions in the sentence, using the abbreviations *adj. cl.* (adjective clause), *adv. cl.* (adverb clause), and *n. cl.* (noun clause).

31. *As scientists have recently discovered,* chameleons are not the masters of disguise they have long been reputed to be.
32. *Their changes of color are not attempts at camouflage;* they are responses to changes in light and temperature.
33. Chameleons, *which dislike any contact,* even with other lizards, will tolerate it for the purpose of breeding.
34. *When two chameleons cross paths,* they do their best to terrorize each other by hissing, snapping, and changing color.
35. Some scientists think *that such encounters with other chameleons control the chameleon's change in color.*
36. Males occasionally fight, but *most chameleons avoid physical confrontation.*
37. Almost all of the species *that make up the chameleon family* live in trees.
38. *Because the chameleon moves slowly,* it would become an easy prey without its natural green and brown coloration.
39. *The chameleon's tongue is sticky and has numerous folds and furrows* that are lined with hooklike cells.
40. The tongue is propelled by a set of muscles *that can extend it as far as one and one half times the length of the chameleon's body.*

F. KINDS OF SENTENCES. Number your paper 41–50. After the proper number, identify each of the following sentences as simple, compound, complex, or compound-complex.

41. During her lifetime, Edna St. Vincent Millay published eleven volumes of poetry and several plays and short stories.
42. She was probably the best-known literary figure of her day, and she epitomized the perfect poet to many of her readers.
43. Because her poems reflected the changing social values of the 1920's, other readers found them shocking.
44. Her popularity grew, and she was awarded the Pulitzer Prize in 1923 for *Ballad of the Harp-Weaver.*
45. Although she wrote about every aspect of life, love and nature are recurring themes in her poetry.
46. Perhaps her best-known poem, "Renascence," was entered in an anthology contest when she was nineteen.

47. The unpublished poem was retrieved from a wastebasket where an editor had accidentally thrown it.
48. It did not win a prize, but it attracted critical attention and a patron who sent her to Vassar.
49. "Renascence" was inspired by an experience in the mountains near her home, and it marked the starting point of her literary life.
50. Since it was first published, it has been regarded as a masterpiece; moreover, it still ranks as Edna St. Vincent Millay's finest work.

PART TWO

USAGE

CHAPTER 5

The English Language

HISTORY AND USAGE

THE HISTORY OF ENGLISH

The Early Beginnings

In the world today more than 2,500 different languages are spoken. In studying the world's many languages, linguists (language scholars) have found that they can be divided into groups called *language stocks*. Each of these stocks, according to scholars, was once a single language, spoken by a group of people who lived in a common homeland. At some point during prehistoric times, speakers of this common language separated into smaller groups, many of whom migrated away from the homeland. Over the years there were changes in how each new group spoke what was once the common language. Eventually these changes resulted in "new" languages.

The following diagram shows that English derived from the Indo-European language stock. What other languages from this stock do you recognize?

Languages from a common stock may not seem on the surface to be related, especially if you have struggled to learn a second language such as German, French, or Spanish. This lack of apparent similarity is due to changes in the common language after members of the group separated. As much as the individual languages have changed over the years, however, languages derived from a common stock still share certain related words, as well as features in grammar and syntax. For example, notice how the word *mother* appears in eight languages from the Indo-European stock.

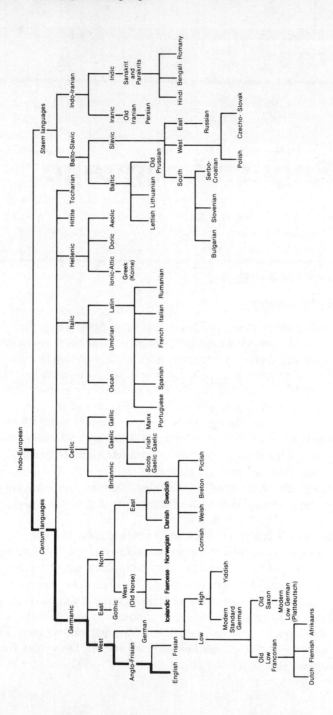

Indo-European languages

English	mother	Greek	meter
Sanskrit	mata	Italian	madre
French	mère	Latin	mater
German	Mutter	Russian	mat'

Because written records were not kept at that time, language scholars do not know exactly what the Indo-European language was like. However, by studying languages that evolved from this parent tongue, they have developed some theories about our ancestor language and about the features of this distant language that survive in our English of today. They know, for example, that such basic words as *heart, lung, head, mother, father, sun, moon, star,* and the numerals from one to ten were all used—in a different form, of course, by the Indo-Europeans. This form, called the Indo-European *base,* is indicated in most dictionaries with an asterisk: **bhero-s* (bear). The asterisk indicates that scholars believe that Indo-Europeans used this form but that they cannot know for certain.

EXERCISE 1. Investigating the Indo-European Language. As your teacher directs, use your school library to find information on the Indo-European language stock. Look for answers to questions such as the following ones:

1. What evidence did scholars use to establish the Indo-European homeland in northern Europe?
2. What was Indo-European life like? How does what scholars know about the Indo-European language enable them to make statements about the life of the people who spoke that language?
3. The language stock from which English developed—the Indo-European—is only one of the known language stocks. What other stocks are there? What are some languages that have developed from these stocks?

EXERCISE 2. Applying Knowledge of Word Origins. Each of the following words has its origins in the Indo-European language. Using a dictionary that shows word origins, find the Indo-European base form for each word. Find also the meaning that scholars believe the word had for the Indo-Europeans.

1. mother	3. cup	5. two	7. head	9. moon
2. sun	4. sky	6. heart	8. weave	10. wolf

Old English

The English that was spoken from the year 450 to the year 1066 is known as Old English. In about 500 B.C., a group of Indo-Europeans called the Celts crossed the English Channel, settling in the countries today called England, Scotland, and Ireland. For many years the Celts lived a relatively calm existence, protected from hostile invaders by the Roman soldiers who occupied the Celtic land at that time. By A.D. 450, however, the situation had changed. As the Roman Empire weakened, the Roman soldiers were withdrawn, leaving the Celts to fight off border raids from the Picts and Scots, their neighbors to the north. For assistance, the Celts looked to three groups of Germanic peoples who lived across the North Sea from them. These people did indeed give the help asked of them but, at the same time, used the opportunity to invade and conquer the Celtic homeland. By the year 600, these three groups of people—the Angles, the Saxons, and the Jutes—were securely established in the country we know today as Great Britain.

In addition to conquering their country, the Angles, Saxons, and Jutes also conquered the language of the Celts. By the year 700, the Celtic language was not much used in England; instead, a blending of the languages spoken by the Angles, Saxons, and Jutes was heard throughout the country. This is the language we know today as *Anglo-Saxon,* or *Old English.*

Although it is the ancestor of our modern English, Old English looks and sounds very different. It had sounds that don't even exist in today's English, and all vowels and syllables of Old English were pronounced. Also, the order used in Old English sentences varied much more than the word order of modern English sentences. This variation was possible because Old English nouns and verbs had endings that indicated their function. A noun did not have to be in "subject" or "object" position as nouns in modern English do. Endings on nouns varied according to their gender. (Old English nouns were masculine, feminine, or neuter, as nouns in modern German are today.)

During the years that it was known as Old English, the pronunciation, vocabulary, and grammar of the language continued to change. One major change began around A.D. 600 when a group of missionaries, led by St. Augustine, came to Christianize the people of Britain. Successful in their mission, St. Augustine's group managed to leave behind not only their religion but also a great deal of their language. In addition to influencing the grammar of Old English, the missionaries were responsible for a large influx of words from Latin (the language of the Church) into the English vocabulary.

EXERCISE 3. Applying Knowledge of Word Origins. Each of the following words came into English through Latin. Using a dictionary that shows word origins, look up each of the words. Write down both the word and its oldest meaning in Latin or Greek. Be prepared to explain how the meaning of the word has changed over the years.

(Note: Dictionaries vary widely in the thoroughness with which they treat word origins. For this and other word origin exercises in this chapter, use your school library resources to consult several dictionaries, including at least one unabridged dictionary. As your teacher directs, bring your research with you to class for discussion.)

1. angel
2. candle
3. disciple
4. hymn
5. cleric
6. martyr
7. mass
8. minister
9. devil
10. priest

Middle to Modern English

The English language between 1066 and 1450 is known as Middle English. The Old English period ended with the defeat of the king of England ("Angle-land") by a Frenchman from Normandy, a province in France, known as William the Conqueror. For the most part, the working classes, who least felt the presence of the French, continued to use the English language. For several hundred years, though, French was the official language of the French court and of the government. As such, it was widely used in literature and in government documents and by British nobles who wished to cultivate the French rulers. During this period of French conquest, more than ten thousand French words became a part of the English language.

As it had during the Old English period, Middle English underwent constant change. For the most part, English became simpler during this period: Nouns, verbs, and adjectives lost many of their inflected endings, nouns lost their gender, and word order in sentences became more regular. Indeed, the English of this period is more recognizable than is Old English. The following lines, for example, were written during the Middle English period. The excerpt, from *The Canterbury Tales,* begins the story of a group of pilgrims on their way from London to a saint's shrine in Canterbury. In the lines printed here, the narrator describes how he happened to meet the other pilgrims while he stopped at an inn (the Tabard) overnight. As you read the excerpt, try to translate the lines into modern English. Notice how similar vocabulary and word order are to today's English.

> Bifel that, in that sesoun on a day,
> In Southwerk at the Tabard as I lay
> Redy to wenden on my pilgrymage
> To Caunterbury with ful devout corage,
> At nyght was come into that hostelrye
> Wel Nyne and twenty in a compaignye,
> Of sondry folk, by aventure yfalle
> In felaweshipe, and pilgrymes were they alle,
> That toward Caunterbury wolden ryde.
> The chambres and the stables weren wyde,
> And wel we weren esed atte beste.
> And shortly, whan the sonne was to reste,
> So hadde I spoken with hem everichon,
> That I was of hir felaweshipe anon,
> And made forward erly for to ryse,
> To take oure wey ther as I yow devyse.

The Middle English language was greatly influenced by several events. One horrible event was the Black Death, a bubonic plague that killed as many as 50 percent of the population in some areas of Europe and Asia during the fourteenth century. With its population decimated, England suffered from a crucial shortage of labor, and the skills of the working classes who survived the plague were in great demand. As a result, members of the working classes gained a new importance in England, and their language—English—once again became a widely respected and used language.

A second, happier event that affected the English language during this period was the Renaissance, a three-hundred-year revival of interest in classical Latin and Greek learning. From the fourteenth through the seventeenth centuries, classical Greek and Latin literature, art, music, and philosophy were explored and much discussed. To talk about many of their new findings, Renaissance scholars adopted many Greek and Latin words and phrases. Consequently, many Greek and Latin words, especially ones related to these particular fields, were brought into the English language at this time.

In addition to the plague and the Renaissance, a new period of world exploration and trade embarked on by the British also influenced the English language. Eventually all of Europe as well as Asia,

Africa, and the Americas had cultural as well as linguistic influences on England. And, of course, one of the most significant influences on the English we use in the United States today took place in 1607 when Captain John Smith arrived at Jamestown to begin the first permanent English colony in the New World. For many years, the new Americans would cling to the English language they had brought with them. Eventually, however, cut off as they were from their native land and with a world of new experiences open before them, the new Americans were influenced by the languages of the native Americans and by those of settlers from many other nations. In this way, the British English that came to this country with the early colonists became the language we know today as American English.

EXERCISE 4. Applying Knowledge of Word Origins. Each of the following words came into English during the French rule of England. Using a dictionary that shows word origins, look up each of the words. Write the French word and its original meaning in either French or Latin. Be prepared to explain how the word's meaning changed as it came into the English language.

1. court
2. council
3. power
4. realm
5. fete
6. countenance
7. jury
8. plaintiff
9. prison
10. robber

EXERCISE 5. Applying Knowledge of Word Origins. Each of the following words came into English during the Renaissance. Using a dictionary that shows word origins, look up each of the words. Write the word as it appeared in Greek or Latin as well as the oldest Greek or Latin meaning shown. Be prepared to explain how the word's meaning changed as it came into the English language.

1. arithmetic
2. logic
3. geometry
4. comedy
5. tragedy
6. nucleus
7. ignoramus
8. radius
9. virus
10. formula

EXERCISE 6. Investigating Word Origins. One of the native Americans' greatest influences on the English language was in place names. More than half our states, for example, have Indian names, as do many lakes, rivers, and mountains. Using a map of your state, locate as many names as possible—of cities, lakes, rivers, mountains, and so on—that were originally Indian names. Since many of the names will have changed in form, use a dictionary to find the original American Indian words.

REVIEW EXERCISE A. Reviewing the History of English. As your teacher directs, give answers to the following questions.

1. What is a language stock?
2. What is the *Indo-European* language? How have linguists been able to learn what they have about the Indo-European language?
3. How is it possible to say that such different languages as Sanskrit and English are related?
4. Who were the Celts? What happened to their language?
5. Describe briefly how Old English became the language of Great Britain.
6. What influence did St. Augustine have on the English language?
7. Why did so many French words become a part of the English language after the year 1066?
8. In what ways did English become less complex during the Middle English period?
9. How did the Black Death and the Renaissance help to influence the English language?
10. How did the settlement of the Jamestown colony help to shape the English we use in the United States today?

USAGE

Regional Dialects

A *dialect* is a form of language that varies in its vocabulary, grammar, and pronunciation from other forms. A *regional* dialect is a variation of language shared by a group of people living in a geographical area.

Even if you have never traveled from one part of the country to another, you are probably aware, from radio and television, that many people living in the South speak differently from those in other parts of the country, that New Englanders may speak differently from inhabitants of the Western states, and so on. Regional dialects in this country began when the British settled in what would eventually become the United States. Much of what is now New England, for example, was originally settled by residents of London (southern England) who used a dialect of English different from that of the British in other parts of England. Later, British inhabitants from northern parts of England, who spoke yet another dialect, began to settle an area that now forms the southern United States.

In this way, as settlement of the New World continued, separate dialect areas established themselves. Later, as western migration began, dialects were dispersed throughout the rest of the country.

Linguists today recognize three major dialect areas: Northern, Midland, and Southern. (Many other smaller and often quite distinctive dialect areas, such as the Appalachian, are also recognized by scholars.) In each of these areas, speakers share features of pronunciation, vocabulary, and grammar. In the Northern area, for example, speakers tend to drop the r and lengthen the /a/ sound so that barn sounds like /bahn/. In the Midland and Southern areas, an r sound is inserted into such words as wash so that the word sounds like /warsh/.

Differences in grammar include the Southern "sick at my stomach" and the Northern "sick to my stomach." Differences in vocabulary are probably the most noticeable. In the Northern area, for example, a certain insect may be called a "darning needle"; in the Midland area, the same insect may be called a "snake doctor," and in other areas, a "mosquito hawk" or "dragonfly." The object that is referred to in the Southern area as a "skillet" may in the Midland area be called a "frying pan" and in the Northern area a "spider."

Differences in regional dialects are not as clear-cut as they may seem. Not everyone in the Southern dialect area, for example, refers to a "skillet," nor may everyone in the Midland area say /warsh/ for wash. Today, because travel is much more frequent, people are exposed to many different dialects, with the result that dialect differences tend to become less pronounced. The effect of radio and television has also been to promote a kind of "national" dialect, one that lacks distinctive features of grammar, vocabulary, and pronunciation. This is the dialect you hear spoken by radio and television commentators.

With a few exceptions, it is difficult to identify any distinctive Northern, Midland, or Southern dialect features in the speech of any of these announcers.

EXERCISE 7. Evaluating Features of Regional Dialects. The characters in the following dialogue are from the play *The Homecoming* made famous in the television show "The Waltons." In this part of the play, which takes place on Christmas Eve, 1933, the mother, Olivia, and the children discuss a cardinal they see outside and their father's late arrival. In the play the family lives in the Virginia mountains, and their speech contains Appalachian dialect features. What features of vocabulary, grammar, and pronunciation do you find in this excerpt? Which features differ from those of your own regional dialect? What vocabulary, grammar, and pronunciation features would you use to express the same thought?

> **Luke:** That red bird is goen to freeze tonight.
> **Olivia:** He won't freeze. Not that bird.
> **Clay-Boy:** Looking back, I don't know if Nana was talking about the cardinal, or if she was trying to say something to her red-headed children.
> **Olivia:** A red bird has got the knack of surviving winter. He knows it, too. Otherwise, he'd of headed South with the wrens and gold finches and the bluebirds back when the leaves started to turn.
> **Luke:** But the red birds don't have to?
> **Olivia** (Touching his hair): Because they've got the knack of surviving.
> **Shirley:** I wish my daddy could fly. Then he wouldn't have to wait for the bus.
> **Mark:** If Daddy goes flyen around, somebody's liable to think he's a turkey buzzard and shoot him down.
> **Olivia** (Emphatically): Don't you worry about our daddy. He's goen to be home for Christmas. You stop fretten about it.

EXERCISE 8. Evaluating Features of Regional Dialects. As your teacher directs, look through your literature textbook or use your school library to find examples of regional dialects. (Hint: Look especially for stories or plays with dialogue.) What regional dialects do you find? What features do you find in these regional dialects that are not in your own? What vocabulary, grammar, and pronunciation features would you use to express the same thoughts?

Standard to Nonstandard English

Standard English is the most widely used dialect of English. Standard English is the English most often used in books and magazines, on radio and television, and in the business and academic communities. There has not always been one such standard form of English. In fact, it was not until after the fifteenth century that English became "standardized" with a designated set of language features. At that time, people living in different parts of England spoke many different dialects of English, each with its own variety of grammar and usage features. In the fifteenth century, however, William Caxton invented the printing press, an accomplishment that, for the first time, allowed the average person access to books. At the time the printing press was invented, London was the cultural and commercial center of the English world. The city, and consequently the form of English used there, was widely admired. Thus when books began to be printed in the city, it was only natural that they be printed in the London dialect of English. It is this same dialect, with a few features added over the years, that has come down to us as "standard" English.

The features that mark standard English are those described in the Usage part of this textbook. These features include the following ones:

1. Singular subjects take singular verbs; plural subjects take plural verbs.

2. Some indefinite pronouns are always singular and take a singular verb.

3. Subjects joined by *and* take a plural verb.

4. The title of a work of art takes a singular verb.

5. A pronoun agrees with its antecedent in number and gender.

English that does not conform to the kinds of features listed is termed "nonstandard" English. It is important to know that the characterizations "right" and "wrong" do not properly apply to standard and nonstandard English. Standard English, through a kind of historical accident, is simply the most widely used form of English. It is also the English most often taught in schools and colleges.

It is also important to know that standard and nonstandard English are not rigidly separated categories into which language neatly fits. Instead, any one person's use of English moves closer to one or the other category, depending on the features of standard English it contains. Almost everyone, at one time or another, uses a feature that is not a part of standard English. This happens more often when you speak than when you write and more often when you speak to close friends than with people you do not know so well. Also, features that were at one time considered features of nonstandard English may gradually, over the years, become a part of standard English. Many linguists believe today, for example, that the distinction between *who* and *whom* is becoming less important as a feature of standard English. At one time, the usage "Who are you calling?" would have been considered nonstandard. Many scholars now, however, believe that this use of *who* is becoming accepted as a part of standard English.

EXERCISE 9. Analyzing the Use of Standard/Nonstandard English. The following paragraph has a mixture of standard and non-standard features. Which words and phrases are nonstandard? Which ones are considered standard? Revise the paragraph, changing all nonstandard features to standard features. For help, refer to the Usage part of this textbook.

This club ain't going to get nowheres except us members cooperate. For one thing, we have to start getting more enthused about coming to the meetings. Also, there's been too many absences, with too many excuses like "I could of come, but I had to feed my dog." We meet only once a month, and everyone knows about the meeting ahead of time, so it's kind of dumb to say that you don't. Another thing is that the members they should sort of take part of the responsibility for the club. The same people hadn't ought to be always taking care of refreshments, planning the program, and making arrangements with the school for the meeting room. I don't mean to infer that you're all deadbeats, but we've got a ways to go to get this club straightened out.

Formal to Informal English

Language use may vary from the very formal to the very informal. Any two people using standard English might still be speaking or writing very differently. One reason for this possible difference is that a user's English might vary from formal to informal, depending on the occasion, audience, and purpose. Differences in formal and informal English include those listed here:

Very Formal:	*Very Informal:*
More often used in writing than in speech	More often used in speech than in writing
More often used for highly ceremonial occasions	More often used on casual occasions
Sentences more often long and complex	More often used with personal friends and small audiences
Sentences more often complete	Sentences more often shorter, less complex, even incomplete
Vocabulary more often precise and complex	Vocabulary more often general and imprecise
Little if any use of slang, colloquialisms, or idiom	More likely to have slang, colloquialisms, and idiom

Formal English

Very formal English is most often used for formal occasions such as weddings, bar mitzvahs, and inaugurations. It is also used at times when the speaker wants to lend a note of dignity and solemnity to the moment. Very formal English is also the form in which most legal documents are written, including constitutions. The following excerpt, for example, is part of Amendment 25 to the Constitution of the United States. This is the amendment that establishes the procedure in the event that a President dies or becomes disabled during his term of office.

> Whenever the Vice-President and a majority of either the principal officers of the executive departments or of such other body as Congress may by law provide, transmit to the President pro tempore of the Senate and the Speaker of the House of Representatives their written declaration that the President is unable to discharge the powers and duties of his office, the Vice-President shall immediately assume the powers and duties of the office as Acting President.

Notice how specifically this section is written: "either the principal officers of the executive departments *or* of such other body"; "the powers *and* duties." Notice also the specific terminology: "transmit" rather than "send," "written declaration" rather than "letter," "discharge" rather than "perform."

Informal English

While formal English is used for solemn, dignified occasions, informal English is most often used for everyday matters. This kind of English is more often used in speaking than in writing. Because of this, it is often called *conversational English*.

Informal English includes colloquialisms and slang. A *colloquialism* is a word or expression used in informal conversation, but not accepted as good usage in formal written English. If you say that someone is "down in the mouth," you are using a colloquialism. *Slang* is highly informal. It is generally considered acceptable when used only in the most informal situations. To use the word *bread* to refer to money is to use slang. (See pages 644–46 for further treatment of colloquialism and slang.)

Remember that as with standard and nonstandard English, formal and informal English are not separate categories; instead, think of very formal and very informal English as being at opposite ends on a line that runs between them. Anyone's use of English tends to move along the line, closer at any given time to one end or the other, depending on the audience, purpose, and occasion.

Language tends to be closer to the informal end when it is spoken and to move closer to the formal end when it is written. Similarly, language tends to be closer to the formal end when the audience is a person or people not known to the user and to move closer to the informal end when the audience is well known. The possible points on this language line are referred to as *levels of usage*. However, since the best choice a writer can make is the one most appropriate to the occasion, the term *levels of usage* is somewhat misleading. On some occasions, formal English is most appropriate; on others, the appropriate choice is informal. The effective writer is one who knows the choices and the appropriate times to use them.

EXERCISE 10. Evaluating Language Use. The purpose and audience for each of the following selections is indicated. Read each selection, noting the features of formal or informal usage that it contains. Be prepared to characterize each selection as very formal, very informal, or somewhere in between. How appropriate is the language in each selection to the purpose and audience? Be prepared to give reasons for your answers.

1

From the keynote address to the 1976 Democratic Party Convention by Congresswoman Barbara Jordan.

In this election year we must define the common good and begin again to shape a common future. Let each person do his or her part. If one citizen is unwilling to participate, all of us are going to suffer. For the American idea, though it is shared by all of us, is realized in each one of us.

And now, what are those of us who are elected public officials supposed to do? We call ourselves public servants but I'll tell you this: we as public servants must set an example for the rest of the nation. It is hypocritical for the public official to admonish and exhort the people to uphold the common good if we are derelict in upholding the common good. More is required of public officials than slogans and handshakes and press releases. More is required. We must hold ourselves strictly accountable. We must provide the people with a vision of the future.

If we promise as public officials, we must deliver. If we as public officials propose, we must produce. If we say to the American people it is time for you to sacrifice, if the public official says that, we [public officials] must be the first to give. We must be. And again, if we make mistakes, we must be willing to admit them. We have to do that. What we have to do is strike a balance between the idea that government should do everything and the idea, the belief, that government ought to do nothing. Strike a balance.

2

From an article explaining why the colonists did not adopt the American Indian word for turkey, but chose instead to name the bird after that far-away country.

In any event, the sixteenth- and early-seventeenth-century English bred these birds that they thought came from Turkey and so were well acquainted with them by the year 1620. Thus, on that first Thanksgiving Day at Plymouth, Massachusetts, in 1621—featuring Gov. William Bradford, Miles Standish, Priscilla Mullins, John Alden, and all that crowd—when the Wampanoag chief Massasoit came forward and offered a wild bird for the feast, saying, "This bird is mighty good eating, folks— it's called a *neyhom*," the Pilgrims no doubt made a reply something like this: "Gee, thanks, Chief. We'll pluck this bird and roast it right away. These birds are well known to us in England; we call them *turkeys*."

EXERCISE 11. Rewriting Formal and Informal English. Select the passage from Exercise 10 that is informal and rewrite it in more formal language. Then rewrite the formal passage in informal language. Are the rewritten passages more or less suitable for the intended purpose and audience? Give reasons for your answers.

REVIEW EXERCISE B. Evaluating the Use of Language. The paragraphs in Exercise 16 of Chapter 12 in this book were written to tell about a student's first day in high school. Read the paragraphs, looking for features of standard or nonstandard, formal or informal English. When you have finished, discuss (in writing, if your teacher directs) the following questions.

1. Is the article written in standard or nonstandard English? Give examples of features of standard or nonstandard English that support your answer.
2. Is the article written in formal or informal English? Does the language in the article actually fall somewhere in between formal and informal usage? Give examples of features of either formal or informal usage that support your answer.
3. What, if any, examples of slang do you find in the article? What, if any, examples of colloquialisms affect the formal/informal usage level of the article? (See pages 644–46 for additional help with this.)
4. This article was written for a student audience. How appropriate is the language use for such an audience? Give reasons to support your answer.
5. Select one paragraph from the article, and rewrite it so that the formal or informal features are changed in the opposite direction. For example, if the paragraph is moderately informal, rewrite it so that it is moderately formal. How appropriate is the new level of usage to the intended audience and purpose? Give reasons to support your answer.

CHAPTER 6

Agreement

SUBJECT AND VERB, PRONOUN AND ANTECEDENT

Agreement, as it is used here, refers to the fact that certain closely related words in sentences have matching forms. Subjects are closely related to their verbs, and a careful speaker makes them agree with each other by matching verb forms to subject forms. In the same way, pronouns and their antecedents are closely related and must be made to agree with each other by matching forms. When such words are correctly matched, we say that they *agree*. When they fail to match, we say there is an error in *agreement*.

DIAGNOSTIC TEST

A. Selecting Verbs That Agree with Their Subjects. Number your paper 1–10. For each sentence choose the verb in parentheses that agrees with the subject of the sentence. Write the verb after the proper number on your paper.

EXAMPLES 1. Neither of the coats on display (is, are) the color I want.
   1. *is*
   2. Both coats (is, are) on sale this week.
   2. *are*

1. The jury (has, have) been paying close attention to the evidence in this case.
2. There (is, are) four herbs that any gardener can grow: basil, thyme, marjoram, and oregano.

141

3. All of these old letters (was, were) tied with ribbon and stored in a trunk in the attic.
4. Each of them (is, are) penned in bold, flowing handwriting, embellished with many flourishes.
5. Alicia and Isabel (thinks, think) that the former owner of the house put the letters in the attic.
6. Neither of them (knows, know) for sure who wrote them.
7. It (doesn't, don't) seem right to read letters addressed to someone else.
8. *Archy & Mehitabel* (is, are) a series of poems about a cockroach that lives in a newspaper office and his friend, a cat.
9. Here (is, are) the latest scores of today's baseball games.
10. Neither potatoes nor corn (is, are) grown on this farm.

B. Writing Verbs That Agree with Their Subjects and Pronouns That Agree with Their Antecedents. In many of the following sentences, either a verb does not agree with its subject, or a pronoun does not agree with its antecedent. Number your paper 11–20. After the proper number on your paper, write the correct form of the incorrect verb or pronoun. If a sentence is correct, write *C*.

EXAMPLES 1. The flock of birds, almost blackening the sky, were an awe-inspiring sight.
1. *was*

2. Only a decade ago their number was declining.
2. *C*

11. The meeting got out of hand when the discussion period began, since everyone tried to express their opinion at the same time.
12. There on the corner of your desk is the books that I returned and that you claimed you never received.
13. Two students from each class is going to the state capital to attend a special conference on education.
14. Each of them are expected to bring back a report on the objectives of the conference so that classmates can get firsthand information.
15. Since they will be on vacation next month, neither Miguel nor his sister are going to enter the mixed-doubles tennis tournament.
16. The audience expressed their admiration for the dancer's grace and skill by applauding wildly.

17. After the senator had read the proposed amendment, anyone who disagreed with the ruling was allowed to state their reason.
18. When she saw the locker room, Ellen became angry because not one of the children had picked up after themselves.
19. She is one of those competitive people who perform best under pressure.
20. Although she owns several pieces of fine china, her most prized possession are the little cups inherited from a great-aunt.

SINGULAR AND PLURAL NUMBER

6a. When a word refers to one person or thing, it is *singular* in number. When a word refers to more than one, it is *plural* in number.

The boldfaced words below agree in number.

EXAMPLES **One** of the players **was** not wearing **his** glove. [singular]
Several of the players **were** not wearing **their** gloves. [plural]

Nouns and pronouns have number. The following nouns and pronouns are singular because they name only one person or thing: *airplane, child, I, idea.* The following are plural because they name more than one person or thing: *airplanes, children, we, ideas.*[1]

EXERCISE 1. Identifying Words as Singular or Plural in Number.
List the following words on your paper. After each plural word, write *P* for plural; after each singular word, write *S* for singular.

1. books	5. people	9. ability	13. both
2. one	6. mouse	10. area	14. data
3. several	7. many	11. mathematics	15. woman
4. lights	8. civics	12. love	

AGREEMENT OF SUBJECT AND VERB

Verbs, too, have number; certain forms are used when a verb's subject is singular and others when the subject is plural. In standard English, verbs agree with their subjects.

[1] For rules regarding the formulation of plurals of nouns, see pages 827–29.

6b. A verb agrees with its subject in number.

(1) Singular subjects take singular verbs.

EXAMPLE Marcia **attends** college, but Laura **goes** to computer school. [The singular verb *attends* agrees with the singular subject *Marcia;* the singular verb *goes* agrees with the singular subject *Laura.*]

(2) Plural subjects take plural verbs.

EXAMPLE Marcia and Laura **attend** college, but the other girls **do** not. [The plural verb *attend* agrees with the plural subject *Marcia and Laura,* and the plural verb *do* agrees with the plural subject *girls.*]

In general, nouns ending in *s* are plural (*aunts, uncles, towns, crimes*) but verbs ending in *s* are singular (*gives, takes, does, has, is*). Singular *I* and *you,* however, generally take verbs that do not end in *s* (*I think, you think, I am, you are*).

☞ NOTE The form *were* is normally plural except when used with the singular *you* and in sentences like the following:

If I were in charge, I would make some changes.
Were Albert home, he could fix this.

EXERCISE 2. Selecting Verbs That Agree with Their Subjects.
Decide which one of the verbs in parentheses should be used to agree with the subject given.

1. student (walks, walk)
2. one (is, are)
3. several (runs, run)
4. it (works, work)
5. Joan (was, were)
6. Carol (sings, sing)
7. many (looks, look)
8. two (was, were)
9. people (plays, play)
10. they (writes, write)
11. houses (stands, stand)
12. the result (is, are)
13. both (believes, believe)
14. crews (sails, sail)
15. women (seems, seem)
16. a person (thinks, think)
17. geese (waddles, waddle)
18. we (talks, talk)
19. the star (glitters, glitter)
20. all men (buys, buy)

6c. The number of the subject is not changed by a phrase following the subject.

Do not be confused when a phrase comes between the subject and the verb. Since the subject is never a part of a phrase, a word in a phrase cannot influence the verb.

EXAMPLE   **One** of the women **is singing.** [The phrase *of the women* does not affect the number of the subject *one: one is,* not *women are.*]

EXAMPLE   Both **women** from the senate **were** at the meeting. [The phrase *from the senate* does not affect the number of the subject *women: women were,* not *senate was.*]

Even prepositional phrases beginning with expressions like *with, together with, in addition to, as well as,* and *along with* do not affect the number of the verb.

EXAMPLES   Tammy, along with her mother and aunt, **is** going to the concert. [Tammy . . . is]
The wind, together with the rain and fog, **was** making navigation difficult. [The wind . . . was]
Jack's imagination, as well as his sense of humor, **was** delightful. [Jack's imagination . . . was]

The logic of this will be clearer to you if you rearrange the first sentence about Tammy.

EXAMPLE   Tammy **is** going to the concert along with her mother and aunt.

Another source of trouble is the negative construction. When such a construction comes between the subject and its verb, it is often mistakenly allowed to affect the number of the verb and throw it out of agreement with its proper subject. Treat negative constructions exactly like phrases following the subject.

EXAMPLE   Carl, not Juan and I, is doing the artwork.

EXERCISE 3. Selecting Verbs That Agree with Their Subjects. In each of the following sentences, you have a choice of verbs. Write the subject of each verb on your paper. Select the one of the two verbs in parentheses that agrees in number with the subject. Remember that the verb and subject must agree in number.

1. Two of these cassettes (is, are) mine.
2. A heaping basket of beets, carrots, and peas (was, were) on the counter.
3. Disregard for the rights and comforts of others (is, are) rude.
4. The community college course on collecting stamps and coins (attracts, attract) many people.
5. The members of the family (meets, meet) for a reunion every year.
6. The roar of the waves (was, were) deafening.
7. Lois, as well as Tricia and Raphael, (has, have) volunteered to count votes.
8. That big tree with the oddly shaped leaves (seems, seem) to be dying.
9. The carpeting in the upstairs and downstairs rooms (is, are) worn.
10. The price of haircuts (is, are) going up again.
11. The package of radio parts (was, were) smashed in the mail.
12. These jars of mustard (is, are) broken.
13. The cost of two new snow tires (was, were) more than I expected.
14. Burt, not Anne and Laura, (has, have) the bicycle pump.
15. The three boxes of dried mint (fits, fit) easily on the bottom shelf.
16. The members of the winning band (feels, feel) jubilant.
17. The escape of three snakes from the laboratory (has, have) created quite a stir.
18. The chief, along with two of the firefighters, (gives, give) lectures on home safety.
19. In the movie, a ring of dancers (performs, perform) a folk dance.
20. Participation in class discussions, not just high test scores, (counts, count) toward one's final grade.

6d. The following pronouns are singular: *each, either, neither, one, everyone, everybody, no one, nobody, anyone, anybody, someone, somebody.*

These words are called *indefinite pronouns* because they refer only generally, indefinitely, to some thing or person. Very often they are followed by a prepositional phrase containing a plural word. When this situation occurs, be sure to make the verb agree with the indefinite pronoun, not with a word in the prepositional phrase.

NONSTANDARD   One of the guitar strings were broken. [The verb *were* does not agree with the singular subject, *one*.]

STANDARD   **One** of the guitar strings **was** broken. [The verb agrees with the subject.]

Read the following pairs of sentences aloud, stressing the subjects and verbs in boldfaced type.

EXAMPLES   **Neither was** sure of the answer.
Neither of the scientists **was** sure of the answer.

Each was called.
Each of the numbers **was** called.

No one leaves early.
No one except the band members **leaves** early.

Someone raids the refrigerator at night.
Someone among the guests **raids** the refrigerator at night.

6e. The following pronouns are plural: *several, few, both, many.*

EXAMPLES   **Several** of the women **were** joggers.
A **few** in the crowd **are** troublesome.
Both have tried harder.
Many of the tourists **stop** here and **rest.**

6f. The pronouns *some, all, any, most,* **and** *none* **may be either singular or plural, depending on the meaning of the sentence.**

A writer may use either a singular or a plural verb to agree with the words *some, all, any, most,* and *none,* depending on the meaning of the sentence. These words are plural if they refer to a plural word; they are singular if they refer to a singular word.

SINGULAR   **Most** of the day **was** gone. [*Most* refers to *day,* which is a singular word.]

PLURAL   **Most** of the steers **were** grazing. [*Most* refers to *steers,* which is a plural word.]

SINGULAR   **Has any** of the shipment arrived? [*Any* refers to *shipment,* which is a singular word.]

PLURAL **Have any** of the coins been spent? [*Any* refers to *coins*, which is a plural word.]

SINGULAR **None** of the damage **was** serious. [*None* refers to *damage*, which is singular.]

PLURAL **None** of the students **have** finished. [*None* refers to *students*, which is plural.]

In each of the last six examples, the prepositional phrase following the subject provides a clue to the number of the subject. You may think of this as an exception to rule 6c. These pronouns can also be used without a prepositional phrase after them.

EXAMPLES Most were grazing. [a number of horses, steers, cows, etc.]
Most was interesting. [a portion of a book, movie, conversation, etc.]

EXERCISE 4. *Oral Drill.* Stressing Subjects and Verbs in Sentences.
Repeat each of the following sentences aloud three times, stressing the italicized words.

1. *One* of those cups *is* broken.
2. Either *one* of the bikes *is* ready to go.
3. A *few* of the girls *are* experienced riders.
4. *Each* of them *has* a complete set of maps.
5. *One* of them *works* for the city.
6. *Some* of the mice *were* caught.
7. *Most* of the milk *is* gone.
8. *Neither* of the cars *has* a radio.
9. Every *one* of the packages *is* heavy.
10. *Either* of those workers *does* a good job.

EXERCISE 5. Writing Sentences with Verbs That Agree with Their Subjects.
Rewrite each of the following twenty sentences according to the directions in parentheses. If necessary, change the number of the verb to agree with the new subject or to accord with the altered sense of the sentence.

1. Everyone quickly understands the rules of this game. (Change *everyone* to *most people*.)
2. Neither of the actresses was nominated. (Change *neither* to *both*.)
3. There is fried chicken for everybody. (Change *chicken* to *potatoes*.)

4. Some of the trees were destroyed. (Change *trees* to *crop*.)
5. Have any of the apples been harvested? (Change *apples* to *wheat*.)
6. Nobody visits that haunted house. (Change *nobody* to *many of our neighbors*.)
7. Each is well trained. (Change *each* to *both*.)
8. Each of the tires needs air. (Change *each* to *several*.)
9. All of the fruit was eaten. (Change *fruit* to *pears*.)
10. Has each of your cousins had a turn? (Change *each* to *both*.)
11. Some of the positions have been filled. (Change *some* to *neither*.)
12. Nobody lives there anymore. (Change *nobody* to *few of our friends*.)
13. Either of these books is helpful. (Change *either* to *each*.)
14. Several of the experiments are completed. (Change *several* to *not one*.)
15. All of the rides were exciting. (Change *all* to *one*.)
16. Most of the livestock was valuable. (Change *livestock* to *mares*.)
17. Neither of your shoes is tied. (Change *neither* to *both*.)
18. A box of firewood was by the stove. (Change *firewood* to *kindling sticks*.)
19. Do all of the word processors work? (Change *all* to *either*.)
20. Neither of those answers is correct. (Change *neither* to *some*.)

EXERCISE 6. Identifying Subject-Verb Agreement in Sentences.
Number your paper 1–20. Read each of the sentences carefully. If the verb and subject agree, write a + after the proper number on your paper. If the verb and subject do not agree, write a 0 after the proper number.

1. Each of the knives are dull.
2. Not one of the keys fits.
3. Several of the crew was commended by the captain.
4. One of the cartoonist's favorite characters was Delbert Duck.
5. Most of the questions on the test was hard.
6. Neither of the coaches were happy with the decision.
7. Each of us are going to make a poster for the election.
8. Some of the ice cream has started to melt.
9. Every one of the entrants have to pass a special exam.
10. Either of those albums are good background music.
11. All of the seats were too near the movie screen.

12. Each one of the machines are thoroughly tested at the factory.
13. Does both of those games require special equipment?
14. Either of the assistants goes for the mail.
15. Each of the ingredients is carefully measured.
16. None of the buildings were damaged by the hail.
17. None of the food has been frozen.
18. Neither of the book reports were finished on time.
19. Every one of the players gets a trophy.
20. Most of the birds were quiet.

The Compound Subject

6g. Most compound subjects joined by *and* take a plural verb.

EXAMPLES Ramon and she **like** hiking.
Her brother and her cousin **are** teachers.

A few compound subjects joined by *and* name a single person or thing and therefore take a singular verb.

EXAMPLES Pork and beans **goes** well with hot dogs. [one dish]
Rock and roll **is** here to stay. [one kind of music]

6h. Singular subjects joined by *or* or *nor* take a singular verb.

EXAMPLES Neither Mark nor Donna **knows** the address.
Does either Father or Mother have the key?
Neither our phone nor our doorbell **was** working.

Note that the word *either* may be omitted, but the number of the subject is not changed so long as the parts are joined by *or*.

EXAMPLE Jim or Peggy **is** taking the letters to the post office.

Note also that this use of *either . . . or, neither . . . nor* should not be confused with that of the correlative conjunction *both . . . and*, which takes a plural verb.

EXAMPLES Both the scout and the counselor **were** part of the emergency drill.
Neither the scout nor the counselor **was** part of the emergency drill.

6i. When a singular and a plural subject are joined by *or* or *nor*, the verb agrees with the nearer subject.

EXAMPLES   Either Horace or his aunts **were** up to something.   [aunts were]

Neither the potatoes nor the roast **seems** done. [roast seems]

In the first sentence *aunts* is nearer to the verb *were* than *Horace,* the other part of the compound subject. The verb must be plural to agree with the nearer subject, *aunts.* Likewise, in the second sentence the verb *seems* must agree with *roast,* since this singular part of the compound subject is nearer to it. This kind of construction is often awkward, however, and it is usually best to avoid it.

EXAMPLES   Either Horace **was** up to something, or his aunts **were**.

The potatoes **do** not seem done, and neither **does** the roast.

EXERCISE 7. *Oral Drill.* Stressing Subjects and Verbs in Sentences.   Repeat each of the following sentences aloud three times, stressing the italicized words.

1. Every *one* of the kittens *has* been given away.
2. A *few* of us *are* going to Chicago.
3. *Each* of the photographs *was* in black and white.
4. *Neither* Sam *nor* Miguel *likes* sports.
5. *Either* Judy *or* Claudia *does* the dishes tonight.
6. Not *one* of the stations *is* coming in clearly.
7. *Several* of the plates *were* cracked.
8. *Both* Marilyn *and* Marge *have* summer jobs.
9. *Either is* acceptable.
10. Each *one* of the statues *is* different.

EXERCISE 8. Selecting Verbs That Agree with Their Subjects.
Number your paper 1–20. For each sentence choose the verb in parentheses that agrees with the subject of the sentence. Write the verb after the proper number on your paper.

1. Neither my brother nor I (has, have) a car.
2. Marlon and she (is, are) the dance champions.
3. Our relatives and theirs (is, are) having a picnic together.
4. Both John and his mother (plays, play) a good game of tennis.
5. Either the director or the actors (is, are) going to have to compromise.
6. Neither the grapes nor the cantaloupe (was, were) ripe.
7. Both the Los Angeles Lakers and the Boston Celtics (is, are) popular with fans.

8. Our class or theirs (is, are) going to sponsor the dance.
9. Either the faucet or the shower head (leaks, leak).
10. Either a transistor or a capacitor (has, have) burned out in this receiver.
11. A fish or a lizard (makes, make) a quiet pet.
12. Trolleys and cable cars (is, are) growing rarer nowadays.
13. The boxers and the referee (wants, want) the videotape to be reviewed.
14. Both oats and hay (is, are) good for horses.
15. Either my team or my sister's (plays, play) yours next week.
16. The chairs and the table (matches, match) the china cabinet.
17. Neither the senator nor her aides (likes, like) the proposed law.
18. Tina or Laurie (does, do) those problems easily.
19. The most grueling event of the Olympics (is, are) the marathon.
20. Either a patch of poison ivy or a clump of poison oak (is, are) growing near here.

Other Problems in Agreement

6j. **Collective nouns may be either singular or plural.**

You may be in doubt at times about the number of a word that names a group of persons or objects. This kind of word is known as a *collective noun*.

A collective noun is singular and takes a singular verb when the group is thought of *as a unit or whole*.

A collective noun is plural and takes a plural verb when members of a group are thought of *as individuals acting separately*. Study the following pairs of sentences.

The class **has** a substitute teacher. [*Class* is thought of as a unit.]
The class **were** disagreeing with one another about **their** answers. [*Class* is thought of as a number of individuals.]

Kathy's club **is** visiting the museum. [*Club* is a unit.]
Kathy's club **are** all wearing **their** new uniforms. [The *club* is thought of as individuals.]

The team **is** on the bus. [*Team* is thought of as a unit.]
The team **write** to **their** friends back home. [*Team* is thought of as a number of individuals.]

The following is a list of some collective nouns:

army	club	family	jury
audience	committee	flock	swarm
choir	crowd	group	team
class	faculty	herd	troop

EXERCISE 9. Writing Sentences with Collective Nouns. Select five collective nouns, and write five pairs of sentences like those on page 152, showing clearly how the words you choose may be either singular or plural.

EXERCISE 10. Writing Sentences with Verbs That Agree with Their Subjects. Rewrite the following ten sentences according to the instructions in parentheses, changing the number of the verb if necessary.

1. Both of the records are in the top forty. (Change *both* to *neither.*)
2. The choir has been arguing with the conductor. (Change *with the conductor* to *among themselves.*)
3. Either my cousins or Julie is bringing the pizza. (Reverse the order of the subjects.)
4. Neither Carrie nor Jana is in the Pep Club. (Change *neither . . . nor* to *both . . . and.*)
5. Jerry and Manuel are going to win. (Change *and* to *or.*)
6. All of your papers were graded. (Change *all* to *each.*)
7. Some of the time was needlessly wasted. (Change *time* to *supplies.*)
8. The delighted team was waving and grinning widely. (Change *waving and grinning widely* to *assembling to accept their medals.*)
9. Everybody in the chorus is trying out for the play. (Change *everybody* to *no one.*)
10. Macaroni and cheese always tastes good. (Change *and* to *or.*)

6k. A verb agrees with its subject, not with its predicate nominative.

In the following examples the subject is marked s and the predicate nominative PN.

EXAMPLES
      S   PN

The greatest **threat** to campers **is bears.**

     S   PN

Bears are the greatest **threat** to campers.

            S   PN

The main **ingredient** of my hot sauce **is** jalapeño **peppers.**

        S   PN

Jalapeño **peppers are** the main **ingredient** of my hot sauce.

Often this kind of agreement problem can be avoided by changing the sentence so as to avoid using a predicate nominative:

EXAMPLE **I use** jalapeño **peppers** as the main ingredient of my hot sauce.

6l. When the subject follows a verb, as in sentences beginning with *there* **and** *here,* **be careful to anticipate the subject, and make sure that the verb agrees with it.**

NONSTANDARD Here is the brushes you need. [not *brushes . . . is*]

STANDARD Here **are** the brushes you need. [*brushes . . . are*]

EXERCISE 11. Identifying Sentences with Subject-Verb Agreement.
Number your paper 1–20. Read each sentence aloud. If the verb agrees with the subject, put a + on your paper after the proper number. If the verb does not agree with the subject, write a 0 after the proper number. Be ready to explain the reasons for your choice.

1. Soap and water is the best cleanser for my face.
2. There's the boats I told you about.
3. Both my father and sister wants to see the Cubs game.
4. Either the twins or Jamie are playing a practical joke.
5. How was the swimming and sailing at the beach?
6. Ham and eggs are a great combination for breakfast.
7. Neither the windows nor the door is locked.
8. Each of the newspapers have clippings cut out.
9. There's always dozens of football games on television on New Year's Day.
10. Each of the dogs have to get a rabies shot.
11. Where's my socks?
12. There's more than enough booklets to go around.
13. Does all of your photographs come out this well?
14. Lyn, along with Anne and Beverly, has decided to attend this meeting.

15. Neither of the candidates has run for office before.
16. Are each of the paintings in the collection an original?
17. Neither Connie nor Rita wants to swim today.
18. My six cousins, the visiting in-laws, together with the five people in our own family, is making the house seem crowded.
19. Was any of our news stories nominated for awards?
20. Either Miss Fleury or her students are bringing the slides.

6m. Words stating amount are usually singular.

EXAMPLES Two years **is** a long time.
Fifty cents **was** the price.
Ninety percent of the student body **is** present.

When the sense of the sentence indicates that the subject designates a collection of individual parts rather than a single unit or quantity, the verb must be plural in number.

EXAMPLES Sixty short minutes **fly** by.
Three quarters **were** in my pocket.
Ninety percent of the students **are** present today.

Two such amount-stating expressions deserve special mention: *the number of* and *a number of*. They should not be confused. *The number of* takes a singular verb, and *a number of* takes a plural verb.

EXAMPLES **The number of** female athletes **is** growing.
A number of girls **like** strenuous sports.

6n. *Every* or *many a* before a word or a series of words is followed by a singular verb.

EXAMPLES **Every** mother, father, and grandparent **is looking** on proudly.
Many a hopeful performer **has** gone to Broadway in search of fame.

6o. The title of a work of art, literature, or music, even when plural in form, takes a singular verb.

EXAMPLES Paul Laurence Dunbar's *Majors and Minors* **is** a collection of his poetry.
Millet's *The Gleaners* **is** a famous nineteenth-century French painting.
Gertrude Stein's *Three Lives* **has** influenced many writers.

6p. *Don't* **and** *doesn't* **must agree with their subject.**

With the subjects *I* and *you,* use *don't* (*do not*); with other singular subjects use *doesn't* (*does not*); with plural subjects use *don't* (*do not*).

EXAMPLES **I don't** have any paper.
You don't need special permission.
It (he, she) doesn't show up in this picture.
They don't feel nervous.

Do not use *don't* after *he, she,* or *it.*

NONSTANDARD It don't look right.

STANDARD It **doesn't** look right.

NONSTANDARD He don't like spinach.

STANDARD He **doesn't** like spinach.

EXERCISE 12. Using *Don't* and *Doesn't* Correctly in Sentences.
Number your paper 1–10. After the proper number, write the correct form (*don't* or *doesn't*) for each of the following sentences.

1. The calf —— look very strong.
2. It —— matter if the weather is bad.
3. She —— play racquetball.
4. He —— write many letters.
5. I —— mind helping out.
6. You —— have to watch the program.
7. Loretta —— enjoy cleaning house.
8. A few of the contests —— award cash prizes.
9. —— it arrive soon?
10. —— he tinker with cars?

EXERCISE 13. Selecting Verbs That Agree with Their Subjects.
Number your paper 1–10. After the proper number, write the correct one of the two verbs given in parentheses in each of the following sentences.

1. The coach, along with two assistants, (was, were) yelling at the players.
2. Georgia O'Keeffe, of all painters, (captures, capture) the mystery of the West.
3. They (wasn't, weren't) interested in learning the accordion.

4. Carlos, not Martha or Jan, (was, were) answering all the letters.
5. Many of them (has, have) already read the novel.
6. *The Birds* (was, were) one of Hitchcock's great movies.
7. Samantha, a Persian cat with expensive tastes, (is, are) partial to lobster.
8. That collection of short stories (is, are) fun to read.
9. Mrs. Williams, as well as two of her neighbors, (is, are) on the budget committee.
10. A few of the men, including Mr. Gomez, (isn't, aren't) convinced the mayor is right.
11. Could it be that nobody among all the world's animal lovers (wants, want) to take these puppies off my hands?
12. (Doesn't, Don't) Chuck want to join the Air Force when he graduates?
13. Caroline, like most of her classmates, (wishes, wish) vacation could last forever.
14. A package of nuts and bolts (was, were) delivered to the hardware store.
15. There (is, are) some good programs on educational television.
16. Neither of his teammates (was, were) open for the pass.
17. The collection of Jill Krementz' photographs (is, are) drawing large crowds at the gallery.
18. It (doesn't, don't) look good for our baseball league this season.
19. (Doesn't, Don't) all of you remember your very first swimming lesson?
20. Both of the skaters (is, are) hoping to become members of the Olympic team.

WRITING APPLICATION A:
Using Subject-Verb Agreement to Make Your Writing Clear

Who are your two favorite teachers? Are these two teachers alike in some ways? Are they unlike in other ways? Being able to write about how people, things, or ideas are alike and unlike is an important skill. It requires careful checking of subject-verb agreement.

Writing Assignment

Pointing out likenesses is generally called comparing. Pointing out differences is generally called contrasting. Write a paragraph in which you compare and contrast two people, things, or ideas. In the paragraph, use at least three of the following expressions, making sure subject and verb agree. When you use the expressions, underline them.

1. each of
2. both of
3. neither of
4. one of
5. either of
6. several of

EXAMPLE   One of my favorite teachers is a fifth-grade teacher.

REVIEW EXERCISE A. Making Verbs Agree with Their Subjects.

In some of the following sentences, the verbs agree with their subjects; in others, the verbs do not agree. Number your paper 1–25. If the verb and subject agree in a sentence, write C after the proper number. If the verb does not agree with its subject, supply the correct form of the verb after the proper number.

1. Each of you are invited.
2. Barbara, along with her cousin, wants to visit Washington, D.C.
3. Not one of those pictures or plaques is hung straight.
4. Neither the class nor Ms. Johnson have heard the news.
5. There are a strain of measles that lasts only three days.
6. Where's the best bargains in clothing in town?
7. Few objections, besides the one about chartering the bus, was raised.
8. *Six Characters in Search of an Author* is a modern play that raises many interesting questions about art and reality.
9. Some of this land is far too hilly to farm.
10. Either he or she are doing the advertising layouts for the paper this week.
11. One of the orangutans have escaped from the cage!
12. Fifteen dollars is a lot to pay for an album.
13. Every one of these handy mango peelers come with a one-year guarantee.
14. In Maine there's many miles of rocky coastline.
15. The committee is prepared to hold its elections.
16. Not one of the eggs in the damaged cartons were broken.
17. Four minutes were his record time in that race.
18. It don't really make any difference.

19. Two thirds of a cup of flour is needed for this recipe.
20. The band was tuning their instruments nervously.
21. There are, in my opinion, a number of good reasons for the change.
22. Every student, teacher, and administrator are contributing to the fund-raising drive.
23. Here is one book of tickets we have left over.
24. It often doesn't snow here until December.
25. A few of the students are in the library.

AGREEMENT OF PRONOUN AND ANTECEDENT

Personal pronouns (*I, you, he,* etc.) have matching forms that must agree with their antecedents. The antecedent is the word to which a pronoun refers.

6q. A pronoun agrees with its antecedent in gender and number.

A small number of nouns in English name persons or things that are clearly masculine: *father, ram, stallion.* About the same number name persons or things that are clearly feminine: *mother, ewe, mare.* Most nouns name persons or things that may be either masculine or feminine (*adult, reader*) or to which the idea of gender does not apply (*town, report*). Nouns that apply to both masculine and feminine, or that do not carry any idea of either masculine or feminine, are said to be *neuter* or to have *common gender.*

Personal pronouns usually match the gender of their antecedents.

EXAMPLES Does **Margaret** like **her** dance class? [The pronoun *her* is feminine to agree with *Margaret.*]

Because the **car** would not start, **it** had to be towed. [The pronoun *it* agrees in gender with *car.*]

Personal pronouns also have forms that reflect the number of their antecedents.

EXAMPLES The **riders** readied **their** horses. [The pronoun is plural to agree with *riders.*]

The **rider** adjusted **his** stirrups. [Because the antecedent is singular now, the pronoun is singular.]

(1) The words *each, either, neither, one, everyone, everybody, no one, nobody, anyone, anybody, someone, somebody* **are referred to by a singular pronoun:** *he, him, his, she, her, hers, it, its.*

The use of a phrase after the antecedent does not change the number of the antecedent.

EXAMPLES **Each** of the teams had **its** mascot at the game.
Someone in the class left **his** notes behind.
Everybody on the bus is supposed to stay in **his** seat.

When the antecedent can be either masculine or feminine, as in the last two examples, it has been standard formal usage to use only the masculine pronoun. However, more writers are beginning to use both the masculine and feminine forms of pronouns in such cases.

EXAMPLE **Everybody** has **his or her** card.

You can avoid the awkward *his or her* construction by rephrasing the sentence using the plural form of the pronouns.

EXAMPLE **All** students have **their** cards.

In conversation, you might find it more convenient to use a plural personal pronoun when referring to singular antecedents that can be either masculine or feminine.

EXAMPLES **Nobody** rode **their** bikes.
Everybody brought **their** fishing rods.

☞ **USAGE NOTE** On certain occasions when the *idea* of the sentence (the meaning of the antecedent) is clearly plural, you must use the plural pronoun even though the singular form of the pronoun is called for grammatically. For example, to use a singular pronoun in the following sentence would be absurd.

When **everybody** has arrived, explain the situation to **them** [not *him*].

It is usually possible to avoid such constructions.

BETTER When **all** the people have arrived, explain the situation to **them**.

(2) Two or more singular antecedents joined by *or* or *nor* should be referred to by a singular pronoun.

EXAMPLE Neither Heidi nor Beth took **her** umbrella with **her**.

(3) Two or more antecedents joined by *and* should be referred to by a plural pronoun.

EXAMPLE   The guide and the ranger wrapped **their** rain ponchos in **their** saddle rolls.

(4) The number of a relative pronoun (*who, which, that*) is determined by the number of the word to which it refers—its antecedent.

EXAMPLES   Miriam is one of those **students who are** always striving to do **their** best. [*Who* is plural because it refers to *students*. Therefore, the plural forms *are* and *their* are used to agree with *who*.]
Anyone who wants to volunteer should raise **his** hand. [*Who* is singular because *anyone* is singular. Therefore, the singular forms *wants* and *his* are used to agree with *who*.]

EXERCISE 14. Selecting Pronouns That Agree with Their Antecedents.
Number your paper 1–20. For each blank in the following sentences, select a pronoun that will agree with its antecedent, and write it after the proper number on your paper.

1. After the hike, all of the scouts complained that —— feet hurt.
2. Either Camille or Rose will bring —— cassette player.
3. Everyone at the campground will need to bring —— own tent and bedroll.
4. Some of the women wrote to —— local newspapers about the pollution problem.
5. Every driver checked —— car before the race.
6. Each of the actors had —— own odd superstition.
7. Both of the girls practiced —— dives off the high tower.
8. Marcia and her brother are saving money to have —— car repaired.
9. Someone has parked —— car in my space.
10. All of the girls knew —— parts perfectly by opening night.
11. Neither of the sweaters had —— price tag removed.
12. Everybody should exercise —— right to vote.
13. Many of the crew got —— first case of seasickness during the violent storm.
14. Gina and her grandfather proudly showed us —— fine string of trout.
15. One of the houses had —— windows broken by the hail.

16. Everyone bought —— own copy of the textbook.
17. The President and the Vice-President expressed —— separate opinions about the issue.
18. Anyone who needs a pencil should raise —— hand.
19. Either Stu or Mike will lend me —— fishing gear.
20. Each of the cars had —— own parking place.

EXERCISE 15. Using Forms of *Be* Correctly in Sentences.

Number your paper 1–10. After the proper number, list the singular or the plural form of the verb *be* for the sentences that require verbs. List a singular or plural pronoun for the sentences that require pronouns.

1. One of the lucky entrants —— going to win a trip to Hawaii.
2. Neither of us —— able to ski.
3. Some of the students finished —— assignments early.
4. Each actress spoke —— own lines.
5. Here —— your hat and jacket.
6. If anybody bothers you, tell —— to go away.
7. One of these documents —— a forgery.
8. Since one of the Cub Scouts —— sick, we drove him home.
9. Neither he nor his sister —— vacationing with the rest of the family.
10. Someone in the band left —— trumpet case here.

WRITING APPLICATION B:
Using Pronoun-Antecedent Agreement to Make Your Writing Clear

Good writers have different and individual ways of thinking. This is a characteristic of creativity. One way to develop your creative thinking ability is to ask questions that start with "What if . . . ?"

Writing Assignment

Write ten questions that begin with "What if . . . " In at least five of the questions, include a pronoun that must agree with its antecedent, as illustrated below. Underline the pronoun and its antecedent when they occur.

EXAMPLE What if a girl discovered that her exact twin was sitting across the table in the cafeteria?

REVIEW EXERCISE B. Identifying Subject-Verb Agreement and Pronoun-Antecedent Agreement in Sentences. In some of the following sentences, either a verb does not agree with its subject or a pronoun does not agree with its antecedent. Number your paper 1–20. If a sentence is correct, write a + after the proper number; if it is incorrect, write a 0.

1. Both Sid and Nikki like their new neighborhood.
2. Neither of the transmitters were affected by the storm.
3. Antonio, in addition to the other singers, were ready for the competition to start.
4. One of the police officers was the top scorer on the rifle range.
5. Neither John nor Bruce has recovered from their disastrous camping trip.
6. *The Three Little Pigs* are my young nephews' all-time favorite animated feature.
7. There was a set of salt-and-pepper shakers on the counter.
8. Where is the Athletics Department?
9. Each of the waitresses were hurrying as fast as possible.
10. A few of the crowd was murmuring impatiently.
11. Is there any of those peanuts left?
12. Either Lois or Maria is in charge of the equipment.
13. Every one of those cattle are going to have to be rounded up.
14. An additional feature of these models is the built-in stereo-speakers.
15. Somebody has gone off and left their car running.
16. If anybody calls, tell them I'll be back by this evening.
17. Each team has its own colors and symbol.
18. One of the goats were nibbling on a discarded popcorn box.
19. Here's the pair of gloves that you forgot.
20. Are there no end to these questions?

REVIEW EXERCISE C. Selecting Verbs That Agree with Their Subjects and Pronouns That Agree with Their Antecedents. Number your paper 1–20. In each sentence, select the correct one of the two forms given in parentheses, and write it after the proper number on your paper.

1. Neither the manager nor the two salespeople (was, were) prepared for the number of customers.
2. Everybody got to listen to a recording of (his, their) own voice.

3. Each of the cyclists (was, were) beginning to feel the effects of the long trip.
4. If anyone comes in now, (he, they) will see the mess we've made.
5. Neither of the sets of barbells (was, were) easy to lift.
6. Both Karen and the two firefighters (is, are) having difficulty getting the cat out of the tree.
7. Ms. Lo, along with her students, (visits, visit) the museum once a semester.
8. Where (is, are) the box of nails that came with the kit?
9. A few of our classmates (was, were) invited.
10. "Birches" (is, are) a poem by Robert Frost.
11. There (is, are) leftover macaroni and cheese in the refrigerator.
12. If anybody likes a spectacle, (he, they) will love seeing a drum corps competition.
13. Several of the audience (was, were) frightened.
14. Nobody knows what (his, their) future may hold.
15. The great auk, as well as the dodo and the passenger pigeon, (is, are) extinct.
16. Where (has, have) the sports section of my paper gone?
17. Neither of the planes had (its, their) cargo loaded.
18. Anyone who wants (his, their) plate refilled had better hurry.
19. Every one of these mosquitoes (seems, seem) to want to bite me.
20. A philosopher once said that if someone built a better mousetrap, the world would beat a path to (his, their) door.

CHAPTER 6 REVIEW: POSTTEST 1

Selecting Verbs That Agree with Their Subjects and Pronouns That Agree with Their Antecedents. In many of the following sentences, a verb does not agree with its subject, or a pronoun does not agree with its antecedent. Number your paper 1–25. After the proper number on your paper, write the correct form of the incorrect words. If a sentence is correct, write *C*.

EXAMPLES 1. Each leaf, flower, and seedpod were glimmering with a silvery coating of frost.
1. *was*
2. Were any tickets left at the box office for me?
2. *C*

1. There was women, as well as men, who set out on the perilous journey into new territory.
2. Everyone who works at the machines wears goggles to protect their eyes.
3. One of the other safety features is guardrails around all equipment.
4. The test results showed that about 80 percent of the class was in the average group.
5. A hostile crowd gathered outside the courtroom to show their disapproval of the verdict.
6. Many of Gwendolyn Brooks' early poems was printed in the *Chicago Defender.*
7. *Bronzeville Boys and Girls* are a collection of her poems.
8. None of the travelers went to their seats immediately, making passage through the aisle impossible.
9. Jesse, who don't like classical music, was not pleased to learn that the evening's concert was all Haydn.
10. Neither of the candidates has prepared his speech.
11. Their biggest problem are apathy and indecision.
12. Every one of the players are eager to learn.
13. Mr. Ortega, in association with other members of his firm, have established a scholarship fund for art students.
14. To apply for the scholarship, a student must submit at least four samples of their work.
15. Either Justin or Colin are to present the award at the assembly.
16. Every teacher in the audience hopes that their pupil will win.
17. Chester or Nina, I think, have the best chance of winning.
18. Only this week the committee announced its decision after a month of deliberations.
19. About half the dog owners at the dog show was complaining about the judges' incompetence and threatening to remove their dogs if a change was not immediately made.
20. For Ellen, one of those exasperating people who is always late, eight o'clock means half past nine.
21. Mr. Johnson and Mr. Golding is repairing the roof now.
22. There are 1,000 people at this concert tonight.
23. My committee is preparing their speeches for Tuesday's meeting.
24. Neither the lawyer nor the defendants were satisfied with the judge's decision.
25. All of the bread are on the table.

CHAPTER 6 REVIEW: POSTTEST 2

Writing Sentences with Subject-Verb Agreement and Pronoun-Antecedent Agreement. Number your paper 1–25. After the proper number, rewrite each of the following sentences (1) following the directions in parentheses, (2) changing the number of the verb to agree with the subject, if necessary, and (3) changing the number of the pronoun to agree with its new antecedent, if necessary.

EXAMPLE 1. Both of the sopranos have sung the part of Carmen. (Change *Both of the sopranos* to *Each of the sopranos.*)
   1. *Each of the sopranos has sung the part of Carmen.*

1. Some of the planes were taking off on schedule. (Change *Some of the planes* to *Not one of the planes.*)
2. Neither Cindy nor the Mitchell children know about the surprise party. (Change *Neither Cindy nor the Mitchell children* to *Neither the Mitchell children nor Cindy.*)
3. Mary Lou, along with the hostess, is to be congratulated. (Change *along with the hostess* to *along with the other two hostesses.*)
4. No one in the group volunteered his services. (Change *No one* to *Many.*)
5. Do Scott and Pam have a map to the park? (Change *and* to *or.*)
6. The herd of buffalo was acting uneasy as the storm approached. (Change *The herd of* to *Several of the.*)
7. Most of the players do well at practice. (Change *Most of* to *Neither of.*)
8. A dollar is too much to spend on this book. (Change *A dollar* to *Ten dollars.*)
9. Several of the girls were sitting out the dance. (Change *Several* to *Not one.*)
10. All astronauts have to go through an extensive training program. (Change *All astronauts* to *Each astronaut.*)
11. All of the scouts know how to set up their tents. (Change *All* to *Every one.*)
12. Three flocks of wild geese have made their winter home on our pond. (Change *Three flocks* to *A flock.*)

13. Both my aunt and my cousin are going with us on vacation. (Change *Both my aunt and my cousin* to *Neither my aunt nor my cousin.*)
14. Each of the students is expected to give his book report this week. (Change *Each* to *All.*)
15. Not one of these stories has been published in the magazine this year. (Change *Not one* to *All.*)
16. Neither Juan nor the two crew members were caught in the storm. (Change *Neither Juan nor the two crew members* to *Neither the two crew members nor Juan.*)
17. Each of the dogs stopped in its tracks on command. (Change *Each* to *All.*)
18. No one raised his hand when the captain asked for volunteers. (Change *No one* to *Few.*)
19. The choir has decided to pay its own transportation to the music festival. (Change *The choir* to *Some of the choir.*)
20. Julian, as well as several music students, has received financial aid. (Change *Julian, as well as several music students* to *Several music students, as well as Julian.*)
21. The dollars were counted and placed in a safe under the counter. (Change *dollars* to *money.*)
22. Several of the roses used in decorations for the banquet have wilted. (Change *Several* to *None.*)
23. No one expressed his opinion about raising club dues to pay for travel expenses. (Change *No one* to *Everyone.*)
24. Sara and Yvonne have agreed to give us their allowances to pay for the damages. (Change *Sara and Yvonne* to *Either Sara or Yvonne.*)
25. Neither of the horses in that stall has been given its feed today. (Change *Neither* to *Both.*)

CHAPTER 7

Using Pronouns Correctly

NOMINATIVE AND OBJECTIVE CASE

A small number of pronouns have three forms: a *nominative* form that is used when the pronoun is a subject or predicate nominative; an *objective* form that is used when it is a direct or indirect object or the object of a preposition; and a *possessive* form that is used to show ownership or relationship. These three forms, all called *cases,* are illustrated as follows:

NOMINATIVE CASE   **We** heard from Sheila.
She is staying in Ohio.

OBJECTIVE CASE   I wrote to **her.**
Sheila phoned **me.**

POSSESSIVE CASE   **Her** vacation is almost over.
She is at **their** farm.

DIAGNOSTIC TEST

Using Pronouns Correctly in Sentences.   Number your paper 1–20. After the proper number, write the correct one of the two pronouns in parentheses.

EXAMPLE 1. Was it (he, him) driving the car when the accident occurred?
     1. *he*

1. Francis said that in a few years he would give his stamp collection to his brother and (I, me).

2. I need to know today if you and (she, her) plan to go with the children to the zoo.

3. Everyone was waiting impatiently to find out (who, whom) the new cheerleader would be.

4. I am going to vote for (whoever, whomever) can present the best solution to environmental problems.

5. After he had spoken at the assembly, the senator agreed to meet with our class president and (we, us).

6. My little sister is a much better chess player than (I, me).

7. She is one of those people (who, whom) can analyze opponents' moves quickly.

8. After the bake sale, give the remaining cookies and cakes to everyone (who, whom) worked.

9. We found that it was (she, her) who called twice while we were out of town.

10. Before the debate started, I noticed that my opponent was as nervous as (I, me).

11. She is the teacher (who, whom) will coach the golf team this year.

12. The teacher said that (whoever, whomever) was ready could give a speech first.

13. As the runners approached the finish line, we saw Lisle and (he, him) break ahead of the others.

14. An argument broke out between Mr. Morales and (they, them) over the location of the property lines.

15. Although her grandfather was the person for (who, whom) the town was named, she moved away immediately after graduation.

16. Noticing that a new car with an out-of-state license plate was parked outside my house, I ran inside, and (who, whom) do you think was there?

17. My coach, Mr. Lopez, said that he would choose between Leslie and (I, me) for the starting position.

18. Please give my message to (whoever, whomever) answers the phone.

19. Mrs. Martin and (she, her) have been friends since childhood.

20. For (who, whom) is this criticism intended?

CASE FORMS OF PERSONAL PRONOUNS

Personal pronouns change form in the different persons.

First person is the person speaking: *I* (*We*) do.
Second person is the person spoken to: *You* were doing.
Third person is a person or thing other than the speaker or the person spoken to: *He* (*She, It, They*) will do.

Study the following list of personal pronouns, noticing the changes in person and case form.

Personal Pronouns

Singular

	NOMINATIVE CASE	OBJECTIVE CASE	POSSESSIVE CASE
FIRST PERSON	I	me	my, mine
SECOND PERSON	you	you	your, yours
THIRD PERSON	he, she, it	him, her, it	his, her, hers, its

Plural

	NOMINATIVE CASE	OBJECTIVE CASE	POSSESSIVE CASE
FIRST PERSON	we	us	our, ours
SECOND PERSON	you	you	your, yours
THIRD PERSON	they	them	their, theirs

Two of the pronouns in the list above—*you* and *it*—have the same form in the nominative and objective case; therefore, they present no special problems. Ignore these two and concentrate on the following forms:

NOMINATIVE CASE	OBJECTIVE CASE
I	me
he	him
she	her
we	us
they	them

EXERCISE 1. Identifying the Case of Pronouns. On your paper, write the case of each pronoun listed here. If you find that you need to consult the list of pronouns presented earlier, you should review the nominative and objective forms until you know them thoroughly.

1. me   3. she   5. them   7. we   9. he
2. him   4. I   6. her   8. they   10. us

EXERCISE 2. Personal Pronouns. Write from memory the following personal pronouns.

1. First person plural, objective case
2. Third person singular, nominative case, feminine
3. Third person plural, nominative case
4. First person plural, nominative case
5. Third person singular, possessive case, masculine
6. First person singular, objective case
7. Third person singular, objective case, feminine
8. Third person plural, objective case
9. First person singular, nominative case
10. Third person singular, possessive case, neuter

THE NOMINATIVE CASE

7a. The subject of a verb is in the nominative case.

EXAMPLES   Both **he** and **I** solved the problem. [*He* and *I* are subjects of the verb *solved.*]
Her brothers and **she** cleaned the house. [*She* is the subject of *cleaned.*]
They knew **we** were going. [*They* is the subject of *knew,* and *we* is the subject of *were going.*]

Most errors involving pronouns as subjects arise when the subject is compound. People who would never say "Me went to the movies" often do make the mistake of saying "George and me went to the movies." The best way of avoiding this error is to try each subject separately with the verb, adapting the verb form as necessary. Your ear will tell you which form is correct.

NONSTANDARD   Her and me study English. [*Her* studies English? *Me* study English?]

STANDARD   **She** and **I** study English. [*She* studies English. *I* study English.]

The pronouns *we* and *they* frequently sound awkward as part of a compound subject. In such cases, it is usually easy enough to revise the sentence.

AWKWARD   We and they will go to the movie.

BETTER   We will go to the movie with them.

Pronouns are sometimes used with a noun appositive:

We road racers run every day.

To determine the right case form to use in such a situation, try reading the sentence without the appositive:

We run every day.

EXERCISE 3. *Oral Drill.* Stressing Pronouns in the Nominative Case. Read each of the following sentences aloud several times, stressing the italicized words.

1. *She* and *I* gave the dog a bath.
2. Irving and *he* plan to try out for the soccer team.
3. *We* sophomores organized the drive.
4. Wendy and *she* can help you in the lab.
5. Are *you* and *she* doing the report?
6. Either *we* or *they* may go to the championship finals.
7. The drill team and *we* band members took the bus.
8. Will *she* and *I* get to go?
9. The twins and *they* go everywhere together.
10. After the game, *he* and *she* walked home.

EXERCISE 4. Using Pronouns in the Nominative Case to Complete Sentences. Number your paper 1–15. Choose correct pronouns for the blanks in the following sentences. Vary your pronouns. Do not use *you* or *it*.

1. The judge and —— studied the evidence.
2. Ted and —— took the wrong train.
3. Linda and —— are planning a party.
4. —— students are having a science fair.
5. Either Carol or —— will give you a ride.
6. —— and —— have been rivals for years.
7. I'm sure —— and —— knew about the meeting.
8. The nun asked if —— would like to tour the church.
9. Soon —— and —— will be graduating.
10. Miss Arami said that —— and —— would be nominated.
11. —— Girl Scouts helped at the Immunization Clinic.
12. —— and —— have overdue library books.
13. —— football players had a tiring practice session.
14. Diana and —— repainted the bedrooms.
15. Julius and —— folded the flag.

EXERCISE 5. Writing Sentences with Pronouns in the Nominative Case.   Use the following subjects in sentences of your own.

1. We teen-agers
2. My family and I
3. He and his friends
4. Liz, Michelle, and she
5. They and their classmates

EXERCISE 6. Using Pronouns in the Nominative Case Correctly in Sentences.   Number your paper 1–20. Read each of the following sentences *aloud*. Decide whether the italicized pronouns are in the correct case. If all of them in a sentence are correct, write a + after the proper number on your paper; if any one of them is not, write a 0 followed by the correct form of the incorrect pronoun.

EXAMPLES   1. Stuart and *she* have studied as hard as you and *I* have.
      1. +
      2. Mrs. Jackson said that you and *me* wrote vivid descriptions.
      2. 0, I

1. I heard that Kate and *she* were home again.
2. Lenny and *he* arrived before Kevin and *I* did.
3. *Him* and *me* went downtown last Saturday.
4. *Us* music students give a recital every spring.
5. You and *I* have to cut up a frog in biology soon.
6. Sharon and *her* missed their bus this morning.
7. *He* and the professor were intently discussing the new discovery.
8. We thought you and *her* were related to each other.
9. *She* and *they* wrote the words and music.
10. You and *he* can help us carry these costumes to the drama room.
11. Did *him* and his coach disagree about the play?
12. *Her* and my uncle met each other at Polly's wedding.
13. How will Nora and *she* get to practice?
14. Ike and *them* promised to give us their support.
15. Did you guess that Ruth and *him* were the winners?
16. The seamstress and *he* worked until midnight.
17. Will you and *she* hand out the papers?
18. *We* shop students are getting some new equipment.
19. Jane and *me* made a mistake in chemistry lab.
20. Tell the band director that Jerry and *I* have the flu.

7b. A predicate nominative is in the nominative case.

A predicate nominative is a noun or pronoun in the predicate that refers to the same thing as the subject of the sentence. It follows a linking verb. The exercises and examples in this chapter concentrate on pronouns as predicate nominatives, since nouns in this position present no problem.

COMMON FORMS OF *be*		PREDICATE NOMINATIVE
am		I
is, are		he
was, were	*are*	she
may be, can be, will be, etc.	*followed*	we
may have been, etc.	*by*	you
want to be, like to be, etc.		they

EXAMPLES It was **I** who chopped down the cherry tree.
The winner might be **he.**
Could the caller have been **she?**

☞ **USAGE NOTE** It is now perfectly acceptable to use *me* as a predicate nominative in informal usage: *It's me.* (The construction rarely comes up in formal situations.) The plural form *(It's us)* is also generally accepted. However, using the objective case for the third person form of the pronoun *(It's him, It's them)* is still often regarded as unacceptable. When you encounter any of these expressions in the exercises in this book or in the various tests you take, you will be wise to take a conservative attitude and use the nominative forms in all instances.

EXERCISE 7. Using Predicate Nominatives in Sentences. Remembering that a predicate nominative is in the nominative case, supply the pronouns specified for the following:

1. Do you think it was ——? (third person singular, masculine)
2. It must have been ——. (third person singular, feminine)
3. Good friends are ——. (third person plural)
4. The pranksters were ——. (first person plural)
5. It was —— at the door. (third person plural)

REVIEW EXERCISE A. Using Pronouns in the Nominative Case Correctly in Sentences. Number your paper 1–20. After the proper number, complete each of the following sentences by writing an appropriate pronoun for each space. Try to use as many different pronouns as you can. Do not use *you* or *it*. Be ready to explain the reasons for your choices.

1. I couldn't believe it was —— .
2. My brother and —— won the road rally.
3. —— art students are making posters for the play.
4. It was Pilar and —— who won the award.
5. Everyone applauded when Pat and —— took a bow.
6. Have you asked if —— and —— can come with us?
7. Where did Barry and —— go after school?
8. Jimmy and —— caught the runaway piglets.
9. The tuba players are —— and —— .
10. Nellie and —— made waffles for breakfast.
11. It is —— that you need to see.
12. Skip argued that it was Lana and —— who made the error.
13. Was it Terry or —— who hit the home run?
14. Either David or —— might be able to do it.
15. It was decided that —— girls could play in the softball tournament.
16. —— and —— both forgot their lunches today.
17. My sister and —— are going to visit Provo, Utah.
18. —— linemen have to practice our plays.
19. I believe that the Masked Marvel has to be —— .
20. Do you think —— and —— can work well together?

THE OBJECTIVE CASE

The pronouns *me, him, her, us,* and *them* are in the objective case. These pronouns are used as direct and indirect objects and as objects of prepositions.

7c. The object of a verb is in the objective case.

EXAMPLES Our coach has been training **us.** [direct object]
I paid **him** a compliment. [indirect object]

As with the nominative forms, the objective forms are troublesome mainly in compound constructions. It is unnatural to say, "The explosion frightened *I*,'' but you might carelessly say, ''The explosion frightened Jim and I.'' Once again, the solution is to try the parts of the compound object separately.

Pronouns in the objective case may also have noun appositives. Whenever a pronoun is used with a noun in this way, you can always determine the case by omitting the noun.

Everyone knows **us** pranksters. [They know *us,* not *we.*]

EXERCISE 8. Using Pronouns in the Objective Case in Sentences.

Number your paper 1–20. Remembering that pronoun objects are always in the objective case, supply appropriate pronouns for the blanks in the following sentences. Use a variety of pronouns. Do not use *you* or *it.*

1. The old sailor warned —— about the danger.
2. The city awarded —— its highest honor.
3. You could ask Deborah or —— .
4. The crowd cheered —— heartily.
5. Be sure to ask —— for her social security number.
6. The shark in that movie didn't scare —— at all.
7. How can I recognize —— ?
8. We saw Norman and —— in their horse costume.
9. Did you give Paula and —— their assignments?
10. I bought my father and —— birthday presents.
11. She told Helen and —— about the parking regulations.
12. We nominated Gretel and —— as class representatives.
13. The long, pointless story didn't amuse —— or —— .
14. Have you invited Francesca and —— to the band picnic?
15. Will the director cast Linda or —— in the leading part?
16. The doctor commended Roger and —— for their quick thinking.
17. The violent weather forced Lydia and —— to cut their trip short.
18. The choir director gave —— baritones a suspicious glance.
19. My aunt sent my sisters and —— a post card from New Orleans.
20. Their story didn't convince either the authorities or —— .

EXERCISE 9. Writing Sentences Using Pronouns in the Nominative and Objective Cases.

Write ten sentences using personal pronouns (except *you* and *it*). Include three using pronouns in compound subjects of verbs, three using pronouns in compound predicate nominatives, and four using pronouns in compound objects of verbs.

EXERCISE 10. Writing Sentences Using Pronouns in the Objective Case. Write ten sentences, each using a different one of the verbs on the following list. After each verb use a pronoun in a compound direct or indirect object. Do not use *you* or *it*.

1. awarded	4. write	7. choose	10. persuade
2. ordered	5. bought	8. showed	11. found
3. bother	6. passed	9. invite	12. presented

REVIEW EXERCISE B. Selecting Pronouns in the Nominative or Objective Case to Complete Sentences. Number your paper 1–10. Select the correct one of the two pronouns in parentheses, and write it after the proper number on your paper. Be ready to explain your answers.

1. Last fall, Tina talked Susan and (I, me) into going on a canoe trip.
2. My father told Susan and (I, me) to wrap our food and equipment well.
3. He warned both Tina and (we, us) that we would probably get a good dunking before we were through.
4. When we first started, Susan and (I, me) could barely steer our canoe.
5. We watched another canoeist and saw how (she, her) and her partner maneuvered their craft.
6. They and (we, us) both did well until we hit the rapids, or rather, the rapids hit (we, us).
7. Susan grabbed for our sleeping bags, and (she, her) and (I, me) both scrambled for our food cooler.
8. All of (we, us) would-be campers were drenched, but no quitters were (we, us).
9. My father's warning haunted all of (we, us) as (we, us) starved adventurers stared at waterlogged hot dogs, soaked rolls, and biscuits with tadpoles in them.
10. Later, Susan and (I, me) discovered that our bedrolls had become portable water beds; after a squishy, cold night I decided wise are (they, them) who heed the voice of experience.

REVIEW EXERCISE C. Using Pronouns in the Nominative and Objective Cases in Sentences. Number your paper 1–10. After the proper number, write the personal pronoun that can be substituted for each italicized expression. In those sentences calling for a first person pronoun, use the appropriate one of the following pronouns: *I, we, me, us*.

EXAMPLES 1. Did you see Judy or *Faye?*
           1. *her*
           2. Both Ray and [first person pronoun] are related.
           2. *I*

1. Coach Welber showed Rita and *the other girl* the new play.
2. Walt gave her and [first person pronoun] some sound advice.
3. The cooks will be Charlie and *Al.*
4. The pilot and *navigator* were puzzled by the readings.
5. Give Bob or [first person pronoun] your dirty dishes.
6. Did my brother tell you and *Jennifer* about the dance?
7. Could it have been *Larry* that called?
8. How soon do you want to see Claire and [first person pronoun]?
9. In charge of entertainment will be Tom and *Wally.*
10. You can bet that if anybody can do it, it is *Wes and Craig.*

REVIEW EXERCISE D. Writing Sentences Using Pronouns in the Nominative and Objective Cases. Using the pronouns listed, write ten correct sentences of your own. Include sentences with pronouns used as subjects, predicate nominatives, and objects of verbs. After each sentence, tell how the pronouns are used.

1. Corrie and me
2. he and Kurt
3. you and I
4. we girls and they
5. my sister and he
6. him and me
7. Don and they
8. him and them
9. you and we
10. us players

7d. The object of a preposition is in the objective case.

A prepositional phrase begins with a preposition and ends with a noun or pronoun that is the *object of the preposition*. When the object of a preposition is a pronoun, it must be in the *objective* case.

EXAMPLES to them, for you and us, with him

    Errors in usage occur most often when the object of a preposition is compound. You can usually tell the correct pronoun by trying the parts of the compound object separately.

EXAMPLES   We spoke with Gwen and (she, her).
            We spoke with she. [nonstandard]
            We spoke with her. [standard]
            We spoke with Gwen and her.

Try this test on the following correct examples:

EXAMPLES   I sent cards to my *uncle* and *him*.
            The hostess brought menus for *Franny* and *me*.
            We can ride with *Joan* and *her*.

EXERCISE 11. Selecting Pronouns in the Objective Case to Complete Sentences.   In the following sentences, pick out the prepositions that take pronoun objects and list them on your paper. After each, write the correct one of the two pronouns given in parentheses.

1. The salesperson showed the computer to Patsy and (I, me).
2. There's some mail for Jeanette and (she, her).
3. The officer gestured toward Bill and (I, me).
4. This matter is strictly between Mary Anne and (she, her).
5. Nobody remembered except Wade and (he, him).
6. Did you see the news story about Trudy and (he, him)?
7. Just set the recorder down by Jack and (I, me).
8. The principal spoke with Cassie and (he, him).
9. You register right after Connie and (I, me).
10. The director gave solo parts to Brent and (I, me).

EXERCISE 12. Selecting Pronouns in the Objective Case to Complete Sentences Correctly.   Select the correct one of the two pronouns in parentheses, and write it on your paper.

1. The referee called fouls on (he, him) and (I, me).
2. Maggie is off fishing with grandfather and (he, him).
3. We didn't want to leave without you and (she, her).
4. They assigned the same locker to (they, them) and (we, us).
5. The duke directed a haughty sneer at the jester and (he, him).
6. A package arrived for Pat and (he, him).
7. Nobody understood the problem but Kevin and (he, him).
8. The player tried to dodge between Sherrie and (I, me).
9. The wary skunk circled around (she, her) and (I, me).
10. Uncle Vic will get the details from you and (she, her).

EXERCISE 13. Writing Sentences Using Pronouns in the Objective Case. Write sentences of your own, using each of the following prepositions with a compound object, at least one part of which is a pronoun.

1. beside	6. between
2. toward	7. for
3. from	8. by
4. against	9. over
5. without	10. except

EXERCISE 14. *Oral Drill.* Stressing Prepositions and Their Pronoun Objects. Read *aloud* five times each of the following sentences, putting the stress on the italicized words.

1. The blame was *on* Amy and *me.*
2. There were calls *for* Walker and *us.*
3. This message is *from* Delores and *her.*
4. We sat *with* Arnie and *them.*
5. Sara looked *after* Holly and *me.*
6. Margo looked *toward* Sue and *me.*
7. They gave copies *to him* and *me.*
8. This drawing is *by* either Max or *him.*
9. Don't hold this *against* Barb and *her.*
10. I walked *between* Vince and *him.*

WRITING APPLICATION A:
Considering Your Audience by Using Pronouns Correctly

Some games have an unwelcome "tilt" light that appears when you do something wrong. When this happens, everything just shuts down and you have to start over. Unfortunately, similar situations occur in writing. If your readers stumble across a glaring error, their concentration goes "tilt." Careful and considerate writers try to avoid causing their readers' thinking to be distracted by such errors.

TILT   Mrs. Smith promised my sister and *I* a baby-sitting job every weekday morning this summer.

Writing Assignment

A narrative relates a series of events. When you write a narrative, you usually explain what happened, when it happened, and to whom it happened. The narrative can be either a true story or an imaginary one. Write a narrative, either truth or fiction, about something that happened to you and another person. In your narrative, illustrate the following use of pronouns:

1. pronoun in compound subjects of verbs
2. pronoun in compound objects of verbs
3. pronoun in compound objects of prepositions

SPECIAL PROBLEMS IN PRONOUN USAGE

Who and Whom

The use of *who* and *whom* in questions can no longer be reduced to a strict law. In modern spoken English the distinction between *who* and *whom* is gradually disappearing altogether, and *whom* is going out of use. *Who do you mean?* and *Who do you know?* are standard, even though, according to the rule you have learned about the case of the object of a verb, the speaker should say *whom* in these sentences. For the exercises in this book, follow the rules of standard formal usage. However, the rules are applied strictly only in formal writing.

Using *who* and *whom* in subordinate clauses, however, is a different matter. In subordinate clauses the distinction between *who* and *whom* is generally observed in both formal and informal writing.

7e. The use of *who* and *whom* in a subordinate clause is determined by the pronoun's function in the clause.

EXAMPLE   Dani is the actress **who played the lead.**

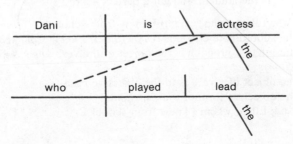

EXAMPLE   Dani is the actress **whom the audience applauded most loudly.**

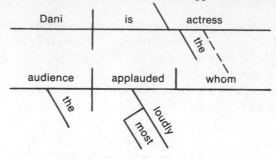

EXAMPLE   She was the student **about whom the story was written.**

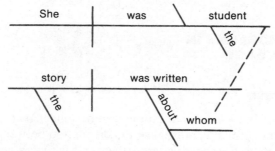

Follow these steps in deciding whether to use *who* or *whom* in a subordinate clause:

1. Pick out the subordinate clause.
2. Decide how the relative pronoun is used in that clause.
3. Determine the case of the pronoun according to the usual rules.
4. Select the correct form of the pronoun.

PROBLEM   Alex is the student (who, whom) got a perfect score.
Step 1   The subordinate clause is *(who, whom) got a perfect score.*
Step 2   The relative pronoun is the subject of the clause.
Step 3   Since it functions as a subject, the pronoun must be in the nominative case.
Step 4   The nominative form is *who.*
SOLUTION   Alex is the student **who** got a perfect score.

PROBLEM   I saw Ellen, (who, whom) I knew from school.
Step 1   The subordinate clause is *(who, whom) I knew from school.*
Step 2   The relative pronoun is the object of the verb *knew: I knew (who, whom).*
Step 3   The object of a verb is in the objective case.
Step 4   The objective form of *who* is *whom.*
SOLUTION   I saw Ellen, **whom** I knew from school.

PROBLEM Do you know (who, whom) she is?
  Step 1 The subordinate clause is *(who, whom) she is.*
  Step 2 The relative pronoun is the predicate nominative: *she is (who, whom).*
  Step 3 A predicate nominative is in the nominative case.
  Step 4 The nominative form is *who.*
SOLUTION Do you know **who** she is?

It is important to remember that no words outside the clause affect the case of the pronoun. In the third problem, the whole clause *who she is* is the object of the verb *know* in the independent clause. Within the subordinate clause, however, *who* is used as a predicate nominative and takes the nominative case.

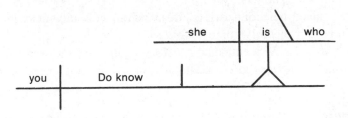

┌───┐
│ ☞ **USAGE NOTE** *Whom* is often omitted (understood) in subordinate clauses. │
└───┘

EXAMPLE The actor [whom] I wrote to sent these photos.

EXERCISE 15. Determining the Use of *Who* and *Whom* in Subordinate Clauses.

Number your paper 1–10. After the proper number, write the subordinate clause containing *who* or *whom* in each of the following sentences. Then tell how the relative pronoun (*who* or *whom*) is used in its own clause—as subject, predicate nominative, object of a verb, or object of a preposition.

EXAMPLE 1. She is someone whom we all admire.
    1. *whom we all admire, object of verb*

1. The people who are born in Puerto Rico live in a commonwealth, with its own senate, supreme court, and governor's cabinet.
2. In 1969 the governor needed a secretary of labor on whom he could depend.

3. The person whom he appointed would occupy the most difficult and sensitive position in the cabinet.
4. Do you know who the choice was?
5. The choice fell to Mrs. Julia Rivera De Vincenti, who became the first woman to occupy a cabinet post in her country.
6. Mrs. De Vincenti, on whom Cornell University had bestowed a Ph.D. in management and collective bargaining, was a good choice.
7. Mrs. De Vincenti, who was later appointed to the U.S. Mission to the UN, was the first Puerto Rican to serve in that capacity.
8. She addressed the General Assembly and showed that she was a woman who knew her job well.
9. She praised her compatriots, from whom new advances in agriculture had recently come.
10. And Mrs. De Vincenti made history again, for she was the first woman who ever wore a pantsuit to address the General Assembly!

EXERCISE 16. Selecting *Who* or *Whom* to Complete Sentences Correctly. Number your paper 1–10. After the proper number, write the use of the relative pronoun in parentheses. After the use, write the correct form of the pronoun.

EXAMPLE 1. This is the story of a woman (who, whom) overcame many difficulties to study science.
    1. *subject—who*

1. Do you know the mathematician (who, whom) Albert Einstein respected most?
2. It was Amalie Noether, (who, whom) was born in Germany in 1882.
3. She was tutored in mathematics by professors with (who, whom) her father taught at the University of Erlangen.
4. In Germany women scientists, for (who, whom) there were few opportunities, had a difficult time.
5. However, Noether was a person (who, whom) truly loved her field, and she studied for her doctorate.
6. At last the University of Göttingen made her a professor, but one to (who, whom) no salary was paid.
7. Later she was one of the people (who, whom) the Nazis did not allow to work or teach.

8. She came to the United States and worked at Princeton with Einstein, from (who, whom) she received high praise.
9. He said she was a creative genius (who, whom) discovered new methods of "enormous importance."
10. Other modern women (who, whom) have increased our knowledge of mathematics are Mina S. Rees and Mary H. Budenbach.

WRITING APPLICATION B:
Using *Who, Whoever, Whom,* and *Whomever* Correctly

Though you may use *who* and *whoever* for *whom* and *whomever* in spoken English, you should always follow the rules for standard English usage for *who* and *whoever* in your school writing.

NONSTANDARD *Who* did you call?

STANDARD *Whom* did you call?

In addition, always observe standard English usage for *who* and *whoever* when you use them in subordinate clauses.

INCORRECT I asked her *who* she had spoken with.

CORRECT I asked her *whom* she had spoken with.

Writing Assignment

Write ten sentences according to the following guidelines:

1. Use *who* as the subject of the subordinate clause.
2. Use *who* to begin a question.
3. Use *whom* as the object of the preposition in a sentence.
4. Use *whom* as the direct object in a sentence.
5. Use *whomever* as the direct object in a subordinate clause.
6. Use *whomever* as the object of the preposition in a subordinate clause.
7. Use *whom* to begin a question.
8. Use *whom* as the direct object in the subordinate clause.
9. Use *whoever* to begin a question.
10. Use *whomever* as the object of the preposition in a sentence.

REVIEW EXERCISE E. Selecting Pronouns to Complete Sentences Correctly. Number your paper 1–20. After the proper number, write how the pronoun in parentheses is used. Use the abbreviations *s.* (subject), *p.n.* (predicate nominative), *d.o.* (direct object), *i.o.* (indirect object), *o.p.* (object of preposition). Following the abbreviation, write the correct pronoun.

1. Did you get the post card from Margaret and (I, me)?
2. We all knew (who, whom) the winner would be.
3. Will Meg and (she, her) run the concession stand?
4. The coach asked you and (I, me) a question about the equipment.
5. Becky and (she, her) rode their bikes to the meeting.
6. Grandfather joked with my sister and (I, me).
7. The lighting crew for the play was Manuel and (I, me).
8. (He, him) and (I, me) were watching the soccer game.
9. They treat (whoever, whomever) they hire very well.
10. We didn't see (whoever, whomever) had knocked.
11. Could it be you or (she, her) that called me?
12. Everyone except Louis and (he, him) was watching.
13. Who is that writer (who, whom) you were with?
14. They met Jennie and (she, her) at the airport.
15. The hostess and (he, him) greeted everyone.
16. The cheerleaders teased Matt and (I, me) about the fumble.
17. I didn't know (who, whom) to give the letter to.
18. I think that the people who were costumed as pirates are (they, them).
19. I looked for someone (who, whom) could give me directions.
20. My aunt and (we, us) went swimming last weekend.

REVIEW EXERCISE F. Selecting Pronouns to Complete Sentences Correctly.   Number your paper 1–20. Write the correct pronoun after the proper number.

1. Did you ask (who, whom) was there?
2. Those are the musicians with (who, whom) we were playing.
3. We gave the papers to Burke and (he, him).
4. This information is just between you and (I, me).
5. Nan can invite (whoever, whomever) she wants.
6. We'll congratulate (whoever, whomever) wins.
7. (We, Us) students are learning computer programming.
8. Was the winning pitcher you or (he, him)?
9. Mort and (we, us) like to fish for perch.
10. Marcie dedicated the next record to Tabitha and (I, me).

11. Sometimes I wonder just (who, whom) she thinks she is.
12. The chairperson appointed Mindy and (I, me).
13. Don't you know (who, whom) he invited?
14. Someone left a mysterious note for him and (I, me).
15. The officers asked Clint and (I, me) to help.
16. You can give Dorothy or (I, me) your receipts.
17. Did you see (who, whom) made the basket?
18. Sit with (whoever, whomever) you like.
19. I wonder if Joey and (he, him) have their music memorized yet.
20. (We, Us) mermaids have the most uncomfortable costumes of anybody else in the play.

REVIEW EXERCISE G. Determining Proper Case of Pronouns in Sentences. Number your paper 1–20. For each sentence in which the pronouns are all in the proper case, write a + after the corresponding number on your paper; for each incorrect sentence, write a 0.

1. Be careful who you tell.
2. Will Marie and I be in the outfield?
3. My brother and me like water-skiing.
4. My family goes to the dentist who Ms. Calhoun recommended.
5. They will be going in place of Charlie and me.
6. Coretta said there would be other flag bearers in addition to Hugh and I.
7. The disc jockey gave Eileen and I each a free record.
8. Have you shown your new card to Linda and he?
9. At the head of the parade were us Girl Scouts.
10. The mayor awarded Marcus and him citizenship medals.
11. Maybe you should ask Rene or he.
12. Nobody except Josh and him finished the marathon.
13. Sonia and I want to work at Graceland next summer.
14. We wish we had neighbors like Sylvia and him.
15. Should you and me sign up for that course?
16. Did your father and them reach an agreement about the boundary dispute?
17. Joanne and us found a great beach.
18. Marilyn told Emily and me about her test.
19. There were us girls with a flat tire and no spare.
20. The incident happened after he and I had left.

The Pronoun in Incomplete Constructions

7f. After *than* and *as* in an incomplete construction, use the form of the pronoun you would use if the construction were completed.

The following are examples of incomplete constructions. In each one, part of the sentence is omitted and is included in the brackets.

> She is taller than **I**. [than *I* am tall]
> The news surprised Andrea more than **me**. [than the news surprised *me*]

From these two examples of an incomplete construction, you will notice that you should use the form of the pronoun you would use if you completed the sentence. Thus in the first sentence *I* is correct because it is the subject of the clause *I am tall*. In the second sentence *me* is correct because it is the object of the verb *surprised* in the clause *the news surprised me*.

Now examine this pair of sentences:

> I understand Mac better than **he**. [than *he* understands Mac]
> I understand Mac better than **him**. [than I understand *him*]

As you can see, the case of the pronoun depends on how the sentence is completed. Both these sentences are correct, but they are quite different in meaning; they are completed in different ways.

EXERCISE 17. Selecting Pronouns to Complete Incomplete Constructions in Sentences. Number your paper 1–10. After the proper number, write out each of the following sentences, supplying the omitted part and using the correct form of the pronoun. After the sentence, write the use of the pronoun in its clause. Some of the sentences may be completed in two different ways.

1. We played defense better than (they, them).
2. Margo works as slowly as (I, me).
3. Nobody tried harder than (she, her).
4. You are a month younger than (he, him).
5. I know Millie better than (she, her).
6. Did you get as far in that book as (I, me)?
7. Richard wanted more tickets than (we, us).
8. Bianca lives farther away than (we, us).
9. She visited Lisa more than (I, me).
10. I hope you aren't as sick as (she, her).

REVIEW EXERCISE H. Selecting Pronouns to Complete Sentences. Number your paper 1–20. Select the correct one of the two pronouns given in parentheses, and write it after the proper number on your paper. Be prepared to give reasons for your answers.

1. Heather and (he, him) live on a blueberry farm.
2. The teacher gave the assignment to (whoever, whomever) was absent yesterday.
3. The supporting players were Dina, Janelle, and (she, her).
4. Do you intercept passes as well as (she, her)?
5. We took Megan and (he, him) for a boat ride.
6. We wondered (who, whom) started the rumor.
7. I was standing in line right behind Dave and (he, him).
8. You and (I, me) could do a cartoon strip for the school paper.
9. You did as well on the test as (she, her).
10. We knew you'd arrive sooner than (he, him).
11. The skit was written by Cy and (he, him).
12. Aunt Stephanie brought Jack and (I, me) some mangoes from Florida.
13. Kathleen struck out Karen and (I, me).
14. The electrician warned (he, him) and (I, me) about the frayed wires.
15. These apricots are for (he, him) and (we, us) to share.
16. You sing much better than (I, me).
17. Did the bus leave without Zack and (he, him)?
18. Can you run the two hundred meters as fast as (they, them)?
19. The author, (who, whom) the critics had praised, autographed a copy of his novel for me.
20. The sleet whirled about George and (he, him) until they could barely see.

CHAPTER 7 REVIEW: POSTTEST 1

Selecting Pronouns to Complete Sentences. Number your paper 1–25. Select the correct one of the two pronouns in parentheses, and write it after the proper number on your paper.

EXAMPLE   1. None of the candidates is better qualified for this office than (she, her).
     1. *she*

1. Was it Gordon or (he, him) that you wanted to see?
2. He is the teacher to (who, whom) the yearbook was dedicated.
3. When we arrived at the roadside park, we saw that (whoever, whomever) had been there last had failed to clean the tables.
4. Did you tell Marion and (she, her) about the dance?
5. Mother asked if Mike and (he, him) were going to the game.
6. (Whoever, Whomever) took the reference book from the shelf is asked to return it.
7. It took me so long to knit this sweater for the baby that it is now too small for (she, her).
8. Usually this race is won by (whoever, whomever) is in the best physical condition.
9. She was disappointed to learn that the one for (who, whom) her letter was intended did not read it.
10. As soon as I heard off-key singing, I knew it was (he, him).
11. By the time summer was over, everyone except (I, me) had learned to swan dive.
12. Did he tell you (who, whom) would give the opening address?
13. How do you know that everyone (who, whom) she selects is prejudiced?
14. She told me the soloists were to be Mr. Grant and (I, me).
15. A stern-looking woman in the office asked me, "(Who, Whom) did you wish to see?"
16. It's not fair that Deborah and (she, her) were not given a chance to try out for that role in the play.
17. After cooking all morning, Mrs. Watson served (whoever, whomever) came to the table at noon.
18. Judge Johnson, (who, whom) has served twenty years, is retiring next month.
19. The man (who, whom) you recommended for the job was highly qualified and went to work immediately.
20. To (who, whom) shall I give my new address so that my mail can be forwarded without delay?
21. You were told to give the instructions to Bruce and (I, me) as soon as you received them.
22. She said that (we, us) older girls would be responsible for the entire program.
23. Was it Megan or (he, him) who won the tennis championship?

24. Those dogs bark at (whoever, whomever) comes inside the fence.
25. Isn't Mrs. Henry the one (who, whom) bought that picture?

CHAPTER 7 REVIEW: POSTTEST 2

Determining the Proper Case of Pronouns in Sentences. Number your paper 1–25. If a sentence contains an incorrect pronoun, write the correct form after the proper number on your paper. For each correct sentence, write *C* after the proper number.

1. Del can't do math any better than her.
2. If anyone calls, ask whom it is.
3. You and him will guard their center.
4. There was some misunderstanding between him and his brother.
5. We saw Mike and he at the clambake.
6. The lab assistant gave Nora and I our equipment.
7. To who was the letter addressed?
8. Inez is better at physics than me.
9. Mona and me stopped to talk to Miss Kim.
10. Give a program to whoever asks for one.
11. I showed the negatives to Debbie and she.
12. Do you know whom will be the speaker at the assembly?
13. It can't be they; that's not their car.
14. The amplifier was assembled by Ricki and she.
15. Ben and you can come with me and them.
16. Here's a list of people whom we can invite.
17. Did everyone finish the experiment except Donna and I?
18. Juanita and him showed us how to start the motor.
19. We band members have to be at school early to practice marching.
20. We saw Carla and her at the auto show.
21. He's the sportscaster who irritates the viewers with his pretentious talk.
22. Will she help you and I work on our catching?
23. Martin and me performed as professionally as them.
24. She can ask Harry and I what the assignment is.
25. If you expect we band members at the rally, you will have to provide a bus.

CHAPTER 8

Using Verbs Correctly

PRINCIPAL PARTS, TENSE, VOICE

People frequently use verbs in a nonstandard way when they speak. You may hear someone say, "He has brang," "She had drank," or "The tree is laying in the middle of the road." Fiction writers sometimes use nonstandard speech to add lifelike detail to dialogue. Although nonstandard verb usage may occur in everyday speech, it is not always appropriate, especially on occasions, such as job interviews, when formal standard English is expected. This chapter will help you learn the standard usage of verbs in speaking and writing.

DIAGNOSTIC TEST

A. Writing the Past or Past Participle Form of Verbs. Number your paper 1–15. After the appropriate number write the past or past participle of the verb given at the beginning of the sentence.

EXAMPLE 1. *do* Because he —— his work so well, his employer raised his pay.
       1. *did*

1. *write* Although Emily Dickinson —— poetry most of her life, very little of her work was published until after her death.
2. *drink* When he saw that the animals had —— all the water from the pails, he refilled them at the faucet.

3. *throw*   Regarding weeds as unwanted intruders, she pulled them from the ground and ―― them over the fence for the cows to eat.

4. *take*   We could not find our literature books because someone ―― them to the wrong classroom by mistake.

5. *fall*   Autumn leaves ―― in colorful drifts, covering the ground with a crazy-quilt pattern of reds and yellows.

6. *swim*   The water was cold and daylight was fading, so he ―― only a short distance before turning back to shore.

7. *freeze*   The dew ―― during the night, covering each twig and blade of grass with a silvery coating.

8. *lay*   The students ―― their books on the grass.

9. *give*   After my brother had ―― his new puppy a bath, he seemed to be wetter than the dog.

10. *speak*   She ―― in such a low voice that the audience strained to hear her remarks.

11. *rise*   The sun ―― at 6:15 A.M.

12. *shrink*   Frightened by the strangers who crowded around, the deer ―― back in its cage.

13. *ride*   Leading the parade was an officer who ―― a prancing black horse.

14. *see*   Because of the dense fog, no one ―― the car backing out of the driveway.

15. *ring*   When the church bell ―― , the villagers became alarmed.

B. Revising Verb Tense or Voice.   Revise the following sentences, correcting verbs that are in the wrong tense or use an awkward passive voice. If a sentence is correct, write *C* after the proper number.

16. Geraldine A. Ferraro was born on August 26, 1935, in Newburgh, New York.

17. She attends Fordham University Law School and received a J.D. degree from the Law School in 1960.

18. In 1974 she becomes an assistant district attorney of Queens, New York.

19. She ran against Republican Alfred A. DelliBovi in the Congressional race in 1978; she defeats him and became the Democratic congresswoman for Queens, New York.

20. Reelection to this office was won by Geraldine Ferraro in 1980 and 1982.

KINDS OF VERBS

All verbs help to make a statement about their subjects. *Action* verbs do so by expressing an action performed by the subject:

ACTION VERBS Ruth **swims** every day.
Ulysses **knew** the sirens' power.

As the second example indicates, the action expressed may be mental as well as physical: *remember, plan,* and *hope* are action verbs, just as *walk, leap,* and *dive* are.

Some verbs help to make a statement by linking with the subject a word in the predicate that explains, describes, or in some other way makes the subject more definite. Such verbs are called *linking* verbs.

LINKING VERBS Our team **was** victorious. [The adjective *victorious* describes the subject *team*.]
Catfish **are** scavengers. [The noun *scavengers* gives information about the subject *catfish*.]

Some verbs can be either action or linking verbs, depending on the way they are used.

ACTION VERB We **felt** the cold wind on our faces.

LINKING VERB We **felt** chilly.

There are not many linking verbs in English; you will find a list of the commonly used ones on page 16. If you can recognize the difference between linking verbs and action verbs, you will be able to choose the appropriate form of a pronoun that follows the verb. (See pages 174–75.)

PRINCIPAL PARTS

Verbs have four basic forms from which all other forms are made. These are called the *principal parts* of the verb.

8a. The principal parts of a verb are the *infinitive*, the *present participle*, the *past*, and the *past participle*.

INFINITIVE	PRESENT PARTICIPLE	PAST	PAST PARTICIPLE
walk	(is) walking	walked	(have) walked
see	(is) seeing	saw	(have) seen

The words *is* and *have* are included to remind you that the present participle is used with some form of the helping verb *be* and the past participle mainly with a form of the helping verb *have*.

Regular Verbs

8b. A *regular verb* is one that forms its past and past participle by adding –ed or –d to the infinitive form.[1]

INFINITIVE	PAST	PAST PARTICIPLE
work	worked	(have) worked
receive	received	(have) received
saddle	saddled	(have) saddled

Irregular Verbs

8c. An *irregular verb* is one that forms its past and past participle in some way other than a regular verb does.

Some irregular verbs form the past and past participle forms by changing the vowels, some by changing the consonants, and others by making no change at all.

INFINITIVE	PAST	PAST PARTICIPLE
bring	brought	(have) brought
begin	began	(have) begun
fly	flew	(have) flown
burst	burst	(have) burst
sit	sat	(have) sat
tear	tore	(have) torn

Since irregular verbs form their past and past participles in unpredictable ways, there is nothing to do but memorize the forms of at least the most common ones. You doubtless already know most of the irregular verbs on the list that follows. Nevertheless, you should study all of them carefully, concentrating on the ones that give you trouble.

---

[1] A few regular verbs have an alternative past form ending in *–t;* for example, it *burns* (present), it *burned* or *burnt* (past), and it has *burned* or *burnt* (past participle).

Common Irregular Verbs

INFINITIVE	PRESENT PARTICIPLE	PAST	PAST PARTICIPLE
begin	(is) beginning	began	(have) begun
blow	(is) blowing	blew	(have) blown
break	(is) breaking	broke	(have) broken
bring	(is) bringing	brought	(have) brought
burst	(is) bursting	burst	(have) burst
choose	(is) choosing	chose	(have) chosen
come	(is) coming	came	(have) come
do	(is) doing	did	(have) done
drink	(is) drinking	drank	(have) drunk
drive	(is) driving	drove	(have) driven
fall	(is) falling	fell	(have) fallen
freeze	(is) freezing	froze	(have) frozen
give	(is) giving	gave	(have) given
go	(is) going	went	(have) gone
ride	(is) riding	rode	(have) ridden
ring	(is) ringing	rang	(have) rung
run	(is) running	ran	(have) run
see	(is) seeing	saw	(have) seen
shrink	(is) shrinking	shrank	(have) shrunk
speak	(is) speaking	spoke	(have) spoken
steal	(is) stealing	stole	(have) stolen
swim	(is) swimming	swam	(have) swum
take	(is) taking	took	(have) taken
throw	(is) throwing	threw	(have) thrown
write	(is) writing	wrote	(have) written

EXERCISE 1. Writing the Past and Past Participle Form of Irregular Verbs.

Your teacher will dictate to you the first principal part of the twenty-five irregular verbs listed above. Write from memory the past and the past participle. Placing *have* before the past participle will help you to learn that this is the form used with *have, has,* and *had.*

EXERCISE 2. Writing the Past or Past Participle Form of Irregular Verbs to Complete Sentences.

Number your paper 1–25. After the appropriate number, write the correct form (past or past participle) of the verb given at the beginning of the sentence. If necessary, refer to the list above.

1. *blow*   All last night the wind —— wildly.
2. *shrink*   Mrs. Ming feared that the jeans she washed had —— .

3. *begin*   I had already —— my homework.
4. *steal*   Did you see how Lou —— second base yesterday?
5. *freeze*   Last winter the rosebushes ——.
6. *tear*   Oops, I think my jacket has ——.
7. *do*   Look what that nuisance of a cat has —— now.
8. *fly*   Last summer we —— in a lighter-than-air balloon.
9. *sit*   During my last class, someone —— on my lunch.
10. *come*   Yesterday afternoon the mail —— late.
11. *write*   She has —— a letter to the newspaper.
12. *see*   When Clark was on vacation, he —— Mount Rushmore.
13. *ride*   Nobody except Walt has ever —— that horse.
14. *take*   My sister has —— that course.
15. *burst*   When she stuck the pin into the bubble, it ——.
16. *choose* Which college has Mickey ——?
17. *bring*   Hadn't she —— her sleeping bag?
18. *drink*   Bill —— three glasses of orange juice at breakfast.
19. *swim*   Every day on vacation my mother —— a mile.
20. *ring*   No one has —— the bell yet.
21. *fall*   He had —— on the icy walk.
22. *throw*   The horse had —— its shoe.
23. *go*   The teachers had —— to a meeting.
24. *break*   We hoped we hadn't —— the machine.
25. *speak*   Last semester our teacher —— about England and Wales.

EXERCISE 3. Selecting the Past or Past Participle Form of Verbs. Number your paper 1–25. Choose the correct one of the two verbs in parentheses, and write it after the proper number. When your paper has been corrected, read each sentence to yourself several times, using the correct word.

1. The robot glided into the control room and (began, begun) blinking its lights.
2. She had (wrote, written) her ideas on scraps of paper.
3. Someone actually (threw, throwed) a chocolate cream pie at the actor.
4. We (did, done) everything we could to help him.
5. Who has (drank, drunk) the rest of the orange juice?
6. My sister (came, come) into my room to remind me to clean up the mess in the kitchen.

7. Last night I (saw, seen) a TV show about whales.
8. Someone has already (tore, torn) out the coupon.
9. Who's (took, taken) the phone off the hook?
10. Once again the cat has (broke, broken) the lamp.
11. Who (give, gave) you the right to mark up my book?
12. She (ran, run) the copying machine last week.
13. I wish you had (spoke, spoken) to me about it sooner.
14. I dived off the high board and (swam, swum) the length of the pool.
15. You must have (rang, rung) the doorbell when I was out.
16. They just (came, come) back from the rink.
17. They could have (went, gone) to the movies.
18. Nancy had never (ate, eaten) a tamale before.
19. Lois (blowed, blew) up the balloon.
20. Suddenly the balloon (burst, bursted).
21. Ice cream that has (froze, frozen) is like a rock.
22. Joyce was (chose, chosen) to represent our school.
23. Marc's puppy was (brought, brung) back by a neighbor.
24. We were (drove, driven) to the train station in a taxi.
25. My suitcase had (fell, fallen) off the luggage rack.

EXERCISE 4. Writing the Past and Past Participle Form of Verbs.
Number your paper 1–20. If the first principal part (infinitive form) is given, change it to the past form. If the past form is given, change it to the past participle. Write *have* before the past participle form.

EXAMPLES   1. fly
          1. *flew*
          2. began
          2. *have begun*

1. break	6. rode	11. drank	16. throw
2. climbed	7. steal	12. fall	17. write
3. swam	8. rang	13. shrink	18. brought
4. drive	9. blew	14. do	19. go
5. chose	10. froze	15. spoke	20. took

TENSE

Verbs change form to show the time of the action or the idea they express. The time indicated by the form of a verb is called its *tense*. There are six tenses, each of which is formed in one way or another from the principal parts of the verb. A systematic listing of the verb forms used in the six tenses is called a *conjugation*.

The conjugations that follow for the verbs *talk* and *throw* illustrate the tense forms of two common verbs, one regular and the other irregular.

8d. Learn the names of the six tenses and how the tenses are formed.

Conjugation of the Verb Talk

Present infinitive: *to talk*   Perfect infinitive: *to have talked*

Principal Parts

INFINITIVE	PRESENT PARTICIPLE	PAST	PAST PARTICIPLE
talk	talking	talked	talked

Present Tense

Singular	Plural
I talk	we talk
you talk	you talk
he, she, it talks	they talk

Present progressive: *I am talking,* etc.[1]

Past Tense

Singular	Plural
I talked	we talked
you talked	you talked
he, she, it talked	they talked

Past progressive: *I was talking,* etc.

Future Tense

(*will* or *shall* + the infinitive[2])

Singular	Plural
I will (shall) talk	we will (shall) talk
you will talk	you will talk
he, she, it will talk	they will talk

Future progressive: *I will (shall) be talking,* etc.

[1] The present progressive is not a separate tense but a form of the present tense since it shows present time. There is a progressive form for each of the six tenses.

[2] For discussion of the use of *shall* and *will*, see page 251.

Present Perfect Tense

(*have* or *has* + the past participle)

Singular	Plural
I have talked	we have talked
you have talked	you have talked
he, she, it has talked	they have talked

Present perfect progressive: *I have been talking*, etc.

Past Perfect Tense

(*had* + the past participle)

Singular	Plural
I had talked	we had talked
you had talked	you had talked
he, she, it had talked	they had talked

Past perfect progressive: *I had been talking*, etc.

Future Perfect Tense

(*will have* or *shall have* + the past participle)

Singular	Plural
I will (shall) have talked	we will (shall) have talked
you will have talked	you will have talked
he, she, it will have talked	they will have talked

Future perfect progressive: *I will (shall) have been talking*, etc.

Conjugation of the Verb Throw

Present infinitive: *to throw*   Perfect infinitive: *to have thrown*

Principal Parts

INFINITIVE	PRESENT PARTICIPLE	PAST	PAST PARTICIPLE
throw	throwing	threw	thrown

Present Tense

Singular	Plural
I throw	we throw
you throw	you throw
he, she, it throws	they throw

Present progressive: *I am throwing*, etc.

Past Tense

Singular	Plural
I threw	we threw
you threw	you threw
he, she, it threw	they threw

Past progressive: *I was throwing,* etc.

Future Tense

(will or *shall* + the infinitive)

Singular	Plural
I will (shall) throw	we will (shall) throw
you will throw	you will throw
he, she, it will throw	they will throw

Future progressive: *I will (shall) be throwing,* etc.

Present Perfect Tense

(has or *have* + the past participle)

Singular	Plural
I have thrown	we have thrown
you have thrown	you have thrown
he, she, it has thrown	they have thrown

Present perfect progressive: *I have been throwing,* etc.

Past Perfect Tense

(had + the past participle)

Singular	Plural
I had thrown	we had thrown
you had thrown	you had thrown
he, she, it had thrown	they had thrown

Past perfect progressive: *I had been throwing,* etc.

Future Perfect Tense

(will have or *shall have* + the past participle)

Singular	Plural
I will (shall) have thrown	we will (shall) have thrown
you will have thrown	you will have thrown
he, she, it will have thrown	they will have thrown

Future perfect progressive: *I will (shall) have been throwing,* etc.

8e. Learn the uses of the six tenses.

Each of the six tenses has its own uses. Sometimes the tense of a verb expresses time only; at other times tense may tell whether or not the action is still going on. Study the following explanations and examples carefully; then refer to these pages frequently as you work to complete the exercises.

(1) The *present tense* is used to express action (or to help make a statement about something) occurring now, at the present time.

EXAMPLES Sonja **owns** a calculator.
Larry **is** in the Chess Club.
We **are rehearsing** the play.

☞ **NOTE** The third example illustrates the present progressive tense. Each tense has a progressive form which is used to indicate that the action expressed by the verb is continuing.

In addition to indicating present time, the present tense has some special uscs. It is used to indicate habitual action:

He **runs** two miles a day.

The present tense is also used to express a general truth—something that is true at all times.

Gary believed that the pen **is** [not *was*] mightier than the sword.

(2) The *past tense* is used to express action (or to help make a statement about something) that occurred in the past but did not continue into the present. The past is regularly formed by adding –d or –ed.

EXAMPLES I **lunged** toward the door.
I **was lunging** toward the door.
They **passed** the dish to me.

(3) The *future tense* is used to express action (or to help make a statement about something) that will occur at some time in the future. The future tense is formed with *will* or *shall*.

EXAMPLES I **will read** a lot.
I **will be reading** a lot.

There are several other ways of indicating future time.

EXAMPLES   I **am going to read** a lot this week.
I **leave next month.** [present tense with another word or phrase clearly indicating future time]

(4) The *present perfect tense* is used to express action (or to help make a statement about something) that occurred at no definite time in the past. It is formed with *have* or *has*.

EXAMPLE   She **has visited** Chicago.

The present perfect tense is also used to express action (or to help make a statement about something) that occurred in the past and continues into the present.

EXAMPLES   She **has worked** there several years. [She is still working there.]
I **have been playing** guitar for six months. [I am still playing it.]

(5) The *past perfect tense* is used to express action (or to help make a statement about something) completed in the past before some other past action or event. It is formed with *had*.

EXAMPLES   After she **had revised** her essay, she handed it in. [The action of revising preceded the action of handing it in.]
When he **had washed** the dishes, he sat down to rest. [He washed the dishes before he rested.]

(6) The *future perfect tense* is used to express action (or to help make a statement about something) that will be completed in the future before some other future action or event. It is formed with *shall have* or *will have*.

EXAMPLES   By the time I leave, **I will have packed** all my clothes. [The packing will precede the leaving.]
At the end of next year, I **shall have been going** to school for eleven years.

EXERCISE 5. Explaining the Uses of the Tenses of Verbs in Sentences.   Explain the difference in meaning between the sentences in the following pairs. Both sentences in each pair are correct. Name the tense used in each sentence.

1. When you get here, I will start work.
   When you get here, I will have started work.
2. How long have you been a pilot?
   How long were you a pilot?

3. What happened at the game?
   What has been happening at the game?
4. She lived in Cleveland for four years.
   She has lived in Cleveland for four years.
5. Clea knew the old table was valuable.
   Clea knew the old table had been valuable.
6. Has he taken the pictures?
   Had he taken the pictures?
7. When I am seventeen, I will get a driver's license.
   When I am seventeen, I will have gotten a driver's license.
8. I knew them well.
   I had known them well.
9. Lynette was a cheerleader for one semester.
   Lynette has been a cheerleader for one semester.
10. The doctor said that Earl had an allergy.
    The doctor said that Earl had had an allergy.

EXERCISE 6. Using the Different Tenses of Verbs in Sentences.
Number your paper 1–10. After the proper number, write the following
sentences on your paper, changing the tenses of the verbs as indicated.

1. Otto lived here a month. (Change to past perfect.)
2. When the alarm goes off, I will get up. (Change *will get* to future
   perfect.)
3. Is she sleeping? (Change to present perfect progressive.)
4. When I get back, will you go? (Change *will go* to future perfect.)
5. Were they at the party? (Change to past perfect.)
6. Were you invited? (Change to present perfect.)
7. The soloist sings well. (Change to present perfect.)
8. By the time you get here, Cammi will find out. (Change *will find*
   to future perfect.)
9. The bus arrives on time. (Change to future.)
10. Ken was in town all summer. (Change to past perfect.)

Consistency of Tense

Young writers, especially when writing essays or narratives, sometimes begin their compositions in one tense and then lapse into another
tense. Such lapses are due largely to carelessness, for students usually
understand the error when it is pointed out to them.

8f. Do not change needlessly from one tense to another.

CARELESS Roy *past* raised his telescope and *present* sees a large bear as it *past* raced back to the woods. [mixture of past and present tenses]

CORRECT Roy *past* raised his telescope and *past* saw a large bear as it *past* raced back to the woods. [past tense throughout]

CORRECT Roy *present* raises his telescope and *present* sees a large bear as it *present* races back to the woods. [present tense throughout]

EXERCISE 7. Identifying Verbs in the Wrong Tense.   Number your paper 1–20. After the proper number, list the verbs that are in the wrong tense. After each, write the appropriate tense form. If there are no incorrectly used verbs in a particular sentence, write *C*.

1. One of the most important battles of the Revolutionary War occurred in September and October 1777 at Saratoga, New York. 2. The leader of the British troops, General John Burgoyne, had set up camp near Saratoga and is planning to march south to the city of Albany.   3. Burgoyne's army has been recently weakened by an attack from an American militia, which had ambushed some of his troops at Bennington, Vermont.   4. Although the march to Albany is dangerous, Burgoyne decided to take the risk because he feels bound by orders from the War Office in London.

5. Meanwhile, also near Saratoga, the American troops under General Horatio Gates and General Philip Schuyler gather reinforcements and supplies.   6. The American forces outnumbered their British enemies by a margin of two to one.   7. The Americans are much better equipped than the British, whose provisions are badly depleted.

8. In spite of these disadvantages, the British open an attack on the Americans on September 19, 1777.   9. After four hours of fierce fighting, the Americans, led by Benedict Arnold (who later became an infamous traitor to the American cause), withdraw.   10. The British, however, have suffered serious losses, including many officers. 11. Burgoyne quickly sends a message to the British command in New York and asked for new orders.   12. He never received a response from his superiors, possibly because the message is intercepted. 13. Burgoyne's tactics became desperate.   14. He boldly leads a fresh attack against the Americans on October 7.   15. This time, however, his troops endure even worse casualties, and the next day Burgoyne prepares to retreat.

16. The Americans surround Burgoyne's army before it leaves Saratoga. 17. Trapped and helpless, Burgoyne begins negotiating his surrender. 18. The Convention of Saratoga, by which Burgoyne gave up his entire force of six thousand troops, is signed on October 17. 19. Saratoga becomes a turning point in the Revolutionary War. 20. Six years later, in 1783, the British signed a peace treaty with the Americans, and the Revolutionary War ended.

WRITING APPLICATION A:
Avoiding Unnecessary Shifts in Tense

The purpose of most writing is to communicate—an idea, a feeling, a mood—to your audience. To achieve this purpose, your writing must be as clear as possible. One important way to achieve clarity in your writing is to select a tense and to avoid shifting tense unnecessarily.

Writing Assignment

Write an essay explaining why you think a particular historical event occurred. Be sure to limit your topic for the length of your essay. Use the past tense, and avoid shifting tense unnecessarily.

ACTIVE AND PASSIVE VOICE

In most English sentences the subject performs the action of the verb. If there is a receiver of the action, it is expressed by the object of the verb, as in this example:

	S	V		O	

EXAMPLE The blazing fire **blistered** the outside walls. [The subject, *fire*, performs the action; the object, *walls*, tells what was blistered.]

A verb that expresses action performed by the subject is said to be in the *active voice*.

For reasons of emphasis, however, such sentences are often switched around so that the object becomes the subject:

	S	V	

EXAMPLE The outside walls **were blistered** by the blazing fire.

Notice that the object has been moved forward to the subject position and that the original subject is now expressed in a prepositional phrase. In addition, the verb has been changed from *blistered* to *were blistered*. Verbs that express action performed *upon* their subjects are said to be in the *passive voice*. The passive verb is always a verb phrase consisting of some form of *be* (*is, was,* etc.) plus the past participle.

ACTIVE She **grows** tomatoes and corn on her farm.
PASSIVE Tomatoes and corn **are grown** on her farm.
ACTIVE She **will plant** the corn in two weeks.
PASSIVE The corn **will be planted** in two weeks.

Notice that these passive sentences do not give the performer of the action. When it is important to know who or what performed the action in a passive sentence, the performer is named in a prepositional phrase.

Although the passive construction is useful in situations in which the performer of the action is unknown or unimportant, it can easily be overused. A succession of passive sentences has a weak and awkward sound and should be avoided.

WEAK PASSIVE The party was enjoyed by all the guests.

BETTER All the guests enjoyed the party.

AWKWARD PASSIVE When the blizzard struck, the fire in the fireplace was started by her.

BETTER When the blizzard struck, she started a fire in the fireplace.

EXERCISE 8. Identifying Sentences in the Active or Passive Voice. Number your paper 1–10. After the proper number, indicate whether the sentence is active or passive.

1. The art of Lucia Wilcox was admired by artists around the world.
2. Her blindness during her last years made her final works particularly interesting.
3. Dufy, Leger, Motherwell, and Pollock were among her teachers and friends.
4. Exhibits of her paintings were shown all over the art world.
5. Her blindness was sudden, though not wholly surprising.
6. It was caused by a tumor near the optic nerve.
7. After she became blind, she claimed she had better sight than anyone else.
8. Her vision and her mind were "free of static and distractions."

9. Her style was altered from energetic silhouettes to larger canvases in lush spreading colors.
10. These visions during her period of blindness were imitated by many well-known artists.

EXERCISE 9. Revising Sentences in the Passive Voice Using the Active Voice. There are five sentences in the passive voice in Exercise 8. Revise each one using the active voice.

WRITING APPLICATION B:
Using the Passive Voice to Create Suspense

In many of the art forms, it is fairly easy to establish mood. If a film director wants the mood to be frightening, for example, he may select eerie music. He may show a dark, rainy night with the wind blowing long, stringy moss that is hanging from old trees. If a dancer wants the same mood, her dance movements become sharp and fragmented. The canvas artist can use deep, dark tones, close to blackness. All of these artists can create sights or sounds or both to reinforce mood. In writing, however, you have to use words alone. One technique in creating suspense in a written work is to keep the performer of the action unknown by using the passive voice, as in the following examples.

EXAMPLES Julie was alone upstairs when she heard the kitchen door *being* quietly *closed*.
The detective entered the room just as the window was being opened.

Writing Assignment

Think of a situation in which suspense is created because the audience does not know who is performing the action—a door slowly opening, a creaking stairway, a car pulling into the driveway. Write a narrative paragraph telling what happened. Use the passive voice to keep the performer of the action unknown. Your aim is to create suspense.

SIX TROUBLESOME VERBS

There are three pairs of verbs in English that account for many usage errors: *lie—lay, sit—set,* and *rise—raise*. Because the meanings of each pair are related and their forms are similar, it is easy to get them mixed up. The exercises in this section will help you to keep these common verbs straight.

Lie and Lay

The verb *lie* means "to recline" and does not take an object. Its principal parts are *lie, (is) lying, lay, (have) lain.*

The verb *lay* means "to put or place" and takes an object. The principal parts of lay are *lay, (is) laying, laid, (have) laid.*

INFINITIVE	PRESENT PARTICIPLE	PAST	PAST PARTICIPLE
lie (to recline)	(is) lying	lay	(have) lain
lay (to put or place)	(is) laying	laid	(have) laid

EXAMPLES   The cat **lies** on the porch, sunning itself.
A thick fog **lay** over the city.
The old papers **had lain** on the desk for months.

Lay your packages down here.
The masons **laid** the bricks.
He **had laid** his keys on the ledge.

When faced with a *lie—lay* problem, ask yourself two questions:

1. What is the meaning I intend? (Is it "to be in a lying position" or is it "to put something down"?)

2. What is the time expressed by the verb? (Only one of the principal parts that you have memorized will express this time accurately.)

PROBLEM   Feeling drowsy yesterday, I (lay, laid) on the couch.
Question 1:   The meaning is "to remain in a lying position."
Therefore the proper verb is *lie.*
Question 2:   The time is past. Therefore, the proper principal part is *lay* (lie, *lay,* lain).
SOLUTION   Feeling drowsy yesterday, I **lay** on the couch.

PROBLEM   The teacher (lay, laid) the cards on the desk.
Question 1:   The meaning is "to put." Therefore, the proper verb is *lay.*
Question 2:   The time is past. Therefore, the proper principal part is *laid* (lay, *laid,* laid).
SOLUTION   The teacher **laid** the cards on the desk.

EXERCISE 10. *Oral Drill.* **Stressing the Correct Forms of** *Lie—Lay* **in Sentences.**   Read each of the following sentences aloud three times, stressing the italicized verbs. Be able to explain, in the light of the information given, why each verb is correct.

1. The ketchup bottle should *lie* on its side.
2. A light haze *lay* over the hills.
3. The cat *laid* its toy on the doorsill.
4. Someone's books are *lying* in the hall.
5. She had *lain* down for a nap.
6. We *laid* new tiles in our kitchen.
7. *Lay* the material on the counter.
8. You could *lie* down and relax.
9. He *laid* his hand over his heart and made a vow.
10. The gifts were *lying* by the fireplace.

EXERCISE 11. Selecting the Correct Form of *Lie—Lay* **to Complete Sentences.**   Number your paper 1–20. Select from each sentence the correct one of the two words in parentheses, and write the word after the proper number on your paper.

1. He (lay, laid) out the silverware.
2. Don't (lie, lay) your books in that puddle.
3. The pasture (lies, lays) in the valley.
4. A sheet (lay, laid) over the rug to catch the paint.
5. The clothing had (lain, laid) strewn about the room all week.
6. Kitty (lay, laid) the book down.
7. Marty had (lain, laid) in the sun too long.
8. The theories developed by Albert Einstein (lay, laid) the groundwork for many later scientific discoveries.
9. The treasure (lay, laid) hidden beneath the waves.
10. The cat has been (lying, laying) on my coat.
11. How long have those newspapers (lain, laid) there?
12. The truce hasn't (lain, laid) our fears to rest.
13. (Lying, Laying) the tip by my plate, I rose to leave the restaurant.
14. (Lie, Lay) the wet sweaters out on these towels.
15. The town of Hooksett (lies, lays) between Manchester and Concord.
16. If I think about that scary movie, I'll (lie, lay) awake all night.
17. She (lay, laid) that carpet all by herself.

18. Are you out there (lying, laying) by the pool?
19. The rusty parts had (lain, laid) out in the rain.
20. Marita (lay, laid) her receipt on the counter.

EXERCISE 12. Writing the Correct form of *Lie—Lay* in Sentences. Number your paper 1–10. After the proper number, write the correct form of *lie* or *lay* for the blank in each of the following sentences.

1. Yesterday morning the snow —— fresh and clean on the hillside.
2. The dog has —— by the fire all evening.
3. I had —— the letters on the table.
4. That old rope has —— in the corner for a week.
5. The child didn't want to —— down and sleep.
6. I —— my keys on the hall table.
7. —— in the grass, the snake was almost invisible.
8. I was —— in my tent, swatting insects.
9. Have you —— the new floor covering yet?
10. The President will —— great emphasis on tax reform.

EXERCISE 13. Determining the Correct Use of *Lie—Lay* in Sentences. Number your paper 1–20. Read each of the following sentences, and determine whether the verb is correctly used. If it is correct, write a + after the proper number on your paper; if it is incorrect, write a 0. Think of the *meaning* of the verb.

1. She had just lain down with a good book when the phone rang.
2. The towels laying in the corner all need to be washed.
3. The patient laid on the operating table.
4. Did you ever lay down on a water bed?
5. After lunch he will lay down and take a nap.
6. After I had tripped, I sat there feeling embarrassed, my groceries lying all around me.
7. Exhausted, she crossed the finish line and laid down in the grass.
8. The peddler lay out his wares.
9. The fox was lying hidden in the thicket.
10. She found the dog laying under the porch.
11. Saturday all we did was lie around and play records.
12. He was lying under the car tinkering with the muffler.
13. The factory has lain off several workers.
14. The sun worshipers were lying on the beach.

15. My gym bag was laying right where I had left it.
16. Last week he lay great emphasis on footnote form.
17. I laid the pie crust in the pan carefully.
18. The cougar was laying in wait for its prey.
19. She sighed and lay down the phone receiver.
20. As I remember it, he laid the bills in a desk drawer.

Sit and Set

The verb *sit* means "to be in a seated position." The principal parts of *sit* are *sit, (is) sitting, sat, (have) sat.*

The verb *set* means "to put," "to place (something)." The principal parts of *set* are *set, (is) setting, set, (have) set.*

INFINITIVE	PRESENT PARTICIPLE	PAST	PAST PARTICIPLE
sit (to rest)	(is) sitting	sat	(have) sat
set (to put)	(is) setting	set	(have) set

Study the following examples:

| You may **sit.** | The cars **sit** in the lot. |
| You may **set** your books here. | We **set** the stand on the street. |

You will have little difficulty using these verbs correctly if you will remember two facts about them: (1) Like *lie*, the verb *sit* means "to be in a certain position." It almost never has an object. (2) Like *lay*, the verb *set* means "to put (something)." It may take an object. *Set* does not change form in the past or the past participle. Whenever you mean "to place" or "to put," use *set*.[1]

EXERCISE 14. *Oral Drill.* Stressing the Correct Forms of *Sit— Set* in Sentences.

Read each of the following sentences aloud three times, stressing the italicized verb.

1. *Set* the groceries on the counter.
2. *Sit* down anywhere you like.
3. Would you *set* the table?
4. The bird *sat* on the wire.
5. Rosita *set* her watch.
6. We had *sat* in the lobby an hour.

---

[1] Several uses of the verb *set* do not mean "to put" or "to place"; for example: *the sun sets, setting hens, set your watch, set a record, set out to accomplish something.*

7. They have been *sitting* on the porch.
8. They came in and *sat* in the front row.
9. Jill *set* a new record in track.
10. We *sat* by the sea.

EXERCISE 15. Selecting the Correct Form of *Sit—Set* to Complete Sentences.   Number your paper 1–10. Select from each sentence the correct one of the two words in parentheses, and write it after the proper number.

1. A few of us were (sitting, setting) at our desks.
2. He (sat, set) in the rocker, reading.
3. He (sat, set) the package on the doorstep.
4. Ida was (sitting, setting) out the chips and dip for the guests.
5. We had been (sitting, setting) on a freshly painted bench.
6. They (set, sat) the seedlings in the window boxes.
7. She (sits, sets) in front of me.
8. He (set, sat) the mousetrap, baiting it with peanut butter.
9. I could (sit, set) and watch the sunset every evening.
10. Mick and Sheila (sat, set) the dials on the machine.

REVIEW EXERCISE A. Selecting the Correct Form of *Lie—Lay* and *Sit—Set* to Complete Sentences.   Number your paper 1–20. Choose the correct verb in parentheses, and write it after the proper number on your paper.

1. (Sitting, Setting) on the table was a pair of scissors.
2. Please (sit, set) the carton down carefully.
3. She (lay, laid) in the hammock, watching the clouds.
4. (Sit, Set) all the way back in your seat.
5. The dirty dishes had (lain, laid) in the sink for hours.
6. Yesterday Tom (lay, laid) the blame for his lateness on his alarm clock.
7. The cat always (sits, sets) on the couch.
8. If only we could have (lain, laid) our hands on that buried treasure!
9. My eyeglasses were (sitting, setting) right where I left them.
10. King Tut's tomb (lay, laid) undisturbed for centuries.
11. Have you ever (sat, set) around with nothing to do?
12. She (sat, set) down at her desk with her checkbook and calculator in front of her.

13. The two children were (sitting, setting) in the playpen.
14. The beached rowboat (lay, laid) on its side.
15. She (sat, set) looking toward the horizon.
16. Laura had just (sat, set) down when the phone rang.
17. Julie (lay, laid) her handbag on the counter.
18. Pieces of the jigsaw puzzle were (laying, lying) on the floor.
19. Jack was (sitting, setting) outside on the top step.
20. Were you (laying, lying) down for a while before dinner?

Rise and *Raise*

The verb *rise* means "to go in an upward direction." It is an *irregular* verb. Its principal parts are *rise, (is) rising, rose, (have) risen.*

The verb *raise* means "to move something in an upward direction." It is a *regular* verb. Its principal parts are *raise, raising, raised, (have) raised.*

Study the following:

INFINITIVE	PRESENT PARTICIPLE	PAST	PAST PARTICIPLE
rise (go up)	(is) rising	rose	(have) risen
raise (force upward)	(is) raising	raised	(have) raised

Just like *lie, rise* never has an object. Like *lay* and *set, raise* may have an object.

EXERCISE 16. Selecting the Correct Form of *Rise—Raise* to Complete Sentences.   Number your paper 1–10. Select from each sentence the correct one of the two words in parentheses, and write it after the proper number on your paper.

1. Has the moon (risen, raised) yet?
2. The tower (rose, raised) high into the darkening air.
3. The temperature (rose, raised) as the sun climbed higher.
4. When speed limits go up, the number of accidents (rises, raises).
5. A serious problem has (risen, raised).
6. Trails of mist were (rising, raising) from the lake.
7. How much did the river (rise, raise) during the flood?
8. Has anyone (rose, raised) that question before?
9. The butterfly (rose, raised) from the leaf and flitted away.
10. The dough was (rising, raising) in the bowl.

EXERCISE 17. Writing the Correct Form of *Rise—Raise* to Complete Sentences. Number your paper 1–10. For each sentence, write the correct form of *rise* or *raise,* whichever is required by the meaning.

1. If you know the answer, —— your hand.
2. —— the flags higher, please.
3. The tide —— and falls because of the moon.
4. Last year Marietta —— money for the charity by baking cookies.
5. Up toward the clouds —— the jet.
6. The crops we —— were sugar beets and corn.
7. Prices have —— in the last few years.
8. The traffic officer —— his hand to signal us.
9. Sonia —— before the sun came up this morning.
10. A question was —— by a member of the council.

REVIEW EXERCISE B. Determining Correct or Incorrect Use of *Lie—Lay, Sit—Set,* and *Rise—Raise* in Sentences. Number your paper 1–10. Read each of the following sentences, and determine whether it is correct. If it is correct, write a + after the proper number; if it is incorrect, write a 0.

1. Set down the eggs carefully.
2. The frog was setting on the lily pad, croaking loudly.
3. The judge studied the papers, then lay them beside her gavel.
4. The cattle were lying in the shade by the stream.
5. Is the thermometer raising, or do I just think it's hotter?
6. Wanda sat out the equipment for the experiment.
7. Why don't you lie those things down?
8. Instead of laying down, you should be getting some type of strenuous exercise.
9. A strange noise raised from the motor.
10. Set down for a while and relax.

REVIEW EXERCISE C. Writing the Correct Forms of Verbs to Complete Sentences. Number your paper 1–25. After the proper number on your paper, write the correct one of the two words in parentheses.

1. Have you (wrote, written) the address down?
2. Little Billy was (lying, laying) in wait for us.
3. Why don't you (lie, lay) the towels over the railing to dry?
4. We had (took, taken) our visitors to the World Trade Center.
5. He had accidentally (thrown, throwed) his homework away.
6. The spilled laundry (lay, laid) in a wet heap.
7. We ate until we almost (burst, bursted).
8. The kitten (shrank, shrunk) back from the barking dog.
9. We need to (lie, lay) out the plans and discuss them.
10. The pack rat had (stole, stolen) my watch during the night.
11. Haven't you ever (swam, swum) in a lake before?
12. They certainly have (ran, run) a successful campaign.
13. When the winners appeared, a cheer (rang, rung) out.
14. When we arrived, the movie had already (began, begun).
15. I put the juice in the freezer to cool, and when I remembered it, it had (froze, frozen).
16. We should have (gone, went) with the first bus.
17. Have you ever (rode, ridden) a roller coaster?
18. I knew I should have (brought, brung) my camera.
19. In New York, we (saw, seen) a Broadway play.
20. Uh-oh, I think this phone is (broke, broken).
21. A strange figure (rose, raised) up out of the mist.
22. The tree was (lying, laying) across the road.
23. It had (fell, fallen) during the storm.
24. I accidentally (sat, set) the dripping cup on the clean tablecloth.
25. We just (did, done) what we had to do.

CHAPTER 8 REVIEW: POSTTEST 1

A. Revising Verb Tense or Voice.   Rewrite the following sentences, correcting verbs that are in the wrong tense or use an awkward voice. If a sentence is correct, write *C* after the proper number.

EXAMPLES   1. The Congressional Medal of Honor was received by Mary Walker, one of the first women doctors, who served as a surgeon during the Civil War.

     1. *Mary Walker, one of the first women doctors, who served as a surgeon during the Civil War, received the Congressional Medal of Honor.*

2. The mason poured the cement between the bricks and then smoothes it.
2. *The mason poured the cement between the bricks and then smoothed it.*

1. Captain Cook, one of the greatest explorers of all time, sailed large areas of the Pacific Ocean and makes accurate maps of the region.
2. Cook joins the navy as a seaman in 1755 and many promotions were received by him before becoming a master of his own ship in 1759.
3. Because of his knowledge of mathematics, astronomy, and geography, he is selected to lead a scientific expedition to the Pacific.
4. The purpose of the expedition is to observe the passage of Venus between the earth and sun, a very rare occurrence.
5. On the voyage, Cook wins a battle against scurvy, a serious disease caused by lack of vitamin C.
6. Raw cabbage, which was rich in vitamin C, was eaten by the sailors to prevent scurvy.
7. By the time the voyage is over, the ship traveled around Cape Horn to Tahiti in the Pacific Ocean.
8. After he observes the passage of Venus, Cook sails off to explore the east coast of New Zealand, which was claimed by him for England.
9. On a second voyage, the Hawaiian Islands were discovered by Cook, which were named the Sandwich Islands by him.
10. In a dispute over a canoe, Cook was killed by island inhabitants and in naval tradition was buried at sea in 1779.

B. Determining Correct or Incorrect Use of *Lie—Lay, Sit—Set,* and *Rise—Raise* in Sentences.
Number your paper 11–25. Read each of the following sentences, and determine whether it is correct. If it is correct, write a + after the proper number; if it is incorrect, write a 0.

11. During our break, we laid under a tree and caught our breath.
12. You can sit the wastebasket in the corner.
13. Interest rates at the bank have been raised.
14. Everyone rose when the judge entered the courtroom.
15. The king was setting on the throne, looking bored.
16. What time does the sun rise today?
17. The grizzly bear suddenly raised up from the shadows.

18. Aunt Bea sat the pie on the windowsill to cool.
19. I like to lay out under the stars and just think.
20. The price of tires raised again.
21. We had just lain out the blueprints for the architect.
22. A shark raised from the depths with its jaws open.
23. The electric fan lay unused during the cold weather.
24. You can sit those boxes up in the attic.
25. The longer we set waiting, the more bored we became.

CHAPTER 8 REVIEW: POSTTEST 2

Revising Verb Tense or Voice. Revise the following sentences, correcting verbs that are in the wrong tense or use an awkward voice. If a sentence is correct, write *C* after the proper number.

EXAMPLE 1. Yesterday Marcia gives a report about Sacajawea, the Shoshone Indian woman who guided Lewis and Clark on their expedition in 1805.

1. *Yesterday Marcia gave a report about Sacajawea, the Shoshone Indian woman who guided Lewis and Clark on their expedition in 1805.*

1. Harriet Tubman, who was a courageous leader of the antislavery struggle, takes more than three hundred slaves to freedom through the underground railroad.
2. When she was a slave in Maryland, she is named Araminta but later is given the name of Harriet, after her mother.
3. She married John Tubman, but he refuses to join her when she flees north to freedom.
4. With her two brothers, she ran away, traveling by night.
5. Soon she became active in the underground railroad and makes at least fifteen trips back to the South to help others escape.
6. She travels the back country at night and signaled the people by singing.
7. Over the years, Harriet Tubman works with many white men and women, who gave her help in hiding slaves traveling the route to freedom.

8. Using the North Star as her guide, many slaves were led by her to safe houses of white abolitionists.

9. In spite of a reward of $40,000 for her capture, she never shrank from her undertaking, saying she was going where God sent her.

10. So successful was she in leading people through the underground railroad that it is said she never loses a man, woman, or child.

11. On one trip her own parents were brought back by her.

12. One of her confederates was John Brown, the Kansas abolitionist who believes that slavery must be abolished by force.

13. Although Harriet Tubman probably knows about his plan to raid Harpers Ferry, illness prevented her from joining him.

14. When the Civil War began, she chooses to work as a nurse, spy, and scout for the Union army.

15. After the Civil War, Harriet Tubman's ''autobiography'' was written by someone else because she was illiterate.

16. Using profits from the autobiography, she works to help children and the elderly in Auburn, New York, where she lived her last days.

17. Called ''the Moses of her people,'' Harriet Tubman lies under an evergreen tree in a grave in New York, a symbol of all who have risked everything for freedom.

18. I chose this book about Harriet Tubman because I had been given the assignment by my teacher to read a biography.

19. After I had checked it out, I lay it down in my room and forgot about it until my report was almost due.

20. I think I did an excellent report because the book was liked by me.

21. Over the past years I have discovered that I enjoy reading biographies.

22. In fact, yesterday I borrow another biography from the library.

23. Tomorrow I set some time aside to begin reading about Martin Luther King, Jr.

24. I know from history class that Martin Luther King, Jr., had been a great American civil rights leader until his death on April 4, 1968.

25. He is deeply concerned about equal rights for all people.

CHAPTER 9

Using Modifiers Correctly

COMPARISON; PLACEMENT OF MODIFIERS

DIAGNOSTIC TEST

A. Correcting Errors in the Use of the Comparative and Superlative Forms. The following sentences contain errors in the use of comparison modifiers. Number your paper 1–10. After the proper number, write the incorrect words from the sentence. Then write the correct form, adding words if necessary.

EXAMPLES 1. I was more hungrier than I thought, so I ordered three hamburgers.
    1. *more hungrier—hungrier*
    2. This storm was even badder than the last one.
    2. *badder—worse*

1. During the Middle Ages, Richard the Lion-Hearted of England was known as the most bravest champion of English chivalry as well as a noble Crusader.
2. He was the more able and intelligent of King Henry II's three sons.
3. John was Richard's youngest brother, and the favorite of their father.
4. While Richard was away fighting in one of the Crusades, John

took over the reins of government and ruled in the disagreeablest manner his subjects had known.

5. After Diego had started lifting weights, he bragged that he was stronger than any man in town.

6. People who live along this road complain because it is the worstest in the entire township.

7. Floyd and his brother are landscape designers who are famous throughout the United States, but Floyd is the best known in this area.

8. Now that the band has practiced together, their music sounds more better.

9. When I had a choice of chocolate or vanilla, I took vanilla because I like it best.

10. Looking across the water at sunset, you can see the beautifullest view you can imagine.

B. Revising Sentences by Correcting Dangling and Misplaced Modifiers.

Each of the following sentences contains a dangling or misplaced modifier. After the proper number, revise each sentence, arranging the words so that the meaning is logical and clear. You may have to add or delete some words.

EXAMPLE 1. The class sent a get-well message to their teacher on a balloon.
    1. *The class sent their teacher a get-well message on a balloon.*

11. Running in circles, they saw that the dogs could herd the sheep into the pen.

12. The winners marched onto the stage carrying ribbons and trophies.

13. A police officer warned students who drive too fast about accidents during the defensive-driving class.

14. After walking through the park, a cold drink was needed.

15. A brightly colored watercolor was hanging on her wall depicting the four seasons.

16. Mother found a package outside our house tied with ribbons.

17. Maria took some close-up photographs of a lion with a telephoto lens.

18. Sitting in a tree outside my window, I see a small brown bird, apparently building a nest on one of the limbs.

19. A young woman knocked on the door wearing a suit and a hat.

20. Walking in the sunshine, it felt warm to the children.

Knowing when to use an adverb and when to use an adjective is not just a matter of form but of meaning. Notice the difference in meaning in the following two sentences.

Lisa does **strenuous** exercise. [adjective]
Lisa exercises **strenuously.** [adverb]

A modifier is a word or a group of words that makes the meaning of another word more definite. Two parts of speech are used as modifiers: the adjective, which modifies a noun or pronoun, and the adverb, which modifies a verb, an adjective, or another adverb.

ADJECTIVE AND ADVERB FORMS

You will have little difficulty using most adjectives and adverbs correctly. Almost the only common problem in distinguishing an adverb from an adjective concerns the following three pairs: *bad—badly, good—well,* and *slow—slowly.* The problem is to learn when to use the adverb form and when to use the adjective form.

Apply the following rule to the three troublesome pairs.

9a. If a word in the predicate modifies the subject of the verb, use the adjective form. If it modifies the verb, use the adverb form.[1]

EXAMPLES The swimmer was **careful.** [The adjective *careful* modifies the noun *swimmer: careful swimmer.*]
He swims **carefully.** [The adverb *carefully* modifies the verb *swims: swims carefully.*]

Linking verbs are usually followed by a predicate adjective. The following are the most commonly used linking verbs: *be, become, seem, grow, appear, look, feel, smell, taste, remain, stay, sound.*

In general, a verb is a linking verb if you can substitute for it some form of the verb *seem.*

She **felt** happy. [She seemed happy.]
The car **appeared** abandoned. [The car seemed abandoned.]

Because many verbs may be used as either linking verbs or action verbs, you must be able to tell which way a verb is used in a particular sentence.

---

[1] Most adjectives become adverbs by adding *–ly: nice—nicely, vague—vaguely, incidental—incidentally.* A few adjectives, however, also end in *–ly (lively, lonely, friendly),* so you cannot always be sure that an *–ly* word is an adverb.

LINKING   The bell **sounded** loud. [verb followed by an adjective modifying the subject: The bell *seemed* loud.]

ACTION   The bell **sounded** loudly. [verb modified by an adverb]

LINKING   The calf **grows** fat. [verb followed by an adjective modifying the subject: The calf *seems* fat.]

ACTION   The calf **grows** quickly. [verb modified by an adverb]

LINKING   The tiger **looked** fierce. [verb followed by an adjective modifying the subject: The tiger *seemed* fierce.]

ACTION   The tiger **looked** fiercely through the bars. [verb modified by an adverb]

Bad and Badly

Bad is an adjective; in most uses *badly* is an adverb.

EXAMPLES   The dog was **bad.** [bad dog]
The dog behaved **badly.** [adverb modifying the verb *behaved*]
The milk smelled **bad.** [After the linking verb *smelled*, the adjective *bad* modifies the subject *milk*.]
The roof leaked **badly.** [The adverb *badly* modifies the verb *leaked*.]

With linking verbs the adjective form is used.

NONSTANDARD   The medicine tasted badly.

STANDARD   The medicine tasted **bad.** [The adjective *bad* modifies the subject *medicine*.]

NONSTANDARD   The spilled garbage smelled badly.

STANDARD   The spilled garbage smelled **bad.** [The verb *smelled* is a linking verb. *Bad* modifies the subject *garbage*.]

☞ **USAGE NOTE**   One prominent exception to this rule is the use of *badly* after the sense verb *feel*. In informal English either *bad* or *badly* is acceptable after *feel*.

He feels **bad** about the accident.
He feels **badly** about the accident. [informal]

However, formal English calls for *bad* after *feel*.

> He feels **bad** [not *badly*] about the accident.

Follow the rules for formal written English in doing the exercises in this book.

Well and Good

Well may be used as either an adjective or an adverb. As an adjective, *well* has three meanings:

1. To be in good health:

> Fran is well.
> She seems well.

2. To appear well dressed or well groomed:

> She looks well in red.

3. To be satisfactory:

> Everything is well.
> That is well.

As an adverb, *well* means *capably:*

> The house was built well.

Good is always an adjective. It should not be used to modify a verb.

NONSTANDARD   She sings good.

STANDARD   She sings **well.**

NONSTANDARD   The car runs good.

STANDARD   The car runs **well.**

STANDARD   The color looks **good** on you. [adjective following linking verb]

☞ **USAGE NOTE**   *Well* is also acceptable in sentences like the last example above: That color looks *well* on you.

Slow and Slowly

Slow is used as both an adjective and an adverb. *Slowly* is always an adverb.

EXAMPLES Go **slow.** [*Slow* is an adverb modifying *go.*]
Go **slowly.** [*Slowly* is an adverb modifying *go.*]

In most adverb uses (other than *go slow* or *drive slow*), it is better to use the form *slowly* as an adverb instead of *slow.*

EXAMPLE **Very slowly** the tiger crept forward.

☞ USAGE NOTE Certain words like *loud, hard, deep,* and *fast* may be used as adverbs without changing their forms.

EXAMPLES Samantha laughed **hard.**   The band played **loud.**

EXERCISE 1. Selecting Adjectives or Adverbs to Complete Sentences. Number your paper 1–20. Select the correct one of the two words in parentheses, and write it after the proper number on your paper.

1. I can't hear you (well, good) when the water is running.
2. The opening paragraph is written (well, good).
3. The situation looks (bad, badly).
4. Why does ketchup come out of the bottle so (slow, slowly)?
5. She certainly plays the marimba (well, good).
6. Can you dance as (well, good) as you sing?
7. These shoes don't fit (bad, badly) at all.
8. Our gym teacher told us to do the exercise (slow, slowly).
9. Did you do (well, good) on the last algebra test?
10. The chef at the corner cafe cooks very (bad, badly).
11. Your orange shirt goes (well, good) with those pants.
12. The bus moved (slow, slowly) in the rush-hour traffic.
13. This furniture polish smells (bad, badly).
14. I can ice-skate really (well, good).
15. Those boots don't look too (bad, badly) to me.
16. We felt (bad, badly) that you missed the class trip.
17. He can't draw as (well, good) as his brother.
18. The line was moving so (slow, slowly) that we thought we would miss our train.
19. Our dress rehearsal didn't go (well, good) at all.
20. For emphasis, the police officer spoke (slow, slowly).

EXERCISE 2. Using Adjective and Adverb Forms Correctly in Sentences. Number your paper 1–20. If the sentence is correct, write a + after the proper number; if it is incorrect, write a 0.

1. All went well at the interview.
2. Raising the camera slow, he tried not to startle the animal.
3. That new hair style looks well on Pat.
4. You had better start slow.
5. He was panting so bad that he had to sit down.
6. Marquita felt bad about her lost pet.
7. You sing so good that you could go on the stage.
8. He read slow, wanting to be careful.
9. The boat cruised slow out of the harbor.
10. The train seemed slow, but it was actually ahead of schedule.
11. She studied good for that test.
12. Joe did bad on the first test, but he improved on others.
13. You certainly hit that ball good.
14. Marcie played as well as any other member of the team.
15. The motor doesn't work as good as it used to.
16. Don't feel bad about not being able to take typing this year.
17. All of his repair work was done good.
18. This juice doesn't taste very well.
19. The truck inched along slow over the rutted road.
20. Walk as slow as you can, and try not to make any noise.

COMPARISON OF MODIFIERS

Adjectives state qualities of nouns or pronouns:

an **expensive** jacket   **fluffy** clouds   **shiny** metal

You can show the degree or extent to which one noun has a quality by comparing it with another noun that has the same quality. For instance:

This jacket is **larger** than the other.

Similarly, you can show degree or extent by using adverbs to make comparisons:

I ran well, but you ran **better**.

9b. The forms of modifiers change as they are used in comparison.

There are three degrees of comparison: *positive, comparative,* and *superlative*. Notice how the following forms of modifiers change to show comparison:

POSITIVE	COMPARATIVE	SUPERLATIVE
low	lower	lowest
fearful	more fearful	most fearful
promptly	more promptly	most promptly
bad	worse	worst
good	better	best

Regular Comparison

(1) A modifier of one syllable regularly forms its comparative and superlative by adding –er and –est.

POSITIVE	COMPARATIVE	SUPERLATIVE
thin	thinner	thinnest
small	smaller	smallest

(2) Some modifiers of two syllables form comparative and superlative degrees by adding –er and –est; other modifiers of two syllables form comparative and superlative degrees with more and most.

In general, the *–er* and *–est* forms are used with two-syllable modifiers unless they make the word sound awkward. The *more* and *most* forms are used with adverbs ending in *–ly.*

POSITIVE	COMPARATIVE	SUPERLATIVE
lovely	lovelier	loveliest
tricky	trickier	trickiest
awkward	more awkward	most awkward
quickly	more quickly	most quickly

Some two-syllable modifiers may use either *–er* and *–est* or *more* and *most*: *able, abler, ablest,* or *able, more able, most able.*

(3) Modifiers of more than two syllables form their comparative and superlative degrees by means of more and most.

POSITIVE	COMPARATIVE	SUPERLATIVE
catastrophic	more catastrophic	most catastrophic
predictably	more predictably	most predictably

(4) Comparison to indicate less or least of a quality is accomplished by using the words *less* and *least* before the modifier.

POSITIVE	COMPARATIVE	SUPERLATIVE
frequent	less frequent	least frequent
helpful	less helpful	least helpful

Irregular Comparison

Adjectives and adverbs that do not follow the regular methods of forming their comparative and superlative degrees are said to be compared irregularly.

POSITIVE	COMPARATIVE	SUPERLATIVE
bad	worse	worst
good } well }	better	best
little	less	least
many } much }	more	most

Caution: Do not add *–er, –est* or *more, most* to irregular forms: *worse,* not *worser* or *more worse.*

EXERCISE 3. Writing the Comparative and Superlative Forms of Modifiers. Write the comparative and superlative forms of the following modifiers:

1. little
2. fundamental
3. humid
4. unbearable
5. smart
6. full
7. good
8. complex
9. congenial
10. expensive
11. loud
12. well
13. likely
14. silly
15. bad

Use of Comparative and Superlative Forms

9c. Use the comparative degree when comparing two things; use the superlative degree when comparing more than two.

The comparative form of a modifier is used for comparing two things, as these examples indicate.

EXAMPLES   Our old house was **larger** than this one.
Omaha is **nearer** than Joplin.
Roberto studies **harder** than Dick.

The superlative form of a modifier is used for comparing three or more things.

EXAMPLES   The whale is the **largest** animal.
                  Meg is the **worst** person in our family to try to awaken.
                  Which of these four shirts costs the **least**?

In informal speech it is common to use the superlative for emphasis, even though only two things are being compared.

EXAMPLES   May the **best** person [of two] win.
                  Put your **best** foot forward.

In writing, however, you will do well to observe the distinction stated in rule 9c.

EXERCISE 4. Writing Sentences Using the Comparative and Superlative Forms of Modifiers.   Write five sentences correctly using adjectives or adverbs to compare two things, and write five sentences using the same adjectives and adverbs to compare three or more things.

9d. Do not omit the word *other* or *else* when comparing one thing with a group of which it is a part.

It is absurd to say "Stan is taller than anyone in his class." Stan must obviously be a member of the class himself, and he can hardly be taller than himself. The word *else* should be supplied: "Stan is taller than anyone else in his class."

> ABSURD   Our school is smaller than any in the county. [This would mean that the school is smaller than itself.]

> ACCURATE   Our school is smaller than any **other** in the county.

> ABSURD   Lucy is funnier than anybody in her group. [This means that Lucy, a member of her group, is funnier than herself.]

> ACCURATE   Lucy is funnier than anybody **else** in her group.

> ABSURD   Rhode Island is smaller than any state in the Union.

> ACCURATE   Rhode Island is smaller than any **other** state in the Union.

9e. Avoid double comparisons.

A double comparison is one in which the comparative or superlative is incorrectly formed by adding *-er* or *-est* in addition to using *more* or *most*.

NONSTANDARD The second movie was more scarier than the first one.

STANDARD The second movie was **scarier** [or *more scary*] than the first one.

NONSTANDARD What is the most deadliest snake?

STANDARD What is the **most deadly** [or *deadliest*] snake?

9f. Be sure your comparisons are clear.

In making comparisons, you should always state clearly what things are being compared. For example, in the sentence "The climate of Arizona is drier than South Carolina," the comparison is not clear. The climate of Arizona is not being compared to South Carolina, but rather to the climate of South Carolina. The sentence should read: "The climate of Arizona is drier than that of South Carolina."

AWKWARD The Millers would rather plant and harvest their own vegetables than canned ones.

CLEAR The Millers would rather plant and harvest their own vegetables than buy canned ones.

Often an incomplete clause is used in making comparisons. Both parts of the comparison should be fully stated if there is any danger of misunderstanding.

NOT CLEAR We know her better than Dee.

BETTER We know her better than we know Dee.
We know her better than Dee does.

EXERCISE 5. Using Modifiers Correctly in Sentences. Number your paper 1–20. If the sentence is correct, write a + after the proper number on your paper; if it is incorrect, write a 0. Be prepared to explain your answers.

1. Laurie is more friendlier than she used to be.
2. The hiker stopped, sat, and examined the sorer of his feet for blisters.
3. Which of the four seasons do you like better?
4. I never saw a countryside more flatter.
5. Margaret Mead was one of the world's most famous anthropologists.
6. Who is tallest, Jim or Jerry?
7. The room looked more brighter after we had painted it.

8. Which is the fastest way to get there?
9. Of the two albums, this was the least expensive.
10. The cheetah is the world's most fastest running animal.
11. The muscles of the leg are stronger than the arm.
12. The right glove of that pair is the most seriously soiled.
13. Denver has a higher elevation than any major city in the United States.
14. The beach was more hotter than we had expected.
15. Which is largest, St. Louis or Pittsburgh?
16. This flood was much worser than the last.
17. He is taller than any member of his family.
18. We moved more closer so we could hear the speaker.
19. If you get two job offers, take the one with the highest pay.
20. My sister and I are less alike than any other twins we know.

REVIEW EXERCISE. Correcting Errors in the Use of Comparative and Superlative Forms.   Most of the following sentences contain errors in the way modifiers are used. Number your paper 1–10. After the proper number, write the correct form of the incorrect words. If a sentence is correct, write *C*.

EXAMPLES   1. After we had heard the dog howling, we became fearfuller.
    1. *more fearful*
    2. The child was toddling so slow that his sister soon was far ahead.
    2. *slowly*

1. Ida Wells, who spoke out brave for civil rights from 1892 to 1931, was one of the founders of the National Association for the Advancement of Colored People.
2. In the Northern Hemisphere, days in June are warmer than November.
3. The governor considered our proposal more favorably than the one written by the other group.
4. She felt badly because she had not recovered from the illness and could not play with the team.
5. That blue suit looks good on Father, but I like the brown one best.
6. Coming in from the cold, they appreciated the fire that burned brightly in the old iron stove.
7. Finding that the new map was usefuller to me than my old one, I took it with me in the car.

8. I like Heather better than Carla.
9. The red apples in that basket are more sweeter than the green ones you bought yesterday.
10. Because his old car ran so good, he decided not to buy a new one.

WRITING APPLICATION A:
Using Comparative and Superlative Degrees to Make Comparison Clear

Have you ever heard someone talk and talk and not seem to say anything? Meaningless chatter does not really give the listener anything to think about and respond to. Occasionally writers produce many words but say little because they omit details or reasons.

> I prefer to live in the city instead of the suburbs for many reasons. Cities are interesting. I really enjoy the things available in cities. Cities have lots of advantages.

Writing Assignment

Use one of the following ideas for a comparison. Be sure to support your opinion with clear reasons. Include each of the three degrees of comparison: positive, comparative, and superlative. Underline and label each when you use it.

EXAMPLE Autumn is <u>more beautiful</u> than winter because of the colorful foliage.
[comparative degree]

IDEAS two sports   the beach versus the woods
city and country   freshman year/sophomore year

DANGLING MODIFIERS

9g. A phrase or clause that does not clearly and sensibly modify a word in the sentence is a *dangling modifier.*

A modifier consisting of a phrase or a clause may be momentarily confusing to a reader if it appears to modify a word that it cannot sensibly modify. Verbal phrases are particularly likely to dangle, since they have only a loose grammatical relationship with the rest of the sentence.

CONFUSING Looking back over my shoulder, the team went into a huddle. [The participial phrase seems illogically to modify *team*.] Towed away by the truck, I sadly watched my car. [The participial phrase seems to modify *I*.]

In both examples the participial phrase appears to modify a word that it cannot logically modify. The word that each phrase is supposed to modify has been omitted from the sentence. Compare the following correct examples.

CLEAR Looking back over my shoulder, I saw the team go into a huddle.
I sadly watched my car being towed away by the truck.

Dangling modifiers can be corrected by rearranging the words in the faulty sentence or by adding words that make the meaning clear and logical.

CONFUSING Going to the store, a building was on fire.

CLEAR Going to the store, I saw a building on fire.

CONFUSING While frying the bacon, the eggs were scrambled.

CLEAR While frying the bacon, Cindy scrambled the eggs.

CLEAR While Jo was frying the bacon, Cindy scrambled the eggs.

CONFUSING To qualify for the Olympics, many trial heats must be won.

CLEAR To qualify for the Olympics, a runner must win many trial heats.

CLEAR Before a runner may qualify for the Olympics, he must win many trial heats.

EXERCISE 6. Revising Sentences by Correcting Dangling Modifiers.

Revise each sentence so that the modifier *clearly* and *sensibly* modifies a word in the sentence. You may have to supply some words to fill out the sentence properly.

1. Sitting on the telephone wire, he saw a meadowlark.
2. Looking through the telescope, the moon seemed enormous.
3. While out running, his mouth got dry.
4. Going around the bend, the ocean came into view.
5. Doing a few tap dance steps, the floor got scratched.
6. Carefully cleaning her whiskers, we watched the mother cat.
7. To grow plants successfully, light, temperature, and humidity must be carefully controlled.

8. After doing the housework, the room almost sparkled.
9. To make manicotti, pasta must be stuffed with cheese.
10. Concluding her speech, the jury looked at her in awe.

EXERCISE 7. Revising Sentences by Correcting Dangling Modifiers. Follow the instructions for Exercise 6.

1. After finishing our dinner, fruit and cheese were served.
2. While popping the corn, the electricity went off.
3. Having helped Brice with the paint job, the looks of the car made me proud.
4. While doing the dishes, a mouse ran across the floor.
5. After putting in a long day's work, the bed looked good.
6. To drive safely, the brakes should be checked regularly.
7. Listening to the radio, the storm was coming closer.
8. To go fishing there, a permit is needed.
9. To repair miniaturized circuits in home appliances, patience is required.
10. After putting out the cat, the doors were locked.
11. When doing a difficult task, concentration is required.
12. Having seen the dentist, my tooth no longer hurt.
13. Before viewing the exhibit, your umbrella must be left with the attendant.
14. When making pizza, the dough must be spread carefully.
15. Scurrying into the anthill, I watched the ants with amazement.

MISPLACED MODIFIERS

9h. Modifying words, phrases, and clauses should be placed as near as possible to the words they modify.

Most of the errors in modification in the above examples resulted from the omission of the word that was supposed to be modified. Unclear sentences can also result from placing modifiers too far away from the words they modify.

Misplaced Phrase Modifiers

(1) Modifying phrases should be placed as near as possible to the words they modify.

The following sentences will indicate the importance of observing this rule.

CONFUSING   Who is the person with the dog in the sports jacket?

CLEAR   Who is the person in the sports jacket with the dog? [The phrase *with the sports jacket* obviously modifies *person*. Otherwise it appears to modify *dog* and gives the impression that the dog was wearing the sports jacket.]

CONFUSING   We learned that Pearl Buck wrote *The Good Earth* in our English class.

CLEAR   In our English class we learned that Pearl Buck wrote *The Good Earth*.

CONFUSING   We rented a boat from my cousin with two motors.

CLEAR   We rented a boat with two motors from my cousin.

CLEAR   From my cousin we rented a boat with two motors.

EXERCISE 8. Revising Sentences by Correcting Misplaced Phrase Modifiers.   Read each of the following sentences. Pick out the misplaced phrase, decide what word the phrase should modify, and revise the sentence, placing the phrase near this word.

1. Charlene likes to walk on the lawn without shoes.
2. We found the injured sparrow on the way to school.
3. We saw several blue jays looking out our front window.
4. He praised the new mayor with great sincerity.
5. She photographed a strange reptile with her disc camera.
6. Mrs. Barry drove downtown after her husband had left for the factory to do some shopping.
7. I found a huge boulder taking a shortcut through the woods.
8. Mr. Tate noticed some caterpillars pruning his fruit tree.
9. We saw a woman with her elkhound in high-heeled shoes.
10. Missie saw a heron driving over the bridge.
11. We noticed several signs riding down the highway.
12. We could see corn growing from our car window.
13. Barking wildly and straining at the chain, the letter carrier was forced to retreat from the dog.
14. I met a woman on the plane in a mink coat.
15. He recounted an incident about a nuclear chain reaction during his chemistry lecture.

16. They were shown a house by the real estate agent with a grove of tall trees.
17. At the pet store we were shown a parrot in a cage with colorful feathers.
18. They arrived just as the meeting began on bicycles.
19. Sitting on the porch swing, the wasp startled the couple.
20. We were given a map by the guide made of green paper.

Misplaced Clause Modifiers

In using modifying clauses, follow the rule for phrases.

(2) Place the clause as near as possible to the word it modifies.

The following sentences will show you how a misplaced clause may make a sentence ridiculous.

AWKWARD   There was a building in the city that was condemned.

CLEAR   There was a building that was condemned in the city.

The modifying clause *that was condemned* modifies *building,* not *city.* In the second sentence the clause has been put next to the word it modifies.

AWKWARD   The letter was in the mailbox which bore a foreign stamp.

CLEAR   The letter, which bore a foreign stamp, was in the mailbox.

AWKWARD   Lyn got a package from one of the stores we visited that she hadn't ordered.

CLEAR   From one of the stores we visited, Lyn got a package that she hadn't ordered.

EXERCISE 9. Revising Sentences by Correcting Misplaced Clause Modifiers.
Read each of the following sentences. Take out the misplaced clause, decide what word the clause should modify, and revise the sentence, placing the clause near this word. If you find a misplaced phrase, correct it.

1. We put the clothing in the cellar that we had outgrown.
2. I gave olives to my friend that I stabbed with my fork.
3. The plane landed on the runway that had the engine trouble.
4. The picture was hanging on the wall that we bought in Canada.
5. I ignored any topics in the book that we covered in class.

6. They showed us a camera on the bus that works underwater.
7. We washed the dishes with sudsy water that had been stacked in the sink all day.
8. They took the cat to the manager's office that had been lost.
9. Jan showed the rooms to her visitors that she had painted.
10. We ran after the dog into the street that had escaped.

WRITING APPLICATION B:
Using Modifiers to Make Your Writing Clear

Dangling or misplaced modifiers do not belong where they are placed. Notice how the misplaced modifier in the following sentence makes the meaning unclear.

EXAMPLE While studying for biology, the ice cream tasted good.

Think about the meaning of this sentence. Can ice cream study? How would you correct this sentence?

Writing Assignment

Complete each of the following sentences. If the modifier does not start with a capital letter, place it at the end of your sentence. Make sure you review your sentences for dangling or misplaced modifiers.

1. wandering around the school grounds
2. Hoping my parents wouldn't be angry
3. after taking the test
4. Placing the assignment on her desk

CHAPTER 9 REVIEW: POSTTEST 1

A. Selecting Adjectives or Adverbs to Complete Sentences.
Number your paper 1–5. For each sentence, select the correct word and write it next to the proper number.

1. The players felt (bad, badly) about losing their last game.
2. She appears so (nervous, nervously) that I am afraid she will forget her lines when the curtain goes up.
3. Speaking (nervous, nervously), he approached the frightened horse and tried to calm it.

4. Our efforts to raise money for the charity fund turned out (good, well).
5. By driving very (slow, slowly), he was able to travel the icy road without sliding into the ditch.

B. Correcting Errors in the Use of Comparative and Superlative Forms.

Most of the following sentences contain errors in the use of modifiers. Number your paper 6–15. If the modifier is incorrect, write the correct form after the proper number on your paper. If a sentence is correct, write *C* after the proper number.

EXAMPLES 1. Elizabeth Cady Stanton was one of the earliest and most influential leaders for women's rights.
1. *C*
2. Early in her life she learned that the rights of women were not equal to men.
2. *equal to the rights of men* [or *equal to those of men*]

6. After he had attended cooking school, my brother soon earned the reputation for making the bestest cakes in town.
7. The climate of San Diego is more moderate than Omaha.
8. For a vacation, DeWayne and Roberto prefer backpacking in the mountains to crowded resorts.
9. Alexander the Great conquered more countries than any other king in the ancient world.
10. Handsome and gifted, he not only was the dazzling hero of his time but also remained a legendary figure long after his death.
11. He was one of the few kings whose deeds were more greater than his legends.
12. Alexander's teacher, Aristotle, was the greatest philosopher in the world.
13. Aristotle knew more about science, geography, and history than anyone of his time.
14. Alexander preferred Greek art to Persia, India, or Africa.
15. As a result of his conquests, the best aspects of the Greek civilization were shared by people outside Greece.

C. Revising Sentences by Correcting Dangling and Misplaced Modifiers.

Most of the following sentences contain dangling or misplaced modifiers. Revise the sentences so that their meaning is logical and clear. If a sentence is correct, write *C* after the proper number.

EXAMPLE   1. Alice found out that she was on the wrong bus from the driver.
  1. *Alice found out from the driver that she was on the wrong bus.*

16. The car belongs to a sales representative with wire wheels and a black top.
17. After taking vigorous exercise, a shower and a good breakfast are appreciated by them.
18. Published in 1938, *The Yearling* became Marjorie Kinnan Rawlings' best-known work.
19. Ten students were injured, according to Mrs. Harris, sliding on the ice.
20. Rowing across the lake, the cabins can be seen from a distance.
21. Did anyone leave a purse on the bus with a broken clasp?
22. Reading my lessons and taking notes, a sudden knock at the door startled me.
23. Mr. Morse got a job driving a truck through a local employment agency.
24. Giving in to every complaint, poor results were obtained from the student action committee.
25. Leading a crusade for women's rights in the nineteenth century, Lucy Stone became known as the voice of women's suffrage.

CHAPTER 9 REVIEW: POSTTEST 2

Revising Sentences by Correcting Errors in the Use of Modifiers. Most of the following sentences contain errors in the use of modifiers (words, phrases, clauses). Revise such sentences, correcting the faulty modifiers. If a sentence is correct, write *C* after its number on your paper.

1. While riding my motorcycle, the neighbor's dog chased me.
2. I bought these clothes with my birthday money that I'm wearing.
3. Adrianne is better at chemistry than anybody in her class.
4. Grading all the papers, the teacher was pleased to see that the students had done better than they had on any previous assignment.
5. I think that kale is more tastier than spinach, but some people don't like either one very good.
6. By eating too quickly, my lunch disagreed with me.

7. Hank worked rather hasty so he could catch up with Clay and Nina.
8. We bought this cat from a farmer that really catches mice good.
9. Thundering over the plains, a herd of buffalo was a sight that could not fail to impress the viewer.
10. Although Mitzi Akira is shorter than any player on her volleyball team, she's the best of the top two scorers.
11. Although Marian felt bad about losing the game, she knew things could be worser.
12. Millie can dance as well as Scott, but of the two, his singing is best.
13. Looking out across the sea from the rail, the whales rose to the surface, spouted, and disappeared once more.
14. By playing carefully, the game was won.
15. To economize during cold months, weatherstripping should be used for all loose-fitting windows with an adhesive backing.
16. Wearily struggling into my boots and parka, a sudden cold wind out of the northeast was faced grimly.
17. Although it is more difficult, this trail is the shorter of the four leading down the mountain.
18. I found a seashell on the beach with beautiful scalloped edges.
19. To develop photographic prints, a source of water and a room that can be darkened completely are needed.
20. Because one carton of chemicals smelled badly, it was examined for contamination before being used in the laboratory.
21. Although Helen is the better actress, Wenona will probably get the leading part because she is more reliable.
22. Requiring a previous course in drawing, I could not enroll in the museum's advanced art course.
23. Mr. Coleman, a woodcarver, thinks a hand chisel is more usefuller for this delicate work than power tools.
24. Keeping a watch throughout the night, all channel markers were carefully recorded on his chart for the return trip.
25. Nero earned the reputation of being one of Rome's worstest rulers.

CHAPTER 10

Glossary of Usage

COMMON USAGE PROBLEMS

This chapter contains a short glossary of English usage to supplement the materials in Chapters 5–9. You may wish to work right through the chapter, using the exercises to test your ability to use these expressions correctly. However, the glossary is intended mainly for reference. Get in the habit of referring to it whenever you are uncertain about a point of usage.

Several kinds of usage problems are treated here. In some, a choice is described between standard and nonstandard ways of phrasing things. In such cases you will be advised to follow the standard practice. Other choices are between formal and informal usages. Here you should follow the formal practice in doing the exercises. Problems arising from the confusion of similarly spelled words are treated in Chapter 32.

DIAGNOSTIC TEST

Revising Expressions by Correcting Errors in Usage. In each of the following sets of expressions, one expression contains an error in usage. After the proper number, rewrite these expressions correctly, using standard formal usage.

EXAMPLE 1. (a) She taught me to sing. (b) fewer letters in the box
        (c) Set down in the shade and rest.
    1. *(c) Sit down in the shade and rest.*

1. (a) anywheres you travel (b) as fast as sound travels (c) Learn French cooking from him.
2. (a) affect the outcome (b) candidate implied in his speech (c) among his two opponents
3. (a) made illusions to the Bible (b) fewer participants in the contest (c) replied to her grandmother respectfully
4. (a) family emigrated from Germany (b) should of gone yesterday (c) discovered a new planet
5. (a) Try and win the game. (b) draw as well as her mother (c) that kind of car
6. (a) Let the dog out. (b) an effect of cold weather (c) books, pencils, papers, and etc.
7. (a) not excepted by the club (b) among all athletes (c) Bring your records with you.
8. (a) less money than last year (b) can't hardly tell the difference (c) Lay the book on the shelf.
9. (a) picture fell off the wall (b) What kind of a dog is that? (c) larger than he
10. (a) sitting beside the tree (b) going a little ways (c) not reality but illusion
11. (a) coat doesn't fit well (b) an immigrant to this country (c) inside of the cabinet
12. (a) car looks like it had been wrecked (b) chair that was blue (c) water jug that burst
13. (a) She effected an improvement. (b) divide an estate between two children (c) Less students joined the club this year.
14. (a) Take the package to the mailroom. (b) Apples fell off of the tree. (c) will scarcely be enough food for all of them
15. (a) invented a better safety device (b) No one beside my aunt knows. (c) played well in the tournament
16. (a) Funds were allotted among six counties. (b) Where is my hammer at? (c) This is as far as the fence extends.
17. (a) going nowheres (b) Doesn't he know the way? (c) She finished reading; then she wrote her essay.
18. (a) Read the book and report on same. (b) Try to learn this poem. (c) Leave the green grapes on the vine.
19. (a) Set the brake on the car. (b) The fog will rise from the lake. (c) One of them glasses broke.
20. (a) It was an illusion caused by light on the surface.

(b) Their report implies a need for funds. (c) That dog he limps.
21. (a) no exception to this rule (b) being that she is the oldest (c) Bring your own tools with you.
22. (a) Set a good example. (b) looked like it had been burned (c) They ought to study before the test.
23. (a) The ice bursted a pipe. (b) Lie on the couch and rest. (c) emigrate from their birthplace
24. (a) Leave me have my turn. (b) Ellen, Jose, and Kim, respectively (c) somewhat cold for swimming
25. (a) haven't only three days of vacation (b) the effect of smoking on the lungs (c) learned that the winner had been announced

---

a, an   These short words are called *indefinite articles*. They refer to one of a general group.

EXAMPLES   **A** salesperson walked to the counter.
The tourists are looking for **a** hotel.
June has **an** appointment next week.

Use *a* before words beginning with a consonant sound; use *an* before words beginning with a vowel sound. In the examples above, *a* is used before *hotel* because *hotel* begins with a consonant sound. *An* is used before *hour* because *hour* begins with a vowel sound.

accept, except   *Accept* is a verb; it means "to receive." *Except* may be either a verb or a preposition. As a verb it means "to leave out"; as a preposition it means "excluding."

EXAMPLES   Gary could not **accept** that he had lost.
If you were absent, you will be **excepted** from this test.
Everybody knew **except** Chrissie.

affect, effect   *Affect* is usually a verb; it means "to influence." *Effect* used as a verb means "to accomplish" or "to bring about." Used as a noun, *effect* means "the result of some action."

EXAMPLES   The heat did not seem to **affect** them.
Did the drug **effect** a cure?
The director wanted to create a special **effect.**

all the farther, all the faster   These expressions are used informally in some parts of the country to mean "as far as" and "as fast as." In formal English, *as far as* and *as fast as* are the correct expressions.

NONSTANDARD This is all the farther we can go.

STANDARD This is **as far as** we can go.

allusion, illusion An *allusion* is a reference to something. An *illusion* is a "false, misleading, or overly optimistic idea."

EXAMPLES She made an **allusion** to the poem.
The magician was a master of **illusion**.

and etc. Since *etc.* is an abbreviation of the Latin *et cetera*, which means "and other things," you are using *and* twice when you write "and etc." The *etc.* is sufficient.

anywheres, everywheres, nowheres Use these words and others like them without the *s*.

EXAMPLE **Anywhere** [not *anywheres*] you travel, you see the same hotels.

at Do not use *at* after *where*.

NONSTANDARD Where's the main office located at?

STANDARD Where's the main office **located**?

being as, being that Avoid each; use *since* or *because*.

NONSTANDARD Being that he was late, he had to stand.

STANDARD **Since** he was late, he had to stand.

NONSTANDARD Being as her grades were so high, she got a scholarship.

STANDARD **Because** her grades were so high, she got a scholarship.

beside, besides *Beside* means "by the side of"; *besides* means "in addition to."

EXAMPLES He nervously glanced at the person **beside** him.
Did anybody **besides** you see what happened?

between, among *Between* implies two people or things; *among* implies more than two. This distinction in meaning is usually observed in formal English; however, use *between* when you are thinking of two items at a time, regardless of whether they are part of a group of more than two. (See third example below.)

EXAMPLES The twins had a strong bond **between** them.
The basketball team talked **among** themselves.
There were differences **between** Massachusetts, Vermont, and Connecticut. [*Between* is correct because the speaker is thinking of differences between *two* states at a time.]

There was a friendly agreement **between** the people of our town and those of the neighboring town. [Although more than two people are involved, the agreement is between two groups.]

bring, take *Bring* means "to come carrying something." *Take* means "to go away carrying something." The situation is complicated by the fact that a speaker, out of politeness, sometimes adopts the point of view of the person being spoken to: "Shall I bring you something to eat?" Usually it is helpful to think of *bring* as related to *come* and *take* as related to *go*.

EXAMPLES **Bring** your radio when you come.
Don't forget to **take** your coat when you go.

bust, busted Avoid using these words as verbs. Use a form of either *burst* or *break*.

NONSTANDARD I busted the switch on the stereo.

STANDARD I **broke** the switch on the stereo.

NONSTANDARD The water main busted.

STANDARD The water main **burst**.

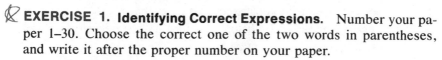 **EXERCISE 1. Identifying Correct Expressions.** Number your paper 1–30. Choose the correct one of the two words in parentheses, and write it after the proper number on your paper.

1. The tasks were divided (among, between) the two scouts.
2. He didn't seem to be (affected, effected) by the news.
3. Penicillin has (affected, effected) some remarkable recoveries.
4. No one (accept, except) the sophomores is supposed to attend.
5. Is that (all the faster, as fast as) you can walk?
6. Please (bring, take) these papers when you leave.
7. The clown distributed the treats (between, among) the many children.
8. Everybody knew about the quiz (accept, except) Larry.
9. We were afraid that the bull had (busted, broken) loose.
10. Ask Ginny to (bring, take) me her new record album.
11. The candidate made a sneering (allusion, illusion) to his opponent's speech.
12. (Being that, Since) everyone is here, let's begin.
13. They graciously (accepted, excepted) my halting apology.
14. I wonder where the mustard (is, is at).

15. Your sock has (a, an) hole in it.
16. (Everywhere, Everywheres) in Hot Springs there are interesting old buildings.
17. I couldn't find the cat (anywhere, anywheres).
18. Somebody (beside, besides) Nancy should help with the cleanup tasks.
19. He is (a, an) ardent supporter of the mayor.
20. When you go to the bank, will you (bring, take) this check for me?
21. Did the dogs (bust, break) out of their pen again?
22. The crosslike rays radiating from the moon were an (allusion, illusion) caused by the screen door.
23. The excessive humidity (affected, effected) all of us.
24. (Bring, Take) your radio with you when you come to my house.
25. Somebody (beside, besides) Julie must have picked up the tickets.
26. This is (all the farther, as far as) that rumor should go.
27. Winning the championship didn't (affect, effect) Terry's ego adversely.
28. When the dam (busted, broke), the villagers had to flee.
29. The seniors are (accepted, excepted) from that ruling.
30. The speaker made an (allusion, illusion) to a statement in Ralph Ellison's book.

can't hardly, can't scarcely   See **The Double Negative** (page 256).

could of   *Could have* sounds like *could of* when spoken. Do not erroneously write *of* with the helping verb *could.* Use *could have.* Also avoid *ought to of, should of, would of, might of,* and *must of.*

EXAMPLE   Muriel could **have** [not *of*] gone with us.

discover, invent   *To discover* means "to find something that already exists." *To invent* is "to be the first to make something not known before."

EXAMPLES   Sarah Boone **invented** the ironing board.
Columbus **discovered** America by accident.

don't   A contraction of *do not, don't* should not be used with a singular noun or a third person singular pronoun (*he, she, it*). Use *doesn't.* See page 156.

NONSTANDARD   He don't like to eat parsnips.

STANDARD   He **doesn't** like to eat parsnips.

NONSTANDARD   It don't matter at all.

STANDARD   It **doesn't** matter at all.

effect   See **affect, effect.**

emigrate, immigrate   *Emigrate* means "to go from a country to settle elsewhere." *Immigrate* means "to come into a country to settle there."

EXAMPLES   My great-grandfather **emigrated** from Norway.
Much of Australia's population is composed of people who **immigrated** there.

everywheres   See **anywheres.**

except   See **accept, except.**

fewer, less   In standard formal English, *fewer* (not *less*) is used before a plural noun. *Less* is used before a singular noun.

EXAMPLES   There are **fewer** [not less] whales than there used to be.
We should have bought **less** meat [but **fewer** eggs].

good, well   *Good* is an adjective. Do not use it to modify a verb.

NONSTANDARD   They skate good.

STANDARD   They skate **well.**

Well is an adverb except in three uses: (1) when used to mean "healthy," (2) when used to mean "neatly groomed" or "attractively dressed," and (3) when used to mean "satisfactory." In all of these instances, *well* is an adjective.

EXAMPLES   The car ran **well.** [adverb]
I didn't feel **well.** [adjective]
They looked **well** in their new outfits. [adjective]
All seems **well.** [adjective]

had of   See **of.**

had ought   See **ought.**

hardly   See **The Double Negative** (page 256).

he, she, they   Do not use unnecessary pronouns. This error is sometimes called the *double subject.*

NONSTANDARD My father he works downtown.

STANDARD My **father works** downtown.

illusion See **allusion, illusion.**

immigrate See **emigrate, immigrate.**

imply, infer *Imply* means "to suggest something." *Infer* means "to interpret" or "to derive a certain meaning from a remark or an action."

EXAMPLES In her speech, the candidate **implied** that she was for tax reform. From other remarks that she has made, I **infer** that she feels that certain taxes are unfair.

EXERCISE 2. Identifying Correct Expressions. Number your paper 1–20. Choose the correct form in parentheses, and write it after the proper number on your paper.

1. My sister's statement (implied, inferred) that she was displeased with the cut in her allowance.
2. Was it George Washington Carver or Thomas Edison who (invented, discovered) all those uses for peanuts?
3. From his letter I (implied, inferred) he would be away all summer.
4. He (don't, doesn't) always say what he means.
5. She read the poem aloud, interpreting it very (good, well).
6. (My aunt, My aunt she) lived a year in San Juan.
7. Few people can play the trumpet as (good, well) as he can.
8. (Emigration, Immigration) to Alaska was spurred by the gold rush.
9. Explorer Jebediah Smith (discovered, invented) the first overland route to California.
10. The heat has affected the growing season; we'll harvest (fewer, less) crops this year.
11. Many French Canadians (emigrated, immigrated) from Quebec to work in the industries of New England.
12. In spite of losing our center just before the tournament, we played (good, well) and won.
13. Mary Beth Stearns (discovered, invented) a device to study electrons.
14. Study this chapter (good, well) and you should master many rules of usage.

15. This year at the shore we saw (less, fewer) gulls than usual.
16. If she (don't, doesn't) show up, we shall leave without her.
17. You could (have, of) borrowed the books from me.
18. To prevent cavities, one should eat (fewer, less) sugar.
19. Audrey must (have, of) taken my jacket by mistake.
20. Those who (emigrate, immigrate) to New Zealand find a land of spectacular beauty.

invent   See **discover, invent.**

kind of, sort of   These expressions, used in informal English, mean "rather" or "somewhat." Avoid them in formal English.

INFORMAL   She seemed kind of bored.

FORMAL   She seemed **rather** bored.

INFORMAL   The waves were sort of rough.

FORMAL   The waves were **rather** [or *somewhat*] rough.

kind of a, sort of a   The *a* is unnecessary. Leave it out.

EXAMPLE   This job takes a special **kind of** screwdriver.

learn, teach   *Learn* means "to acquire information." *Teach* means "to instruct" or "to give out knowledge."

EXAMPLES   She **learned** how to saddle the horse.
The stable owner **taught** her how.

leave, let   *Leave* means "to go away." *Let* means "to allow" or "to permit."

EXAMPLES   **Let** [not *leave*] them find their own way.
We **let** [not *left*] the trapped bird go free.

lie, lay   See page 209.

like, as   *Like* is usually a preposition. *As* is usually a conjunction.

EXAMPLES   The animal looked **like** a fox. [prepositional phrase]
The animal ran and dodged **as** a fox might. [This is a subordinate clause introduced by a conjunction. In this construction, *like* is often used informally, but *as* is preferred in formal English.]

like, as if   Phrases such as *as if* and *as though* are used as conjunctions to introduce a subordinate clause. In writing, avoid using *like* in place of these conjunctions.

INFORMAL   This looks like it might be the right place.

FORMAL   This looks **as if** [or **as though**] it might be the right place.

might of, must of   See **could of.**

nowheres   See **anywheres.**

of   Do not use *of* with prepositions such as *inside, off,* and *outside.*

EXAMPLES   **Outside** [not *outside of*] the building was a patio.
The diver jumped **off** [not *off of*] the board.

Of is also unnecessary with *had.*

EXAMPLE   If **I had** [not *had of*] remembered my keys, I would have been able to open this locker.

off of   See **of.**

ought   The verb *ought* should never be used with *had.*

NONSTANDARD   Nikki had ought not say such things.

STANDARD   Nikki **ought** not say such things.

NONSTANDARD   They had ought to have thought of that sooner.

STANDARD   They **ought** to have thought of that sooner.

respectfully, respectively   *Respectfully* means "with respect or full of respect." *Respectively* means "each in the order given."

EXAMPLES   The reporters listened **respectfully** to the senator's request.
Nick, Margo, and Ted are nineteen, seventeen, and fifteen, **respectively.**

EXERCISE 3. Identifying Correct Expressions.   Number your paper 1–20. Choose the correct form in parentheses, and write it after the proper number on your paper.

1. Will your parents (leave, let) you go to the game?
2. This is a powerful machine, so treat it (respectfully, respectively).
3. Hilary jumped down (off, off of) the horse.
4. We went to the hardware store for a special (sort of, sort of a) wrench.
5. You can do (like, as) you like, but you should do (like, as) you think best.

6. (Leave, Let) us stop and rest a minute.
7. The council said they (respectfully, respectively) refused to hear further debate on the subject.
8. (Leave, Let) me take my share now.
9. Rachel Carson (learned, taught) me to care about ecology.
10. (Leave, Let) us listen without any interruptions.
11. Adelita stayed (inside, inside of) the building until the rain stopped.
12. The muskrat slipped (off, off of) the bank smoothly and swam away.
13. We could (of, have) left earlier, I suppose.
14. If you (leave, let) me stay home, I can study.
15. How long does it take you to (learn, teach) somebody to use a word processor?
16. Why did she feel (like, as if) she'd said something wrong?
17. T. J. (ought, had ought) to see this program.
18. We should mind our own business and (leave, let) that porcupine mind his.
19. John was trying in vain to (learn, teach) me some new dance steps.
20. We didn't want to take the boat out because the waves looked (sort of, rather) choppy.

rise, raise   See page 214.

same   *Same* is used as an adjective (the *same* day, the *same* person) and as a pronoun (more of the *same*). In the latter use, *same* should always be used with *the*. Such uses as the following one should be avoided.

EXAMPLE   We located the plant known as the Lousewort and photographed same. [In this sentence, *it* is preferable.]

shall, will   There was a time when careful speakers and writers used *shall* in the first person (*I shall, we shall*) and *will* in second and third persons (*you will, he will, they will*). Today, however, this distinction is not observed. *Will* is considered as correct as *shall* in the first person.

STANDARD   I **shall** return.

STANDARD   I **will** return.

sit, set   See page 212.

so In writing, *so* is often overworked as a conjunction meaning "therefore." Avoid using *so* excessively.

POOR The meeting was over at noon, so Karen came home early.

BETTER Since the meeting was over at noon, Karen came home early.

some In writing, do not use *some* for *somewhat* as an adverb.

NONSTANDARD This medicine will help your cough some.

STANDARD This medicine will help your cough **somewhat.**

sort of See **kind of, sort of.**

take, bring See **bring, take.**

than, then Do not use *then* in the place of *than*. *Than* is a conjunction used in comparisons.

EXAMPLE She is younger **than** you.

Then is an adverb telling when.

EXAMPLE Jake swept the floor; **then** he emptied the trash.

them *Them* is not an adjective. Use *these* or *those*.

NONSTANDARD It's one of them fancy show dogs.

STANDARD It's one of **those** fancy show dogs.

this here, that there *Here* and *there* are unnecessary.

NONSTANDARD This here fooling around has got to stop.

STANDARD **This** fooling around has got to stop.

try and In formal writing the correct form is *try to*.

INFORMAL When you're at bat, you must try and concentrate.

FORMAL When you're at bat, you must **try to** concentrate.

way, ways Use *way*, not *ways*, in referring to distance.

EXAMPLE She lives quite a **way** [not *ways*] from here.

what Do not use *what* to mean *that*.

EXAMPLE This is the book **that** [not *what*] I told you about.

when, where Do not use *when* or *where* incorrectly in writing a definition.

NONSTANDARD   S.R.O. is when all tickets have been sold, and there is standing room only.

STANDARD   S.R.O. means that all tickets have been sold and there is standing room only.

where   Do not use *where* for *that.*

EXAMPLE   I read **that** [not *where*] the renovation of the town hall was turned down by the voters.

where ... at   See at.

which, that, who   *Which* is used to refer only to *things. That* is used to refer to either *people* or *things. Who* is used to refer only to *people.*

EXAMPLES   The hat **which** I want is now on sale.
There is the tube **that** needs replacing.
There is the woman **that** won the medal.
There is the woman **who** won the medal.

who, whom   See pages 181–83.

EXERCISE 4. Revising Sentences by Correcting Errors in Usage.   The following sentences contain examples of the errors listed after Exercise 3. Revise each sentence correctly, and then practice saying aloud the corrected form.

1. I see where the governor says taxes will have to be raised again.
2. A solar eclipse is when the moon comes between the earth and the sun.
3. The workers which put up this building were certainly fast.
4. I found the right equipment in the catalog and ordered same.
5. I really like them science fiction movies.
6. A run-on sentence is where two sentences are erroneously joined as one.
7. When the bell finally rang, I felt relieved some.
8. Them mosquitoes can drive a person nearly crazy.
9. Aline used a lever to get the rock to move some.
10. They were the very ones which complained about the test.
11. Betty heard on the radio where the mayor is going to Washington about the redevelopment project.
12. We met them girls last summer at camp.
13. We saw them lobster boats a long ways out in the cove.

14. Margarita will probably be here sooner then Billy.
15. I'm tired of trying to cut the grass with this here old lawn mower that should be in an antique exhibit.
16. The police officer spotted the suspicious vehicle and reported same.
17. We've got to try and find Algernon, our escaped boa constrictor.
18. I read where a teacher is going to be picked to go to the moon.
19. Instant replay is when they repeat a certain action in slow motion on television.
20. This here camera makes taking pictures very easy.

REVIEW EXERCISE A. Identifying Correct Expressions. Number your paper 1–10. Choose the correct form in parentheses, and write it after the proper number on your paper.

1. Thanks to modern medicine, there are (fewer, less) cases of tetanus and diphtheria nowadays.
2. I tried to (learn, teach) my dog to do tricks, but he just sits and stares at me.
3. I see (where, that) pandas are an endangered species.
4. Cape Porpoise is (somewhere, somewheres) near Portsmouth.
5. Priscilla wrote a much longer paper (than, then) Tammy.
6. I have to go home and feed the cats, dust the furniture, take out the garbage, load the dishwasher, defrost the chicken, (and etc., etc.).
7. We (hadn't ought to, ought not) decide until we know more facts.
8. It (don't, doesn't) make any difference if we finish today or tomorrow.
9. Someone must (of, have) left the door unlocked.
10. Was it Benjamin Franklin who (discovered, invented) electricity?

REVIEW EXERCISE B. Writing Sentences Using Expressions Correctly. Write twenty original sentences correctly using the following words or phrases.

1. the effect
2. as if
3. not accepting
4. not excepting
5. brought
6. taken
7. beside Janice
8. besides Janice
9. ancestors emigrated
10. ancestors immigrated
11. among the three sisters
12. between the two sisters

13. as though
14. leave her
15. let her
16. Carol and I respectfully

17. Carol and I respectively
18. it affected
19. it effected
20. like

REVIEW EXERCISE C. Selecting Appropriate Expressions.
Number your paper 1–30. For each sentence, choose the correct form in parentheses, and write it after the proper number on your paper.

1. Andy might (of, have) left for school early today.
2. Loretta said she couldn't (of, have) done the job so (good, well) without your help.
3. When E. E. Cummings published his strangely punctuated poetry, many readers were not sure what (kind of, kind of an) experiment he was up to.
4. He (don't, doesn't) give true-false tests.
5. (Inside, Inside of) the box was a heap of glittering gems.
6. After our slumber party, my room looked (like, as if) a tornado had swept through it.
7. Mary could (of, have) written a thank-you note.
8. The five hikers divided the camping equipment (between, among) themselves and loaded their packs.
9. She shouldn't (have, of) driven all by herself when she could (of, have) joined our car pool.
10. Linda (doesn't, don't) enjoy doing (them, those, that) sort of exercise.
11. May I (imply, infer) from your yawns that you are bored?
12. My great-grandmother (emigrated, immigrated) from Italy as a young woman.
13. How do you suppose the director achieved that interesting (affect, effect) in the movie?
14. Please (accept, except) this check for one million dollars.
15. (Being that, Because) school was canceled today, we are going out sledding.
16. Those events happened in 1949 and 1952, (respectfully, respectively).
17. (Beside, Besides) speaking Spanish, Vera can speak Portuguese.
18. He wanted to be (learned, taught) to fly helicopters.
19. Far before us on the desert, a lake seemed to sparkle, but it was only an (allusion, illusion).

20. Diane looked (as if, like) she wanted to say something.
21. Please leave at once, and (bring, take) your pet skunk with you.
22. This water shortage will (affect, effect) the whole county.
23. I don't think my parents will (leave, let) me borrow the car in this kind of weather.
24. How the mayor resolves this problem will (affect, effect) the outcome of the next election.
25. She was taught to speak to all of her elders (respectfully, respectively).
26. We couldn't find a trace of the lost steer (anywhere, anywheres).
27. What (sort of, sort of a) dog is the one with the long ears, sad eyes, and drooping jowls?
28. We made (this, this here) maple syrup on our own farm.
29. San Diego is quite a (way, ways) from here.
30. Because of the indiscriminate slaughter, each year there were (fewer, less) buffalos.

The Double Negative

A *double negative* is a construction in which two negative words are used when one is sufficient. Before the eighteenth century, two or more negatives were often used in the same sentence to make the meaning more emphatic. Standard modern English no longer uses this method of gaining emphasis, and a double negative is generally considered to be nonstandard.

can't hardly, can't scarcely The words *hardly* and *scarcely* should not be used with *not* (or the contraction of *not*, *n't*).

EXAMPLES   You **can** [not *can't*] **hardly** see ten feet in front of you.
We **had** [not *hadn't*] scarcely enough time to finish our essay test.

haven't but, haven't only In certain uses, *but* and *only* convey a negative meaning and should not be used with *not*.

EXAMPLES   We **have** [not *haven't*] **but** three more days.
We **have** [not *haven't*] **only** a dollar between us.

no, nothing, none Do not use these negative words with another negative.

NONSTANDARD   There isn't no reason to be nervous.

STANDARD   There **is no** reason to be nervous.

STANDARD   There **isn't any** reason to be nervous.

NONSTANDARD   I didn't hear nothing.

STANDARD   I **heard nothing.**

STANDARD   I **didn't hear anything.**

NONSTANDARD   We searched the playground for clues but didn't find none.

STANDARD   We searched the playground for clues but **found none.**

STANDARD   We searched the playground for clues but **didn't find any**.

EXERCISE 5. Revising Sentences by Correcting Errors in Usage.
The following sentences contain many of the usage errors covered in this chapter. Rewrite each sentence correctly. Practice saying *aloud* the correct sentences.

1. They haven't only one more chance to score before the buzzer sounds.
2. My uncle finished the canoe race, but he was sort of tired.
3. Mother told us we hadn't ought to have played our radio so loudly.
4. I might of gone to the concert if I'd of heard about it earlier.
5. Pam and her sister Stacey look so much alike that you can't hardly tell them apart.
6. My cousins didn't hardly know how to swim, but they wouldn't of missed going to the lake.
7. We told the usher which handed out the programs that we didn't need but two more.
8. Them reference books in the library are kept in some kind of a special section.
9. This here is the car what I told you about.
10. Hadn't you ought to try and help them?
11. I wonder where them fishing poles are at.
12. That don't hardly seem fair to me.
13. We don't live in that there neighborhood no more.
14. We might of gone on the tour, but we wouldn't of had no camera to take pictures.
15. Ellen didn't have nothing to say.
16. A foot fault in tennis is when the server steps over the base line before hitting the ball.
17. Since there wasn't scarcely any rain last spring, there are less mosquitoes this summer.

18. When the play was over, the audience seemed sort of subdued.
19. I saw on the news where manufacturers will start putting them air bags into all the new cars.
20. That tree has grown some since we were here last.
21. She don't know nothing about football, and she don't like nothing about football.
22. Miss Kim likes to give those kind of surprise quizzes.
23. Let's try and finish early so we can relax some.
24. Leave us work a while longer on the motor; we can't hardly leave it this way.
25. Susan don't have but one cousin.

WRITING APPLICATION A:
Using Standard English to Make Your Writing Acceptable to the Audience

If you had to give someone directions from the school to your home, you might have to decide which route to describe. Usually, you can take any one of several different ways to end up at the same place. In writing, you also have many choices. You may choose between the word *buy* and the word *purchase,* for example. One of the choices you do *not* have in writing, however, is whether to use standard or nonstandard English. Although nonstandard English might be all right in casual conversation, it is usually not acceptable in formal situations. Nonstandard English is acceptable in writing only when imitating dialect.

Writing Assignment

Using standard English, write an original sentence with each of the following words or phrases. Underline the word or phrase in your sentence.

1. can hardly	6. than
2. have only	7. somewhat
3. burst	8. ought not
4. where is	9. nowhere
5. set	10. respectively

CHAPTER 10 REVIEW: POSTTEST 1

Revising Expressions by Correcting Errors in Usage. In each set of expressions, one expression contains an error in usage. Write the expression correctly, after the proper number, using standard formal usage.

EXAMPLE   1. (a) Her speech implies that a change is needed. (b) Leave me have some oranges, too. (c) This house is somewhat larger than our old one.
   1. (*b*) *Let me have some oranges, too.*

1. (a) wasn't no reason (b) words had no effect (c) can hardly wait
2. (a) families immigrated from Europe (b) sail as far as the channel marker (c) made allusions to classical literature
3. (a) being that he was alone (b) The people accepted new ways. (c) the woman who was elected
4. (a) From the newspaper article you may infer his reasons. (b) acts like a child (c) can't hardly hear the music
5. (a) what kind of gloves (b) There is overtime besides the regular work. (c) an historic moment
6. (a) Listen respectfully to the sermon. (b) her head raised from the pillow (c) the chair that you repaired
7. (a) the man for whom you voted (b) the police officer which is on duty (c) the house beside the church
8. (a) Leave the broken glass alone. (b) Leave him have his own way. (c) Leave the door open when you go.
9. (a) To return, take the same road. (b) Their gifts were the same. (c) Buy this pen and write your lessons with same.
10. (a) Teach your dog this trick. (b) I'm feeling kind of ill. (c) might have been too late
11. (a) are the winners of first, second, and third prizes, respectively (b) Take the books off of that shelf. (c) The bag burst, spilling groceries.
12. (a) invented less expensive fuel (b) had ought to try harder (c) raised the heavy timbers
13. (a) This is all the farther he had gone. (b) creating an optical illusion (c) His coaching effected a change.
14. (a) fewer stamps in the collection (b) Bring the tray to the kitchen when you come. (c) He works like he will never tire.

15. (a) accepted the offer on this contract (b) made no exceptions to his terms (c) proudly excepted the blue ribbon
16. (a) They took all the peaches, besides taking the pears. (b) The seller he said that the car had low mileage. (c) It costs less to drive a small car.
17. (a) Strong rivalry grew among the two athletes. (b) He doesn't want to go. (c) They should have called.
18. (a) After his vacation he looked good. (b) Children can't hardly reach that bookshelf. (c) The rule takes effect soon.
19. (a) Paintings, photographs, drawings, and etc. will be displayed. (b) The blue dress is somewhat more expensive than the black one. (c) "The golden touch" is an allusion to King Midas.
20. (a) a rabbit hiding among the trees (b) a rose growing beside the cabin door (c) a stack of busted bicycles
21. (a) It could of been worse. (b) Hardly any money was taken. (c) That kind of house suits me.
22. (a) The mayor inferred that he would run for reelection. (b) made fewer mistakes on the final exam (c) Clothes lay on the floor of their room.
23. (a) Let me go with you. (b) The dog is walking like its leg is broken. (c) He might win first place this time.
24. (a) taller than her sister (b) Dough will rise in a warm place. (c) We read where the damage was extensive.
25. (a) Try to be on time. (b) They walked a long way. (c) Them stairs are dangerous and need repairs.

CHAPTER 10 REVIEW: POSTTEST 2

Revising Sentences by Correcting Errors in Usage. The following sentences contain many of the common errors you have been studying. Revise the sentences correctly.

1. A sight gag is when comedy depends on action, not on speech.
2. Being that the lights were out, we thought nobody was at home.
3. My sister she can't hardly stand the sight of spiders, so my brother he loves to try and tease her with them.
4. We hadn't ought to of bought this kind of car; we should of bought one who has less things wrong with it.

5. Haven't I seen you before somewheres?
6. The audience was laughing so loudly we couldn't hardly hear the lines of the play.
7. If we hadn't of had jobs last summer, we couldn't of bought the hockey equipment what we wanted.
8. You can't hardly get water out of this faucet; it must be busted.
9. This here lotion ought to of helped your poison ivy some.
10. He jumped off of the diving board, made some kind of a wrong movement, and scraped his back some.
11. My grandmother she likes watching music videos, but you can't hardly get her to admit it.
12. We don't have but one canteen of water left; we'd better try and make it last.
13. These old magazines what she's been saving aren't good for nothing, are they?
14. My baby sister tries to help some, but she's kind of clumsy.
15. Is this here all the further the bus goes, or does it go on a ways?
16. We couldn't hardly get all them bricks loaded into the wheelbarrow; there was scarcely no room.
17. Being that this is a holiday, hardly none of them stores are open.
18. There isn't no kind of fish I can't catch with these here special worms.
19. I read in this here book that there's a new way what dogs can be trained.
20. My father he knew he couldn't hardly check all them figures by himself.
21. Hadn't you ought to try and make less mistakes?
22. This here is a person which can do them jobs good.
23. It don't seem right that Judy she always has to do all them dishes.
24. I might of left my books in the band room because I left there in a sort of a hurry.
25. With those there players, there wasn't nobody we couldn't of beaten.

USAGE
MASTERY REVIEW: Cumulative Test

A. AGREEMENT. In some of the following sentences either a verb does not agree with its subject, or a pronoun does not agree with its antecedent. Number your paper 1–10. If a sentence is correct, write a + after the corresponding number; if it is incorrect, write a 0.

1. One of the dresses are blue.
2. The display of antique watches are new.
3. Several in the audience like the performance.
4. Have any of the performers arrived?
5. Each of the students should carry their own books.
6. Either Alan or his brother drives his sister to school.
7. Neither Mary nor Janet has her books.
8. Everyone on the committee are prepared to speak.
9. Juanita is one of the reporters who likes her assignments.
10. There is just a few people in the theater.

B. CORRECT PRONOUN USAGE. After the proper number, write the correct one of the two pronouns given in parentheses.

EXAMPLE   1. This information is intended only for you and (I, me).
　　　　　 1. *me*

11. I asked my mother (who, whom) it was that called last night after I had left the house.
12. The argument between Thomas and (he, him) soon grew into a major contest between rival factions.
13. The woman (who, whom) you choose will be the leader on the day hike.
14. If it had not been for Louis and (he, him), the fund-raising project would have failed.
15. She is a better swimmer than (I, me), but the coach said she needed both of us on the team.
16. I will support (whoever, whomever) is selected by the class for president.
17. It is not fair to let all the boys except (they, them) go on a holiday.
18. (Who, Whom) is the teacher supervising the drama festival this year?

19. Before going on the trip, you need written permission from your parents and (I, me).

20. Everyone finished the test before (they, them).

C. USING THE CORRECT FORM OF THE VERB. Number your paper 21–30. After the number of the corresponding sentence, write the correct form of the verb given at the beginning of each sentence. In some instances you will have to add *have, has,* or *had*.

EXAMPLE 1. *fly* Now that summer is over, many birds —— south.
  1. *have flown*

21. *blow* After the storm we discovered that several large trees —— down and were blocking the road.

22. *break* Flying debris —— most of the windows and littered the floors.

23. *lie* An hour ago he —— down to watch television, but he fell asleep.

24. *ride* After they —— several miles in silence, they started to sing.

25. *drink* Hot and dusty from the long walk through the barren fields, the men seized the water jugs and —— every drop.

26. *lay* Picking the sleeping child up gently, she —— him on the bed and covered him with his blanket.

27. *take* She —— advantage of every opportunity to remind us of our mistakes.

28. *rise* At every meeting several people —— to object to the arrogance of the chairman, who ignored their complaints.

29. *shrink* The flimsy material —— in the hot water and was no longer useful.

30. *burst* When heavy rains continued day after day, the water —— through the dam and flooded the fields.

D. CORRECT USAGE OF MODIFIERS. In the following sentences, modifiers are either incorrect or misplaced. After the proper number, write the correct word, or revise the sentence to make the meaning clear and logical. If the sentence is correct, write *C*.

EXAMPLES 1. The gift was more costlier than I had expected it to be.
  1. *more costly*
  2. A blue girl's coat has been found.
  2. *A girl's blue coat has been found.*

31. Seeing that no damage was done, the cars drove away in opposite directions.
32. Working long hours and taking few vacations, the success that he longed for came to him after many years.
33. Walking very careful over the broken cobblestones, the old woman made her way from one end of the lane to the other.
34. By standing on the balcony and looking through a telescope, the far shore could be seen dimly.
35. For hours afterward I worried about that test because I thought the questions were more harder than usual.
36. I feel worser when I don't make good grades in any of my classes, especially in one that is my favorite subject.
37. Waiting nervously the next day, my paper was the last one the teacher returned.
38. How surprised I was when I saw my grade; it was higher than any other grade in the class.
39. Of the two exams I took on the same day, this was my best grade.
40. To tell the truth, I prefer writing essays or discussing the subject to tests.

E. STANDARD FORMAL USAGE OF EXPRESSIONS. Most of the following sentences contain errors in usage. After the proper number, write the correct form of the words or expressions. If a sentence is correct, write *C*.

EXAMPLE 1. Being as I like to read about knights, I checked out a book about King Arthur of England.
      1. *Since I like to read*

41. I can't hardly believe what this book says about King Arthur.
42. It says that there wasn't no real King Arthur who ruled England during the Middle Ages.
43. Arthur was actually a kind of a chieftain, a powerful leader during the Dark Ages.
44. The author infers that the legend of a noble king who introduced chivalry into England is the work of storytellers.
45. Most of the illusions to the Round Table are based on a work by Sir Thomas Malory, *Morte d'Arthur*.
46. Some of the legends say that Arthur accepted almost a thousand knights for membership at the Round Table.

47. Although it might of been true, Malory's version says there were two hundred and fifty knights who earned the right to set at the Round Table.
48. Some of the most famous contests were among Sir Mordred, a wicked man, and Sir Lancelot, a brave defender of honor.
49. When Arthur laid dying, the magician Merlin appeared and brought Arthur away to the magical island of Avalon.
50. This is all the farther the story goes; it infers that Arthur will come again to inspire noble deeds.

PART THREE

COMPOSITION:
Writing and Revising
Sentences

CHAPTER 11

Writing Complete Sentences

SENTENCE FRAGMENTS AND RUN-ON SENTENCES

Two of the most common errors in student writing result from care-lessness in marking the end of one sentence and the beginning of the next. The first kind of error, the *sentence fragment,* occurs when a part of a sentence—a phrase or subordinate clause, for example—is written as a complete sentence. The second, the *run-on sentence,* occurs when two or more sentences are run together with only a comma, or no punctuation at all, between them.

SENTENCE FRAGMENTS

11a. A *sentence fragment* **is a group of words that does not express a complete thought. Since it is only a part of a sentence, it should not be allowed to stand by itself but should be kept in the sentence of which it is a part.**

A group of words is not a sentence unless it has both a subject and a verb and expresses a complete thought. The following examples are fragments because they fail to meet one or both of these conditions.

FRAGMENT The referee calling the foul. [The *–ing* form of a verb cannot function as the verb in a sentence unless it has a helping verb with it.]

269

FRAGMENT Because the referee was calling the foul. [The subordinating conjunction *Because* signals that what follows is only part of a larger sentence. Taken by itself, the fragment does not express a complete thought.]

Both of the fragments just illustrated are really parts of a longer sentence.

EXAMPLES The referee calling the foul was waving her arms in the air.
Because the referee was calling a foul, she was waving her arms in the air.

Good writers sometimes punctuate fragments as sentences for stylistic reasons. For example, you may sometimes notice a fragment like this in a story.

FRAGMENT Paul rides to school every day. *On his younger brother's tricycle.*

The second part is not a complete sentence. It is only a prepositional phrase. The writer used a capital letter at the beginning and a period at the end of the phrase for humorous effect, thinking that the point would be otherwise lost to the reader.

Paul rides to school every day on his younger brother's tricycle.

A better solution might have been to use a dash, thus gaining the desired emphasis while remaining within the limits of conventional punctuation.

Paul rides to school every day—on his younger brother's tricycle.

Although the use of fragments can be justified, the practice requires experience and judgment, and the beginning writer will do well to avoid it.

The Phrase Fragment

A phrase is a group of words acting as a single part of speech and not containing a verb and its subject.

You will recall from your study of verbals (pages 74–86) that present participles and gerunds are words ending in *–ing*. Words ending in *–ing* cannot be used as verbs unless they follow a helping verb. With a helping verb like *am, are, has been, will be,* etc., they become complete verbs. It is the same with infinitive phrases. Like participial and gerund phrases, infinitive phrases can never stand alone. In order to make sense, they must be attached to a preceding or following sentence or be completed by being developed into a proper sentence.

A participial phrase must not be written as a sentence.

FRAGMENT   The woman giving us directions. [a phrase; no verb]

CORRECTED   The woman **was giving** us directions. [The present participle has been made into a complete verb by the addition of the helping verb *was*.]

FRAGMENT   We admired the seascape. Painted and signed by Winslow Homer. [The participial phrase modifies the word *seascape*. It must be included in the sentence with the word it modifies.]

CORRECTED   We admired the seascape **painted and signed by Winslow Homer.** [The fragment is corrected by including the participial phrase in the sentence with the word it modifies.]

A gerund phrase must not be written as a sentence.

FRAGMENT   Many of us dislike working in the kitchen. Cleaning and scrubbing objects that in a few hours will be dirty again. [Here a gerund phrase functioning as an appositive of *working* is cut off from it by the period. It must be reconnected.]

CORRECTED   Many of us dislike working in the kitchen, **cleaning and scrubbing objects that in a few hours will be dirty again.** [The gerund phrase fragment is corrected by including it in the sentence.]

An infinitive phrase must not be written as a sentence.

FRAGMENT   You must first learn to float. To swim properly and with confidence. [The phrase cannot stand alone. It should be attached to the preceding sentence.]

CORRECTED   **To swim properly and with confidence,** you must first learn to float.

A prepositional phrase or a succession of prepositional phrases must not be written as a sentence.

FRAGMENT   The post office is two blocks from here. Near the corner on the north side of the street. [Here three successive prepositional phrases are isolated. They make sense only when included in the sentence.]

CORRECTED   The post office is two blocks from here **near the corner on the north side of the street.**

In the examples above, the sentence fragments were cut off from the sentences they were part of by improper punctuation. To correct this kind of mistake attach the phrase to the parent sentence.

EXERCISE 1. Correcting Phrase Fragments. Convert each of the following phrase fragments into a complete sentence by using one of two methods as shown in the example: (1) attach the fragment to an independent clause, or (2) develop the phrase into a complete sentence.

EXAMPLE 1. putting on her jacket
  1. *Putting on her jacket, Cindy left the theater.* [attached]
    or
  1. *Cindy was putting on her jacket.* [developed]

1. standing on the deck beside the captain
2. to make set shots consistently from outside the pivot position
3. on lower Main Street under the Lexington Bridge
4. puzzled by the question
5. to stay alert
6. finishing her assignment
7. murmuring something about a meeting
8. burned and blistered by the sun
9. playing tennis in the hot sun
10. performing the chemistry experiments

The Appositive Fragment

An appositive is a noun or pronoun that follows another noun or pronoun to identify or explain it. An appositive phrase is made up of an appositive and its modifiers; it should not be written as a separate sentence.

EXAMPLES Mike, **the best mechanic in the garage,** worked on my car. [*The best mechanic in the garage* is an appositive. It is in apposition with *Mike.*]

In two years I will graduate from Madison High School, **a red brick building with a golden dome.** [*A red brick building with a golden dome* is in apposition with *Madison High School.*]

Sometimes a hasty writer will treat an appositive phrase as a complete sentence and leave it standing alone, even though it lacks a verb and subject and does not express a complete thought.

FRAGMENT The amateur boat-builder was constructing a simple model. A small outboard cruiser of conventional design.

CORRECTED The amateur boat-builder was constructing a simple model, **a small outboard cruiser of conventional design.** [The appositive phrase has been attached to the sentence in which it belongs.]

EXERCISE 2. Correcting Appositive Phrase Fragments. Number your paper 1–10. If an item consists of a sentence followed by an appositive fragment, write the last word in the sentence and follow it with a comma and the first word of the appositive. If an item consists of two sentences, write *C*.

1. Before railroads, much inland transportation of freight was done by means of canals. Hand-dug, water-filled ditches that connected natural waterways.
2. Between 1790 and 1850, Americans constructed a canal network totaling 4,400 miles. A distance greater than that between New York and San Francisco.
3. An essential feature of the canals was their locks. Devices by which boats were raised or lowered from one level to another to accommodate changes in the terrain.
4. Where locks were not practical, boats were moved up or down on an inclined plane. A short boat railway on which a boat was raised or lowered by cable.
5. Canal boats were towed by horses walking on towpaths alongside the canals. This was a slow method of transportation.
6. The horses were driven on the paths by youths between the ages of twelve and seventeen. They were called loggees.
7. On the Erie Canal in 1850, a thousand people were employed as loggees. They were exposed to rough weather and, if they let their towlines become tangled with those of a passing boat, to the wrath of boat captains.
8. Some boats were passenger boats. The so-called fast packets, which moved at a speed of five miles an hour.
9. In good weather, passengers enjoyed watching the slowly passing landscape from the roof of the boat's cabin. The only suitable deck space.
10. At night the cabin was a common bedroom. The author Nathaniel Hawthorne named it a "chamber of horrors."

The Subordinate Clause Fragment

Although the subordinate clause does have a verb and a subject, it depends upon the independent clause of a sentence to complete its meaning. Standing alone, a subordinate clause suggests a question which it does not answer.

EXAMPLES Because the machine is so dangerous. [Well . . .? What will happen?]
If you do not know how to operate it. [Well . . .? What will happen?]

An isolated subordinate clause must be attached to an independent clause in order to complete its meaning. It should not be written as a sentence.

FRAGMENT Television make-up differs from stage make-up. Because it must withstand the intense heat from the studio lamps.

CORRECTED Television make-up differs from stage make-up **because it must withstand the intense heat from the studio lamps.**

FRAGMENT Lamps that burned fat or olive oil served as the only source of artificial light until 1600. When petroleum was discovered.

CORRECTED Lamps that burned fat or olive oil served as the only source of artificial light until 1600, **when petroleum was discovered.**

☞ NOTE   In combining an adverb clause with an independent clause, the adverb clause may either precede or follow the independent clause.

EXAMPLES **If you bring your guitar to the picnic,** we can have some music. [adverb clause first]
We can have some music **if you bring your guitar to the picnic.** [adverb clause last]

EXERCISE 3. Revising by Correcting Subordinate Clause Fragments.

The following paragraphs contain several sentence fragments. They are all subordinate clauses that should be attached to an independent clause. Copy the paragraphs, changing the punctuation to eliminate the subordinate clause fragments.

Have you ever taken a course in film history? Some film historians believe that Alice Guy Blache was the first person. Who used the medium of motion pictures to tell a story. After she had worked as a director for

Gaumont in Paris. She came to the United States. Where she formed her own production company in 1919. When she closed it down and began making films for Metro and Pathé. She returned to France in 1922. Since she was unable to find work in France. She retired from the cinema industry. Still in existence are some of this enterprising woman's American films. Which were made under the Solax company name. Alice Guy Blache died in an American nursing home in 1968 at the age of ninety-five. Her death received little public notice.

In the opinion of many critics, Sarah Maldoror is one of the most important of the film makers. Who are emerging from the Third World. Among her best films is *Sambizanga.* Which is set in Angola during the period before the uprising against Portuguese rule in 1961. *Sambizanga* deals with the conflicts between the Angolans and the Portuguese.

Do you know what a documentary film is? Have you ever seen one? While some people use the camera to present a fictional story. Others use the camera to try to capture life exactly as it is. In this latter category is Chick Strand, another important film maker. Whose films are part documentary and part personal interpretation of people and events. Her deep concern with anthropology and ethnography is reflected in each of her films. Which attempt to present all of the elements that will enable the viewer to see the people she is filming exactly as they are.

Check your local papers and see if you can find a showing of films by any of these three women.

EXERCISE 4. Using Subordinate Clauses in Sentences. Add an independent clause either at the beginning or at the end of each of the following subordinate clauses to make ten complete sentences. When an adverb clause comes at the beginning of a sentence, it should be followed by a comma.

1. if we do well on the test
2. when they send the message
3. who can play several musical instruments
4. which I have never read
5. as we shut off the motor
6. what you forgot to say
7. before you do anything impulsive
8. that he was your brother
9. until she has finished her assignment
10. while I was in the dentist's office

EXERCISE 5. Identifying and Correcting Fragments. Some of the following groups of words are complete sentences. Others are fragments. On your paper, mark the complete sentences with an *S*, and correct the fragments by making them parts of complete sentences.

1. Furnished with beautifully finished cottages, the resort was one of the finest in the area.
2. Running and dodging are features of lacrosse. Whose original object among its creators seems to have been the development of endurance and agility.
3. If you decide to go.
4. The friends shopped all day at the new shopping mall.
5. Elected by an overwhelming number of the students.
6. As she opened the door and peered out.
7. Because it was foggy and the visibility was poor.
8. Located in the middle of a swamp. The cabin was four miles from the highway.
9. Driving at night can be dangerous. Blinded by the lights of an approaching car. We almost hit a tree.
10. Because they wanted to escape the heat. They left for the mountains. Setting out in the early part of August.
11. To climb up the steep cliff with a heavy pack and camera slung on his back was difficult.
12. He was plagued with difficulties. Losing his way, running out of water, and falling over vines and creepers.
13. How he envied the hawk. Gliding effortlessly high over the tangle of the swamp and thickets.
14. To break through the last thicket of brambles and dwarf cedar into the clearing. This was the hope that drove him on.
15. This was the Maine wilderness. Through which Arnold and his men had dragged cannon and other heavy equipment on their way to Quebec.

THE RUN–ON SENTENCE

11b. Avoid the run-on sentence. Do not use a comma between sentences. Do not omit punctuation at the end of a sentence.

There are two main ways in which independent clauses can be combined in a single sentence: (1) by means of a comma plus a word like *and* or *but;* (2) by means of a semicolon. The following examples illustrate these two methods.

> Peanuts were more than just food to George Washington Carver, and in his laboratory he used them to make such things as ink and shampoo. [A comma plus *and* is used to join the two independent clauses.]
> Peanuts were more than just food to George Washington Carver; in his laboratory he used them to make such things as ink and shampoo. [A semicolon is used to join the clauses.]

The colon or the dash is sometimes used, but a comma alone is never enough between independent clauses. Using a comma or no punctuation at all in this situation results in the run-on sentence.

> Peanuts were more than just food to George Washington Carver, in his laboratory he used them to make such things as ink and shampoo.

The run-on sentence is used effectively by experienced writers, especially when its parts are very short. A famous example is the translation of Caesar's boast "I came, I saw, I conquered."

An easy test for spotting run-on sentences consists of simply reading your compositions aloud. The rise or fall of your voice and the pause you make at the end of a sentence sound quite different from the intonation and pause that a comma usually signals.

EXERCISE 6. Revising by Correcting Run-ons. The following passages contain a number of run-on sentences. Determine where each sentence properly begins and ends, and write the last word in the sentence with the proper mark after it. Then write the first word of the following sentence with a capital letter.

1

Having been excused early, we hurried to the locker room and changed to our uniforms, when the coach called us, we were ready to go the big bus drew up in the drive, and just as we had done a dozen other times, we piled in and took our usual seats this trip was different, however, everybody knew how different it was we would return either as champions of the state or as just another second-rate team.

2

It was the hottest day we could remember, coming down the street, we were sure we could see heat waves rising from the sidewalk, we felt as though we'd never get home we ambled up the street in a daze, hoping we'd last just one more block, we knew if we could make it there would be large bottles of ice-cold soda awaiting us.

3

Working on a lake steamer all summer was monotonous, it was also better than any other job I could have obtained, I loved the water and the ships and the rough and ready crew with whom I worked, the food was good the work was not too strenuous, if it hadn't been for the sameness of the routine day after day, I would probably never have left.

REVIEW EXERCISE. Revising Paragraphs by Eliminating Fragments and Run-ons. Read the following paragraphs carefully. They contain sentence fragments and run-on sentences. Rewrite the passage, removing all fragments and run-ons by changing the punctuation and capital letters whenever necessary.

Our national bird is the great bald eagle. As most Americans know. Similar to the bald eagle is the golden eagle. Which has a wingspread up to seven-and-a-half feet. The national bird is protected by law, but the golden eagle is not, the result is that hunters are rapidly diminishing the number of these great birds. If the golden eagles are not also given the protection of the law, they may become extinct. In a few years.

The National Audubon Society says that the annual slaughter of golden eagles is a national disgrace. Some hunters bagging hundreds of eagles a year. Texas and Oklahoma are the principal hunting territories, the birds are often shot from airplanes by gunners. Who are paid both by sheep ranchers and by manufacturers. Who want the feathers. Sheep ranchers claim the eagles menace sheep, tourists buy the feathers. Protecting the golden eagle will also provide further protection for the bald eagle. Because hunters often mistakenly kill bald eagles. Which, at a certain stage in growth, resemble golden eagles.

The golden eagle migrates to Texas and Oklahoma from northern regions. Such as Canada, Alaska, and our other Northwestern states. Golden eagles will be protected. If Congress amends the Bald Eagle Act. To include golden eagles.

CHAPTER 12

Writing Effective Sentences
SENTENCE COMBINING
AND REVISING

Although a knowledge of grammar and punctuation is of obvious help in learning to write correct sentences, there is much more to effective writing than avoiding errors in sentence structure. Effective writing is not a matter of correctness, but a matter of *style*.

Style is a hard word to define exactly, but its essential meaning is "a way of doing something."/The idea of style can be applied to many other things besides writing. For example, a professional basketball player and an ordinary player perform essentially the same operations in dribbling the ball, yet even a spectator who knows little about the game can usually see a difference. In basketball, and in most other things, there is a difference between doing things well and doing them any old way.

There are probably more ways of writing a sentence than there are ways of dribbling a basketball. In the pages that follow, you will find principles that will help you to write sentences that are more varied and therefore more interesting for your readers.

SENTENCE COMBINING

Short sentences are often effective in a composition, but a long series of short sentences tends to irritate readers. Notice how the short, choppy sentences in the following paragraph sound immature and make the paragraph less interesting to read.

> The first person to go over Niagara Falls in a barrel and live was Annie Edson Taylor. She was a schoolteacher. She was from Michigan. On September 24, 1901, she entered the upper Niagara River. She entered the river above the Horseshoe Falls. The Horseshoe Falls drops 51 meters to the lower Niagara River. Seventeen minutes passed. Then Canadian rescuers pulled Annie from the river. She was badly bruised and shaken. She had escaped serious harm. Annie did not gain fame for her dangerous act. She did not gain fortune. Years later she died in a poorhouse.

Notice how the short, choppy sentences in the previous passage can be combined into longer, smoother sentences.

> The first person to go over Niagara Falls in a barrel and live was Annie Edson Taylor, a schoolteacher from Michigan. On September 24, 1901, she entered the upper Niagara River above the Horseshoe Falls, which drops 51 meters to the lower Niagara River. After seventeen minutes had passed, Canadian rescuers pulled Annie from the river. Badly bruised and shaken, she nevertheless escaped serious harm. Annie did not gain fame or fortune for her dangerous act, and years later she died in a poorhouse.

A number of sentence-combining devices have been used to rewrite the original passage. For example, the first three sentences have been combined through the use of an appositive phrase. Other sentences in the original passage have been combined through the use of coordination and subordination.

12a. Combine short, related sentences by inserting adjectives, adverbs, or prepositional phrases.

TWO SENTENCES The coach praised the players.
The coach was delighted.

ONE SENTENCE The **delighted** coach praised the players. [adjective]

TWO SENTENCES The tired fans left the stadium.
The fans left quietly.

ONE SENTENCE **Quietly,** the tired fans left the stadium. [adverb]

THREE SENTENCES The deer were feeding.
The deer were on the hill.
The hill was behind our house.

ONE SENTENCE The deer were feeding **on the hill behind our house.**
[prepositional phrases]

When you join short sentences by inserting adjectives, adverbs, or prepositional phrases, you may invent different ways of combining the same sentences. In such instances, the choice of word order is up to you, the writer. The combined sentences, however, should not change the meaning of the original sentences, nor should adjectives, adverbs, or prepositional phrases be misplaced within the combined sentences.

EXERCISE 1. Combining Sentences by Inserting Adjectives, Adverbs, or Prepositional Phrases. Combine each group of short, related sentences into one sentence by inserting adjectives, adverbs, or prepositional phrases. There may be more than one correct way to combine the sentences.

EXAMPLE 1. The basketball game will be televised.
The game is tonight.
The game is in the school gym.
   1. *The basketball game tonight in the school gym will be televised.*

1. Basketball has a history.
   The history is interesting.
2. The inventor was James Naismith.
   He was the inventor of basketball.
   He was from Springfield, Massachusetts.
3. In the first games, players shot a soccer ball at a peach basket.
   There were nine players on each team.
   The peach basket was suspended.
4. Basketball rules have changed.
   The rules have changed since 1891.
   The rules have changed greatly.
5. Basketball is popular.
   It is popular today.
   It is popular among men and women.
   It is popular all over the country.
6. Women basketball players compete.
   They are professional players.
   They compete before large crowds.
   They compete regularly.
7. The speed of modern basketball is surprising.
   It is often surprising.
   It is surprising to the spectator.

8. Dribbling, leaping, and shooting are the skills players practice.
   Dribbling, leaping, and shooting are skills in basketball.
   Most players practice these skills.
   They practice them for many hours.
9. Players concentrate on passing, shot blocking, and play making.
   They concentrate during team practice.
   They concentrate under a coach's direction.
   They usually concentrate.
10. Players may organize a play and then execute the play.
    They may organize a play for hours.
    They execute the play during the game.
    They execute the play in seconds.

12b. Combine short, related sentences by using participial phrases.

A participial phrase (see pages 78–80) is a group of related words that contains a participle and that acts as an adjective, modifying a noun or a pronoun. In the following examples, all the words in boldfaced type are part of participial phrases.

EXAMPLES **Galloping across the meadow,** the horse neared the forest.
Elated by the news, we prepared a celebration.

Two closely related sentences can be combined by making one sentence a participial phrase.

TWO SENTENCES The dogs yelped loudly.
The dogs ran down the trail.

ONE SENTENCE **Yelping loudly,** the dogs ran down the trail.

A participial phrase must be placed close to the noun or pronoun it modifies. Otherwise the phrase might confuse the reader.

MISPLACED **Flying overhead,** we saw an eagle.

CORRECTED We saw an eagle **flying overhead.**

EXERCISE 2. Combining Sentences by Using Participial Phrases. Combine each of the following groups of sentences into one sentence by using a participial phrase. There may be more than one correct way to combine the sentences. Add commas where necessary. (See pages 689–90 for the use of commas to set off introductory phrases.)

EXAMPLE 1. His radio blared.
       It woke up the house.
       1. *His blaring radio woke up the house.*

1. Music is an ancient word.
   It originates in the Greek word *mousikos*.
2. In Greek, *mousikos* is an adjective.
   It means "concerned with the Muses."
3. The Muses of Greek mythology ruled over the arts.
   They inspired artists in their work.
4. The halfback was evading the tacklers easily.
   The halfback scored a touchdown.
5. Juanita Platero writes about Navajo culture.
   The writing describes the conflict between old and new ideas.
6. Richard Wright was born a sharecropper's son.
   He fought valiantly for an education.
7. *Meridian* was written by Alice Walker.
   It is a novel about hope and courage.
8. Eudora Welty's stories are full of eccentric characters.
   The stories are set in rural places.
9. The memoir *An Unfinished Woman* lay on the table.
   It was assigned last week.
10. James Baldwin's essays depict his youth in Harlem.
    These essays are very popular.

12c. Combine short, related sentences by using appositive phrases.

Appositive phrases (see pages 87–88) are useful for explaining or identifying nouns or pronouns. The following sentence contains an appositive phrase in boldfaced type.

EXAMPLE The poodle, **a very intelligent dog,** is the most popular breed in the
       United States today.

Two related sentences can be combined by using an appositive phrase.

TWO SENTENCES The Shetland stands about one meter tall at the shoulders.
           The Shetland is the smallest of ponies.

ONE SENTENCE The Shetland, **the smallest of ponies,** stands about one meter
          tall at the shoulders.

EXERCISE 3. Combining Sentences by Using Appositive Phrases. Combine each pair of sentences by turning one sentence into an appositive phrase. Be sure to put the phrase next to the noun or pronoun it identifies. Punctuate the sentence correctly. (See pages 692–93 for the use of commas to set off appositive phrases.)

EXAMPLE 1. The kiwi has a strong sense of smell.
The kiwi is a flightless bird of New Zealand.
1. *The kiwi, a flightless bird of New Zealand, has a strong sense of smell.*

1. The railroad worm looks like a train with a red headlight.
The railroad worm is actually a light-producing beetle.
2. The weaver may build nests measuring five meters across.
The weaver is a sparrowlike African bird.
3. Koalas carry their young in pouches.
Koalas are living models of the teddy bear.
4. On my travels to South America I saw an Araucana.
An Araucana is a hen that lays blue-and-green eggs.
5. The Atlantic bay scallop may have as many as a hundred eyes.
The Atlantic bay scallop is a delicious shellfish.
6. The flounder is a flat fish that swims on its side.
The flounder has both eyes on one side of its head.
7. The walking catfish can survive on land for a long time.
This catfish is a recent import to North America.
8. Prairie dogs greet each other with a kiss.
The kiss is a touching of their noses and front teeth.
9. The zoo has a colony of animals that never need to drink water.
The animals are kangaroo rats.
10. That noise sounds like a barking dog.
It is the voice of a barking frog.

12d. Combine short, related sentences by using compound subjects and compound verbs.

Compound subjects and compound verbs (see page 43) are joined by conjunctions such as *and*, *but*, or *or* and by correlative conjunctions such as *either—or, neither—nor,* or *both—and.*

EXAMPLES Mom **and** Dad took us to see Williamsburg.
The committee could **neither** agree on the amendment **nor** vote on the motion.
Both students **and** teachers arrive early **and** leave late.

Short, related sentences may often be combined by using a compound verb, compound subject, or both.

TWO SENTENCES   We went to the movie theater.
We saw the new horror film.

ONE SENTENCE   We went to the movie theater **and** saw the new horror film.

FOUR SENTENCES   The players rushed to home plate.
The coach rushed to home plate.
The players protested the umpire's call.
The coach protested the umpire's call.

ONE SENTENCE   **Both** the players **and** the coach rushed to home plate **and** protested the umpire's call.

EXERCISE 4. Combining Sentences by Using Compound Subjects and Compound Verbs. Combine the following groups of sentences into one sentence by using compound subjects and compound verbs. Be sure the subjects and verbs agree in number.

1. Refined sugar is not necessary in a healthful diet.
   Too much salt is also not necessary in a healthful diet.
2. We should include a food from the bread group in every meal.
   We should avoid overeating carbohydrates.
3. A healthy person eats a varied diet.
   A healthy person exercises regularly.
   A healthy person gets enough sleep.
4. Meat provides essential protein.
   Beans provide essential protein.
   Rice provides essential protein.
5. Long-distance runners control their diets.
   Football players control their diets.
   The runners drink plenty of fluids.
   Football players drink plenty of fluids.

REVIEW EXERCISE A. Revising a Paragraph by Combining Sentences. Revise the following paragraph so that it is appropriate for an English report to be read to your class. Combine short and choppy sentences.

Romeo and Juliet are two young people from rival families. They fall in love. They marry secretly. Romeo is exiled for killing Juliet's cousin in a duel. Romeo returns at night. He finds Juliet lying in a deep coma.

Romeo thinks she is dead. Romeo kills himself with poison. Juliet awakens. She discovers Romeo's corpse. She kills herself with his dagger. Their senseless deaths stun the rival families. The deaths bring reconciliation.

12e. Combine short, related sentences by writing a compound sentence.

A compound sentence (see page 108) is really two or more simple sentences joined together by the conjunctions *and, but, or, nor, for, so,* or *yet.*

EXAMPLE We started for home, **but** the rain made travel difficult.

When writing a compound sentence, be sure the ideas you connect are related and equal in importance. Unrelated or unequal ideas should not be combined in a compound sentence.

UNRELATED IDEAS The actors rehearsed their lines, and snow fell in record amounts.

RELATED IDEAS The actors rehearsed their lines, and the musicians tuned their instruments.

EXERCISE 5. Combining Sentences into a Compound Sentence.
Five of the following groups of sentences contain two or more closely related ideas. Combine these ideas into a compound sentence, using *and, but, or, nor, för,* or *yet.* Two groups contain unrelated ideas. They should not be combined. Add commas where necessary. (For the use of commas in a compound sentence, see pages 684–85.)

1. The *Voyager* space probes have discovered much about Jupiter.
   We still have much to learn.
2. Earlier pictures had suggested that Jupiter's atmosphere was calm.
   The *Voyager* craft uncovered high-speed winds.
3. *Voyager* photographs showed lightning flashes.
   Scientists detected a new moon orbiting the planet.
4. Jupiter has several moons.
   Scientists are especially interested in the moon named Io.
5. *Voyager* passed close to Io.
   Scientists wanted a clear look at this small moon.
6. Volcanoes erupt on Io's surface.
   Geology includes the study of volcanoes.
7. Space probes may one day encounter life in another part of the universe.
   So far, there have been no signs of life.

12f. Combine short, related sentences into a complex sentence by putting one idea into a subordinate clause.

A complex sentence (see page 109) has an independent clause and at least one subordinate clause.

(1) Use an adjective clause to combine sentences.

An adjective clause (see pages 99–102) is a subordinate clause that, like an adjective, modifies a noun or a pronoun. In the following example, the adjective clause is in boldfaced type.

EXAMPLE   We found a book **that had been printed more than two hundred years ago.**

Adjective clauses begin with one of the relative pronouns: *who, whom, whose, which,* or *that.*

To combine two sentences with an adjective clause, supply the necessary relative pronoun.

TWO SENTENCES   The driver reported the accident.
The accident had blocked traffic in both directions.

ONE SENTENCE   The driver reported the accident, **which** had blocked traffic in both directions.

EXERCISE 6. Combining Sentences by Using an Adjective Clause.   Combine each of the following groups of sentences into one sentence by using an adjective clause. Add commas where necessary. (For the use of commas with nonessential clauses, see pages 686–87).

1. Sacajawea guided Lewis and Clark.
Lewis and Clark explored the Louisiana territory.
2. Matthew Henson was among the first explorers to reach the North Pole.
Robert Peary chose Henson as his chief assistant.
3. Margaret Mead studied families in Samoa, Bali, and New Guinea.
Her books are very popular today.
4. E. A. Martel pioneered in cave exploration.
He charted deep vertical caves in Europe.
5. Amelia Earhart tried to fly around the world at the equator.
She crashed into the Pacific Ocean.
6. Silvia Earle tests diving suits.
The suits enable her to descend 380 meters.

7. Heinrich Schliemann unearthed an ancient city.
   This city, he believed, was the Troy of Homer's *Iliad*.
8. Inez Mexia was a famous botanical explorer.
   She spent months in the jungles of South America.
9. Antarctica has a harsh climate.
   It has never been fully explored.
10. Tenzing Norgay finally scaled Mount Everest.
    He had been climbing mountains for many years.

(2) Use an adverb clause to combine sentences.

An adverb clause (pages 102–103) is a subordinate clause that, like an adverb, modifies a verb, an adjective, or an adverb.

EXAMPLE **If the team scores this goal,** it will win the divisional championship.

Adverb clauses, like adverbs, may tell *when, how, where, to what extent,* or *under what condition* an action is done. An adverb clause begins with a subordinating conjunction. Study the following list:

Common Subordinating Conjunctions

after	before	than	whenever
although	if	unless	where
as	since	until	wherever
because	so that	when	while

When you combine two short sentences by turning one of them into an adverb clause, be careful to choose the correct subordinating conjunction.[1] Because a subordinating conjunction shows the relationship between clauses, a poorly chosen conjunction will show a false or meaningless relationship. For example, a number of subordinating conjunctions could be used to join these two sentences, but not all of them would show a relationship that makes sense.

TWO SENTENCES At camp we get up.
              The sun rises.

    UNCLEAR   At camp we get up until the sun rises.

      CLEAR   At camp we get up **when** the sun rises.

EXERCISE 7. Combining Sentences by Using an Adverb Clause.
Combine each of the following groups of ideas into one sentence by putting one idea into an adverb clause. Refer to the list of subordinat-

[1] Choosing a subordinate conjunction is further discussed on pages 298–99.

ing conjunctions on page 288. Vary the conjunctions you choose. Add commas where necessary. (For the use of commas with introductory clauses, see page 690.)

1. A bill begins its passage into law.
   A representative sends a bill to the clerk of the House.
2. The Speaker of the House routes all bills to House committees.
   Relatively few bills pass beyond the committee stage.
3. A committee sends the approved bill to the full House.
   All representatives can have a vote.
4. The House passes the bill.
   It must also win the approval of the Senate.
5. A Senate committee approves or amends a similar bill.
   It moves to the full Senate.
6. The Senate bill is approved.
   The bill must agree with the House version.
7. The two bills go to a House-Senate conference committee.
   A compromise bill is agreed to.
8. A bill passes both the Senate and the House.
   It goes to the President to be signed into law.
9. The bill becomes law.
   The President vetoes it.
10. A vetoed bill can become law.
    A two-thirds majority in both House and Senate can override the President's veto.

(3) Use a noun clause to combine sentences.

Noun clauses (see pages 105–106) are usually introduced by *that, what, whatever, who, whoever, whom,* or *whomever.*

EXAMPLE The jury decided **that the defendant was innocent of the charges.**

Two ideas can be combined by using a noun clause.

TWO SENTENCES The doctor said something about nutrition.
It was important.

ONE SENTENCE **What the doctor said about nutrition** was important.

EXERCISE 8. Combining Sentences by Using a Noun Clause.
Combine each of the following groups of ideas into one sentence by turning one of the ideas into a noun clause.

1. We are going to the fair tonight.
   Nancy told me.
2. The wheel was invented long ago.
   Exactly when is still unknown.
3. The ticket seller refused to admit us.
   My father wanted to know why.
4. Bernie told us something.
   We wanted to hear it.
5. Fifteen players were injured.
   This fact did not affect the coach's game plan.

REVIEW EXERCISE B. Combining Sentences. Combine each of the following groups of sentences into one sentence. There may be more than one correct way to combine them. Add commas where necessary.

1. American artists have various backgrounds.
   The artists are modern.
   The artists come from many different places.
2. Marisol Escobar spent her childhood in Venezuela.
   She moved at the age of eleven.
   She moved to the United States with her family.
3. Marisol prefers to use only her first name.
   She has displayed her work at the Museum of Modern Art.
   She has displayed her work in a special room at the museum.
4. Gwendolyn Brooks was born in Kansas.
   She was raised in Chicago.
   She was the first black woman to receive the Pulitzer Prize.
   The prize she won was for poetry.
5. Miss Brooks has been recognized as a major American poet.
   She has been recognized for a long time.
   She has been elected to the National Institute of Letters.
6. Hiroko Yajima is originally from Tokyo.
   She is a young violinist.
   She came to New York.
   There she made her professional debut.
7. She has been praised for her sensitivity.
   She has been praised for her agility.
   She has been praised for her accurate pitch.
   She has become a favorite of the critics.

8. Fernando Bujones has lived in New York City.
   He is Cuban-born.
   He has been a dancer with the American Ballet Theater.
9. Cicely Tyson is a native-born American.
   She has appeared on television.
   She appeared as a young African woman.
   This woman refused to adopt Western culture.
10. Miss Tyson is best known for something.
   It is her portrayal of Rebecca.
   Rebecca is the resilient young mother in the movie *Sounder.*

REVIEW EXERCISE C. Revising a Paragraph by Combining Sentences. Revise the following paragraph by combining short sentences into longer sentences. There may be more than one correct way to combine the sentences. Add commas where necessary.

The volcanic explosion of Krakatoa produced a noise. Krakatoa is an Indonesian island. The noise was one of the loudest ever heard. People claimed the noise sounded like a cannon. The people were on the island of Rodriguez. Rodriguez is over 5,000 kilometers away. The volcanic explosion caused tidal waves. The tidal waves traveled over 1,300 kilometers. The tidal waves killed over 36,000 people. For three years people all over the world saw exceptionally brilliant sunsets. Fine dust scattered by the volcano into the atmosphere caused the brilliant sunsets. Krakatoa's explosion, however, had only one fifth the force of the eruption at Thera. Thera is an island in the Aegean Sea. This eruption probably destroyed the Minoan civilization in 1470 B.C.

VARYING SENTENCE BEGINNINGS

12g. Vary the beginnings of your sentences.

The usual way to form an English sentence is to begin with the subject and end with the predicate. Any piece of writing in which most of the sentences depart from this natural order is certain to strike a reader as artificial. However, an unbroken sequence of subject-predicate sentences may result in another stylistic fault—monotony. Such a sequence is monotonous because it lacks the logical connections and special emphasis that variation in sentence structure can provide.

Compare the following versions of the same paragraph. In the first, each sentence begins in the same way. In the second, an attempt has been made to achieve emphasis and clarity by varying sentence beginnings.

NOT VARIED

The trial had been scheduled for two o'clock. The audience was noisily settling itself in the courtroom for the coming show. The lawyers were quietly talking and shuffling piles of papers at the polished tables in the front of the room. The bell in the courthouse tower struck two in resounding tones. Judge Perez, dignified in her long black robe, walked slowly to her bench. The clerk rasped out, "Everyone rise." The room seemed suddenly to lift for a moment; then it settled back into an ominous silence. The judge opened the case of *The People v. John Strong* in a manner which seemed to imply that such trials happened every day of her life.

VARIED

The trial had been scheduled for two o'clock. In the courtroom the audience was noisily settling itself for the coming show. At the polished tables in the front of the room, the lawyers were quietly talking and shuffling piles of papers. When the bell in the courthouse tower struck two in resounding tones, Judge Perez, dignified in her long black robe, walked slowly to her bench. "Everyone rise," rasped the clerk. Suddenly the room seemed to lift for a moment; then it settled back into an ominous silence. In a manner which seemed to imply that these trials happened every day of her life, the judge opened the case of *The People v. John Strong*.

You need not avoid the normal order of sentences merely for the sake of variety, but often you can increase the force and clarity of a statement by beginning it with an important modifier.

The exercises that follow are intended to give you practice in using different kinds of sentence openers. Used sparingly, such devices will improve your writing.

(1) You may begin a sentence with a single-word modifier—an adverb, an adjective, or a participle.

EXAMPLES   **Instantly** I felt better. [adverb]
          Thick and slimy, the mud oozed from under the wheels. [adjectives]
          Grinning, Myra tuned in her favorite program. [present participle]
          Dejected, the coach sat on the bench and brooded over his team. [past participle]

EXERCISE 9. Revising Sentences by Beginning with Single-Word Modifiers.
The following sentences, all of which begin with simple subjects, contain single-word modifiers that can be placed at the beginning of the sentences. Find this modifier in each one and rewrite the

sentence, placing the modifier first. The sentences in this and the following exercises are good sentences. You are asked to rewrite them so that you will learn a variety of ways of expressing the same idea. (For the use of commas with introductory single-word modifiers, see page 689.)

EXAMPLE 1. Our system of measurements will eventually be changed.
  1. *Eventually our system of measurements will be changed.*

1. The United States is planning cautiously to introduce the metric system.
2. This system, unfamiliar and different, will change American habits quite a bit.
3. Our vocabulary of measurement will gradually be replaced by a new one.
4. The metric system, tested and refined, has been in use in Europe and most of the rest of the world since the early nineteenth century.
5. The standard unit of measurement until then, surprisingly, was a person's hand or foot.
6. This obviously is not a standard size.
7. The metric system, comprehensive and orderly, includes measurements of length, weight, volume, and temperature.
8. An inch converts metrically to 2.54 centimeters; an ounce to 28.3 grams; a quart to .946 liters; and 32° Fahrenheit to 0° Celsius (or Centigrade).
9. The notion of changing to another system once seemed forbidding.
10. Anyone, informed and willing, can make conversions with ease.

EXERCISE 10. Writing Sentences That Begin with Single-Word Modifiers. Write five sentences of your own beginning with single-word modifiers. Include at least one adjective, one adverb, and one participial modifier.

(2) You may begin a sentence with a phrase: a prepositional phrase, a participial phrase, an appositive phrase, or an infinitive phrase.

EXAMPLES **At the sound of the bell,** the teacher collected the papers. [prepositional phrase]
  Having examined the records, the lawyer prepared a new deed. [participial phrase]

An excellent example of modern architecture, the new city hall is a favorite tourist attraction. [appositive phrase]
To learn to swim better, we took lessons at the pool. [infinitive phrase]

EXERCISE 11. Revising Sentences by Beginning with Phrase Modifiers.

The following sentences, all of which begin with the subject, contain phrase modifiers that can be placed at the beginning of the sentences. Revise each sentence by placing the modifying phrase at the beginning. Place a comma after each introductory phrase.

1. Pompeii was a well-to-do commercial city at the foot of Mt. Vesuvius.
2. Its population at the time of its destruction was about 30,000.
3. Archaeologists have discovered many facts about the life and times of ancient Pompeii to add to our knowledge of bygone days.
4. Wealthy Romans, attracted by the beauty of the location and healthfulness of the climate, built many villas there.
5. The streets, paved with blocks of lava, were usually wide and straight.
6. The Forum was a square, completely surrounded by temples and public buildings, near the western edge of the city.
7. Mt. Vesuvius had never given any indication of its volcanic character up to the year A.D. 63.
8. The inhabitants, still rebuilding their city from the ravages of earthquakes, were overwhelmed by the sudden eruption of August 24, A.D. 79.
9. The people fled the city to save their lives.
10. The existence of Pompeii was forgotten during the Middle Ages, and it was not until 1763 that excavations of the city began.

EXERCISE 12. Revising Sentences by Beginning with Single-Word and Phrase Modifiers.

You will not hold your audience's interest if all of your sentences begin with the subject. Revise the following sentences so that each begins with either a word or a phrase modifier. In revising keep the original meaning. Hints are given for the first five.

EXAMPLE 1. We were tired and decided to leave the party early.
     1. *Tired, we decided to leave the party early.*

1. Tommy flopped into the nearest chair, kicking off his shoes. [Begin with *kicking*.]
2. He looked through the program to find what songs Chita Rivera would sing. [Begin with *to find*.]
3. The program about Roberto Clemente began at seven o'clock sharp. [Begin with *at*.]
4. We scraped the old bureau down to the natural wood and discovered that it was real mahogany. [Begin with *scraping*.]
5. Our boat, trim and fast, won the race. [Begin with *trim*.]
6. My car was greased last week, and now it runs perfectly.
7. The stage crew, working evenings after school for weeks, completed the sets on schedule.
8. The band marched around the field and entertained the spectators during the half.
9. Garden City High School has good school spirit and always has a large attendance at football games.
10. The light bulb, flickering on and off for several seconds, finally went out.

(3) You may begin a sentence with a subordinate clause.

EXAMPLES I was unable to attend the Junior Prom because I had the flu.
Because I had the flu, I was unable to attend the Junior Prom.

Katsura was interested in joining the Masquers Club and the Film Group, but she did not have time to attend the meetings.

Although Katsura was interested in joining the Masquers Club and the Film Group, she did not have time to attend the meetings.

Subordinate clauses at the beginning of sentences usually begin with a subordinating conjunction. For a list of subordinating conjunctions, see page 288.

EXERCISE 13. Revising Sentences by Beginning with Subordinate Clauses.
Revise each sentence so that it begins with a subordinate clause instead of the subject. Place a comma after an adverb clause coming first in the sentence.

1. The praying mantis is a welcome guest in any garden because it destroys many harmful pests. [Because . . .]
2. The insects are not large in this country, but their South American relatives are big enough to devour small birds. [Although . . .]

3. The mantis was once highly regarded, and its landing on any person was considered a token of saintliness and an omen of good fortune. [Since . . .]

4. They watch patiently for their prey, and these creatures hold their claws in a kind of praying position. [When . . .]

5. Superstitious people believed these insects to be engaged in prayer, and so mantises were often called soothsayers or prophets. [Because . . .]

6. This insect can fly, but it prefers to wait on shrubs for its unsuspecting dinner to come by.

7. The mantis moves quietly and carefully, and seldom does its prey get away.

8. The forelegs shoot out like lightning, and the victim is caught in the mantis' trap.

9. The female lays small groups of eggs, and she attaches these to boards or twigs.

10. The eggs hatch in May or June, and the small mantises look almost exactly like their parents.

11. The baby mantises develop wings as they mature.

12. The female mantis harbors no love for her mate, and a male mantis may find himself his wife's dinner if he is not fast on his feet.

13. These voracious eaters of destructive pests are protected by law in many areas, and a person may be fined for harming them.

EXERCISE 14. Revising Sentences by Beginning with Single-Word, Phrase, and Clause Modifiers. Change each of the following sentences in the manner suggested.

1. The steak was thick and juicy, and it just seemed to melt in my mouth. [Begin with single-word modifiers.]

2. The batter swung wildly at the ball. [Begin with a single-word modifier.]

3. The Student Council elected a parliamentarian to settle all disputes about conducting a meeting. [Begin with an infinitive phrase.]

4. Myron forgot his lines in the middle of the second act. [Begin with prepositional phrases.]

5. The house was appraised at $40,000 last year and sold for $45,000 this week. [Begin with a past participial phrase.]

6. The bookstore in our town gives special discounts at Christmas time. [Begin with a prepositional phrase.]

7. The coach was annoyed at Christine's failure to show up for practice and benched her for two games. [Begin with a past participial phrase.]

8. Ms. Wentworth came into the room and told us to report to the auditorium for our seventh-period class. [Begin with a subordinate clause.]

9. We rowed across the lake and camped at Paradise Point. [Begin with a participial phrase.]

10. I liked *A Separate Peace* very much and have recommended it to all my friends. [Begin with a subordinate clause.]

VARYING SENTENCE STRUCTURE

12h. Vary the kinds of sentences.

You learned in Chapter 4 that, when classified according to their structure, there are four kinds of sentences: *simple, compound, complex,* and *compound-complex.* If you are not sure of the characteristics of each of these, you should turn back to pages 108–10 and refresh your memory before going further.

Just as it is possible to achieve variety in your writing by varying the beginnings of your sentences, it is also possible to achieve variety by varying the kinds of sentences you use. Using simple or compound sentences all the time tends to make your style monotonous. For example, read the following paragraph composed almost entirely of simple and compound sentences.

1. My parents always get a yearning for a family reunion just before Thanksgiving.   2. At this time, the magazines show smiling families sitting around tables laden with the most massive turkeys outside a zoo.   3. I smile bravely at their resolution and resign myself.   4. I sit there and glower.   5. The magazines never really show the "before and after" of sitting down to consume the traditional fare.   6. My parents have a mania for cleanliness.   7. With company coming, we will turn the house upside down to create a good impression.   8. We will rearrange the house thoroughly and clean silverware and do other odd jobs.   9. These tasks finally completed, we will stagger to the door to greet our guests.   10. Then we will put a sizable dent in the turkey; then we will have endless varieties of leftover food.   11. We will have hot and cold turkey sandwiches, creamed turkey, turkey hash, turkey surprise, and finally turkey soup.   12. Eventually we will throw out the skeletal remains and feel the strangest urge to gobble.   13. I must not forget one thing.   14. I will have a gala time with the pots and pans.   15. I would like to change the routine.   16. I hate drudgery.

Now read the next paragraph, which tells the same tale but contains many complex sentences (the new subordinate clauses are italicized). You will see the superiority of this version over the first one.

1. My parents always get a yearning for a family reunion just prior to Thanksgiving *when the magazines show smiling families sitting around tables laden with the most massive turkeys outside a zoo.* 2. I smile bravely at their announcement and say, "Sounds great." 3. Actually, I sit there and glower. 4. The magazines never really show *what goes on before and after the merry throng sits down to consume the traditional fare.* 5. *Because my parents have a mania for cleanliness,* we will turn the house upside down to create a good impression for the expected company. 6. We will rearrange the house thoroughly and clean silverware and do other odd jobs. 7. These tasks finally completed, we will stagger to the door to greet our guests. 8. *After we have put a sizable dent in the turkey,* we will have endless varieties of leftover food. 9. We will have hot and cold turkey sandwiches, creamed turkey, turkey hash, turkey surprise, and finally turkey soup. 10. *Before the skeletal remains are thrown out,* we will feel the strangest urge to gobble. 11. I must not forget to mention *that I will have a gala time with the pots and pans.* 12. Do you think for one instant *that I would change the family routine in spite of the drudgery?* 13. You bet your life *I would!*

Actually, all that had to be done to break the monotony of the first version was to change some of the less important ideas from independent clauses to subordinate clauses. A subordinate clause in a sentence makes the sentence complex.

Using subordinate clauses not only gives variety to your writing but also helps you to show how the ideas in a sentence are related. One idea may be the cause or the result of another idea in the sentence, or it may give the time of the other. Study the following pairs of sentences. The first sentence in each pair is compound; the second is complex. Notice that in the second sentence the relationship between ideas is clearer than in the first sentence.

EXAMPLES   Our school is very crowded this year, and most of the study halls are in the auditorium.
Because our school is very crowded this year, most of the study halls are in the auditorium. [The first idea expresses the *cause* of the second.]

The Cabinet met in emergency session, and the President consulted his staff.
Before the Cabinet met in emergency session, the President consulted his staff. [One idea gives the *time* of the other.]
The band members rehearse every day after school, and then they can give a good performance at their concert.

> The band members rehearse every day after school **so that they can give a good performance at their concert.** [The idea in the subordinate clause states the reason for the idea in the independent clause.]

The following words, when used at the beginning of a subordinate clause, help to make clear the relationship between the sentence ideas:

CAUSE because, since, as

RESULT OR REASON so that, in order that

TIME when, while, as, since, until, after, before, whenever

Whenever you are combining ideas, make sure that your connectives are appropriate.

EXERCISE 15. Changing Compound Sentences into Complex Sentences. Change each of the following compound sentences into a complex sentence by expressing one of the ideas in a subordinate clause. Begin each subordinate clause with a word that will show how the ideas in the sentence are related: cause, result or reason, time.

1. Last week I visited New York City with my parents, and we saw the Dance Theater of Harlem at the Uris Theater.
2. Melva Murray-White danced in *Don Quixote,* and I was fascinated by her performance.
3. She danced with a powerful grace, and her movements radiated energy and exhilaration.
4. The dancers performed *Romeo and Juliet,* and I became even more entranced.
5. My favorite dance was *Agon,* and I enjoyed its theme of life and combat.
6. It remarkably traced the path of movement in time and space, and I came to admire Balanchine and Stravinsky, who created this dance.
7. Its movements were like flashes of electricity, and the dancers darted back and forth across the stage with computerlike precision and timing.
8. I watched the dances, and I concluded that the group combines jazz movements with classical ballet.

9. I had not known dancers could convey such joy, but then I saw this marvelous group.
10. I will get an advance schedule next year, and I will surely see a dance by Geoffrey Holder.

EXERCISE 16. Revising a Composition by Changing or Combining Sentences into Complex Sentences.

The following paragraphs consist chiefly of simple and compound sentences. Revise them, varying the style by changing or combining some of the sentences into complex sentences. Do not try to make all your sentences complex, for your purpose is to achieve sentence variety.

1. My first day in high school was one of the most hectic days of my life. It all seems ridiculous now, but it was no joke then. With my heart in my mouth, I boarded the school bus that morning. Many of my old friends from junior-high days were seated there, but for some strange reason they did not want to talk very much. Everybody was abnormally quiet, and the air was electric with the tension. Gus, the bus driver, must have enjoyed the ride. Usually he has to tell us about twenty times to pipe down.

2. The silent bus soon arrived at the high school, and we filed quickly into the courtyard. For the tenth time in five minutes, I looked at my instructions for the first day. These instructions had come in the mail the week before, and by now I had practically memorized them. Still, I did not want to lose them. "Proceed to the student lobby and check your name on the lists posted there," stated the valuable paper. To make a long story short, I did just that and soon located my name on the bulletin board. The next step was to find Room 134, my official homeroom according to the list on the wall.

3. I wandered all over the school looking for Room 134. I should have asked for directions and saved myself a lot of trouble, but I was too stupid. At least, that's my excuse today. I bumped into Ray and Mike, my best friends last year. They were looking for Room 147. They didn't know the location of 134, but Ray did have a map of the school. I looked at it closely and found that Room 134 was right next to the student lobby.

4. I entered Room 134 slowly and glanced around. There wasn't a familiar face in sight. Where could all these strange people have come

from? A short, red-haired man strode toward me and told me to take a seat. Sitting in the front makes me feel very conspicuous, so I selected a choice spot in the back of the room. I just can't stand a million eyes bouncing off the back of my head. The red-haired man was our homeroom teacher, and he explained about fire drills, cafeteria procedure, absentee notes, and countless other school rules. He was wasting his time. It sounded like mumbo jumbo to me, and it went in one ear and right out the other. Soon he distributed the program cards and a map of the school and told us to report to the first class at the ringing of the bell. The bell cut the silence of the room, and off I went on my big adventure.

5. The rest of the day was a real nightmare. I got lost many times, I got pushed around in the halls, and I felt like a rat prowling around in a gigantic maze. Some upperclassmen, chuckling to themselves, tried to sell me a ticket to the swimming pool on the third floor. I didn't fall for that, however. There isn't any swimming pool, and there isn't any third floor. I met all my new teachers, and each one kindly presented me with a book weighing about three pounds. I could hardly walk around. The books kept slipping out of my arms. And so I came to the end of that first day and boarded the bus with my head swimming with *do*'s and *dont*'s. The ride home was just like old times. It wasn't quiet, and sure enough, Gus had to exercise his lungs and tell us to pipe down.

REVIEW EXERCISE. Writing a Composition Using a Variety of Sentence Structures. Write a narrative composition about one of your own experiences. The purpose of your writing is to show that you can avoid a monotonous style by varying the form of your sentences. Before writing, review the three ways of beginning a sentence. Include some complex sentences in your composition.

PART FOUR

COMPOSITION:
The Writing Process

CHAPTER 13

Writing and Thinking

THE WRITING PROCESS

Whenever you write a paragraph or an essay, you are involved in an ongoing process that involves thinking, making decisions, and rethinking. Writing is not something that happens all at one time. Rather, many steps are required from the time you first think about a piece of writing until the time you consider yourself finished. In this chapter, you will learn about five stages in the writing process and the many steps that make up each stage.

THE WRITING PROCESS

PREWRITING—Identifying your purpose and audience; choosing a subject; considering attitude and tone; limiting a subject; and gathering, classifying, and ordering information

WRITING A FIRST DRAFT—Expressing your ideas in sentences and paragraphs

REVISING—Improving the content, word choice, and sentence structure in a draft

PROOFREADING—Checking the revised version to correct inaccuracies in grammar, usage, and mechanics

WRITING THE FINAL VERSION—Preparing a final version and proofreading it

PREWRITING

The first stage in the writing process is called prewriting. During this stage you make decisions about four important questions: Why am I writing? For whom am I writing? What will I write about? What will I say?

THE WRITER'S PURPOSE

13a. Have in mind a clear purpose for writing.

Every piece of writing has a purpose—sometimes more than one purpose. If you write an essay about the forms of government in your community, your purpose is to give information or explain. If you write a paragraph about something funny that happened to you when you went to pay a library fine, your purpose would be to tell a story.

Most writing has one of the following four purposes:

1. Narrative writing tells a story.

EXAMPLES   An essay about your experiences on a shopping expedition
           A letter to a friend about your first day in a new school

2. Expository writing gives information or explains.

EXAMPLES   A paragraph about the history of the Statue of Liberty
           An essay question defining what genes are

3. Descriptive writing describes a person, place, or thing.

EXAMPLES   An essay describing the view from a skyscraper
           A letter to a pen pal describing your room

4. Persuasive writing attempts to persuade or convince.

EXAMPLES   A letter to the editor about the need for a teen recreation center
           A brochure encouraging residents to donate blood

EXERCISE 1. Identifying Purposes for Writing.   Decide what the writer's purpose is in each of the following paragraphs.

1

The outcome of presidential elections is decided not by popular vote but by the election of members of the electoral college. On Election Day voters determine which candidate will receive each state's electoral votes. The number of electoral votes for each state is equal to the total of its members in the Senate and in the House of Representatives. Tennessee, for example, has eleven electoral votes; Illinois has twenty-four. Alaska has the smallest number—three electoral votes. Following the November presidential election, Congress meets on January 6 for a formal count of the electoral votes.

2

According to the National Centers for Disease Control, lung cancer will soon become the leading cause of all cancer deaths among women. Until now, many fewer women than men have suffered from lung cancer because fewer women smoked. The epidemic of lung cancer among women is especially tragic because, according to the National Centers for Disease Control, it is preventable: Approximately 85 percent of all lung cancer cases are directly caused by cigarette smoking. In recent years women have been striving for equal rights with men. Let's not make that equality in lung cancer, too. If you are already smoking cigarettes, it's not too late to stop. If you have not yet started, stay smart—and don't!

3

When the frame of a tall building is complete, construction workers hold a ceremony called "topping out." A fir tree (sometimes a flag) is hoisted to the building's top to signal that the framework is complete. During the 1930's this custom was known in New York City as a "roof-tree raising" or "roof-bush raising." Most builders believe that the custom originated in Scandinavia and dates back as far as A.D. 700. According to Scandinavian mythology, spirits lived within each tree. The topping-out ceremony was an attempt to appease the anger of the tree spirits for having chopped down trees for lumber. In Norway today the topping-out ceremony takes place in the building of homes as well as public buildings.

EXERCISE 2. Identifying Purposes for Writing. Identify the purpose you would have in writing about each of the topics on the following page. Number your paper 1–10. After the proper number, write the letter of the appropriate purpose. (Some items may have more than one purpose.)

a. To tell a story   *c.* To describe
b. To inform or explain   *d.* To persuade

1. History of the Alamo
2. What the town you were born in looks like
3. Why the legal drinking age should be twenty-one
4. What happened when you tried to ice skate for the first time
5. The earliest history of your community
6. What your best friend looks like
7. Why high schools should add an extra period to each day's schedule
8. What happened when your tent collapsed during the middle of the night on a recent camping trip
9. Why people who live in apartments should (or should not) be allowed to have dogs or cats
10. What a chinchilla looks like

CRITICAL THINKING:
Analyzing How Purpose Affects Writing

Analysis is the critical thinking skill that you use when you think about how a whole can be broken into its smaller parts. When you narrow a broad, general subject into a limited, more specific topic, you use analysis. Analysis is also the skill that you use when you think about how the parts of a whole are related to each other and how each part affects the whole. During the prewriting stage, you analyze how audience and purpose will affect your finished piece of writing.

The purpose that you choose will affect both the content of your writing and the words you choose to express your ideas. If your purpose is to inform, you will include many specific details and write in fairly formal language.

EXAMPLE   The preparation for any bicycle tour—and the fun—begins with planning a route. The first source of information is a good motoring atlas, like Rand McNally's. It indicates the location and size of settlements, classifies highways and points out landmarks and other places of interest that might be worth a visit. Upon request, local chambers of commerce will furnish brochures about particular areas and calendars of local events.

GWEN BALLARD

However, if you are writing to tell a story, you will use less formal language and choose details or events that will amuse your reader.

EXAMPLE   When my brother Larry persuaded me to join him on a two-day bicycle trip, I should have known better. I had been used to bicycling back and forth to school (about two miles each way), but I'd never really bicycled for a long distance. Also, my bike is an old clunker—a heavy five-speed that no matter what I do seems to have only two speeds. We set out one Saturday morning before dawn. Larry zipped along in the dark on his ten-speed, while I pedaled furiously to keep him in sight. I yelled at him to slow down, but he either ignored me or pretended not to hear. If I'd had any sense at all, I'd have turned back and missed the weekend's disasters; but somehow I was into "proving" myself, so I kept on madly pedaling.

If your purpose is to persuade, you will use formal language to express specific opinions, reasons, and evidence. Your writing style will be concise, and you will concentrate on expressing your ideas as clearly as you can.

Descriptive writing uses less formal language and a looser, freer writing style. Your description will include specific, concrete, and sensory details as you try to create a vivid image for your reader.

For each writing purpose, you will use a different combination of language and details.

Purpose:	Language:	Details:
To persuade	Formal	Specific, precisely stated opinions, reasons, and evidence
To inform	Formal	Specific facts, examples, information
To tell a story	Informal	Important details and events; often includes description
To describe	Informal	Specific and vivid concrete and sensory details

EXERCISE 3. Analyzing How Purpose Affects Writing.

Each of the numbered items on the next page identifies a topic and an audience plus two purposes for writing. Consider how each purpose would affect the piece of writing. For example, for each purpose think about what specific aspect of the topic you might choose to write about. Decide also what kinds of details you might include in your writing. Be prepared to discuss your answers.

1. *Topic:* Washing clothes
   Audience: Class of sixth-graders
   Purpose: a. To inform   b. To tell a story
2. *Topic:* Registering to vote
   Audience: A group of eighteen-year-olds
   Purpose: a. To inform   b. To persuade
3. *Topic:* Designing the car of the future
   Audience: A group of tenth-graders
   Purpose: a. To describe   b. To inform
4. *Topic:* Forming a Neighborhood Watch club
   Audience: A group of homeowners
   Purpose: a. To tell a story   b. To persuade

THE WRITER'S AUDIENCE

13b. Identify the audience for whom you are writing.

It is always helpful to think about the different audiences for whom you may be writing. An essay about the dangers of fad diets, for example, may be written for any of the following audiences: a group of overweight teen-agers, parents of dieters, members of a health class, a group of sixth-graders. For each of these audiences, your essay will be different.

EXERCISE 4. Identifying Purpose and Audience. List at least seven different pieces of writing that you have read during the past few weeks. You may include articles in magazines and newspapers, instructions and directions, novels, and short stories. Be prepared to tell both the main purpose and what you think is the intended audience for each piece of writing.

CRITICAL THINKING:
Analyzing How Audience Affects Writing

The following paragraphs were written for an audience of educated adult readers:

> One of the country's leading authorities on hieroglyphics received a $128,000 award in February to pursue any work he chose over the next

five years. "It's really a shock—still a little hard to comprehend," said the recipient, 18-year-old David Stuart of Silver Spring, Md.

Mr. Stuart became interested in hieroglyphics—or "glyph," as the cognoscenti sometimes call them—at 8, when he accompanied his father, George, an archaeologist, to the Yucatan Peninsula. In February, the youth became the youngest person to win a MacArthur Foundation award.

"It hasn't really changed things in the short run," he says. "Right now I'm working on a book on hieroglyphic writing—Maya stuff." He doubts it will be a best seller, although it is aimed at "a very general audience."

"I suppose I know about roughly the state of knowledge on it now," he says of Mayan hieroglyphics, but he observes that "no one is really able yet" to interpret the glyphs fully. There is no Rosetta Stone to unravel the Mayan puzzle, he says, adding, "I'm working slowly to break little pieces here and there."

RICHARD HAITCH

If you were to rewrite this same information for an audience of ten-year-olds, what changes would you make? First you would explain certain references that the writer of this article assumes the reader knows. For example, you would need to explain what hieroglyphics are, what an archaeologist does, where the Yucatán Peninsula is, where and when the Mayan culture existed. You would also need to give some background information about the Rosetta Stone, a tablet of black stone containing ancient Egyptian and Greek inscriptions that enabled scholars to decipher Egyptian hieroglyphics. Next, you would turn your attention to vocabulary and sentence length. You would replace the difficult word *cognoscenti* with an easier word, such as *experts*. You might also change the word *comprehend* to the easier word *understand*.

Audiences vary widely—in age and background, in knowledge and interests, and in the opinions and feelings they have about a topic. An audience may be biased (prejudiced) either in favor of a topic or against it. To understand how your audience affects your writing, consider each of the following questions. You will use the answers to these questions to adapt your writing to a specific audience.

1. Is the audience made up of friends, acquaintances, or strangers? Is it made up of some combination of these groups?

2. What background information does the audience already have about the topic? What background information will you need to supply? (For example, will you need to explain the history of a topic or references to unfamiliar people or places?)

3. What terms will be unfamiliar to the audience? Which of these terms will you need to define? Which ones can be replaced by easier words or expressions that will not need to be defined?

4. Does the audience have any bias (strong feelings either for or against) toward the topic? If so, what is the bias—violently opposed, moderately opposed, or in favor?

EXERCISE 5. Analyzing a Selection. Read the following paragraphs carefully; then answer the questions that follow them.

Qin Shi Huangdi was a man in a hurry. In 221 B.C., while the king of Qin, he conquered the six other feudal states of China, becoming its first emperor and the ruler of what he and his people regarded as the civilized world. His reign lasted fifteen years, but its impact on his country cannot be exaggerated. He standardized China's written language, its monetary system, and even the width of the axles on its carts.

A ruthless and oppressive dictator, he immediately embarked on several of the most ambitious public works in ancient times. He consolidated and extended the various sections of the Great Wall. According to records from the time, he had constructed at the city of Xian a mausoleum for himself, studded with precious stones that represented the sun, the moon, and the stars. The mausoleum was so large that more than 700,000 people spent thirty-six years building it. It was ransacked shortly after his death and has not yet been excavated.

Apart from his role in construction of the Great Wall, Qin's most stunning known achievement is perhaps the massive group of vaults filled with terra-cotta bodyguards who were destined to serve their ruler in his afterlife.

1. Who would you say is the intended audience for this article?
2. What is the writer's purpose?
3. Make a list of at least five words you would have to define or replace if you were writing this information for an audience of second-graders.
4. Which of the following items do you think you would give background information about if your audience were a group of fifth-graders?
   a. Feudal states
   b. The axles on carts
   c. The Great Wall of China

EXERCISE 6. Rewriting Paragraphs for a Different Audience.
Try rewriting the three paragraphs in Exercise 5. Choose one of the

following audiences, and rewrite the paragraphs for that audience. At the beginning of your paper, identify your audience.

a. A group of aliens from a different planet
b. A group of fifth-graders
c. A group of citizens in the year 3010
d. A group of tenth-graders in a world history class

EXERCISE 7. Analyzing How Audience Affects Writing. For each numbered item, answer each of the following questions. Be prepared to discuss your answers.

a. Which audiences would have the most knowledge of the topic? Which would have the least knowledge?
b. For which audiences would technical terms need to be defined?
c. For which audiences would background information be necessary?
d. Which audiences might be biased in favor of the topic? Which against the topic?
e. Which audience would you choose to write for? Why?

1. *Topic:* How to insert new material when revising on a word processor
   Purpose: To inform
   Audiences: (a) Members of a word processing class, (b) a group of your friends, (c) members of a club called Society Against Word Processors and Personal Computers, (d) members of your high school's track team
2. *Topic:* Why people should voluntarily give up driving their cars one day each week to reduce air pollution in this city
   Purpose: To persuade
   Audiences: (a) People who drive to work every day, (b) people who take public transportation to work every day, (c) people who do not own cars, (d) a group of air-pollution experts
3. *Topic:* The first time you failed the test for a license
   Purpose: To tell a story
   Audiences: (a) A group of your friends, (b) a group of inspectors who test new drivers and decide whether to pass or fail them, (c) a group of third-graders, (d) a group of persons who have been injured in automobile accidents caused by drivers from sixteen to eighteen years of age

314 < Writing and Thinking

4. *Topic:* A painting of a mother and young child by the American artist Mary Cassatt
   Purpose: To describe
   Audiences: (a) A group of professional artists, (b) members of a high-school painting class, (c) a group of senior citizens, (d) a group of high-school mathematics teachers

CHOOSING A SUBJECT

13c. Choose a subject that is appropriate for your audience.

You can probably write about any subject for any audience if you are willing to spend the time and energy necessary to explain terms and give background information. For example, you could conceivably explain a complicated scientific theory, such as Einstein's theory of relativity, to an audience of fourth-graders. However, you would have to know your subject very well in order to simplify it enough for a young audience. Whenever possible, avoid choosing a subject that is too difficult for your audience.

Your subject should also be appropriate to the audience's interests. For instance, people who live inland and have never sailed will probably not be interested in the latest design improvements in catrigged sailboats, but the topic will have great appeal to present catboat owners. Similarly, a discussion of the goals of the Gray Panthers, a senior citizens' lobby group, may not interest an elementary-school audience, but it would be appropriate for a group of retired men and women.

EXERCISE 8. Choosing a Subject Appropriate for an Audience.
Decide whether each of the following subjects is appropriate for the intended audience. Number your paper 1–10. After the proper number, write *A* for "appropriate" or *N* for "not appropriate."

1. *Subject:* The training of Seeing Eye dogs
   Audience: Parents of blind children
2. *Subject:* Changes in income-tax laws for the current year
   Audience: Members of the high-school Drama Club
3. *Subject:* Growing vegetables without soil
   Audience: Members of a gardening club
4. *Subject:* Raising bridge and highway tolls
   Audience: Readers of a local newspaper

5. *Subject:* Latest research in heart-transplant operations
   Audience: College students interested in becoming doctors
6. *Subject:* The ten best tennis rackets, as selected by tennis pros
   Audience: Tennis team at a local high school
7. *Subject:* A discussion about Shakespearean comedy
   Audience: Class of third-graders
8. *Subject:* History of American women's fight for the right to vote
   Audience: American history class in high school
9. *Subject:* Cost-of-living increases for Social Security recipients
   Audience: Members of a junior-high English class
10. *Subject:* Sports injuries
    Audience: Members of high-school football and track teams

EXERCISE 9. Choosing Subjects for Writing.   Read the following list of broad subjects. Choose five about which you would be interested in learning more, or choose five subjects of your own.

1. Football
2. Silent movies
3. Classical music
4. Cars of the future
5. Stage fright
6. Marriage
7. Computers
8. Medical research
9. World War I
10. The Civil War
11. The stock market
12. Oceanography
13. Baseball
14. How television works
15. Raising livestock
16. Colonies in space
17. Thoroughbred horses
18. Gardening
19. Child development
20. The state legislature

CREATING TONE

13d. Identify your attitude toward your subject, which will be expressed through the tone of your writing.

Part of the task of choosing a subject involves deciding what your attitude or point of view toward that subject will be. Your attitude toward a subject may be positive (favorable) or negative (unfavorable), humorous or serious, angry or enthusiastic. An awareness of your attitude will help you to make choices about which details to include in your writing. For example, if you had a humorous attitude about learning to play golf, you would choose humorous incidents rather than serious advice from a golf pro.

Your attitude affects not only the details that you choose but also the language that you use to express your ideas. Your choice of language will help to create a *tone* that is serious or humorous, formal or informal, personal or objective.

Consider, for example, the informal tone of the following paragraph. What would you say is the writer's attitude toward her subject?

> Though Faith Ringgold, artist and activist, has traveled everywhere, she's never really left Harlem. She was born at Harlem Hospital (in 1930), grew up in the areas known as the Valley and Sugar Hill, and lives today on West 145th, in Dinah Washington's old apartment. She studied art at City College, whose nearby Gothic buildings she views affectionately from her apartment window. She and her second husband first met as kids in the neighborhood; together they brought up in Harlem, too, her own two daughters by an earlier marriage. To Mrs. Ringgold, who smiles at "a sort of backwardness" in herself that keeps her there, Harlem is a small town that radiates warmth and a sense of shelter, and its life and people loom very large in her art. So it's only fitting that this summer a local institution, the Studio Museum in Harlem, is devoting its main exhibition galleries to a Faith Ringgold retrospective, celebrating 20 years of her art (through Sept. 4).
>
> GRACE GLUECK

What would you say is the tone of the following paragraphs? What is the writer's attitude toward his subject?

> Intent and Good Faith are central ideas in law and morality. We all make mistakes, sometimes egregious,[1] often with terrible consequences. We punish ourselves inwardly, or suffer obloquy[2] from our fellows or ridicule from the public, but are not punished by the law because our intent was not malicious.
>
> The general who ordered the Union troops to assault the heights at Fredericksburg, with disastrous results, was relieved and disgraced, but not court-martialed; he erred with the intent to win.
>
> The doctor who undertakes a risk operation, the lawyer who gambles on an unorthodox defense to save his client, the businessman who bets the company on a new product, all have one great limitation on their

[1] *egregious:* outstandingly bad
[2] *obloquy:* censure

liability: If they took their chance in good faith, "if they failed while daring greatly," they may ruin themselves in the profession or the marketplace but face no further punishment in law.

WILLIAM SAFIRE

EXERCISE 10. Identifying Tone. Bring to class three examples of paragraphs from different sources, such as newspapers, magazines, books, or short stories. Identify the tone of each paragraph and the author's attitude toward the subject.

LIMITING THE SUBJECT

13e. Limit your subject so that it can be covered adequately in the form of writing you have chosen.

A *subject* is a broad, general area of knowledge, such as "music" or "car repairs." A *topic,* on the other hand, is a limited subject—one that is specific enough so that it can serve as the basis for a paragraph or a composition. "The development of the first electric guitar" and "how to change a flat tire on a car" are limited subjects, or topics.

A topic for a paragraph is necessarily more limited than a composition topic, because in a paragraph you have only a few sentences in which to develop your ideas. In a composition you have anywhere from several paragraphs to several pages, so a composition topic can be less limited than a paragraph topic. Remember, however, that your topic must be one that you can cover adequately in the length of the paper you are writing.

EXERCISE 11. Distinguishing Between Subjects and Topics. Number your paper 1–10. After the proper number, identify each item as either a broad, general subject (*S*) or a topic (*T*) that is suitably limited for a composition of a single paragraph or several paragraphs.

1. Mountains
2. The sculptured faces on Mount Rushmore, South Dakota
3. What to look for when buying a used car
4. Caring for a pet boa constrictor
5. Modern American literature

6. Major themes of *My Ántonia* by Willa Cather
7. American women in politics
8. Latest national unemployment statistics
9. Types of penalties in basketball
10. Three requirements for a good quarterback

CRITICAL THINKING:
Analyzing a Subject

A broad, general subject may be analyzed (divided and subdivided) into its smaller parts. Depending on the subject, the basis for the first set of divisions may be any of the following ones: time periods, examples, features, uses, causes, history, types.

EXAMPLES 1. *Subject divided into time periods*
         Subject: Government in Alaska
         Main divisions: As a Russian territory—before 1867
                         As a U.S. territory—from 1867 to 1959
                         Since statehood—from 1959 to present
    2. *Subject divided into examples*
       Subject: American folk heroes
       Main divisions: John Henry
                         Paul Bunyan
                         Johnny Appleseed
    3. *Subject divided into features*
       Subject: Photography
       Main divisions: History of earliest photography
                         Equipment needed to take a good photograph
                         Advice to beginning photographers
                         Famous photographers

Sometimes the first division of your subject will yield a topic that is suitably limited for the form in which you are writing. Usually, however, you will need to continue dividing and subdividing into smaller parts. The diagram on the next page shows how a writer divided the broad, general subject "photography" into more specific parts. The topics that are labeled 4 are limited enough to be covered adequately in a short composition.

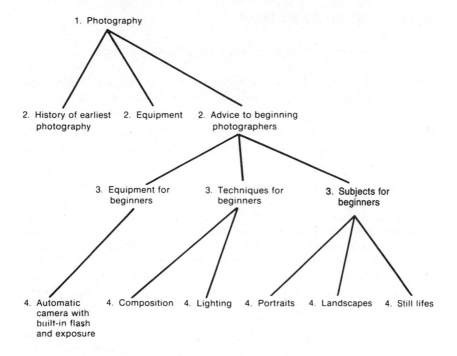

EXERCISE 12. Analyzing Subjects to Develop Topics. From the following list of subjects, choose the five that interest you most. Analyze each of these subjects by dividing it into at least three smaller parts. (*Note:* There is no single "right" way to analyze a subject. For each subject, many different analyses are possible.)

1. United Nations   6. Education   11. History of Mexico
2. Basketball   7. Holidays   12. Songs
3. Field and track events   8. Clothing   13. Airplanes
4. Cooking   9. Popularity   14. Wars
5. Careers   10. Eskimos   15. Health

EXERCISE 13. Limiting a Subject to Develop Topics Suitable for Paragraphs. Choose one of the subjects that you analyzed into smaller parts for Exercise 12. Could each of these smaller parts be covered adequately in a paragraph of seven or eight sentences? If not, continue dividing the parts until you have at least three topics that could each be covered in a paragraph. Show your analysis in the form of a diagram like the one on this page.

GATHERING INFORMATION

13f. Gather information appropriate to your writing purpose.

The kinds of details that you choose to include in your writing are largely determined by your purpose. For example, if your purpose were to describe a rock concert, you would note specific details that would help your readers picture the sights and sounds of the audience, the performers, and the stage. Notice these details in the following description of a jazz-rock concert in Tokyo, Japan.

> Some ten thousand young people had arrived promptly at six-thirty for Hino's concert, settling into the giant arena as gently as snow. The jazz-rock star was a slight, almost fragile-looking young man with a small face, which puffed out as he played his trumpet. ("Like a blowfish" was how Miyake described Hino's cheeks at full toot.) Wearing black leather pants, a samurai dagger, and a particolored wing-shoulder wetsuit-fabric jacket, Hino was holding his own against an elaborate backup band and a set with energetic lighting in which the words "Damon," "Pyramid," and "Hino" blinked, coursed, and pulsed in a ceaseless show of vivid color. "He was also a Suntory Personality," Miyake said to me, whispering, as though we were sitting at a string-quartet recital. Around us, indeed, were very few weaving heads or tapping feet; the audience seemed almost eerily calm. The lit-up words clashed brightly on in a swirl of colored-smoke effects, like Hades. In shafts of purple air, the band turned blue, Hino red, and the teetering brass cymbals magenta.
>
> KENNEDY FRASER—*THE NEW YORKER*

If your purpose is to give information, the kinds of details you would look for are specific facts, statistics, examples, and quotations. The following paragraph about firefighting in Montana contains a quotation by an expert followed by some historical facts to explain the statement made in the paragraph's last sentence.

> What is often forgotten about fires and forests is that what is natural is the fire and what is unnatural is man's attempt to stop it. "Nature is eventually going to take its course," said David Turner of the United States Forest Service. "It is a cataclysmic event for humans. But this is a dry habitat. Fire has been sweeping through this land for centuries." The flames are part of a cleansing process with real benefits, a lesson the Indians learned long ago to their hunting advantage but forest officials came late to. Now, in part due to budget restrictions, they do not rush in to fight every blaze everywhere. Some isolated fires are left to burn themselves out, naturally.
>
> ANDREW H. MALCOLM

On the following pages you will learn about many techniques for gathering information for your writing. You may use a combination of methods as you gather information for a particular writing assignment, or you may decide to use only one technique. Practice with all these techniques will help you decide which ones you find most useful and easiest to work with.

Direct and Indirect Observation

(1) Use your powers of observation to note specific details.

Whenever your observations are from firsthand experiences (through your senses of sight, smell, sound, taste, and touch), they are called *direct observations*. From the following paragraph, you can tell that Roger Angell observed the scene carefully. He observed specific details about the scene, a baseball cap, a baseball player's gestures and movements, and the sound of the audience's applause.

> Carl Yastrzemski, encircled for the last time by the Fenway Park multitudes, stood at a microphone in the first-base coaching box before the game and waved his cap to the crowd. He turned slowly to face the left-field stands, the cap held high, with the green of the underside of its bill showing, and then slowly back in the other direction, toward right field, and then to face out toward the bleachers, and the waves of clapping and cheers seemed to move and swirl around him, almost visible in the damp afternoon air. He gestured toward the home dugout, and his teammates came up and out onto the field, in their white uniforms and shiny dark warmup jackets, to surround him and shake his hand, and he and Jim Rice embraced; then the Red Sox pitchers and catchers and coaches left the bullpen and came walking and running across the grass to join him and be near him. The cheering rose again (it went on all afternoon, really), and Yaz approached the microphone with a piece of paper in his hand. "Thank you very much," he said, but then he stopped and walked a little distance out onto the diamond and waved his hand, with his head down. He was crying.
>
> ROGER ANGELL—*THE NEW YORKER*

If your observations are not made directly through your senses, they are called *indirect observations*. When you listen to someone else's experiences or read about them, you are making an indirect observation. For example, Roger Angell wrote about his direct observations at Fenway Park in the model paragraph above; for you, the reader, these are indirect observations.

CRITICAL THINKING:
Observing Specific Details

Observing involves carefully noting the specific details that make up an experience. Obviously, you cannot possibly notice everything all at once, but you can work toward improving your powers of observation. Concentrate on paying attention to as many specific details as possible.

EXERCISE 14. Testing Your Powers of Observation.   Answer each of the following questions from memory.

1. Whose face is on the United States quarter? The penny? The five-dollar bill?
2. Is the name of your school displayed anywhere outside the school? If so, where?
3. What is the number on the uniform of your favorite baseball (or football) player?
4. How tall is your best friend? How much does he or she weigh?
5. What color stripe is at the top of the American flag? What color stripe is at the bottom?
6. On an AM radio dial, what number is the smallest number shown (all the way to the left-hand side)? What is the largest number?
7. What does a fire hydrant in your community look like? Draw one.
8. Draw a picture of a stop sign. What color is it?
9. How many windows are there in your home?
10. On a traffic signal, what color light is at the top? At the bottom?

A Writer's Journal

(2) Keep a writer's journal to record your thoughts and feelings about your experiences.

A writer's journal is useful in two ways: It can be a source of ideas for writing topics, and it can help you to recall specific details about an experience. In your journal you can write about your ideas and your experiences as well as your reactions to other people and to events. You may include in your journal opinions about music, movies, books, and TV shows; you may also include quotations or sayings that you like. Your writer's journal should contain only ideas, experiences, and feelings that you want to share with others. You might consider also keeping a private journal for your personal use.

EXERCISE 15. Using a Journal Entry to Gather Ideas for Writing.
Read the following journal entry; then answer the questions that follow it.

> Sunday—October 5
>
> Went on a three-hour canoe trip on the Fox River yesterday with Lynette and her dad. We drove in two cars. First, Lynette's dad put the canoe in (it's called "put in") at Lookout Park. He lifted the canoe all by himself from the car's top. Then he parked his car seven miles downstream, and we all drove back to the park in Lynette's car. Lynette's dad steered the canoe by paddling in back. Lynette in front—I was in the middle. We paddled slowly; sometimes we just drifted. Bright, sunny day. Smell of cool, fall leaf mold. Very quiet—no birds, no wildlife, no other river traffic. Part through densely overgrown river banks. When we got to where his car was parked, Lynette's dad hauled the canoe up and put it back on top of his car. He's been a Boy Scout leader for forty years and is one of a group that goes canoeing and birding before dawn every other week. He knows a lot about birds of north-central Illinois. Unfortunately, he didn't warn me about poison ivy on the river bank, and I have an awful case on my ankles and legs.

1. On the basis of this journal entry, the writer decided she could write a narrative essay about the canoe trip. Reread the entry and think of at least two other topics, suggested by the entry, that she might write about. List as many topic ideas as you can think of.
2. Think of at least three questions you could ask Lynette's dad about one of the topics you listed in question 1. Write as many questions as you can think of.

Brainstorming and Clustering

(3) Use brainstorming and clustering to find writing ideas.

Both brainstorming and clustering are techniques used to generate a free flow. You may use these techniques to think of topics for writing or to generate specific details to develop a topic you have already chosen.

When you *brainstorm,* you concentrate on a particular subject or topic and write down every idea, word, and phrase that comes to mind. At the top of a blank piece of paper, write the subject or topic that you are going to begin with, and list under it whatever ideas come to mind. Work as quickly as possible, jotting down every idea that occurs to you. Keep going until you run out of ideas.

As you brainstorm, do not stop to judge or evaluate the ideas that you are listing; your purpose is simply to write down all the ideas you can think of. Only when you have finished brainstorming should you stop to evaluate the material you have listed. If you started with a subject, decide which of the items on your list might be usable topics for writing, and circle them. If you started with a limited topic, decide which specific details might be useful in developing the topic, and circle them. These circled topics or details may help you to think of other ideas to add to your list.

Here is a list of brainstorming notes on the subject of the composition of portrait photographs taken outdoors during the summer. The parenthetical notes show the writer's evaluation of the ideas after the list was complete.

composition (arrangement of the elements within a photograph)
three main things to consider
brightest part of photograph (center of light; eyes drawn to center of light)
lines that draw the eye into a photograph (leading lines)
outdoor portrait photos during the summer
examples of good photos (Franny at beach; Lou in sleeping bag)
bad photos (faces shaded; too dark or too bright—but why?)
balance in photograph
rule of thirds (diagram photo as framed in viewfinder into thirds)
type of camera

Clustering (or, as it is sometimes called, *making connections*) is similar to brainstorming. Unlike brainstorming, however, clustering groups related ideas in the form of a diagram instead of a list. Begin by writing a subject or a limited topic in the center of a piece of paper, and draw a circle around it. Think about the circled item, and write around it whatever related ideas come to mind. As you add each new idea, circle it and draw a line connecting it either to the subject in the center or to a related idea already on the paper. Continue to write whatever new ideas occur to you, circling them and drawing lines to connect them to ideas already on your paper.

Here is a clustering diagram for the same subject, "composition of portrait photographs taken outdoors during summer."

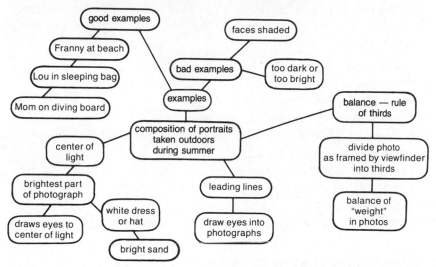

EXERCISE 16. Using Brainstorming or Clustering to Gather Information. Choose one of the topics you developed in Exercise 13 on page 319, or choose another limited topic. In this exercise you will generate specific ideas and information to develop the limited topic. Use either brainstorming or clustering to gather information about the topic you have chosen.

Asking the 5 *W-How?* Questions

(4) Gather information and ideas by asking the *5 W-How?* questions.

Asking the basic *Who? When? Where? What? Why?* and *How?* questions can help you to gather specific details to use in your writing. Not every question will apply to every topic.

EXAMPLE *Topic:* What the Olympic Games were like
        Who? Who participated in the original Olympic Games?
        What? What events were included in the original Olympic Games?
        Where? Where were they held?
        When? When were the first Olympic Games held?
        Why? Why were they held?
        How? How were the events different from events today?

EXERCISE 17. Gathering Information by Asking the 5 W-How? Questions. Use the *5 W-How?* questions (*Who? When? Where? What? Why? How?*) to gather information about one of the following topics or a topic of your own. Write the questions that you ask as well as the answers to the questions. (You may need to do some research to find the answers.) Some of the *5 W-How?* questions may not apply to the topic you have chosen.

1. Required insurance for drivers in your state
2. History of basketball
3. An ideal holiday meal
4. Early life of an American hero or heroine
5. Pros and cons of a national seventy-mile-per-hour speed limit
6. Design for a space station
7. Why I would (or would not) volunteer to live in a space colony
8. My earliest memory
9. Something I would like to change if I could
10. A proposal for solving a specific community problem

Asking Point-of-View Questions

(5) Gather information and ideas by viewing the subject from different points of view.

Another questioning technique for gathering information about your topic requires that you consider the topic from different points of view. Three basic questions (What is it? How does it change or vary? What are its relationships?) allow you to ask many additional questions, which will help you to generate information and specific details.[1]

1. *What is it?*
    In this first point of view, you will focus on the topic itself. If your topic is a place, person, or object, you may ask questions that will elicit information about what the topic looks like, what it does, and how it is different from others of its kind.

EXAMPLE   *Topic:* How to prepare a résumé [What is a résumé? What is it used for? What does it look like? What information should it contain? How should the information be organized?]

---

[1] This technique is based on ideas in *Rhetoric: Discovery and Change* by Richard E. Young, Alton L. Becker, and Kenneth E. Pike (New York: Harcourt Brace Jovanovich, 1971).

The *What is it?* question can be useful even when your topic is an abstract idea. This question will help you define your topic and understand how it is different from other, similar ideas or topics.

2. *How does it change or vary?*

The second point-of-view approach helps you to focus on how a topic changes over a period of time. Such questions help bring out information about the topic's history and about its future.

EXAMPLE *Topic:* Types of phonograph records [What were the first phonograph records like? When were they made? What are 78-rpm and 45-rpm records? What other ways are there of recording sound? What are compact disc (CD) recordings? What will records be like ten years from now? A hundred years from now?]

From this point of view, you also consider how the topic keeps its identity even while it varies. The following example poses questions about the characteristics of abstract painting. What do the thousands of paintings that are very different from each other have in common that allows critics to classify them as abstract painting?

EXAMPLE *Topic:* Characteristics of abstract painting [What are the characteristics of abstract painting? What is the difference between abstract painting and expressionist painting? What, if anything, do they have in common? Who are some famous abstract painters? What do they have in common? How do they differ? What are some examples of abstract painting?]

3. *What are its relationships?*

For the third point of view, you focus on how the topic's various parts, or aspects, are related to each other and to the topic as a whole. (Note that this approach is similar to the critical thinking skill of analysis: breaking a whole into its parts and seeing how the parts are related.)

EXAMPLE *Topic:* The story behind a successful Drama Club presentation [What jobs are necessary for producing a student play? What are the responsibilities of each type of job? Which jobs are most important, or are they all equally important?]

When you consider the topic from this point of view, you may also consider how the topic is related to other, similar topics.

EXAMPLE   *Topic:* A movie that you think is terrible [What type of movie is it: comedy, drama, historical drama, movie with a message, movie about a real person, etc.? How is it different from good movies of the same type? What makes this movie worse than others of the same type?]

EXERCISE 18. Gathering Information by Asking Point-of-View Questions.

Using the three different point-of-view questions (What is it? How does it change or vary? What are its relationships?), ask questions that will help you gather information about two of the following topics. In addition to your answers, write all the questions you think of.

1. A specific sports team (high-school, college, or professional)
2. A specific place or neighborhood
3. A government body (student council, city council, state legislature, etc.)
4. A specific animal or species of animal
5. A character in a play
6. A specific car
7. A person whom you know well
8. A specific house or apartment building
9. A type of hobby
10. A type of job

CLASSIFYING INFORMATION

13g. Classify your ideas and information by grouping related ideas.

The next step in the writing process is to classify, or group, the ideas you have gathered. In effect, grouping related items will result in an informal outline of your topic.

CRITICAL THINKING:
Classifying Ideas

When you *classify,* you identify details that are similar in some way, and you group similar items under a heading that explains what they have in common. For example, what do the following details have in common?

EXAMPLE   Discounts at some movie theaters
Discounts on airlines
No fees at some banks for checking accounts
In some communities, eligibility for free classes at colleges
Reduced fares on public transportation
Eligibility for Medicare

You probably guessed that what these details have in common is that they are all advantages that senior citizens can enjoy. They may be grouped under the heading "Advantages for Senior Citizens."

Of course, it is a more difficult task to "see" several possible headings or groupings when you look at a jumbled list of details or notes. The following questions will help you to classify ideas and information.

1. Among the items listed, are there any that can be grouped under a larger heading? What do the items have in common?

2. Do some of the items seem more important than others? Which are the most important (or main) ideas?

3. Which items seem to be subdivisions (examples, parts, etc.) of the main ideas? If you have not listed any of these subdivisions for your main ideas, what do you think they might be?

Remember that the basic task of classifying is to group related ideas. Do not hesitate to discard, at this point in the writing process, items that do not seem to fit into any of your groups or headings.

EXERCISE 19. Classifying Ideas and Information. Use the following four main headings to classify the items and information on the following list. (*Note:* One item will not fit under any of the main headings.)

Expedition to Ocean's Bottom
Discovery of Exotic Species of Life
Location of Discovery
Water Temperature

Redheaded worms discovered—up to 5 feet long
Water measured at 293° Centigrade
Deep-sea dive in submarine *Alvin*
Photosynthesis—process that lets plants use energy from sunlight
Water heated by vents miles below water's surface; vents lead to
    molten rock beneath ocean floor

Part of gigantic undersea mountain ridge
4,000-foot crater of axial volcano, underwater
Unusual species of clams discovered
Alvin holds three scientists: oceanographers (scientists who study the ocean) and geophysicist (scientist who studies the physics of the earth and ocean)
These animals feed on poisonous chemicals (sulfur compounds) in ultrahot water in deep ocean

EXERCISE 20. Classifying Ideas and Information. Look carefully at the following list of ideas for a composition on how to study for a test. First, decide which ideas can be grouped because they are related. Then decide on the main headings that will show what the ideas have in common. (*Note:* The headings are not included in this list.) On a separate sheet of paper, write the ideas you have grouped under their main headings. You may discard any items that do not seem to fit.

Memorize dates, formulas—whatever needs to be memorized
Last math test I got 79
Spend enough time
Find a quiet place with good lighting
Charts and diagrams
Notes from classes
Restate in your own words most important ideas covered
Chapters in textbook
Define important terms and symbols
Final exam in English next Tuesday
No TV or radio

ARRANGING INFORMATION

13h. Arrange your ideas in order.

Once you have classified your ideas under main headings, consider what is the best order in which to present these ideas to your readers. Often the order will be suggested by your purpose. For example, if you are explaining how to stir-fry vegetables in a wok, you will probably follow chronological (time) order, in which you describe each step in the order it should occur. If, however, you are trying to persuade your readers to sign a petition for more after-school activities, you will probably arrange your ideas in the order of importance—with the most important reason last.

Sometimes background information is necessary so that the reader can understand the ideas you wish to present. Background information along with terms that need to be defined should be presented first. If your purpose or the ideas themselves do not suggest an order, arrange your ideas in the order that you think will be clearest and most interesting for your audience. (You will learn more about different types of order in Chapter 14.)

REVIEW EXERCISE A. Following the Steps for Prewriting. Prepare to write a paragraph on a topic of your choice. (If you wish, you may use any of the topics that you have not already worked with in this chapter.) Choose a subject, and limit it to a topic that can be covered adequately in a single paragraph. Decide on your purpose and your audience. Using at least one of the techniques for gathering information, make a list of specific details to include in your paragraph. Classify the details into related groups, and make up the main headings. Decide how to arrange the information in an appropriate order.

WRITING A FIRST DRAFT

All of the many prewriting activities you have practiced so far in this chapter have taken you, finally, to the point where you are ready to begin writing the first draft. This second stage in the writing process is sometimes called *drafting*.

Writing a First Draft

13i. Write a first draft, keeping your audience and purpose in mind.

Remember that a first draft is not the final version of your writing. You will revise your first draft several times, making changes in both content and wording. You will also spend time proofreading your revised version to correct mechanical errors in usage, punctuation, and spelling.

As you write, keep in front of you the list of details that you have classified and arranged. Try to express your ideas as clearly as possible, and remember to choose specific details and language that are appropriate both for your audience and your purpose.

CRITICAL THINKING:
Synthesis

Synthesis is the putting together of separate parts, or elements, to create a new whole. The word *synthesis* comes from two Greek words that mean "to place together." All writing is a kind of synthesis, for writers put words and ideas together in new ways to create letters, paragraphs, compositions, poems, stories, and plays.

As you write your first draft, you will be rethinking all your earlier decisions about content and organization. Perhaps you will decide that a term you earlier thought would be clear to your audience needs to be defined and explained. Occasionally you may change the order in which you decided to present your ideas. You may make whatever changes seem appropriate to you, even while you are shaping each sentence in the first draft.

EXERCISE 21. Analyzing a First Draft. Read this first draft, and answer the questions that follow it.

One day more than thirty years ago, two cardiologists, Dr. Meyer Friedman and Dr. Ray Rosenbaum, in San Francisco noticed something strange about the chairs in their waiting room. Some of the chairs the patients sat in had fabric that was being worn out. The doctors wondered if perhaps this had something to do with the nervous, hurry-up, take-charge personality traits associated with Type A personalities. They decided to do a study to see if the behavior patterns of Type A patients could be changed and if such changes in behavior would decrease the chance of a second heart attack.

Dr. Friedman studied more than eight hundred men who had had heart attacks. Some of them went to group counseling meetings to learn how to stop being competitive, aggressive, and hurried. They actually learned to change their personalities and to calm down. They also watched themselves on videotape and saw how nervous they were. Dr. Friedman also had a control group, and he compared the results of the two groups. After three years, 79 percent of those who had gone for group counseling had changed their Type A behavior and had become more calm and relaxed. Only 9 percent of this group had a second heart attack. In the control group, after three years only 49 percent had changed their behavior, and 19 percent had suffered coronaries. Both groups were given advice on diet and the importance of exercise.

1. What would you say is the writer's purpose?
2. Who do you think is the intended audience for these paragraphs? How can you tell?
3. Which of the following words or terms do you think need to be defined or explained?

   a. cardiologists   c. group counseling   e. aggressive
   b. Type A personalities   d. control group   f. coronaries
4. Suppose the audience for these paragraphs is a group of third-grade science students. How appropriate for the audience is the writing? What would need to be changed? Now suppose that the audience for these paragraphs is a group of cardiologists. How appropriate is the writing for this audience? What needs to be changed or added?
5. What is the topic of this first draft? Is the topic limited enough for two paragraphs?
6. The writer did not summarize the results of Dr. Friedman's study. Would a sentence be sufficient to summarize the results, or would a concluding paragraph be needed? Write your concluding sentence or paragraph.
7. If you could ask Dr. Friedman two questions about this study, what questions would you ask? Write the questions.
8. What is the tone of these paragraphs? Is the tone appropriate for the writer's apparent audience and purpose?
9. The writer considered adding this sentence: "Each of the guys in the study worked hard to learn how to goof off instead of being up-tight all the time." What is wrong with this sentence? Rewrite the sentence so that it is appropriate for the paragraphs. Where would you place this sentence?
10. There are two basic personality groups, Type A and Type B personalities. On the basis of what you have learned in these paragraphs, what traits would you guess are associated with Type B personalities? Which group would you guess is more prone to having heart attacks?

EXERCISE 22. Writing a First Draft. Using the prewriting notes you developed for Review Exercise A (page 331), write a first draft of a paragraph. Refer to the Guidelines for Writing and Revising Paragraphs (page 381) for some extra help before you begin writing.

REVISING

Many writers actually do some revising as they write the first draft. They may, for example, substitute precise words for vague ones, change sentence beginnings, or cross out entire sentences. Even if you do make changes as you write, you will still need to spend considerable time revising. Reread your first draft many times, concentrating on how to improve it.

REVISING YOUR FIRST DRAFT

13j. Revise your first draft.

Revising requires several rereadings of the first draft. First, consider each sentence in relation to the paragraph and to the writing as a whole. For a composition, you will need to judge how effectively each paragraph contributes to the total work. In all of these cases, the major questions to ask are these: Is the main idea adequately developed or supported? Is the development or support clear and logical? Next, look closely at each sentence to see how well it expresses what you intended to say. Finally, concentrate on each word in each sentence. Which words, if any, are unnecessary and should therefore be deleted? Which words need to be more precise?

An important part of the revising process is rethinking your writing once more in terms of purpose, audience, and tone. Remember that purpose, audience, and tone affect both the content of your writing and the language you use.

At some point during the revising stage, many teachers ask students to exchange papers and comment on each other's first drafts. The purpose of responding to a classmate's writing is to make helpful suggestions, such as pointing out ideas that are not developed fully. If you are asked to respond to another writer's paper, be honest but tactful in your comments. A writer should not be so discouraged by others' negative comments that he or she sees no way to make a paper better. One good technique for commenting on another person's paper is to mention a strength for every weakness that you cite.

You can use the Guidelines for Revising on pages 336–37 of this chapter with almost any form of writing. On page 341 you will find a set of revising and proofreading symbols that will help you make changes on your first draft. As your teacher directs, copy the Guidelines for Revising and the Revising and Proofreading Symbols into your notebook, and use them whenever you revise your own work.

You will learn more about revising in the chapters on paragraphs and compositions. Detailed guidelines are provided for each form of writing (paragraph, composition, letter) and each kind of writing (expository, descriptive, narrative, and persuasive).

CRITICAL THINKING:
Evaluating Words and Ideas

The critical thinking skill that you use when you revise is called *evaluating,* or judging. To be well grounded, such judgments should be made on the basis of carefully developed *criteria,* or standards. Throughout the composition chapters of this book, you will find guidelines that express the criteria for the specific forms and kinds of writing. (See page 420, for example, for Guidelines for Writing and Revising Narrative Paragraphs.)

EXERCISE 23. Analyzing a Writer's Revisions. In revising the following paragraph, the writer used the Guidelines for Writing and Revising Expository Paragraphs on pages 412–13. Read the paragraph, noting the changes made by the writer (the changes are in handwriting). Then, using the guidelines on pages 336–37 and 412–13, answer the questions that follow the paragraph.

We owe the idea of standard time to the nation's railroad companies.
In the good old days before November 18, 1883, passengers traveling from Maine to California on a railroad train had to set their watches back and forth almost a hundred times. *Because* Almost every city and state ran on *a* different local time*s.* Not only that. To make things *even* more confusing, every railroad clock was a little bit different*;* Clocks were not *yet* synchronized.

~~Railroads got together and somebody had a very bright idea.~~ Railroad
on November 18, 1883,
company executives created the idea of "standard time" ∧ and divided the

United States into four time zones ∧ ~~Today we have~~ Eastern ∧ ~~Time;~~ Central ∧
Pacific
~~Time, Rock;~~ Mountain ∧ ~~Time,~~ and ∧ ~~one other time zone—I forget which.~~
also
They ∧ synchronized the clocks in all of the railroad stations ∧ Within each
station's   *so that*
time zone every railroad ∧ clock showed the same time. This ∧ helped ~~them~~
run   efficiently, but also allowed
~~to run~~ the railroads ∧ more ∧ ~~better and to allow~~ passengers to follow exact
timetables.   *which*
railroad ∧ ~~schedules.~~ Congress passed the Standard Time Act of 1918 ∧ ~~This~~
zones
made the railroad time ~~changes~~ official for the whole country.

1. What do you think is the writer's purpose?
2. Who do you think is the writer's audience?
3. What is the writer's main idea? Is it adequately and clearly developed?
4. The writer crossed out two sentences in revising the paragraph. Why were the two sentences omitted?
5. What specific information did the writer add to the revision?
6. Find three examples of sentences the writer combined to make the paragraph read more smoothly.

EXERCISE 24. Revising a First Draft. Revise the first draft in Exercise 21 for an audience of high-school students. Use the Guidelines for Revising on this page and the next as you consider each word and each sentence. Reread your draft several times as you revise it.

REVIEW EXERCISE B. Revising a First Draft. Revise the first draft that you wrote in Exercise 22, or revise another composition.

GUIDELINES FOR REVISING

Content

1. Is the content suited to the purpose and audience? Are unfamiliar terms explained and background information supplied when necessary? (pages 306–312)

2. Is the subject appropriate for the audience? Does the writer know more about the subject than the audience? Is the writer's tone appropriate to the topic and the purpose? (pages 314–16)

3. Is the subject suitably limited for the form? (pages 317–19)

4. Is the topic adequately developed with information and ideas suitable for the purpose and form? (pages 320–28)

5. Are the ideas clearly organized?

6. Have all ideas that do not directly relate to the main idea been omitted?

Word Choice and Sentence Structure

1. Does the writing contain precise, specific words rather than vague words? (pages 630–32)

2. Does the writing contain no unnecessary words? (page 643)

3. Are the ideas smoothly joined with transitional words and phrases? (pages 365–67)

4. Do sentence beginnings vary, as appropriate to meaning? (pages 291–95)

5. Do sentence structures and lengths vary, as appropriate to meaning? (pages 279–89 and 297–99)

PROOFREADING

When you are satisfied that your revision is as good as you can make it, you turn to the next stage in the writing process: *proofreading*. In this stage you look for and correct inaccuracies in grammar, usage, and mechanics (spelling, capitalization, and punctuation).

PROOFREADING YOUR WRITING

13k. Proofread your revised version.

If possible, let some time elapse before you proofread your revised version. When you see it again after a short time, you will view it more objectively and will be more likely to spot inaccuracies. One technique that will help you to focus on each word and mark of punctuation separately is to cover all of your paper below the line you are proofreading with a plain sheet of paper. When you finish proofreading a line, lower the cover sheet one more line. This method keeps you from reading ahead and overlooking inaccuracies.

CRITICAL THINKING:
Applying the Standards of Written English

The purpose of proofreading is to apply the standards of written English to your writing. These standards, sometimes called *conventions,* are the rules of written English that are generally used in books, magazines, and newspapers. The main reason for applying these standards is to prevent your reader from being confused about what you mean or distracted by inaccuracies. The Guidelines for Proofreading on page 339 summarize the standards of written English, which are explained in greater detail in Parts 1, 2, 5, and 6 of this book. Refer to those parts whenever you are not sure whether you have applied the standards of written English correctly.

EXERCISE 25. Applying the Standards of Written English. Each of the following sentences has an error in grammar, usage, or mechanics. Rewrite each sentence, correcting the error. If you cannot correct an error, follow the instructions in parentheses, using the index of this book to find the explanation of the standard. Then make the correction.

1. Each of the topics have been limited adequately. (See the rule on subject-verb agreement with indefinite pronouns.)
2. The young woman, who is standing next to Maria, has just moved to Dallas from New York City. (See the rule on punctuating restrictive adjective clauses.)
3. Just between you and I, Lisa is a better tennis player than he. (See the rule on using the objective case of pronouns for the object of a preposition.)
4. When does the Book Fair exhibit open. (See the rule for punctuating questions.)
5. If you are going to the concert on Saturday night next week. (See the rule about sentence fragments.)
6. First, think about the answers that seem possible, then choose the best one. (See the rule about run-ons.)
7. She had never before swam in an icy mountain lake. (See the rule on forming the past participle of an irregular verb.)
8. I'm real glad that you called. (See the rule on using adjectives and adverbs correctly.)

9. Fred has laid in the sun all morning and is badly sunburned. (See the rule for the correct use of *lie* and *lay*.)

10. Meet me at the Commercial bank building on Thirty-eighth Street. (See the rule for capitalizing names of specific buildings.)

EXERCISE 26. Proofreading a Revised Draft.   Proofread the draft you revised for Review Exercise B (page 336) or another paper you have revised. The Guidelines for Proofreading follow.

GUIDELINES FOR PROOFREADING

1. Is every sentence a complete sentence? (pages 269–78)

2. Does every sentence end with a punctuation mark? Are other punctuation marks used correctly? (pages 675–755)

3. Does every sentence begin with a capital letter? Are all proper nouns and appropriate proper adjectives capitalized? (pages 655–74)

4. Does every verb agree in number with its subject? (pages 143–59)

5. Are verb forms and tenses used correctly? (pages 192–219)

6. Are personal pronouns used correctly? (pages 168–91)

7. Does every pronoun agree with its antecedent in number and in gender? Are pronoun references clear? (pages 159–61)

8. Are frequently confused words (such as *lie* and *lay, fewer* and *less*) used correctly? (pages 241–65)

9. Are all words spelled correctly? Have spellings been checked in a dictionary? (pages 821–43)

10. Is the paper neat and free from obvious crossed-out words and erasures? (page 340)

WRITING THE FINAL VERSION

CORRECT MANUSCRIPT FORM

13l. Write the final version, following correct manuscript form.

The last step in the writing process is to prepare a clean copy of your carefully revised and proofread draft. There is no single correct way to prepare a manuscript, but the following standards are widely used and accepted.

1. Use lined composition paper or, if you type, white $8\frac{1}{2} \times$ 11-inch paper.

2. Write on only one side of a sheet of paper.

3. Write in blue, black, or blue-black ink, or typewrite. If you type, double-space the lines.

4. Leave a margin of about two inches at the top of a page and margins of about one inch at the sides and the bottom. The left-hand margin must be straight; the right-hand margin should be as straight as possible.

5. Indent the first line of each paragraph about one-half inch from the left margin.

6. Follow your teacher's instructions for placing your name, the class, the date, and the title on the manuscript.

7. If the paper is more than one page long, number the pages after the first one. Place the number in the upper right-hand corner, about one-half inch from the top.

8. Write legibly and neatly. If you are using unlined paper, try to keep the lines straight. Form your letters carefully, so that *n*'s do not look like *u*'s, *a*'s like *o*'s, and so on. Dot the *i*'s and cross the *t*'s. If you are typing, do not strike over letters or cross out words. If you have to erase, do it neatly.

9. Before handing in your final version, proofread it carefully to make certain that your recopying has been accurate.

EXERCISE 27. Writing the Final Version. Write the final version of the paper you proofread for Exercise 26. Use the rules for correct manuscript form or rules your teacher provides. Be sure to proofread this version carefully before you hand it in.

CHAPTER 13 WRITING REVIEW

Practicing the Writing Process. As directed by your teacher, write a paragraph on a topic of your choice. Complete each of the parts of the prewriting stage. Write a first draft. After you have written your first draft, let it sit for at least a few hours, preferably a whole day. Then look at the first draft carefully to see how you can improve it. As you revise the paragraph, keep your audience and purpose in mind. Consider how clearly the ideas are expressed and whether or not the sentences read smoothly. For help in revising the first draft, refer to the Guidelines for Revising on pages 336–37. Proofread your revised version before you prepare a final copy, using the Guidelines for Proofreading on page 339. Be sure to proofread the final copy once again before turning it in.

REVISING AND PROOFREADING SYMBOLS

Symbol	Example	Meaning of Symbol
≡	Maple High school	Capitalize a lower-case letter.
/	the First person	Lower-case a capital letter.
∧	the first May	Insert a missing word, letter, or punctuation mark.
∧	seperate	Change a letter.
ℓ	Tell me the the plan.	Leave out a word, letter, or punctuation mark.
⌒	an unusual idea	Leave out and close up.
◡	a water fall	Close up space.
∽	recieve	Change the order of the letters.
tr.	the last Saturday of September in the month	Transfer the circled words. (Write tr. in nearby margin.)
¶	¶"Help!" someone cried.	Begin a new paragraph.
⊙	Please don't go	Add a period.
⋏	Well what's new?	Add a comma.
#	birdcage	Add a space.
⨀	the following ideas	Add a colon.
⋏⁒	Houston, Texas; St. Louis, Missouri and Albany, New York	Add a semicolon.
=	two teenagers	Add a hyphen.
∨	Sallys new job	Add an apostrophe.
stet	An extremely urgent message	Keep the crossed-out material. (Write stet in nearby margin.)

CHAPTER 14

Writing Paragraphs

STRUCTURE OF PARAGRAPHS

A paragraph is a physical division of a composition, marking a stage in the writer's thought. It is possible for a reader to struggle through a long piece of writing not divided into paragraphs, just as it is possible for a motorist to drive over unmarked roads to a destination. But like the motorist, the reader hopes to find an occasional signpost pointing the way. In a composition of several paragraphs, the indentation, or spacing, that marks the beginning of a paragraph is a signpost that signals a change in the direction of the writer's thought—a new idea; a change in place, time, or situation; a slightly different point of view.

Paragraphs differ in length, content, and organization, but it is possible to form an idea of the kind of average paragraph that you will be asked to write in school assignments. It is likely to be from 100 to 150 words long, to consist of a general statement supported by specific statements, and to have a single unifying idea. This chapter provides you with instructions, examples, and practice to help you master the writing of an effective paragraph. The work is important preparation for Chapters 16, 17, 18, 19, and 20, which deal with writing compositions of many paragraphs.

14a. A paragraph is a series of sentences that develop one main idea about a topic.

A paragraph is a unit of thought that focuses on one main idea. In the following paragraph by Dr. Martin Luther King, Jr., which sentence states the paragraph's main idea that violence is both impractical and immoral? How do the other sentences develop that idea?

> Violence as a way of achieving racial justice is both impractical and immoral. It is impractical because it is a descending spiral ending in destruction for all. The old law of an eye for an eye leaves everybody blind. It is immoral because it seeks to humiliate the opponent rather than win his understanding; it seeks to annihilate rather than to convert. Violence is immoral because it thrives on hatred rather than love. It destroys community and makes brotherhood impossible. It leaves society in monologue rather than dialogue. Violence ends by defeating itself. It creates bitterness in the survivors and brutality in the destroyers. A voice echoes through time saying to every potential Peter, "Put up your sword." History is cluttered with the wreckage of nations that failed to follow this command.   MARTIN LUTHER KING, JR.

In this paragraph, after stating the main idea in the first sentence, the writer supports the idea by stating reasons for the impracticality and immorality of violence. The paragraph (from a longer article on nonviolent resistance) makes a forceful, unified plea against violence.

PREWRITING

THE TOPIC SENTENCE

14b. The sentence that states the one main idea of a paragraph is called the topic sentence.

Most paragraphs, like the one written by Dr. Martin Luther King, Jr., have a general statement, or *topic sentence,* giving the main idea. (Descriptive paragraphs and paragraphs in stories often do not have a topic sentence, but they are a special case.) The topic sentence usually comes at the beginning of the paragraph, so that the reader can immediately tell exactly what the paragraph is about. Notice that the topic sentence comes at the beginning of the model paragraph above. Putting the topic sentence at the beginning can be a help to the writer, too, since a clear statement of an idea at the outset can prevent the writer from wandering from the subject.

Occasionally the topic sentence appears in the middle of the paragraph, and sometimes it comes at the end. Coming at the end, the topic sentence often serves as the climax to the series of details that lead up to it. It is a conclusion based on the evidence presented in the paragraph.

Read the following paragraphs, noting the topic sentences in bold-faced type.

> CRIPPLEHORSE CREEK, Mont.—With the slow brightening of the sky in the east shortly after 4 A.M., the ragged hulks of the mountains, some still carrying snow, start to take on shape. Gradually, the black mountainsides turn green as the sun touches thousands of towering pines with more and more light. The shape of the forest emerges to roll on as far as the eye can see in this isolated northwest corner of Montana. **Dawn has come that way to many of these trees more than 30,000 times in the near century since they were seedlings.**
>
> ANDREW MALCOLM

> The fourteenth century opened with a series of famines brought on when population growth outstripped the techniques of food production. The precarious balance was tipped by a series of heavy rains and floods and by a chilling of the climate in what has been called the Little Ice Age. Upon a people thus weakened fell the century's central disaster, the Black Death, an eruption of bubonic plague which swept the known world in the years 1347–1349 and carried off an estimated one-third of the population in two and a half years. **This makes it the most lethal episode known to history, which is of some interest to an age equipped with the tools of overkill.**
>
> BARBARA TUCHMAN

Topic and Restriction Sentences

Sometimes a paragraph's main idea is not completely stated in a single sentence. Instead, two sentences work together to reveal the paragraph's central idea. The first sentence announces or introduces the paragraph's topic, and the next sentence restricts or further limits that topic by telling what particular aspect of the topic the paragraph will be about. These two sentences are called *topic* and *restriction* sentences.

EXAMPLE [Topic] Calligraphy is the art of decorative handwriting.
[Restriction] In recent years it has become an extremely popular hobby. [The paragraph goes on to discuss the popularity of calligraphy.]

EXAMPLE [Topic] Communicating about feelings is quite difficult for many people. [Restriction] Yet without such communication, there is little hope of two people gaining real understanding and knowledge of each other. [The paragraph goes on to discuss the reasons why communicating about feelings is essential to understanding and knowledge.]

In the following paragraph, notice that the first two sentences work together to state the paragraph's central idea.

[Topic] *This farm, which was situated two miles west of the village, immediately won our love.* [Restriction] *It was a glorious place for boys.* Broad-armed white oaks stood about the yard, and to the east and north a deep forest invited exploration. The house was of logs and for that reason was much more attractive to us than to our mother. It was, I suspect, both dark and cold. I know the roof was poor, for one morning I awoke to find a miniature peak of snow at my bedside. It was only a rude little frontier cabin, but it was perfectly satisfactory to me.

EXERCISE 1. Identifying Topic Sentences.
Identify the topic sentence or topic and restriction sentences in each of the following paragraphs.

1. Morrisonville had not developed the modern disgust with death. It was not treated as an obscenity to be confined in hospitals and "funeral homes." In Morrisonville death was a common part of life. It came for the young as relentlessly as it came for the old. To die antiseptically in a hospital was almost unknown. In Morrisonville death still made house calls. It stopped by the bedside, sat down on the couch right by the parlor window, walked up to people in the fields in broad daylight, surprised them at a bend in the stairway when they were on their way to bed.

   RUSSELL BAKER

2. People who say they do not want to pick flowers and have them indoors (the idea being, I suppose, that they are more "natural" in the garden than in the house) don't realize that indoors one can really look at a single flower, undistracted, and that this meditation brings great rewards. The flowers on my desk have been lit up one by one as by a spotlight as the sun slowly moves. And once more I am in a kind of ecstasy at the beauty of light through petals . . . how each vein is seen in relief, the structure suddenly visible. I just noticed that deep in the orange cup of one of these flat-cupped daffodils there is translucent bright green below the stamens.

   MAY SARTON

3. Americans have a long tradition of moving toward nature, beginning with the Puritan errand into the wilderness and continuing with the great westward expansion of the nineteenth century. Crèvecoeur held that after the love of newness, what most animated Americans was the desire to be close to nature. Even after the frontier closed, wealthy men built mansions out in the country and commuted by rail to work in the city. When the middle classes discovered the automobile, they moved out too. By the 1960s even industry, wary of the social decay and growing taxes of the inner cities, followed the workers to the suburbs. Today, people are living far beyond the suburbs and commuting to workplaces in the greenbelts.

PETER STEINHART

4. American Sign Language substitutes for speech a dizzying combination of animated hand gestures, facial expressions and body movements. In a signed performance of *Little Shop of Horrors,* for example, Carl Chopinsky and Marie Taccogna of Theater Access Project mouthed all of the words spoken or sung in perfect synchrony with the actor he or she was interpreting. Simultaneously, with their hands, each signer delivered the dialogue and, in time to the music, the lyrics. When a trio sang a song à la the Supremes, the interpreters, their hips rolling and swaying, created the harmonies by singing in unison. Their hand movements were clipped and hiccuping, or rolling and sustained, mimicking the sound of the voices. At the climax of the show, when Audrey II, a huge man-eating plant, advanced toward the audience and the music swelled, the interpreters' signs grew broader, extending farther from their bodies, engulfing more space.

ELEANOR LUGER

5. Fretting parents and educators can no longer accuse television writers of influencing the behavior of inner-city teenagers. The violence of day-to-day urban reality far exceeds any cruelties, atrocities or mayhem depicted in the current crop of television crime and adventure series, with the sole exception of the 6 o'clock news, which dramatically portrays the horrors of urban living. What is the most immediate consequence of a vicious murder committed by a young mugger, who is subsequently apprehended? The answer is instant stardom by way of the 6 o'clock news and the evening headlines. Regardless of the severity of the ensuing punishment, he had his moment of infamous glory.

CLAUDE BROWN

WRITING AND REVISING

Writing an Effective Topic Sentence

As you may have seen, the topic sentence not only states the paragraph's main idea but also restricts or limits the paragraph. The topic sentence announces to the reader: "This is what the paragraph will be about; the rest of the sentences in the paragraph will tell you more about this idea." Because it performs these two functions—announcing the main idea and limiting the scope of the paragraph—the topic sentence is the most important sentence in the paragraph.

To be effective, a topic sentence must meet the following three requirements.

(1) A topic sentence should be neither too limited nor too broad.

A topic sentence that merely states a fact is too limited because that fact cannot be developed further. Once you have stated a limited and specific fact, there is nothing more to say.

TOO LIMITED   Indira Gandhi served as Prime Minister of India.

TOO LIMITED   Indira Gandhi was the daughter of Jawaharlal Nehru, India's first Prime Minister.

SUITABLE   Indira Gandhi learned many of her leadership skills from her father, Jawaharlal Nehru, who also served as Prime Minister of India. [Paragraph goes on to talk about specific leadership skills Indira Gandhi learned from her father.]

A topic sentence that is too broad is not sufficiently limited for a paragraph. To develop the central idea in such a topic sentence, you might need a long essay or a whole book.

TOO BROAD   Women have proved themselves to be effective as national leaders.

TOO BROAD   India has had many important leaders.

SUITABLE   Indira Gandhi faced several complex economic problems during her years as Prime Minister of India. [Paragraph goes on to identify several of these economic problems.]

(2) A topic sentence should state the paragraph's main idea precisely.

As you try out various ways of wording a topic sentence, begin by stating the main idea as directly and as clearly as you can. Eliminate wordiness and unnecessary phrases such as "I am going to tell you about . . ." and "In this paragraph I will explain . . ." These expressions weaken a topic sentence and make the main idea harder for a reader to find. A topic sentence should not be vague; it should be clear and easy for a reader to understand.

WEAK   In this paragraph I am going to explain why trains should not sound their whistles while people are asleep.

IMPROVED   This community should pass a law that will prevent train engineers from sounding train whistles at railroad crossings between 11:00 P.M. and 7:00 A.M.

WEAK   Scuba diving is a fascinating sport.

IMPROVED   Scuba diving opens up a whole new world: the underwater world of plants and animals that are vastly different from those we see on land.

(3) A topic sentence should arouse the reader's interest.

A topic sentence should intrigue the reader enough so that the reader wants to finish the whole paragraph. Although it is not always possible to write a topic sentence with a clever twist, try to catch the reader's attention—perhaps with a specific detail, perhaps by involving the reader directly in the topic.

WEAK   Our long-distance bicycle trip was fun.

IMPROVED   If you've ever had aching muscles and a hard time sitting, you have some idea of the aftereffects of my thirty-five-mile bicycle trip last weekend.

WEAK   Making a list helps people remember what they have to do.

IMPROVED   If you have sixteen things to do and you can't even remember half of them, make a list.

EXERCISE 2. Improving Topic Sentences.   Some of the following topic sentences are too broad for a paragraph; some are too narrow. Rewrite each topic sentence so that it is an effective topic sentence for a paragraph. You may make up any information you need or use reference books to find more information.

1. Many sports require special equipment.
2. The original name of Sojourner Truth, an important abolitionist who led many slaves to freedom, was Isabella.
3. People are really funny.
4. The Great Wall of China is about 2,420 kilometers long.
5. Movies make you forget about your problems.
6. John Henry is an American folk hero.

7. Some days are better than others.
8. Weather affects how people feel.
9. The Latin expression *in loco parentis* means "in the place of a parent" and refers to someone other than a parent exercising authority over a child.
10. A divining rod is a forked stick or branch used to locate underground water.

EXERCISE 3. Improving Topic Sentences. Each of the following topic sentences needs to be made more clear, more interesting, or both. Rewrite each topic sentence so that it is an effective topic sentence for a paragraph. You may either make up any information you need or use reference books to find out more information.

1. The Eskimos are an interesting people.
2. Roses have many different uses.
3. I plan to tell you in this paragraph about some of the myths from many different cultures that explain the Big Dipper and Little Dipper constellations.
4. People can suffer from poor nutrition even though they eat a lot.
5. In this paragraph you will find out about the order in which colors appear in a rainbow (from violet at the top to red at the bottom) and why.
6. I want to tell you a funny story that happened to me when I visited Mammoth Cave National Park in southwestern Kentucky.
7. Using a trampoline is a lot of fun.
8. Many fairy tales teach something.
9. Life in the Pueblo villages of the Southwest (such as those of the Zuñi, Hopi, and Tewa tribes) was different.
10. Woodworking is a good hobby.

REVIEW EXERCISE A. Writing Topic Sentences. For each of the following lists of details, write an effective topic sentence that will be the first sentence in the paragraph. (You will not necessarily use all the details in a paragraph.)

1. *Details:* New service for joggers in Eugene, Oregon: rent a Doberman pinscher
Dogs trained to protect female joggers
Women joggers rent fierce-looking dogs

Service started several years ago; 12 large black Doberman pinschers

Isolated female runners vulnerable to attack and harassment

Not one assault reported by joggers with rented Doberman pinschers

Joggers hold dog on leash

Amazon Trail—6½-mile jogging trail along Willamette River

2. *Details:* Ideas for improving corporation's relationship with its employees

Certain amount of time off each week for employees' exercise activities

Days off as reward for employees who don't use up "sick days"

Flexible hours so employees can meet personal responsibilities

Bonus or time off as reward for employees who quit smoking cigarettes

10-minute relaxation or exercise breaks

3. *Details:* Kayaking an Olympic sport since 1936; women kayaking in Olympics since 1948

Kayaks first used by Eskimos for transportation

Olympic kayaks made of laminated wood or fiberglass; Eskimo kayaks made of sealskin stretched over wood frame

Paddler sits in middle of kayak, an enclosed shell

Olympic paddlers use double-bladed wood paddle; may average two strokes a second

White-water kayaking on rivers with rapids; Olympic kayaking races are flat-water (no rapids)

4. *Details:* In New York City since 1970's, "educational option" high schools providing training in broad career areas—each school specializing in one area

Existing programs in commercial art, business and banking, health professions

Open to high-school students in city

More than 28,000 applications to one high school, half of them for computer science program

Schools usually take only about 1,000 applicants

Local high schools losing best students to educational op-

tion schools; beginning to develop own specialized programs
Two thirds of city's high schools have or are developing
such programs
5. *Details:* Good-will packages sent by American communities to communities in Soviet Union
Attempt to make direct contacts between American and
Soviet peoples
Packages of photos, post cards, drawings, letters
800 packages sent to Soviet Union; more than 27 received
from Soviet Union
One Russian mother wrote: "They say that from the cosmos our planet appears a tiny speck. Let us take care of
our common home in which live our children and their
children's children."
A 15-year-old Russian girl wrote: "The earth is our mother.
She fed us and raised us, so let's be grateful to her for
this."

CRITICAL THINKING:
Forming a Generalization

A *generalization* is a universal statement about a whole group of
people, events, things, or places. Generalizations apply to every specific individual or instance within the group.

EXAMPLES   All birds have wings.
All whales are mammals.
All tortillas are made from either cornmeal or flour.

The following statements are *not* generalizations because they
cover one specific instance, not a whole group.

EXAMPLES   Our pet parrot has wings.
This whale is a mammal.
Teresa makes her tortillas from either cornmeal or flour.

In the chapter on persuasive writing, you will see that a sound
generalization is a conclusion based on many observations or experiences. A *hasty generalization* is made after only one or two experiences; it is not valid (true) and is considered a fallacy in logical
thinking. (See page 527.)

People make many generalizations that they use every day. For example, suppose you have spent two weeks catching a 4:00 bus that has never yet arrived at your bus stop before 4:15. Based on your two weeks of experience waiting for the bus, you will make the following generalization: "The 4:00 bus does not arrive at my bus stop before 4:15." Having concluded this, you will no longer rush to reach the bus stop at 4:00. Or suppose that you have gone to see five or six films that the movie critic in the local newspaper has recommended highly. To your surprise, you found that you did not like these films at all. You will make the generalization "This movie critic's taste is very different from mine." You will probably not pay much attention to what the critic says about films in the future.

Learning to form generalizations is a critical thinking skill that is necessary for writing paragraphs because the topic sentence of a paragraph often states a generalization.

EXAMPLES   Violence as a way of achieving racial justice is both impractical and immoral. [Dr. Martin Luther King's statement covers all specific instances of violence to achieve racial justice—in the past, present, and future.]

American Sign Language substitutes for speech a dizzying combination of animated hand gestures, facial expressions, and body movements. [Eleanor Luger makes this generalization about every specific instance of the use of American Sign Language.]

In a paragraph, the rest of the sentences provide examples, facts, or reasons that prove that the generalization made in the topic sentence is true.

EXERCISE 4. Identifying Generalizations.

Some of the following topic sentences are generalizations about a whole group of people, events, places, or things; some of the sentences are not generalizations. Identify all the generalizations. Be prepared to explain your answers.

1. It is much better for elderly people to live in their own environment or as part of a family unit than in a caretaking facility such as a nursing home.
2. The ability to play music "by ear" is a gift that some people have and most do not; it is not a skill that can be learned through practice.
3. The capital of Oklahoma is Oklahoma City.

4. For income tax purposes, it is better to own a home than to rent one.
5. Jane Austen wrote *Pride and Prejudice, Sense and Sensibility,* and *Emma.*
6. It is better to give than to receive.
7. Water is essential to life.
8. Some form of daily exercise will benefit your health.
9. Latin is seldom taught in public schools.
10. Fear of the dark is the most common fear of young children.

EXERCISE 5. Identifying Generalizations. Look at all the topic sentences in the model paragraphs in this chapter. Identify all the topic sentences that you think are generalizations. Be prepared to explain your answers.

EXERCISE 6. Evaluating Generalizations Based on Data. Use the following chart to decide whether the generalizations given after the chart are true or false. If you cannot tell whether the generalization is true on the basis of the information given in the chart, write *can't tell.* Number your paper 1–10. After the proper number, write *true, false,* or *can't tell.* Remember that the generalization must be drawn only from information given in the chart.

NUMBER OF RESTAURANTS IN A MICHIGAN CITY

(BY ETHNIC BREAKDOWN)

	THIS YEAR	LAST YEAR	THE YEAR BEFORE
Asian	14	8	4
French	3	4	8
Spanish	9	2	0
Italian	10	10	9
Jewish	3	4	4
Soul food	8	7	7
Russian	0	0	1
Hungarian	2	2	2
Scandinavian	1	1	0

1. Asian food is becoming increasingly popular in this city.
2. Spanish food has become increasingly popular in this city.

3. There are more fast-food restaurants in this community than all the ethnic restaurants combined.
4. The Hungarian restaurants are very expensive.
5. People in this community are not as interested in French food as they were two years ago.
6. Soul food is more popular in this community than Scandinavian food.
7. There are more Spanish-speaking people living in this city than there are people from the various Asian nations.
8. Interest in Italian, Jewish, and soul food has increased considerably during the past three years.
9. Russian food is too expensive.
10. Italian food is often very spicy.

EXERCISE 7. Forming Generalizations Based on Data. For each of the following charts, write at least two generalizations based on the data given in the chart. (If you can write more than two, write as many as you can.)

1. ESTIMATED ADVERTISING EXPENDITURES IN THE UNITED STATES
(Including all types of local and national advertising)

MILLIONS OF DOLLARS	1950	1955	1960	1965
	5,700	9,150	11,960	15,250

MILLIONS OF DOLLARS	1970	1975	1980	1982
	19,550	27,900	53,550	66,580

2. TOTAL DEATHS FROM ACCIDENTS IN THE UNITED STATES, 1960–1980
(By type of accident; from 1970 on, figures include only U.S. residents)

TYPE OF ACCIDENT	YEARS				
	1960	1965	1970	1975	1980
Motor vehicle accidents	38,137	49,163	54,633	45,853	53,173
Water transport accidents	1,478	1,493	1,651	1,570	1,429
Air and space transport accidents	1,475	1,529	1,612	1,552	1,494
Railway accidents	1,023	962	852	508	632
Accidental falls	19,023	19,984	16,926	14,896	13,294
Accidental drowning	5,232	5,485	6,391	6,640	6,043
Accidents caused by:					
Fires and flames	7,645	7,347	6,718	6,071	5,822
Firearms	2,334	2,344	2,406	2,380	1,955
Electric current	989	1,071	1,140	1,224	1,095

SUPPORTING SENTENCES

14c. Other sentences in the paragraph give specific information that supports the main idea stated in the topic sentence.

It is easy to make general statements; it is harder to find the specific details, examples, or reasons that are needed to back up such statements. The details may be of many kinds—facts, examples, incidents, or reasons. (You will learn more about each of these kinds of details in Chapter 15.) The details, however, must be there, and they must clearly support the topic sentence.

The following paragraph does not develop its topic sentence. Instead, it merely restates its main idea several times in different words. Saying something over and over does not, of course, make it any clearer or truer than saying it once. Details are needed to support the generalization in the first sentence.

> In my opinion, running daily is the best exercise you can do to become physically fit. People today talk a great deal about physical fitness, but there would not be so many people in poor physical condition if everyone ran a mile every day. It is our responsibility to take care of our bodies. We cannot do this without exercising. No one has found a better or more efficient means of exercising than running. Therefore, everyone should practice running, since it is the best exercise you can do to become physically fit.

In the following paragraph, notice the way in which each of the sentences supports the main idea as it is stated in the topic sentence.

[1]For a long time, the hardware store has been playing upon the secret feeling of many men that the only thing that stands between them and expert performance is the right tool. [2]Men with an 18 handicap almost always play with clubs that are every bit as good as Tom Watson's. [3]Weekend tennis players carry Prince graphites. [4]In the same way, the suburban handyman stands in the hardware store thinking that if he just had the right tool there would never again be a time when he would cut his hand and, at the same time, worm the head off a screw while trying to change a sim-

(1) topic sentence

(2, 3) examples of "right tools"

(4) examples of "inexpert performance"

ple door latch. [5]Standing in the store, studying the
64-piece socket set, the miter box and the apparatus that will hold a rattail file at exactly the
correct angle, he can imagine himself capable, feel
his ability. [6]Because of this, more tools are bought
than used.

(5) examples of "right tools"

(6) result

GEOFFREY NORMAN

Sentences 2 and 3 make a comparison with the main idea of tools
in a hardware store by giving specific examples of men who imagine
that the best "sports tools" will help them perform expertly. Sentence
4 actually restates the central idea of the topic sentence and, at the
same time, gives two examples of "inexpert performance" with hard-
ware-store tools. The fifth sentence again refers to the topic sentence,
but this time adds specific examples of "right tools." The last sentence
tells what happens as a result ("Because of this . . .") of the idea in
the topic sentence.

14d. **The topic sentence must be supported with sufficient details.**

A paragraph with only one or two supporting details is not an effective
paragraph. You need to have at least three or more details (ideas,
examples, facts, statistics, reasons) to support the main idea. The
following example paragraphs describe the writer's first experience
parachuting in tandem with Manning, a parachute instructor. Compare
the two versions, noticing how the addition of specific details strength-
ens the second version.

WEAK   After 15 seconds of free fall, I feel a tug at my harness. Manning
gives me some ropes to hold, which steer the parachute. I've never
seen such a beautiful day.

IMPROVED   After what seems like several seconds of free fall, but is actually
15, the wind starts to quiet down and I feel a gentle tug at my
harness. I look up at the spreading blue and white canopy. Manning
asks how I'm doing. I just couldn't be better. I yell to him
needlessly, like a drunk who has lost all volume control. I think
my head will probably fall off if I don't stop smiling so hard.
Manning gives me some ropes to hold, which steer the parachute.
If you pull down on the left one, that side dips and you soar in a
wide circle—like a BIRD. It's great. I've never seen such a beautiful

day, but that's probably just one of the temporary illusions that results from thinking you're going to die and then getting another chance.

AMANDA WOOD

EXERCISE 8. Adding Supporting Information. For each of the following topic sentences, one or two supporting details have been given. Write as many other details as you can think of that can be used to support the topic sentence. Try to have at least three details for each topic sentence.

1. *Topic sentence:* Next time you run a fever and feel terrible, remember these time-tested remedies.
   a. Drink plenty of fluids.
2. *Topic sentence:* If you think the volume of your stereo isn't loud enough, remember that studies show that long-term exposure to loud noises can cause permanent hearing loss.
   a. Workers who use jackhammers—portable hammers used for drilling rock and concrete
3. *Topic sentence:* Children who own dogs and cats may think of themselves as lucky, but they're actually having some important learning experiences as well.
   a. Learning about an animal's habits
4. *Topic sentence:* Even though she is a talented photographer, Julie has had difficulty earning a living as a photographer.
   a. Won prizes in several photo contests during last three years
   b. Sold some photos to local weekly newspaper
5. *Topic sentence:* We planned the surprise birthday party in great detail, but not the things that went wrong.
   a. Severe electrical storm knocked out power for four hours.
6. *Topic sentence:* A newspaper editor tries to balance stories of tragic events that happen every day with cheerful material.
   a. Feature stories about women and men accomplishing good things
   b. Gossip column and society news
7. *Topic sentence:* No matter what your tastes in music are, a simple flip of the radio dial can satisfy your listening desires.
   a. Classical music 24 hours a day on WTMI
8. *Topic sentence:* Letter writing is a disappearing art—a form of communication rarely practiced in modern times.
   a. Everyone likes to receive letters from friends and family.
   b. Few people take the time to write letters.

9. *Topic sentence:* A psychologist has seriously advised that everyone develop at least one P.A. (positive attitude), a daily need for doing something that is good for you.
   a. Exercise such as walking
10. *Topic sentence:* Credit cards may be convenient, but they should be used with care, for they can cause great difficulties.
    a. Interest rates are very high.

EXERCISE 9. Improving a Weak Paragraph.   The following paragraph is weak because it does not have enough supporting details. Study the paragraph and the questions that follow it. Then use your answers to the questions to rewrite the paragraph so that it has sufficient information to support the central idea as stated in the topic sentence. You may revise the topic sentence also. Write your revised paragraph on a separate piece of paper.

> Being outdoors just before sunrise, as the sky begins to lighten, is a special feeling. The streets are almost empty. Several cats are in front of the houses. Everything is very quiet.

1. Is the neighborhood a city neighborhood, a suburban one, or a country one? What kinds of houses are on the street? What do the houses look like in the early morning? Are there any lights in the houses?
2. Are there any signs of human life in the houses or on the streets? Are there joggers, walkers, bicyclists?
3. Are there cars parked on the streets? What do they look like in the early morning?
4. What do the cats do so early in the morning? Are they moving or at a standstill? If they move, what do they seem to be doing? How do they move? If they are still, where are they? What do they seem to be doing?
5. What noises can you hear? Are there any traffic noises in the distance? Are there other sounds of human life?
6. How does being alone outdoors at this time of day make you feel? Is it a good feeling or a bad feeling? Do you ever feel this way in other circumstances? If so, list those circumstances.

REVIEW EXERCISE B. Improving Weak Paragraphs.   Revise each of the following weak paragraphs by adding sufficient supporting details to develop the paragraph's idea. You may also revise the topic sentence to make it more precise or more interesting. Write the revised paragraphs on a separate sheet of paper.

1

One of the most important things that people need to learn is being responsible. Keeping promises is part of being responsible. You also need to do the things that must be done—even if it's no fun doing them. (*Hint:* Add specific examples of keeping promises and things that need to be done. Add other aspects of being responsible, and give examples for each.)

2

Imagine what your life would be like if you had no "best" friend. Everyone needs someone with whom to share feelings and with whom to go places. (*Hint:* Add specific details and examples, and think of other functions that a best friend serves.)

3

Last Saturday's football game was the most exciting game I have ever seen. Our team played badly during the first half. In the last ten minutes of the game, we scored 14 points. We won 14–12. (*Hint:* Add specific details about the action of the game, the players, how the fans reacted to the scores. You might even tell what the weather was like.)

4

Grandparents have much to offer their grandchildren. They can teach the children skills and crafts and tell them stories. They usually have more time and are patient with their grandchildren. They are usually very affectionate.

5

Words have fascinating histories. For example, the word *tragedy* comes from ancient Greek and means literally "the song of the goat."

THE CONCLUDING, OR CLINCHER, SENTENCE

14e. A paragraph may end with a clincher sentence.

Sometimes you may wish to reemphasize the main point of a paragraph by restating it in a concluding sentence. This kind of restatement is called a *clincher sentence*. A clincher sentence may also summarize specific details or suggest a course of action.

Not all paragraphs have or need a clincher sentence, however. A clincher is unnecessary, for example, in a very short paragraph. A poor clincher is one that seems to be tacked on just for its own sake to a paragraph that is complete and effective without it.

In the following paragraph, both the topic sentence and the clincher sentence are printed in boldfaced type. The paragraph is from Pauline Kael's review of *Never Cry Wolf,* a movie about a young biologist named Tyler, who spends a year in the Arctic trying to study the habits of wolves.

The cruel fact is that more wolves would have helped; wolves that were more accommodating would have helped, too. The animals on the screen	topic sentence
just don't seem eager to act out their roles, and	detail 1
they're not strong in the grandeur department—	detail 2
they look sort of scroungy. Children who went to see *The Black Stallion* could believe in that myth-	detail 3
ological horse because Ballard [the director] had fully created him; the wolves here are never char-	
acters. Despite the names that Tyler gives them, they have no discernible personalities, and noth-	detail 4
ing really happens between Tyler and the wolves.	
These long-legged creatures with tiny, sharp eyes are playing out a script of their own devising.	clincher sentence

EXERCISE 10. Writing Clincher Sentences. For each of the following paragraphs, write a clincher sentence. Try writing several versions for each paragraph; then choose the one that you think is most effective.

1

Like many other workers, lumberjacks have a colorful language all their own. Lumberjacks are people who cut down trees for a living, but they never refer to themselves by that name. They call themselves *sawyers, fallers,* or *gypos* (short for *gypsies,* independent truckers). Lumberjacks have other words that most people do not know. A *widowmaker* is a huge tree limb that crashes silently to the ground from high above. *Skidding* is dragging chain-wrapped felled trees with a tractorlike piece of equipment through the forest to the roadside.

2

Since 1978 New York City's Ethnic Advisory Council has promoted understanding and peaceful accord among the city's 150 or so ethnic groups. Representatives for each of the twenty-five largest ethnic groups meet once a month to discuss problems in New York's diverse communities. Although the council advises the mayor and the groups that come before it, the council has no real power. The Korean representative, Mrs. Grace Lyu-Volckhausen, believes that the council would be more effective if it had legal powers. However, the council has had some real successes, according to Indian leader Swami G. Jagdishwaranand. Acting on the council's suggestion, the Indian community contacted the public schools and local organizations to help end a four-year period of violence against Indians in a Queens neighborhood.

REVIEW EXERCISE C. Writing Paragraphs. Look back at Review Exercise A on pages 349–51. Using the topic sentence that you developed for each set of details, write a paragraph for each numbered item. Add a clincher sentence to each paragraph if you feel that it improves the paragraph.

UNITY IN THE PARAGRAPH

14f. Every sentence in a paragraph should be directly related to the main idea.

A paragraph in which every sentence supports the main idea is said to have *unity*. A unified paragraph is a forceful unit because all of the sentences have a common purpose: to develop the general statement made by the topic sentence. It is possible to measure the unity of a paragraph by testing the relationship of each sentence to the main idea. As you write a paragraph, ask yourself this question: How is each detail related to the topic sentence? Study the following paragraph, noting how its unity has been broken.

¹American bald eagles, once an endangered species, are making a gradual comeback across the country. ²~~You can see the bald eagle on the United States coat of arms on the back of a dollar bill.~~ ³During the 1970's the bald eagle (or American eagle, as it is sometimes called) was put on the endangered species list because its numbers had steadily decreased and sightings of these ea-

(1) topic sentence

(2) unrelated fact breaks paragraph unity

(3, 4) history of bald eagles as an endangered species

gles were extremely rare. ⁴After the insecticide DDT was removed from use, their numbers slowly began to increase. ⁵This year during the annual midwinter census taken by the National Wildlife Federation, almost 12,000 bald eagles—many of them immature birds—were counted in forty-two of the original forty-eight states. ⁶In 1979, during the first bald eagle census, only 20 percent of the eagles counted were young birds; now 30 to 35 percent are. ⁷~~You can recognize an immature eagle by its brownish black head; a mature eagle has a snowwhite head.~~ ⁸The fact that the percentage of immature birds has been steadily increasing through the 1980's is a sign that the overall eagle population is growing and that the birds are producing healthier offspring.

(5) statistics and other specific information about the eagles' comeback

(6) statistics developing idea in sentence 5

(7) related fact but breaks paragraph unity

(8) conclusion based on sentences 5 and 6

The two sentences that are crossed out interrupt the paragraph's logical flow of ideas. Sentence 2 states a fact about the bald eagle, but this fact has nothing to do with the paragraph's main idea (that bald eagles were disappearing but now are making a comeback). The fact stated in sentence 7 is somewhat related to the previous sentences, which mention immature and young birds, in that it tells how to recognize an immature bird. But placed as it is, this idea interrupts the logical flow of thought. One way of adding this information to the paragraph would be to put it in parentheses in sentence 6:

In 1979, during the first bald eagle census, only 20 percent of the eagles counted were young birds (recognizable by their brown-black heads, unlike the adults' white heads); now 30 to 35 percent are.

But it would be better to omit this information altogether. The reader does not need to know how young eagles are recognized in order to understand the central idea of this paragraph.

EXERCISE 11. Identifying Sentences That Destroy Unity. Examine each of the following paragraphs to test its unity. One or more sentences in each are not closely related to the topic. Find these sentences, copy them onto your paper, and be ready to explain how they break the unity of the paragraph.

1

When backpacking in Glacier National Park in northwestern Montana, hikers are advised not to disturb the grizzly bears that live in the park. Because grizzlies have been known to react violently when surprised by visitors, hikers wear bells that jingle as they march, warning any bears in the vicinity that intruders are coming. The black bears found in Yellowstone Park do not have the same frightening reputation as the grizzlies. Although there are only about two hundred grizzlies in Glacier National Park (the park is larger than the state of Rhode Island) and although the chances of being attacked are about a million to one, visitors are uneasy because the grizzly has traditionally been considered America's fiercest and most dangerous animal. Even today a grizzly will occasionally attack a human being—with painful or fatal results.

2

If you have paddled a canoe, you know that paddling is a skill that must be learned. Since a canoe can be pushed from its course by a slight breeze, the paddlers must sit in such a way that the bow will not be forced too high out of the water, where it will catch too much wind. In calm weather the canoeists should sit in the stern, but in windy weather they should kneel just aft of the middle, for in this position they can control their craft with less effort. They should paddle on the side opposite the direction of the wind because the wind then actually helps them to hold to a straight course. Canoeists who are white-water canoeing in a river with rapids and falls should wear life jackets in case the canoe overturns. Try to float on your back with your feet pointed downstream so that your head does not smash against a rock. Steering a canoe is done by a twist of the paddle at the end of each stroke, the extent of the twist depending on the force of the stroke and the strength of the wind against the bow.

3

Annie Peck's career as a mountaineer was astonishing for a woman who began climbing mountains in the nineteenth century. This internationally acclaimed climber first became interested in mountaineering when she saw the majesty of the Matterhorn in the Alps. She climbed Mount Shasta in California and then, in 1895, ascended the Matterhorn. Climbing Mount Orizaba in southern Mexico won her recognition for achieving the highest point in the Americas reached by a woman up to that time. Peck was not satisfied with achieving something no woman had ever achieved before; she wanted to reach a height no person had ever reached before. Some people considered her climbing costume as daring as her accomplishments. She continued searching for the right mountain, and she finally climbed the north peak of Huascarán in central Peru. This peak was named Huascarán Cumbre Ana Peck in her honor. Peck continued to be an active mountaineer until her death at the age of eighty-four.

4

Walking is one of the best and cheapest forms of recreation—one that will benefit you no matter what mood you are in. When you are feeling lonely and depressed, a long walk in the crisp air helps to cheer you up. Then again, if you're filled with the glorious feeling that everything is perfect, you enjoy a walk outdoors where everything in nature seems to be happy with you. On hikes through wild country, campers make many wonderful and surprising discoveries, enjoying the peaceful feeling of direct contact with the natural world. Nervous business people, waiting to hear whether the stock market has gone down another point, put their hands behind them and pace impatiently up and down a room. Bicycling and running are also good for you. Next time you are bored or happy or unhappy or worried, take a walk.

REVIEW EXERCISE D. Writing a Unified Paragraph. Look carefully at the list of details that follows, and choose sufficient details to write a unified paragraph. First, write a topic sentence that expresses the paragraph's main idea. Then select and arrange enough details to support that idea in five or six sentences. (You do not need to use all of the details.) Once you have written a first draft of your paragraph, go over it carefully to check on the logical flow of ideas. Check also to see that each sentence supports the paragraph's main idea. Cross out or revise any sentence that breaks the paragraph's unity.

Details: Forest fires—part of natural cycle
Recent forest fires in Montana—400 square miles destroyed
New forest ready for harvesting for lumber in 22nd century
Fire started by lightning during thunderstorm; timber very dry in seasons without rain
Dry grass and layers of sticks, dried needles as fuel
After fire some roots and seeds survive
Scorching and nutrients in ash stimulate growth of grasses
Seeds sprout in spring of first year after fire; lodgepole pines first trees, their seed cones melted by heat of fire
In conifers (family of gymnosperms)—such as pines, firs, cedars, spruce—reproduction by means of seeds in pine cones and windblown pollen
In Montana fast-growing forest of lodgepole pine and Western larch first 20 years after fire
In 100 years after fire, fir trees replacing lodgepole and larch
Completes the natural cycle of fire, destruction of forest, new growth, development of new forest
Conifers provide about 75% of all lumber

COHERENCE IN THE PARAGRAPH

Coherent paragraphs are easy to read. The relationship of ideas is clear, and the train of thought moves easily and naturally from one sentence to the next. Coherence is achieved in two ways: (1) providing clear transitions or links between ideas and (2) arranging ideas in a logical order. In this section, you will see how pronouns and transitional expressions are used to link the ideas in a paragraph. On pages 368–77, you will learn about four types of logical order.

Using Pronouns and Phrases

14g. Strengthen a paragraph by linking ideas clearly to one another.

The most useful words for this purpose are the pronouns: *he, she, they, this, that, these, those, them, it,* etc. When pronouns appear in a paragraph, they serve to remind the reader of their antecedents—the words, expressions, and ideas to which they refer. As reminders, they help to bind together more tightly the ideas in the paragraph.

(1) Keep the thought of a paragraph flowing smoothly from sentence to sentence by using pronouns and phrases that refer to words and ideas in previous sentences.

As you read the following paragraphs, notice how the italicized pronouns and phrases refer to an idea that comes earlier in the passage.

A hundred years ago, the average workweek in the United States was about seventy hours. Today, *it* is about forty hours—and experts say that in the next decade or so *it* will be cut again, the predictions ranging from thirty-seven hours or thereabouts down to twenty or even less. *This reduction* might come as a shorter workday, fewer workdays per week, or longer—very much longer—vacations.

What shall we do with *all that free time*? Many people are profoundly troubled about *this question*. *They* feel that, far from being a blessing, the change may prove a catastrophe. Certainly, the growth of leisure time is an extremely serious matter. *It* deserves far more attention than *it* is getting.

EXERCISE 12. Analyzing Paragraphs for Coherence.   The following paragraphs are about Eleanor Roosevelt, yet her name is mentioned only twice. Make a list of the pronouns and phrases the writer used to refer to Eleanor Roosevelt to avoid repeating her name.

It was a childhood you wouldn't wish on anyone. The girl was born on October 11, 1884, into a confounding world of privilege and deprivation. She was rejected by a mother who called her "granny." She idolized a father who was at once loving and unstable. Orphaned by the age of 10, she went to live under the roof and rules of a grandmother so rigid that the girl rebelled by adding a bit of warm water to a cold bath.

The creature of this comfortlessness later described herself as "a solemn child, without beauty. I seemed like a little old woman entirely lacking in the spontaneous joy and mirth of youth." As a cousin put it, "It was the grimmest childhood I had ever known."

Yet, out of this, Eleanor Roosevelt became, quite simply, the greatest American woman of the century.

Those of us who pay homage at the centennial of this woman's birth, those of us who admire her, live now in a rampantly psychiatric age. We have the conceit that adult life is predictable to any nursery-school observer. Yet who could have predicted Eleanor, the First Lady of the World?

ELLEN GOODMAN

Using Transitional Expressions

(2) Keep the thought and purpose of the paragraph flowing smoothly from sentence to sentence by the use of transitional expressions.

As you can see from the following chart, transitional expressions can indicate different relationships among ideas.

To add an idea to one already stated:

moreover	likewise	besides	too
further	also	and	again
furthermore	nor	then	in addition
equally important	in the same fashion		

To limit or contradict something already said:

but	still	although
yet	nevertheless	otherwise
and yet	on the other hand	at the same time
however	on the contrary	

To show an arrangement of your ideas by time or place:

first	meanwhile	next	here
second (etc.)	later	presently	nearby
finally	eventually	at length	opposite to
at this point	sooner or later	afterward	adjacent to

To exemplify some idea or to sum up what you have said:

for example	to sum up	in any event
for instance	in brief	in any case
in other words	on the whole	as I have said
in fact	in short	as a result

One mark of a good prose style is care in the choice of transitional expressions. Many expressions do approximately the same job. For instance, you can add an idea to those already mentioned in a paragraph by introducing it with *furthermore* or *in addition*. You can use *consequently* and *therefore* to show that one idea is the result of the previous idea. You can use *however* or *nevertheless* to make clear that you are about to introduce a contrasting idea. Which connective you use depends on the logical relationship of the sentences.

In the sections on logical order, you will find lists of transitional expressions that are appropriate to each type of order.

EXERCISE 13. Choosing Appropriate Transitional Expressions. From the choices given in parentheses, choose the transitional expression that you think links the ideas most effectively. Write the sentences on a separate sheet of paper, and be prepared to explain your choices.

1. Norrine enjoys playing the French horn. Unfortunately, (on the other hand, however, for instance), she has no place where she can practice without disturbing others.
2. (Because, Although, While) human beings have no gills, they cannot stay underwater for long periods of time without special breathing equipment.
3. Many adults discover talents that they never knew they had. Mother's cousin Ralph, (as a result, consequently, for example), became an accomplished metal sculptor in his fifties even though he had no formal training.

4. No one wearing street shoes is allowed to enter the Norikami Museum. If you wish to enter, (therefore, nevertheless, on the other hand), you must leave your shoes outside and wear paper slippers.

5. Kerri and Mitch were wearing their seat belts when a driver crashed into the rear of their car. (As a result, In addition, Finally), they were not injured badly, (although, while, and) their car was totaled.

LOGICAL ORDER IN THE PARAGRAPH

The word *logical* means "reasonable" or "orderly." When ideas are arranged logically, one idea flows smoothly into the next, and the paragraph is easy to understand and follow. In the following pages, you will study four plans for organizing your ideas: chronological order, spatial order, order of importance, and comparison and contrast.

14h. Strengthen a paragraph by arranging the ideas in a logical order.

Chronological Order

(1) Details in a paragraph may be arranged in chronological order.

Whenever you are telling a story or telling about an event that actually happened, the most logical way to organize your information is to use *chronological order*—the order in which events happened in time. You begin with the first event and go on to narrate what happened next, after that, and next, and, finally, last.

The following paragraphs describe a series of actual historical events that happened over a six-year period. Notice that the italicized expressions help the reader to follow the events and to understand when they occurred.

> *In 1853* Commodore Matthew C. Perry steamed into what is now called Tokyo Bay with his "black ships." *Then* as now trade was the source of American discontent with Japan. *After* delivering a missive from the President of the United States demanding the opening of trade relations, Perry repaired to sunny Okinawa for the winter.
> *When* he returned *in February 1854,* the Emperor's court, recognizing that Japan had nothing to match Perry's guns, signed a treaty with the Americans. The first ports opened were Shimoda and Hakodate on the northern island of Hokkaido. But other treaties *followed,* opening ports closer to Japan's major centers of commerce and, *by 1859,* foreign residents

were allowed to live in what was to become the most important of these ports, Yokohama, then a tiny fishing village.

STEVE LOHR

The following transitional expressions are often used to show chronological order:

after	earlier	moments later
afterward	finally	next
as soon as	first	since
at first	formerly	soon
at last	in the beginning (end)	then
at the same time	in the meantime	until
before	later	when
during	meanwhile	while

Chronological order is also used in paragraphs that describe the steps in a process. Each step must be done in the right order to achieve the desired result. In the following paragraph, identify each step in the traditional Indian manner of baking salmon. How many transitional expressions can you find?

Salmon at its finest was traditionally baked over alder wood coals by Northwest Indians. The fish was split down the back and laid flat, then pressed between the parts of a split-cedar stake. It was held in place by thin cedar strips, like a sail on a mast; then the stake was pounded into the ground near the coals, leaning slightly over the smoke. The fish was baked until it was cooked through but still moist. Sometimes the salmon was brushed with seal oil to enhance its succulence.

EXERCISE 14. Writing a Paragraph with Chronological Order.
Use the following information to write a paragraph in which the details are arranged in chronological order. Write a first draft of your paragraph. Then see if you can improve the paragraph by adding transitional expressions that make clear the order in which the events happened. You may reword the sentences in any way you choose.

Topic sentence: During last week's game with the Panthers, the Leesberg Eagles scored three runs in the last few minutes of the ninth inning, winning the game 3–2.

a. Milewski advanced to third, and Goldstein slid safely into second.
b. Then the pitcher walked Milewski, the first-base player, putting an Eagles runner on base for the first time in the game.

c. The first Eagles batter struck out, and the second batter popped out to first.

d. Milewski and Goldstein trotted home, while Washington went around the bases to roaring applause.

e. The fourth batter, Goldstein, hit a long, hard drive that careered off the center-field wall.

f. Tension mounted as the rookie Panthers pitcher finished warming up, with Washington, the Eagles center fielder, waiting near the batter's box.

g. On the first pitch, Washington hit a long drive to left field that landed in the upper deck.

h. With two players on base and only one out to go, the Panthers coach replaced the tired pitcher.

EXERCISE 15. Writing a Paragraph That Explains a Process.
Write a paragraph telling how to do something. The process that you choose to explain should be one that you are familiar with and one that can adequately be explained in a single paragraph.

Purpose: To explain a process
Audience: Members of your English class

PREWRITING Begin by choosing the process that you will write about. You may write about how to build a bookcase, how to cook a special dish, how to tie-dye a shirt, how to catch a trout, or any other "how to" that is appropriate for your audience. List all the details in the process that you can think of; then arrange them in the order in which they should be done. Be sure that you do not leave out any essential details.

Ask yourself the following questions to elicit specific and concrete details for the paragraph you will write.

1. What equipment is necessary to do this process?
2. What is the end result of the process?
3. In what order do I perform the steps in this process? Is this the necessary and essential order, or is some other order possible? What is the best way to carry out the process?

WRITING THE FIRST DRAFT Write a topic sentence that will catch your reader's attention and tell what the paragraph is about. As you write, consider your audience and whether you need to provide any additional background information; perhaps you will need to define some unfamiliar terms.

REVISING AND PROOFREADING Reread the first draft several times to make sure that the process is clearly explained and that the steps in the process are easy to follow. Do the sentences read smoothly? Consider adding appropriate transitional devices (such as *first, second, next, finally*) to clarify the order in which the steps must be done. Review the Guidelines for Revising on pages 336–37 and decide how your paragraph can be improved.

Use the Guidelines for Proofreading on page 339 to make sure that your paragraph is free from inaccuracies. Then prepare a final copy of the paragraph, and proofread that copy once more before you turn it in.

Spatial Order

(2) The details in a paragraph may be given in spatial order.

When a place is the subject of a description, the details may be arranged in spatial order, which means that the writer is careful to give the location of each part of the place. For example, if you were to describe your school building, you might first describe the entrance; then, as you enter the building, you would tell what is on your left, on your right, and straight ahead. The following brief description of Mark Twain's boyhood home, Hannibal, Missouri, follows spatial order. Expressions used to locate details are italicized.

> One morning I stood *atop* 200-foot-high Cardiff Hill and surveyed the scene that stretched *before* me. Hannibal—an active town of 20,000 people that today is an agricultural, rail and light manufacturing center—*nestles in* a mile-and-a-half-wide fan-shaped valley. It rises gradually *from the river up to residential areas in* the low hills and knolls *a mile or two off to the west. Above* the riverfront's cobblestone levee *below to my left* towered the white silos of the Hannibal Grain Terminal, while directly *in front of me* Main Street passed *through the center* of the grid-like downtown area *on its way toward* Lover's Leap, the high bluff that *overlooks* the river *to the south.*

Spatial order is also used in paragraphs that describe objects, as in the following description of a Sioux cradle.

> The babe was done up as usual in a movable cradle made from an oak board two and a half feet long and one and a half feet wide. *On one side of it* was nailed with brass-headed tacks the richly embroidered sack which was open in front and laced up and down with buckskin strings. *Over the arms of the infant* was a wooden bow, the ends of which were firmly attached to the board, so that if the cradle would fall the child's head and

face would be protected. *On this bow* were hung curious playthings—strings of artistically carved bones and hoofs of deer which rattled when the little hands moved them.

CHARLES A. EASTMAN [OHIYESA]

As you write, try to include transitional expressions that clarify the position of objects being described. The following transitional expressions are used in paragraphs with spatial order:

above	below	in front of	throughout
across	beneath	in the middle	to the side of
against	beside	inside	toward
alongside	between	near	under
among	beyond	next to	underneath
around	down	on	up
at	facing	opposite	upon
before	in a corner	outside	within
behind	in back of	over	without

EXERCISE 16. Writing a Paragraph with Spatial Order. Use some of the following details to write a paragraph using spatial order. (You do not have to use them all.)

Details:

View from observation deck at airport, looking toward the bay

Busy traffic; airplanes coming and going every few minutes

Directly below observation deck: jumbo jet being loaded with baggage and cargo; red-and-white jet backing away from terminal for takeoff

At eastern edge of airport, hangars like huge garages; fleet of small private planes looking like toys

To the west: skyline of downtown partly hidden by rain and mist

Looking off into the distance: two planes approaching for landing; small private plane climbing after takeoff; sailboat traffic on the bay; bridge across the bay; dark clouds

To the east: multicolored houses on steep hills; city streets end in the distance; houses dot heavily forested hills

PREWRITING Begin by deciding what general impression you want to give of the scene from the observation deck, and write a topic sentence stating that impression. Then decide whether you want to describe the scene from east to west, near to far, or far to near. Arrange the details so that they follow the logical progression you have chosen. Develop each detail into an interesting sentence.

WRITING THE FIRST DRAFT As you write the first draft, check to see that you have followed the order of the approach you selected. Make sure that the paragraph has enough detail to make the description interesting. If not, consider what kinds of details might be added. Do the sentences read smoothly? Are the ideas clearly expressed? Refer to the Guidelines for Revising on pages 336–37 and when your revised version is complete, refer to the Guidelines for Proofreading on page 339.

EXERCISE 17. Writing a Paragraph with Spatial Order. Choose one of the following topics or a topic of your own, and write a descriptive paragraph using spatial order.

1. A football stadium
2. A baseball stadium
3. The inside of a car
4. The inside of a post office
5. The kitchen in your home
6. The school cafeteria
7. The inside of a movie theater
8. The view from a mountaintop
9. The view of a busy city street as seen by a dog
10. The view from a goldfish bowl as seen by a goldfish

Order of Importance

(3) The details in a paragraph may be given in the order of their importance.

Suppose that you are writing an expository paragraph and you have three pieces of information to give in support of your topic sentence. You will have to decide which idea or piece of information to give first, which to give second, and which to give third. You may decide to put the most important first, followed by the idea second in importance and the idea that is least important. Or you may reverse this order, placing the most important last, where it will come as a kind of climax. The point is that your paragraph should follow a logical order.

The ideas in the paragraph on the next page are arranged by *order of importance,* with the most important idea first, directly following the topic sentence.

Specialists in children's television viewing suggest a number of ways parents can control their children's viewing. Most important, they say, is setting time limits, such as one hour a day, no viewing on school nights, or two or three hours on weekends. Another suggestion is that parents discuss with the children which television programs to select. It is important that children learn to choose their programs instead of just watching whatever happens to be on. It is generally agreed that parents should watch with their children occasionally. Viewing programs together leads to discussion of the programs and to rating them fairly. It may also bring the family closer together and increase understanding of different points of view.

most important suggestion

second most important suggestion

least important suggestion

Reasons in a persuasive paragraph may also be given in the order of importance. In general, it is better to begin with the least important reason and build up to the most important one, thus achieving a conclusion. In some situations, however, especially when the writer may have one very important reason and several less important ones, it may be appropriate to give the most compelling fact or reason first and then support it with the less important details.

The following transitional expressions are used to indicate order of importance:

above all	in the first place
also	more important
another	moreover
besides	most important
finally	next
first (second, third, etc.)	of greater (greatest) importance
for one reason	of less (least) importance
furthermore	to begin with
in addition	

EXERCISE 18. Writing a Paragraph with Order of Importance.

Choose one of the following topic sentences (either *should* or *should not*). Then decide which of the reasons listed support your topic sentence. You may add other reasons of your own, if you wish. List your reasons in order of importance, from least important to most important. Then write a paragraph based on this list of reasons. As you write, try to develop each reason into a sentence that is interesting to read.

Topic sentence: Every young adult (should, should not) learn to drive a car.

Details: You never know when it will be necessary to drive, in case of a sudden and severe emergency.

Some people who never learned to drive are too frightened to learn in later life.

Not everyone has a car; not everyone can afford to own a car.

Many people have no need to drive; they use public transportation.

Some jobs require being able to drive a car.

Driving is fun.

Many people are not suited temperamentally to drive—they are too nervous or too aggressive.

If everyone learned how to drive, roads would be more crowded and the air more polluted.

EXERCISE 19. Writing a Paragraph with Order of Importance.
Write a paragraph in which you organize information by means of the order of importance. You may use one of the following topics or one of your own.

1. Three advantages (or disadvantages) of going to college at night
2. Three advantages (or disadvantages) of being left-handed
3. Three reasons for learning to speak standard English
4. Reasons for not smoking cigarettes
5. Reasons why people should use seat belts when they are in a car
6. The advantages (or disadvantages) of living in a big city
7. The responsibilities (or advantages) of being an American citizen
8. Reasons for learning a foreign language
9. The advantages of knowing one's family history
10. Three characteristics necessary for success in the business world

Comparison and Contrast

(4) The details in a paragraph may be given in order of comparison or contrast.

You may develop a paragraph by means of *comparison* (showing how things are alike) or *contrast* (showing how they are different). Facts, incidents, concrete details, or examples may be used to point out the similarities or differences between the two subjects. Sometimes you may include both comparison and contrast in the same paragraph, as in the following example.

Termites are not true ants, though many people call them "white ants." Like the ant, the termite has only two body sections, although the thorax of the termite is not so clearly separated from the abdomen. Most ants are shiny and dark in color, but termites are soft and pale. Termites also differ from ants in matters of colony life. Worker ants are all wingless females, but workers in a termite colony may be either male or female.	topic sentence comparison contrast 1 contrast 2 contrast 3

The paragraph about termites used the *point-by-point* or *alternating method* of development. For each feature that is compared or contrasted, both subjects (termites and ants) are mentioned. For example, the second sentence discusses the body sections and thorax of both the ant and the termite. The third sentence talks about the color of both insects, and the fifth sentence talks about the sexes of both ant and termite workers.

You may also use the *block method* of development when you are using a comparison or contrast. In this organization, all the ideas about one subject are presented first, followed by all of the ideas about the second subject. The following paragraph, comparing caring for puppies and two-year-olds, uses the block method of development.

In one way, baby-sitting for a two-year-old child is like dog-sitting for a two-month-old puppy. You cannot trust either of them out of your sight.	topic and restriction sentences

Puppies must be watched constantly because their   subject 1
curiosity is endless and their teeth are sharp.
Nothing they can reach is safe. They can happily
destroy a shoe or a pillow or a book in a few
minutes. If you don't know where a puppy is, you
had better worry. Silence doesn't necessarily
mean sleep. Similarly, two-year-olds are never   subject 2
still. They run, climb, fall down, throw things,
disappear suddenly. They try to put everything
into their mouths. If you can't see or hear them,
you had better investigate. Silence often means
mischief.

Some of the transitional expressions that may be used in a paragraph of comparison or contrast include these words:

COMPARISON		CONTRAST	
also	just as	although	on the other hand
and	like	but	unlike
besides	similar	by contrast	whereas
both	similarly	however	while
in the same way			

EXERCISE 20. Analyzing a Comparison. Read the following
paragraphs about teaching drawing; then answer the questions that
follow them.

In many ways, teaching drawing is somewhat like teaching someone
to ride a bicycle. It is very difficult to explain in words. In teaching
someone to ride a bicycle, you might say, "Well, you just get on, push
the pedals, balance yourself, and off you'll go." Of course, that doesn't
explain it at all, and you are likely finally to say, "I'll get on and show
you how. Watch and see how I do it."

So it is with drawing. Most art teachers and drawing textbook authors
exhort beginners to "change their ways of looking at things" and to "learn
how to see." The problem is that this different way of seeing is as hard to
explain as how to balance a bicycle, and the teacher often ends by saying,
in effect, "Look at these examples and just keep trying. If you practice a
lot, eventually you may get it." While nearly everyone learns to ride a
bicycle, many individuals never solve the problems of drawing. To put it
more precisely, most people never learn to *see* well enough to draw.

1. What is teaching drawing compared to in these paragraphs?
2. The writer says that the two subjects are somewhat alike "in many ways." Name all of the ways mentioned in these paragraphs in which the two subjects are alike.
3. According to the last paragraph, the two subjects are different in one important way. How are they different?
4. Which of the following features of learning to ride a bicycle might also be a point of comparison or contrast with learning to draw? For each feature that might "work" in the paragraph, write a sentence making the comparison or contrast with learning to draw.
   a. Learning to ride a bicycle is fun.
   b. Learning to ride a bicycle can be dangerous.
   c. Learning to ride a bicycle provides good exercise for the body.
   d. Some people learn to balance so well that they can ride a bicycle without using their hands.
   e. When you are learning to ride a bicycle, you must observe certain rules for your own safety.

EXERCISE 21. Writing a Paragraph of Comparison and Contrast.   Use the following information to write a paragraph comparing and contrasting helium and hydrogen. You may use either the point-by-point method or the block method. You do not have to use all the information provided on the chart.

SUBJECTS	HYDROGEN	HELIUM
Natural state	Colorless gas	Colorless gas
Weight	Lightest known substance	Second-lightest known substance
Ability to burn	Can burn	Cannot burn
Boiling point	−252.8° C	−268.9° C
Melting point	−259.14° C	−272.2° C
Uses	Combines with other elements to form water, carbohydrates, fats, oils, acids, bases; used in nuclear materials	Used for inflating balloons, for low-temperature work, as a part of "air" supplied to deep-sea divers

EXERCISE 22. Writing a Paragraph of Comparison or Contrast.
Use one of the following topics to write a paragraph of comparison or contrast, or choose a topic of your own. Organize your points of comparison or contrast in either the block method or the point-by-point method.

1. Playing tennis and playing racquetball
2. A city skyscraper and an ancient pyramid
3. Paddling in a canoe and rowing a rowboat
4. Swimming underwater and swimming at the water's surface
5. A photograph and a painting (or drawing) of the same scene or person
6. A whale and an elephant
7. A trumpet and a trombone
8. A television situation comedy and a half hour in the life of an average family
9. A television news broadcast and a daily newspaper
10. Saving money and spending money

REVIEW EXERCISE E. Choosing an Order for Developing a Topic. For each of the following topic sentences, indicate the kind of order (chronological, spatial, order of importance, or comparison and contrast) that you would use in writing a paragraph based on the topic sentence. Be prepared to give the reasons for your choice.

1. Last year the political issues were much less complicated than they are this year.
2. Three factors will affect the outcome of this year's election.
3. The process for converting solar energy into electricity involves a great number of steps.
4. In the past few years the pollution of local rivers and streams has been steadily decreasing.
5. In every corner of her room and on every wall and table, Nora displayed her interest in biology.
6. On a clear day from atop Point Jarvis in New Jersey, you can see three different states.
7. Italian and Spanish, which are both Romance languages, are alike in several respects.
8. Though both use the same equipment, cross-country skiing and downhill skiing are vastly different sports.

9. Long before we reached the door of the farmhouse, we could tell that no one had lived on the farm for many years.
10. To bake a perfect muffin, you must follow these directions exactly.

REVIEW EXERCISE F. Evaluating and Revising Paragraphs.
Read the numbered paragraphs carefully. As you read, consider what is wrong with each paragraph and how it can be improved. Use the following questions to help you decide how the paragraph might be improved.

1. Does the paragraph have a topic sentence that states the main idea clearly and precisely? How effective is the topic sentence?
2. What is the writer's purpose?
3. Does the paragraph contain sufficient details to support the main idea?
4. Does the paragraph contain any sentences that destroy the paragraph's unity?
5. Are the paragraph's ideas presented in a logical order?
6. If you could add information or details, what would you add?
7. Does the paragraph have a clincher sentence? How effective is it? If you think a paragraph that does not have a clincher sentence would benefit from one, try to write several versions.

Revise all three paragraphs, and write your revised versions on a separate sheet of paper. When you have improved each paragraph as much as possible, proofread your revised paragraphs before making final copies.

1

Civilization has come such a long way that it is now possible to spend several hundred dollars on kitchen gadgets. If advertisers have their way, the days of "hands-on" food preparation are on their way out. Gone are the days of hand-operated can openers, hand kneading of dough, and slicing vegetables by hand. Food processors are an expensive kitchen gadget. They knead, chop, grate, slice, blend, stir, and whip in seconds. Microwave ovens are another expensive piece of kitchen equipment. People who use these expensive gadgets swear that they cannot do without them.

2

Portable stereo radios and tape cassettes that are worn with earphones can be dangerous. They do provide wonderful sound, however, as you know if you have ever tried one. Joggers and walkers who wear them while they use or cross city streets cannot hear approaching cars or bicyclists. Drivers who wear them cannot hear car horns or sirens if the volume is up too high. A recent law in this county makes people who bicycle in the streets while wearing such earphones liable to a ticket with a fifty-dollar fine.

3

Graphology is the study of handwriting. Graphologists are experts in handwriting. They believe that they can analyze people's personalities by studying samples of their handwriting. To read a person's character traits, they look carefully at the slant of the writing and the spacing between words. They analyze the size of the letters, the shape of loops and cross-bars, end strokes, and punctuation. My handwriting teacher, Mr. Smith, used to be furious at students who wrote small circles over their lower-case *i*'s and *j*'s instead of simply dotting them. The worst offense, according to Mr. Smith, was not crossing our *t*'s. According to graphologists, a straight capital *I* with no loops or curves suggests that a person is extremely confident. A person whose handwriting looks almost like printing is said to be creative, witty, and independent.

GUIDELINES FOR WRITING AND REVISING PARAGRAPHS

1. Does the paragraph have a topic sentence that clearly states the paragraph's main idea?
2. Does the topic sentence arouse the reader's interest?
3. Do supporting sentences develop the paragraph's main idea with sufficient detail?
4. Would the paragraph be improved by adding a concluding, or clincher, sentence that restates the main idea, summarizes specific details, or suggests a course of action?
5. Does every sentence in the paragraph relate directly to the main idea? Have all sentences that destroy the paragraph's unity been eliminated?
6. Are the ideas in the paragraph arranged logically according to a definite plan?
7. Does the paragraph contain pronouns and transitional expressions that clearly link ideas to one another?

CHAPTER 14 WRITING REVIEW

Developing a Paragraph. Choose a topic that may be organized chronologically, spatially, by order of importance, or by comparison or contrast. You may choose a topic of your own or one of the following topics: "packing a canoe with supplies," "frying chicken," "pruning a tree," "executing a football play," "comparing or contrasting two kinds of pasta," "two varieties of roses," or "the African elephant and the Indian elephant." When you have selected your topic and determined the order you will use, plan your paragraph: Write an effective topic sentence; list supporting information; write a possible clincher sentence; eliminate any supporting information that might destroy the paragraph's unity; arrange the supporting information in a clear order; make a list of transitional expressions you might use. Then, if your teacher directs, write a first version of your paragraph.

CHAPTER 15

Writing Paragraphs

DEVELOPMENT OF PARAGRAPHS

You have seen in Chapter 14 that paragraphs are made up of topic sentences, supporting sentences, and sometimes clincher sentences. These are the three basic ingredients of a paragraph. You have also seen that effective paragraphs must have the two qualities of unity and coherence.

In this chapter, you will review the steps in the writing process as they apply specifically to the paragraph form. You will also practice writing four different types of paragraphs: expository, narrative, descriptive, and persuasive.

THE DEVELOPMENT OF A PARAGRAPH

Like any other form of writing, paragraphs do not happen all at once. When you write a paragraph, you use the basic writing and thinking steps—no matter what type of paragraph you are writing. You begin by asking, "What am I going to write about?"

PREWRITING

Choosing and Limiting a Topic

15a. Develop a limited topic that is suitable for a paragraph.

Paragraphs, as you have discovered from your reading of newspapers and magazines, vary in length from one or two sentences to sometimes ten or twelve. The paragraphs that you will practice writing in this chapter will be about 150 to 200 words in length and consist of six to eight sentences. Since the paragraph form has such definite space limitations, the topic that you choose must be limited enough so that it can be adequately developed in a single paragraph.

In Chapter 13, you practiced limiting a broad subject by analyzing it into its smaller parts. The following diagram shows how the broad subject "mystery stories" can be limited to a topic suitable for a paragraph.

EXAMPLE

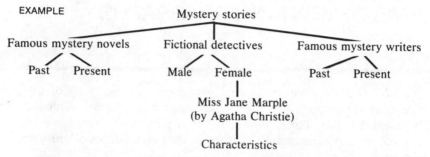

The writer has analyzed the broad subject "mystery stories" into three basic parts and further broken down each part into at least two other parts. The idea of famous female detectives seemed most appealing, so the writer thought of one specific example, Miss Jane Marple. Realizing that even this was too broad a topic for a paragraph, the writer further limited the topic to "the characteristics of Miss Jane Marple."

A broad subject may be limited by focusing on a specific example, aspect, time, part, or use, as in the following examples.

TOO BROAD Disc jockeys

SUITABLY LIMITED Qualities that make a disc jockey successful [Specific aspect of the job]

TOO BROAD Problems of a single parent

SUITABLY LIMITED How Rusty Lester, a single parent, holds weekly family meetings with her children [Specific example]

TOO BROAD Immigration to the United States

SUITABLY LIMITED Numbers of Haitians immigrating to the United States during the 1980's [Specific example and specific time]

EXERCISE 1. Limiting a Broad Topic. For each numbered item, provide at least two topics that are limited enough for a single paragraph.

EXAMPLE 1. Air conditioning
1. *How a room air conditioner removes moisture from the air*

1. Caring for a pet
2. Holiday celebrations in our home
3. My hobbies
4. Women in American politics
5. Early exploration of America
6. Coretta Scott King
7. Nuclear arms race
8. My goals
9. American folk tales and legends
10. Hawaii

EXERCISE 2. Choosing and Limiting a Topic. Select a subject that interests you. Then divide the subject into smaller parts, and continue subdividing until you have three limited topics that are suitable for paragraphs. If you wish, you may use a subject from the list above.

Considering Purpose and Audience

15b. Determine your purpose for writing the paragraph.

Before you begin writing, make sure that you have a clear understanding of *why* you are writing. Is your purpose to *explain* an idea or some facts, or are you writing to *describe* a scene or person? You may be writing to tell a story or to persuade your audience to do something. Occasionally you may write for a combination of purposes, as, for example, when you describe a dangerous intersection and then try to persuade the city council to put up a traffic light at that intersection. Knowing what your purpose is will help you to keep firm control over the content of your paragraph.

In the paragraph on the next page, the writer's purpose is to describe the sounds and sights in a kitchen on a warm summer day. Being aware of her purpose enabled the writer to eliminate any details and information that were not directly related to that purpose.

It was warm in the kitchen. A blow-fly buzzed, a fan of whity steam came out of the kettle, and the lid kept up a rattling jig as the water bubbled. The clock ticked in the warm air, slow and deliberate, like the click of an old woman's knitting needle, and sometimes—for no reason at all, for there wasn't any breeze—the blind swung out and back, tapping the window.

KATHERINE MANSFIELD

15c. Consider how your audience will affect your writing.

Your audience will affect your writing in three important ways. First, your audience will affect the limited topic that you choose; you will want to choose a topic that interests your audience and is not beyond their understanding. Suppose, for example, that you decide to write about blue jeans. Will an audience of tenth-graders be more interested in a paragraph about how the first Levi's were invented and why they are called Levi's, or will they prefer to read about how to repair the machinery on which denim is woven? The first topic will probably have much more appeal for your audience.

Second, your audience will affect the kinds of details and information that you include in your paragraph. You must provide whatever background information the audience needs to understand the ideas in the paragraph, and you may also have to define unfamiliar or technical terms. For instance, if you were writing for an audience of seventh-graders about the death of the last passenger pigeon in 1914, you would provide background information about how abundant passenger pigeons once were in America. If your audience were a group of second-graders, you might need to define the terms *species* and *extinct*.

Finally, your audience will affect the language you use to express your ideas. Although you need to write simply and clearly for all audiences, you would probably use short sentences and an easy vocabulary for an audience of second-graders. For an audience of adults, your sentences would be longer and more complex to avoid the monotonous, singsong effect of a string of short declarative sentences. (See pages 279–91 on combining sentences.)

EXERCISE 3. Rewriting Paragraphs for a Different Audience.

Rewrite the following paragraphs for the audiences specified. Pay attention to vocabulary, sentence length, and the way in which ideas are presented. If you need to add any additional background material or to define unfamiliar terms, use reference books to find the information that you need.

1. The following paragraph appeared in a special section on future careers in *The New York Times,* written for adults. Rewrite the paragraph so that the same ideas are expressed for a class of fourth-graders.

> People who are adept at dealing with other people will find a wealth of jobs open to them by the turn of the century, predicts Christopher Dede, past president of the World Future Society and a visiting scientist at M.I.T. The need for their services, he said, will be largely a response to the problem of having so many jobs dependent upon computer interaction all day long. This, he said, will create a need for intensive human contact in every other sphere of life, helped along by professions. His list of such people includes therapists of all kinds, educators, people in dating services, and negotiators and conciliators to bring more disputes out of the courts and into mediation.
>
> ANDREE BROOKS

2. The following paragraph is from *The Trumpet of the Swan* by E. B. White, a novel for young readers. Rewrite the paragraph for an audience of adults.

> Months went by. Winter came to the Red Rock Lakes. The nights were long and dark and cold. The days were short and bright and cold. Sometimes the wind blew. But the swans and geese and ducks were safe and happy. The warm springs that fed the lakes kept the ice from covering them—there were always open places. There was plenty of food. Sometimes a man would arrive with a bag of grain and spread the grain where the birds could get it.
>
> E. B. WHITE

Gathering Information

15d. Gather information about the limited topic of your paragraph.

Chances are that most of your one-paragraph compositions will be about your own experiences, observations, and ideas. For such paragraphs, you need not do any research. You can gather all the information you will need either by sitting down with a piece of paper and a pencil and thinking about your topic or by making some new observations. Brainstorming and clustering are two techniques for getting onto paper ideas and specific details that are already in your head.

Your journal will also help you to remember an event or observation and will remind you of specific details that you can convey to your reader. (On pages 320–28 of Chapter 13, you learned about these and other techniques for gathering information. You may want to review these pages at this time.)

Other ways to gather information include asking yourself questions about the topic. The *5 W-How?* questions (*Who? What? Where? When? Why?* and *How?*) will help you gather specific details, although not all of the questions will apply to every topic. Other questions that you may ask include "What is it?" "What is its relation to its surroundings?" and "How does it change or vary?" You may need to turn to sources outside yourself to find the answers to some of these questions. Talking to others and using reference books will enable you to fill in any missing information.

As you gather information for your paragraph, be sure to put all your ideas into writing—either in the form of a list or as notes. Only when you have completed the longest list you feel you can produce should you go back and decide which ideas are usable and which ones should be eliminated. The following list shows how one writer evaluated information for a paragraph on a September evening visit to Faneuil Hall in Boston.

Details: Crowds of people, mostly young
        Hundreds of restaurants and food stalls—all kinds of foods, foods from all nations
        Ate a Greek souvlakia
        Friedman's bakery—one of best in Boston
        Stopped to eat a boysenberry frozen yogurt
        Shops and pushcarts—all kinds of clothing and souvenir items; some clothing stores very expensive
        Crowds gathered around juggler and comedian in open square
        Brick sidewalks; trees and benches
        Few elderly people
        Bought a T-shirt for my brother
        Had a photograph taken of me wearing 1890's costume
        Young woman playing guitar and singing folk songs
        Cool, clear fall night
        Brilliant colors of banners, flowers, people's clothing
        Greenhouse area of plants and flowers

EXERCISE 4. Gathering Information for a Paragraph.   Choose three of the following limited topics (or choose three of your own), and for each topic write a long list of details and information you might use for a paragraph. You may use any of the techniques for gathering information discussed on pages 320–28.

1. The last birthday celebration you remember (your own or someone else's)
2. What you did on New Year's Day this year
3. Something you hope to accomplish this year
4. What you value most about your best friend
5. A career that might interest you
6. Your favorite musical group or performer
7. A hobby or sport that you would like to try someday
8. A famous person no longer living about whom you would like to know more
9. A time when you laughed very hard—what happened to make you laugh
10. A place that you would like to visit someday

EXERCISE 5. Gathering Information for a Paragraph. Choose a limited topic, and use one or more of the information-gathering techniques to compile a long list of information for that topic. If you wish, you may use one of the topics in Exercise 4 that you have not already used. When your list is as long as you can make it, go over your list carefully, and cross out any ideas or details that are not directly related to the topic. You will use the resulting list as a basis for a paragraph you will write later in this chapter.

Ways of Developing a Paragraph

15e. Choose an appropriate method of development for your paragraph.

What goes into the supporting sentences that develop the paragraph's main idea? The kinds of details you can put into these sentences include concrete and sensory details, facts and statistics, reasons, examples, causes and effects, and incidents. On pages 399–425 you will practice using each of these types of details to develop the paragraph's main idea.

Although you will practice using these methods of paragraph development one at a time, the actual paragraphs that you write may use a combination of methods. For example, when you are writing a persuasive paragraph, you may include reasons to support your position as well as facts, statistics, and examples to support each reason. A narrative about an exciting event not only may tell about a specific incident but also may use concrete and sensory details to describe the setting and the characters.

15f. Write an effective topic sentence.

You have already learned that an effective topic sentence states the paragraph's main idea as precisely as possible. The topic sentence also limits the paragraph's content because everything that is included in the paragraph must directly support the main idea as it is stated in the topic sentence. An effective topic sentence should be clearly worded and should, whenever possible, arouse the reader's interest and curiosity. For practice in writing effective topic sentences, review the material on pages 346–51 in Chapter 14.

Developing a Working Plan

15g. Develop a working plan for your paragraph.

When you have decided on the ideas you will include in the paragraph, arrange the ideas in the order you think is most effective, and then write a sample outline of your paragraph. Examine the following outline of a paragraph.

Topic sentence: People vary a great deal in the conditions they require for efficient study.
Details: Some want silence and solitude.
 Others want noise and company.
 Some want the radio on.
 Some want the same conditions day after day.
 Some can study anywhere.

EXERCISE 6. Making a Paragraph Outline. Make a paragraph outline for each of the following topic sentences. The items in the outline need not be in sentence form. Copy the topic sentence first; then list the details you would use in your paragraph.

1. Anyone planning a trip from New York to San Francisco can find several ways to make the journey.
2. There are many reasons people would rather attend a spectator sport than watch it on television.

3. In every home certain jobs should be delegated to the children.
4. You will find some of the same types of teachers in any high school.
5. All tenth-graders must make some important decisions that will affect their future lives.

EXERCISE 7. Making a Paragraph Outline. Write a topic sentence for the limited topic you chose for Exercise 5. Then arrange your details in the order you wish to present them, and make a paragraph outline.

WRITING

WRITING THE FIRST DRAFT

15h. Write a first draft of your paragraph.

The main task involved in writing the first draft is expressing the paragraph information in sentences that are easy to understand. If your ideas in the paragraph outline are already expressed in sentences (as on page 390), writing the first draft should be a simple task. If, however, you are writing from a list of details, you will need to think of how best to express your images and ideas in complete sentences.

Remember that the first draft is *not* the finished version of your paragraph. When you revise the paragraph, you will spend time trying to improve content, word choice, and organization. A final step will be proofreading the paragraph to make sure that it conforms to the conventions of written standard English.

Here is the first draft of a paragraph based on the list of details on page 388.

On a cool September evening, Boston's Faneuil Hall and Quincy Market are very crowded. It must be the busiest place in Boston. Inside the marketplace, hundreds of young people stroll and visit the restaurants and food stalls, sampling foods from all nations. The smell of Greek souvlakia mingles with Belgian waffles, Israeli falafel, pizza, and Indian curry. Hundreds of restaurants and booths tempt the stroller with both ethnic foods

and typical American foods. When they are not eating, strollers eye the passing crowds, looking for familiar faces or perhaps someone to meet and talk
with. Outside the hall, in the cool, dark night, applause and laughter float
on the air from the crowd that circles a mime and a juggler onstage in the
courtyard between the two main buildings. Away from the entertainment,
crowds browse through the dozens of pushcarts that line the sidewalks
and streets. (It is possible to buy rugs from Peru, Boston T-shirts, mufflers
from Scotland—anything from anywhere.) The trees and branches cast
shadows on the brick sidewalks, the strollers, and the bench sitters. Above,
brightly colored banners wave gently in the night air. The whole area seems
ablaze with color and movement as the crowds of people move, stop, and
move again. Serious shoppers enter the expensive and moderate-priced
shops that line the sidewalks or browse the windows of closed stores.

EXERCISE 8. Writing a First Draft. Use the following list of details
to write the first draft of a paragraph about different types of dreams.
You do not have to use all the details, and you may change examples
or make up additional details of your own.

Details: Don't always remember dreams, but sometimes jot them down right
after waking
Keeping a journal of dreams
In most I am main character
Some nightmares—being chased by large animal in pitch-black night
Some pleasant, wishes come true: winning an award or large sum of
money; dreams of romance and adventure
Some recur—unable to open school locker and remember combina-
tion
Some remembered in vivid color; some with sound
Sometimes friends and family appear

EXERCISE 9. Writing a First Draft. Write a first draft of the paragraph you outlined in Exercise 7.

REVIEW EXERCISE A. Writing a First Draft. Choose a limited
topic, and go through all of the prewriting steps outlined on pages 383–
90. Then write a first draft of your paragraph. Before you begin writing,
make sure that you have arranged your ideas in a logical order. Begin
by writing a topic sentence. Follow the topic sentence with five to
seven sentences that provide adequate supporting details. Consider
whether a clincher sentence will strengthen the paragraph, and, if so,
write one.

REVISING

15i. Revise the first draft of your paragraph.

Your writing task does not stop once you have completed your first draft. The next stage of the writing process, revising, requires that you reread the first draft several times as you evaluate different aspects of the paragraph. You need not do each step in the suggested order, but each step must be completed before you can consider your paragraph finished. Experienced writers know that it is impossible to "see" six different things at once and that reading for revising should focus on only one thing at a time.

You may begin by deciding whether your topic sentence is as effective as you can make it or whether it can be improved. Does it clearly express the paragraph's main idea? Is it interesting enough to make a reader want to find out what is in the rest of the paragraph? Then consider whether or not the paragraph has enough supporting information. Have you added enough specific details, reasons, or examples to support the topic sentence? Have you left out any important information that would strengthen the paragraph? Consider once more the purpose and the audience as you read the paragraph as a whole. How well does the paragraph accomplish your intended purpose? How appropriate is the language for the audience? As you revise, read through the paragraph once again to make sure that it does not contain ideas, words, or phrases that destroy the paragraph's unity. Check also on coherence: how effectively the ideas are organized and how smoothly the sentences flow together. Finally, focus "up close" on each word and phrase as you decide whether you can replace a word or phrase with one that is more precise or vivid.

GUIDELINES FOR REVISING PARAGRAPHS

1. Does the paragraph contain a topic sentence that accurately and clearly expresses the paragraph's main idea?
2. Is there sufficient supporting information to develop the main idea?
3. Do all sentences in the paragraph support the paragraph's main idea? Are all ideas directly related to the main idea?
4. Does the paragraph contain a concluding, or clincher, sentence to summarize the main points or restate the main idea?

5. Is the writer's purpose clear to the reader? Has the paragraph achieved that purpose? Is the language in the paragraph appropriate for the intended audience?

6. Are the ideas arranged in a logical order?

7. Does the paragraph contain transitional words, synonyms, pronouns, and repetition of key words to tie the sentences together smoothly?

8. Have any words and phrases that are awkward, vague, or confusing been replaced with specific, clear language?

The following example shows the changes the writer made in revising the first draft of the paragraph on pages 391–92.

On a cool September evening, Boston's Faneuil Hall and Quincy Market *teem with activity.* ~~are very crowded. It must be the busiest place in Boston.~~ Inside the marketplace, ~~hun~~-dreds *thousands* of *mostly* young people ~~stroll and visit the restaurants~~ and food stalls, ~~sampling~~ *sample* foods from all nations. The *savory aromas* ~~smell~~ of Greek souvlakia mingles with *the hot, sweet smell of* Belgian waffles, *and caramel apples and the spicy smells of* Israeli falafel, pizza, and ~~Indian~~ curry. Hundreds of restaurants and booths tempt the stroller with both ethnic foods and *apple-pie* ~~typical~~ American foods. When they are not eating, ~~strollers~~ *those who walk or stand still or sit* eye the passing crowds, looking for familiar faces or perhaps someone to meet and talk with.

Outside the hall, in the cool, dark night, applause and laughter float on the air *A laughing* ~~from the~~ crowd ~~that~~ circles a mime and a juggler *onstage* in the courtyard between the two main buildings. Away from the entertainment, *tourists and shoppers* ~~crowds~~ browse through the dozens of pushcarts that line the sidewalks ~~and streets~~.

Margin notes:

Use more precise wording.

Eliminate dull, uninteresting sentence.

Eliminate unnecessary and weak phrases.

Add more precise details.

Replace bland word with more colorful one.

Avoid repeating *strollers:* use more precise description of what crowds are doing.

Break up long sentence into two shorter ones.

Replace vague word with more precise one.

There one can

(~~It is possible to~~ buy rugs from Peru, Boston T-shirts,

scarves

^~~mufflers~~ from Scotland—anything from anywhere.) The

trees and branches cast shadows on the brick sidewalks,

the strollers, and the bench sitters. Above, brightly

colored banners wave gently in the night air. The whole

area seems ablaze with color and movement as the

on

crowds of people move, stop, and move ^again. ~~Serious~~

~~shoppers enter the expensive and moderate-priced~~

~~shops that line the sidewalks or browse the windows of~~

~~closed stores.~~

Replace awkward wording.

Replace unfamiliar word with more familiar one.

Use more precise wording.

Delete unnecessary sentence.

CRITICAL THINKING:
Evaluating Word Choices

In order to revise a paragraph, you must be able to decide whether one word or phrase is better than another word or phrase. This process of judging whether something is better or worse involves the critical thinking skill called *evaluating*.

Evaluating is developed through practice and experience. For example, you are much better at judging a topic sentence today than you were as a seven-year-old. The more you actually practice writing, the more you sharpen your skills of evaluating what you write and what others write. Evaluating skills are also developed by exposure to good writing, which is why the model paragraphs in this book are by professional writers. If you had never read an example of a good paragraph, how could you be expected to know if a paragraph is good or bad?

In this chapter and throughout the composition section, the word *effective* is used to indicate writing that is good. An effective topic sentence, for example, does all that it is supposed to do and is interesting to read besides. Take a look at the examples on the next page, and see if you can judge which one is most effective.

EXAMPLES   1. Many employers are encouraging their employees to develop healthy habits.
2. At Johnson & Johnson headquarters in New Brunswick, New Jersey, employees can take lunch-hour exercise classes.
3. Lunch-hour exercise classes at Johnson & Johnson and free physical exams at IBM are part of a growing nationwide movement in which employers offer fitness programs to their employees.

Of the three topic sentences, the third is most effective because it interests the reader with two specific examples and then goes on to state precisely the paragraph's main idea. The first example states the main idea but is not interesting to read; the second is interesting to read but does not state the main idea.

Choices in wording involve making judgments about how precisely and clearly the word expresses the intended meaning. Another consideration in choosing the words to express an idea is the paragraph's intended tone—whether it is formal or informal (see pages 315–17).

EXERCISE 10. Evaluating Word Choices.   In the following paragraph, certain word choices are given in parentheses. For each one, choose the word or phrase that you think would be effective in the paragraph. Be prepared to explain why you made each choice.

Lunch-hour exercise classes at Johnson & Johnson and free physical exams at IBM are part of a growing nationwide (interest, trend, increase) in which employers offer "wellness programs" to their employees. Such programs are (hoped, planned, designed) to improve employees' physical health and, (in part, as a result, on the other hand), to decrease absenteeism and increase productivity. Company officials (say, think, report) that existing fitness programs have (hopefully, already, probably) saved them millions of dollars' worth of lost work time and employee (medical expenses, doctors' bills, hospital bills). Exercise classes and weight-loss programs are (usually, sometimes, often) found in large companies, some of which also have programs to help (attack, eliminate, target) employees' smoking and alcoholism. Smaller companies that do not have their own exercise programs often pay all or part of employees' (money, bills, expenses) at private classes, such as those (offered, run, done) by the Y.M.C.A. Workers say that exercise classes and other wellness programs not only make them feel good about themselves but also make them feel (good, proud, friendly) about their employers.

EXERCISE 11. Revising a First Draft. Revise the following first draft of a paragraph about a fingerprinting program for children. Copy the paragraph on a separate sheet of paper; then revise it step by step as you go through the revision guidelines on pages 393–94 one question at a time. You may add whatever additional details or information you think would improve the paragraph. When you feel that the paragraph is as good as you can make it, copy the revised version on a separate sheet of paper.

A chain of grocery stores is cooperating with the police department in order that a missing children-identification program can be created in order to protect the children of this community. Every parent or guardian should have every child's fingerprints (all ten are suggested) on file and identification on the same form. Along with a current photograph and information about an accurate description. The grocery store supplies the form, and it also has a black square that can be used for fingerprinting. And there are also instructions on how to do the fingerprinting. Forms available from grocery stores ask for the child's full name and nickname, birthday, race, sex, eye color, height, and weight. They want to know about medications, allergies, scars, and additional identifying information. Parents should keep these forms on file so that they will be available to police just in case a child becomes missing. If a child becomes missing, parents are supposed to call the local police and the county sheriff's office, they should call a special toll-free number for the Missing Children's Information Center that has an office in the state capital.

REVIEW EXERCISE B. Revising a First Draft. Revise the first draft of the paragraph you wrote for Review Exercise A. Refer to the Guidelines for Revising Paragraphs on pages 393–94. When you have finished revising the paragraph, copy the revised version on a separate sheet of paper.

PROOFREADING

When you proofread, you correct inaccuracies in grammar, usage, and mechanics (spelling, capitalization, punctuation). Be sure to refer to the Guidelines for Proofreading on page 339 and to proofread your paragraph several times.

EXERCISE 12. Proofreading a Paragraph. Proofread the following paragraph, and write it on a separate sheet of paper. Your proofread version should follow all of the conventions of standard written English. Refer to the Guidelines for Proofreading on page 339.

Something must be done about the empty lot across from the Department of Sanitation on Twelfth avenue and West 56th street, the lot is so full of litter that it looks like a dumping ground for the city's garbage trucks. Actually, litter has simply accumulated there over the year, blown by winds or thrown by humans. Because it is not city property, the city itself is not responsible for cleaning up the lot. However a city official in the proper department should notify the owner of the lot that it must be cleaned up within a certain time limit. Perhaps two weeks. If the owner does not clean up the lot, the city should hire a cleanup crew or use volunters from a local charity. The city could then bill the lots owner for the amount paid to the workers or to the charity. Vacant lots must be kept clean to keep the city attractive and to avoid rats and other health problems.

FOUR TYPES OF PARAGRAPHS

15j. Learn to write four types of paragraphs: expository, descriptive, narrative, and persuasive.

Like longer forms of writing, which you will study in later chapters, most paragraphs can be classified into four types: expository, descriptive, narrative, and persuasive. The type of paragraph you write often depends on your purpose in writing.

For each type of paragraph, certain methods of paragraph development and certain types of order (methods of arranging supporting details) are appropriate. You have already studied four types of paragraph order on pages 368–77. In the following sections, you will practice using six different types of paragraph development in the four paragraph categories.

1. An *expository paragraph* informs or explains.

EXAMPLE A paragraph explaining how Mother's Day came to be a national holiday

2. A *descriptive paragraph* describes a particular person, place, or object.

EXAMPLE   A paragraph describing the flower garden you planted as a Mother's Day gift

3. A *narrative paragraph* tells a story.

EXAMPLE   A paragraph about how Mother's Day was celebrated in your home last year

4. A *persuasive paragraph* attempts to convince the reader that an opinion is true or persuade the reader to perform a specific action.

EXAMPLE   A paragraph persuading students to make their own greeting cards for Mother's Day

The Expository Paragraph

When you write an expository paragraph, your purpose is to give information, to explain something, or to do both. The writer of the expository paragraph on page 400, for example, gives a great deal of specific information about the shark-fin industry in Hong Kong. Expository paragraphs may be developed with facts and statistics, examples, or causes and effects.

You have read about four types of order (chronological, spatial, order of importance, and comparison and contrast) on pages 368–77. Each of these types of order may be used in an expository paragraph, depending on the writer's purpose and subject matter. For example, when the purpose of a paragraph is to explain how to do or make something or how something works, it is only natural to give the steps of the process in the order in which they must be performed. This is chronological order, the order in which events happen in time. In the following paragraph about the stages in setting up a space station, the details are given in chronological order.

[1]After blasting off, the booster rockets the entire double assembly up into the final reaches of the earth's atmosphere. [2]Having achieved proper altitude and velocity, the booster separates from the orbiter stage. [3]Then the booster extends its wings and, guided by its two-man crew, returns to earth in normal airplane fashion, using auxiliary jet engines as necessary. [4]The second stage, which

(1) topic sentence

(2) first step

(3) second step

(4) third step

carries the payload of personnel and supplies, takes up where the booster stage lets off. ⁵It ac-celerates on into orbit and makes a rendezvous with the space station. ⁶After transferring its crew and cargo, and picking up whatever personnel or equipment is scheduled for a return to earth, the orbiter casts off for the journey home. ⁷Owing to its unique design, which includes small wings and efficient control surfaces, it is able to spiral down-ward and reenter the atmosphere at a safe, gentle angle, unthreatened by extreme friction heat.

(5) fourth step

(6) fifth step

(7) concluding sen-tence

Developing a Paragraph with Facts and Statistics

(1) An expository paragraph may be developed with facts and statistics.

If your purpose is to explain or to provide information, it is natural that you develop your topic sentence with facts and statistics. A *fact* is a statement that can be proved to be true. Historical events and dates are facts, as are scientific findings that can be checked or repro-duced. It is a fact, for example, that the earth is one of nine planets that revolve around the sun. It is also a fact that the Bill of Rights (the first ten amendments to the United States Constitution) was adopted on December 15, 1791.

Statistics are facts that are expressed in numbers and have been accurately collected and recorded. In the following paragraph, the writer uses both facts and statistics to develop the central idea.

In Hong Kong the shark fin is so important a luxury food that an industry worth more than $10 billion a year has grown up around its capture, sale and preparation. Many Hong Kong fishermen make their living catching sharks in the South China Sea and other waters near Hong Kong. And because the fins are so highly regarded, their importation from such places as India, Singapore, the Philippines, Taiwan, Japan, Norway, Mexico and South America is a big business. Fins are auctioned twice daily in Hong Kong, and more than 3,000 tons a year find their way to the city's restaurants through its 20 auction houses and more than 100 profes-sional buyers.

EILEEN YIN-FEL LO

In a paragraph developed by facts and statistics, simpler facts should be given before those that are harder to understand. As you write such a paragraph, think of yourself as a teacher. Ask yourself, "What do I need to explain first? What do I need to explain next?"

The tone of an expository paragraph should be factual and unemotional. This can be accomplished by using clear and precise language to present your facts. Such a tone will influence the reader to believe that the information you are presenting is true and accurate. Expository paragraphs should also be objective; that is, you, the writer, should not intrude your personality into the paragraph. The following sentence would be inappropriate in an expository paragraph because it destroys the factual, impersonal tone.

INAPPROPRIATE TONE   When I was mining for rubies in North Carolina, I spent two disgusting hours in the boiling-hot sun sifting through six buckets of mud, and I didn't find a single ruby.

APPROPRIATE TONE   Visitors to the ruby mines just north of Franklin, North Carolina, pay two dollars a bucket for the privilege of sifting through mud and clay dug from the ruby mines.

CRITICAL THINKING:
Distinguishing Between Facts and Opinions

The difference between a fact and an opinion is a simple one: A *fact* is a statement that can be proved to be true, whereas an *opinion* is a statement that cannot be proved. To write effective expository and persuasive paragraphs, you must be able to distinguish between facts and opinions. As a reader and as a listener, also, it is essential to know when you are being given an accurate, true, verifiable fact and when you are listening to someone's ideas or opinions.

FACT   The capital of Alaska is Juneau.
OPINION   Alaska is the most beautiful state in the United States.

FACT   Almost three fifths of the earth's surface is covered by water.
OPINION   Everyone should learn to swim.

FACT   Ella Fitzgerald was born in Newport News, Virginia, on April 25, 1918.

OPINION   Ella Fitzgerald is the greatest female jazz singer of the twentieth century.

If you look carefully, you can see that opinions often use "judgment" words, such as *most, should, should not, greatest,* and *best.* Everyone has opinions about people, things, and events—and opinions are perfectly acceptable; but they should never be confused with facts. An opinion cannot prove anything; facts can.

EXERCISE 13. Distinguishing Between Facts and Opinions. Some of the following statements are facts, and some are opinions. Number your paper 1–10. After the proper number, write *F* for each fact and *O* for each opinion. (Assume that the statements that are written as facts are true.)

1. Booker T. Washington, an American educator, lived from 1856 to 1915.
2. The constellation Orion is named for a giant hunter in Greek mythology.
3. Greek myths are more interesting to read than Roman myths.
4. If anything can go wrong, it will.
5. A gargoyle is a grotesque human or animal figure that functions as a rain spout, carrying water away from the roof.
6. Greta Garbo was the most talented silent-film star.
7. Each of the signs of the zodiac is the name of a constellation.
8. Cigarette smoking is dangerous to human beings' health.
9. Everyone should be able to speak at least one foreign language, preferably two.
10. Carry Nation was an American reformer who led the movement for prohibition.

EXERCISE 14. Writing an Expository Paragraph Developed with Facts and Statistics. Write a paragraph based on one of the following topic sentences. You may need to do some research to gather facts and statistics to develop the topic sentence. If you prefer, you may write a paragraph on a topic of your own, using facts, statistics, or both to develop the main idea.

1. One of the greatest problems in the world is the nuclear arms buildup.
2. Many popular beliefs about wild animals are completely wrong.
3. Sports in this country are more popular than ever before.
4. In the past twenty-five years the percentage of American women in the labor force has steadily increased.
5. A volcanic eruption is perhaps the most destructive force on earth.
6. No one knows exactly why it is so, but women in the United States have a significantly longer life span than men do.
7. The average age at which women and men marry has been rising steadily.
8. For the past five years, the school's tenth-grade students have scored higher (lower) than the national average on tests of verbal and math abilities.
9. Experts who predict what the job market will be like ten years from now are able to identify the jobs and professions for which there will be a high demand.
10. Television has become so much a part of the American way of life that it is difficult to imagine a time or a place without TV.

PREWRITING To gather facts and statistics for most of these topics, decide first exactly what kind of information you are looking for. For sentence 10, for example, you might try to find statistics on the number of television sets per home today and the number of homes without any television sets. You might also try to find out how these numbers have changed over time—for example, how the percentage of homes without television sets today compares with the percentage twenty years ago. You will need to look for such information in an almanac or other reference book, such as *Statistical Abstracts of the United States*. Ask your reference librarian for help in finding information on the topic that you have chosen. If you are lucky, you will find more information than you can use in a single paragraph. When you decide what information you will use, you may reword the topic sentence any way you wish to adjust it to the information that you actually find. Arrange your ideas in what seems to be a logical order.

WRITING If you are using statistics, try not to use too many in a single paragraph. You do not want to overwhelm your reader with numbers. You may also use facts to break up the statistics. If your paragraph is made up mostly of factual information, a few statistics will support the factual statements and help make them more believable. Concentrate on expressing your ideas clearly in fairly formal language.

REVISING AND PROOFREADING For a paragraph developed with facts and statistics, ask someone else to read your paragraph and tell you whether or not it is easy to understand. Such feedback will help you to make sure that you have expressed your ideas clearly. Follow the Guidelines for Writing and Revising Expository Paragraphs on pages 412–13, and refer to the Guidelines for Proofreading on page 339.

EXERCISE 15. Writing an Expository Paragraph Developed with Facts and Statistics. The following graph shows clearly the rise and fall of unemployment between the years 1965 and 1978. In a one-paragraph report, tell what trends the graph illustrates for unemployment for these years.

As your teacher directs, research the unemployment figures for the years 1975 to 1986. Prepare a graph similar to the one in this exercise. Write a one-paragraph report telling what trends your graph illustrates for unemployment for those years.

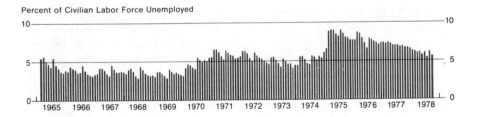

Percent of Civilian Labor Force Unemployed

Developing a Paragraph with Examples

(2) An expository paragraph may be developed with examples.

Sometimes a topic sentence states a general idea that can best be supported by a number of specific examples. If carefully chosen, each specific example will make the topic sentence clearer for the reader. In the following paragraph, how many examples does the writer give to demonstrate the idea in the first sentence (the topic sentence)?

William Golding's *Lord of the Flies* is an interesting book not only because of its unusual plot but also because of the constant suspense Golding creates. For example, there is always the question of whether or not the boys will find adult help before they destroy themselves. Then, too, there is the problem of the beast. Is the beast real or is it imaginary? If real, what kind of creature is it, and how should it be dealt with? An event that adds to the suspense is the chase near the end of the book when Ralph is being hunted down by Jack and his fierce band.

The following paragraph uses a combination of facts and examples to develop the central idea stated in the topic sentence.

The English language has its peculiarities, —topic sentence
some of which make the language difficult for
speakers of another language to learn. In English, fact 1
the position of a word is very important. By plac- example
ing the word *only* before a different one of the
seven words in the following sentence, you can
change the meaning of the sentence seven times:
"She told me that she loved me." English has a fact 2
number of words that can be used with opposite
meanings. *Seeded* rye has caraway seeds in it, but examples
seeded raisins have had the seeds removed. A *fast*
horse runs, but a *fast* color does not. When plants
are *dusted,* chemical dust is sprayed on them, but
when furniture is *dusted,* the dust is wiped off.
Another source of confusion is the fact that in fact 3
English the pronoun *I* has the plural form *we,* but
the pronoun *you* is the same in the plural as in the
singular.

EXERCISE 16. Analyzing an Expository Paragraph Developed with Examples.
Read this paragraph, and answer the questions that follow it.

Our lives are a series of births and deaths: we die to one period and must be born to another. We die to childhood and are born to adolescence; to our high-school selves and (if we are fortunate) to our college selves and are born into the "real" world; to our unmarried selves and into our married. To become a parent is birth to a new self for the mother and father as well as for the baby. When Hugh and I moved from the city to

live year round at Crosswicks, this was death to one way of life and birth
to another. Then nine years later when we took our children, aged seven,
ten, and twelve, out of a big house, a quiet village, a small country school,
and moved back to New York and the world of the theatre, this was
another experience of death and birth.

MADELEINE L'ENGLE

1. What is the topic sentence in the paragraph? How effective do
   you think it is?
2. Does the paragraph have a clincher sentence? If so, what is it? If
   not, try writing at least two possible clincher sentences for this
   paragraph.
3. List all the examples the writer gives of dying and being born to
   another self.
4. Based on your own observations and experiences, can you think
   of other examples the writer might have added to this paragraph?
5. Part of the paragraph is a series of generalizations about all people.
   At what point in the paragraph does the writer begin to give
   specific details about her own life? Do you think these specific
   details improve the paragraph or detract from it? Explain your
   answer.

**EXERCISE 17. Writing an Expository Paragraph Developed with
Examples.**   Choose one of the following topics or a topic of your
own, and write a paragraph using examples to illustrate the paragraph's
central idea.

1. Problems caused by crowding in school classrooms
2. Inspiring, amazing athletes
3. Professional athletes who continue to play (whatever sport) well
   beyond an age when most athletes retire
4. Free or inexpensive places to take a date
5. Current diets to lose weight (or to stay healthy)
6. The best mystery novels (or science fiction novels) of all time
7. Current movies definitely worth seeing (or worth missing)
8. The best jazz musicians playing today
9. Problems caused when people do not communicate well
10. Some of the most common fears

PREWRITING Begin by listing details that you might include in your
paragraph. Many of these details should be examples; some may be

information that supports or explains the examples. Focus your paragraph more clearly by writing an interesting topic sentence that states the paragraph's main idea. Then go back over your list of details, and cross out those that do not seem effective, keeping only the most effective ones—those you can say the most about. Try to have at least two or three examples to support the topic sentence. Decide in which order you want to arrange the examples.

WRITING AND REVISING See if your topic sentence can be improved in any way as you write your first draft. If any of your examples need explaining or additional information, be sure to include these points before going on to the next example. You may have as many as two or three sentences for each example. When you have finished your first draft, go back over it several times, checking for content, style, and organization. Use the Guidelines for Revising Paragraphs on pages 393–94 and the Guidelines for Proofreading on page 339.

EXERCISE 18. Revising Expository Paragraphs Developed with Examples. Both of the following paragraphs are weak because insufficient details and information are included for the examples given. Revise both paragraphs by adding specific information for each example. You may also improve the paragraphs by adding transitional expressions such as *for example, for instance, in addition, too,* and *also.*

1

You have probably sat in the audience to watch a school play, but unless you have ever worked on one, you may not be aware of the long and hard efforts of the invisible specialists who never appear on stage. The director directs the actors, and the stage manager is in charge of everything else. A crew of people sets up and operates the lights. There are a costume crew and a stage crew. There are the publicity committee and a whole lot more people involved.

2

Even before people speak, they give messages to others about the kind of person they are. Their clothes reveal a lot about their tastes and personalities. Their hair styles and jewelry send a message. Their facial expressions and the way they move their bodies say a lot even without words. All of these are part of nonverbal communication—communication without words.

Developing a Paragraph with Causes and Effects

(3) An expository paragraph may be developed by discussing cause and effect.

One kind of explanation that an expository paragraph may give is in answer to the question *Why?* You may write a paragraph explaining a scientific or natural phenomenon, such as how the moon's gravity causes the rise and fall of the tides. You may write a paragraph explaining the causes of someone's behavior, such as why some people seem to lie easily and often. Whenever a paragraph is developed by means of cause and effect, it is necessary for the reader to distinguish easily between what is a cause and what is an effect. A *cause* is an event or situation that produces a result. An *effect* is anything brought about by a cause.

CAUSE   Marcie slips on the wet floor in a supermarket and falls.
EFFECT   Marcie breaks her wrist when she falls.

CAUSE   There are twelve inches of rain over a twenty-four hour period.
EFFECT   The river overflows and the downtown area is flooded.

When you write a cause-and-effect paragraph to explain why something has happened, you begin by stating the effect and going on to mention the cause or the causes. Often, as you know, more than one cause is involved in a complex event or situation. The following paragraph begins with a topic sentence that states the effect.

For the past two years, school officials have   effect
noted that fewer students are participating in after-
school activities. One of the reasons for this de-   cause 1
cline is that many students rush off to jobs that
begin immediately after school lets out. More than
half of the 150 tenth-grade students surveyed recently said they work after school or must go
home to take care of younger brothers and sisters.
Other students who responded to the survey said   cause 2
they go home right after school to watch favorite
TV shows, such as "General Hospital," which are
immensely popular with college students as well

as high-school students. Still others said that the   cause 3
reason they do not participate in after-school activities is that they are dependent for transportation
on school buses, which leave immediately after
school. Finally, some students said that they are   cause 4
just "not interested" in activities such as Drama
Club, marching band, and the school newspaper.
Perhaps the time has come to create some new   proposed solution
after-school activities that will interest more of the   to problem
students who have free time in the afternoons.

Another way to organize a cause-and-effect paragraph is to state a
cause in the topic sentence and then to describe the effects or results
of that cause. Such a paragraph does not answer the question *Why?*
but discusses the consequences of a particular situation or action.

American society has become so mobile in the   cause
twentieth century that in any given year many
families move, usually because of a job change or
a search for work. Often the move is a considerable one, involving a change of state or a change
from one region of the country to another. One of   result 1
the results of this vastly mobile society is that
most children change school systems frequently
as they grow up. Few students graduate from the
same system in which they began their schooling,
which means that young adults do not often maintain friendships from their early years. Another   result 2
result of frequent moves is the loss of a sense of
"roots" as fewer and fewer adults remain in the
same place where they were born and their par-
ents and grandparents lived. Perhaps the most se-   result 3
rious consequence of our highly mobile society,
however, is that families are widely separated as
children move to different parts of the country,
marry, and have families. Because travel is

expensive, families do not regularly get together for holidays and other family occasions, and children grow up never really knowing their cousins, aunts, uncles, and grandparents.

If you write a paragraph using the cause-and-effect method of development, you need to make clear to the reader which statements are causes and which are results. Some words and phrases that help to make your ideas clear to the reader include the following ones:

WORDS THAT INDICATE CAUSES AND EFFECTS

because	since	as a result	effect
cause	so that	thus	if
reason	unless	consequently	therefore

EXERCISE 19. Planning a Cause-and-Effect Paragraph. Each of the following topic sentences states a cause. For each topic sentence, make a list of all the possible effects (or results) that you can think of. Write each effect in a complete sentence.

EXAMPLE   *Cause:* Enrollment in an already crowded high school increases by 10 percent in September.
         Effects: a. Class sizes are larger.
               b. Halls are more crowded between classes.
               c. The cafeteria is so crowded during lunch hour that some students have no place to sit.

1. *Cause:* The high-school football team is having a spectacular season, winning all of the games played so far this year.
2. *Cause:* Three new industries come to your community, employing a total of 1,350 new workers.
3. *Cause:* Legislation strictly controlling the disposal of toxic wastes is passed in your community.
4. *Cause:* A time machine suddenly propels you two thousand years into the future.
5. *Cause:* The national driving speed limit is raised to 75 miles per hour.

EXERCISE 20. Planning a Cause-and-Effect Paragraph. Each of the following numbered items makes a statement about a situation. For each situation, think of as many possible causes as you can. Remember that the causes will answer the question *Why?* about the situation. Write each cause in a complete sentence.

EXAMPLE   *Effect:* New car sales are less than half what they were a year ago.
   Causes: a. People have less money to spend on luxury items.
   b. People are repairing their old cars instead of buying new ones.
   c. New cars are too expensive.
   d. Interest rates on car loans are at an all-time high.

1. *Effect:* Only a small percentage of students are taking two years of a foreign language in high school.
2. *Effect:* Each year an increasing number of high-school students enroll in combined work-study programs, which allow them to spend half a day at work.
3. *Effect:* The percentage of men and women 65 years old and older in the American population is increasing each year. (In 1920, 5 percent of the population was over 65; in 1950, 8 percent; in 1978, 11 percent.)
4. *Effect:* Only slightly more than half of the citizens eligible to vote actually cast their votes in the last presidential election.
5. *Effect:* More women are working than ever before.

EXERCISE 21. Writing a Cause-and-Effect Paragraph.   Write an expository paragraph in which you use cause and effect as the method of development. You may choose one of the topics from Exercise 19 or Exercise 20, or choose a topic of your own.

   PREWRITING   Begin by looking carefully at the topic sentence (the numbered item) and the list of causes or effects that you have developed for the exercise. Do you have at least two causes or effects? (Your paragraph will be stronger with three or four.) Which of the causes or effects that you have listed do you think is the strongest? You may wish to put that one last. Write a brief paragraph outline, indicating your topic sentence and the supporting details in the order in which you plan to present them. Consider whether you want to reword the topic sentence to make it clearer or more interesting, and try writing one or two versions of a clincher sentence for your paragraph.

   WRITING   Follow the paragraph outline (topic sentence, list of causes or effects, clincher sentence) that you have developed. As you write, try to make the sentences read smoothly and, at the same time, express your ideas as clearly as possible. You may add specific information (facts, statistics, examples) to back up each of the causes or effects you plan to discuss.

REVISING AND PROOFREADING Look at the first draft to check whether the ideas are arranged in the strongest possible order. Make sure that the reader can distinguish between causes and effects. Would the paragraph be improved by adding transitional expressions such as *as a result of, consequently, because,* or *effect?* As you revise, refer to the Guidelines for Writing and Revising Expository Paragraphs on this page and the next. Before you turn your paragraph in, check the Guidelines for Proofreading (page 339).

EXERCISE 22. Revising a Weak Cause-and-Effect Paragraph.
Read the following paragraph carefully, and answer the questions after it. On the basis of your responses, revise the paragraph on a separate sheet of paper.

> Some teen-agers lie easily and often and do not seem to care about getting caught in a lie. Such people want the "easy way out." Often they have a poor self-image and do not really care what others think about them.

1. What is the topic sentence? Does the topic sentence state a cause or an effect?
2. Do the other sentences in this paragraph state causes or effects?
3. Think of a specific example to illustrate sentence 2. (You may make up an incident, using a fictional name.)
4. Think of a specific example to illustrate sentence 3. (Again, you may use a fictional example.)
5. Can you think of additional reasons why some people lie easily and often? If so, state each reason in a single sentence.
6. Which of the following information would improve this paragraph?
   a. A statement from a psychologist or psychiatrist about why young adults lie
   b. An analysis of four different types of lies
   c. A discussion of the need for honesty in business and politics
   d. A discussion of how to train young children not to lie
   e. The results of a poll of two hundred teen-agers on why teen-agers lie

GUIDELINES FOR WRITING AND REVISING EXPOSITORY PARAGRAPHS

1. Is the topic of the paragraph limited to an idea or event that can be adequately explained in a single paragraph?

2. Does the paragraph contain a topic sentence that clearly expresses the paragraph's main idea? Is the topic sentence one that will arouse the reader's interest?

3. Does the paragraph contain sufficient details to support the main idea in the topic sentence?

4. Are the supporting ideas arranged in a logical and effective order?

5. Is the paragraph clear and easy to understand? Is the language appropriate for the intended audience?

6. Does the paragraph contain whatever background information is necessary for the audience to understand the paragraph's ideas? Has the writer defined all terms that the audience might not understand?

7. Does the paragraph contain transitional expressions that make the ideas easy to follow? Do the sentences in the paragraph flow easily from one to another?

8. If appropriate, does the paragraph contain a clincher sentence?

REVIEW EXERCISE C. Writing an Expository Paragraph. Choose one of the following limited topics (or choose a topic of your own), and write an expository paragraph. Remember that your purpose is to inform or to explain. Develop the main idea of the paragraph by means of facts and statistics, examples, or cause and effect.

1. High-school dropouts in tenth grade this year
2. Attendance at school events (sports, dances, plays)
3. Newest clothes fads
4. Dangers of anorexia among young adults
5. What teen-agers spend their money on

The Descriptive Paragraph

A writer who wants to tell a reader exactly what something looks, tastes, smells, feels, or sounds like uses description, the type of writing that appeals chiefly to the senses. A paragraph-length description usually concentrates on one subject: a place, an object, a person, or an event.

Developing a Paragraph with Concrete and Sensory Details

(4) A descriptive paragraph may be developed with concrete and sensory details.

In the following paragraph, the writer describes an event—a Pueblo Corn Dance. The writer includes many concrete and sensory details that help the reader to picture the dance. Which concrete and specific details tell about the way the dancers are dressed? Notice how many times the writer mentions specific colors. Which sensory details appeal to the reader's sense of hearing?

> The men dance together in double file, big-bellied men and skinny boys, toddlers and elders with gray hair flowing to the waist. Their torsos are painted with ocher clay, for these are the Squash People, who lead the dance. The Turquoise People, who follow, will be painted blue-gray. On their breasts are bandoleers of seashells and loops of turquoise and silver. High moccasins are on their feet, parrot feathers in their hair. Pine branches are tied to their upper arms. Their white wool kilts are tied by a long fringed sash, symbolic of rain, and by a belt of jingling sleigh bells. Fox furs hang down their backs like tails. In one hand each carries a rattling gourd; in the other a branch of evergreen. As they dance they will shake down the waters of the sky with their gourds and beat forth the waters of the earth with their feet.
>
> BETTY FUSSELL

Some paragraphs concentrate on only one of the senses. In the following paragraph, notice how all of the sentences appeal to the reader's sense of hearing.

> On a broiling afternoon when the men were away at work and all the women napped, I moved through majestic depths of silences, silences so immense I could hear the corn growing. Under these silences there was an orchestra of natural music playing notes no city child would ever hear. A certain cackle from the henhouse meant we had gained an egg. The creak of a porch swing told of a momentary breeze blowing across my grandmother's yard. Moving past Liz Virts's barn as quietly as an Indian, I could hear the swish of a horse's tail and knew the horseflies were out in strength. As I tiptoed along a mossy bank to surprise a frog, a faint splash told me the quarry had spotted me and slipped into the stream. Wandering among the sleeping houses, I learned that tin roofs crackle under the power of the sun, and when I tired and came back to my grandmother's house, I padded into her dark cool living room, lay flat on the floor, and listened to the hypnotic beat of her pendulum clock on the wall ticking the meaningless hours away.
>
> RUSSELL BAKER

In the following paragraph, the writer describes bus travel in rural India. As you read, note that the details appeal to the reader's senses of sight and touch. In the last sentence, the details appeal exclusively to the sense of touch.

> I have not yet traveled on a bus in India that has not been packed to the bursting-point, with people inside and luggage on top; and the buses are always so old that they shake up every bone in the human body and every screw in their own. If the buses are always the same, so is the landscape through which they travel. Once a town is left behind, there is nothing till the next one except flat land, broiling sky, distances and dust. Especially dust; the sides of the bus are open with only bars across them so that the hot winds blow in freely, bearing desert sands to choke up ears and nostrils and set one's teeth on edge with grit.
>
> RUTH PRAWER JHABVALA

Supporting details in a descriptive paragraph are often arranged in spatial order, which moves the reader's attention from left to right, near to far, top to bottom, and so on (see pages 371–73). In his paragraph on sounds, Russell Baker uses an unusual kind of spatial order: one that represents a journey around the neighborhood. He begins with the outdoor sounds on his grandmother's farm, then mentions sounds heard while walking through the neighborhood, then returns to his grandmother's house and the sounds inside the house. Ruth Prawer Jhabvala's paragraph about the bus journey in India uses the spatial order of inside to outside and back to inside again. She begins with a description of the inside of the bus, goes on to describe the landscape outside the bus, and ends by describing the dust inside the bus.

In a descriptive paragraph, the topic sentence often reveals a main impression of the subject being described. For example, Russell Baker's topic sentence mentions "silences so immense," and the sounds described in the paragraph are almost all quiet, "silent" sounds. The first sentence in the paragraph about bus travel in India gives an impression of the great discomfort of riding in such a bus, and the paragraph goes on to develop this idea of discomfort.

GUIDELINES FOR WRITING AND REVISING DESCRIPTIVE PARAGRAPHS

1. Is the paragraph's topic limited to a single person, place, object, or event?

2. Does the paragraph contain a topic sentence that identifies the subject being described and states a main impression?
3. Does the paragraph contain enough specific and concrete details to bring the topic to life?
4. Does the paragraph contain sensory details that appeal to more than the sense of sight?
5. Are the details in the paragraph arranged in a logical order?
6. Does the paragraph present the reader with vivid images of the subject?

EXERCISE 23. Revising a Weak Descriptive Paragraph. The following descriptive paragraph is weak because it does not contain sufficient concrete and sensory details. Use your imagination to add enough specific details to make the paragraph interesting. Write your revised paragraph on a separate sheet of paper.

> Jenny came out of the house. She was tall and thin. She wore a pair of jeans and a T-shirt. It was a hot summer day. Jenny sat on the front steps and waited. She heard a lot of sounds. She watched some people go by and said "Hello" to two of them. After a while she looked at her watch and frowned.

EXERCISE 24. Writing a Descriptive Paragraph. Use the following list of details to write a descriptive paragraph about the United States one-dollar bill. You do not have to use all of the details, and you may use others of your own. Arrange the details in any order you find effective. (You will probably benefit from your own close observations of a dollar bill.) Write an appropriate topic sentence for the paragraph.

> *Details:* George Washington, wise and serious-looking; labeled by his last name in case you don't recognize him
> Signature of the secretary of the treasury
> Front printed in black except for two green serial numbers and green seal of Department of the Treasury; seal has balanced scale above a key
> Back printed all in green
> Heavy, pleasant-feeling paper; crisp when new; limp and

rather tan and creased when old

Two seals on back

In one seal, eagle holds 12 arrows in one claw and a branch in other; in its beak a banner "E Pluribus Unum," which means "Out of many, one "

Another mysterious-looking seal: cut-off pyramid, topmost part has one eye surrounded by glowing light. Wording on this seal: "Annuit Coeptis," which means, "He [God] has smiled on our undertakings"; "Novus Ordo Seclorum," which means "A new order of the ages"

Fine network of spiderwebs and curlicues, leaves, and border designs

EXERCISE 25. Writing a Descriptive Paragraph. For this assignment, choose a place somewhere in your school. Write a descriptive paragraph about that place, using concrete and sensory details to make the scene come alive for your readers.

PREWRITING Spend some time actually observing the place you are going to write about. Take a pencil and paper with you, and jot down as long a list as possible of concrete and sensory details. Decide in advance whether you are going to describe the place when there are people in it (during school hours) or when it is empty (before or after school). As you take notes, ask yourself questions that will help you gather a list of details. For example, if you are describing the empty gym, what sounds can you hear? What do your footsteps sound like? What smells are there? Is the floor polished? Are the foul lines clearly painted, or are they dull? What colors do you see? Is the room dim or brightly lit?

WRITING Concentrate on including in your paragraph numerous concrete and sensory details that will create a vivid picture for the reader. Your topic sentence should reveal the subject of your description and indicate the main impression you want to create. Consider whether it will be helpful to organize your description by means of spatial order (left to right, near to far, top to bottom, and so on) or whether some other order is more effective for your particular subject.

REVISING AND PROOFREADING Refer to the Guidelines for Writing and Revising Descriptive Paragraphs (pages 415–16) and the Guidelines for Proofreading (page 339).

The Narrative Paragraph

If you want to develop a topic by relating a story or a series of events, you will write a narrative paragraph. Your purpose is to tell the reader a story either to illustrate a point stated in the topic sentence or just to entertain by telling a story.

A paragraph-length narrative usually focuses on one action or one series of events.

Developing a Paragraph with an Incident

(5) A narrative paragraph may be developed with an incident or an anecdote.

When a paragraph is developed by means of a brief story, or anecdote, the topic sentence usually states a generalization that the story illustrates. Often that incident is drawn from the writer's personal experiences. The writer, in effect, is telling the reader, "This is what I learned about life (topic sentence), and this is how I learned it (the incident or anecdote in the rest of the paragraph)."

In the following selection, Harry Crews tells about an experience with a car he once owned. Why does he tell his story? What point is the writing making?

The 1953 Mercury was responsible for my ultimate disenchantment with cars. I had already bored and stroked the engine and contrived to place a six-speaker sound system in it when I finally started to paint it. I spent the better half of a year painting that car. A friend of mine owned a body shop, and he let me use the shop on weekends. I sanded the Mercury down to raw metal, primed it, and painted it. Then I painted it again. And again. And then again. I went a little nuts, as I am prone to do, because I'm the kind of guy who if he can't have too much of a thing doesn't want any at all. So one day I came out of the house (I was in college then) and saw it, the '53 Mercury, the car upon which I had heaped more attention and time and love than I had ever given a human being. It sat at the curb, its black surface a shimmering of the air, like hundreds of mirrors turned to catch the sun. It had twenty-seven coats of paint, each coat laboriously handrubbed. It seemed to glow, not with reflected light, but with some internal light of its own. I stood staring, and it turned into one of those great scary rare moments when you are privileged to see into your own predicament. Clearly, there were two ways I could go. I could sell the car, or I could keep on painting it for the rest of my life. If 27 coats of paint, why not 127? The moment was brief and I understand it better now than I did then, but I did realize, if imperfectly, that something was dreadfully wrong, that the car owned me much more than I would ever own the car, no matter how long I kept it. The next day I drove to Jacksonville and left the Mercury on a used-car lot. It was an easy thing to do.

HARRY CREWS

Harry Crews does not tell everything about the 1953 Mercury. He does not, for example, tell how many miles the car had when he bought it, how much it cost, or how much he sold it for. Instead, he focuses on his obsession with painting the car and how he dealt with that obsession.

Another reason for writing a narrative paragraph is to look back on a past experience in order to understand it better. In the following paragraph, Agatha Christie remembers an incident she experienced as a child and how it made her feel.

The next morning the three horses arrived, and off we went. We zigzagged along up the precipitous paths, and I enjoyed myself enormously perched on top of what seemed to me an immense horse. The guide led it up and, occasionally picking little bunches of flowers, handed them to me to stick in my hatband. So far all was well, but when we arrived at the top and prepared to have lunch at the plateau there, the guide excelled himself. He came running back to us bringing with him a magnificent butterfly he had trapped. "Pour la petite mademoiselle," [French for "For the little miss"] he cried. Taking a pin from his lapel he transfixed the butterfly and stuck it in my hat! Oh, the horror of that moment! The feeling of the poor butterfly fluttering, struggling against the pin, the agony I felt as the butterfly fluttered there. And of course I couldn't say anything. There were too many conflicting loyalties in my mind. This was a kindness on the part of the guide. He had brought it to me. It was a special kind of present. How could I hurt his feelings by saying I didn't like it? How I wanted him to take it off. And all the time, there was the butterfly, fluttering, dying. That horrible flapping against my hat. There is only one thing a child can do in these circumstances. I cried.

AGATHA CHRISTIE

The order of ideas in a narrative paragraph is usually chronological, the order in which events occur in time. If you have ever listened to someone tell a joke or relate a story but confuse the proper order of events, you will understand how important chronological sequence can be in a narrative paragraph. Since the narrative paragraph must tell its story briefly, it must never risk confusing the reader.

GUIDELINES FOR WRITING AND REVISING NARRATIVE PARAGRAPHS

1. Does the writer make clear at the beginning of the paragraph all of the essential information (characters, setting, place) that the reader will need to follow the events being described?
2. Does the paragraph contain a topic sentence or clincher sentence that reveals how the writer feels about the incident or what the writer learned from it?
3. Are events organized in chronological order?
4. Does the paragraph contain specific details to make the story interesting?
5. Does the paragraph contain any details or incidents that distract the reader from the main point of the story?
6. Is the language appropriate for the intended audience?
7. Does the paragraph contain concrete and sensory details that can enhance the reader's understanding?

EXERCISE 26. Writing a Narrative Paragraph. Use the following list of details to write a paragraph developed with an incident. The list provides information in chronological order. Write a topic sentence, and then write a paragraph.

Details: Took four-year-old cousin Annie to Sea World one day on a holiday weekend—very crowded

Annie pleasant company—curious, lively, self-confident

Went to buy Annie a cold drink, waited in line

Turned around, Annie gone; nowhere in sight

Called her name; searched the dolphin area where we had just been

Panicky—asked a guard to help me find Annie

Annie's name and description broadcast on loudspeakers throughout park

Waited for what seemed like hours, actually about 20 minutes; imagining her eaten by sharks or drowned in one of the pools

Tear-stained Annie brought in by guard

She had wandered into a training area for seals; guard found her asking baby seal how to get home

EXERCISE 27. Writing a Narrative Paragraph. Find a photograph in a newspaper or magazine, and write a paragraph telling about an incident that happened just before the photograph was taken or just after the photograph was taken. Make up a specific setting and characters as well as events, and provide enough specific details to make the story interesting. If you prefer, you may write a paragraph about an incident that happened just before or after a family snapshot was taken. Attach the photograph to your paper.

PREWRITING Make a list of details that the reader will need to know to understand the incident. Where does the event take place? If it is outdoors, what is the weather like? Who are the main characters? How can you describe or identify them briefly yet interestingly? Where will you begin the story? Make a list of the separate actions that take place that are necessary to understanding the incident. Consider how you (or the imaginary main character) feel about the incident or what you learned from the experience, and write a topic sentence, or a clincher sentence, that comments on the meaning of the incident.

WRITING As you write, concentrate on adding specific details that will make the story interesting. Try to vary sentence beginnings and structure, avoiding sentences that begin, "And then I . . ."

REVISING AND PROOFREADING Read the first draft carefully, checking to see whether you can add any additional specific details to make the paragraph more interesting. See if transitional expressions are needed to clarify the order of events in the story. Reread the paragraph, finally, to see how smoothly the sentences work together. Refer to the Guidelines for Writing and Revising Narrative Paragraphs (page 420) and the Guidelines for Proofreading (page 339) before you write your final version.

EXERCISE 28. Writing a Narrative Paragraph. Write a paragraph in which the main idea or topic is developed with a brief story. Be specific about time, place, and characters. Use one of the following topics (or a topic of your own).

1. The best things in life, it is said, are free.
2. Anger is one of the most difficult emotions to learn to handle well.
3. When it comes to a test of willpower—especially regarding food and TV—more often than not I fail.

4. My mother always tells me that if something is worth doing, it is worth doing right.
5. In every family there are certain classic stories about something funny that a family member did or said.

The Persuasive Paragraph

The purpose of persuasive writing is to state an opinion and to support it so effectively that the reader will accept the opinion as correct. Sometimes a persuasive paragraph attempts also to convince the reader to perform a specific action, such as making a contribution to a charity or joining a neighborhood cleanup day. The topic sentence in a persuasive paragraph states the writer's opinion, and the supporting sentences are reasons.

Developing a Paragraph with Reasons

(6) Develop a persuasive paragraph with reasons.

The limited topic for a persuasive paragraph should be an opinion about a debatable issue. An effective topic focuses on an important and meaningful issue rather than a personal preference. The first two options are not appropriate topics for a persuasive paragraph because they state personal preferences.

NOT APPROPRIATE   Country music is better than rock music.

NOT APPROPRIATE   Maya Angelou is the best writer.

APPROPRIATE   Citizens should sign a petition to recall the mayor.

APPROPRIATE   TV commercials should be banned on children's programs.

The topic sentence of a persuasive paragraph should state the writer's opinion as clearly and succinctly as possible. The topic sentence should not be so brief, however, that it is uninteresting.

EFFECTIVE   For years, motorists have been offered a choice of leaded (regular) and unleaded gasoline, but it is time to eliminate leaded gasoline from the market.

TOO BRIEF   Leaded gasoline should be eliminated from the market.

TOO BRIEF   Leaded gasoline should be banned.

To develop a persuasive paragraph, you give reasons as to why you hold the opinion stated in the topic sentence. Reasons are most convincing when they are supported by facts, as in the following example paragraph. Notice that each reason is supported by a sentence or two providing additional facts and information.

For years, motorists have been offered a   –topic sentence
choice of leaded (regular) and unleaded gasoline,
but it is time to eliminate leaded gasoline from the
market. Lead is a substance that is highly poison-   reason 1
ous to human beings. It can do considerable damage to the brain, especially in young children.
Some learning experts have even speculated that
a certain percentage of learning disabilities may
be caused by lead poisoning. Lead levels in the   reason 2
air are increasing, especially in urban areas. The
lead content in the atmosphere is caused by emis-
sions from automobiles using leaded gasoline.
Leaded gasoline is supposed to be used only in   reason 3
cars built before 1974, but many car owners buy
converter attachments for the pump nozzles so
that leaded gas can be pumped into newer cars
designed to use only unleaded gas. These car owners do not care about the environment or hazards
to public health; they care only about the money
they save by using the cheaper leaded gasoline.
Since voluntary controls for the use of leaded gas-   reason 4
oline are not effective, leaded gasoline should be
removed from the market. Just as leaded paint
was removed from the market when scientists
found that children who ate chips of leaded paint
suffered from lead poisoning and brain damage,
so, too, we must eliminate the hazards of lead in
our air by stopping the production of leaded gasoline.

One type of reason that you may use to support an opinion is a statement made by an *authority,* an expert in the field being discussed.

The following paragraph gives reasons and cites authorities to support the main idea that women are better suited than men to some endurance sports.

Dr. Nicholas and several other doctors agreed   −topic sentence
that physiological differences make women best
suited for sports that call upon endurance, like
marathons and English Channel swims, and those
that require balance, like certain gymnastics
events and skiing. They are least suited for events
that require upper body strength, such as the discus or the pommel horse in gymnastics, or those
that require bursts of speed, like sprint races.
Many experts tentatively speculate that once   reason 1
women catch up in opportunity or training, they
will surpass men in endurance events. "Because   reason 2
of their lighter bones," Dr. Marshall wrote, making the comparison between aluminum and steel,
"women have a chance to end up better mara-
thoners."

JANE GROSS

Reasons in a persuasive paragraph are usually given in the order of importance. In general, it is better to begin with the least important reason and build up to the most important one, thus achieving a vigorous conclusion. In some situations, however, especially when you have one very important reason and several less important ones, it may be appropriate to do just the opposite—to give the most important reason first and follow it with the less important details. Whether you choose one order or the other, the reader must be able to distinguish important from less important details in a persuasive paragraph.

Tone is especially important in a persuasive paragraph because readers need to feel that the writer is being fair and reasonable in presenting the argument. To be most convincing, a persuasive paragraph should be unemotional. Avoid referring to the opposing view by calling names or by using words with negative connotations, such as *ignorant, liar,* and *unpatriotic*. The reasonable tone of a persuasive paragraph depends on the logical presentation of sufficient reasons and facts to back up your opinion. Be as specific as you can, and be accurate. Concentrate on expressing your ideas in clear, forceful, but unemotional language.

Some paragraphs that are developed with reasons are actually expository paragraphs, as is the paragraph on pages 408–409. In such paragraphs, reasons are given to explain a situation or event rather than to persuade the reader.

GUIDELINES FOR WRITING AND REVISING PERSUASIVE PARAGRAPHS

1. Is the topic of the paragraph one that is debatable and important?
2. Does the paragraph contain a topic sentence that states the writer's opinion clearly and succinctly? Is the topic sentence interesting?
3. Is the writer's opinion supported with at least two reasons?
4. Is each reason supported with facts, statistics, examples, quotations from an authority, or some other kind of specific information?
5. Are the reasons arranged in order of importance—usually with the most important reason given last?
6. Are the ideas in the paragraph easy to follow and understand? Is the language appropriate for the intended audience?
7. Is the tone of the paragraph reasonable and fair? Does the paragraph contain emotional language that might detract from the argument?

EXERCISE 29. Writing a Persuasive Paragraph. From the following list of reasons, write a paragraph developing the main idea stated in your topic sentence.

Topic sentence: Students should (should not) be allowed to drive their own cars to high school.

Reasons:
Too many accidents involving students' cars in parking lot and on local streets near high school
Students use parking lot as hangout—often cut classes
Parking lot area could be used to build new gym
School bus transportation available to all students who live more than a mile from school
Pressure on students to own cars
Many students have after-school jobs and need cars to get to work on time
Busing requires leaving home too early; cars more convenient

Many students have worked hard to pay for owning and driving cars; deserve to use them as they wish

Fewer students will need school buses, thus saving city money

PREWRITING Begin by deciding which position you want to take, "should" or "should not." Then read through the list of reasons to find those that support your position. Select the three or four you think are strongest. (You may make up and use any additional reasons you think strongly support your position.) Outline your arguments, and arrange the reasons you select in the order of importance. You may wish to give the reason you think most important last. Think of evidence (facts, statistics, examples) to support each reason, and plan a sentence or two of additional evidence to follow each reason. You may reword the topic sentence to make it more interesting. Be sure to write a clincher sentence for your paragraph.

WRITING Follow the paragraph outline (topic sentence, reasons plus evidence, clincher sentence) that you have prepared. As you write, concentrate on expressing your ideas clearly and unemotionally.

REVISING AND PROOFREADING It may be helpful to have another person read your first draft to give you feedback on how convincingly you have stated your argument. Check the tone of your writing. Does it seem reasonable and logical? Are the reasons and evidence presented unemotionally, without any wasted words? Refer to the Guidelines for Writing and Revising Persuasive Paragraphs (page 425) and the Guidelines for Proofreading (page 339).

EXERCISE 30. Analyzing a Persuasive Paragraph. Read this paragraph, and answer the questions that follow.

The many successful horror movies of recent years—both realistic movies about human and natural disasters and movies about fantastic supernatural events—are sheer moneymakers. They have little or no meaning or social value. Movies should convey some sort of meaningful message, yet we come away from a horror movie merely feeling glad that the scary events pictured on the screen did not happen to us. Nothing about such movies makes us better human beings. By boycotting mindless horror films, moviegoers can send a clear message to movie producers: that they want quality films that are meaningful as well as entertaining.

1. What is the topic sentence? How effective is it? Try writing at least two other topic sentences for this paragraph.
2. What is the writer's opinion about horror films? Do you agree or disagree with the writer's opinion?

3. How many reasons does the writer give to support the opinion? Does the writer give separate reasons, or is the same reason repeated in different words?
4. Can you think of any additional reasons to add to the paragraph? Write a sentence for each additional reason.
5. What does the writer urge the reader to do?
6. Which of the following specific pieces of information would strengthen the paragraph?
   a. References to scary children's stories and fairy tales
   b. Statistics on (1) percentage of box-office successes that are horror movies, and (2) percentage of movies produced each year that are horror movies
   c. Detailed discussion of different types of horror movies
   d. Examples of specific titles and plots of recent horror movies
   e. Quotations from a movie critic on why horror movies are so successful
   f. Quotation from a psychologist about why horror movies are so successful
   g. Poll of movie viewers' reactions after seeing a particular horror movie
7. Does the paragraph have a clincher sentence? If so, what is it and how effective is it? Try writing one or more clincher sentences for this paragraph.

EXERCISE 31. Revising a Persuasive Paragraph.   Rewrite the paragraph in Exercise 30, adding reasons to strengthen the argument and some of the kinds of information suggested in question 6. You may make up any information that you need. If you prefer, you may write a paragraph defending the opposite view: that horror movies are worth seeing. Be sure to state your opinion in a topic sentence and provide several clearly stated reasons to support that opinion. Whenever possible, each reason should have one sentence of additional information (details, facts, statistics, or examples).

CHAPTER 15 WRITING REVIEW

Writing a Paragraph.   Write a paragraph based on one of the following limited topics or a topic of your own. Begin by identifying for yourself the type of paragraph (expository, narrative, descriptive, or persuasive) that you plan to write. Then identify the audience for your paragraph. List your ideas, and organize them into a brief paragraph outline. Begin writing your first draft with a topic sentence that effectively expresses the paragraph's main idea and arouses the reader's interest. When you have finished the first draft, revise it carefully. Proofread your revised paragraph before and after copying it on a separate sheet of paper.

1. Need for a stricter dress code in high school
2. A movie review
3. Close-up of a green pepper (or any other vegetable or fruit)
4. A proposed solution for a specific problem
5. Explanation of time zones in the United States
6. Story about something funny you did when you were very little
7. A favorite elderly relative or neighbor
8. Accomplishments of a modern hero or heroine
9. Explanation of the difference between ice hockey and field hockey
10. An annoying advertisement

CHAPTER 16

Writing Expository Compositions

PLANNING AND WRITING THE LONGER COMPOSITION

In this chapter you will study how to use the writing process to write expository compositions. A composition consists of several paragraphs—arranged as an introduction, body, and conclusion—that develop a single topic. The expository composition, like other forms of exposition, specifically aims to inform an audience about a topic or to explain a topic to an audience.

Writing an effective expository composition entails many of the same procedures as writing an effective paragraph. Like the paragraph, the composition has a central, controlling idea that must be developed by means of smaller, more specific ideas. These specific ideas must be carefully chosen and organized in a logical way, and their relation to each other and to the central idea must be made clear. Since the idea for a composition is necessarily broader than the main idea of a paragraph, a composition calls for more planning and more writing.

PREWRITING

SEARCHING FOR SUBJECTS

16a. Search for subjects for your expository composition.

Exposition, because it explains or informs, is what you most often write in school. For example, your teacher may ask you to explain photosynthesis or to discuss why *Julius Caesar* is a tragedy. Such assignments often provide specific topics for you to write about. Frequently, however, your teachers will assign expository compositions without also assigning specific and limited topics. Then, responsibility for discovering suitable subjects to write about falls to you. In those instances, searching for subjects—discovering something to write about—is your first step toward writing an expository composition.

Keeping in mind exposition's explanatory or informative purpose, you can use your own experiences, knowledge, and interests to begin the search for subjects. You may realize that good writing depends on knowing your subject. In addition to what you have learned in school, you have a great deal of knowledge that has come from other sources. Your own special interests have already taught you many things. Your interest in places has acquainted you with the people, the sights, and the experiences associated with another town, city, or country. Your hobbies—collecting stamps, coins, stones, or seashells; practicing a musical instrument, singing, or dancing—have developed your interests and increased your knowledge. By participating in family, school, neighborhood, and community life, you have acquired a variety of experiences. When you must search for something to write about, these personal resources are an ideal place to begin.

You need not, of course, limit yourself to subjects you know well already. In addition to familiar material from your own experience, there may be subjects that pique your interest even though you do not know much about them. Such subjects may make excellent material for expository compositions, provided that you are willing to seek—through reading and investigation—the information necessary to write about them. Writing is an intense and stimulating activity; new ideas that you have mastered sufficiently to write about are likely to become a permanent part of your stock of knowledge and can extend your interests. In other words, writing a composition is not just a way to show what you know already; it can be a way for you to learn new things.

EXERCISE 1. Discovering Your Personal Resources. Answer each of the following questions about your personal resources. Your answers will constitute a personal resource inventory to which you may refer as you search for subjects for expository compositions.

1. What do you know a great deal about?
2. What would you like to be able to do very well?
3. What things can you do very well?
4. What unusual experiences have you had?
5. What unusual experiences would you like to have?
6. If you could do anything at all, what would you do?
7. What is your favorite school subject?
8. What do you most like to read about?
9. What do you most like to watch on TV or in movies?
10. What are your hobbies and out-of-school activities?

Tapping Your Personal Resources

As you write your first expository composition, you will probably wish to use a subject derived completely from your own interests, knowledge, and experiences. Three techniques enable you to tap these resources: keeping a writer's journal, brainstorming, and clustering.

A *writer's journal,* in which you record your ideas, thoughts, and experiences, can be a significant source of subjects to write about. As you review and react to your journal entries, you might find many possible subjects for expository compositions. For example, an entry about visiting the Grand Canyon might suggest the following subjects: natural wonders in the United States, formation of the Grand Canyon, disadvantages of organized sightseeing tours, and benefits of traveling.

Another useful technique is *brainstorming,* in which you generate as many ideas as possible without evaluating them. Suppose, for example, that you have an open-ended assignment to write an expository composition about any subject. To search for possible subjects, you might brainstorm by asking, "What interests me?" Your brainstormed list might resemble what follows; any item is a possible broad subject for an expository composition.

> painting with watercolors
> drawing still lifes of animals and insects
> listening to rock music
> exploring junk shops and flea markets
> backpacking and hiking in wilderness areas
> collecting family stories from relatives
> playing computer games
> reading about space travel

watching tennis matches on TV
collecting minerals

You can also brainstorm by asking, "What have I experienced?" and "What do I know about?" Once again you might list as many ideas as you can think of in response to each question. Whether you focus on your interests, knowledge, or experiences, brainstorming about yourself can be an excellent place to begin in the search for subjects.

Clustering, a more focused and visual form of brainstorming, enables you to generate ideas and to make connections between them. To use clustering, you begin by writing and circling a word or phrase, then writing and circling each other word or phrase that subsequently occurs to you. You connect these circled words and ideas with lines; these connections allow you to follow your train of thought, seeing how one idea suggests another, then another, and so on. By enabling you to follow your thought processes, clustering can also be a useful technique in searching for subjects.

In the following example, the writer starts by thinking about the seashore, then uses clustering to continue a search for subjects based on this word. Each of the circled phrases or words is a possible subject for an expository composition.

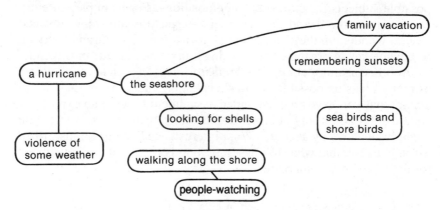

EXERCISE 2. Using a Writer's Journal to Search for Subjects.
For three to five days, keep a writer's journal that you are willing to share with others. If you already keep such a journal, you may select several entries to use in this exercise. By reviewing and reacting to your journal entries, list at least five possible subjects for expository compositions. Remember that you may choose to use any one of these subjects in later exercises in this chapter.

EXERCISE 3. Brainstorming to Search for Subjects. For each of the following questions, brainstorm at least five possible subjects for expository compositions. You may find it helpful to refer to the personal resource inventory you developed in Exercise 1 before you begin brainstorming. As noted in Exercise 2, you should retain these brainstormed subjects for use in later chapter exercises.

1. What interests me?
2. What do I know about?
3. What have I experienced?

EXERCISE 4. Brainstorming in a Group. Brainstorming can be a very productive strategy to use with a group of people, because one person's idea stimulates another idea in someone else in a kind of creative chain reaction. As your teacher directs, form a small group. With these fellow students, select one of the following subjects; then brainstorm as many possible composition subjects as you can think of together. After you have completed your brainstorming, answer the following two questions: How does brainstorming with a group differ from brainstorming by yourself? Which brainstorming arrangement do you prefer, and why?

1. Travel   5. Television   8. Animals
2. Relatives   6. Clothing   9. Buildings
3. Careers   7. Friends   10. Fads
4. Music

EXERCISE 5. Using Clustering to Search for Subjects. Select any one of the subjects on the following list. Then use the clustering technique to search for subjects for an expository composition.

1. Holidays   5. Foods   8. Movies
2. Brothers and sisters 6. Hobbies   9. Books
3. Vacations   7. Sports   10. School
4. Seasons

EXERCISE 6. Using Discovery Techniques. Use a writer's journal, brainstorming, or clustering to search for subjects for an expository composition of your own. Keep the subjects you discover in your notebook; you may choose to use any one of them in later exercises in this chapter.

SELECTING AND LIMITING SUBJECTS

16b. Select and limit your subject.

By using yourself as a source, you have generated many possible subjects to write about. Now you should select one subject to write about and limit that subject to a topic manageable in an expository composition.

Selecting a Subject

The same resources that guided your search for subjects—your interests, knowledge, and experiences—can direct your choice of one subject to write about. Several questions, related to these resources, can be especially helpful at this stage of the writing process.

1. What interests me the most? What interests me the least? Why?
2. What have I experienced firsthand? What experiences have I heard about or read about? What experiences have I learned about through TV, movies, or radio?
3. What do I know about? What special knowledge have I gained through hobbies, after-school or leisure activities, personal reading, or talking with others?

By applying these questions to each subject you have discovered, you can select one subject to write about. This is possible because it is unlikely that every subject in your lists is one that you are simultaneously interested in, know about, and have experience with.

Consider, for example, the list of subjects brainstormed on pages 431–32. You might be very interested in playing computer games, yet you might not know enough to be able to explain how they are played. Similarly, you might be very interested in collecting family stories without ever having actually tried to do so. Therefore, you probably lack both the experience and the knowledge necessary to explain this subject to someone else. By contrast, you might know a great deal about local flea markets and junk shops because you visit them regularly. Because your knowledge, interest, and experience all come together on this subject, you could select "junk shops and flea markets" as a broad subject for an expository composition.

EXERCISE 7. Selecting Subjects. Study the following list of subjects. Think about your interests, knowledge, and experiences; then select five possibilities that you think you would enjoy writing about.

For each subject you choose, phrase several questions you think a composition on the subject should answer. If your teacher so directs, submit your list to your teacher for suggestions and comments. When you get this list back, keep it in your notebook for future use.

EXAMPLE   1. Science fiction writers
　　　　　1. *a. Who are the most popular science fiction writers?*
　　　　　　b. Are these writers scientists?
　　　　　　c. Are they hopeful about the future of humanity?
　　　　　　d. What were the earliest science fiction stories about?
　　　　　　e. Have science fiction themes changed?

1. The moon's resources
2. Skin diving
3. Two authors with different attitudes toward youth
4. Modern sculpture
5. The electric car
6. Financing your own college education
7. High-school spirit
8. The tragic side of a comic character in a novel or play
9. Origins of place names in your area
10. Collecting records
11. Talking to chimps and dolphins
12. The importance of physical fitness
13. Wildlife conservation
14. Computers for home use
15. Characteristics of science fiction
16. Popular novels and the movies made from them
17. New steps in dancing
18. Training for the Olympics
19. New horizons in science
20. How advertisers attract customers

EXERCISE 8. Selecting a Subject.   Using the lists of subjects you developed in earlier exercises, select one subject for an expository composition. Remember that the subject you select might be the one you will decide to write about in later exercises in this chapter. Ask yourself the following questions in order to select a subject.

1. What interests me the most? What interests me the least? Why?
2. What have I experienced firsthand? What experiences have I heard about or read about? What experiences have I learned about through TV, movies, or radio?
3. What do I know about? What special knowledge have I gained through hobbies, after-school or leisure activities, personal reading, or talking with others?

Limiting a Subject

After you have selected a subject, you should limit that subject to a size that is manageable for an expository composition. Most of your composition assignments will call for a paper four to five paragraphs long. You can see that if you choose a subject like "skin diving" (about which whole books have been written), you must severely limit your treatment to some specific aspect of the sport to avoid writing mere generalities. Even one aspect—such as how Jacques Cousteau and Emil Gagnan invented scuba diving equipment for the French navy during World War II—offers more to write about than can be covered by a short composition.

To limit your subject to a manageable size, you should analyze it, or break it down into its smaller parts. The limited subject that results is called a *topic*. Notice how the following broad subjects may be subdivided into more limited topics. Any of these topics might be covered fully in a short composition, whereas the general or broad subject would require several more pages of development. Think of the general subject as the title of the book and each of the topics as the chapters. Your expository composition then would make a very short chapter or even part of a chapter.

Broad Subject: Skin diving
Limited Topics:
1. Nitrogen poisoning: what it is and how to avoid it
2. Are sharks really dangerous?
3. The advantages of the wet suit
4. Scuba diving in nearby Marion Pond

Broad Subject: Movie stars
Limited Topics:
1. Have the top movie stars attended drama school?
2. How do movie stars prepare for each movie?
3. How do movie stars feel about their fans?
4. What happens to young movie stars when they grow up?

Broad Subject: Walking
Limited Topics:
1. Walking for exercise
2. What to look for when walking through woods
3. Last summer's disastrous hike to Elk Creek
4. Walking in the city

As these examples illustrate, limiting a subject involves focusing on its parts or aspects.

EXERCISE 9. Limiting Subjects for Compositions. Using the questions about your interests, experiences, and knowledge, select five of the following broad subjects. Then, by analyzing each broad subject, list three limited topics for each subject you selected. Remember that each limited topic should lend itself to the purpose of exposition: to inform or to explain.

1. Cars	11. Money
2. Sports	12. Television
3. Family life	13. Books
4. Our town	14. Hobbies
5. Clothes	15. Politics
6. Popularity and unpopularity	16. Travel
7. Things I wish were different	17. Jewelry
8. World leaders	18. Food
9. Women athletes	19. Movies
10. Technology	20. Pets

EXERCISE 10. Limiting Your Own Subject. Limit the subject you selected in Exercise 8. To do so, you should break it down into its smaller parts or aspects, any one of which should be a suitable size for an expository composition.

CONSIDERING PURPOSE, AUDIENCE, AND TONE

16c. Evaluate your topic: consider purpose, audience, and tone.

How well your topic is limited will affect how easily you can proceed through subsequent steps in the writing process. Thus, you should now determine if you have sufficiently limited your topic in terms of purpose, audience, and tone.

Considering Purpose

The purpose of your composition clearly affects how you limit your topic. One way purpose affects your topic is by determining which aspects of the topic your composition should discuss. For instance, different purposes influence how you might limit one topic, "the popularity of jogging." Notice how each of the following examples focuses on a different aspect of the topic, in keeping with a specific purpose.

To amuse: "the ridiculous side of jogging enthusiasts"
To persuade: "jogging to lose weight and get into shape"
To inform: "differences in the quality and price of running shoes"

Purpose also affects limiting a topic by determining how extensively a topic can be discussed, that is, how many of its features can be explained. In writing exposition, your aim is to inform or to explain. You must therefore sufficiently limit the topic so that you can, in fact, explain it in the paragraphs available to you. For example, it would be very difficult (if not impossible) to explain the following topic in a single expository composition: "differences in quality and price of jogging equipment." Jogging equipment simply includes too many items to explain thoroughly and clearly in one composition: running suits, socks, running shoes, sweat suits, rain suits, shorts and tops, safety clothing, and so on. By contrast, "differences in quality and price of running shoes" is a manageable size for a composition because the topic can be explained within a composition's limits.

To determine if you have sufficiently limited your topic for an expository composition, ask one question: Is this topic limited enough that I can explain it clearly and thoroughly in several paragraphs?

EXERCISE 11. Evaluating Topics According to Purpose. Indicate which of the following topics are limited enough to be explained clearly and thoroughly in an expository composition. Write *L* for topics that are sufficiently limited and *NL* for those that are not.

1. Boring TV shows
2. Why I prefer first-run movies over made-for-TV movies
3. Making holiday decorations from bread dough
4. How rainbows form
5. Preparing picnics
6. Developing itineraries for visiting national parks in the West
7. Phases in spontaneous combustion
8. Community activities
9. After-school jobs
10. How magicians make rabbits disappear

EXERCISE 12. Developing Limited Topics. Develop three limited topics for each topic you judged as too broad in Exercise 11. For example, the topic "weekend chores" can be further limited into the following topics: "why doing weekend chores builds a teen-ager's character," "how to start a weekend job service in your neighborhood," and "the weekend chores I most dislike." Notice that each topic focuses on a more specific aspect of "weekend chores" and can, therefore, be explained clearly and thoroughly in an expository composition.

Considering Audience

The goal of expository writing is to explain a topic *to someone*. This "someone"—your particular audience—also influences how your topic should be limited, that is, which aspects of the topic you ought to explain. Different audiences can differ greatly in what they bring to understanding your topic. You must therefore consider your audience's characteristics—their background, knowledge, viewpoints, and information needs—and limit the topic with this particular audience in mind.

Suppose, for example, that you are preparing to write a composition about school fund-raising. For your classmates, you might limit this topic to "organizing simple weekend fund-raisers." This topic is limited to reflect your audience's particular needs and characteristics: Your classmates might want to know how to *organize* a fund-raiser; they might want to know what activities they can execute *easily;* and they might want to know what activities can be done in their *free time.* By contrast, for parents who want to become involved in school activities, you might limit your topic to "three ways parents can help with school fund-raisers." Parents and classmates differ markedly, so the topic is limited differently for each particular audience.

Several questions can help you evaluate your limited topic in terms of your audience. Ask yourself:

1. What does my audience *already know* about this topic?
2. What does my audience *want to know* or *need to know* about this topic?
3. What aspect of this topic *may interest* my audience?
4. What will my audience *be able to understand* about this topic?
5. What *viewpoints* does my audience have about this topic?

Notice, too, that by asking these questions you will begin to consider what kind of information will develop your topic best for your particular audience. This will be useful to you when you are actually writing your composition.

EXERCISE 13. Selecting an Audience. Several topics for expository compositions are listed. Following each topic are three different audiences. Indicate which audience the topic fits *best*. Be prepared to explain your choices.

1. Advanced resuscitation techniques
   a. Intermediate swimming students
   b. Lifesaving instructors
   c. Hospital emergency-room attendants
2. How to write a limerick
   a. Fifth-graders
   b. College poetry class
   c. Poetry society members
3. Economic difficulties of New England's fishing industry
   a. High-school social studies students
   b. National sports-fishing association
   c. Advisers to state governors in the Northeast
4. Recreational opportunities through local colleges
   a. Foreign travelers
   b. Tourist bureau members
   c. Community newcomers
5. Job application procedures for June graduates
   a. High-school seniors
   b. Parents of high-school seniors
   c. Teachers of high-school seniors

EXERCISE 14. Limiting Topics for Audiences. Limit each of the topics on the next page for the audience given. For example, notice how the topic "travel advice" is limited differently for the following two audiences.

   a. For experienced travelers: Traveling the back roads of France
   b. For inexperienced travelers: How to make flight reservations to France

Remember, too, that each topic is being limited for an expository purpose.

1. *Topic:* Rules for basketball
   Audience: a. Elementary-school students
   b. Members of the National Basketball Association (NBA)
2. *Topic:* Preparing nutritious lunches
   Audience: a. School cafeteria personnel
   b. Your classmates
3. *Topic:* Symbols of community pride
   Audience: a. Community newcomers
   b. High-school social studies teachers
4. *Topic:* American presidential elections
   Audience: a. Foreign tourists
   b. Readers of the local newspaper
5. *Topic:* The pleasures of reading
   Audience: a. Your classmates
   b. Adults learning to read

Considering Tone

Considering tone is another aspect of evaluating your topic. Tone is a writer's attitude, or point of view, toward a topic. Anyone can hold many different outlooks, so there can also be many different tones: serious or humorous, formal or informal, personal or impersonal. You might realize that you have different attitudes about any given topic. That is, you may have both a serious outlook and a humorous outlook on the same topic because you are able to see the topic from different angles. For instance, consider your responsibilities at home. Sometimes you might see them as significant burdens, yet at other times you are able to make light of them. If you write about these responsibilities from each outlook, an audience will clearly notice the difference in your attitude.

When you are writing an expository composition, ask two questions to determine if you have limited your topic to reflect the tone or attitude you want to convey to your audience.

1. What attitude do I want to convey?
2. Have I limited my topic to reflect this tone?

To determine if your topic is limited to reflect the tone you want, consider how you have worded your topic. For example, the topic "decisions that changed my life significantly" reflects a serious and straightforward tone. This topic can also be worded—and therefore limited—to reflect another point of view. To reveal a humorous tone, for instance, you might limit the topic to "decision making through coin flipping." As you can see, tone is revealed through the language you use.

As you evaluate your topic in terms of tone, you must also consider two additional points. First, ask yourself if the tone you have decided to convey is appropriate for your expository purpose. If, for example, you are going to explain how to perform cardiopulmonary resuscitation (CPR), it would be inappropriate to adopt a humorous tone. CPR is a complex process used for a very important reason—to save lives. To treat CPR lightheartedly could detract from explaining it clearly and thoroughly. Thus, a humorous tone would not enable you to fulfill your expository, or explanatory, purpose. Similarly, you should consider whether your tone, or point of view toward the topic, is appropriate for your particular audience. For instance, suppose you are writing a paper to inform your classmates about student elections. Given that your audience is people of your own age whom you probably know well, it would be inappropriate to adopt a formal or impersonal tone. "Appropriate procedures for participating in student government" would be too formal for this audience; by contrast, "voting in this year's student elections" reflects a more appropriate personal tone. Be sure to consider tone when you evaluate your topic.

EXERCISE 15. Identifying Tone. Identify the tone of each topic listed. Remember that tone can be serious, impersonal, formal, critical, humorous, enthusiastic, personal, informal, and so on. For example, the topic "jiffy hints for easy shopping" has an informal tone, whereas "building evacuation procedures" has a formal tone.

1. How to perform the Heimlich maneuver
2. Three fantastic ways to achieve popularity
3. How you can become a superstar
4. Three reasons for my amazing academic success
5. Camping without millions of "creepy-crawlies"
6. Basic equipment for downhill skiing
7. Similarities between *Romeo and Juliet* and *West Side Story*
8. Widespread causes of teen-agers' academic difficulties
9. Growing vegetables for fun and profit
10. Favorite local sports facilities

EXERCISE 16. Limiting Topics to Convey Different Tones. Select any five topics from Exercise 15. Rewrite each selected topic to convey a different tone from the one you identified. For example, "three famous aviators," which has a serious tone, can be rewritten as "three fliers who conquered that wild blue yonder" to convey an informal tone.

EXERCISE 17. Limiting Topics According to Tone. Limit each of the following topics to the tone indicated. For example, for a formal tone, the topic "lifesaving techniques" can be limited to "vital resuscitation procedures." For an informal tone, the same topic can be limited to "ways to save a life."

1. *Topic:* Causes of personal success
   Tone: a. Serious
   　　　 b. Humorous
2. *Topic:* Community theater events
   Tone: a. Formal
   　　　 b. Informal
3. *Topic:* Organizing a savings plan
   Tone: a. Personal
   　　　 b. Impersonal
4. *Topic:* How to read a play
   Tone: a. Serious
   　　　 b. Humorous
5. *Topic:* Two women writers: Charlotte Brontë and George Eliot
   Tone: a. Formal
   　　　 b. Informal

REVIEW EXERCISE A. Evaluating Your Own Topic. Evaluate a topic of your own in terms of purpose, audience, and tone. The topic you choose to evaluate may be one that you have selected and limited in earlier exercises. Use each of the following questions to evaluate your topic:

1. Is this topic limited enough that I can explain it clearly and thoroughly in several paragraphs?
2. What does my audience already know about this topic?
3. What does my audience want to know or need to know about this topic?
4. What aspect of this topic may interest my audience?

5. What will my audience be able to understand about this topic?
6. What viewpoints does my audience have about this topic?
7. What attitude toward this topic do I want to convey?
8. Have I limited my topic to reflect this tone?

CHOOSING A TITLE

16d. Choose a title that reflects your purpose and topic.

Once you have evaluated your limited topic, a title for your composition may suggest itself quite naturally. Remember that a good title gives both topic and purpose in one phrase. It catches the audience's interest and suggests what the composition is about. Take, for example, the topic "the popularity of jogging." Different titles reflect different purposes for a composition on this topic. If you were writing to amuse an audience, you might choose the title "Jogging: Flashy Outfits and Sore Feet." For a persuasive composition, you might choose the title "Run Today for a Healthful Tomorrow." On the other hand, for an expository composition you might choose the title "Dollars and Sense for Running Shoes." Notice that each title clearly reflects the topic and purpose of each composition.

If you cannot immediately think of the "right" title, it is no great matter. You will probably think of a suitable one later, perhaps when you are developing an outline for your composition. Also note that a title written now is tentative, subject to later revision. After you develop an outline or write a first draft, you may decide to rewrite your title so that it better reflects what your composition is about.

EXERCISE 18. Writing Titles. Titles do not always tell everything, but sometimes a title can suggest what follows. For each of the following topics, write a title that reflects both the topic and the writer's expository, or explanatory, purpose. For example, a possible title for the topic "avoiding an exhausting vacation" might be "Coming Home Refreshed."

1. Preparing lunches with fruits and vegetables
2. The benefits of summer travel
3. How the New York Stock Exchange works
4. Changes in fashions since 1900
5. My favorite record albums
6. Opportunities for young people's involvement in our community
7. Our school's grading system

8. How to start any collection
9. Planning a satisfying family holiday
10. Organizing a class trip

EXERCISE 19. Writing Your Own Title. Write a title for a topic of your own. You may, of course, write a title for a topic you have selected, limited, and evaluated in earlier exercises. Remember that this is a *tentative* title that you may decide to revise at a later stage in the writing process.

GATHERING INFORMATION

16e. Gather information on your topic.

Having evaluated your limited topic, you can now gather information—that raw material of your composition. Several strategies will enable you to discover what you already know about your topic. This will be the information you will include in your expository composition.

The *writer's journal,* helpful in the search for subjects, can also be a valuable source of information on your topic. Suppose, for example, that one entry in your writer's journal details the time you assembled your ten-speed bicycle. If you were writing a composition, you might use this journal entry as a source of information—that is, specific details—on "how to assemble bicycles." If one entry does not contain all the information you need, you might review several entries to gather the information you need. For example, several consecutive entries about a trip to the Florida Keys would probably contain enough information for a composition on "visiting literary landmarks in a tropical setting." A writer's journal, then, can be an important place to gather information on topics drawn from your own knowledge, interests, and experiences.

Several *questioning strategies* can also be useful in gathering information on your topic. The *5 W-How? questions* enable you to assemble a range of information about any topic: *Who? What? When? Where? Why? How?* Similarly, with the *point-of-view questions* you can gather information about your topic by considering it from three different perspectives: What is it? How does it change or vary? What are its relationships? You can also ask a series of *questions about a topic:* What is it? What are its parts? How is it put together? How is it made or done? What do I think about

it? What is its value? What is it good for? Any of these three questioning strategies will enable you to gather a great deal of information
about any topic.

Brainstorming, a technique you might have used to search for
subjects, is also a helpful information-gathering strategy. Your aim in
brainstorming is to stimulate a free flow of thought. You should list
all the ideas you have on a topic, as rapidly as they come to you and
without any regard for their order or importance.

Suppose, for example, that you are gathering information on the
topic "the appeal of cave exploring." To brainstorm about this topic,
you should record every idea, impression, and recollection about exploring caves that might occur to you. This list of ideas and details
constitutes the raw material of your composition. Also remember that
this list of ideas and details, although it is spontaneously produced, is
not solely the product of one session of silent thought. It is also the
outgrowth of many activities: your personal reading on the topic, talks
with fellow cave explorers, and, perhaps, other investigations (such
as a trip to the library or a call or letter to an organization of cave
explorers)—in short, all that you already know about the topic. The
following list might result from brainstorming about cave exploring.

the darkness of caves
graffiti in caves and my anger at it
formation of caves—geology
appeal of darkness in caves
the sense of timelessness in a cave
the preservation of footsteps in a cave's protected atmosphere
dangers—flash floods and unmarked passages
age of caves in the United States
experienced climbers descend in groups
cracks in ceilings—water seeping through
the beauty of cave formations
animal life in caves—insects and bats
the growing popularity of cave exploring
discovering, as astronauts and pioneers might
limestone mountains in the South
appeal to the senses—crisp sounds, pure air
rock-climbing experience a requirement?
stalactites and stalagmites—magnificent formations
climate in caves—coldness and dampness
equipment needed for cave exploration
physical requirements—strength for climbing and crawling

Regardless of which information-gathering technique you decide to use, the ideas and details you collect will later be classified and arranged to develop your topic in your expository composition.

EXERCISE 20. Gathering Information on a Topic.   Select any three topics from the following list; then use a different technique to gather information for each topic. Be prepared to explain why, in your opinion, each technique did or did not work well for that particular topic. Keep the information you gather for use in later exercises in this chapter.

1. Local facilities for water sports
2. Why personal talents need nurturing
3. Variations on basic omelets
4. Simplified foreign language study
5. Significant state historical figures
6. Differences between household chores and after-school jobs
7. Preparing for careers in the arts
8. Similarities between badminton and tennis
9. The excitement of rock music
10. How to vote intelligently
11. School applications of personal computers
12. How TV and movies differ
13. My most courageous moment
14. Why I cherish a family heirloom
15. Productive uses for leisure time

EXERCISE 21. Comparing and Contrasting Information-Gathering Techniques.   As your teacher directs, form a small group with three to four classmates and compare the information you gathered in Exercise 20 with what your classmates gathered. Be prepared to determine and to explain whatever similarities and differences exist between the information you and your classmates have gathered on the same topics, particularly noting similarities and differences when *different* information-gathering techniques are used on the *same* topic.

EXERCISE 22. Gathering Information on Your Own Topic. Gather information on a topic of your own, using any one of the information-gathering techniques. You may, of course, use a topic you have developed in earlier exercises. Keep the information you gather for use in later exercises in this chapter.

CLASSIFYING AND ARRANGING IDEAS

16f. Classify and arrange your ideas.

After gathering information on your topic, you should classify and arrange these ideas and details. Scrutinize the information you have gathered in order to sort out the three or four major ideas—or main headings—under which everything else may be organized. These headings will be the major steps in the unfolding of your explanation. Under each of these headings you will group the information you have gathered—examples, incidents, facts, or observations—necessary to develop the main heading clearly and thoroughly. By grouping ideas and details to discover main headings, you will be *classifying,* or organizing according to relationships.

For the sample brainstormed list on the topic "the appeal of cave exploring," you might classify ideas and details according to what kind of appeal they explain. This might result in the following groupings of ideas and details.

Ideas and details:	*Main headings:*
formation of caves—geology age of caves in the United States limestone mountains in the South	record of earth's history inside a cave
dangers—flash floods and unmarked passages experienced climbers descend in groups physical requirements—strength for climbing and crawling rock-climbing experience a requirement?	dangers of caving
the sense of timelessness in a cave appeal of darkness in caves discovering, as astronauts and pioneers do	appeal to human need for adventure
the beauty of cave formations climate in caves—coldness and dampness stalactites and stalagmites—magnificent formations appeal to the senses—crisp sounds, pure air	cave's beauty and appeal to the senses

Notice how these groupings and main headings reflect the relationships among the ideas and details gathered about the appeal of cave exploring.

Through classifying, you have developed several main headings to organize information for your composition. Your next step is to arrange the main headings into the order in which you will discuss them in your composition. Usually this order will suggest itself merely from an examination of the main ideas in light of your purpose for writing. A composition explaining an opinion, for example, proceeds logically—usually from least important reason to more important reason to most important reason, or vice versa. An explanation of a process goes from simple to complex or according to chronological or sequential order. For some compositions, the writer must determine what the most logical order is for that particular topic. For example, for the appeal of cave exploration, the order might proceed from what you see as the simplest appeal to the most complex. Accordingly, you might arrange the four main headings in this order:

> dangers of caving
> cave's beauty and appeal to the senses
> record of earth's history inside a cave
> appeal to human need for adventure

Any composition is clearest when its elements are arranged in the right order; it is your task as the writer to determine what that order is. To do so, you should experiment with the raw material of your own list. Rearrange the items under your main topic until each has found its proper place and appears to belong nowhere else. As the example clearly indicates, some ideas and details will have to be rephrased, others combined, and still others—those that do not fit anywhere or are too long and complicated to be treated adequately—will have to be eliminated entirely. This rephrasing, combining, and eliminating process is natural, something that all writers experience. Items that are eliminated are not necessarily lost forever, however. They might be good points to include in the composition's introduction or conclusion.

EXERCISE 23. Classifying and Arranging Ideas and Details.   In Exercise 20 you gathered information on three topics you selected from the list provided. For these same three topics, classify and arrange the ideas and details you gathered using the various information-gathering techniques. Remember that *classifying* involves grouping related ideas and details under main headings and that *arranging* involves organizing these main headings into the most logical order for your composition.

EXERCISE 24. Classifying and Arranging for Your Own Topic.
Classify and arrange the ideas and details you have gathered for any
topic of your own. Keep these arranged main headings in your notebook for use in later exercises in this chapter.

Developing a Topic Outline

By classifying and arranging ideas and details, you have produced an
informal plan, or outline, for your expository composition. This informal plan can also be written more formally as a *topic outline*, which
is characterized by a specific format for writing main headings and
details about a topic. The various items in a topic outline (main topics
and subtopics) are single words or phrases, not complete sentences,
and are arranged so that the main ideas stand out. You should observe
the following rules for form as you develop a topic outline for your
own expository composition.

(1) Place the title and the statement of purpose above the outline.

**(2) Use Roman numerals for the main topics. Subtopics are given cap-
ital letters, then Arabic numerals, then small letters, then Arabic numerals in parentheses, then small letters in parentheses.**

Title: ***Correct Outline Form***
Purpose:
  I.   Main topic
    A.   Subtopics of I
    B.
       1.   Subtopics of B
       2.
          a.   Subtopics of 2
          b.
            (1)   Subtopics of b
            (2)
               (a)   Subtopics of (2)
               (b)
 II.   Main topic

**(3) Indent subtopics. Indentations should be made so that all letters or
numbers of the same kind will come directly under one another in a
vertical line.**

(4) When subtopics are included in an outline, there must always be more than one subtopic. Because subtopics are divisions of the topic above them, you must have at least two parts when you subdivide.

If you find yourself wanting to use a single subtopic, rewrite the topic above it so that this "sub-idea" is included in the main topic.

INCORRECT   D. The study of French culture
                1. The study of the French language
CORRECT   D. The study of French culture and language

(5) For each number or letter in an outline, there must be a topic.

Never place an *A,* for instance, next to *I* or *1* like this: *IA* or *A1*.

(6) A subtopic must belong under the main topic beneath which it is placed. It must be closely related to the topic above it.

(7) Begin each topic and subtopic with a capital letter. You should not place a period after a topic because it is not a complete sentence.

(8) The terms *introduction, body,* **and** *conclusion* **should never be included in the outline.**

Of course, you may have an introduction and a conclusion in your composition, but these terms themselves are not topics you intend to discuss.

Refer to the following sample topic outline as you develop an outline for your expository composition.

Sample Topic Outline

CAVE EXPLORING: A TRIP INTO DARKNESS
AND DANGER

Purpose: To explain why people risk danger to explore the dark, mysterious world of caves

  I. Dangers for cave explorers
     A. Unmarked passages
     B. Flash floods
     C. Exploring alone
     D. Being out of condition

II. Caves' appeal to senses
    A. Cool, clean air
    B. Crispness of sounds
    C. Beautiful formations
        1. Stalactites
        2. Stalagmites

III. Geology of caves
    A. Southern caves in limestone mountains
    B. Water tables over centuries
    C. Markings etched onto cave walls by water

IV. Caves as frontiers of exploration
    A. Similarity to astronauts' mission
    B. Similarity to pioneers' adventure

EXERCISE 25. Writing a Topic Outline. Copy carefully the skeleton outline given at the right, and place each of the items in the list at the left in its proper position in the outline.

Title: Pleasures of travel
Purpose: To explain three enjoyable aspects of travel

Eiffel Tower in Paris	I.
Swiss cable cars	A.
Seeing natural wonders	B.
California's giant sequoias	C.
Toronto's CN Tower	II.
Seeing wonders created by human beings	A.
Victoria Falls in Africa	B.
Golden Gate Bridge in San Francisco	C.
Dog sleds in Alaska	D.
Aurora borealis	E.
Using unusual transportation	III.
Mexican pyramids	A.
Venetian gondolas	B.
Chesapeake Bay Bridge-Tunnel Complex	C.
Camelback in Egypt	D.

EXERCISE 26. Developing a Topic Outline. In Exercise 23 you classified and arranged information you previously gathered on three topics. For each topic, write a topic outline, following correct topic outline form and using the classifications and arrangements you

developed earlier. Keep your work for use in a later exercise in this chapter.

EXERCISE 27. Writing Your Own Topic Outline. In Exercise 24 you classified and arranged ideas and details for a topic of your own. Write these same ideas and details as a formal topic outline. Keep this topic outline in your notebook for later use when you write your expository composition.

CRITICAL THINKING:
Synthesizing to Write a Thesis Statement

16g. Write the thesis statement.

Having gathered, classified, and arranged information on your topic, you should now write a thesis statement for your expository composition. A *thesis statement,* like the topic sentence in an expository paragraph, indicates the composition's purpose and suggests what the composition will discuss. Notice, however, that the thesis statement pertains to an *entire* composition, whereas a topic sentence presents the main idea for one paragraph only. Thus, the thesis statement focuses both the writer's and the audience's attention on specifics, that is, the composition's content.

To write a thesis statement, you employ the critical thinking skill called synthesis. *Synthesis* comes from Greek words meaning "to place together." Placing together is exactly what you do in writing a thesis statement: You synthesize what you know or understand about your topic, expressed in one sentence called the thesis statement.

You have acquired this knowledge or understanding of your topic by progressing through each prewriting step in the composing process. As you limited your subject for a particular audience, purpose, and tone, you also focused on its specific parts. This focus on specifics continued as you evaluated your topic and gathered information. Through classifying and arranging your ideas and details, you perceived relationships among these ideas and details. The thesis statement finally brings together what you now understand as a result of prewriting: what the specific aspects of your topic are and how they are related to each other. You have arrived at the understanding expressed in your thesis statement by synthesizing, or placing together, the insights and information you have gained through prewriting.

Through synthesizing, you might develop the following thesis statement for "the appeals of cave exploring": *This paper will explain that cave explorers are searching for adventure and for a strange beauty unknown in the "upper" world of light.* This statement, which should appear in the composition's introductory paragraph, states the composition's purpose (to explain) and suggests what aspects of the topic the composition will discuss (searching for adventure and for a strange beauty).

EXERCISE 28. Writing Thesis Statements. Using the three topic outlines you wrote in Exercise 26, write a thesis statement for each topic. As your teacher directs, exchange papers with a classmate and review the thesis statements you have written on the same topics. Be prepared to explain why similarities and differences, if any, exist between the thesis statements you have each written.

REVIEW EXERCISE B. Writing Your Own Thesis Statement. Using the topic outline you wrote for your own topic, write a thesis statement for your expository composition. Remember that this thesis statement should state the composition's purpose and should suggest what aspects of your topic the composition will be about.

WRITING

WRITING THE PARTS OF A COMPOSITION

16h. Write the parts of your composition: the introduction, the body, and the conclusion.

If you have carefully completed each of the preceding steps in the writing process, you will find that many of the problems of writing have been solved in advance. You know your topic and your purpose in writing about it. You have gathered information about your topic and have arranged it in what you see as the correct order for presentation. Now, using your thesis statement and topic outline as guides, you can concentrate on actually writing your composition.

An expository composition has three principal parts: a beginning (the introduction), a discussion of the topics in the outline (the body), and an ending (the conclusion). Each part plays a specific role.

Writing the Introduction

(1) The introduction arouses the audience's interest and states the main idea of the composition.

Although the introduction does not appear as a heading in the topic outline, it is nevertheless a very important part of an expository composition. The introduction should give the audience a preview of what the composition is about. It should clearly indicate the topic and your purpose in writing about it, and it should catch your audience's interest. In a short composition, the introduction may consist of only a sentence in the first paragraph. In longer compositions, a short paragraph may serve this purpose. Regardless of its length, however, the introduction should include your thesis statement—either as originally written or in a revised form.

Following are five ways to write the introduction for an expository composition. Notice how each arouses the audience's interest and indicates what the composition will be about.

1. *Begin with an anecdote or example.* The following paragraph relates an anecdote to illustrate how sensitive an instrument the harpsichord is.

> Lemon or no, the harpsichord is the tetchiest instrument ever invented, bar none, and keeping one in working condition is a drain on anybody's time. Because it contains so many wooden moving parts, the instrument is extremely sensitive to changes in humidity and temperature. Once, as a reviewer, I attended one of those oh-so-important debut recitals where everything had to be just so, and for this occasion the artist had selected (that is, borrowed) a brand-new and magnificent Hubbard. It was an unseasonably hot night in October, and because the people were suffering, somebody opened a window, letting humanity off the hook but putting the harpsichord in a draft. When the harpsichordist tore into his opening Couperin group, he found his whole upper keyboard in the terminal stages of harpsichord pneumonia, with many of the notes more than a whole tone out of tune and one whistling away an octave and a half out of sight. The show was wrecked. Luckily, the man's career was not; but for all the labor that went into it, this recital did him no good.
>
> ROBERT EVETT

2. *Begin with a question.* Notice how the following essay begins with a question, which the writer thoroughly answers in his introduction.

What has the telephone done to us, or for us, in the hundred years of its existence? A few effects suggest themselves at once. It has saved lives by getting rapid word of illness, injury, or famine from remote places. By joining with the elevator to make possible the multistory residence or office building, it has made possible—for better or worse—the modern city. By bringing about a quantum leap in the speed and ease with which information moves from place to place, it has greatly accelerated the rate of scientific and technological change and growth in industry. Beyond doubt it has crippled if not killed the ancient art of letter writing. It has made living alone possible for persons with normal social impulses; by so doing, it has played a role in one of the greatest social changes of this century, the breakup of the multigenerational household. It has made the waging of war chillingly more efficient than formerly. Perhaps (though not provably) it has prevented wars that might have arisen out of international misunderstanding caused by written communication. Or perhaps—again not provably—by magnifying and extending irrational personal conflicts based on voice contact, it has caused wars. Certainly it has extended the scope of human conflicts, since it impartially disseminates the useful knowledge of scientists and the babble of bores, the affection of the affectionate and the malice of the malicious.

JOHN BROOKS

3. *Begin with a direct statement of the topic.* In the following introduction, the first sentence directly states the essay's topic.

In the folklore of the country, numerous superstitions relate to winter weather. Back-country farmers examine their corn husks—the thicker the husk, the colder the winter. They watch the acorn crop—the more acorns, the more severe the season. They observe where white-faced hornets place their paper nests—the higher they are, the deeper will be the snow. They examine the size and shape and color of the spleens of butchered hogs for clues to the severity of the season. They keep track of the blooming of dogwood in the spring—the more abundant the blooms, the more bitter the cold in January. When chipmunks carry their tails high and squirrels have heavier fur and mice come into country houses early in the fall, the superstitious gird themselves for a long, hard winter. Without any scientific basis, a wider-than-usual black band on a woolly-bear caterpillar is accepted as a sign that winter will arrive early and stay late. Even the way a cat sits beside the stove carries a message to the credulous. According to a belief once widely held in the Ozarks, a cat sitting with its tail to the fire indicates very cold weather is on the way.

EDWIN WAY TEALE

4. Begin with a statement opposite to your thesis, followed by a positive or direct statement. The following paragraph begins with two statements that contradict the writer's thesis.

> There are two popular views of animal aggression. One is that animals in the wild spend all their time fighting. The other is that if wild animals are not interfered with they will never fight. Both ideas have been perpetuated by Walt Disney's films, and they are as wrong as they are different. They do grave injustice to the richness of animal behavior patterns and serve only to confuse those who turn to animals to seek knowledge of human aggression. So before starting we must dispose of some hoary old myths.
>
> ROBIN CLARK

5. Begin by providing general background information. The following paragraph introduces an essay that explains how the first transatlantic cable was laid. Notice how this introduction discusses events that preceded the transatlantic cable.

> For thousands of years, communication moved only as fast as a horse could run or a ship could muster subject to the vagaries of the wind. But in the 19th century, an invention popularly attributed to Samuel F. B. Morse suddenly transcended the miles, within countries and beyond. Miraculous wires began to creep over Europe and the more settled regions of North America. By mid-century the telegraph system was proliferating rapidly, defying distance and shrinking the vast earth, which would diminish further with the telephone, automobile, and airplane. In 1850 a telegraph cable was laid across the English Channel and was promptly followed by a link between Dover, England, and Ostend, Belgium; four between England and Holland; and a spanning of the Black Sea in 1855 to enhance British communications in the Crimean War.
>
> CAROLINE SUTTON

These introductory forms offer you several alternatives for writing your composition's introduction. Regardless of which way you decide to write your introduction, however, be sure to maintain a consistent tone in your writing. The tone of your introduction, which reveals your attitude toward your topic, should mirror the point of view you decided on earlier in the writing process.

EXERCISE 29. Writing Introductory Paragraphs. Select two thesis statements from the following five thesis statements. Then write two introductory paragraphs for each thesis statement, using a different approach for each. Be sure to refer to the examples just given, and remember that the purpose of an introductory paragraph is to state the composition's main idea—usually by including the thesis statement somewhere in the paragraph—and to arouse the audience's interest.

1. Creativity demands both inspiration and discipline.
2. Rock musicians often combine musical talent with dramatic flair and a sense of poetry.
3. Establishing a school choral group involves finding a willing faculty sponsor and gathering interested and talented classmates.
4. Our community leaders are notable for their resourcefulness, farsightedness, and sensitivity.
5. I enjoy fishing because it is relaxing, rewarding, and challenging.

EXERCISE 30. Writing Your Own Introductory Paragraph. Write an introductory paragraph for your own expository composition, using the thesis statement and topic outline you have developed for a topic of your own. Decide which one of the ways to write an introduction will suit your composition best; consider how you can best arouse your audience's interest and state the composition's main idea. Also be sure to include in this introduction your thesis statement, either as originally written or slightly altered.

Writing the Body

(2) The body states and develops the main ideas in the outline.

The body is the heart of the composition. It fulfills the promise of the introduction and consists of several paragraphs that develop the topic, as stated in your thesis statement. The nature of your subject and your specific purpose will determine the exact length of the body of your composition.

As you write your first draft, you must decide at which points new paragraphs must be started. The way you paragraph should show your reader the successive stages of your thinking. It may be that you can devote one paragraph in your composition to each of the main headings in your topic outline or to each point in your thesis statement. This simple solution usually works out well in shorter compositions. In longer compositions, however, you will often find that you need to devote a paragraph to certain subheadings in your outline, or that a major point in your thesis statement would be developed best in two paragraphs. In any case, each of your paragraphs should be built around a single idea or aspect of your topic. Every time you take up a new idea, begin a new paragraph that develops and supports your thesis statement. In this way your composition will be unified.

Each paragraph within the body should itself be well developed; that is, each paragraph should have a topic sentence supported by specific details, facts and statistics, examples, reasons, or incidents. Each paragraph's topic sentence should address one point of your thesis statement, and each should be supported by one of the methods of paragraph development. Each paragraph may also end with a clincher sentence. Use your topic outline, which includes the main ideas in your thesis statement and the details to support each, to write each paragraph in the composition's body.

Achieving Coherence and Emphasis

As you draft the body of your composition and join the body to the introduction and conclusion, you must also be concerned with achieving coherence and emphasis. By arranging paragraphs in a logical order and making connections between ideas from paragraph to paragraph, you will achieve *coherence,* or a logical flow of ideas. By indicating to your audience that some points are more important than others, you will achieve *emphasis* in your composition.

(2a) Arrange your ideas to achieve coherence.

You considered the order of ideas earlier when you arranged items for your topic outline. The paragraphs that form the body of your composition should also be arranged in a logical order. The order you choose depends on the topic you are explaining. For example, in compositions that explain how to make or do something, paragraphs should be arranged in chronological or spatial order. Compositions that explain opinions often use order of importance, progressing from the least important idea to the most important idea, or just the opposite. For some topics, the order of paragraphs simply depends on which ideas are necessary for understanding later points and, therefore, should precede them. By arranging the paragraphs in the body in a logical order, you will achieve coherence, or the smooth and logical flow of ideas, in your composition. For a more extensive discussion of arranging ideas coherently, see pages 365–77 of Chapter 14.

(2b) Connect your ideas to achieve coherence.

In an effective composition the current of thought flows smoothly throughout the composition. It is not interrupted by the divisions between paragraphs; it is helped easily over these divisions by certain *transitions:* transitional expressions, direct pronoun references, and repetition of key words. By using these transitions, the writer indicates how ideas in one paragraph connect to ideas in another paragraph. Transitions also enable a writer to indicate how ideas are related within a single paragraph.

Transitional Expressions

To indicate another point: after that, also, another, at last, at the outset, further, besides, finally, first (second, etc.), furthermore, in addition, in conclusion, in other words, in the next place, lastly, moreover, then, then again, to begin with, too, to sum up

To indicate place or position: above, across from, adjacent to, around, before, below, beside, beyond, here, in the distance, nearby, next, on my left, on my right, opposite to, there, to the left, to the right

To indicate results: accordingly, as a result, as might be expected, consequently, hence, therefore, thus

To indicate time order or sequence: afterward, again, at last, at the present time, at the same time, at this point, eventually, finally, first (second, etc.), meanwhile, next, not long after, presently, soon, sooner or later, then, thereafter, thereupon

To introduce examples: an example of this, for example, for instance

To show comparison: again, also, and, besides, in addition, in a like manner, likewise, moreover, similarly, such, too

To show contrast: but, however, in spite of, instead, nevertheless, on the contrary, on the other hand, opposite to, otherwise, whereas, yet

To show order of importance: after that, also, equally important, furthermore, in addition, in conclusion, in the first (second, etc.) place, then, to begin with, to sum up

EXAMPLES   Day after day the drought continued.
On the thirtieth day, **however,** the wind changed. It blew cool against the face and carried a faint breath of something new.

. . . scientists found that dolphins were intelligent.
An example of this intelligence is the way in which dolphins once avenged themselves on fishermen. A fishing boat in the Pacific had killed several dolphins. The next day about two hundred dolphins surrounded the fishing boat, stranding the fishermen aboard.

. . . it was the hottest day of the year.
The mayor, **accordingly,** declared a heat emergency.

Direct Pronoun References

EXAMPLE   . . . The lamb was uneasy too. **It** started violently at unexpected noises and cried piteously when left alone.
This was not the worst burden on **its** owner, however. . . .

Repetition of Key Words

EXAMPLES   . . . What is more, the car will accelerate from 0 to 60 miles per hour in only five seconds.
This blistering acceleration, however, is not its best feature. . . .

. . . A further advantage of using the play by Lorraine Hansberry is that it would require only a small cast of talented actors.
Having a small cast would allow us to increase our profits by at least 10 percent, a major goal since we are donating the proceeds to charity. Since our overhead costs . . .

(2c) Arrange your ideas to achieve emphasis.

All the parts of your composition are not necessarily equally important in explaining your topic to your audience. That is, the introduction and the conclusion are less important to the development of your ideas than is the middle section, or body, of your composition. Within the body, some points may also be more important than others. Therefore, as you write your composition, you also must arrange your ideas to achieve emphasis. How you develop the paragraphs in the composition's body should clearly indicate to the reader which ideas and details receive the strongest emphasis. You can usually achieve emphasis in one of the following three ways:

1. *Direct statement.* By using phrases like "the most important reason," "the major step in the process," and "the most significant result," you state directly which ideas you think are most important and should therefore receive the greatest emphasis.

2. *Emphasis by position.* Ordinarily the strongest positions in the composition's body are the first and last parts. Ideas and details you want your audience to notice particularly should be placed in these positions. Another type of emphatic organization frequently used is the *order of climax,* which moves from weakest to strongest idea or reason.

3. *Emphasis on proportion.* This is the most important kind of emphasis, for the amount of space you devote to a part of your topic reflects its importance. If you tell your audience that a given topic is important, they will expect that topic to be given extensive treatment. Thus the more important the topic, the more space you devote to it.

In writing your composition, remember that the number of subtopics a topic has in an outline does not necessarily determine the amount of emphasis the topic should eventually receive. Sometimes a topic with several subtopics may concern the least important idea in your composition, while a topic with few subtopics may address the most important idea.

EXERCISE 31. Evaluating Coherence and Emphasis. In a magazine or newspaper that you may cut up, find three to five paragraphs written on one topic. Paste these paragraphs neatly on a sheet of paper. Underline the transitions and summarize what kinds of transitions the writer uses, and why these are or are not appropriate for the excerpted paragraphs. Be prepared to discuss how the writer has or has not arranged ideas in a logical order. Also indicate if the

writer has achieved emphasis by position, proportion, or direct statement and if the writer has successfully indicated which ideas and
details should receive the strongest emphasis. Be prepared to explain
your answers.

EXERCISE 32. Writing the Body of Your Composition. Write the
body for a composition on a topic of your own. Using your topic
outline and thesis statement as guides, write one paragraph for each
main topic in your outline. Be sure to support the topic sentence in
each paragraph with specific details, facts and statistics, examples,
incidents, or reasons—the subtopics in your topic outline. Achieve
coherence by connecting ideas with transitions, and achieve emphasis
by direct statement, position, or proportion. As you write, remember
that the body of the composition is the sole place where you can
develop the main idea stated in the thesis statement.

Writing the Conclusion

**(3) The conclusion clinches or extends the main points made in the
body of the composition.**

One way to end a composition is simply to stop writing. Although this
method is an easy one, it has the disadvantage of suggesting that you
have given up. A better way to end a composition is by recalling the
purpose of the composition and the information set forth to develop
the topic. At the same time, however, the conclusion should not merely
repeat the introduction and the body. That is, it should go beyond
simply restating what the audience has already read in the composition. Rather, the conclusion should make a final statement that is an
outgrowth of the points discussed in the body. In so doing, you will
leave your audience with a final impression of your topic.

The conclusion may be only a few sentences, or it may be a whole
paragraph. In either case, it should tell your audience that you have
completed your composition, not abandoned it.

Notice how the following conclusion brings the writer's discussion
of American Indians' rights to a definite close.

> The "vanishing Indian," the stereotype of the late nineteenth-century,
> is far from vanishing. Reservation home rule is more solidly established
> than ever, Indian self-esteem is on the rise, and the Indian world is in
> ferment. Where this will lead is anybody's guess, but at this writing the
> Indian's future, if not bright, certainly seems brightening. Alexander

Pope's "poor Indian! whose untutor'd mind/Sees God in clouds, or hears him in the wind" has become a sophisticated and successful practitioner of the art of survival in the modern world.

ROBERT A. HECHT

EXERCISE 33. Evaluating a Conclusion. In a magazine or newspaper you may cut up, find a conclusion to an expository article or essay. Paste this concluding paragraph on a sheet of paper. Explain why this conclusion does or does not provide an effective and definite ending to the article. Ask yourself the following questions to evaluate the conclusion: What final impression does the concluding paragraph leave on the reader? How is the conclusion related to the body of the article or essay? Does the conclusion summarize the article's main points without exactly repeating them? Does the conclusion go beyond the points developed in the body? What could the writer add or subtract to make the conclusion more effective?

EXERCISE 34. Writing Your Own Concluding Paragraph. Write the concluding paragraph for the expository composition you are writing on your own topic. Asking one question may help you as you write the conclusion: What do I want my audience to remember about this topic when they have finished reading this composition?

STUDYING A SAMPLE COMPOSITION

At the end of this paragraph is a sample expository composition on the topic "the appeal of cave exploring." As you read the composition, pay particular attention to how its various parts explain the topic. The introduction catches the audience's interest and states what the composition will be about, with the thesis statement as this paragraph's last sentence. The body develops the main headings in the topic outline, with four separate paragraphs discussing the special appeal of cave exploration. The conclusion leaves the audience with a final impression by emphasizing that cave exploring satisfies the human need to seek adventure. Keep these points in mind as you read the composition.

CAVE EXPLORING: A TRIP INTO DARKNESS
AND DANGER   title

    Caves are dark, cold tunnels inhabited by ants,   introduction
lizards, insects, and eyeless fish—weird, colorless
creatures that have never seen sunlight. Little   specific details to
from the world above can penetrate the black   arouse audience
   interest in topic

space of caves, except for water that seeps through cracks, occasional threads of light that sneak between rocks—and human beings who descend bravely into the dark. Every year, more and more people become interested in the unique hobby of cave exploring. What lures them into the murky depths? What pleasure do they get from crawling along narrow, jagged passages? <u>As we will see they are searching for adventure and for a strange beauty unknown in the "upper" world.</u>

> thesis statement

<u>For would-be adventurers, cave exploring offers unusual dangers.</u> Cave passages are seldom marked; therefore, it is quite easy to lose all sense of direction. Water often fills caves during flash floods, drowning anyone inside. Because of these dangers, explorers must never risk entering a cave alone. They also must be in good physical condition because maneuvering inside a cave requires strength for climbing and crawling.

> body
> topic sentence: states main topic I
>
> specific details delineate dangers of cave exploring

Once the explorer enters a cave's deep vaults, <u>however</u>, all the difficulties seem worthwhile. Cave air is cool and clean. Sounds echo crisply through the vast emptiness. Magnificent rock creations, shaped over centuries by drops of water seeping through the earth, dominate the interior. Like exotic sculptures in a secret museum, formations called stalactites droop ominously from a cave's ceiling, while stalagmites rise in massive pointed shapes from the floor. <u>For the cave explorer, the underground is a hidden realm of beauty.</u>

> main topic II
> transitional word
>
> specific details illustrate appeal to the senses
>
>
>
>
>
> topic sentence

<u>Many explorers know another secret hidden inside caves: a sense of intimacy with earth's geologic past.</u> The caves of the Carolinas and Georgia, for example, were originally formed out

> topic sentence: states main topic III; also includes transition

of limestone mountains. They were created by water tables—levels of water in the ground—that rose and fell over centuries, slowly dissolving the limestone bases of the mountains. The high, dry spaces left when the waters receded are the caves we know today. The explorer sees these water markings etched into the cave's floors and walls. They are vivid reminders of the earth's transformation and development.

Even more impressive than a cave's beauty or its record of the past is its pull on the human imagination. A cave is a frontier of adventure, a last unexplored wilderness. Like an astronaut, a cave explorer is a wanderer into an alien world. Every "caver" has the pioneer dreams of being the first to find a new passageway and to take a fresh step into an undiscovered cavern. It is this call of the unknown that lures an explorer into the earth's depths—to enter a world where space, darkness, and the human imagination merge.

[margin annotations:]
transition; also indicates emphasis

topic sentence: states main topic IV

examples illustrate caves' pull on human imagination

conclusion clinches composition

EXERCISE 35. Evaluating an Expository Composition. Answer each of the following questions about the sample composition. You may find it helpful first to review the explanations on the introduction, body, and conclusion found on pages 454–64.

1. According to what method is the introductory paragraph written?
2. How effective, in your opinion, is this introduction in arousing audience interest and in stating the composition's main idea? Be prepared to explain your answer.
3. Review each paragraph in the body. What other details, if any, do you think the writer could have included to support each topic sentence better?
4. Is there a concluding or clincher sentence in each paragraph? Does its presence or absence add to the paragraph's development and effectiveness? How?

5. How effective is the composition's conclusion? What final impression does it leave on you as an audience? How does this final impression relate to the thesis statement in the introduction?

6. What changes, if any, have been made from the writer's topic outline on pages 451–52? Why do you think the writer did or did not make changes?

7. How does the writer achieve coherence in the composition?

8. How does the writer achieve emphasis in the composition?

9. If you were to revise this composition, what additional information would you include to support the thesis statement better? What information would you omit without weakening the development of the thesis statement?

10. How might you rewrite the title to make it more interesting or indicative of the composition's content?

GUIDELINES FOR WRITING EXPOSITORY COMPOSITIONS

PREWRITING

1. Select a topic you understand well enough to explain. If you do not understand the topic, you may find it difficult to explain it to someone else.

2. Be sure to limit your topic well. Although you have several paragraphs to present information about your topic, you should limit the subject so that you can discuss specific aspects in the available space.

3. Pay special attention to gathering information for your topic. Ask yourself what someone unfamiliar with this topic might need to know or might want to know about it. Because your purpose is to give information about a particular topic, you need to have both the *right kind* of information and *enough* information to explain the topic well to your audience. Depending on your topic and audience, gather facts, statistics, specific details, examples, or incidents.

4. Determine if any technical terms or unusual vocabulary needs to be defined in your composition. Remember that your audience may need help with specialized uses of words.

5. Carefully organize the information you gather. If you are to present this information clearly and directly, it must be organized so that your audience will understand it. Keep in mind that your purpose is to explain your topic as well as possible; then group and arrange related ideas and details into

an informal plan or topic outline. Use this outline or plan to draft a thesis statement.

WRITING

6. Select one of the methods for writing an introductory paragraph. Be sure the introduction includes a thesis statement that clearly and directly indicates what the composition will be about.

7. Use your topic outline or informal plan as you draft the body of your composition. Write one paragraph for each main topic in your outline, supporting the topic sentence for each paragraph with ideas or details from your outline. Be sure to arrange the paragraphs in the body in some kind of logical order. Use transitions to show how ideas and paragraphs are related, and achieve emphasis through position, statement, or proportion.

8. As you write, be aware of the tone of your writing, and choose words that accurately convey your attitude toward the topic and are appropriate for your particular audience. Also continue to consider what language will best explain the topic to your audience.

9. Write a concluding paragraph that clinches the composition. It should restate your topic and leave your reader with a final impression about your topic.

REVISING AND PROOFREADING

10. After you have written your composition, determine if you have included enough information and the right kind of information to explain this topic as well as possible to your particular audience. Also consider if the paragraphs in the body are arranged so as to explain your topic as thoroughly and clearly as possible. Reevaluate your choice of words by considering how appropriate your language is for your audience and for the tone you wish to convey. Be sure to proofread for inaccuracies in spelling, grammar, usage, and mechanics. Proofread again after you prepare a final draft to catch any accidental mistakes made in recopying.

REVIEW EXERCISE C. Writing an Expository Composition. Select a topic of your own for an expository composition. Then, by following the Guidelines for Writing Expository Compositions, write an expository composition on this topic. Be sure to follow each step in the writing process as you write your composition.

REVISING

16i. Revise your composition by evaluating content, organization, and style.

Shakespeare is supposed to have written whole plays and changed only a few lines. That is not the way it goes for most of us. Most of the time, second thoughts are better than first ones; a thoughtful and critical reading of first drafts produces a stronger and clearer final draft.

Revising your composition follows the preparation of your initial draft. The object in revision is to see the composition as much as possible through the eyes of your audience. To revise, therefore, you review your composition to determine what changes would improve the way you explain the topic to your audience. Specifically, evaluate three aspects of your composition: content, organization, and style.

To revise for *content,* you consider topic development. Remember that the purpose of an expository composition is to explain or to inform a particular audience about your topic. To do so, each paragraph in your composition should perform a particular role. The introduction should attract your audience's attention and present your thesis statement. Each paragraph in the body should develop one aspect of the thesis statement. The concluding paragraph should clinch or extend the composition. The topic sentence within each paragraph should be supported with specific details, facts, statistics, incidents, reasons, or examples. Most important, the paragraphs in your composition—individually and together—should all discuss the one topic your composition is about.

To revise for *organization,* you evaluate how the paragraphs in your composition are arranged and related. Determine if you have arranged paragraphs in the logical order most appropriate for this particular composition—that is, the order that presents information about this topic in the clearest, most logical, and most easily understood way. You should also consider how ideas between and within paragraphs are related. Through the use of transitions, one paragraph should flow smoothly and logically to the next; similarly, details within each paragraph should be logically related to one another. You should also determine if you have achieved emphasis, either by direct statement, position, or proportion.

To revise for *style,* you evaluate the language in your composition. Above all, the language you use should be clear. The composition should contain sentence variety and words that are appropriate for your particular audience, and technical terms or unusual vocabulary should be clearly explained. Evaluating the tone of your writing is particularly important. Consider if you have clearly indicated your tone, or point of view, toward the topic in language appropriate for your particular audience. You should also determine if the tone itself is appropriate for your audience and if you have maintained a consistent tone throughout your composition.

Three strategies may be helpful as you evaluate your composition's content, organization, and style. First, if possible, lay your first draft aside for a while before you begin the process of revision. Revising is different from writing; it requires a little detachment, which the passage of time helps you to achieve. Second, read your first draft aloud to yourself. Reading aloud can help you locate places in your composition where you should make changes to explain your topic more clearly or thoroughly. If something sounds confusing or awkward or if you have difficulty following your ideas, it is possible that the same thing will happen to the reader. Third, at your teacher's request, exchange compositions with a classmate. Another reader who is not familiar with your composition might be able to provide very helpful ideas for revising—perhaps by suggesting where an additional transition would connect one paragraph more logically to the next, by indicating where more specific details would explain a point more clearly, or by noting what terms seem unclear or inappropriate for your intended audience. These suggestions can be very helpful when you revise, just as reading someone else's draft can help you see how another writer tackles and solves writing problems.

Here are some general guidelines for revising any expository composition. Be sure to ask yourself each question as you evaluate your expository composition.

GUIDELINES FOR REVISING EXPOSITORY COMPOSITIONS

1. Does the introduction include a thesis statement and attract the audience's attention?
2. Does each paragraph in the body discuss only one main idea?
3. Is each paragraph in the body well developed; that is, does each paragraph have a topic sentence supported with specific details, facts and statistics, examples, incidents, or reasons?

4. Does each paragraph in the body contribute to developing the topic; that is, does each paragraph explain one aspect of the thesis statement?

5. Is the topic sufficiently developed; that is, are enough points included to support the thesis?

6. Does the concluding paragraph go beyond the points developed in the body to make a final impression on the audience? Does it clinch the composition?

7. Does the conclusion logically relate to the thesis statement?

8. Does the composition follow a logical order of development, that is, chronological or spatial order or order of importance?

9. Are transitions used to link ideas within each paragraph?

10. Are transitions used to join paragraphs to each other so that there is a smooth and logical flow from one paragraph to another?

11. Is emphasis achieved by direct statement, position, or proportion?

12. Is the composition's language appropriate for the audience? Does the composition include clear and specific words and avoid wordiness?

13. Are technical terms or unusual vocabulary defined and explained?

14. Does word choice reflect the writer's tone or point of view toward the topic? Is this tone consistent throughout the composition? Is this tone appropriate for the intended audience?

15. Are sentences clear, varied, and appropriate for the audience?

16. Is the title interesting, and does it suggest the composition's main idea and purpose?

EXERCISE 36. Revising Paragraphs. The following paragraph is a revised draft of the sample composition's fourth paragraph, seen in its final form on pages 465–66. Study the changes the writer made; then, answer the questions about the revisions.

Many explorers *know another secret hidden inside* ~~get something from~~ caves: a sense of intimacy with
geologic
earth's past. The caves of the Carolinas and Georgia *for example* were originally formed
out of limestone mountains. They *created* were ~~made~~ by water tables that rose *– levels of water in the ground*
over centuries *dissolving*
and fell ~~for years~~, slowly ~~breaking up~~ the limestone bases of the mountains.

~~Limestone is a kind of rock~~ composed of the organic remains of sea animals. The explorer sees these water markings, all kinds of crazy-looking tr squiggles, etched into the cave's floors and walls. The high, dry spaces left behind when the waters receded are the caves we know and love, today. They are *vivid* reminders of *the* earth's transformation and development.

1. The writer has made several deletions—of words, phrases, or sentences. What deletions were made and why—for example, to achieve unity? To avoid redundancy? To express ideas more concisely?

2. In which instances did the writer add transitions to improve the logical flow of ideas in the paragraph? Are those additions effective? Why or why not?

3. Which words or phrases were either added or substituted for others? How did making these changes improve the development of the topic sentence, alter the paragraph's tone, or provide additional information for the audience?

4. The writer rearranged, or reordered, two sentences in the paragraph. How does this change improve the paragraph?

5. What revisions, in your opinion, could still be made to improve the paragraph? What changes did the writer make that did not substantially improve the paragraph? Be prepared to explain and support your answers.

EXERCISE 37. Revising Your Own Composition.   Revise any expository composition you have written in this chapter, referring to the **Guidelines for Revising Expository Compositions** on pages 470–71. As you revise, keep in mind that your goal is to make sure that your thesis statement is thoroughly and logically supported and that your topic is fully developed for your particular audience. Remember, too, that reading this composition aloud may help you determine where you should revise. As your teacher directs, you might exchange compositions with a classmate, who may offer useful suggestions for revision as well.

PROOFREADING

16j. Proofread your composition for inaccuracies in spelling, grammar, usage, and mechanics.

After revising your composition for content, organization, and style, you should proofread for any inaccuracies that might confuse or distract your audience—inaccuracies in spelling, punctuation, capitalization, grammar, and usage. Expository writing, if it is to fulfill its explanatory purpose, must be clear and precise. If a run-on sentence, misplaced comma, or misspelling confuses your audience, they might miss the point of your exposition. By avoiding and correcting such inaccuracies, you can make your expository composition more effective.

Use the following list of proofreading guidelines to proofread any expository composition you write.

GUIDELINES FOR PROOFREADING EXPOSITORY COMPOSITIONS

1. Is the paper neat, legible, and free from obvious corrections?
2. Are all words spelled correctly?
3. Does every sentence begin with a capital letter? Are all proper nouns and proper adjectives capitalized?
4. Are there any sentence fragments or run-on sentences?
5. Does each sentence end with the correct punctuation mark? Are other punctuation marks—such as commas or apostrophes—used correctly?
6. Is there correct subject-verb agreement?
7. Are verb forms and verb tenses used correctly?
8. Are subject and object forms of personal pronouns used correctly?
9. Do pronouns agree with their antecedents? Are pronoun references clear?
10. Are frequently confused words—such as *lie* and *lay,* or *fewer* and *less*—used correctly?

11. Are abbreviations used correctly?
12. Are words divided correctly at the ends of lines?
13. Do indentations show where new paragraphs begin?
14. Are there proper margins?

EXERCISE 38. Proofreading a Paragraph. Proofread the following paragraph, which contains inaccuracies in spelling, grammar, punctuation, capitalization, or usage. Locate each inaccuracy; rewrite the paragraph correctly on your own paper. Underline each correction.

Less than 60 years ago, physicists considered it prooved that, because of the nature of light no microskope could ever be built, that would yield higher magnification then the best compound microskopes. Then come the electron microscope with it's magnification of fifty thousand times and more the electron microscope uses electrons instead of light. Physisists at once accepted the new facts and changed there previous ideas. If all sientists had stuck to the old idea about microscopes would the electron microscope have been discovered. Can you think of any curent example in which sticking to an old believe may blocking a search for new discoveries?

EXERCISE 39. Proofreading Your Expository Composition. Proofread any expository composition you have written in this chapter. Indicate where there are inaccuracies in spelling, grammar, usage, or mechanics, and indicate how you can correct them for your final draft. Be sure to refer to the Guidelines for Proofreading Expository Compositions that begin on page 473.

You may find it helpful to refer to the chapters on spelling, grammar, punctuation, capitalization, and usage found throughout this book. You can also refer to the list of proofreading symbols found on page 341. As your teacher directs, you might find it helpful to exchange compositions with a classmate in order to double-check your proofreading.

WRITING THE FINAL VERSION

16k. Prepare the final draft of your composition.

After you have proofread your revised draft, you are ready to prepare the final draft, or final version, of your expository composition. As you realize, a composition requires a considerable amount of effort. By the time you come to the preparation of the final draft, most of this work is behind you. Your main concern now is to put your composition in a neat and attractive form that reflects the thought and care you have devoted to the whole undertaking. Follow correct manuscript form (see Chapter 23) or your teacher's specific instructions for this assignment. After writing the final draft, proofread again. Check for omitted words and additional inaccuracies in spelling or punctuation accidentally made in recopying.

EXERCISE 40. Preparing Your Final Draft.   Prepare a final draft of any expository composition you have written in this chapter. Be sure to proofread again after recopying this revised and proofread version of your composition.

CHAPTER 16 WRITING REVIEW 1

Writing Expository Compositions.   Select a topic of your own. Following the Guidelines on pages 467–68, write an expository composition on your topic. Also be sure to refer to the revision and proofreading guidelines on pages 470–71 and 473–74 of this chapter.

CHAPTER 16 WRITING REVIEW 2

Using the Writing Process.   Review the writing you do in a school subject other than English—perhaps a science or social studies class. Select any long piece of exposition you have written in this class. Evaluate this composition, applying the guidelines for writing and revising expository compositions that appear on pages 467–68 and 470–71 of this chapter. Rewrite the composition, incorporating changes that your evaluation suggests are necessary. As your teacher directs, you may exchange papers with a classmate. Do so in order to determine how applying your knowledge of the writing process can affect the expository writing you do in your other classes.

CHAPTER 17

Writing Expository Compositions

SPECIFIC EXPOSITORY WRITING ASSIGNMENTS

The general principles of exposition discussed in Chapter 16 apply to most of the writing assignments you are likely to be given in school. There are, however, certain specific kinds of expository compositions that come up often enough to require special treatment: process explanations, critical reviews, and essays of literary analysis. These kinds of compositions may play an increasingly important part in your classroom assignments from now on. As your teacher directs, concentrate on one type at a time, and remember that the general ideas about using the writing process to write expository compositions apply to all expository writing.

PROCESS EXPLANATIONS

The explanation of a process gives a complete presentation of the steps that must be followed either (1) to make or do something, or (2) to understand how something works. You have probably read and followed process explanations in do-it-yourself instructions, recipes, or repair guides.

A process explanation limits the discussion of your subject to a step-by-step account of its stages or parts. When explaining a process, you must pay particular attention to the logical sequence that connects all of the steps, so that you do not confuse your audience. The hints, model, and guidelines that follow will help you plan and write an effective process explanation.

Prewriting Hints for Process Explanations

1. *Select and limit your subject.* For your subject, choose a process you can clearly explain in a paper that contains an introduction, three or more paragraphs of explanation, and a concluding paragraph (or sentence). You could not fully explain the process of "how a car works" in a few paragraphs. You would need to limit this subject to a more manageable topic, such as "how a radiator cools an engine." In giving an explanation of your topic, you assume a position of authority. Therefore, be certain that you are fully informed on your subject before you begin to explain it.

2. *Gather sufficient information on your topic.* You cannot assume that your audience is already familiar with your topic. Try to anticipate questions that someone might have. A good way to do this is to use one of the information-gathering techniques described in Chapter 16, especially the questions about a topic (pages 445–46). Ask yourself: What are my topic's parts? How is it put together? How does it work? How is it made or done? Be sure that you give every step and that you do not include unnecessary steps that will confuse your audience.

3. *Organize your information in a logical plan.* When you have listed all the steps in your process, arrange them in chronological order. Read them over again. Could someone follow this plan to make or to understand what you are explaining? If not, you will need to add information or clarify what you already have, or perhaps you may even need to delete something. In any case, you will find it easier to organize your information by arranging the steps of your process in a topic outline (see pages 450–52).

4. *Use the proper tone and language for your audience.* While you can assume that your audience is not familiar with your topic, do not "talk down." Do not oversimplify or use childish language; instead, treat your audience with respect by using specific words that show the relationships between the steps in the process.

5. *Define special terms.* Be sure that you explain any technical or special terms to your audience.

6. *Specify any materials, supplies, or tools that are needed.* Give exact amounts, measurements, descriptions, etc., of any supplies or equipment needed in the process you are explaining.

7. *Include special cautions and notes.* Be sure to tell your audience about any special instructions or cautions. For example, if you were

explaining how to service an automobile radiator, you would want to warn your audience about the danger of removing the radiator cap before the radiator is cool.

Writing Process Explanations

The following is a process explanation of how to carve a wooden egg. After specifying what materials will be needed, the explanation proceeds through a careful step-by-step presentation of what the audience would need to do to carve a wooden egg. A number of transitions have been marked to show how the writer has tied together the separate parts of her explanation so that the audience can easily follow along.

Also note that the introduction states the purpose of the process, which is not simply to carve the egg, but further, to get good practice in woodcarving. This purpose is then restated in the conclusion, with an additional note on the value of doing a project by yourself. In this way, the writer has announced her purpose, shown when it has been achieved, and told the audience its value.

CARVING A WOODEN EGG FOR PRACTICE

Whether or not you have carved wood before, this practice project is a good way to begin. Use a block of wood of any kind (without knots) about 1 ½ inches thick by 1 ½ inches wide by 2 ½ inches long, with the grain running the long way. — *introduction / gives specific measurements / gives special instructions*

If you cannot find wood this thick, you can make such a block from two pieces of standard ¾-inch board, each 2 ½ inches long. Measure and mark with the ruler and pencil the 2 ½-inch lengths. Clamp the board in the vise of C-clamps, and with the crosscut saw cut off the measured pieces, then glue them with the flat sides together, using a thin coat of white glue. Press them in the vise or clamp them together, but not *too* tightly or all the glue will squeeze out. Let them dry for at least an hour, then use the piece exactly as if it were a single solid block. This method of gluing is called *laminating* wood, and although the joint — *body / topic sentence / (1) first step / gives special equipment / signals transition / gives special instructions / defines special term that is emphasized* may show a little, it will give you no trouble in carving if the two pieces are of the same kind of hardness of wood. All wood can be glued easily and permanently with the *flat sides* (long grain) together, but it is almost impossible to glue two *cut* ends (end grain) together to stay.

gives special instruction emphasis: draws attention to definition of special terms

Now you need to make a simple pattern for the wooden egg. On a piece of the cardboard measure off and mark with ruler and pencil the 1 1/2-inch by 2 1/2-inch rectangle of one side of your block. In that rectangle, draw freehand the shape of an egg that almost touches each of the four sides. Now, using the scissors, cut out the cardboard-egg pattern and draw around it with the pencil on each of the four sides of your wooden block. To start work on the egg, first shave away with the knife the four corners of the block outside the drawn lines and then slowly shape the piece into an egg just like those in the refrigerator. We are not going to give you a single further hint or bit of instruction. You are on your own to experiment and to learn some of the things about using your knife and about carving wood that you must find out for yourself. Try using first one blade and then the other to discover how your knife works. This practice is more important than it is to make a perfectly oval-shaped egg, so don't worry too much if the wood splits, or if you finally wind up with nothing but a scrap of wood. This is an important way to learn—to do a project by yourself in your own way.

signals transition (2) second step

gives specific measurements; repetition for coherence

signals transition

(3) third step; signals first operation

signals next operation

conclusion; final advice

FLORENCE H. PETTIT

EXERCISE 1. Writing Your First Draft. Choose one of the following topics and develop it into a process explanation five to seven paragraphs long. Before you begin writing, review the Prewriting Hints for Process Explanations and the model above.

1. *How to make or do something:* how to tie a bowline (or some other) knot, how to can or freeze fruit or another food, how to hang wallpaper, how to clean fish (game), how to use a dictionary, how to buy a specific piece of stereo equipment, how to enjoy a movie (TV show or recording)

2. *How something works:* how a lightning rod works, how an electric eye works, how a thermostat controls temperature, how a vacuum cleaner works, how a microwave oven cooks food, how muscles coordinate to move a finger (arm or leg)

3. *A topic of your own:* Under your teacher's direction, select, limit, and develop a subject of your own that clearly involves a process explanation. Be sure to select a topic you know well and can therefore explain more easily.

GUIDELINES FOR REVISING PROCESS EXPLANATIONS

Revising requires several rereadings of the first draft. As you reread the first draft you prepared for Exercise 1, keep the following guidelines in mind, making any necessary notes for revision.

1. Is the topic limited to a process that can be explained adequately in a few paragraphs?

2. Are all materials, along with specific amounts and descriptions, included, as well as all steps the audience will need to know to follow the process?

3. Are the steps in the process, including any special cautions or notes, presented in chronological order?

4. Are transitional expressions used to make clear to the audience the order of the steps in the process?

5. Are any terms that might be unfamiliar to the audience explained in appropriate language?

6. Is the explanation written in clear, varied sentences that are appropriate for the audience?

7. Are there any sentences that should be rewritten or omitted because they do not contribute to the unity of the explanation?

8. Can sentences or details be repositioned to make the explanation more coherent?

9. Does the explanation end with a concluding paragraph or sentence?

EXERCISE 2. Preparing Your Final Draft. Use the following suggestions to prepare a final draft of the process explanation that you wrote for Exercise 1.

1. Using the Guidelines for Revising Process Explanations, revise your first draft for content, organization, and style.
2. Referring to the Guidelines for Proofreading (page 339), proofread your revised draft for any inaccuracies.
3. As you write the final draft, follow correct manuscript form (see Chapter 23) or your teacher's specific instructions.
4. Before giving your final version to your audience, proofread it once again for any omissions or inaccuracies made in recopying.

CRITICAL REVIEWS

The critical review is written to enable your audience to decide whether or not they could use or would enjoy the particular work being reviewed. Works to review might include books, films, recordings, TV programs, or any other creative forms. A critical review does not necessarily find fault with a work, although it may. Your critical review should include (1) a concise summary of the work's subject, main thesis, or story line, (2) an examination of major points or elements in the work, and (3) an evaluation of the work's success in presenting its subject or story.

A critical review calls for both objective and subjective analysis. You should give a factual, objective report of the work's contents. Then, you should offer your subjective impression of the work's effectiveness.

Prewriting Hints for Critical Reviews

1. *Identify and limit your subject.* When reviewing a work, begin by classifying it according to one or more categories, such as subject matter (fiction or nonfiction), type (comedy, tragedy, documentary, etc.), genre (western, science fiction, biography, etc.), or audience (adults, teen-agers, historians, etc.). Next, to determine the content of your summary, jot down the main sections or scenes of the work.

Remember that your summary must be short, only one or two paragraphs, so limit your notes to the central topic or story.

To determine what is central to the work, ask yourself: What information or action is necessary to understanding what this work is about?

2. *Gather sufficient information on your topic*. Be certain that you are totally familiar with the work you are reviewing. This will mean, for example, rereading parts or all of a book and, if possible, seeing a film more than once. Jot down specific quotes that you can use to express or support your views. Determine what the author's, director's, or artist's purpose was in creating the work. To do this, ask yourself: What elements of the work are repeated? What elements are given the most space or time? What elements are emphasized (for example, with italics, boldfaced type, or other highlighting devices in a book; with slow motion, music, or other attention-getting devices in a film)? When reviewing a nonfiction work (biography, history, science, current affairs), it is often helpful to look into the author's background so that you can determine whether the work is likely to be authoritative, biased, or the like.

3. *Organize your information in a logical plan*. Present the information in your summary in the same order in which it appears in the work you are reviewing. Then organize your list of major points and elements either in the order in which they appear, in order of importance, or in chronological order. Conclude your review with a statement of your evaluation of the work. Ask yourself: Has the work made me aware of something I did not know or feel? Has the work presented a convincing argument or dramatization that changed or confirmed my views? Would I recommend this work to someone else? Be sure that you list specific information from the work itself to support your answers to these questions.

4. *Give your audience an accurate representation of the work*. Your audience is relying on your review to provide an accurate representation of the content and effectiveness of the work you are reviewing. So, be sure that you include all important points and that you do not distort the work's content, style, or theme.

5. *Describe any special features of the work*. Nearly all works have special features that will be of interest to your audience. When reviewing a book, for example, mention if it is illustrated, has an index, offers a bibliography, is footnoted (specify whether the footnotes are helpful, distracting, confusing, etc.), contains charts or similar aids, and anything else you think would make the book more— or less— useful to your audience. In the case of a film, note whether

it is color or black and white, is in English or has subtitles, has a soundtrack, uses distinctive techniques (time-lapse photography, 3-D, fade-outs, etc.), contains special effects, or has other distinctive features that are important to enjoying or understanding the film.

6. *Give your individual response to the work.* Do not simply state, "This is a good book" or "I think this was a bad movie." Instead, look over your summary and your list of major points and decide exactly what makes the work effective or ineffective, enjoyable or unenjoyable. Then use specific details about the work to state your judgment of it. Generally, it is wise to moderate approval or criticism unless you have strong objective support for your view. Give a reasoned appraisal of the worth of the work you are reviewing.

Writing Critical Reviews

Two critical reviews follow: the first of a nonfiction book and the second of a film. Notice that each review is preceded by the work's title. In a book review, the author's and publisher's names and the date of publication are usually given. Film reviews are less standardized than book reviews; however, the film's title is often accompanied by the director's name, along with the names of the production company, the starring actors and actresses, and sometimes the screenwriter or author, especially if either is well known.

The following review of *Shinohata* begins with an introduction that gives some background about the book's subject, life in Japan, and indicates why there is an audience for books like this. In the second paragraph the reviewer states her purpose and gives specific support from the book. Notice that the reviewer also discusses how the author gained firsthand information for *Shinohata,* which helps establish his authority on his subject. The review ends with several specific reasons for the reviewer's conclusion that *Shinohata* is a worthwhile book. Take special note of how the reviewer uses pronouns and modifiers to create interesting sentences packed with information.

Shinohata
by Ronald P. Dore
Pantheon © 1978

title, author, and publisher

The Western vision of Japanese society rarely goes much further than picturing the entire nation

introduction

uniformly dressed in dark suits and shiny slim ties, walking submissively behind a tour leader with a pennant in his hand. The other more congenial, but equally superficial, impression of the Japanese comes from the foreign traveler who has returned home laden with gifts, praising Japanese hospitality, the Tokyo taxi drivers who refuse tips, the friendly natives who ever so politely offer directions at Ginza street corners. Excluded, coddled, taunted, charmed, confused Westerners shift between enchantment at the warm mysteries of the Japanese sensibility and anger at what frequently seems a spitefully unapproachable, thoroughly hermetic society.

audience

In his chatty, friendly description of life in the village of Shinohata, Ronald P. Dore has done much to give us the brains and blood and humor of the puzzling Japanese. When Dore, an eminent Japanologist, visited Shinohata in 1955, the villagers were finally recovering from the ravages of the war, and upon his return in 1975, he found the people prospering from the Japanese industrial boom. Tracing the effects of the development upon his old friends, Dore makes a fascinating exploration of the changes in farming techniques, transportation, land ownership, and family life. Economic well-being has brought farm machinery, color televisions, indoor toilets, and automobiles to many Shinohata families, but some old-timers complain that wealth has destroyed reverence for small, lovingly tended details: There is a particularly Japanese regret for the loss of "the preciousness of things."

purpose

indicates author's authority on topic

summary of contents

specific examples used to present one element of conflict explored in the book

Shinohata lives most vividly in the talk of the villagers, which Dore has transcribed verbatim.

discussion of distinctive elements of the book accompa-

We hear the lament of the mother-in-law, once the all-powerful tyrant over her daugher-in-law's existence, who complains about the disobedience of the new, independent brides. Or the modern farmer, his nose too sensitized to bear the smell of cow manure ("The stink gets into your clothes and into your hair. . . ."), now completely dependent upon manufactured chemical fertilizer. Comfortable with the Japanese and their language, Dore has combined the precision of a scholar, the anecdotal talents of a novelist, and the heart of a humanist. He could have given his hosts in Shinohata no greater gift than this affectionate and informative portrait of their lives.

nied by specific examples

specific quote from the book

general evaluation

personal response

PHYLLIS BIRNBAUM

The next review deals with the film *The Last Starfighter*. The introduction presents the main idea or premise that the movie develops, identifies the opposing forces, and states the primary plot conflict. The second paragraph offers more information about the plot through a discussion of one of the characters, who is evaluated favorably by the reviewer. In the third paragraph the reviewer details additional main scenes and gives his critical opinion of one of the actors, the writer, the director, the musical score, the sets and props, and the film in general. The reviewer states his criticisms effectively.

THE LAST STARFIGHTER

Nice idea: a video game that is designed not merely as an amusement for idle teen-age reflexes but as aptitude test and recruiting device for Starfighters. These warriors are needed to defend a space frontier, maintained by the Star League, an interplanetary alliance threatened by the dread, yucky Ko-Dan.

introduction

film's main premise

main plot conflict

Nice performance: Robert Preston as a sort of intergalactic Music Man who markets the games here below and lures earthlings skyward to battle

character discussion

more about plot

for righteousness. After almost a half-century, Preston's energy and infectious pleasure in performance remain delightful.

evaluation of actor

Curious lapse: once young Alex Rogan (Lance Guest) reluctantly leaves his dismal trailer park and his pert girlfriend (Catherine Mary Stewart) and arrives on Rylos, staging area for the paltry battle to come, he is either too polite or too dense to mention its uncanny resemblance to the mechanical landscapes scattered about the *Star Wars* galaxy. Of course, he can't hear the score (marked down John Williams) and is perhaps too caught up in the action to notice how much everyone and everything he meets resembles software, hardware and ideas people have all had just about enough of. Inexpressively written by Jonathan Betuel and languidly directed by Nick Castle, Jr., *The Last Starfighter* offers the audience little more than the pleasure of naming its previous movie bases as it touches them. Let's see: *TRON* . . . *E.T.* . . . *Close Encounters* . . . and so to sleep.

character identification
plot development

evaluation of character

opinion of music

response to costumes, props, and sets
evaluation of scriptwriter
evaluation of director
response to movie in general

RICHARD SCHICKEL

EXERCISE 3. Writing Your First Draft. Choose one of the following topics and develop it in a critical review three to five paragraphs long. Before you begin writing, review the Prewriting Hints for Critical Reviews on pages 481–83 and the two models above.

1. *Nonfiction book review:* Write a critical review of a nonfiction book that either (1) you have used as a reference or read in another course, such as history, science, or social studies; or (2) you would recommend to someone else or to a committee that was selecting "The Best Book for High-School Students."
2. *Film review:* Write a critical review of a film that you have seen.
3. *Record review:* Write a critical review of a recording.
4. *A topic of your own:* Review any creative work you wish.

GUIDELINES FOR REVISING CRITICAL REVIEWS

Reread the first draft of your critical review several times. Using the following guidelines, revise your first draft to correct and improve your review.

1. Does the review give an accurate, complete presentation of the work's subject, main thesis, or story line?

2. Is the audience given enough information about the major elements of the work to understand what it covers?

3. Does the review mention distinctive features of the work, such as illustrations and reference aids in a book, and elaborate sets or unique camera angles in a film?

4. Is the review presented in a consistent, coherent order that the audience can follow?

5. Are specific elements of the work used to support critical evaluations and opinions?

6. Have all quotations from the work been enclosed in quotation marks and cited word for word?

7. Are transitions used effectively to help the audience see connections between statements and supporting quotations and details?

8. Is the sentence structure clear and varied sufficiently to keep the audience on track and interested?

9. Are the language and tone of the review appropriate for the audience?

10. Does the review help the audience decide whether the work is worthwhile?

11. Does the review offer the reviewer's personal response, and is this response logically related to other information in the review?

EXERCISE 4. Preparing Your Final Draft. Use the following suggestions to prepare a final draft of the critical review that you wrote for Exercise 3.

1. Use the Guidelines for Revising Critical Reviews to make revisions of your draft. Check content, organization, and style.

2. Refer to the proofreading guidelines (page 339) while you proofread your revised draft for any inaccuracies in spelling, punctuation, grammar, and usage. Pay special attention to the rules governing quotation marks and other marks of punctuation with quotation marks.

3. Follow correct manuscript form (see Chapter 23) or your teacher's specific instructions when you write your final draft.

4. Proofread your final draft one last time to catch any possible inaccuracies made in recopying before you submit it to your audience. If possible, have someone else also read it.

ESSAYS OF LITERARY ANALYSIS

The purpose of the essay of literary analysis is to expand knowledge about a literary work so that the work can be better understood and appreciated. As the writer of such an essay, you will broaden your knowledge through your close analysis of the literary work. Thus, your task will be to focus your studies into a specific thesis that you will present in your essay, thereby passing along part of your knowledge to your audience. Knowing more about a literary work enhances appreciation of it by revealing meanings, allusions, and other insights that give it added dimension.

Before you begin your literary analysis, become familiar with the major literary elements of the work you will be studying. In analyzing a short story, for example, you would examine plot, setting, character, dialogue, and other elements that apply to fiction. In the case of a poem or a song, you would consider rhyme scheme, meter, scansion, and elements of poetry. Some elements, such as imagery, symbolism, allusion, theme, and point of view, apply to nearly all literary works and should be examined in all cases.

Like all expository essays, the essay of literary analysis contains an introduction, body, and conclusion. In your introduction, identify the work that will be the subject of your literary analysis, and introduce your thesis. Use several paragraphs in the body of your essay to present your analysis of the work. In the conclusion, summarize the findings of your analysis and complete your explanation of how your analysis supports your thesis; then, finally, close with a suggestion of further areas of study or further implications of your analysis.

Prewriting Hints for Essays of Literary Analysis

1. *Identify and limit your subject.* In the space of a short essay you obviously cannot fully discuss a literary work. Therefore, you will need to limit your subject, the work you are analyzing, to a specific

topic by categorizing it according to areas of study. You might focus on a literary category (such as plot, imagery, rhyme scheme, etc.), a sociological category (social class, family relations, criminal codes, etc.), a psychological category (emotion, motivation, intelligence, etc.), or any other category of human activity. Generally, you will want to limit your subject by applying more than one category, for example, how a particular character (literary category) is motivated (psychological category) to be a criminal (sociological category). No matter which categories you choose, however, you will always be working with one or more literary categories in your analysis. One way to generate ideas for topics is to think of the topic as a problem to be solved. As you are reading the work or as your class is discussing it, questions about it may occur to you. By using precise terms to state one of these questions, you are likely to create a suitably limited topic. Before you use this topic as your thesis, examine the literary work to make certain you can gather enough information to support that thesis.

2. *Gather sufficient information on your topic.* Gathering sufficient information will require that you reread the work at least once or, usually, several times. Analyze the work carefully. Take it apart; reexamine its plot, theme, figurative language, and other literary elements. Note all ideas, images, quotations, and specific information applying to your topic. You can list these on a sheet or two of paper or on index cards under group headings or separately. Keep in mind that using index cards makes rearranging your information easier. At this stage do not be selective; gather all relevant information you can find. Whenever you copy a passage or phrase word for word, be sure that you do not change anything and that you use quotation marks.

3. *Organize your information in a logical plan.* To organize the information that you will use to develop your analysis, group together related details and quotations from the work. When grouping information, you will almost always have stray passages and details that do not fit in anywhere. Do not try to force them into a group; instead, just let them drop and turn your attention to your ordered information, which will make up your outline. As you organize the information you will use in your analysis, relationships between specific details and between groups of details will become apparent. One common relationship is a comparison, in which likenesses are established between separate items. Related to the comparison is the contrast, which entails

pointing out differences between like items. (For further discussion of comparison and contrast see Chapter 14, pages 376–77.) Your analysis might also seek to explain, or clarify, a specific aspect, such as character, theme, or connotative meaning, of the work. Another way to analyze the work is to interpret it, which means to give the meaning or to offer a particular reading of a work. When analyzing a poem, you might give an explication, in which a short passage or an entire poem is examined line by line in order to illuminate its content and technique. Make sure that your analysis expands knowledge about the work. Providing only a simple summary of the work's plot, theme, or content adds little, if anything, to your or your audience's knowledge. Your analysis should investigate some aspect of the work in such a way that you and your audience gain insight into the work's meaning, significance, or composition. This insight will become the predicate, or what you say about the subject (the work itself), in your thesis statement.

4. *Consider your audience's familiarity with the work.* Before you can add to your audience's knowledge, you first need to have an idea of what your audience already knows. Determine whether your audience is familiar with the work you are analyzing. If so, you need not give any summary of the work and can simply refer to it in your essay. If not, give your audience a brief summary of the main elements of the work, such as its plot, theme, characters, and other significant components that are necessary to the meaning and characteristic identity of the work. You will probably want to present a large part of this summary in a paragraph at the beginning of your essay and then give additional specific summary information at appropriate points in your analysis. As in most expository essays, use a serious, factual tone.

5. *Support your analysis with specific information from the work.* Each point that you develop in your analysis should be supported by a specific quotation or reference from the work you are analyzing. When you use direct quotations, make sure that they fit smoothly and correctly into your sentences. For example, if you were discussing Gwendolyn Brooks' poem "One Wants a Teller in a Time like This," you could use the title in making the statement: In this poem Gwendolyn Brooks describes how a teen-age girl faced with the uncertainties of adolescence "wants a teller in a time like this." Notice that the subject "girl" agrees with the quoted verb "wants." Make sure that the sentence elements within quotations always agree with the sentence elements within your own text.

Writing Essays of Literary Analysis

Read the following poem:

GOD'S WORLD

O world, I cannot hold thee close enough!
    Thy winds, thy wide grey skies!
    Thy mists, that roll and rise!
Thy woods, this autumn day, that ache and sag
And all but cry with colour! That gaunt crag
To crush! To lift the lean of that black bluff!
World, World, I cannot get thee close enough!

Long have I known a glory in it all,
    But never knew I this:
    Here such a passion is
As stretcheth me apart—Lord, I do fear
Thou'st made the world too beautiful this year;
My soul is all but out of me—let fall
No burning leaf; prithee, let no bird call.

                  EDNA ST. VINCENT MILLAY

    A literary analysis of "God's World" could focus on the poet's use of distinctive language, on a theme in the poem, on the poem's symbolism, or on any number of aspects of the poem. The analysis in the following essay is an explication that explores the relationship between the emotions expressed by the poet and her controlled use of poetic elements. The first step in explicating a poem is to reread it several times, both silently and aloud, to familiarize yourself with its content and sound. During each reading, make notes of passages and details that you think are significant. For example, if you were explicating "God's World" to investigate the relationship between emotion and poetic control, you would want to note specific statements of emotion in the poem, such as the poet's response to the beauty of an autumn day, the poet's wonder and delight in the natural landscape, the poet's desire to embrace this beauty, and the poet's asking God to withhold additional beauty because of the unbearably intense ecstasy that she feels. In any explication, attention is always given to how language is used in the poem. In this case, you might note the immediacy that is created by the poet's addressing the world as if it were alive, the use of exclamation, the direct expression of intense feelings, the use of overstatement to heighten emotional intensity, the use of repetition for emphasis, and the relationship between emotion and pain expressed in specific words, such as *ache, cry,* and *crush.*

Another element of a poem that is usually examined in an explication is structure. "God's World" contains fourteen lines divided into two stanzas with a pair of short lines appearing in the same place in both stanzas. The rhyme scheme is *abbccaa*. The regularity of pattern in the poem imposes tight control over the powerful emotions that are being expressed, preventing them from becoming excessive and unrestrained. You might conclude from these notes that Millay successfully balances content and form by giving the effect of an outpouring of intense feeling while at the same time exercising strict artistic control over her materials. You could organize these notes into an outline under the statement of the thesis that you discovered through your analysis of the poem. Your thesis and outline of specific supporting information could then be developed into an essay of literary analysis such as the one that follows.

POETIC CONTROL OF EMOTION IN
"GOD'S WORLD" — title

The apparent subject of the lyric "God's World," by Edna St. Vincent Millay, is the beauty of nature. However, the center of the poem is not the autumn landscape but the intense personal emotion that it arouses in the poet. Millay's artistry lies in giving the effect of a spontaneous outpouring of feeling while she exercises strict control over her materials. — introduction / thesis

The poet's response to the autumnal scene is so ecstatic that the experience is painful. In the first ten lines the poet addresses the world and expresses her wonder and delight in the unspoiled natural landscape. The scene she describes is romantic, with its gray skies, rolling mists, and spectacular crags and cliffs. The poet desires to embrace this beauty, to draw near to it. At the same time, the experience is so intense that it causes her pain: "Here such a passion is/As stretcheth me apart." In the last four lines, the poet addresses God and asks that He withhold any more beauty from the scene. The ecstasy she feels — topic sentence / body / supporting details from work / specific supporting quotation from work is already so intense that a single leaf or bird call will be unbearable. The poem ends with an expression of the poet's reverence for God and nature.

The language of the poem conveys the emotional intensity of the poet's feelings. The apostrophe to the world (in lines 1 and 7), as if it were alive, adds immediacy to the poem. Every statement in the first stanza is an exclamation, an outcry of emotion. The poet relies on the direct expression of her feelings and on overstatement. Her use of exaggeration is a means of achieving emotional intensity: she cannot get <u>close enough</u>; the world is <u>too beautiful</u>; the woods *all but cry;* her soul is *all but out* of her. The poet chooses words that have connotations of pain or effort: *ache, sag, cry, crush, stretcheth, apart, burning.* She also uses repetition for emphasis in the opening and closing lines of the first stanza.

topic sentence

specific supporting details from work

The powerful emotions of the poem do not seem excessive or unrestrained because the poet imposes control through regular patterns of rhyme and rhythm. The rhyme scheme, *a b b c c a a,* is strictly adhered to in both stanzas. The basic iambic pentameter pattern is varied in both stanzas by the trimeter couplet (lines 2–3; 9–10). This contraction and expansion of the line not only adds metrical variety to the poem, but suggests the way the poet's emotions are pulled.

topic sentence

In "God's World," Millay successfully balances content and form. The result is a poem that communicates a fresh and genuine experience.

conclusion

EXERCISE 5. Writing Your First Draft. Choose one of the topics on the next page and develop it into an essay of literary analysis. Before you begin writing, review the Prewriting Hints for Essays of Literary Analysis and the model above.

1. Analyze the main character, the setting, or the plot from a short story of your own choosing.
2. Analyze the figurative language, imagery, or symbolism in a poem of your own choosing.
3. Analyze a main theme in either a short story or a poem of your own choosing.
4. Analyze any significant aspect of a literary work of your own choosing.

GUIDELINES FOR REVISING ESSAYS OF LITERARY ANALYSIS

Read through the first draft of your essay of literary analysis. Then, read the following guidelines and apply them to your first draft.

1. Does the introduction give the author's name, the title of the work, and a specific thesis that states how the work will be analyzed and what the analysis will attempt to show?
2. Does the body of the essay present a complete and convincing analysis that develops the thesis stated in the introduction?.
3. Are specific details and quotations from the work given to support each point in the analysis?
4. Have all quotations been given word for word as they appear in the work and been enclosed in quotation marks?
5. Does the conclusion summarize how the analysis has developed the idea(s) stated in the thesis?
6. Are transitions used to help the audience see the relationships between the ideas and information and between the sentences and paragraphs of the essay?
7. Has the audience's familiarity with the work been considered so that neither too much nor too little summary of the work has been given?
8. Are varied sentence structures used in order to present ideas and information as clearly as possible and to make the essay interesting to read?
9. Have definitions been given for all words, images, characters, and other elements that the audience might not know?
10. Is the essay headed by an informative title that tells the audience what to expect in the literary analysis that follows?

EXERCISE 6. Preparing Your Final Draft. Refer to the following suggestions at each stage of preparing the final draft of the essay of literary analysis that you wrote for Exercise 5.

1. Use the Guidelines for Revising Essays of Literary Analysis to make revisions of your draft. Go over your essay several times; on each reading, check a different area of your content, organization, and style.

2. As you proofread your revised draft for inaccuracies in spelling, punctuation, grammar, and usage, keep the Guidelines for Proofreading (page 339) beside you for ready reference. Be especially careful that all quotations are given exactly as they appear in the work and are enclosed in quotation marks.

3. Follow correct manuscript form (pages 339–40) or your teacher's specific instructions when you write the final draft of your essay of literary analysis.

4. Before you submit your essay of literary analysis to your audience, proofread it once more to be certain that you have not made any errors recopying it. It may be helpful to cover your essay with a blank sheet of paper that you can move down the page one line at a time as you read very slowly, frontward and backward, across the line. Doing this will help prevent your natural tendency to read quickly, which can cause you to skip over inaccuracies, especially at the beginnings and ends of lines.

Writing Persuasive Compositions

BUILDING AN ARGUMENT

Persuasive writing requires that you learn to think clearly about what you believe is true. The ability to build an argument (a logical and convincing presentation of ideas) is the basis for all good persuasive writing. Besides deciding what you think about a given issue, you will need to back up your opinion with reasons and back up your reasons with evidence.

As you develop skills in building an argument, you will improve your ability to listen critically to anyone trying to convince you to do something. You will learn, for example, how to evaluate the argument of an advertiser or of a candidate trying to get your vote. You will also improve your ability to be convincing when you speak. For instance, you will learn how to use specific reasons and evidence when you present an opposing point of view on an important issue.

PREWRITING

CHOOSING A FORM AND AN AUDIENCE

One type of persuasive essay is the letter to the editor, a brief essay that appears on the editorial page of a newspaper. If you send a letter to the editor of your school newspaper, you can asssume that the audience is a group of peers (people your own age), although the letter is likely also to be read by teachers, administrators, and some parents. If you send a letter to the editor of a local newspaper, your audience will be the general public, a cross section of the adult population of your community.

A persuasive composition, which is longer than a letter to the editor, is usually made up of at least five paragraphs: an introductory paragraph, three paragraphs in the body, and a concluding paragraph. Unless you identify a specific audience for your essay of opinion, you may assume that your audience is made up of the members of your English class and your teacher. Occasionally it may be necessary for you to plan an essay of opinion for a specific audience. For example, an essay about the need for increasing city real estate taxes might be directed to any one of the following audiences:

1. Members of a homeowners' association, who must pay the tax increase
2. Members of a renters' association, who will not be directly affected by the tax increase
3. Group of store owners and apartment-house owners, who will pay large increases because their property is so valuable
4. Members of the city council, who must decide whether or not to pass the proposed real estate tax increase

You might guess that most of these audiences would have a particular bias (already held ideas for or against a topic) toward the tax increase. The homeowners, store owners, and apartment-house owners, for example, would be likely to oppose the increase because they do not want to pay more taxes. City council members, on the other hand, knowing the need for more funds, might be biased in favor of the increase. Members of the renters' association, because they do not feel directly involved in the issue, might have no bias for or against the tax increase. The argument that you present to each of these four audiences would be tailored in some way to appeal to the interests and needs of the particular audience.

EXERCISE 1. Identifying an Audience's Attitudes and Biases.
Think carefully about what attitude or bias each of the following audiences is likely to have. Which of the following audiences are likely to be opposed to the opinion stated in the position statement? (*Hint:* Some questions may have more than one answer.)

1. *Position statement:* Students in this high school must have at least a B+ average in all of their classes to be eligible to participate in a sport.
   a. Members of the football team
   b. Coaches for all the athletic teams
   c. Members of the general student body
   d. Members of the committee to improve excellence in academic subjects in the high school
2. *Position statement:* All male students attending this school should be required to wear slacks, shirts, and ties. Female students should be required to wear knee-length skirts and tailored blouses.
   a. Parents of tenth-graders
   b. Class of tenth-graders
   c. Teachers in this school
   d. Grandparents of tenth-graders
3. *Position statement:* All adults who work in the United States should be required to donate one day's pay a month to local charities.
   a. Workers in a local factory
   b. Retired workers
   c. Sixth-grade class
   d. Workers in an organization devoted to helping poor families in the community
4. *Position statement:* The state should provide a free, four-year college education to any high-school graduate who qualifies for college by means of an entrance exam.
   a. Parents of students who plan to attend college
   b. Students who plan to attend college
   c. State legislators who know what such a program would cost
   d. Students who do not plan to attend college

CHOOSING A TOPIC

18a. Choose a limited topic that is debatable.

The topic for a persuasive essay must be about an issue that is debatable, that is, an issue on which reasonable arguments can be made on both sides. The topic, therefore, must state an opinion and not a fact. A fact is a statement that can be proved and is, by definition, not debatable. You cannot, for example, debate whether carbon dioxide is made up of carbon and oxygen. An opinion, on the other hand, is a statement that cannot be proved. Opinions can be supported only by means of evidence (facts, statistics, examples, quotations by experts, incidents) that make them seem likely to be true.

NOT SUITABLE   Surgeons can transplant corneas to restore a person's vision. [fact]

SUITABLE   You should carry a donor card giving permission for your cornea to be used in a transplant operation in the event of your sudden death. [opinion]

NOT SUITABLE   Puerto Rico is an island. [fact]

SUITABLE   Puerto Rico should become the fifty-first state. [opinion]

The opinion that serves as the basis for a persuasive essay must be about an issue that is important or significant. It should not merely state a personal preference.

NOT SUITABLE   Parrots are better pets than parakeets. [personal preference]

NOT SUITABLE   Boxing is a more interesting sport than wrestling. [personal preference]

SUITABLE   People who live in apartment houses should not be allowed to have dogs or cats.

SUITABLE   Boxing should be completely outlawed.

EXERCISE 2. Identifying Suitable Topics for a Persuasive Essay.

Each numbered item states a limited topic. Number your paper 1–10. Decide whether each topic is suitable for a persuasive essay or not, and after the proper number write *S* for suitable or *NS* for not suitable.

1. Every school should have a psychologist available for students who feel they have problems they want to talk about.
2. Penalties for drunk driving should be increased.
3. The United States should spend more money on defense.
4. Sales of personal and home computers have been decreasing in recent years.
5. Every high-school student should be required to pass a test of physical abilities.
6. Susan B. Anthony was the greatest American leader of the women's rights movement.

7. In tests of mathematics ability, junior-high-school students have the most difficulty in adding and subtracting fractions.
8. Every student in an English class should be required to write at least one essay a week.
9. Avocados taste better than tomatoes.
10. The city council should have one member under twenty years of age to represent the teen-agers in this city.

EXERCISE 3. Thinking of Suitable Topics for a Persuasive Essay. For each of the following broad subjects, write a limited topic that would be suitable as the basis for a persuasive essay. Write the limited topic in a statement that expresses an opinion.

EXAMPLE *Broad subject:* City income taxes
Limited topic: All major cities should impose city income taxes to fund their services.

1. Sports
2. Nuclear arms race
3. Election campaigns
4. Traffic problems
5. Jobs for teen-agers
6. Movies
7. Air pollution
8. Education
9. Government
10. Military service

WRITING A POSITION STATEMENT

18b. Express your opinion clearly in a single sentence.

Now that you have chosen a limited topic, you need to write a single sentence that expresses your opinion on the limited topic. Such a sentence is called a *position statement* or *thesis statement*. A position statement should appear in the introductory paragraph of a persuasive essay so that your reader knows where you stand on the issue being discussed.

EXAMPLES Employers should make special efforts to hire handicapped persons who are able to work effectively.
During presidential elections, polls should be open for a twenty-four-hour period.

CRITICAL THINKING:
Evaluating Position Statements

In a persuasive composition, the position statement should be as specific as you can make it. Consider, for example, the following three statements. Which one is the most general? Which is the most specific?

1. Maybe changing the day on which school dances are held would increase attendance.

2. Something needs to be done about school dances to increase attendance.

3. For the next two months, school dances should be held on Saturday night instead of Friday night to see if this increases attendance.

Of the three, statement 2 is the most general and far too vague to be useful as a position statement. Statement 1 focuses on the idea of changing the day but is not at all specific about the proposed change. Also, statement 1 begins with the word *maybe,* which makes it weak and ineffective. Statement 3 is the most specific, mentioning a detailed proposal that includes the change of day and the length of time for such a change. Statement 3 is, therefore, an acceptable position statement.

EXERCISE 4. Making Position Statements Specific.   Each of the following statements is unacceptable as a position statement because it is too vague or general. Make up any information that you need to make the statement specific enough to serve as the position statement in a persuasive essay.

1. Many students object to the dress code.
2. The high-school curriculum needs to be improved.
3. Something should be done about the litter in the school parking lot.
4. Taxes are too high.
5. What can we do to stop vandalism in schools?
6. I don't like the commercials shown in movie theaters before the feature film.
7. It would be nice to have outdoor concerts during the summer.
8. Whether to build a nuclear power plant in this community is a serious problem.
9. It is really a shame that some of the city's parks are so run down.
10. Something should be done to get more eighteen-year-olds to register to vote.

REVIEW EXERCISE A. Analyzing a Letter to the Editor.   Read the following letter to the editor, and answer the questions that follow.

To the Editor:

I live near the high school on Twelfth Avenue and N.E. 171st Street. Before and after school each day, student drivers speed up and down Twelfth Avenue. Even though this is a residential area, and 30-mile-per-hour speed limit signs are clearly posted, many drivers (and not just students) use Twelfth Avenue as a highway, averaging 50 to 55 miles per hour.

Yesterday my dog was hit by a speeding car. An eyewitness reported that the car slowed briefly, then sped away. My dog was killed, but not instantly. She was in terrible pain before she died.

Something must be done immediately to stop the speeding cars. Next time it could be a child or an elderly person that is killed.

The city should put up two four-way stop signs along Twelfth Avenue in the ten blocks between N.E. 175th Street and the high school. This will slow the traffic, provided, of course, that drivers stop at the stop signs. I urge that police officers patrol the area (especially before and after school) to ticket drivers who do not stop at the new stop signs.

If you are concerned about life-threatening traffic in residential neighborhoods, write to your city council representative to ask for stop signs and police patrols. Come to next Tuesday's council meeting to demand safety for our neighborhood streets.

YOLANDA DOWNS

1. What is the limited topic of this letter to the editor?
2. What is the writer's opinion about that topic? State the opinion in your own words.
3. Does the letter contain a position statement? If so, write the sentence that states the writer's opinion. (*Hint:* There may be more than one sentence.) If you think the letter does not have a position statement, write one.
4. Who would you say is the intended audience for this letter?
5. Is the tone of the letter serious or humorous? Formal or informal? How appropriate is the tone to the letter's topic?

BUILDING AN ARGUMENT

To be convincing when you write and when you speak, you need to back up your opinion with reasons and evidence. Nobody is going to believe that what you say is true just because you say it. You need to build a sound, logical argument, consisting of your opinion, reasons, and evidence.

Reasons

18c. Support your opinion with reasons and evidence.

In Chapter 15 you saw that a persuasive paragraph is developed by means of reasons that support the opinion stated in the position statement (see pages 422-25). A reason is a statement that explains to the reader why you hold that position and why the reader, too, should hold that position.

CRITICAL THINKING:
Evaluating Reasons

An argument is convincing if the reasons are relevant and distinct. Each reason should state a fact that directly explains or justifies the writer's opinion. Such reasons are said to be *relevant*. A reason that is irrelevant has nothing to do with the argument. A reason is distinct if it does not simply rephrase the opinion in the position statement or a reason already given. For example, consider the following argument.

Position statement: Every elementary-school child should have his or her fingerprints on file with the local police department.

STRONG REASONS   Fingerprints are the most accurate way to identify a human being.
Fingerprints would help identify a missing child. An increasing number of children disappear each year.

These two reasons give strong support for the position statement because each reason is distinct and relevant to the argument.
All of the following, however, are weak reasons. If you were to include them in a persuasive essay, they would weaken your argument and make it less convincing.

WEAK REASONS   Police departments should have access to fingerprints of your children. [restates position statement]
Fingerprints are fun to take. [not relevant to the argument]
All criminals have fingerprints on file. [not relevant to the argument]
Every human being has unique fingerprints. [restates first strong reason]

EXERCISE 5. Evaluating Reasons. For each of the numbered position statements, decide which reasons strongly support the opinion. Write the letter of the reasons you would choose in outlining an argument to support the position statement. Some of the reasons given are not relevant to the argument, and some repeat the opinion in the position statement.

1. *Position statement:* Workers should not be forced to retire when they are sixty-five years old.
   a. Many workers are productive and capable at sixty-five and well past that age.
   b. Workers at sixty-five sometimes have health problems.
   c. Workers at sixty-five are usually highly paid.
   d. In countries where there is no mandatory retirement age, many workers remain productive well into their seventies.
   e. Many workers die long before they reach sixty-five.
2. *Position statement:* The break between class periods should be extended from four minutes to six minutes.
   a. Four minutes is not time enough for students who have to go from one end of the school to the other end.
   b. More students are needed to patrol the halls between periods.
   c. Halls and stairways are so crowded that rushing students can injure other students.
   d. Students are not allowed to use the elevator without a special pass.
   e. Instead of four minutes, students should be given at least six minutes to reach their next class.

EXERCISE 6. Thinking of Reasons.   For each of the following position statements, think of at least two distinct and relevant reasons. (Try to think of as many good reasons as you can.) Write each reason in a complete sentence.

1. All high-school students should be required to take a one-year course in speech.
2. People should not marry before the age of twenty-one.
3. Every car should have its brakes and tires inspected once a year.
4. Every state should have a state income tax.
5. Every adult male and female should be required to serve two years in the armed forces or in the Peace Corps.

Evidence

Evidence is any kind of specific information that you use to back up a reason. Evidence may consist of facts, statistics, examples, incidents, and quotations from experts. Remember that opinions, unlike facts, cannot be *proved* to be true. You can, however, make your opinion *seem believable* if it is supported with strong reasons and if the reasons, in turn, are backed up by evidence. Evidence should either come from a reliable source or be the result of many personal observations— not just one or two. Usually, a mixture of facts, statistics, quotations, and examples is more effective in an argument than only one kind of evidence.

CRITICAL THINKING:
Evaluating Evidence

Just as reasons must be relevant to the position statement, evidence must be relevant to the point being made. A fact, example, or statistic is irrelevant if it is not directly related to the statement that it is supposed to support. Irrelevant evidence should be completely eliminated from the argument. The following excerpt outlines part of an argument for keeping grocery stores open until 10:00 P.M. One reason is given, and several pieces of evidence are suggested. Which of the following pieces of evidence are relevant to the reason?

> *Reason:* Many people who work cannot get to the grocery store before its present closing (at 6:00 P.M.).
> *Evidence:*
> 1. Seventy-two percent of shoppers in a poll taken in the grocery store on Saturday said they cannot get to the store before 6:00 P.M.
> 2. Gas stations in the neighborhood are open till 10:00 P.M.
> 3. Many shoppers say that they try to shop only once a week.
> 4. Mrs. Janet Lopez, who works downtown, does not leave her office till 6:00 P.M.
> 5. Todd Lewis, president of Lakeland Supermarket, says, "We have had hundreds of complaints each month from working people who cannot get to our stores before they close at six."

Only three pieces of evidence (1, 4, and 5) are relevant to the reason given. Items 2 and 3 are irrelevant and should be discarded.

EXERCISE 7. Selecting Relevant Evidence. For each of the numbered items on the next page, decide whether the evidence is relevant or irrelevant to the particular reason given. Write the letter of the evidence that is relevant to the reason.

1. *Position statement:* Employers should allow workers to work flexible hours, not just from 9:00 to 5:00 or 8:30 to 4:30.

   Reason: Flexible work hours would help working mothers of young children.

   Evidence:
   a. Statements by working mothers explaining why they want flexible working hours
   b. Statistics on profits of a particular company during the past five years
   c. Statistics on the number of employees in a particular company during the past ten years
   d. Statement by an industrial psychologist about benefits to employers of allowing working mothers to work flexible hours
   e. Statement by a labor union leader requesting a shorter workweek
   f. Example of how flexible hours benefit a specific working mother

2. *Position Statement:* The faculty advisor should have the power to censor the student newspaper and to take out any material that is not appropriate.

   Reason: Student editors do not have the maturity to decide what is appropriate material for a student newspaper.

   Evidence:
   a. Specific example: the editorial in last week's student newspaper that caused a riot
   b. A statement by the editor of the newspaper about why that editorial was published
   c. Statistics on the number of students who read the school newspaper
   d. Statement by the principal about the role of the student newspaper's editors
   e. Statistics on the number of high-school newspapers that have faculty advisers who censor all material before it is published
   f. Statement by a professor of journalism at a nearby university about the number of students enrolled in journalism courses

EXERCISE 8. Thinking of Evidence. Choose one of the position statements in Exercise 6. Using the two (or more) reasons that you created for that exercise, think of the kinds of evidence you would look for to support such reasons. Write as many kinds of relevant evidence as you can think of for each reason. (*Note:* If you cannot think of any evidence to support your reason, consider changing the reason to one for which you can find evidence.)

EXAMPLE

   Reason: Many students have difficulty in distinguishing facts from opinions.

   Evidence: 1. Statistics on facts and opinions from nationally standardized test
   2. Statement from a reading teacher on students' difficulties in distinguishing facts from opinions
   3. Examples based on personal observations of students who have difficulty distinguishing facts from opinions

OUTLINING THE ARGUMENT

18d. Outline your argument.

The outline for an argument consists of the position statement, followed by reasons and evidence. If there is a call to action at the end of the argument, that, too, is listed in the outline. The following outline is for the letter to the editor on page 502.

   Position statement: The city should put up two four-way stop signs along Twelfth Avenue between N.E. 175th Street and the high school, and the police should patrol the area to ticket drivers who do not stop at the new stop signs.

   Reason 1: Many drivers speed along Twelfth Avenue, which is a residential area.

   Evidence: a. Speeders average 50 to 55 miles per hour in a 30-mile-per-hour zone.
   b. Many of the speeders are high-school students on their way to school or coming from school.

   Reason 2: Speeding in a residential neighborhood is dangerous.

   Evidence: a. My dog was killed by a hit-and-run speeder.
   b. Children and elderly people are at risk.

   Call to action: Write to your city council representative, or come to next Tuesday's council meeting.

Notice that the writer lists two reasons and that each reason is supported with evidence. This argument could be strengthened by adding some of the following specific evidence, which would make the writer's statements seem more factual, more believable.

1. Statistics on the number of drivers who actually speed along Twelfth Avenue
2. A statement by the head of the police department on the number of student drivers who speed before and after school
3. A statement by the head of the traffic safety department on the effectiveness of four-way stop signs in slowing traffic
4. Statistics on the number of accidents caused by speeders
5. Statistics on the number of accidents involving pedestrians injured by speeding cars on Twelfth Avenue

EXERCISE 9. Outlining an Argument. Outline the argument for a persuasive composition. You may use the topic you worked with in Exercise 8, or you may choose an altogether different topic. Make sure that your outline includes the position statement, reasons, evidence, and a call to action (if you plan to ask the reader to take some specific action).

CRITICAL THINKING:
Evaluating an Argument

The critical thinking skill of evaluating an argument can be applied not just to your own writing but also to the persuasive writing that you read and to the persuasive speeches that you listen to. To judge how convincing an argument is, you must first be able to identify the various parts of the argument: the position statement, the reasons, and the evidence. Use the following guidelines to evaluate an argument.

GUIDELINES FOR EVALUATING A PERSUASIVE ARGUMENT

1. Is the writer's opinion clearly stated? What is the position statement?
2. What are the writer's reasons? Are the reasons clearly stated?
3. Is each reason relevant to the argument?
4. Is each reason distinct? That is, do the reasons merely rephrase the position statement or another reason?
5. How many reasons are there? In a persuasive essay, a writer should have at least three relevant and distinct reasons.

6. Is each reason backed up by evidence? Is the evidence relevant to the reason?
7. Does the argument include any weak reasons or any irrelevant evidence?

EXERCISE 10. Evaluating an Argument. Read the following interviews on the issue "Should motorists be forced to wear seat belts?" The interview in favor, with Representative David Hollister, supports the position that a law should be passed requiring all motorists to wear seat belts. In the interview against, Assemblyman Michael Nozzollo gives reasons against such a law. As you read each interview, see if you can discover each person's argument: the reasons that are given to support each position.

Should Motorists Be Forced to Wear Seat Belts?

Interview with David Hollister,. Michigan state representative

PRO

QUESTION: Representative Hollister, why do you favor state laws that require motorists to wear seat belts?

ANSWER: Because studies of 36 counties and municipalities which have laws to that effect show conclusively that there is a dramatic reduction in highway deaths and injuries and large savings of money. In this country, we would save over 12,000 lives each year. In the U.S. each year, there are over 400,000 moderate-to-serious injuries and 2.8 million minor injuries caused by auto accidents. These would be reduced substantially.

QUESTION: The Reagan Administration will start requiring passive restraints, such as air bags or automatic seat belts in new cars, unless states with two thirds of the population pass mandatory seat belt laws. Won't that make ordinary belts obsolete?

ANSWER: By no means. Under the administration's plan, it will take some 10 years before all cars on the road have such passive restraints. Meanwhile, only the rich—the ones who can afford to buy new cars—will be protected. On the other hand, we already have seat belts in virtually all cars, if people would only use them. Besides, while air bags are effective in head-on collisions, they don't give you protection in rollovers, rear-end and side collisions, whereas seat belts do. The ideal protection may be both a seat belt and an air bag, but in a choice between the two I'd pick the belt. The economics and effectiveness are with the belt.

QUESTION: Do mandatory seat belt laws infringe on people's constitutional rights?

ANSWER: Such as the right to go through the windshield? I'm a civil-libertarian myself, but the lives and dollars saved far outweigh the individual rights issue in this case.

QUESTION: Shouldn't people be able to decide for themselves?

ANSWER. No, they should not. Accidents always involve other people. Injuries and death disrupt families. They create major social costs: lost work time, lost wages, high medical bills and welfare outlays. It is estimated that each traffic fatality costs the state and family about $330,000. Injuries and lost wages caused by the non-use of belts cost society $2,500 per accident.

QUESTION: Could such laws be enforced without harassing motorists?

ANSWER: Yes. Our traffic laws are largely self-enforcing. I stop at a stop sign at 3 in the morning not because I think there's a police officer on the corner, but because it's the law. With a seat belt law, a police officer who pulled up alongside of you and saw you weren't buckled up could ticket you—a $10 or $50 fine or whatever amount is set—or just give a warning. Police stopping a driver for any reason would also check for belt use. Not much more would be required.

QUESTION: Why wouldn't education bring about compliance?

ANSWER: Because it has never worked. In this country, voluntary compliance is only about 12 percent. In those countries that have passed mandatory laws, compliance has gone from 11 percent to 70 percent. It would happen here as well.

Interview with Michael Nozzollo, New York state assemblyman

CON

QUESTION: Assemblyman Nozzollo, why do you oppose mandatory seat belt laws?

ANSWER: Because the government has neither the right nor the responsibility to prescribe conduct to its citizens simply because it deems such conduct to be in their best interest.

QUESTION: Doesn't using seat belts greatly reduce injuries and deaths?

ANSWER: I concede that. I wear a seat belt myself. But the government shouldn't prescribe it. What if tomorrow the government ordered everyone to get 8 hours of sleep each night, take a daily dose of vitamins and a daily jog and get an annual medical checkup—on the ground that this could enhance and maybe even save lives?

QUESTION: Don't individuals have to accept reasonable restrictions on their freedom for the common good?

ANSWER: Certainly, up to a point. But there's a difference between restrictions and prescriptions. It's one thing to make motorists stop at a red light or stop sign or impose speed limits; it's quite another to prescribe what individuals must do inside their own automobiles. Furthermore, such laws will be extremely difficult to enforce.

QUESTION: Why?

ANSWER: Because it is easy enough to fool a policeman by quickly buckling up when you see a patrol car approaching. It's harder to cheat with a shoulder harness, so those who have both a harness and a seat belt will face tougher enforcement than those who have a seat belt only.

You're going to see a lot of court litigation on whether or not a driver can be held guilty of negligence if the passengers in his car failed to buckle up and an accident occurred.

New York is the first state to pass a mandatory seat belt law. There will certainly be a lot of confusion for tens of millions of people traveling from other states who drive through New York annually.

Also, I disapprove of diverting the scarce resources of our police away from fighting real crime in order to enforce the seat belt law.

QUESTION: If motorists generally obey laws regarding stop signs even without policemen around, why wouldn't the same hold true for seat belt laws?

ANSWER: Because seat belt laws represent a far greater interference with personal freedom of choice. As such, they're likely to be widely resented, disrespected and disobeyed. Persuasion and education are the right road to follow.

QUESTION: Haven't efforts to encourage voluntary seat belt use been a failure?

ANSWER: Voluntary measures such as public-service announcements and driver-education courses will gradually create a pro–seat belt generation. We're already seeing more seat belt use by young motorists.

1. Having read the interviews carefully, which position do you agree with more: for or against mandatory seat belt laws? Explain why you favor this position.
2. Reread the interview for the position you agree with. Using your own words, summarize the argument given in the interview. Write a position statement and three reasons to support that position.

3. Can you think of any other reasons to support your position that were not mentioned in the article? If so, state each reason in a single sentence.

4. From the reasons you have identified for questions 2 and 3, list the three reasons that you think are the strongest. Of these, which one is the strongest?

5. Now think of what evidence you could use to support each of the reasons you have listed in question 4: facts, statistics, examples, incidents, citing an authority. Where would you look to find such evidence?

6. Which of the following specific pieces of evidence could you use in an essay supporting your position?

    a. Statistics on the number of deaths and injuries from traffic accidents during the last five years

    b. Statistics showing which traffic-accident victims were wearing seat belts and how many were not

    c. Statement on the importance of using seat belts by a police officer who investigates traffic fatalities

    d. Statement on the importance of using seat belts by a doctor who is an expert on deaths and accidents resulting from motorists' being thrown from the car

    e. Eyewitness report from a survivor of a serious traffic accident

    f. Statement on the effectiveness of seat belts by a safety engineer for an automobile manufacturer

    g. Quotation from the Bill of Rights on the government's not making any additional laws to restrict personal freedom

    h. An analysis of other kinds of safety measures, such as air bags

EXERCISE 11. Outlining a Persuasive Argument. Use the list of reasons and suggested evidence that you identified in questions 2–6 of Exercise 10 to outline the argument for a brief essay of opinion. Write a position statement that will be part of an introductory paragraph. Choose three different reasons, saving the most important reason for last. If you wish the reader to take some specific action (such as writing to a congressional or state representative), include this call to action in your outline.

WRITING A FIRST DRAFT

WRITING THE ARGUMENT

18e. Write a first draft.

Your outline of the argument serves as the work plan for your persuasive essay. The essay will include an introductory paragraph, a body, and a conclusion.

Introductory Paragraph

The introductory paragraph will introduce the limited topic and end with the writer's position statement. The introductory paragraph also serves to arouse the reader's interest and to provide any background information that is necessary to understanding the topic. The following paragraph is the introduction to a persuasive composition titled "Driver Training for All."

> On a single weekend last month, there were three serious highway accidents in this county caused by teen-age drivers. One of the results of this tragic weekend was a renewed public demand that high-school students be required to take a course in driver training. True, most of the high schools in this area have offered driver training courses for many years, but these courses have always been elective, rather than required, and sometimes only a small fraction of the student body has actually been enrolled in the course. I believe that a course in driver training should be required for all tenth-grade students.

specific example to arouse reader's interest

background information

position statement

The Body

The middle part of the essay is called the *body*. In a persuasive composition, each reason, together with its supporting evidence, takes up one paragraph in the body of the essay. You may also include in the body arguments against your position; these are called the *opposing viewpoint*. By refuting these arguments (showing why they are not true), you give your reader the impression that you are knowledgeable and have researched your topic thoroughly. This gives credibility to your own argument. Your refutation of the opposing viewpoint may come either before or after your own list of reasons. In the composition about driver training, the writer deals with the opposing argument first. The following paragraphs of the body come right after the introductory paragraph.

Opponents of this idea have argued that providing driver training for every student would be very expensive and that the results would not be worth the price. It is true that the courses would be costly. Our town school board has estimated that to provide driver training for every high-school student, the school would need at least two more full-time instructors and two additional training cars, as well as extra lab space and equipment. However, the cost of this program must be weighed against the much greater cost—both in money and in human suffering—of continuing to allow inexperienced and poorly trained people to join the ranks of licensed drivers. An effective driver training program would certainly be worth the expense. There is little question that the driver training course now offered at our school has been effective. According to Ms. Shue, the instructor in charge of the course, only two of the forty-three students who took and passed the course last year failed to pass the state driver's license examination on the first try; both of them passed on the second try. This compares very favorably with the statewide average of nearly 20 percent failures on the examination. Furthermore, Ms. Shue reports that only one of the students who has completed the course during the past five years has been

opposing viewpoint

refutation of opposing viewpoint

reason 1

statistics

statistics

involved in a serious accident since getting a license and that in this case the other driver was judged at fault. Although Ms. Shue does not have figures for accidents involving students who have *not* taken the course, she says that each year at least three or four such students from our school have been arrested for speeding, while no student who has completed the course has been arrested for any traffic violation.

statistics

Some people grant that driver training courses are effective but still do not feel that driving instruction should be a required subject in a public high school. I think that if we are to turn out a future generation of well-trained drivers, the public school is the logical place to provide the training because all young people are in school until they are at least sixteen. Sixty years ago, driving an automobile may have been a hobby of the rich, but today it is an essential part of nearly every adult's workaday life. It would be in the public interest to train all citizens to drive well and wisely. The only present alternative to teaching driving in the schools is to continue the haphazard practice of leaving the instruction to parents or older friends, a system that in too many cases has proved ineffective.

reason 2

fact 1

fact 2

Concluding Paragraph

The *concluding paragraph* in a persuasive essay may ask the reader to take some specific action. Such a call to action makes an effective and forceful ending for a persuasive essay or for a letter to the editor. The writer assumes that the argument has been so convincing that the reader will be motivated or inspired to do something tangible to bring about the desired end stated in the position statement. A persuasive essay does not always have a call to action. Instead, the concluding paragraph may simply restate the writer's position, or it may summarize the writer's opinion and the main reasons given in the essay to support that opinion.

The schools have shown that they can train good drivers. Since they have access to all of our young people, let's give them the job of teaching all students to drive well. Beginning next semester, driver training should be a required course for all tenth-grade students in this city's public high schools.

summary of position statement and reasons

EXERCISE 12. Writing a Persuasive Essay. Use the argument you outlined in Exercise 11 to write the first draft of a persuasive essay on a mandatory seat belt law. Include a precisely worded position statement in your introductory paragraph. If you have added a call to action in your outline, be sure to make that part of your concluding paragraph. If you wish, you may write a persuasive essay on a topic of your own. Make sure, however, that you outline your argument before you begin to write the first draft.

REVIEW EXERCISE B. Writing a Persuasive Essay. Read the following four brief persuasive essays carefully, and write a brief persuasive essay telling what you think should be done to save the Olympics.

PREWRITING Decide what you think about each of the ideas set forth in the essays. Does one idea seem better than the others? If so, which one? Why do you think it makes more sense or will work better? Perhaps you have an entirely different idea about what should be done to save the Olympics from further boycotting. Or perhaps you think the Olympics should remain as they are. Write a position statement; then outline your argument for a persuasive composition about what should be done to save the Olympics. If you can, think of evidence to support each reason. Before you begin writing, evaluate your argument by referring to the guidelines on pages 508–509.

WRITING THE FIRST DRAFT Plan to have at least four paragraphs in your essay: an introductory paragraph containing the position statement; two reasons, each developed in a separate paragraph; and a concluding paragraph. As you write, concentrate on making the position statement specific and expressing your ideas in the clearest possible way.

REVISING AND PROOFREADING Go back over your essay to make sure that the position statement, reasons, and evidence are all clearly stated. Eliminate any unnecessary words or phrases, expressing your ideas as clearly and briefly as you can. Once again, check to see that the reasons and evidence are relevant and that they strongly support the position statement. Refer to the Guidelines for Proofreading on page 339.

FOUR IDEAS TO SAVE THE OLYMPICS

1. *Return the Games to Greece*   Senator Bill Bradley (Democrat, New Jersey), member of the gold-medal Olympic basketball team in 1964

   Since 1976, I have proposed that the Olympics be moved to a permanent site, preferably Greece, the birthplace of the games. In 1980, when the U.S. boycotted the Moscow Olympics, the Greeks proposed a 1,250-acre site near ancient Olympia, but the idea was opposed by the International Olympic Committee. In the wake of the Soviet boycott, President Constantine Caramanlis of Greece has again called for returning the games to that nation.

   Construction costs for facilities in Greece would be paid by the participating nations. It would be a matter of spending 10 billion dollars once—rather than spending that amount or more every four years.

   Such a step is necessary to spare the Olympics the inevitable political repercussions that come from moving from site to site. If there had been a permanent site, the boycotts of 1980 and 1984 would not have occurred.

2. *Protect the Athletes*   David Scheffer, attorney and associate, Harvard University Center for International Affairs

   A basic principle of the modern Olympics is that the games are designed for individual achievement, not the achievement of nations. The Olympics have moved away from that principle, but they need to return to it through an international treaty.

   Under the treaty, which could perhaps be negotiated through the United Nations, countries would agree to uphold the rights of their athletes. Thus, if a nation determined that it would not officially participate in the Olympic Games, individual athletes would still be allowed to compete on their own, provided that they meet Olympic qualifications and pass the review of an arbitration panel set up to hear complaints of athletes.

   This method would keep countries from pulling the rug out from under qualified athletes at the 11th hour.

3. *Split Up the Games*   Buck Dawson, executive director, the International Swimming Hall of Fame

   I favor decentralizing the Olympics into five separate sets of games—aquatics, winter sports, land individual sports, land team sports and cultural competition—held in five different places. This would be consistent with the Olympic symbol, which is composed of five rings.

Since the whole world would not be congregated in one place, this would reduce the temptation to use the Olympics for political purposes. If a host country tried to politicize the games, you could shift the event somewhere else—something you can't do now with so much preparation and detail involved in one huge Olympics.

Decentralization would also make it possible to expand the number of Olympic events. For instance, at present they don't have the full quota of swimming events because Olympic officials feel that the games are already too big. They're reluctant to take on new sports for the same reason.

In addition, this system would reduce the incredible cost of hosting the games and make it possible for smaller countries to serve as hosts.

4. *Pick a Neutral Site* John Lucas, professor of physical education, Pennsylvania State University

The solution to the political problems that beset the Olympic Games is establishment of a permanent site in a politically neutral country. Central Switzerland would be ideal since it has both snow-capped mountains and an idyllic summer environment. The money for establishing the facilities would come primarily from the huge cache that the IOC [International Olympic Committee] has accumulated over the past 25 years from TV revenue. This location is preferable to Greece where during July and August the temperature reaches 110 degrees in the Peloponnesus, home of the original games. Moreover, Greece is very unstable politically.

So far, the International Olympic Committee has rejected this plan because members feel the games should change sites every four years. But the IOC can't have the chaos that now exists and expect the games to last much longer.

If the IOC won't approve a permanent location, it should at least limit the games to a few already established sites. The summer games could rotate among Tokyo, Montreal and Munich. The winter games could be shifted among some of the European spas, such as Grenoble, France, that have already hosted the Olympics. The important thing is to keep the games away from the territory of the two superpowers.

REVISING

18f. Revise the first draft.

As with any other type of composition, you need to reread the first draft of a persuasive essay several times. With each reading, focus your attention entirely on just one aspect of the composition as you try to improve it.

(1) Focus first on the argument.

Your position statement, reasons, and evidence should be stated so clearly that the reader can easily follow the logic of your argument. Highlight your reasons with transitional expressions such as *first, second, most important,* and *also.* Make sure that you have included sufficient reasons (at least three) to support your opinion and that each reason is supported by some kind of specific evidence. Now is the time to evaluate your argument once again, using the Guidelines for Evaluating Persuasive Argument (pages 508–509). Decide whether each reason and piece of evidence is relevant and distinct. You may decide to replace reasons or evidence that seem weak, or you may decide to change the order of ideas.

(2) Make sure that the tone is formal and the style is concise.

The tone of a persuasive essay should be both serious and formal, which means that you avoid using slang, colloquialisms, or contractions. To give the reader the impression that you are both logical and fair, avoid loaded words and emotional appeals, such as name calling (see pages 522–26); also avoid fallacies or errors in logic such as circular reasoning (see pages 526–28).

The argument in a persuasive composition should be tightly knit; that is, it should not contain unnecessary, awkward, or elaborate words and phrases. Aim for clarity of ideas with no flowery phrases or unnecessary repetition. Eliminating this type of "padding" from a persuasive composition makes the argument easier to follow.

(3) Check the word choice.

Look carefully at each word to make sure that it expresses your ideas precisely. Make sure that you are aware of the connotations (emotional associations) of every word and that you choose only words that will help make your argument convincing. (See page 522, loaded words.)

Study the changes that the writer has made in revising paragraph 3 in the body of the essay on requiring driver's training courses for all tenth-graders.

Some people grant that driver-training courses are effective but still do not believe that driving instruction should be a required subject in a public high school. On the contrary, the public school is the logical place to provide such training because all young people are in school until they are at least 16. One alternative to teaching driving in the schools is to continue the haphazard practice of leaving the instruction to parents or older friends, but this instruction has too often proved ineffective. Another option is to require all young adults to take driving lessons from private driving schools, but most students cannot afford such lessons. It is in the public interest to spend the money to train all citizens to drive well and wisely.

Use the following guidelines in revising your persuasive composition.

GUIDELINES FOR REVISING A PERSUASIVE COMPOSITION

1. Is the topic of the composition a debatable opinion about a serious issue?
2. Does the position statement clearly state the writer's opinion? Does the position statement appear in the introductory paragraph?
3. Is the writer's opinion supported by at least three reasons?
4. Is each reason supported by some kind of evidence, such as facts, statistics, examples, or quotations?
5. Is necessary background information provided for the audience?
6. Is the tone consistently formal and serious?
7. Does the writer consider the opposing viewpoint and refute opposing arguments?
8. Does the concluding paragraph restate the writer's opinion, summarize the argument, or suggest a course of future action?
9. Does the essay contain any fallacies? (See pages 526–28.)
10. Do transitional expressions connect the writer's ideas and make the essay easy to understand?
11. Has the writer eliminated wordiness, vagueness, and unnecessary or distracting information?

EXERCISE 13. Revising a Letter to the Editor. Revise the following letter to the editor of a local newspaper. Pay special attention to tone and clarity. You may make up any additional information you need to strengthen the argument. Make sure that there is a clear position statement and a concluding sentence.

Dear Editor:

I'd like to write something about the new Metrorail system. It's all very nice, but it doesn't run after 8:00 P.M. or on the weekends at all. That's when lots of people like us high-school students would like to ride it. We'd go downtown to movies, museums, and restaurants on dates and stuff. The downtown area, which is totally and really dead at night, would get busy and attract more people if the Metrorail system were open later hours and on weekends.

The guys who head up the transportation department say they're waiting for "public demand" to extend the hours at night and on weekends. Most people are too lazy to give them a call or write a letter, so there never will be enough "public demand." Really, my friends and I would use the Metrorail system if it were open. Just last Saturday we wanted to go downtown to a movie but couldn't. Why don't they try running it on weekends for a couple of months and see if it takes off?

Also, I think the dollar fare is too high and that the Metrorail should service more parts of the city.

DAVID B. SMITH

PROOFREADING

18g. Proofread your revised version to make sure that it agrees with the conventions of standard written English.

Once again, reread the revised version several times, focusing on one particular aspect each time. You might focus first on spelling, stopping to check in a dictionary any word that you suspect might be misspelled. Next, turn your attention to punctuation, and read through the essay to make sure that you have written complete sentences and that punctuation marks are used correctly. Use the Guidelines for Proofreading on page 339 to check all the important aspects of mechanics and usage.

After you have proofread the revised version, write the final version on a separate sheet of paper, following the manuscript form required by your teacher. Be sure to proofread this version once more to make sure that you have not made any mistakes in the final copying.

RECOGNIZING PERSUASIVE TECHNIQUES

Identifying Emotional Appeals

18h. **Learn to recognize emotional appeals.**

Although a persuasive argument should be based almost entirely on logical appeals, you should learn to recognize emotional appeals that may help make your argument convincing. Also, as a reader and as a consumer, you should be alert to emotional appeals that are designed to make you think or act in a certain way.

Loaded Words

Loaded words reveal the writer's opinion and tend to make a reader feel either positively or negatively toward the subject being discussed. *Flag, decency, patriotism, mother, freedom, democracy*, and *the public good* are loaded words and phrases because they are associated with positive feelings. (See pages 632–33 for more information about the positive and negative connotations of words.) *Grotesque, diseased, arrogant,* and *untrustworthy* are examples of loaded words with negative connotations.

In the following paragraph the writer describes the contents of a vacant lot in the middle of a city block and tells what should be done about it. As you read, see if you can identify the loaded words.

> The time has come to do something about the filth that exists in the middle of our city. Wherever there is a vacant lot, people have dumped their refuse. The lot in the middle of the 5400 block of Sherman Street contains six torn, stained mattresses; four broken chairs; a rusty refrigerator; two discarded stoves; one abandoned and rusting bicycle; sixty-seven empty soda cans; and hundreds of pounds of decaying food. People live and work next to these illegal garbage dumps. Pedestrians walk by, cars drive by, businesses carry on nearby, and hundreds of citizens live in neighboring lots, while the garbage rots in their midst. The sanitation department should clean up these vacant lots and bill the owners for their services. Once the lots are clean, law-abiding citizens should organize a "Lot-Watch," reporting to the police anyone who dumps any kind of refuse in a vacant lot. Violators must be promptly punished to the full extent of the law.

Filth, garbage, decaying, and *rots* are loaded words with negative connotations. *Law-abiding citizens* and *full extent of the law* are loaded phrases with positive connotations.

EXERCISE 14. Identifying Emotional Appeals. Analyze the following paragraphs. Be prepared to discuss whether the paragraphs contain any loaded words; some paragraphs may not.

1

When is our school system going to understand that what makes a good student is not the fear of punishment, but the quality of teachers, the exciting methods of teaching subjects and the clever programs of study?

Bored students are always looking for entertainment (from throwing papers to getting into drugs). Give them involving, attractive, creative classes starting in kindergarten (it's important that it starts at the very beginning) and children will become used to being attentive and well-behaved. Give them boring classes and they will be worse every day, no matter how much you punish them. Or, by the way, no matter how many hours you try to teach them.

I say this because they're talking about adding time to school days. If I don't learn what you teach me in six hours, you can bet your life that I'm not going to learn it in 7 or 27. Everything in the world has its limits—even school hours.

ALEJANDRA PINIELLA

2

John Houseman's Acting Company has come and gone. What a joy it was to see its admirable production of *Tartuffe*, translated by Richard Wilbur, of course, and directed by Brian Murray! For the record, Philip Goodwin was Tartuffe, Margaret Reed was Mariane, Richard S. Iglewski was Orgon, and Lynn Chausow was the maid, Dorine. After heaven knows how many exposures to this marvelous play, it struck me for the first time that the scene in the second act in which Tartuffe gets his comeuppance is as deeply, permanently satisfying as the scene in *David Copperfield* in which Betsy Trotwood tells off the Murdstones. At the Wednesday matinee that I saw, most of the audience appeared to be high-school students, and their gleeful surprise and applause would have delighted Molière.

EDITH OLIVER - *THE NEW YORKER*

3

It seems that all sorts of groups object in this case to the killing of a perfectly healthy baboon. On the other hand, medical science backs its position by emphasizing in such instances that it is ethically and morally justifiable to sacrifice a "lesser" species of life in order to save the life of a human child.

My point is not to argue one way or another. Rather, I seek an answer to a question that has perplexed me ever since these same humanitarian and environmental groups vigorously lobbied a few years back to save the seals. Why is it that these same people, and in fact the great majority of all Americans, don't even blink an eye at the thought of sacrificing "lesser" forms of life . . . to satisfy our own palate (which, needless to say, is not a life-threatening situation)?

Is it because the baby seal and baboon are cuter than the cow, chicken, or fish? I, for one, am going to propose to my congressman the passage of a "Save the Cow" bill.

DOUGLAS KRUGER

Bandwagon Appeal

When a writer uses the "bandwagon appeal," the reader is urged to "jump on the bandwagon" before it is too late. In other words, "everyone else" is doing or has already done whatever it is the writer is trying to persuade the reader to do. In order not to feel left out, the reader is urged to take a specific action.

EXAMPLES   Student response to the school play has been overwhelming. Buy your tickets now before they are all gone.

According to our latest figures, 99 percent of all registered voters have already cast their ballots. Polls close in exactly one hour. Don't miss your chance to make your vote count.

Name Calling

In political campaigns, opponents sometimes label an opponent as *radical, liberal,* or *conservative.* Such labels are emotional appeals because they arouse either positive or negative connotations. Without knowing anything specific about the candidate, the reader is already prejudiced by the emotional connotations of the label.

EXAMPLE   Candidate X, my opponent, is a bleeding heart and a big spender. If elected, Candidate X will lead this nation into debt.

Glittering Generalities

Some loaded words have such positive connotations that they are called "glittering generalities." They make the reader feel good without understanding why. Words like *honor, integrity, justice,* and *freedom* are examples of glittering generalities.

EXAMPLE   You know that you are a person of integrity, a person with a sense of social justice. You cannot stand idly by while your neighbors go hungry or have no shelter. It is your duty, therefore, to make your annual contribution to the United Charities drive.

Testimonial

One type of evidence often used in persuasive writing is a quotation by an expert or authority on the subject being discussed. Such a quotation is an acceptable logical appeal because it is reasonable to expect that an expert in the field has information and opinions that are believable. However, when a famous person who is *not* an expert in the field endorses a product or a candidate, such a *testimonial* is an emotional appeal. The glamour or glory surrounding the famous person is not enough of a basis for believing everything the person says. Testimonials are often used in advertising and in politics.

EXAMPLES   Frankie T., the famous rock-jazz guitarist, says: "I always eat this brand of cereal because it is absolutely the most nutritious brand on the market. Look how much energy it gives me!"

Ruthie W., the gorgeous movie star, is voting for Candidate Morrison for state senate, so you should, too.

Plain Folks Appeal

Advertisers use the "plain folks appeal" when they show average-looking, middle- and working-class people using their product and having a wonderful time. Although it is usually never stated directly, the message is that you, too, should buy the product or vote for the candidate because "plain folks" just like you are doing it already.

EXAMPLES   Candidate X is the choice of the people who struggled to build America by working long, hard hours in the factories and on the farms.

Folks in this town know it's important to eat right, so we buy Hometown applesauce—it's just like the kind your grandma used to make.

Snob Appeal

Snob appeal is the opposite of the plain folks appeal. When advertisers show glamorous, well-dressed people using their products, they imply that your life will be more glamorous and exciting if you buy the products that these "beautiful people" are using. Snob appeal also implies that you are one of the special, privileged few.

EXAMPLE Readers of this magazine are among the most successful people in their fields. Doctors, lawyers, and business executives subscribe to our magazine to learn how to make the most of every second of their lives. Subscribe today and find out what these successful people know.

EXERCISE 15. Analyzing Persuasive Paragraphs for Emotional Appeals. Read each of the following paragraphs carefully. Be prepared to identify loaded words and other emotional appeals.

1

Everything in the world can be yours with your World Extravaganza credit card. You can have everything you've always wanted—cars, clothes, houses, travel. Enjoy the finest things in life today and pay for them tomorrow. Be one of the special few who are invited to enjoy the privilege of having a World Extravaganza credit card. Just fill out the enclosed application, and you can start making all your dreams come true.

2

Commissioner Neil Frank should be removed from office by means of the special recall process outlined in our city charter. Commissioner Frank has not served the public well in his year of office. He has been absent from more commission meetings than he has attended, and he has been a consistent troublemaker. Joe O'Rourke, the restaurant owner, and Lisa Craig, the violinist, both believe that Commissioner Frank should be recalled from office. We ordinary citizens of this country, who wholeheartedly believe in good government, must join together to protect our community from this troublemaker. If you are a registered voter, please sign a petition for the recall of Commissioner Frank.

Identifying Fallacies

18i. Learn to identify fallacies and avoid them in your writing.

Persuasive writing, as you have seen, is based on logical thinking. Errors in logical thinking are called *fallacies*. Learning to recognize fallacies will help you to think more clearly and to build more effective arguments for persuasive compositions. Recognizing fallacies will also help you to become a better critical thinker when you read and when you listen to speakers.

Hasty Generalization

A generalization that is made without sufficient evidence to back it up is called a *hasty generalization*. Often, a hasty generalization is made on the basis of only one or two experiences.

EXAMPLES   I have a French pen pal who loves to tell jokes. I guess French people have a terrific sense of humor.

Jeff says, "It's impossible to learn to play a musical instrument once you get past the age of 10. I know this is true because I tried piano lessons for a month last year and just couldn't do it."

A sound generalization is based on a whole series of observations and experiences. The more evidence you gather before making a generalization, the more likely it is that your generalization will be sound.

Stereotype

A *stereotype* is a hasty generalization. According to a stereotype, all members of a particular group share certain qualities or characteristics—usually negative ones. Instead of judging people as individuals, stereotypes "prejudge" individuals by their group membership.

EXAMPLES   Skinny people are too tense and serious.

All college graduates are snobs.

Cause-Effect

The *cause-effect* fallacy occurs when one event is said to be the cause of another just because the two events happened in sequence. You cannot assume that an event caused whatever happened afterward.

EXAMPLES   My brother visited the Modern History Museum on Saturday. On Saturday night he came down with a bad cold that lasted a week. Museums are certainly unhealthy places.

> I bought a new houseplant yesterday, and my bird died last night. That new plant must be giving off poisonous fumes.

Attacking the Person

If you are discussing your opponent's views, your focus should be on the opponent's argument—the reasons and evidence given to support the opposing point of view. If, instead, you attack the opponent's character or situation, you are guilty of the fallacy of *ad hominem—attacking the person*.

EXAMPLES George's ideas about the Presidential candidates shouldn't be taken too seriously. You know that cars and baseball are all that George cares about.

Of course Tara will defend the hospital's position on containing health costs. Her mother's a doctor, isn't she? What else could Tara possibly say?

Circular Reasoning

In *circular reasoning,* you might appear to be giving a reason to support your opinion, but all you are actually doing is restating the opinion in other words. You are saying, in effect, that a statement is true because you say it is true.

EXAMPLES Louis is the best candidate for Student Council treasurer because of all the candidates he is clearly the superior one.

People should not be allowed to smoke cigarettes in public places, such as supermarkets and movie theaters, because smoking should be banned from such places.

Either—Or

The *either—or* fallacy occurs when a person says that there are only two possible causes or courses of action and ignores all other possibilities. To the *either—or* thinker, the world is either good or bad, right or wrong, black or white; there are no in-between "shades of gray."

EXAMPLES If you loved me, you'd do my chores for me. But since you won't, you obviously don't love me.

If I don't get accepted at State University this fall, I will never be able to attend college.

EXERCISE 16. Identifying Fallacies.   Make up an example for each of the following fallacies. Your example may be a sentence or two, or it may be a paragraph. Be sure that the error in reasoning is clearly shown.

1. Circular reasoning
2. Hasty generalization
3. Cause-effect
4. Attacking the person
5. *Either—or* fallacy

EXERCISE 17. Identifying Fallacies.   Identify the fallacy in each numbered item.

1. It's silly to try to talk to JoAnn about sports. You know that women just aren't interested in sports.
2. Either you take this vitamin pill right now, or you will be sick tomorrow.
3. The only time I've been camping, a bear came into the campgrounds and stole someone's food. I'll never go camping again—it's far too dangerous!
4. Whenever I travel by plane (and it's happened to me twice), the airport is closed because of a blizzard. Flying is really an undependable form of transportation.
5. Jason thinks that the United States should retaliate against terrorists, and he has a lot of statistics and examples to prove his point. But everyone knows that Jason has some really weird ideas and a terrible temper, so I wouldn't waste time listening to what he has to say.
6. If I don't learn to ski, I'll never be popular with my classmates.
7. Physical education classes should be required for all four years of high school because I firmly believe that physical education should be mandatory for all students.
8. Chess players are cold and have no sense of humor.
9. Mrs. Applegate should win the Teacher-of-the-Month award because she is the teacher most deserving of the award.
10. The day Jenny broke up with Bob, we had an earthquake; and the night she broke up with Larry, there was a blizzard. There's bound to be some kind of natural disaster the next time Jenny ends a romance.

REVIEW EXERCISE C. Identifying Emotional Appeals and Fallacies. Read the editorials and letters to the editor in several issues of a daily newspaper, a news magazine, or a school newspaper. Bring to class any examples that you find of appeals to emotion or of fallacies. You might display on a class bulletin board the examples that you find.

CHAPTER 18 WRITING REVIEW

Writing to Persuade. Compile a list of debatable issues by consulting current magazines and newspapers, interviewing adults, and talking with classmates and friends. As your teacher directs, use one of these issues as a topic for a persuasive composition. Follow the steps detailed in this chapter: Choose your form and audience; write a position statement; build an argument; write a first draft; revise the draft, paying attention to emotional or logical appeals used; write and proofread a final version.

CHAPTER 19

Writing Narration and Description

STORIES; CHARACTER AND BIOGRAPHICAL SKETCHES

Most of the writing that we call literary writing—novels, short stories, poetry, biographies, personal narratives—is a combination of narration and description. Sometimes narration dominates the work and description is used to add detail and interest. Sometimes description dominates the work and the narration is used to illustrate an idea. Combining narration and description helps writers achieve a great range of emotional responses from their readers.

WRITING CREATIVELY

All writing is creative in the sense that any piece of writing is a creation; it is something that never existed before. However, the expression "creative writing" has a special meaning. It usually means a more personal kind of writing than the kind normally required in school courses and in life after you graduate. It includes stories, personal essays, and poems. Creative writing is literary writing as distinguished from practical workaday writing. It is imaginative rather than factual. It attempts to involve readers, to stir their feelings, and to amuse and entertain them, rather than merely to inform or to explain.

Many of the skills of writing creatively, however, may be used to good advantage in any kind of writing. They enable the writer to add interest and color and life. Furthermore, writing creatively is fun for both writer and reader.

531

Developing the Habit of Close Observation

19a. Develop the habit of close observation.

Because creative writers are mainly concerned with describing the people around them and the world they live in, they must learn to describe accurately whatever they perceive. They must be very close observers of life.

In the following paragraph, Annie Dillard shares with us an experience she enjoyed when visiting the Atlantic coast of Florida. Because she observed closely and remembered what she observed in accurate detail, she is able to convey to us the full excitement of her experience.

EXERCISE 1. Analyzing Descriptive Writing. Read the passage and visualize the scene. Then answer the questions following the passage.

> Another time I saw another wonder: sharks off the Atlantic coast of Florida. There is a way a wave rises above the ocean horizon, a triangular wedge against the sky. If you stand where the ocean breaks on a shallow beach, you see the raised water in a wave is translucent, shot with lights. One late afternoon at low tide a hundred big sharks passed the beach near the mouth of a tidal river, in a feeding frenzy. As each green wave rose from the churning water, it illuminated within itself the six- or eight-foot long bodies of twisting sharks. The sharks disappeared as each wave rolled toward me; then a new wave would swell above the horizon, containing in it, like scorpions in amber, sharks that roiled and heaved. The sight held awesome wonders: power and beauty, grace tangled in a rapture with violence.
>
> ANNIE DILLARD

1. What details does the author include to indicate time and place?
2. What accurate details specify size and shape?
3. Point out a verb and an adjective that you think were particularly well chosen.
4. What comparison does the author use to make the experience vivid?

EXERCISE 2. Writing Vivid Description. Write a paragraph in imitation of Annie Dillard's in which you describe a simple childhood experience, perhaps an exploration of your own, and make clear to your reader what you saw and how you felt.

To sharpen your powers of observation, jot down in your journal or notebook, every day for a week, brief detailed descriptions of things you see, preferably ordinary, unimportant things you may not have observed closely before or, indeed, even noticed at all. Your descriptions need not be written in sentence form. The following examples, all written about things observed on the way to school, will make clear this kind of recording of observations.

1. water standing in the gutter, a film of oil reflecting in rainbow swirls
2. a worker—big stomach like a basketball above his belt—drinking coffee from a white cup held with both enormous hands
3. a metal garbage can, dented, leaning drunkenly by the curb, a greasy bag thrown on top like an afterthought, spilling bits of lettuce, dried bread, eggshells
4. the driver of a car that stopped below my window on the bus, grim, unshaven jaw and a big black pipe protruding from mouth, hairy elbow resting on the window frame
5. a discarded aluminum can on the school lawn, its silver end reflecting in the sun like a bright flashlight

CRITICAL THINKING:
Analysis

When you examine material and determine its parts and their relationship to each other, you are using the critical thinking skill of *analysis*. You analyze when you examine a piece of writing to determine how effectively the writer has used detailed observation.

EXERCISE 3. Analyzing Effective Use of Observation. An example of the effective use of detailed observation is the following description of an old-fashioned oil lamp, the kind of table lamp found in most houses before the advent of gas and electric lighting. The style of this passage is "literary"; you should read slowly and attempt to see the lamp exactly as it is. The authors supply enough details. Prepare answers to the questions that follow the passage.

1. It is of glass, light metal-colored gold, and cloth of heavy thread.

2. The glass was poured into a mold, I guess, that made the base and bowl, which are in one piece; the glass is thick and clean, with icy lights in it. The base is a simply fluted, hollow skirt; stands on the table; is solidified in a narrowing, a round inch of pure thick glass, then hollows again, a globe about half flattened, the globe-glass thick, too; and this holds oil, whose silver line I see, a little less than half down the globe, its level a very little—for the base is not quite true—tilted against the axis of the base.

3. This "oil" is not at all oleaginous,[1] but thin, brittle, rusty feeling, and sharp; taken and rubbed between forefinger and thumb, it so cleanses their grain that it sharpens their mutual touch to a new coin edge, and the odor is clean, cheerful, and humble, less alive by far than that of gasoline, even a shade watery; and a subtle sweating of this oil is on the upward surface of the globe, as if it stood through the glass, and as if the glass were a pitcher of cool water in a hot room. I do not understand nor try to deduce this, but I like it; I run my thumb upon it and smell of my thumb, and smooth away its streaked print on the glass; and I wipe my thumb and forefinger dry against my pants, and keep on looking. . . .

4. In this globe, like a thought, a dream, the future, slumbers the stout-weft[2] strap of wick, and up this wick is drawn the oil, toward heat; through a tight, flat tube of tin, and through a little slotted smile of golden tin, and there ends fledged with flame, in the flue; the flame, a clean, fanged fan.

JAMES AGEE and WALKER EVANS

1. Following the details given in the third paragraph of the description, draw in rough outline a picture of the lamp. Compare your picture with those of your classmates. What information that would be helpful did the authors omit?
2. From paragraph 3, select three or four descriptive details that were most helpful to you when you were drawing the lamp.
3. Is the authors' description of the lamp limited to the nature of the lamp and oil, or does it include their feelings about them? Explain.
4. Explain the meaning of the following pieces of description:

paragraph 2   *solidified in a narrowing*
paragraph 3   *it sharpens their mutual touch to a new coin edge*

[1] *oleaginous:* oily
[2] *weft:* woven

as if the glass were a pitcher of cool water in a hot room

paragraph 4   *In this globe, like a thought, a dream, the future, slumbers the stout-weft strap of wick*

5. Find evidence in the selection to support the following statement: In their description of the lamp, the authors show that they are close observers.

REVIEW EXERCISE A. Writing a Detailed Description.   Take any object that interests you, observe it closely, and write a detailed description of it.

PREWRITING   Your description will be easier to write and more effective if you choose a small object like the lamp, rather than a large object like a car or a plane or a building. You might write about a ballpoint pen, a light fixture, a beat-up book bag, or a classmate's shoe. After you have chosen an object for your description, take some time to observe it closely. Ask yourself questions about the way it looks. Does it have any unusual features? What color is it? What is its shape? What is its size? How do you feel about the object? Do you think of it as something special? Do you have an emotional attachment to it, or do you think of it as something purely practical? Consider organizing the details according to their location on the object.

WRITING AND REVISING   As you write, try to make your description so accurate that a reader could draw a picture of the object. If you can, let the reader know your feelings about the object, as Agee and Evans let you know their feelings about the lamp. After you have finished writing your description, take time to revise and proofread what you have written. Use the Guidelines for Revising on pages 336–37 and the Guidelines for Proofreading on page 339.

Selecting Words That Appeal to the Senses

19b. In descriptive writing, select words that appeal to the senses.

Much of what we experience, we experience through our senses. It is impossible to write a description of anything without appealing to at least one of the five senses: sight, hearing, smell, touch, and taste. The sense most commonly appealed to, of course, is the sense of sight. However, because most experiences involve more than one of the senses, skillful writers increase the effectiveness of their descriptions by referring to as many senses as they can.

To appeal to the senses, writers use words that describe, or identify, the various sights, sounds, smells, tastes, and feelings or physical sensations that they wish their readers to experience.

EXERCISE 4. Identifying Sensory Words. Number your paper 1–20. Copy the following list of words. After each word, write the sense to which it refers. Some may refer to two senses.

1. hot	6. salty	11. whisper	16. glassy
2. spicy	7. icy	12. bitter	17. glittering
3. sour	8. bright	13. tart	18. thump
4. loud	9. roar	14. coarse	19. empty
5. green	10. moist	15. smoky	20. burnt

Describing the Sense of Sound

Most of the words we use to describe sounds are words that suggest in themselves the sounds to which they refer. *Clang,* for example, suggests the sound of metal striking metal; *bong* suggests the sound of a large bell, while *jingle* suggests the sound of a small bell. The use of words of this kind is called *onomatopoeia,* and the words are said to be *onomatopoeic.*

EXERCISE 5. Using Onomatopoeia. Number your paper 1–10. After the proper number, write the entire item on your paper, supplying an onomatopoeic, or sound-imitating, word for the blank. You may, if you wish, qualify the words with adjectives; thus "the crash of thunder" might become the "ear-splitting crash of thunder."

1. the —— of pages being turned
2. the —— of footsteps in the corridor
3. the —— of the wind
4. the —— of wheels on gravel
5. the —— of water dripping
6. the —— of a fire
7. the —— of a piano
8. the —— of distant rifle fire
9. the —— of an opening door
10. the —— of a jet plane

Describing the Senses of Smell and Taste

Since smell and taste are closely related, the same words may be used to describe both. For example, the words *pungent, bitter, musty,* and *stale* may be used to describe both taste and smell.

In the following paragraph, Thomas Wolfe describes the sounds and smells he associated with the arrival of the circus at the railroad station-yard when he was a young boy. Discuss with your classmates the effectiveness of Wolfe's descriptions of smells.

> And to all these familiar sounds, filled with their exultant prophecies of flight, the voyage, morning, and the shining cities—to all the sharp and thrilling odors of the trains—the smell of cinders, acrid smoke, of musty, rusty freight cars, the clean pineboard of crated produce, and the smells of fresh stored food—oranges, coffee, tangerines and bacon, ham and flour and beef—there would be added now, with an unforgettable magic and familiarity, all the strange sounds and smells of the coming circus. The gay yellow sumptuous-looking cars in which the star performers lived and slept, still dark and silent, heavily and powerfully still, would be drawn up in long strings upon the tracks. And all around them the sounds of the unloading circus would go furiously in the darkness. The receding gulf of lilac and departing night would be filled with the savage roar of the lions, the murderously sudden snarling of great jungle cats, the trumpeting of the elephants, the stamp of the horses, and with the musty, pungent, unfamiliar odor of the jungle animals: the tawny camel smells, and the smells of panthers, zebras, tigers, elephants, and bears.
>
> THOMAS WOLFE

EXERCISE 6. Choosing Words to Describe Smell and Taste. Supply an adjective you think appropriate for each blank.

1. the —— taste of coffee
2. the —— odor of strong cheese
3. the —— taste of pickles
4. the —— aroma of fresh bread
5. the —— smell of pizza

Describing the Sense of Touch

Such words as *smooth, rough, icy,* and *slimy* describe the feeling of a surface when we touch it or are touched by it. In the passage on the next page, Lois Hudson recalls the sensations she experienced as a young girl on a North Dakota farm when the temperature one winter night dropped to 50 degrees below zero.

I was well acquainted with the shock of stepping from the warm kitchen into a winter night. But none of the freezing memories of the past could prepare me for the burning air that night. It was like strong hot smoke in my nostrils, so that for one confused instant I thought I was going to suffocate with the cold that was so cold it was hot. I gasped for breathable air, and my father said, "Don't do that! Breathe through your nose—your breath is warmer that way when it gets to your lungs."

We walked carefully down the hill to the barn; then I slithered down the steps, chopped in a snowdrift in front of the door, and slid it open. The barn was very old, but, always before, it had been warm with the heat of the animals kept in it all day long. But that night being inside didn't seem to make any difference. I still had the kind of ache in my temples and cheekbones that I always got when I took too big a mouthful of ice cream.

LOIS HUDSON

EXERCISE 7. Choosing Words to Describe the Sensation of Touch.
Write an adjective or a phrase that describes the sensation of touching each of the following items:

1. velvet	4. corduroy	7. fish	9. baseball
2. marble	5. denim	8. fur	10. tire
3. silk	6. earthworm		

Using Vivid Details

19c. Fill your writing with vivid details.

Most writing, no matter what kind it is, goes from the general to the particular. Whether you are writing a description or telling a story, you make general statements and then back them up with supporting details. Writing shorn of its details is dull and lifeless. Through close observation, a skillful writer sees the details needed to convey a picture clearly.

In the following paragraph, Edmund G. Love recalls the barber to whom he and his brother went when they were children. Find two general statements about Joe Gage, and point out the details that support the general statements.

I do not think Joe Gage overcharged for his haircuts. A boy certainly got his money's worth. He was the first barber I ever knew who gave away lollipops to his customers. He also gave balloons, tops, kites, and baseballs. He entertained his customers as he cut their hair. He would stop in the middle of whatever he was doing and put on the boxing gloves and go a quick round with a boy. He would Indian-wrestle, play mumblety-peg, or teach a boy how to whittle. He would repair a coaster wagon or paint a name on a sled. He was a talented man in many ways. He was the best whistler who ever came to Flushing. He could imitate birds or whistle a song. He could sing. He could tell stories. Sometimes in the middle of a haircut he would get so engrossed in one of his own stories that he would draw up a stool and sit down. When my brother Walter stalked into his shop and asked for a shave, a shave was forthcoming. Joe lathered Walter's face, used the back of a comb to shave off the lather, applied a hot towel, and finished off with a generous application of witch hazel and lilac water.

EDMUND G. LOVE

EXERCISE 8. Writing a Description with Appropriate Details. Each of the following places has its own atmosphere. Select one place—if you prefer, a place not listed here—and write a one-paragraph (approximately 150 words) description conveying its atmosphere. Support your general statements with as many appropriate details as you can. Appeal to as many of the senses as possible. Let your reader know your feelings in this place.

pizza parlor	library
greenhouse	schoolroom
automobile repair shop	zoo
city playground	restaurant
city street	indoor swimming pool

Using Figurative Language: Similes and Metaphors

19d. Use similes and metaphors to make your writing clear and interesting.

Skillful writers give full play to their natural tendency to think in terms of comparison. In the models of good writing in this chapter, we have seen many examples of the use of comparisons. In Annie Dillard's description of an encounter with sharks, you noticed her use of comparison. She writes of *scorpions in amber* when referring to the sharks inside the waves, and she refers to a wave as a *triangular wedge against the sky.*

In their description of a glass lamp, James Agee and Walker Evans said its base was a *fluted, hollow skirt,* thus drawing a comparison between the lamp base and an article of clothing. They say that the lamp wick *slumbers* in oil, comparing the wick to a live thing that is asleep, and they describe the flame at the top of the wick as a *clean, fanged fan*.

Comparisons like those you have been reading are called *figures of speech*, and the language in which they are expressed is called *figurative language*. A figurative expression is the opposite of a literal expression. An expression is literal when it is completely factual. It is figurative when it is imaginative rather than factual, when it compares things that are not alike in reality but are alike in the writer's imagination. For example, a writer describing the sensations of a passenger on the bow of a ship at sea on a winter night might say, "The wind in her face was strong and cold." This would be literal, not figurative, description. On the other hand, the sentence might read, "The wind cut her face like a knife." While there is really no similarity between wind and knife, the comparison does make sense imaginatively.

Comparisons are common features of your speech and writing. You use them often without thinking: "busy as a bee," "hard as a rock," "straight as an arrow." We speak of a person as "a good egg," and we talk about a "flood of words" and "death's door." Such everyday comparisons as these are to be avoided in writing because they are "tired" and commonplace. They have lost their effectiveness as description. The ability to fashion fresh, original comparisons is a very important writing skill.

The two most common figures of speech are simile and metaphor. A *simile* is a comparison between things essentially unlike, expressed *directly* through the use of a comparing word such as *like* or *as:*

> They slept *like* the dead all day.
> The flame rose *like* a pointed flower.
> She is as quick *as* a rabbit.

A *metaphor* is a comparison between things essentially unlike, expressed *indirectly,* without a comparing word such as *like* or *as.* The comparison is suggested rather than stated:

> Between steep walls flowed the *swollen stream* of rush-hour traffic.
> The sun *hammered* at our uncovered heads.
> The blooming orchard *was a pink cascade* on the hillside.

EXERCISE 9. Identifying Similes and Metaphors. Identify each of the following quotations as simile or metaphor by writing *S* or *M* after the proper number. Be prepared to state what things are being compared and to evaluate the effectiveness of the figure of speech.

1. Buildings are waterfalls of stone.—LOUIS GINSBERG
2. The modern racehorse, inbred for speed, carrying the maximum amount of muscle on the minimum amount of bone structure, is as frail as a pastry shell.—ERNEST HAVEMAN
3. A tree of pain takes root in his jaw.—JOHN UPDIKE
4. I could not bear to see her dimmed.—MARY RENAULT
5. Her face was deep-carved stone.—MAURICE WALSH
6. I felt their eyes directed like burning-glasses against my scorched skin.—CHARLOTTE BRONTË
7. An island [Manhattan] uttered incandescent towers like frozen simultaneous hymns to trade.—MALCOLM COWLEY
8. The Possible's slow fuse is lit / By the Imagination!—EMILY DICKINSON

EXERCISE 10. Writing Similes. Using your imagination, complete the following similes in as fresh and original a way as you can. Take time to wait for your imagination. Do not write down the first comparison that comes to mind; it may be a well-known, worn-out expression.

1. Cars climbing the distant hill looked like . . .
2. He had a chin like . . .
3. Bright beach umbrellas like . . .
4. To press his hand was like . . .
5. Trees outlined against the sky like . . .
6. The heavy fog was like . . .
7. High above us a jet plane moved across the sky like . . .
8. The room was as quiet as . . .
9. The clouds were like . . .
10. She looked as happy as . . .

REVIEW EXERCISE B. Writing a Description of an Experience.
Write a three-paragraph composition (approximately 300 words) describing the experience of waking up in the morning or falling asleep at night.

   PREWRITING Whether you choose to describe the experience of waking up or the experience of falling asleep, you should be able to identify several things and people to describe. You may want to look through your journal for any ideas you have noted in the past. You may also want to keep a notebook beside you for a few nights in a row as you go to bed or wake up. Try to observe all that is happening around you: What sounds do you hear? What can you see? Can you smell anything—breakfast cooking, perhaps? Does the air in the room feel crisp and cool or muggy and hot? Jot down your ideas in a notebook before you forget them.

Since you are describing an experience, you may be able to select from more than one method of organization. You could use chronological order, starting with the moment you turn out the light and ending with the moment you fall asleep (or from the moment you first wake up to the moment you get out of bed). You could use spatial order, organizing the details by their physical location in the room. You might, for example, begin by describing what you see on the ceiling and move from there to the walls and the floor. You could also use order of importance, organizing the details from the least to the most important or from the most to the least important. If you use order of importance, first decide which detail you think is most important; then decide whether you want to start with that detail or end with it.

WRITING As you write, remember your method of organization—spatial, chronological, or order of importance. Try to include specific details that show your close observations. As you describe your sensations, remember your notes about senses other than sight. You may do some revising and changing of sentences or words at this time, but concentrate more on creating a first draft.

REVISING AND PROOFREADING After you have finished your first draft, revise carefully. Think about content, organization, and style. Use the Guidelines for Revising on pages 336–37. Before you hand in your final paper, proofread it carefully using the Guidelines for Proofreading on page 339.

WRITING SHORT STORIES

A short story is an imaginative narrative. Good storytellers use all of the elements of creative writing discussed earlier in this chapter: accurate details, words that appeal to the senses, and comparisons. To these ingredients they add the basic elements of plot (what happens), characters (who is involved), setting (the time and place of the action), and point of view (who is telling the story).

PREWRITING

Choosing a Struggle or Conflict

19e. Choose a struggle or a conflict that is appropriate for a short story.

When you look for a subject for a short story, you must find a situation or a problem that could lead to some kind of struggle or conflict. Without a conflict or a struggle, there is no story.

A character can be in conflict with society, with another character, with a natural force, or with competing desires or needs. These conflicts are not necessarily violent, or even physical; they may consist of strong disagreements or tests of will.

Ideas for conflicts that can be imaginatively treated in short stories are all around you. Perhaps you have read a newspaper story about a family attacked by a bear in Yellowstone Park. From reading the newspaper account, you know what happened; by using your imagination, you can create a story about a conflict that *could* happen. In your imaginary story, you might develop a conflict between the people and the park service, rather than between the people and the bear.

Newspapers are only one source of ideas for short stories. You can also find ideas by reading through your journal and recalling your own experiences, by observing the actions of people around you, by reading and watching television, and by interviewing people in your neighborhood and community.

As you use these sources to try to discover problems or situations leading to conflicts appropriate for a short story, remember that a short story is a fictional rather than a true narrative. You may draw on *what happened* for ideas; but to create a good story, you must write a concise, interesting, and suspenseful account of an imaginary happening.

EXERCISE 11. Choosing a Conflict. By watching television, reading the newspaper, reviewing your journal, and observing people around you, develop a list of five conflicts or struggles that actually happened. For each of the five real conflicts, use your imagination to develop two related conflicts that could happen.

EXAMPLE   *Actual conflict:* A conflict between a hotel owner and a fire marshal over fire hazards in a building

> *Imaginary conflict 1:* A conflict between a landlord and a tenant over fire hazards in a building
> *Imaginary conflict 2:* A conflict between a firefighter and a roaring hotel fire that is endangering the lives of several people in the hotel

Identifying Audience and Tone

19f. Analyze how the audience will affect your writing.

Although you may not have a specific audience for your short story, you still must be aware that an audience exists. A short story is written to be read and enjoyed. The readers, whoever they are, must be able to understand the story and must find it interesting.

If you do have a specific audience—the students who read your school magazine, for example—consider how the interests and background of that audience will affect what you should include in your story. If your school is in the city and most of the students lack actual experience in forests, how will you describe a forest fire so they can understand the power and devastation of that natural event? If most of the students in your school have lived in the same neighborhood all their lives, how can you make them understand the fear of a teenager whose family is moving to a foreign country? Even when you are writing for a general audience, remember to think about your readers as real people who may need background information, who may have certain biases, and who will need to find your story interesting.

EXERCISE 12. Analyzing the Effect of Audience. Analyze how the audience will affect the writing of a story on the following conflict: During a blizzard, a woman nearly freezes to death right outside her own front door. Analyze the effect of *each* of the three audiences by answering the following questions. Be prepared to discuss your answers in class.

> *Audiences:* 1. Students in an elementary school
> 2. A group of adults who have lived their entire lives in southern Florida
> 3. A general audience in Nome, Alaska

1. Will this audience have a natural interest in this conflict?
2. What details or actions can be included in the story to make it more interesting to this audience?
3. Will this audience need any special background information in order to understand and appreciate this struggle?

4. What kind of information, if any, will have to be provided to ensure that the audience understands and appreciates this struggle?
5. Will this audience have a natural bias in favor of or against this struggle or the main character involved in the struggle?

19g. Choose a tone that is appropriate for your audience and your purpose.

Your general purpose when you write a short story is to entertain or interest your audience; more specifically, you may want to make your readers laugh, to fill them with suspense and horror, or to help them to understand some basic conflict in everyday life. That specific purpose reflects your own attitude toward the conflict: For example, you want to make your readers laugh because you feel the conflict is humorous. The tone of your story should always be appropriate for your attitude (and your specific purpose). If you want your audience to laugh, you must choose details and language that will convey a humorous tone. If you want your audience to tremble with fear, you must choose details and language that will convey the mystery and horror of the conflict.

In the following excerpt from a short story by Kurt Vonnegut, Jr., the tone is light and humorous. We can tell from these first two paragraphs that Vonnegut is enjoying the characters and the conflict, and he wants the audience to enjoy them also. Read the paragraphs, and think about how Vonnegut has used words and details to reveal his attitude.

> The North Crawford Mask and Wig Club, an amateur theatrical society I belong to, voted to do Tennessee Williams's *A Streetcar Named Desire* for the spring play. Doris Sawyer, who always directs, said she couldn't direct this time because her mother was so sick. And she said the club ought to develop some other directors anyway, because she couldn't live forever, even though she'd made it safely to seventy-four.
>
> So I got stuck with the directing job, even though the only thing I'd ever directed before was the installation of combination aluminum storm windows and screens I'd sold. That's what I am, a salesman of storm windows and doors, and here and there a bathtub enclosure. As far as acting goes, the highest rank I ever held on stage was either butler or policeman, whichever's higher.
>
> KURT VONNEGUT, JR.

1. How does the title of the drama club reflect the tone of this story?

2. If the tone of the story were very serious, how might the last sentence in the first paragraph be rewritten?

3. What word in the first sentence of the second paragraph helps reveal the light tone of this story?

4. How does the phrase *whichever's higher* contribute to the tone?

5. What details about the narrator's occupation contribute to the tone of the story?

When you are preparing to write your own short story, think about its purpose and how you will share that purpose with your audience. Then choose a tone that will accurately reflect your purpose and your attitude toward the conflict.

EXERCISE 13. Analyzing Audience, Purpose, and Tone. From the list of conflicts you identified in Exercise 11, choose one, and answer the following questions.

1. Beyond entertaining my audience, what is my specific purpose in telling this story?

2. What is my attitude toward the conflict?

3. Am I writing this story for a general audience or for a specific audience? If the story is intended for a specific audience, what are the unique needs of that audience?

4. What can I have my characters say or do that will convey my tone and purpose to my audience? What details can I include to reflect the tone of the story?

5. Might the audience be surprised by or concerned about the tone I intend to use in this story? If so, should I consider changing the tone?

Selecting a Point of View

19h. Select a point of view that is appropriate for your story.

Someone must always tell, or narrate, a story. When you plan your own short story, you must decide what kind of narrator will work best.

You may write your story from the first-person point of view, which is the point of view of someone who is either directly involved in the conflict or a witness to the conflict. The advantage of the first-person point of view is that it makes the audience feel close to the action; the disadvantage is that the first-person narrator cannot know what any other character is thinking or feeling.

You may also write a story from the third-person point of view, which is the point of view of someone who is outside the story. The third-person *omniscient* (all-knowing) narrator has the advantage of being able to reveal what is going on in any character's mind and to show what all the characters are saying and doing. The following examples illustrate the differences among the three points of view.

First-person, directly involved in the conflict. The blisters on my feet were raw, and I felt that every step would be my last.

First-person, a witness to the conflict. I saw Jane sprint around the corner into the final stretch of the race, and the pained expression on her face was clearly visible.

Third-person, all-knowing. As Jane rounded the corner into the final stretch of the race, she struggled with the pain, willing herself to keep running. Martin watched from the sidelines, almost unable to bear the pain he saw in his friend's face.

When you choose the point of view for your own story, consider whether you will need to show what more than one character is thinking and feeling. Third-person point of view is frequently used by fiction writers because it gives the writer the most freedom.

EXERCISE 14. Writing from Different Points of View. Using the following situation and characters, write a sentence or two illustrating each of the following points of view: (1) first-person directly involved in the conflict; (2) first-person, a witness to the conflict; (3) third-person, omniscient. You may use the examples above as a model for your own sentences.

Situation and characters: Two teen-agers have spotted what appears to be a spaceship in a clearing in a forest preserve. One teen-ager decides to go up to the ship to investigate while the other remains at the edge of the woods to watch.

Organizing a Plot for a Short Story

19i. Organize a plot for your short story.

The plot of the short story is the plan of action. It consists of the situation or conflict, the series of actions resulting from the conflict, the climax (the moments of greatest interest or excitement) of those actions, and the final resolution or outcome of the conflict. After choosing the basic conflict in the story, a writer must decide how to begin the story, what events to include and in what order, and how to resolve the conflict. Follow these hints when you begin to organize your own plot.

1. The opening of the story establishes the nature of the conflict and stimulates the interest of the audience.

2. The actions are related in chronological (natural order of time) order and should keep the reader interested and in suspense about how the conflict will be resolved.

3. The climax is the highest point of interest for the audience and it should come near the end of the story.

4. The resolution or outcome should occur immediately after the climax. The story may end either happily or unhappily, but the outcome should seem to be the likely result of the actions and events in the story.

In the following very brief short story, observe the beginning, the middle, and the end. As you read the story, be aware that Death is the character telling the story.

AN APPOINTMENT IN SAMARRA

There was a merchant in Bagdad who sent his servant to market to buy provisions, and in a little while the servant came back, white and trembling, and said, "Master, just now when I was in the marketplace I was jostled by a woman in the crowd, and when I turned I saw it was Death that jostled me. She looked at me and made a threatening gesture; now, lend me your horse, and I will ride away from this city and avoid my fate. I will go to Samarra and there Death will not find me." *(beginning: nature of conflict established; interest aroused)*

The merchant lent him his horse, and the servant mounted it, and he dug his spurs in its flanks and as fast as the horse could gallop he went. Then the merchant went down to the marketplace and he saw me standing in the crowd and he came to me and said, "Why did you make a threatening gesture to my servant when you saw him this morning?" *(the middle: actions and events leading to climax)*

"That was not a threatening gesture," I said, "it was only a start of surprise. I was astonished *(the end: outcome of the situation)* to see him in Bagdad, for I had an appointment with him tonight in Samarra.''

Adapted from a work by w. SOMERSET MAUGHAM

EXERCISE 15. Organizing the Plot for Your Short Story. Using one of the conflicts you identified in Exercise 11, or any other conflict of your choice, develop a plot outline or plan. Follow this format as you develop your plan:

1. Describe the event or situation you will use to establish the nature of the conflict and to interest the audience.
2. Make a list, in chronological order, of the actions that lead to the climax. Describe how you will build suspense into the actions.
3. Describe the climax of the action.
4. Describe how the conflict will be resolved—either happily or unhappily.

WRITING

Developing Characters

19j. Develop characters through description, dialogue, and action.

Many readers are more interested in the characters in a story than in the action in a story. The main character of the story always faces the problem—is always involved in the struggle or the conflict. The hero or heroine of the story is called the *protagonist*. Often another character, called the *antagonist*, opposes the plans or wishes of the hero or heroine. A narrative may include other characters, of course, depending on the writer's plan.

When you create characters for your own story, you have a responsibility to your audience to make those characters convincing. As Laurence Perrine noted in *Literature: Structure, Sound, and Sense*,[1] you must do three things in order to make your characters convincing:

1. Make the behavior of the characters consistent. They should not behave one way at one time and another way at another time. For

[1] Laurence Perrine, *Literature: Structure, Sound, and Sense,* copyright © 1978 by Harcourt Brace Jovanovich, p. 68.

example, if you introduce a character as a miser, do not later show that character spending money with abandon.

2. Show motivation for everything the characters do. The reader should be able to understand why characters behave as they do. If the avid mountain climber turns back before reaching the peak, the reader should be shown *why* the character made that decision.

3. Make the characters believable. The reader must feel that these characters could actually exist in real life. If a character is too perfect or too evil, readers will not find the character believable.

To create characters that are convincing and interesting, you will need to use description, dialogue, action, or a combination of these. The following excerpt from ''The Story of Muhammad Din'' illustrates how a writer can combine all three techniques to develop a character.

Next day, coming back from [the] office half an hour earlier than usual, I was aware of a small figure in the dining room—*a tiny, plump figure in a ridiculously inadequate shirt which came, perhaps, halfway down the tubby stomach*. It wandered round the room, thumb in mouth, *crooning to itself as it took stock of the pictures*. Undoubtedly this was the ''little son.'' **[physical description]** **[action]**

He had no business in my room, of course, but was so deeply absorbed in his discoveries that *he never noticed* me in the doorway. I stepped into the room and startled him nearly into a fit. *He sat down on the ground with a gasp. His eyes opened, and his mouth followed suit.* I knew what was coming, and fled, followed by *a long, dry howl which reached the servants' quarters* far more quickly than any command of mine had ever done. In ten seconds Imam Din was in the dining room. Then despairing sobs arose, and I returned to find Imam Din admonishing the small sinner who was using most of his shirt as a handkerchief. **[action]** **[action]** **[action]**

''This boy,'' said Imam Din, *judicially, ''is a budmash*[1]*—a big budmash. He will, without* **[another character describing the character]**

[1] *budmash:* a bad character; a worthless fellow

doubt, go to the jailkhana[2] for his behavior." Renewed yells from the penitent, and an elaborate
apology to myself from Imam Din.

"Tell the baby," said I, "that the Sahib[3] is not
angry, and take him away." Imam Din conveyed
my forgiveness to the offender, who had now gathered all his shirt round his neck, stringwise, and
the yell subsided into a sob. The two set off for
the door. "His name," said Imam Din, as though
the name were part of the crime, "is Muhammad
Din, and he is a budmash." Freed from present
danger, Muhammad Din turned round in his fath-
er's arms, and said gravely, *"It is true that my*   character revealed
name is Muhammad Din, Tahib,[4] but I am not a   through own words
budmash, I am a man!"

RUDYARD KIPLING

In this excerpt, Kipling begins the character development of Muhammad Din with a physical description: *a small figure in the dining
room—a tiny, plump figure in a ridiculously inadequate shirt which
came, perhaps, halfway down the tubby stomach.* Examples of the
child's actions and a discussion between the boy's father and the
narrator continue the character development by showing that the
father thinks his son is a problem. The boy's own words—"It is true
that my name is Muhammad Din, Tahib, but I am not a budmash, I
am a man!"—reveal Muhammad Din's strength of character, his will-
ingness to assert himself, even to an English gentleman. As a result
of what is revealed through the description, the actions, and the dialogue, we see the complexity of the character. Muhammad Din is a
very curious little boy, who, although little more than a baby, is willing
to assert himself to a powerful stranger.

As you develop characters for your own stories, the following
information may help you use description, action, and dialogue.

1. *Description.* Your readers do not need an exact, complete physical description; they need to know only the physical characteristics

---

[2] *jailkhana:* prison, jailhouse
[3] *Sahib:* Master: a title used by natives in addressing European gentlemen
[4] *Tahib:* Muhammad Din's childish mispronunciation of *Sahib*

that are important to *who* the character is. Kipling does not tell the reader Muhammad Din's height, weight, or hair color. The important features reveal that Muhammad Din is little more than a baby—*tiny, plump; tubby stomach; thumb in mouth.*

2. *Action.* In a short story, you may be able to include only one or two actions to reveal character. Those actions must show some important trait or characteristic. Kipling shows Muhammad Din curiously exploring a room and crying with fear and surprise, two actions that reveal important elements of his character.

3. *Dialogue.* Effective dialogue is brief. Sentences are short, and characters usually do not give long speeches. Notice the brevity of the dialogue in the excerpt. Effective dialogue is appropriate to each speaker's age, occupation, and educational background. Muhammad Din's mispronunciation of the words *Sahib* and *Salaam* is appropriate for a young child.

EXERCISE 16. Developing a Character.   Select one of the conflicts you identified in Exercise 11, and assume that you are going to write a short story about it. Think about the main character of the story. Then write two or three sentences in which you give a physical description of the character, a brief description of an action in which the character reveals personality traits, and a brief dialogue or quotation in which the character's own speech reveals personality traits.

Developing Setting

19k. Develop setting with descriptive details.

Short-story writers use descriptive details to let their readers know when and where a story is taking place. Occasionally a writer will include a complete paragraph or two containing only a description of the setting. More often, the details related to setting are sprinkled in with the development of the plot and the action. Notice how Kipling mixes details of setting in with the action in the following excerpt from the same short story.

Heaven knows that I had no intention of touching the child's work then or later; but, *that evening, a stroll through the garden* brought me unawares full on it; so that I *trampled*, before I knew, *marigold heads, dust bank, and fragments*

time and place

action
details of setting

of broken soap dish into confusion past all hope of mending. Next morning I came upon Muhammad Din *crying softly* to himself over the ruin I had wrought. Someone had cruelly told him that the Sahib was very angry with him for spoiling the garden, and had scattered his rubbish, using bad language [all] the while. *Muhammad Din labored for an hour at effacing every trace of the dust bank and pottery fragments,* and it was with a tearful and apologetic face that he said "Talaam, Tahib," *when I came home* from [the] office. A hasty *inquiry resulted* in Imam Din informing Muhammad Din that, by my singular favor, he was permitted to disport himself[1] as he pleased. *Whereat the child took heart and fell to tracing the ground plan of an edifice* which was to eclipse the marigold–polo ball creation.

    For some months, the chubby little eccentricity[2] *revolved in his humble orbit among the castor-oil bushes and in the dust;* always fashioning magnificent palaces from *stale flowers thrown away by the bearer, smooth water-worn pebbles, bits of broken glass, and feathers* pulled, I fancy, from my fowls—always alone, and *always crooning* to himself.

RUDYARD KIPLING

[right margin annotations:]
action

action related to setting

time and action

action related to setting

action related to setting

details of setting

action

EXERCISE 17. Using Descriptive Details for Setting. Using the conflict you selected for Exercise 13 or 15, or any other conflict of your choice, assume that you are going to write a short story. Consider the setting that would be appropriate for that story. Then answer the following questions.

1. Where will the story take place? What country? Will it be in a small town, a city, or the country?

[1] *disport himself:* play.
[2] *eccentricity:* odd person.

2. What is the climate like? What is the weather like on the day or days when the story takes place?
3. What is the relationship, if any, between the conflict and the location of the setting? Between the conflict and the weather at the time?
4. Does the time of day make a difference in the conflict? If so, what time of day is it when the conflict begins? When it ends?
5. What senses—sight, smell, touch, taste, sound—will be important in describing this setting? See pages 535–38 for a discussion of sensory details.

Writing a First Draft of Your Short Story

19l. Write a first draft of your short story.

You write the first draft of a story in the same way you write the first draft of any other kind of writing. After you have thought about your subject and topic (in this case, the conflict) and developed an outline (a plot outline), you are ready to write. Think of the first draft as an opportunity to get your ideas on paper and to begin to think through some of the problems in your writing task. Remember that you will have opportunities to improve the story when you revise.

EXERCISE 18. Writing a First Draft of Your Story.   Write a first draft of your story. Try to create an interesting beginning and to build suspense into the actions leading to the climax. You may use the plot outline, characters, and setting you created in earlier exercises, or you may select a new conflict and develop a new plan.

REVISING AND PROOFREADING

Revising and Proofreading Your Story

19m. Revise and proofread your story.

Professional writers often write many drafts of their stories, and they may write those drafts over a long period of time—sometimes months or even years. The paragraphs on the next page are from the beginning of a short story. Notice the changes the writer made in the revision of the first draft.

"~~Please grip~~ the rope better," Marcia ~~said as~~ she ~~moved up~~ the side of the cliff.

Hang on to ... *yelled struggled for a foothold on*

"Okay! Okay!" I ~~yelled back~~. "Give me t~~he benefit of the doubt~~. My hands are ju~~st too cold to hold on to the rope~~."

grumbled ... *a break!* ... *half frozen!*

~~George's brother was a mountain climber. The man~~ and woman h~~ad been~~ ~~on the mountain for six hours,~~ and neither had much strength or patience le~~ft.~~ ~~George was six feet tall and weighed a hundred and ninety pounds, and Marcia~~ ~~had dark hair and dark eyes. Marcia was strong for her size.~~

Marcia   I   just spent the last six hours trying to move ten feet up the face of that cliff. *Although I was in good physical condition and ~~us~~ Marcia had more endurance than anybody I knew, we both had reached our limits.*

1. Why did the writer change the wording of the first person's dialogue?

2. Why were the words of the second person changed?

3. Why was the first sentence of the last paragraph eliminated?

4. Why were the words "The man and woman" changed to "Marcia and I"?

5. Why did the writer make the changes in the last two sentences?

In your own writing, allow as much time as possible for revising; you should find that your story will improve substantially as it is revised. After you have completed the final version of your story, take time to proofread it carefully and to prepare a clean copy.

GUIDELINES FOR REVISING SHORT STORIES

1. Does the beginning of the story establish the conflict and arouse the interest of the reader?

2. Are the actions in the story clearly organized chronologically?

3. Do the actions leading to the climax develop suspense?

4. Is the point of view consistent throughout the story?

5. Are the characters convincing?

6. Has the main character been fully developed through description, dialogue, action, or a combination of these?

7. Is the dialogue natural and appropriate for the characters?

8. Do the details of setting contribute to the reader's understanding of the character and the conflict?

9. Is there a resolution to the conflict that grows logically out of the actions and characters in the story?

EXERCISE 19. Revising and Proofreading Your Short Story. Revise your story, and proofread your final copy. If you have used dialogue in the story, carefully examine your use of quotation marks, other punctuation, and paragraphing. If you need to review the rules for punctuating dialogue, see page 723. Use the guidelines above, the general revision guidelines on pages 336–37, and the proofreading guidelines on page 339 as you revise and proofread your story.

WRITING CHARACTER SKETCHES AND BIOGRAPHICAL SKETCHES

If you want to tell other people what someone is like or was like, you can write a *character sketch*. If you want to tell other people what someone has done—to relate the major events and accomplishments in someone's life—you can write a *biographical sketch*. Both character sketches and biographical sketches combine narrative and descriptive techniques.

PREWRITING

Choosing a Character and Gathering Information

19n. Choose an interesting character, and gather information for a character sketch or a biographical sketch.

Choosing Characters

Whether your character or biographical sketch will be an individual piece of writing or a part of a larger work such as a short story, an essay, a biography, or a history, the character you write about should be an interesting person. If the character is fictional or imaginary, you have the opportunity to *create* an interesting personality. If you are going to write about a real person, you will do well to choose a character who, because of appearance, individual peculiarities, characteristics, occupation, or achievements, is naturally interesting. Both character sketches and biographical sketches can be written about either imaginary or real characters, but the subject of a biographical sketch is usually a real person.

Gathering Information About People

Whether you are gathering information about a real person or an imaginary person, you need to collect information about physical characteristics and personality traits. For both character sketches and biographical sketches you may also need to gather information about setting and environment and how they relate to the character's personality or achievements. For biographical sketches you will also need to gather information about the major events and achievements in the person's life. For character sketches you will probably want to identify one or two incidents that reveal the dominant personality trait of your character.

The source of information about imaginary characters for either kind of sketch will be your own mind. You might refer to journal notes, literature or history books, or television for ideas, but you will have to create the details out of your own mind and imagination.

Sources of information about real people will vary, depending on the subject. If the person is someone you know, you may find information by reading your own journal, by interviewing friends or family members, or by observing. If the person is someone you do not know, perhaps a contemporary film star or a former king of England, your major source of information will be books or magazines. For biographical sketches you will more than likely have to consult one or more books to gather information about the major accomplishments and events in the person's life.

To gather information about people, you can use the following questions to guide your thinking.

A CHARACTER SKETCH

1. What are the outstanding physical characteristics of this person? What are the person's most striking or most unusual features?

2. What is this person's dominant personality trait? Is the person friendly, generous, outgoing, courageous, domineering, timid, or something else?

3. How does this person act? How does this person talk, dress, move, treat other people? How do other people feel about this person?

4. What events or actions could be used to show what this person is really like?

5. Is there a particular setting that helps reveal the dominant personality trait of this person? What are the features of that setting?

A BIOGRAPHICAL SKETCH[1]

1. When was this person born? In what major period of time did the person live—Civil War, Great Depression, Middle Ages?

2. In what city or what country did this person live?

3. What were the important periods in the person's life?

4. What were the major events in this person's life?

5. What were this person's major achievements? What did this person do that had a real impact on the lives of other people?

6. What did this person look like? How did appearance affect this person's accomplishments?

7. What were the outstanding personality traits of this person? What was the relationship between those personality traits and the person's accomplishments?

EXERCISE 20. Gathering Information for a Character Sketch.
Use prewriting techniques such as brainstorming, observing, or asking questions to identify a real or an imaginary person as a subject for a character sketch. Then use the questions on page 557 to gather information about the person. Write the answers to the questions on a sheet of paper, and be prepared to discuss the personality of the character you have chosen.

EXERCISE 21.   Gathering Information for a Biographical Sketch.
Use prewriting techniques such as brainstorming, observing, reading, or asking questions to identify a subject for a biographical sketch. Use the questions above to gather information about the person. Write the answers to the questions on your paper, and be prepared to discuss the highlights of the person's life.

Considering Audience and Purpose

19o. Consider the purpose and the audience of your character sketch or biographical sketch.

The purpose of a character sketch is to reveal the personality of a character. The purpose of a biographical sketch is to recount the major accomplishments and events of a person's life. For either sketch, the writer may also want to communicate a specific attitude toward the character or person being described. If the writer's attitude is that the person is a scoundrel, a clown, or a saint, the tone of the sketch should

---

[1] These questions will vary somewhat if you are gathering information about a living person.

reflect that attitude. As you write your own character sketches and biographical sketches, consider your attitude toward the person and how you will choose events, details, and language to reflect that attitude or tone.

As for any other kind of writing, you should consider your intended audience when writing character sketches and biographical sketches. Your teacher may suggest a general audience or some specific audience such as the readers of a popular magazine. For any audience, specific or general, think about the background information you might need to provide, the biases the audience might have toward or against the character, and the kinds of details you will need to include to keep a reader interested.

EXERCISE 22. Considering Purpose and Audience. Using the character or person you identified and the information you gathered for Exercise 20 or 21, consider the following questions about purpose and audience. Write your answers on a sheet of paper, and be prepared to discuss them in class.

1. What is my purpose—to reveal this person's character or to highlight the achievements in the person's life?
2. What is my attitude toward this person or character? What do I want my audience to think of this person?
3. What actions and details do I need to include in my sketch in order to share my attitude with my audience?
4. If the subject is a real person or a well-known fictional character, what does my audience already know about this person or subject?
5. What background information will my audience need?
6. How can I interest my audience in this person?

Organizing a Character Sketch or a Biographical Sketch

19p. Organize a character sketch around a dominant personality trait.

Since you will normally not be able to develop a character as fully in a brief character sketch as a novelist would in an entire book, you can avoid painting a jumbled and confused picture by emphasizing one main impression. Your character sketch thus becomes a study in depth of the outstanding quality of the subject.

To decide on the chief impression you want to create, think about the attitude you have formed about the character. Look over the information you have gathered. What kind of picture does the information create? What kind of picture do you want to create? What is the dominant characteristic of this person? Is the person mean, petty, gentle, humble, wise, strong-willed? Once you have decided what impression you want to create, eliminate any details that do not contribute to that impression.

After the unnecessary details have been eliminated, you are ready to decide how to arrange the details logically. You might begin with a revealing incident and then go on to the details of physical characteristics and personal habits. Another logical arrangement might be to group all the physical details at the beginning and all the personality and behavioral details at the end. Read the following character sketch, and analyze the organization that the writer has used.

> The family was at the very core and ripeness of its life together. Gant lavished upon it his abuse, his affection, and his prodigal provisioning. They came to look forward eagerly to his entrance, for he brought with him the great gusto of living, of ritual. They would watch him in the evening as he turned the corner below with eager strides, follow carefully the processional of his movements from the time he flung his provisions upon the kitchen table to the rekindling of his fire, with which he was always at odds when he entered, and onto which he poured wood, coal, and kerosene lavishly. This done, he would remove his coat and wash himself at the basin vigorously, rubbing his hands across his shaven, tough-bearded face with the cleansing and male sound of sandpaper. Then he would thrust his body against the door jamb and scratch his back energetically by moving violently to and fro. This done, he would empty another half can of kerosene on the howling flame, lunging savagely at it and muttering to himself.
>
> Then, biting off a good hunk of powerful apple tobacco, which lay ready to his use on the mantel, he would pace back and forth across the room fiercely, oblivious to his grinning family who followed these ceremonies with exultant excitement, as he composed his tirade. Finally, he would burst in on Eliza in the kitchen, plunging to the heart of denunciation with a mad howl.
>
> His turbulent and undisciplined rhetoric had acquired, by the regular convention of his usage, something of the movement and directness of classical epithet[1]: his similes were preposterous, created really in a spirit of vulgar mirth, and the great comic intelligence that was in the family—down to the youngest—was shaken daily by it. The children grew to await his return in the evening with a kind of exhilaration.
>
> As he stormed through the house, unleashing his gathered bolts, the children followed him joyously, shrieking exultantly as he told Eliza he had first seen her "wriggling around the corner like a snake on her belly," or, as coming in from freezing weather, he had charged her and all the

[1] *epithet:* a word or phrase used to characterize something or someone.

Pentlands with malevolent domination of the elements.

"We will freeze," he yelled, "we will freeze in this . . . cruel and God-for-saken climate. . . . Merciful God! I have fallen into the hands of fiends incarnate, more savage, more cruel, more abominable than the beasts of the field. . . . They will sit by and gloat at my agony until I am done to death!"

As his denunciation reached some high extravagance, the boys would squeal with laughter, and Gant, inwardly tickled, would glance around slyly with a faint grin bending the corners of his thin mouth.

THOMAS WOLFE

1. Why does Wolfe begin this characterization by mentioning the family?

2. Very early in this excerpt, Wolfe announces the dominant characteristic of the person he is describing. What is that dominant characteristic or impression?

3. Wolfe uses a series of typical behaviors to support his impression of the character. What are those behaviors?

4. What is the effect of the one quotation Wolfe uses in the next-to-last paragraph? Why is the quotation placed near the end of the character sketch?

5. What detail at the very end of the selection sums up the dominant characteristic of this person? Why does Wolfe place that detail at the very end of the sketch?

EXERCISE 23. Organizing a Character Sketch. Using the character you identified and the information you gathered in Exercise 20, develop an informal plan for a character sketch. Begin by identifying the dominant characteristic or personality trait you intend to reveal in the sketch. Then make a list of the events, physical traits, personal habits, and other details in an order that seems appropriate for your sketch.

19q. Organize a biographical sketch in chronological order, according to the major periods in the person's life.

Since a biographical sketch highlights the important events in a person's life, the most logical order of organization is chronological. You will want to divide the person's life into major periods or blocks of time such as youth, early adulthood, middle age, and so forth. Once you have identified the major periods of time, you will be able to organize the main events and achievements within each period. Details that reveal the personality and physical characteristics of the person may be included in an introductory paragraph or along with the discussion of the major events and achievements in that person's life.

The following paragraphs are from the beginning of a biographical sketch written by Louis Untermeyer. Notice how the writer begins the sketch with background information on the status of women's rights prior to the efforts of his subject, Susan B. Anthony.

What is perhaps the most radical alteration of social relationships in the last century is already so taken for granted that its newness is generally overlooked. Yet less than one hundred years ago women had no rights. The first organized demand occurred as late as 1848 and asked for such essentials as the right "to have personal freedom, to acquire an education, to earn a living, to claim her wages, to own property, to make contracts, to bring suit, to testify in court, to obtain a divorce for just cause, to possess her children, to claim a fair share of the accumulations during marriage." Only one college in the United States admitted women; there were no women doctors or lawyers in the country. Married women literally "belonged" to their husbands as slaves or chattels. If they earned money or inherited it, legally it was not theirs but their husbands'. Single women had to be represented by male guardians. Obviously, no woman was entitled to vote. Except in ancient Egypt and under Roman law, this approximately had been the status of women from the beginnings of time.

In the second paragraph, Untermeyer introduces the person about whom he is writing. He begins chronologically, providing details about her family and her childhood. He ends by revealing details of Anthony's personality, her *inquiring mind* that *was bound to rebel.*

The dogged seventy-five-year campaign of prodding, petitioning, and pleading that emancipated modern woman owed its strength and its strategy to Susan Brownell Anthony, sometimes called "the Napoleon of Feminism." She was born February 15, 1820, in Adams, Massachusetts, the second child in a family of eight. Her father, Daniel Anthony, was a man of strong intellect and liberal inclinations. Though a Quaker, he was not a conformist. For his wife, he picked Lucy Read, who was not only a Baptist but a young woman of lively disposition. However, when she became Mrs. Anthony she observed all the Quaker customs. Susan was brought up in a household that, in her childhood, wore Quaker clothes, spoke in Quaker terms, and proscribed frivolity. Though Daniel was a prosperous mill owner, it was incumbent on his wife to do all her own work, including farm chores, as well as board and serve the mill hands who lived with them from time to time. The children, particularly the older girls, were trained early in household accomplishments. But their education was far from neglected. Before she was five, precocious Susan could read and write. As her schooling progressed, whenever she came to a subject in which she was interested (such as more and more advanced arithmetic) she insisted on being taught it—even though it was nothing that girls were supposed to know. The early learning was obtained at home from a governess. In her teens, Susan was sent to an inexpensive finishing school near Philadelphia, Miss Deborah Moulson's Select Seminary for Females. Miss Moulson's task, as she saw it, was to mold her pupils in the prevailing forms, rather than direct an inquisitive spirit, and Susan's inquiring mind was bound to rebel.

Untermeyer follows the first two paragraphs of the sketch with a chronological development of Anthony's early years in teaching and in the movement for women's rights. The following paragraphs, taken from the middle of the sketch, relate Anthony's activities and experiences during the Civil War. Notice the concise way in which Untermeyer treats the important events over a period of several years.

Meanwhile, the Civil War was embroiling the nation. Immediately upon Lincoln's election the extreme Abolitionists, with whom Susan had always identified herself, had campaigned—at first against Lincoln who was trying to prevent the war—for immediate emancipation. During the war the women's rights fight was suspended. The New York State legislature took advantage of the situation by repealing that part of the law they had passed two years earlier covering women's rights over children. Susan was immobilized on her father's farm. In her journal she noted: "Tried to interest myself in a sewing society; but little intelligence among them." Besides the farm work, she passed the time reading Elizabeth Barrett Browning and George Eliot, storing up energy towards the next battle. The call for it sounded in the clanging notes of the Emancipation Proclamation. Free the women as well as the slaves, Susan demanded. Let this be a government of the people, by the people, including women, she insisted—assuming that women are people.

Arguing that women's rights could be tied in with Negro rights, Elizabeth Stanton and Susan organized large numbers of women to campaign for a constitutional amendment abolishing slavery; the signatures they succeeded in getting to a petition helped effect the passage of the Thirteenth Amendment. It was with dismay, then, that they read the proposed Fourteenth Amendment and learned that civil rights were reserved for previously disenfranchised *male* citizens only. If they could have that one word struck out of the amendment, then all women, white as well as Negro, would win the vote at one stroke. The amendment, however, was passed as written. Susan retired to home ground, concentrating on the votes-for-women issue in Albany. It was at this time that the famous exchange of discourtesies took place between her and Horace Greeley.

"Miss Anthony," said Greeley with deadly suavity, "you are aware that the ballot and the bullet go together. If you vote, you are also prepared to fight?"

"Certainly, Mr. Greeley," Susan retorted. "Just as you fought in the last war—at the point of a goose-quill."

The writer includes the information about the Civil War and the Thirteenth and Fourteenth Amendments because these political events had a direct impact on the efforts and motivations of Susan B. Anthony. The exchange between Greeley and Anthony serves two purposes: (1) It shows the kind of opposition Anthony was facing, and (2) it reveals her courage and wit.

The following paragraphs are from the end of Untermeyer's sketch of Susan B. Anthony. Notice how these last paragraphs continue the chronological development of Anthony's life but also make a statement about her achievements and contributions to society.

> In 1904, when the International Woman Suffrage Alliance was formed, she was automatically acknowledged by the women of the world as their undisputed leader. Early in 1906, she attended what she suspected would be her last convention and told the delegates: "The fight must not stop. You must see it does not stop!" On her eighty-sixth birthday, she insisted on going to Washington to attend a dinner in her honor and ended her remarks by insisting, "Failure is impossible."
>
> It was success, however, that seemed impossible. When, as the result of a cold caught on the trip to Washington, she died on March 13, 1906, though the country flew its flags at half-mast in grief at her passing, she was eulogized as "The Champion of a Lost Cause."
>
> Thirteen years later, on May 21, 1919, the lost cause was won; an amendment giving women the full rights of citizenship was added to the United States Constitution. It was called the Susan B. Anthony Amendment.

Untermeyer does tell how and when Susan B. Anthony died, but he includes that information in the next-to-last paragraph. In the last paragraph he tells of an event after her death which symbolized the achievements of her life.

1. What is the purpose of the first paragraph in this biographical sketch? Would the sketch be as effective if Untermeyer had eliminated the first paragraph? Why or why not?

2. In the second paragraph, Untermeyer provides some information on Anthony's developing personality. Why does the writer include that information?

3. Untermeyer includes no information about the great battles of the Civil War. Why not?

4. In which sentences does Untermeyer show the impact of the Civil War and the Thirteenth and Fourteenth Amendments on Susan B. Anthony?

5. Would the sketch be as effective without the final paragraph? Why or why not?

CRITICAL THINKING:
Evaluating Information

When you make judgments about the relative value of information, you are using the critical thinking skill of *evaluation*. When you gather information for a biographical sketch, you develop a list of events and achievements, some of which are more important than others. You must evaluate the information on that list, judging whether each individual event or achievement is important enough to include in your sketch.

EXERCISE 24. Evaluating the Importance of Information. The following list of events and achievements is from the life of an imaginary person, a scientist. Evaluate the importance of the information, and divide it into two lists: minor events and achievements and major events and achievements. In evaluating the importance of the information, consider the writer's purpose. Be prepared to discuss your list in class.

Writer's purpose: To show the significance of the scientist's contributions to the scientific world and to society.

Events and Achievements:

4.0 grade average in high school
sixteenth-birthday party
4.0 grade average in college
named to *Who's Who*
became a gourmet cook
invited to make presentation before Congressional committee
a barbecue at the home of a friend
graduation from college, *summa cum laude*
Nobel Prize award ceremony
birth of first child
knee surgery
discovered a cure for cancer
married childhood sweetheart

received National Science Foundation Grant
elected president of college Science Club
death at age 37
appeared on television talk show
received Nobel Prize for Science
received second Nobel Prize
founded a scientific think tank
discovered an unknown bacterium
served in the Air Force
taught science at a university
applied for National Science Foundation grant

EXERCISE 25. Organizing a Biographical Sketch. Using the person you identified and the information you gathered in Exercise 21, evaluate the relative importance of events and achievements, and eliminate the minor ones from your list. Arrange the remaining events and achievements in chronological order under major periods in the person's life. Under each event or achievement, list any related details (physical characteristics, personality traits, setting) that should be included in the sketch.

WRITING

Writing Character Sketches and Biographical Sketches

19r. Write a first draft of your character sketch or biographical sketch.

Writing a First Draft of a Character Sketch

As you write the first draft of your character sketch, keep the following suggestions in mind:

1. When you begin your description, place the character in a setting that either reflects personality or serves as an effective contrasting background. Do not describe the setting in too much detail; a few brief strokes will do. Whenever possible, details of setting should be woven naturally into the rest of the sketch. Notice the brief, natural way in which Wolfe included details of setting in the sketch on pages 560–61.

2. Show your character in action. Show, for example, how the person walks, sits, gestures, and expresses anger, amusement, love, dislike, confusion, and so on. In the sketch by Wolfe, the reader discovers how the character *flung his provisions upon the kitchen table,* how *he would remove his coat and wash himself at the basin vigorously,* how *he would thrust his body against the door jamb and scratch his back energetically.*

3. Use dialogue to contribute to the total picture. Use idioms and expressions that would be characteristic of the person. The model character sketch on pages 560–61 includes only one paragraph in which the character actually speaks, but those few sentences demonstrate his dominant characteristic, "gusto."

4. Include vivid details of physical appearance. You cannot include everything about a person's physical appearance, so you must select the details that contribute most to the dominant impression you are trying to create. In describing features, use striking comparisons whenever possible, but avoid clichés. For help with figurative language, refer to pages 539–40.

5. In describing the setting and the appearance of the character, choose sensory details that will help the reader see, feel, hear, and smell. For additional ideas on how to use sensory details, refer to pages 535–38.

6. Pay special attention to word choice. Use specific and concrete nouns (not ''he wore a sweater,'' but ''he wore a red wool cardigan''). Use active and sharp verbs (not ''walked'' but ''ambled'' or ''strode'' or ''paced''). Use vivid adjectives too, but be careful not to overuse them.

EXERCISE 26. Writing a First Draft of a Character Sketch. Using the informal plan you developed in Exercise 23, write a first draft of a character sketch. Before you begin to write, review the suggestions just listed. Once you begin writing, concentrate on allowing your thoughts to flow freely. You will have an opportunity to check your organization and to give attention to detail when you revise.

Writing a First Draft of a Biographical Sketch

As you write the first draft of your biographical sketch, keep in mind the following suggestions:

1. In your opening paragraph, try to arouse the reader's interest. You might begin with an incident from the person's life, with a summary of the person's accomplishments, with background information related to the person's accomplishments, or with the person's birth. Notice how Untermeyer begins with background information in the sketch on page 562.

2. Include only the events and accomplishments that are significant in the person's life. Remember that they should be organized in chronological order according to the major periods in the person's life.

3. Since you will have a number of events to relate, be as concise as possible. Untermeyer dealt with Anthony's early childhood in one sentence. *Before she was five, precocious Susan could read and write* (page 562).

4. If there is any connection among the events—cause and effect, for example—be sure to show that connection. In Untermeyer's discussion of the Civil War years, he shows the effects of the Emancipation Proclamation on Anthony's campaign for women's rights (page 563).

5. If the person about whom you are writing is no longer alive, you may want to end the sketch with the event of the person's death or with a paragraph that summarizes or ties together the person's major accomplishments. Untermeyer's sketch ends after Anthony's death with the passage of the Susan B. Anthony Amendment (page 564). If the person is still alive, you may want to end with the most recent significant event, with a summary, or with some prediction of what the person might accomplish in the future.

EXERCISE 27. Writing a First Draft of a Biographical Sketch. Using the formal plan you developed in Exercise 25, write the first draft of your biographical sketch. As you write, try to follow your plan, and remember the suggestions for biographical sketches listed on page 558. Do not worry too much about details of organization at this time, however. You will be able to revise your paper later.

REVISING AND PROOFREADING

Revising and Proofreading Character Sketches and Biographical Sketches

19s. Revise and proofread your character sketch and your biographical sketch.

As with any other kind of writing, you should take time to revise your character sketches and biographical sketches. Whenever possible, allow some time between the writing and the revision, and share your draft with friends or classmates. Remember that good writers often revise several times. Proofreading and preparing a final copy are the last stages in the writing process.

The paragraph on the next page begins a character sketch. Think about the changes the writer has made in the first draft.

~~My~~ grandfather was ~~attractive, but he was~~ not handsome. He was too
even scrawny, *was stooped from years of working over a machine in a factory.*
thin ʌand he ~~stooped when he walked. My grandmother was crazy about him.~~
He was attractive, though, and
ʌI think his attractiveness came almost entirely from his personality. What
special   *ability to see the humor in life.*
made my grandfather ~~great~~ was his ~~sense of humor.~~ He was soft-spoken and
a twinkle in his eye and
gentle, but he always had ʌa ~~big~~ smile on his face.
bright

1. Why did the writer shorten the first sentence?
2. Why do you think the writer added the information about working in a factory?
3. Why did the writer eliminate the third sentence?
4. Why did the writer reverse the order of the last two sentences?
5. Why did the writer change the word *great* to *special* and add
the phrase "had a twinkle in his eye"?

GUIDELINES FOR REVISING CHARACTER SKETCHES

1. Is the character shown in action? Are gestures, movements, and
responses pictured vividly?

2. Is speech used effectively to reveal character and feeling?

3. Is the setting sketched in so that it helps the reader see the character?
Is the setting readily visualized?

4. Do the details of the description provide a clear sense of the dominant
characteristic of the character?

5. Does the description make an effective appeal to the senses? Do the
sensory images contribute to the total effect of the description?

6. Are precise, specific, and vivid words—nouns, verbs, and adjectives—
used effectively?

7. Has figurative language (similes and metaphors) been used to make
the description clearer and more colorful?

8. Is the tone of the character sketch appropriate for the subject, the
audience, and the purpose?

The paragraphs on the next page are from the middle of a biographical sketch about an imaginary photographer. Read them carefully, and
study the changes the writer has made in the first draft.

When he was twenty-four,
✓Harold Tinker sailed off to Europe, where he planned to establish his career in photography. After two years of adventure, the money he had inherited from his aunt had disappeared. He ~~had~~ visited cathedrals and museums and castles; he went to *dinner parties, tennis parties, all kinds of* parties. ~~He stayed in touch with his friends back in the United States, even flying home for a good friend's birthday party.~~ While in Europe he kept pace with the European jet set, *he had such wonderful adventures, that he* and had no time for photography.

and He was forced to take photography seriously. He went back to the *cathedrals and the castles,* sights with a *new* eye and determination; ~~His father had taken him to Washington Cathedral when he was a child, and he had never forgotten it.~~ *Still in need of money,* ✓Tinker turned his attention to the photography of people. The resulting collection *of photography* was published under the title *The Eye and the Spirit: Cathedrals and Castles of Western Europe.*

1. Why did the writer add the phrase to the first sentence?
2. Why was the second sentence moved to the beginning of the second paragraph?
3. Why did the writer eliminate the fourth sentence in the first paragraph and the third sentence in the second paragraph?
4. Why did the writer add details to explain the types of parties and the types of sights?
5. Why did the writer move the last sentence to an earlier position in the paragraph?

GUIDELINES FOR REVISING BIOGRAPHICAL SKETCHES

1. Does the beginning of the sketch arouse the reader's interest?
2. Does the sketch include only the *major* accomplishments and events in the person's life?
3. Have the events and accomplishments been arranged chronologically into blocks of time or periods in the person's life?
4. Is the tone of the writing appropriate for the purpose and the audience of the sketch?

5. Does the ending of the sketch satisfy the reader's need to know what happened to the person or where the person's life may be heading in the future?

EXERCISE 28. Revising and Proofreading Your Character Sketch. Using the Guidelines for Revising Character Sketches on page 569, the general Guidelines for Revising on pages 336–37, and the Guidelines for Proofreading on page 339, revise and proofread your character sketch. Follow the standards for manuscript preparation when you prepare your final copy.

EXERCISE 29. Revising and Proofreading Your Biographical Sketch. Using the Guidelines for Revising Biographical Sketches above, the general Guidelines for Revising on pages 336–37, and the Guidelines for Proofreading on page 339, revise and proofread your biographical sketch. Follow the standards for manuscript preparation when you make your final copy.

CHAPTER 19 WRITING REVIEW 1

Writing a Short Story. Write a short story about a struggle or conflict that is not physical. The struggle may be one character's need to make a difficult personal decision. The struggle might be between two characters, perhaps rivals for a political office, for the affection of a third person, or for some medal or award. Write the story from the third-person omniscient point of view.

PREWRITING Look through your journal, read the newspaper or watch television, brainstorm, or talk to other people to gather ideas for situations that could lead to struggles or conflicts. After you have selected a conflict, ask yourself questions about the conflict. What could happen? How could it happen? To whom could it happen? When could it happen? Why could it happen? Think about your leading character or characters and how you will reveal personality. Will you use action, description, dialogue, or all three? What details will you need to include? Organize your information according to what you will include in the beginning, the middle, and the end of the story.

WRITING Follow your plan as you write, but feel free to make changes as you go along. Try to create an interesting beginning and to build suspense or excitement toward the climax or high point of the action. When you are writing dialogue, try to make it brief, natural-sounding, and appropriate for your characters. Make sure that you maintain a consistent third-person omniscient point of view, and remember that the third-person omniscient narrator can know what is happening at any place at any time. Try to keep the actions in logical chronological order so that your readers will understand what is happening. Include any details of setting that are important to the plot.

REVISING AND PROOFREADING Try to give yourself a day or two away from the story before you begin revising. When you do revise, think about organization, character development, interest and suspense, and the beginning and ending. Use the revision guidelines on page 555. When you have completed your revisions and have a final draft, proofread it carefully. Use the Guidelines for Proofreading on page 339, and be sure to prepare a neat final copy.

CHAPTER 19 WRITING REVIEW 2

Writing Character Sketches and Biographical Sketches. Choose a real person who has made some significant contribution to society. The person may or may not be alive today. Write both a character sketch and a biographical sketch of that person.

PREWRITING Choose a person you have read about in a history class or someone you have read about in the newspaper or seen on TV. A subject might be someone from the field of entertainment or athletics; someone from the sciences or professions—a great judge, an astronaut, an educator; someone in the field of business; or someone in the military. Use the questions on pages 557–58 to gather information for both types of sketches. If your teacher has not identified an audience, select an audience that would have a natural interest in the person you are writing about. Organize the information for your character sketch around a dominant characteristic. Organize the information for your biographical sketch chronologically, according to the major periods in the person's life.

WRITING As you write your character sketch, keep the dominant characteristic in mind. Show your character in action, and use description as well as speech to reveal the person's character. Use sensory detail and vivid language to make your character sketch interesting.

As you write your biographical sketch, remember to concentrate on major periods of time and significant achievements. Try to arouse the reader's interest in the beginning. Make sure the ending satisfies the reader's need to know what happened to the person or where that person's life may be headed in the future.

REVISING AND PROOFREADING After you have written the sketches, ask a friend or classmate to read them and make suggestions for changes. Use the revision guidelines on pages 579–71 to check for the problems that might occur in these sketches. After you have completed your revisions, proofread carefully, and prepare a clean copy. Consult the Guidelines for Proofreading on page 339 and the standards for manuscript form on pages 339–40.

CHAPTER 20

Writing a Research Paper

RESEARCH, WRITING, DOCUMENTATION

The research, or library, paper is a relatively long factual paper based on outside sources rather than on your personal knowledge.

A research paper is generally written in language suitable for an educated audience. It tends to be somewhat formal in tone and usually does not include personal comments by the writer. In other ways, however, a research paper is much like any other composition. It should be interesting, well written, and appropriate for its intended audience.

Generally, there are two types of research papers. One brings together and summarizes information on a given topic. Such a paper is one that traces the history, general performance, and problems of women in the national military academies. The sample research paper on pages 603–11 of this chapter is the first type. The second type draws a conclusion from the information presented. This type of paper might answer a question such as "How effective are different approaches to rehabilitation in our prison systems?" Follow your teacher's directions about the type of paper you will write.

Preparing a research paper involves many steps, each of which may be confusing and time consuming. For this reason the steps are presented separately in this chapter, with examples and practice exercises at each stage. In this chapter you will study and practice the steps for writing a research paper.

PREWRITING

BEGINNING WITH A SUBJECT

20a. Begin with an interesting subject that is appropriate to your audience.

Some of the considerations for choosing a research paper subject are the same as those for other types of writing; others are specific to research papers. The following guidelines can help you to select an appropriate subject.

1. *Choose a subject that interests you.* Since preparing a research paper is likely to be time-consuming, choose a subject that you can live with. Also, with an interesting subject, you are more likely to write an effective paper.

2. *If possible, visit your school library before choosing a subject.* By looking through the card catalog's subject cards, you will find a wider selection of subjects than you might otherwise have had. You might also glance through some current magazines and newspapers for subject ideas.

3. *Choose a subject appropriate to your audience.* Unless your teacher specifies otherwise, your research paper will be written for a general audience, including your teacher and classmates. This audience would not be likely to find a technical subject that treats the microcircuitry in the nervous system of the porpoise greatly appealing. On the other hand, the same audience would probably find a subject about Cub Scout history too dull. Before choosing your subject, ask yourself these important questions about your audience: (1) What are their interests? (2) What do they already know? Then select a subject suitable for the interests and knowledge of the audience.

4. *Choose a subject for which there is sufficient information in your school library.* Before making a final decision about your subject, look in the card catalog for books your library has available on your subject. Then, after checking the *Readers' Guide to Periodical Literature* for articles about your subject, ask your librarian which of the periodicals containing the articles are carried by your library. (Many school libraries, for example, do not carry periodicals about highly technical subjects.) If there does not seem to be enough available material, select another subject.

5. *Choose a subject about which your library has current information.* For some subjects, such as new research into brain functions, it is important that the information be up-to-date. Again, check the card catalog and *Readers' Guide* to determine the recency of the library's information about your subject.

EXERCISE 1. Evaluating Subjects for Research. Each of the following subjects is a preliminary choice for a research report. Based on the guidelines for choosing subjects discussed in this section, which of the subjects do you find appropriate? (Assume that your paper is written for a general audience and that your only source of information is your school library.) Be prepared to explain why you do or do not feel that each of the subjects is appropriate for a high-school research report.

1. Discrimination against obese people in the United States
2. Operations in the mechanical drive of the Jarvik-7 artificial heart
3. Quality of life for artificial-heart transplant patients
4. Safe disposal of methyl isocyanate toxic waste
5. Simplified federal income-tax proposals
6. Effectiveness of hijacking-prevention procedures at major U.S. airports
7. Combating street-gang violence in large U.S. cities
8. Lengthening life through macrobiotic dieting
9. Job discrimination against attractive women
10. The new poor in America—the unemployed factory worker

EXERCISE 2. Selecting Subjects for Research. On a piece of paper, write down five preliminary subjects you might choose for a research paper. In making your choice, follow the guidelines on pages 575–76.

LIMITING THE SUBJECT TO A SUITABLE TOPIC

20b. Limit the subject to a topic that can be treated in sufficient detail.

In this textbook the word *subject* refers to a broad area. The word *topic* refers to a much more limited area that can be treated in detail given the length and scope of a piece of writing. In creating a limited topic, remember not only your audience and the resources of your library, but also the limitations of time and space. The general subject of the brain, for example, probably appeals to a wide audience, and it is likely that your library would have many sources with information about it. That subject, however, is obviously too large (a vast number of books have been written on it) and must be limited to a suitable topic. One limitation might be "position emission topography in brain research" (using radioactive substances called "isotopes" to track brain activity). Probably, however, your audience, with its limited general knowledge of the brain and of the radioactive substances called "isotopes," will have difficulty understanding your paper. Also, it is unlikely that your library will have adequate resources for developing this highly technical topic.

As you think about limiting your subject, remember that most subjects are too general for these reasons:

1. The subject covers too many years.

EXAMPLES Two hundred years of space research [Two hundred years is a long time. A suitable topic, which limits the time covered, is the space shuttle, a project developed only within the last twenty years.]

Woman's fashions through the years [*Years* may include every year since the beginning of time. One suitable limited topic is the "dress for success" movement among women during the 1980's.]

History of the United States Postal Service [This subject covers more than two hundred years. An example of a suitable topic is the use of technology (optical scanner, for example) in the postal service today.]

2. The subject covers too great a geographical distance.

EXAMPLES Public-housing problems in the United States [Every major city in the United States has housing supported by city, state, or federal funding; the subject is obviously too large. A suitably limited topic could focus on specific problems in one major city, perhaps your own.]

Fads among the world's teen-agers [Fads differ among teen-agers in such diverse areas as Europe, Asia, Africa, South America, and the United States. Limit the subject to a topic you can treat in enough detail to be interesting, perhaps one discussing the strange fads of American college students during the 1950's, such as swallowing goldfish and stuffing themselves into telephone booths.]

Human rights problems in Africa [*Human rights* is itself a broad subject, and Africa is the world's second-largest continent, having a great many separate countries. A suitably limited topic would be on the governmental policy of apartheid, strict racial segregation and discrimination, in South Africa.]

3. The subject has too many parts, or features.

EXAMPLES The brain [This subject includes such parts as the following ones: brain structure and chemistry, mental retardation, sensory perception, movement, mental illness, creativity, learning and memory, and sleep. An example of a topic that is limited to one part of the brain is the use of recent brain research to improve memory.]

Reducing accidents [Accidents can happen at home, on the job, in public buildings, on public or private transportation, or even in outer space. Limit this subject to one part for a topic such as improving safety records on U.S. commercial airlines.]

Long life [This broad subject includes such parts as people who have lived extraordinarily long lives, reasons for longevity, the practice of cell rejuvenation, and special diets for prolonging life. A limited topic from this subject might be a report on new research about how diet and exercise can prolong life.]

EXERCISE 3. Analyzing Broad Subjects.
Analyze each of the following subjects to decide why it is too broad for a high-school research report. Does the subject cover too many years or too great a distance? Does the subject have too many parts? (The subject may be too broad for a combination of these reasons.)

1. Personal computers
2. Bandits through history
3. High-school grading systems
4. The history of money
5. Americans and their pets
6. The dehumanizing effects of machines
7. Establishing antismoking laws
8. Problems of tampering with public food and medicine
9. Male and female roles in today's society
10. The world black market in video recordings

EXERCISE 4. Developing Limited Topics. From the list of subjects in Exercise 3, select three subjects of interest to you, or use three of the subjects you selected for Exercise 2. For each of the three subjects, develop three limited topics. Before deciding on the topics, think about your audience, the resources of your library, and the length of your paper.

GETTING AN OVERVIEW OF YOUR TOPIC

20c. Use library resources to gather general information about your topic.

The first step in gathering information for your research paper is getting a general overview of the topic. Your purpose is to determine what questions about your topic you want to answer through your research. You may know, for example, that you want to write about the brain's communication system—how signals that control or affect human thoughts, emotions, perceptions, and so on—are sent and received. By getting an overview of the topic, you can determine that you need answers to questions such as the following ones: (1) What roles do both electricity and chemicals play in the brain's communication system? (2) How is the structure of the nerve cell designed for efficient communication? (3) What happens when this vital communication system breaks down?

Begin your overview with sources such as encyclopedias, atlases, and almanacs that specialize in general information. Beginning with general information is especially important if the topic is new to you. Also, look through the subject cards of your library's card catalog for books on your topic. Then, after locating these books on the shelves, quickly scan the book covers, inside jacket flaps (if the book has a jacket), and indexes. For example, on the inside flap of a book titled *The Human Brain,* by Dick Gilling and Robin Brightwell, is the following information: "We meet a Los Angeles housewife who lives an apparently normal life but whose brain is divided into two completely separate halves, with astonishing effect upon her personality." Based on this information, you might pose questions such as, "What roles do the two halves of the brain play in the communication system?" or "How can communication continue when the two halves are split?"

An excellent source for general information on various topics is the *Readers' Guide to Periodical Literature.* This resource gives titles of articles on any number of subjects and topics and sometimes brief descriptions of the articles. Reading through titles on your topic may help you to develop questions for your research. For example, in a recent *Readers' Guide* entry under the subject heading "Word processing" is an article titled "Word Processing: A Road to Management." If your topic were about the field of word processing, you might ask yourself, "How are word processors used as management tools?" Then, in your research, you would look for answers to this question.

DEVELOPING A PURPOSE STATEMENT

20d. Once you know more about the specific information needed to develop your topic, write a purpose statement.

A *purpose statement* is simply one or more sentences that state what you plan to accomplish in your paper.

EXAMPLES I plan to list the causes of the 1984 drought in Ethiopia, Africa, and to discuss steps to prevent future droughts.

I intend to describe some of the serious safety problems in U.S. commercial aviation and to outline what should be done to make the airways safer.

I will explain the basic structure of the brain's nerve cells and discuss how the structure works to send signals back and forth through the brain.

Your purpose statement will not actually appear in your final paper. As you will recall, sentences beginning with phrases such as "I plan to describe . . ." are not effective beginnings for any type of writing. Also, during your research you will probably find or delete information that will change your purpose statement. You might, for example, add a description of the *effects* of the Ethiopian drought on the inhabitants of the country and so revise the purpose statement as follows:

I plan to list the causes of the 1984 drought in Ethiopia, Africa, to describe its effects on the inhabitants, and to discuss steps to prevent future droughts.

The purpose statement is an important part of preparing your research paper because it, like the overview of your topic, will make your research more efficient.

EXERCISE 5. Forming an Overview. For this exercise, select a limited topic for a research paper, perhaps one you developed for Exercise 4. Then follow these directions:

1. Find a general information article about your topic in an encyclopedia. (If you do not find the particular topic, try a slightly different aspect of it.) In two or three sentences, summarize the information about your topic contained in the article.
2. Look up your topic in the most recent issue of *Readers' Guide to Periodical Literature.* Look quickly through the articles about your topic, along with any descriptions of the articles. Then jot down the titles of any two articles that give you ideas of specific questions to answer in your research.
3. Using the subject cards in your library's card catalog, find at least two books on your topic. After locating each book on the shelves (substitute if you cannot find one or both books), scan the cover (front and back), jacket flaps (if there is a jacket), and the table of contents for each book. Then for each book, jot down at least one phrase or sentence that gives you ideas for questions to guide your research.

EXERCISE 6. Applying General Knowledge About Topics. Based on your work in Exercise 5, make a list of five specific questions you will attempt to answer through your research.

EXERCISE 7. Forming a Purpose Statement. Using the topic for which you have made an overview, write a purpose statement. Remember that the sentence or sentences state what you want to achieve in the paper, but they do not actually appear there.

DEVELOPING A PRELIMINARY OUTLINE

20e. Develop a preliminary outline to guide your research.

A preliminary outline, usually informal, is simply a list of topics to be covered in your paper in the order that you plan to cover them. The topics included in this first outline will come from the general information that you gathered during the overview stage and from the purpose statement that you phrased. The outline does not have to be detailed; its purpose, as with the overview, is to help guide and to organize your research.

20f. In developing the preliminary outline, consider the purpose of the paper.

The order of topics in your outline is the result of your paper's purpose. If, for example, you plan to discuss research on communication within the human brain, you might first discuss early research and then proceed chronologically to the present. If you plan to describe the structure of a nerve cell in the brain, you might describe how it appears under an electron microscope as your eye moves from one part of the cell to the other.

As you begin your research, you will find topics that do not belong in this preliminary outline and, as you learn new information, you will find topics that should be added to the outline. Throughout your research, then, you will be adding, deleting, and rearranging material in the preliminary outline.

The following example is a preliminary outline for a research paper on the topic of how brain cells send and receive information.

REACHING ACROSS THE GAP: COMMUNICATION IN THE HUMAN BRAIN

Early knowledge of brain function
    Heart as center of body
    Brain as center of body
Electricity as basis for brain communication
Chemicals as basis for brain communication
Basic nature of nerve cell
    Axon
    Dendrite
    Synapse
Breakdown of brain communication system
    Physical illness
    Mental illness
New research on brain communication system

Notice that this informal outline, unlike the formal outline, does not use a numbering system. Notice also that this outline is a topic, rather than sentence, outline. If your teacher prefers you to use a formal, sentence outline at this stage, review the information on preparing formal outlines in Chapter 16, pages 450-52.

EXERCISE 8. Developing a Preliminary Outline. As your teacher directs, use the topic for your research paper as the basis for this exercise. For your topic develop a preliminary outline, using information you gathered from the overview and from your purpose statement. Use the outline form your teacher prefers.

LOCATING SOURCES AND GATHERING INFORMATION

20g. Locate sources with specific information about your topic.

For the specific information necessary for detailed, interesting writing, you will need such sources as books, magazines, newspapers, journals, governmental and other types of pamphlets, film, radio, and television programs, and so on. You can often begin locating these sources through encyclopedias, where articles on various topics often refer readers to more specific sources. Books themselves usually list bibliographies of other sources on the same topics, and the subject cards in the library's card catalog can again be a valuable aid.

Once you have located a source, always evaluate it first for its usefulness. Is the material current enough for your purposes? (Check the date of copyright on the copyright page.) For example, if you are looking for information on the discovery in 1984 of the first new planet outside the earth's solar system, you could not use a book with a 1983 copyright date. Is the author of the article or book an expert in the field? Can the author be relied on to give you specific, accurate information? (Look for information on the author's credentials on the book cover or on the inside jacket flap.) Also, ask yourself whether or not the source covers any of the topics in your preliminary outline? If it does not, why do you think it will be helpful to you?

For additional help in using the library to locate information on your topic, review Chapter 29, pages 759–79.

COMPILING A WORKING BIBLIOGRAPHY

20h. Prepare a working bibliography.

A working bibliography is a list of sources you consult during your research. For convenience, keep entries in a working bibliography on separate note cards, one card for each source. Each of the cards should have all of the information illustrated below. This information will be extremely important as you prepare the final bibliography for your paper, so check the information carefully against the source. For a book, most of the necessary information appears on the title and copyright pages. General publishing information about a magazine (date, volume, issue) is usually found on the first two or three pages of the issue.

EXAMPLES   *Working bibliography card for a book*

Working bibliography card for an article

Number bibliography cards consecutively in the upper-right corner. Later, when taking notes, you can identify the source of each note by simply repeating the bibliography card source number on the note card. Under the source number on the bibliography card, write each book's call number, if it has one, so that you can easily locate it. At the bottom of the card, write any special information you might need to relocate the source easily.

EXERCISE 9. Evaluating Sources. Using your limited topic, locate at least three books and two magazine articles that give specific information about it. For each source, answer the following questions:

1. What is the copyright date? Is the information current enough for your purposes? If not, why not?
2. Is the author an authority on the subject? What reasons do you have for believing that the information in the source is both specific and accurate?
3. Does the book or article cover one or more topics listed on your preliminary outline? If so, on what pages of the book or article will you find treatment of the specific topic? If the source does not cover a topic on your outline, can it help you to achieve the purpose of your paper? How?

EXERCISE 10. Preparing Bibliography Cards. For each of your sources in Exercise 9, prepare a working bibliography card. For each card, provide the information shown in the examples on page 584.

TAKING NOTES FROM YOUR SOURCES

20i. Take notes on material that relates directly to a topic or subtopic in your preliminary outline.

At this point, discard sources that do not relate to your outline topics or that cannot help you achieve the purpose of your paper. Once you have decided on sources, use note cards as a convenience in recording information. For each note on a different topic or subtopic, use a new card. Change cards also when you move to a different source. Suppose, for example, that your paper is on the topic, "the role of the Confederate secret service during the Civil War." From your first source, an article in *American Heritage* magazine, you take notes on a first-person account of a Confederate soldier who served in his side's secret service. This particular note card is about the attempt on the part of the Confederacy to bring Britain into the war against the

Unionists. In another source, *The American Civil War* by Peter Parish, you read about the same topic—the Confederate attempt to bring Britain into the war. Even though each source treats the same topic, use one note card for the article source and one for the book.

Before taking notes, read quickly over the relevant material in each source. This will help you to absorb general information.

There are three ways to take notes:

1. *Summarize.* Summarize when you need to capture only the main ideas on some information. In summarizing, use your own words.

2. *Paraphrase.* Paraphrase when you want to record all of the ideas in a passage. Again, use your own words.

3. *Quote.* Quote when the author's language, as well as ideas, is important. Copy the author's material word for word.

For more information on summarizing and paraphrasing, review pages 853–57 in Chapter 33.

When quoting material directly, always check your notes against the original material to be certain that you have copied exactly. On your note card, include the exact page or pages from which you have quoted; place quotation marks around the author's exact words.

On each note card, place the same circled number that appears in the upper right-hand corner of the appropriate bibliography card. In the upper left-hand corner, write the name of the topic or subtopic from your outline with which the card deals. (This line is sometimes referred to as the *slug.*) Then, before summarizing, paraphrasing, or quoting, write the page number or numbers from which the material has been taken.

EXAMPLE

Mental illness ②

Schizophrenia may be caused by "overheated" circuits — too many messages sent and received

page 222

EXERCISE 11. Evaluating Notes. For this exercise, refer to the preliminary outline on brain communication on page 582. Then read the note card, on the same topic, that appears below. Based on the topics and subtopics listed in the preliminary outline, is this an appropriate note to have taken? Be prepared to explain your answer.

Happiness ⑧

Too many articles published in newspapers and magazines make Americans believe they should always be happy. This belief — one of the big problems in our society   page 16

EXERCISE 12. Taking Notes. As your teacher directs, take notes on your sources about your topic. Be prepared to indicate, for each note card, whether you have summarized, paraphrased, or quoted the material. Prepare your note cards as directed in the previous section. Follow these directions:

1. Place a circled number in the upper right-hand corner of the card that corresponds to the source number of the appropriate bibliography card.
2. In the upper left-hand corner, identify the topic or subtopic of your preliminary outline that you are treating in the note card.
3. In the bottom right-hand corner, write the page number or numbers from which you take the material.
4. Summarize, paraphrase, or quote the material as it best suits the purpose of your paper.

Indicating Sources on Note Cards

Giving authors credit for their words and ideas is called documentation. Failing to document constitutes plagiarism. (The word *plagiarism* comes from a Latin word meaning "kidnapper.") Whether you summarize, paraphrase, or quote, you must still acknowledge words and ideas that are not your own. It is not necessary, however, to acknowledge the following information:

1. *Information that is general knowledge.* This is information that can easily be found in general reference sources such as dictionaries and encyclopedias. (*Plagiarism* comes from a Latin word meaning "kidnapper." The capital of Mexico is Mexico City.)

2. *Information that most educated people know.* (The brain is made up of nerve cells. Snow is formed when particles of water vapor freeze in the upper air and fall to the ground.)

3. *Information you routinely acquire from public sources such as radio, television, magazines, and newspapers.* (The winter of 1978 was one of the coldest in Chicago's history. Future plans for space shuttles include retrieving communications satellites of various governments.)

In preparing your note cards, be scrupulous in recording source information and page references. Also, in the beginning stages of research paper writing, remember that a good policy to follow is, "When in doubt, document."

PREPARING THE FINAL OUTLINE

20j. Prepare a final outline from which you will write your paper.

A final outline, from which the first draft of your paper is written, is usually a formal outline. (Formal outlines are discussed on pages 450–52 of Chapter 16.) Topics and subtopics of formal outlines are identified with Roman numerals, capital letters, and Arabic numerals, although the outlines may consist of either topics or sentences. (Ask your teacher whether you should prepare a topic or a sentence outline.) As you begin to prepare your final outline, read over your note cards, looking for notes that fall into general categories. Then give each of these categories a heading. For example, a stack of note cards dealing with the early history of research in brain communication might have the heading, "Early history." Next, plan the content of your paper's introduction and conclusion. The words *introduction* and *conclusion* do not actually appear in your outline; instead, the first and last headings will identify the content of those important parts of your paper.

As mentioned earlier, your final outline, because of unrelated material you discarded during your research or new information you learned, will differ from your preliminary outline. However, the final outline, based on the specific material you have located, should have many more details than the preliminary outline. The following example is a final outline for the research paper on brain communication. What are the differences between this outline and the preliminary outline that appears on page 582 of this chapter?

REACHING ACROSS THE GAP: COMMUNICATION IN THE HUMAN BRAIN

I. Early knowledge of human brain
   A. Early belief in heart as center of life
   B. Later discovery of brain as center
II. Knowledge of brain communication process
   A. Galvani's discovery of electricity's role
   B. Woewi's discovery of chemical role
III. Nerve cells as center of brain communication
   A. Structure of cell
     1. Nucleus
     2. Axon
     3. Dendrites
   B. Importance of synapse
     1. Role of electricity
     2. Role of chemicals
IV. Breakdown in brain communication system
   A. Results
     1. Physical illness
     2. Mental illness
   B. Causes
V. New research in brain communication
   A. Research into development of synapses
   B. Applications of knowledge for improving quality of human life

EXERCISE 13. Classifying Note Cards.   Sort through the note cards you have prepared for your research paper, making at least three stacks. Then give each of the three stacks a general heading that describes its contents. Next, decide on the content of your introduction and conclusion, and also give each of these parts a heading. On a piece of paper, write, in the order that you plan to present them, the headings that you have prepared.

EXERCISE 14. Preparing a Final Outline. After studying the material on outlines on pages 588–89, prepare a final outline for your research paper. Before you begin, study the example of a final outline on page 589.

REVIEW EXERCISE A. Analyzing the Steps in Planning a Research Paper. In this chapter each of the steps in planning a research paper is taught in its appropriate order. As your teacher directs, discuss problems you might encounter by omitting or changing any of the steps listed below.

1. Beginning with an interesting subject
2. Limiting the subject to a suitable topic
3. Getting an overview of the topic
4. Developing a purpose statement
5. Developing a preliminary outline
6. Locating sources and gathering information
7. Compiling a working bibliography
8. Taking notes from the sources
9. Preparing the final outline

WRITING

WRITING THE FIRST DRAFT

20k. Know the parts of a research paper.

A research paper consists of the following parts:

1. The paper itself, with an appropriate title
2. Some sort of credit, or documentation, for material used. This documentation may take the form of notes within the paper, called *internal* or *parenthetical* notes, notes at the bottom of each page, called *footnotes,* or notes at the end of the paper, called *endnotes* (these other forms of documentation are discussed in the 1984 edition of the handbook published by the Modern Language Association of America).
3. A bibliography, usually placed at the end of the paper on a separate page, in which you list the sources you have used in preparing the paper

20l. Know the correct form to use for the research paper.

The form of a research paper is the style in which it is prepared. Form usually includes such aspects as how sources are documented, how pages are numbered, how the bibliography is presented, and so on. The form described in this chapter is that of the Modern Language Association of America (MLA), a highly respected organization of English language and literature scholars. There are, however, other acceptable formats for preparing research papers; your teacher may prefer that you use one of these optional styles.

20m. Begin with a rough draft.

The purpose of a rough draft is to record in some appropriate order, on paper, the material that supports your purpose statement. Before you begin this first draft, organize your note cards so that the topics and subtopics follow your final outline. The order in which you arrange your material should be appropriate for the ideas you present. (Ordering ideas is discussed in Chapter 16, pages 459–62.) Once again, discard any material that does not relate to the topics or subtopics of your final outline.

As you write, you may find that each topic or subtopic in your outline develops easily into one or sometimes two paragraphs. Other times, however, you will find that you lack sufficient details on a particular topic and must do more research. If so, stop immediately and gather the additional information.

In writing your rough draft, you should pay particular attention to two matters of format: documenting sources and incorporating quotations.

Documenting Sources

The latest *MLA Handbook* recommends that sources be given in parentheses following the summarized, paraphrased, or quoted material. This parenthetical information is usually very brief; its main purpose is to refer the reader to the more complete source information in the bibliography at the end of the paper. If your teacher approves, use the following MLA guidelines to document sources within your paper:

1. When you use an author's words or ideas, follow them with a pair of parentheses in which you place the author's last name and the page number or numbers from which the information was taken.

592 < Writing a Research Paper

(Remember that complete information about the source is included in the bibliography.) Notice that there is no punctuation between the author's last name and the page reference. Notice also that the words *page, pages,* or their abbreviations do not appear in the parentheses. Place your final punctuation mark after the parentheses. Follow quoted material with closing quotation marks. Then insert the parenthetical information, followed by the closing punctuation mark.

EXAMPLE   The Spanish neurologist Santiago y Cajal once referred to each of the individual cells that make up this network as "the aristocrat among the structures of the body, with its giant arm stretched out like the tentacles of an octopus" (Restak 26).

2. If your bibliography has two or more entries by authors with the same last names, use both the first and last names of each author.

EXAMPLES   (Richard Restak 26)
               (John Restak 93)

3. If a source has two authors, use both last names. If there are more than two, give the last name of the first author listed in the source, followed by the Latin abbreviation *et al.* (and others). Do not use punctuation between *et al.* and the page reference.

EXAMPLES   (Ornstein and Thompson 134–138)
               (Roby et al. 22)

4. If the author's name is used within the text of your paper, you may need only to add parenthetical page numbers to identify the location of the material you used.

EXAMPLE   Ornstein and Thompson point out that the connections that seem actually to determine the quality of life are not simple: "The mind cannot exist in a single identified nerve cell, or even in many thousands of them; it is the product of the interaction among the myriad neurons in the vertebrate brain" (81).

5. Parenthetical information about your source is best placed at the end of the sentence that contains the information, but it should be as close as possible to the material to which it refers. End punctuation for the phrase, clause, or sentence containing the parentheses follows the parentheses.

EXAMPLE This electrical force, Galvani believed, was produced by the brain and stored in the nerve for later use (Restak 31). It seemed that this electrical current, which the French writer Montaigne described as a "miraculous force," was used to send signals by the brain throughout the body (Restak 30).

Before you begin writing your rough draft, study the sample research paper on pages 603–11 for more examples of the documentation described above.

EXERCISE 15. **Preparing Documentation.** Each of the following pieces of material is followed by information about its source. On a piece of paper, follow the directions to summarize, paraphrase, or quote each of the items. Then, in parentheses, place the necessary information about the item's source, as you would in preparing an actual research paper. Information given here about the source may be more than you will actually use.

1. Summarize the following information on internal body rhythms.

   Changes occur routinely in the body throughout the day. One's temperature, for example, reaches a peak early in the evening and a low early in the morning. The level of the hormone cortisol is lowest after midnight and starts to rise again at around 4:00 a.m., whereas the level of the hormone melatonin rises during the night and falls at dawn. Short-term memory deteriorates as the day proceeds, but long-term memory improves. (This excerpt is from an article by Joseph Alper titled, "Biology and Mental Illness," published in *Atlantic Monthly* magazine, December 1984. The material appearing here is from page 72 of that article.)

2. Paraphrase the following information about phobias. Use one quotation from the material.

   He has also found that fear of snakes is fairly general in primates and in man, "but it is difficult to exclude the role of tradition in the origins of this fear," he adds. There is said to be little such fear in two-year-olds, but "by the age of 3 1/2 some caution has appeared and the snake might be only tentatively touched. Definite fear of snakes was often present after the age of four; increased to the age of six (at which stage it is then present in one-third of British children) and then declined to the age of 14. This prevalence is striking when one considers how small the actual danger is from snakes in the British Isles."

(The *he* referred to in this passage is Dr. Isaac Marks, a British psychiatrist and expert on phobias. The excerpt is from pages 17–18 of a book by Fraser Kent, titled *Nothing to Fear: Coping With Phobias.*)

3. Summarize the following information on the history of medicine in the United States. In your summary, use at least one quotation.

> Most ailments were, in the terminology of the day, "self-limited." In the great majority of cases a patient could expect to recover—with or without the physician's ministrations. This was understood and acted upon; even the wealthy did not ordinarily call a physician immediately except in the case of severe injury or an illness with an abrupt and alarming onset. The decision to seek medical help would be made gradually; first a family member might be consulted, then a neighbor, finally perhaps a storekeeper who stocked drugs and patent medicines—all before turning to a doctor. Many housewives kept "recipe books" that included everything from recipes for apple pie and soap to remedies for rheumatism and croup. Guides to "domestic practice" were a staple for publishers and peddlers. It is no wonder that doctors a century ago were so critical of the care provided by what they dismissed as uneducated and irresponsible laymen. (This selection is from page 24 of an article by Charles E. Rosenberg, appearing in the October/November 1984 issue of *American Heritage* magazine.)

Incorporating Quotations

When you use quotations, they should be worked into the general text of your paper. The MLA gives the following guidelines for using quotations:

1. Use quotations sparingly, only when the author's words, as well as ideas, are important.

2. Copy the quotation exactly as it appears in the source, including capitalization and punctuation. Place quotation marks around the author's exact words.

3. If the quotation is a short piece of prose (four lines or less), run it into your text. Remember that you do not always have to quote whole sentences. You may quote only a word or phrase that you place within your own sentence.

EXAMPLE   Joseph Jacobs Thorndike describes his ancestor of eight generations back, George Jacobs. In Salem, Massachusetts, in 1692, Jacobs was accused of witchcraft and brought to court before examining magistrates. As he confronted his accusers, Jacobs said, "You tax me for a wizard. You may as well tax me for a buzzard" (Thorndike 82).

4. Long prose quotations (more than four lines) are set off from the text. Indent the quotation ten spaces from your paper's left margin, without using quotation marks. Introduce the quotation in your own words, followed by a colon. Even if the quotation is a complete paragraph, do not indent the first line.

EXAMPLE In her book *An Unfinished Woman,* Lillian Hellman describes how, as a child, she learned, while sitting in a fig tree, the pleasures of reading:

> It was in that tree that I learned to read, filled with the passions that can only come to the bookish, grasping, very young, bewildered by almost all of what I read, sweating in the attempt to understand a world of adults I fled from in real life but desperately wanted to join in books. (I did not connect the grown men and women in literature with the grown men and women I saw around me. They were, to me, another species) (84).

20n. Remember to use paragraph- and essay-writing skills.

Because there are many technical points involved in writing a research paper, it is sometimes difficult to remember to apply the same paragraph- and essay-writing skills that you would with other types of writing. Your research paper should have an interesting and effective introduction and conclusion; ideas should be arranged in a logical order; and transitions between paragraphs should be smooth. In addition, each topic should be developed with sufficient specific details to make the writing interesting. (Chapter 16, pages 429–74, presents material on writing effective compositions.)

EXERCISE 16. Evaluating a First Draft.   The first draft on the next page is the first two paragraphs of the sample research paper on brain communication. As you read the paragraphs, be prepared to discuss the following questions:

1. How closely does the documentation of sources within the paper follow MLA format? What inaccuracies, if any, are there in the documentation?

2. How accurately, according to MLA format, are quotations placed within the text? What mistakes are there in the use of quotations?

3. Do these paragraphs display effective paragraph- and essay-writing skills? Is the introduction effective? Are ideas arranged in a logical order? How effective are transitions between sentences? Are the transitions between paragraphs smoothly achieved? Is the topic of each paragraph developed with sufficient, specific detail? (Before answering these questions, your teacher may wish you to review the material on pages 454–66.) Be prepared to give reasons for your answers.

4. Are any details included in these two paragraphs of the rough draft that should be omitted because they do not relate to topics in the final outline on page 589? If so, what are the details?

5. What specific suggestions do you have for revising these two paragraphs?

REACHING ACROSS THE GAP:
COMMUNICATION IN THE HUMAN BRAIN

Little was known about the function of the brain until after the 14th century. It was only then that scientists finally understood the basic function of the brain. Before then, scientists believed that the heart, in the center of the body, was the organ that controlled thoughts and feelings. It was an early observation that when the heart stopped beating, the body became cold. The heart had provided heat to all parts of the body. Then scientists learned that blood vessels from the heart went to all parts of the body. Today, scientists know so much about the heart that heart transplants can be performed. (Restak, *The Brain,* pp. 21–24.)

Scientists learned that the brain controlled thoughts and emotions, but how did the brain send this information? Scientists also knew that the brain and the body were made up of individual cells. How did communication take place between the cells? In the 18th century Galvani used the muscles of frogs to show that living creatures contained electricity. (Even then animals were used for scientific experimentation.) It seemed that this electrical current, which the French writer Montaigne described as a "miraculous force" (Restak, 30), could be used to send signals throughout the body. Galvani was not the first to know about electrical forces in living creatures. Pictures on ancient Egyptian tombs proved that Egyptians knew about electric catfish.

EXERCISE 17. Writing a First Draft. Following your final outline, write the first draft for your research paper. Begin by organizing your note cards so that they follow topics as they are listed in your final outline. Follow the MLA format described in this chapter for documenting sources and for incorporating quotations into your text. As you write, pay particular attention to the paragraph- and essay-writing skills you have learned in the composition chapters of this textbook. Before you begin, study the Guidelines for Preparing a Research Paper on page 602.

REVISING

REVISING THE FIRST DRAFT

20o. Revise the first draft for content, organization, and style.

In your first revision, concentrate mostly on content and organization. Think again about details that may not support the purpose of your paper or about topics that lack sufficient supporting details. Are details within a paragraph arranged in a logical order? Are paragraphs arranged in a logical order? Consider your audience once again. Have you given them information they need to understand your topic? Have you defined technical terms they are not likely to know?

The guidelines on page 602 will be helpful to you in revising your first draft.

EXERCISE 18. Evaluating a Revision.   Reread the first two paragraphs of the first draft for the sample research paper, "Reaching Across the Gap: Communication in the Human Brain," that appear on page 596. Then read the corresponding two paragraphs on pages 603–604. As you compare the two versions, prepare to discuss the following questions:

1. What material was deleted from the first draft? Why do you think this was done?
2. In the final draft, what material was added? Did the additions improve the paragraphs? Why?
3. What are several instances in which the wording of phrases, clauses, or sentences was changed from the first to the final draft? How did the rewording help to improve the paragraphs?
4. How effective were transitions between sentences in the first draft? How were transitions improved in the final draft? Give specific examples.
5. How effective was the transition between the two paragraphs in the first draft? How was this transition improved in the final draft?

EXERCISE 19. Revising the First Draft. After reviewing once again the Guidelines for Preparing a Research Report, page 602, revise the first draft of your research paper. Before you begin, you may also wish to review pages 334–37 of Chapter 13 for explanations and examples of revision.

PREPARING A FINAL VERSION

PREPARING THE FINAL COPY

20p. Proofread the final draft. Prepare a clean copy in correct manuscript form.

Preparing the final copy of your paper consists of two stages: proofreading and preparing a clean copy.

Proofreading

Proofreading means checking your paper for inaccuracies in usage and mechanics and then correcting them. The terms *revision* and *proofreading* are sometimes used with the same meaning, but they are very different. Revision is usually the major rewriting that you do to improve the content, organization, and style of your paper. Proofreading is done mostly to correct words and is done after revision is complete.

EXERCISE 20. Proofreading the Final Draft. For this exercise, review the material on proofreading on pages 337–39 in Chapter 13. Using the proofreading guidelines on page 339, check your final draft for inaccuracies in usage and mechanics. As your teacher directs, insert corrections into the final draft.

Preparing a Clean Copy

As your teacher directs, rewrite your final draft, incorporating the changes you made at the proofreading stage. As you prepare this clean copy, use the MLA guidelines on the next page.

1. Type or write your paper neatly and legibly on one side of acceptable paper.

2. Leave one-inch margins at the bottom and sides of your pages and a two-inch margin at the top.

3. Double-space throughout, including title, quotations, and bibliography.

4. As your teacher directs, place your name, information about your class, and the date one inch from the top of the first page, even with the left margin. Double-space between these lines. The title is centered with double-spacing between the information at the top of the page and the title. Double-space again between the title and the first line of your paper. Do not put quotation marks around your title.

5. Number pages consecutively throughout your paper, including bibliography pages. Place page numbers in the upper right-hand corner of each page, one-half inch below the top of the page and fairly close to the right margin. Use a number with or without the words *page*, *pages,* or their abbreviations.

EXERCISE 21. Preparing a Clean Copy.   Prepare a clean copy of your final draft. Follow the MLA guidelines listed in the previous sections or any other guidelines your teacher may prefer. Before handing in this copy, proofread once again. If your teacher permits, insert brief (and very neat) corrections into the clean copy. If you have many corrections, you may need to recopy the paper a second time.

PREPARING THE BIBLIOGRAPHY

20q. A final bibliography is a list of sources you have consulted in preparing your research paper.

The bibliography gives the reader complete information about sources you have listed within your paper. Do not include in your bibliography general reference sources, such as encyclopedias, that you used in your overview. The MLA guidelines for preparing a bibliography follow:

1. Begin the bibliography on a separate page from the text of the paper itself. Continue numbering pages from the text. For example, if your research paper ends on page 13, then the first page of your bibliography will be page 14.

2. Center the word *Bibliography* one inch from the top of the page.

3. Double-space between the title *Bibliography* and the first entry. Begin the first entry even with the left margin. If the entry runs more than one line, indent all other lines five spaces from the left margin. Double-space all lines in entries and double-space between entries.

EXAMPLES Alper, Joseph. "Biology and Mental Illness." <u>Atlantic Monthly</u> Dec. 1984: 70–76.

              Andreasen, Nancy C. <u>The Broken Brain: The Biological Revolution in Psychiatry</u>. New York: Harper & Row, 1984.

4. For books, give information in the following order: author's name, book title, place of publication, name of publisher, and date of publication. Alphabetize entries by the author's last name, followed by a comma and then his or her first name. Place a period after the author's name and skip two spaces before the book's title. Underline the title, placing a period after it. Then skip two spaces and write the city of publication (if more than one city appears on the copyright page, use the first city listed), followed by a colon and the name of the publishing company. Follow this name with a comma and the year of publication. End every entry with a period.

EXAMPLE Andreasen, Nancy C. <u>The Broken Brain: The Biological Revolution in Psychiatry</u>. New York: Harper & Row, 1984.

For a book by two or more authors, list the names as they are shown on the title page (not necessarily alphabetized). Reverse only the name of the first author, and add a comma.

EXAMPLE Wender, Paul H., and Donald F. Klein. <u>Mind, Mood, and Medicine: A Guide to the New Biopsychiatry</u>. New York: Farrar Straus Giroux, 1981.

5. For articles from magazines published every week or every two weeks, you need the following information: the author's name (last name first); the title of the article (in quotation marks); the title of the periodical (underlined); the day, month (abbreviated), and the year of the issue; a colon, a space, and the page number or numbers of the article. Place periods after the author's name, after the title of the article, and at the end of the entry.

EXAMPLE Shreve, Anita. "The Working Mother as a Role Model." New York Times Magazine 9 Sept. 1984: 39–54.

6. For magazines published monthly, give the month or months of publication and the year, but not the day.

EXAMPLE Alper, Joseph. "Biology and Mental Illness." The Atlantic Dec. 1984: 70–76.

7. For newspapers (daily), follow the format for articles published every week or two weeks. If the newspaper appears in sections and each section begins numbering anew, add the section number followed by a colon and the page number or numbers. (See the final entry of the sample research paper bibliography on page 611 of this chapter.)

EXERCISE 22. Preparing a Bibliography. On a sheet of paper, center the heading "Bibliography" (without quotation marks) as the MLA guidelines direct. Then prepare a final bibliography that lists each of the following sources. Alphabetize the entries and use the MLA format for entry content, format, and punctuation.

1. A book by Isaac Asimov published by Houghton Mifflin (Boston) in 1984 titled *Opus 300*
2. An article by Victoria Horstmann titled "Career Metamorphosis," published in the magazine *Working Woman* in the May, 1984, issue on pages 114–117
3. A book published in 1980 by Harcourt Brace Jovanovich (Orlando) titled *A Double Discovery: A Journey,* written by Jessamyn West
4. An article by Herbert R. Lottman published in the weekly periodical *Publishers Weekly* titled "What's New in France's Publishing Capital," appearing on pages 22–40 of the November 9, 1984, issue
5. A book titled *The Careful Writer: A Modern Guide to English Usage,* published by Atheneum (New York) in 1984 and written by Theodore M. Bernstein

EXERCISE 23. Preparing a Final Bibliography. Using your working bibliography cards, prepare the final bibliography for your research paper. Before you begin, study the sample bibliography on page 611 of this chapter. Use the MLA format described in this chapter.

GUIDELINES FOR PREPARING A RESEARCH PAPER

PREWRITING

1. Is the subject interesting and appropriate to the audience?
2. Is the subject one for which there is sufficient and current information?
3. Is the subject limited to a topic suitable to the audience, the available resources, and the length of the paper?
4. Is there an appropriate overview and purpose statement?
5. Does a preliminary outline list topics to be covered in the order in which they will be treated?
6. Are the sources with specific information evaluated for their usefulness? Is the information current, specific, and accurate?
7. Is a working bibliography card prepared for each source? Does the card give author, title, and publication data, as well as a source number?
8. Is the material for notes summarized, paraphrased, or quoted? Is a new card used for notes on each topic, subtopic, or source?
9. Does a final outline list in detail topics to be covered in the paper? Have the words *introduction* and *conclusion* been avoided in the outline?

WRITING AND REVISING

10. Begin the rough draft by organizing note cards into major categories. Follow the final outline in writing the draft.
11. Incorporate sources into the rough draft by using parenthetical information. Follow the MLA guidelines or one your teacher prefers.
12. Incorporate quotations into the text if they are short; otherwise set them off from the text.
13. In writing the paper, use paragraph- and essay-writing skills described in the composition chapters of this textbook.
14. Evaluate your first draft according to these guidelines. Revise the first draft for content, organization, and style.
15. Using the Guidelines for Proofreading on page 339, proofread and correct the final draft.
16. Prepare a clean copy, using the MLA format or one your teacher prefers.
17. According to the appropriate format, prepare a bibliography that lists (other than general reference materials) the sources you consulted in preparing your paper.

A Sample Research Paper

REACHING ACROSS THE GAP:
COMMUNICATION IN THE HUMAN BRAIN

For thousands of years, the mysterious organ known as the brain has been a source of wonder. Protected as it is by the thick bones of the skull, the brain has never been easily studied. In fact, so little was known about the brain that it was not until after the fourteenth century that its basic function was finally understood. Before that time, most scholars believed that the heart, in the center of the body, controlled thoughts and feelings. This belief was reinforced by the early observation that when the heart stopped beating, life stopped, and the body became cold. Such an event seemed to show that the heart, during life, had provided heat to all parts of the body and was thus central to its being. Also, by the fifteenth century, scientists had learned, through dissection, that blood vessels coming from the heart spread out into all parts of the body. Again, this design seemed to confirm the central role of the heart in human life (Restak 21–24).

Only by the eighteenth century did scientists learn that the brain, not the heart, determined thoughts, emotions, movements, and so on. By then they also knew that, in some way, the brain received and processed information from all over the body and then sent back "directions" for action. In addition, scientists, who had known for some time that the brain, like the rest of the body, was made up of individual cells, reasoned that communication was somehow taking place between the cells. The knowledge that remained missing for many more years was exactly how this

leave one-inch margins at top, sides, and bottom; center title; double-space between title and first word of text; double-space paper throughout

parenthetical information includes author's last name and page reference communication was accomplished. How did the brain, in less than a split second, receive a message from a finger touching a red-hot iron and then return the message to the finger, telling it to move? Even more baffling, how did the brain send and receive information that caused one person to behave "normally" and another to hear voices and see images that were not there? The beginning of an answer to these questions lay in, of all things, the leg of a frog.

In the late eighteenth century an Italian scientist named Luigi Galvani, using the leg muscles of frogs, showed that the bodies of living creatures contained electricity. He demonstrated this belief by exposing the muscles on either leg of a frog. When one exposed muscle was placed against another, the second muscle twitched, obviously in response to a force coming from the first muscle. This electrical force, Galvani believed, was produced by the brain and stored in the nerves for later use (Restak 31). It seemed that this electrical current, which the French writer Montaigne described as a "miraculous force," was used to send signals by the brain throughout the body (Restak 30).

Thanks in large part to the work of Galvani, scientists were getting closer to understanding the mystery of communication within the brain. By the end of the nineteenth century, they knew that electricity flowed within the brain and between the brain and other parts of the body, but they still were not certain how information was actually carried by the current. To complicate matters still further, an Austrian scientist named Otto Woewi demonstrated, in 1921, a new piece of information to be fitted into the puzzle. Working with the still-

[margin notes:]
this and the next paragraph develop the second major topic of the final outline

source

source

beating hearts of two newly killed frogs, Woewi showed that brain communication involved chemicals as well as electricity. To prove his point, he placed the two hearts, each still connected to a nerve leading to the brain, into a fluid. Then, in one of the hearts, he stimulated the attached nerve. In a living frog, this particular nerve would send a message to the brain and back, telling the heart rate to slow down. In the heart kept alive by the fluid, the message also arrived, and the heart rate slowed down. As the first heart slowed, Woewi removed some of its surrounding fluid and mixed that fluid with the fluid surrounding the second heart. As the two fluids mixed, the second heart slowed down also. Woewi's explanation, one widely accepted by scientists, was that the brain, in response to a signal from the first heart's nerve, had caused the heart to release a chemical. This chemical had caused the slowdown in the first heart and also in the second heart when the fluid containing the chemical was transferred (Gilling and Brightwell 128).

note the two authors for this source

Brain communication, it was discovered, involves both electricity and chemicals. This electrochemical process begins in each of the ten billion or more nerve cells that make up the brain. Each nerve cell, or *neuron,* consists of a *nucleus,* or center, and a number of fibers. Each cell body has one long, thick fiber called an *axon.* At the other end of the cell, however, numerous, small hair-like fibers called *dendrites* (from the Greek word for "tree") branch out in all directions toward other cells. Under a powerful microscope, this network of fibers, both axons and dendrites, is clearly visible. The Spanish neurologist Santiago Ramon y Cajal once referred to each of the

the words "brain communication" are used as a transition between the previous paragraph and this one individual cells that make up this network as "the aristocrat among the structures of the body, with its giant arms stretched out like the tentacles of an octopus" (Restak 267). Nerve cells within this network do not actually touch each other, however. Instead, each cell is separated from other cells by a gap called the *synapse*. It is across this synapse that communication within the brain actually takes place (Ornstein and Thompson 68).

incorporate quotations into your text, unless more than five lines

final punctuation for this sentence is placed after the parentheses

Communication from cell to cell begins when an electrical impulse travels down the axon of one cell to the synapse. At the synapse (from the Greek word for "handshake"), small sacks of chemicals, called *neurotransmitters* ("neuro" for nerve; "transmitters" for carriers), are stored. Under the right conditions, the sacks of chemicals are released. Once they burst from their sacks, they flow across the synapse to the dendrites of the second cell. In this way the electrical impulse that travels down the axon is translated to a chemical impulse when it reaches the synapse. Upon reaching the second cell, however, the chemical signal is translated back into an electrical impulse (Ornstein and Thompson 77–79).

source

The second cell, the receiver of the electrochemical signal, may or may not respond to the signal sent by the first cell. If it does respond, the cell sends an electrical impulse down its own axon, where the signal is ferried across the synapse in the form of a chemical impulse, and so on. The response of the receiver cell is crucial because without it no communication, and thus no movement, thought, emotion, and so on, takes place.

Spreading into all parts of the body, nerve cells, through electrochemical impulses, send to and receive from the brain the vital information on which life depends. When this communication system works normally, most people give little thought to it. They make up a bed and feed the dog, change oil in a car, decipher a complex math problem, perhaps even compose a piece of music for the guitar. However, if enough parts of this complex system break down or otherwise malfunction, the system can no longer be taken for granted. In fact, if the problem is serious enough, illness may result. One kind of breakdown, for example, occurs when cells in one particular part of the brain become overly sensitive to impulses from other cells and fire too often themselves. As a result, signals are sent so fast and furiously throughout this part of the brain that the brain cannot process them. The person undergoing this electrochemical "storm" goes into convulsions, often falling unconscious to the ground (Andreasen 185). Epilepsy, as this disease is called, has been known at least since the time of Julius Caesar (who himself was epileptic), but only recently have scientists understood the role of the brain's communication system in the disease.

    Another kind of breakdown in the brain communication system results in a condition known as Parkinson's disease. This illness, which most often afflicts older people, causes severe tremor and stiffness throughout the body. Victims of Parkinson's have difficulty beginning or completing any movement, even so simple a one as walking. Scientists now know that a particular part of the brain controls movement, and that a breakdown in this area results in Parkinson's disease. The malfunction is in the chemical messenger, or neurotransmitter, used in this movement area to send and receive signals. In Parkinson's disease

source

this information is easily available in general reference sources victims, there seems to be a lack of the chemical messenger used to ferry messages across the synapses. With this low level of neurotransmitters, cells do not receive strong enough signals and so do not fire properly. Thus, appropriate signals back and forth from the brain to the body that would ordinarily control body movement are neither sent nor received (Andreasen 28–29).   source

Researchers now think that breakdowns in the electrochemical system may result in mental as well as physical illnesses. One of the most serious mental illnesses thought to be caused at least partly by such a breakdown is schizophrenia. This disease, in which patients suffer from such wildly confused thoughts and emotions that they often cannot function outside a hospital, has been known throughout history. Descriptions of the disease, in fact, were found written on papyrus in ancient Egyptian tombs. During the Dark Ages, schizophrenics, who often have hallucinations, seeing and hearing things that are not there, were often burned as witches or demons. Even in more enlightened times, they have been chained, beaten, starved, and otherwise mistreated, only because they were the unfortunate victims of a disease no one understood. Real hope for sufferers of schizophrenia finally surfaced in the 1950's. It was then that scientists, who already knew about the chemical messenger that works in the movement center of the brain, discovered that this same messenger also acts in the part of the brain controlling emotions and personality. Since these areas—emotions and personality—are the first to be affected in schizophrenia, scientists assumed that a malfunction in the chemical messenger also played a role in schizophrenia (Restak 289–291).   source

Researchers are not exactly sure how it happens, but in cases of schizophrenia, there seems to be too much chemical messenger activity in the brain. Rather than failing to fire and send signals, schizophrenic cells fire when they should not, sending too many signals. Patients are thus getting a wildly confusing input of signals—thoughts, feelings, sights, sounds, smells, and so on (Gilling and Brightwell 154–155).

source

Unfortunately, most researchers today believe that the breakdowns that may lead to physical and mental illnesses are more complex than a simple deficiency or excess of a particular chemical messenger. It might be that the cells receiving the messenger are too easily stimulated by the chemical, thus firing too often and sending too many signals. Another possibility has to do with what happens to the chemical messenger after it has carried its signal across the synapse. Normally, the neurotransmitter is reabsorbed by the first cell or broken down by an enzyme. If this process does not work, the excess chemical will continue signaling cells to fire (Restak 288–292). To complicate matters even further, certain researchers believe that a change in any one chemical messenger might affect other neurotransmitters. Even a slight change in the production of one of these chemicals can throw an entire part of the system into chaos (Alper 427). Obviously, this interrelationship means that the system is much more complex than has yet been imagined. It might also mean that a true cure for diseases caused by breakdowns in the electrochemical system is much further away than researchers had hoped.

source

source

In their continuing efforts to unravel the remaining mysteries of the brain's communication system, scientists have looked closely at the nerve cells themselves—how they develop and how they mature. Because the synapses, pathways across which cells communicate, seem so vitally important, they have been of special interest to researchers. For some time scientists have known that all of the nerve cells that the human brain will ever have are formed by the time of birth. From that point on, the human brain is unable to replace damaged or dead cells.

Although the brain does not develop new nerve cells, scientists have discovered that it can establish new synapses, thus creating pathways for new and more complex information to travel through the brain. It is the number and complexity of these synapses, researchers are beginning to believe, that determines the intellectual and emotional richness of life. The connections that seem actually to determine the quality of life are not simple: "The mind cannot exist in a single identified nerve cell, or even in many thousands of them; it is the product of the interaction among the myriad neurons in the vertebrate brain" (Ornstein and Thompson 81).   source

The new pathways in the brain—particular nerve cells and synapses across which electrochemicals move—are formed only when there is sensory stimulation from the environment. Thus, an environment rich in sights, sounds, smells, tastes and textures, one that stimulates thinking and feeling, can actually lead to a more complex brain, capable of a much richer quality of life (Ornstein and Thompson 81).   source

Further research on the brain is almost certain to be on the brain's electrochemical communication system. A better knowledge of how this system works will help scientists to understand better how the brain develops and how it functions to control and affect thoughts, feelings, and sensory information from the outside world. Perhaps, understanding the brain and its communication system can help us to provide the richness and quality of environment that seem the right of every human being.

the last paragraph, the conclusion, develops the final subtopic of the final outline

A Sample Bibliography

BIBLIOGRAPHY

Allen, Oliver E. "The State of Medical Care, 1984: An Interview with Dr. David E. Rogers." *American Heritage* Oct.–Nov. 1984: 32–40.

Alper, Joseph. "Biology and Mental Illness." *Atlantic Monthly* Dec. 1984: 70–76.

Andreasen, Nancy C. *The Broken Brain: The Biological Revolution in Psychiatry.* New York: Harper & Row, 1984.

Gilling, Dick, and Robin Brightwell. *The Human Brain.* New York: Facts on File Publications, 1982.

Ornstein, Robert, and Richard F. Thompson. *The Amazing Brain.* Boston: Houghton Mifflin, 1984.

Restak, Richard. *The Brain.* Toronto: Bantam, 1984.

Wender, Paul H., and Donald F. Klein. *Mind, Mood, and Medicine: A Guide to the New Biopsychiatry.* New York: Farrar Straus Giroux, 1981.

Wolfson, Jill, "Increased Funding Adds Troops to Battle Against Alzheimer's." *Chicago Tribune* 22 July 1984, sec. 6: 1+.

(*Note:* When you study this sample bibliography, refer to pages 600–602. The "1+" in the last entry indicates that the article begins on page one of section six and continues on following pages.)

Helpful Hints for Research Papers

1. Do not return any of the sources you may have used until your fina' draft is complete. As you write, you will probably find information on your note cards that is incomplete or that needs additional checking.

2. As you prepare working bibliography cards, double-check the spelling of such items as authors' names, titles of books and magazines, and names of publishing companies against your original sources. Then, when you transfer the information to your final bibliography, you will need only to check the same information against your bibliography cards.

3. As you insert names of authors and page numbers into your rough draft, check the spellings of authors' names and page numbers against the original sources.

4. In preparing note cards, use special symbols, such as a star (*), to indicate notes you especially want to use. These may include particularly interesting quotations or important definitions.

5. Keep a good dictionary nearby, and use it for more than checking the spelling or definitions of words. For example, the writer of the sample research paper on pages 603–11 needed to understand the basic nature of electricity. This information is concisely explained in a good dictionary under the entry for "electricity."

6. Be especially careful in checking the spelling of foreign words and the meaning and spelling of technical terms. Remember that it is extremely easy to miscopy such items as numbers and dates. Check these carefully in your original sources.

7. Before you begin work on your paper, make a chart for yourself that outlines the steps involved (for example, choosing and limiting the subject, developing an overview of the topic, locating sources and gathering information, filling out bibliography cards). If your teacher has given you a deadline for each step, make a note of those dates. Then check off each step as you complete it.

8. If possible, make a copy of your paper for yourself before handing it in. In this way you not only protect yourself against loss of your paper but also have a model to study for next year's paper.

REVIEW EXERCISE B. Evaluating Your Work in Writing a Research Paper. The following comments are ones your teacher or classmates might make in response to your research paper. Beneath each comment is a list of possible reasons that might have led to the comment. As a means of self-evaluation, first decide whether or not each comment could possibly apply to your paper. If the comment could apply, which of the reasons could have led to the comment? What changes would you need to make to correct the problem?

1. The paper lacks specific detail.
   a. subject too limited

b. no purpose statement formed
c. not enough information gathered on subject
2. This is a poor choice of subject.
   a. audience and purpose not sufficiently analyzed
   b. library resources on subject inadequate
   c. subject uninteresting to writer or audience
3. The paper lacks organization.
   a. note cards not classified according to some logical order
   b. preliminary outline not revised
   c. final outline not followed in rough draft
4. The purpose of this paper is not clear.
   a. purpose statement not formed
   b. overview of topic skipped
   c. preliminary outline not revised
5. The paper is not interesting.
   a. topic inappropriate for audience and purpose
   b. library lacking current information on topic
   c. insufficient gathering of information
6. The use of source material is poor.
   a. too much quoted material
   b. paraphrased material too much in author's own words
   c. main ideas missing in summarized material
7. The relationship of ideas is not clear.
   a. effective transition lacking between sentences
   b. effective transition lacking between paragraphs
   c. ideas not arranged in logical order
8. This paper does not conform to MLA format.
   a. internal documentation incorrect
   b. bibliographic form incorrect
   c. pages not numbered correctly
9. The writing in this paper is weak.
   a. paper lacks effective introduction and conclusion
   b. other paragraph- and essay-writing skills not applied
   c. too little time allowed for revision
10. This paper has many problems in grammar and mechanics.
    a. paper not proofread
    b. too little time allowed for proofreading
    c. specific criteria for proofreading not used

CHAPTER 21

Writing Business Letters

FORM AND CONTENT OF BUSINESS CORRESPONDENCE

A letter speaks for you in your absence. To do its job of representing you well, it must be clear, appropriate in tone, and attractive in appearance. Let us consider these three important qualities individually.

Clarity. Remember that you will not be present when your letter is being read to explain what you mean. The reader will not be able to ask you to clarify your meaning. Obviously, then, you must make your message unmistakably clear. It goes without saying that your letter should be legible, whether handwritten or typewritten.

Tone. When speaking face-to-face with someone, you use your tone of voice to reflect shades of meaning and attitude. Writing, too, has a tone, reflected largely in the words you choose. What will your letter sound like to the recipient? First, be sure that it sounds like you—that it speaks with your voice. Second, be sure that the tone will neither anger nor offend. Unlike spoken words, which are often readily forgotten, letters are permanent records of what you have said.

PREWRITING

APPEARANCE AND FORM OF A BUSINESS LETTER

Appearance and form are the "good manners" of letter writing. This chapter explains the conventions of letter-writing form. If you follow them carefully, even though they may seem unimportant to you now, your letter will have a much better chance of making a good impression. A letter that is neat, free of errors, and in good form will do a fine job of representing you—just as your speech and personal appearance do in a face-to-face relationship.

21a. Observe standard practice in writing business letters.

A business letter is usually written to a firm or an individual in a firm. It must be a combination of clearness, brevity, and courtesy.

Appearance and Stationery

Proper stationery is the first important consideration in a business letter. You should type your letter, if possible, on the usual $8\frac{1}{2} \times 11$-inch plain white paper. The typewritten letter is more legible and therefore more quickly read than a handwritten one. If you write the letter by hand, use the same stationery as for a typewritten letter. Also, remember to write carefully; your best penmanship is a courtesy you owe to anyone to whom you are writing.

Form

The form of a business letter follows a certain pattern. Whether your letter is typewritten or handwritten, the pattern is the same. The semiblock form is used in the illustrations which you will find later in this chapter; however, the full block and the block forms are also acceptable, and an illustration of these forms is also given.

The Letter Picture

Three frequently used forms for the business letter are the full block, the block, and the semiblock. In the full block all typed material is flush with the left-hand margin, and paragraphs are not indented. Such a form is easiest for the typist, since there is no indentation to worry about. Some object to it, however, because it seems unbalanced to the left. The only difference between the block and the full block is the

Model Business-Letter Forms

placement of the heading, closing, and signature; in the block style these are placed just to the right of the center. The semiblock style is similar to the block except that it uses paragraph indentation.

Before beginning your letter, judge the amount of space it will occupy on the page you are using. Center it as nearly as possible by making sure you have approximately the same margin at the top of your page as at the bottom, and the same margin on both the left- and right-hand sides. Never run your letter off the page at the right-hand side, and never finish the body of your letter at the end of a page so that you have nothing left for the second page except the complimentary close and your signature. If the letter is to be very short, it will look better on smaller stationery. Use the $5\frac{1}{2} \times 8\frac{1}{2}$-inch size, which is also acceptable for business letters. For a model letter see page 618.

1. Heading

To begin your business letter, always put your *complete* address and the full date in the upper right-hand corner, beginning no less than one inch from the top of the page. It is better to write this heading without abbreviations.

EXAMPLES   49 Surrey Lane
               Clinton, Iowa   57232
               June 4, 1986

               RFD 4
               Cross Corners, Oklahoma   73028
               September 27, 1986

2. Inside Address

Business firms file copies of the letters they write. Since the copies are filed under the name of the person or firm to which they are written, standard form requires an inside address on every business letter.

The inside address should be placed at the left-hand side of the page, flush with the margin and several spaces (at least four, if the letter is typewritten) lower on the page than the heading. It should include the full name of the company to which you are writing, as well as its full address. If you are writing to an individual in the firm, use the full name and title, with a comma between the two if they are on the same line; if the name and title are too long to be put on one line, put the title on the next line.

EXAMPLES   The Helen Mills Company
               220–224 Center Street
               Waukegan, Illinois   60085

               Ms. Marjorie Berg, Vice-President
               Newland and Company
               40 Fifth Avenue
               Lewiston, Maine   04240

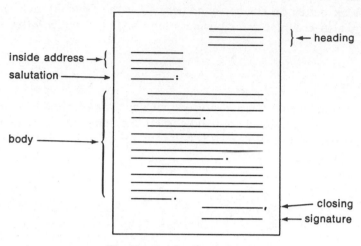

The Parts of a Business Letter

Mr. Reginald B. Macpherson
Secretary to the President
Wilbur Field and Sons
218 South Street
Fort Hamilton, Virginia   24437

Mrs. Susan Barlow, Principal
Lakeview High School
Lakeview, Michigan   48850

3. Salutation

The salutation is placed two spaces below the last line of the inside address and flush with the margin. When writing to an individual within the firm, the correct salutation is *Dear Mr. . . . (Mrs., Ms.,* or *Miss)* followed by a colon. If you are writing to a professional man or woman, use the title instead:

EXAMPLES   Dear Dr. Grayce:
                  Dear President Tyson:

Sometimes you may be writing to an entire group or company, or to an officer whose name you do not know. You may have just "Personnel Department," "President," or "Editor" on the first line of the inside address. You may use an impersonal salutation *(Editor, Personnel Department)* or the traditional salutation *(Dear Sir, Gentlemen)* followed by a colon.

In using traditional salutations it is understood that the group you are writing to may be composed of both men and women.

4. Body

The form of the body of a business letter is the form followed in the body of any letter. A double space is used between paragraphs of a typed letter. If your typewritten letter is short (seven lines or less), you may either put it on a smaller sheet of stationery or double-space the entire body of the letter on 8½ × 11-inch stationery.

5. Closing

The closing of a letter comes between the body of the letter and the signature. In business letters, appropriate closings are limited. *Very truly yours, Yours truly,* and *Yours very truly* are the ones most frequently used. *Sincerely yours* and *Yours sincerely* are also correct. The closing is placed just to the right of the center of the page, two spaces below the last line of the body of your letter. It is followed by a comma.

Avoid ending your letter with an outmoded phrase such as "I beg to remain," "Hoping to hear from you soon, I am," or "Thanking you in advance, I am . . ." End the body of your letter with a *period,* and then begin your closing.

EXAMPLES Very truly yours,
Yours truly,
Sincerely yours,

6. Signature

Sign your full name to your letter. Do *not* put *Mr.* or *Mrs.* or *Ms.* before your name. An unmarried woman writing to a stranger may choose to put *Miss* in parentheses before her signature.

EXAMPLE *(Miss) Margaret Hoyt*

A married woman signs her full name, and if she wishes, she may put her married name in parentheses directly below her signature.

EXAMPLE *Elsie M. Rhoad*
(Mrs. Robert L. Rhoad)

A signature should always be handwritten. If your letter is typewritten, type your name below your signature, flush with the first letter of the closing and far enough below to allow room for your signature.

7. Envelope

For a letter on small stationery, use a small envelope (be sure the letter fits it). A letter on small single-sheet stationery is usually folded twice unless it fits into the envelope without any folding. The folds are made in this way: up from the bottom about a third of the way, then down from the top, so that when it is unfolded it will be right side up for the reader. Note paper or personal stationery is usually folded in half and inserted into the envelope with the fold at the bottom.

Either a small or a large envelope may be used for a letter on large single-sheet stationery. If a large envelope is used, the folding is the same as that of a small sheet for a small envelope. If the envelope is small, fold your letter up from the bottom to within a quarter of an inch of the top; then fold the right side over a third of the way; finally, fold the left side over. Insert in the envelope with the fold at the bottom of the envelope.

Your envelope should carry the same address as the inside address of the letter and also your own name and full address. You may put your return address on the back of the envelope, but the post office prefers that you put the return address in the upper left-hand corner of the envelope on the same side as the address to which it is going. Unless the address to which a letter is being sent is very long, you

Folding the Letter

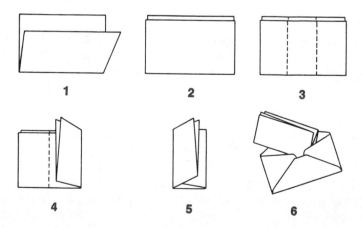

1   2   3

4   5   6

Model Envelope

```
Theodora Jonas
303 Clayton Street
Huntington, West Virginia 25703



              Executive Secretary
              Chamber of Commerce
              Mystic, Connecticut 06355
```

should start it about halfway down the envelope and place it midway between the ends.

The post office also requests that you use your ZIP code number in both the address to which the letter is going and in your return address. The ZIP code should appear on the last line of the address, following the city and state, with a double space left between the last letter of the state and first digit of the code. A comma should *not* be inserted between the state name and ZIP code. Note the examples in the models shown on this and on the following page.

CONTENT OF THE BUSINESS LETTER

Clarity, tone, and form are important in the business letter, since business letters are customarily sent to firms or individuals who do not know you and who have a large amount of mail to handle. No matter how routine your communication is, be sure that your letter speaks well of you.

Even though the tone will be formal, you still should strive for naturalness and simplicity of expression. Come right to the point in your letter; avoid wordy beginnings. Make sure you have supplied all the necessary information. Never use the old-fashioned clichés of business correspondence. Be very certain that you do not close with the expression, "Thanking you in advance." Such a phrase presumes that the recipient will grant your request and seems to indicate that you are too lazy to write a separate thank-you note if some special favor is received.

WRITING

TYPES OF BUSINESS LETTERS

The Request Letter

You have had and will continue to have many occasions to write letters of request: sending for a college catalog, requesting a free pamphlet, arranging for a speaker to talk to your club. First, be reasonable in your requests. If you are asking for information, be very specific about what you want. Do not make yourself look ridiculous by asking, "Please send me all you have about national parks and camping grounds." If asking for a free pamphlet, request only that number which you personally can use. If arranging for a speaker, be sure to write in plenty of time and give all information necessary about time, place, and audience.

Second, be courteous in the phrasing of your request. While you should avoid the "thanking you in advance" expression dicussed previously, it is good form to conclude the request letter with a polite acknowledgment like: "I shall certainly appreciate any help you can give me with this request." Finally, make your request simple and clear. Companies handling a large volume of mail cannot afford to waste time reading lengthy, chatty letters.

Model Request Letter

76 Brixton Place
Phoenix, Arizona   85008
July 8, 1986

Model Airways, Inc.
410–12 Second Avenue
Flagstaff, Arizona   86001

Mail Order Department:

Will you please send me a copy of your latest catalog on model planes?   I have three of your models and would like to add some of the later ones to my collection.

Very truly yours,

Frank Tyndall

Frank Tyndall

EXERCISE 1. Writing a Request Letter. Write to a college, asking for its catalog. If you think the catalog may not include all the information you need, ask specifically for whatever you wish to know.

Another type of request letter is the kind you write when you ask a firm to send a representative to your school for a specific purpose. This kind of letter is a little more complicated to write, because it is *you* who have to give the company information before they reply. Remember to include all the details necessary for the company's complete understanding of the situation.

EXERCISE 2. Writing a Request Letter. Copy in proper form the business letter given below.

420 Jackson Avenue, Iola, Texas 77861, January 8, 1986. Miss R. F. Hawkins, Business Manager, Perry and Company, 480–96 Fuller Street, Fort Worth, Texas 76104. Dear Miss Hawkins: Our junior class of 170 pupils in the Iola High School is to decide this month on our class rings and pins. We expect to have representatives from several companies here on Monday, January 21, to show us samples of the rings and pins their firms make, together with price lists. We'd like very much to have someone from your company here on that date, if possible. Your representative should come to Room 31, any time after 2:45 P.M. Very truly yours, Sarah Porter, Secretary of the Junior Class, Iola High School.

EXERCISE 3. Writing a Request Letter. Using the following information, set up this material in the form of a business letter. You must compose the letter.

Ms. Elsie Dowing of 22 Twin Oaks Road, Carlsburg, Ohio 43316, writes on April 6, 1986, to the George C. Buckeye Company, 240 Lexington Avenue, Cleveland, Ohio 44102, stating that while shopping there the week before, she lost a valuable gold ring. It contained a diamond and two pearls in an old-fashioned setting. She would like to know if it has been found and if so, where she may call for it.

EXERCISE 4. Writing a Request Letter. As head of the student assembly program, you wish to have a neighboring high school send its glee club to perform in one of your assembly periods. Give the time, date, place, length of program, type of song selection (if you wish), and any other information you think is necessary.

EXERCISE 5. Writing a Request Letter. You are interested in art. There is an exhibit to be given in the high-school auditorium of a nearby city. Write to the art department of the high school, requesting information. Ask specific questions about what you want to know—time, admission price, dates of the exhibit, etc.

The Order Letter

If you are writing an order letter, you should list the items you wish, one below the other, with complete information (catalog number, style, size, price, etc.) about each item. The price should be put at the

Model Order Letter

---

                              58 Crane Street
                              Canton, Iowa 52542
                              December 1, 1986

Webb and Sons
140-156 Seventh Avenue
Des Moines, Iowa 50311

Gentlemen:

        I should like to order the following arti-
cles, as advertised in the Des Moines Register
of November 29.

2 white silk scarves, fringed, one with black
    initials A.J., the other with red initials
    M.W., @ $7.98 $15.96
1 size 15-34 Supercron white shirt   16.50
                          Postage   1.20
                          Total $33.66

        I am enclosing a check for $33.66 to cover
the total amount.

                              Very truly yours,

                              Amy Ladd

                              Amy Ladd

---

right-hand side (flush with the right-hand margin), and each amount should be placed directly under the one above, to make it easier to add the prices. List the cost of shipping, if you know it, and include it in the total, unless you know the firm pays for it. Be sure to specify how the articles are to be paid for—check, C.O.D., etc.

EXERCISE 6. Writing an Order Letter. Write a letter to Marshall Field and Company, 111 North Street, Chicago, Illinois 60602, ordering 2 long-sleeved cotton blouses, size 14, 1 plain white, the other French blue, at $10.98, 1 green "Betty-Jo" dress, size 13, at $17.95. Have them sent C.O.D.

EXERCISE 7. Writing an Order Letter. Write to Ritz Camera Center, 1147A Sixth Avenue, New York, N.Y. 10036, a letter ordering the following items: 1 Star D Model D–18 tripod, price $19.75; 3 rolls 35 mm Kodachrome film at $3.50 a roll. Include $1.50 postage. You are enclosing a money order for the amount.

The Letter of Application

The letter of application is one with which you have no doubt had very little experience to date. However, you soon may find that it is one of the most important types of business letters, for it is in the application letter that you try to convince an employer to hire you.

When you apply for a position, your letter of application comes before your personal interview with your prospective employer. It is the first contact the two of you have. Therefore, you must "put yourself across" in a way that will suggest confidence that you can do the job called for. You will also have an added advantage if you can put some original, personal touch into your letter (but only if it comes naturally to you) to distinguish you, favorably, from the rest of the applications this employer may be considering.

Remember to include the following information:

1. Include a statement of the position you are applying for and how you learned about it.

2. Show that you know what qualifications are needed and that you believe you can fill them. State your age, experience, and education.

3. Give references as to your character and ability.

4. Request an interview at the employer's convenience.

Model Letter of Application

---

98 Oxford Street
St. Cloud, Minnesota 56303
April 2, 1986

Mrs. O. A. Lester, Director
Camp Carlson
Oneidaga Lake
Big Pines, Minnesota 56680

Dear Mrs. Lester:

Ben Nichols, one of your regular campers, told me this week that you have a vacancy for a swimming counselor on your camp staff this summer, and I would like to apply for the position.

I am a senior at St. Cloud High School and am eighteen years old. For the last two years I have been the junior swimming counselor at Camp Winnebega, Cauhoga Falls, Wisconsin. I have just received my Examiner's badge in lifesaving and am now certified for the position of senior swimming counselor. If you have junior or senior life-saving classes, I am also qualified to direct them.

The following people have given me permission to use their names as references:

Mrs. J. B. Morse, Director, Camp Winnebega, Cauhoga Falls, Wisconsin.

Mr. Chester Roberts, Principal, St. Cloud High School, St. Cloud, Minnesota.

I will be glad to come for a personal interview at your convenience.

Sincerely yours,

Francine Larson

Francine Larson

EXERCISE 8. Writing a Letter of Application. You have learned from a friend that a couple she knows in another city are looking for a high-school student to spend the summer with their family at their summer home. They want the student to take care of three children, ages two, four, and six. Write to the couple (make up a name and address) and apply for this job. State your qualifications. Try to make your letter interesting as well as informative.

EXERCISE 9. Writing a Letter of Application. A drugstore in a neighboring town needs someone to deliver orders from 4:00 to 6:00 P.M. schooldays and all day Saturdays. Write your letter of application.

☞ **NOTE** The United States Postal Service recommends the use of two-letter codes for states, the District of Columbia, and Puerto Rico. The service also recommends the use of nine-digit ZIP codes. When you use these codes, the address on business correspondence should look like this: **EXAMPLE** Ms. Laura Baverman
72 White Plains Boulevard
Dallas, TX 75231-2424

The two-letter code is in capital letters and is never followed by a period. Refer to the following list of two-letter codes.

Alabama AL	Kansas KS
Alaska AK	Kentucky KY
Arizona AZ	Louisiana LA
Arkansas AR	Maine ME
California CA	Maryland MD
Colorado CO	Massachusetts MA
Connecticut CT	Michigan MI
Delaware DE	Minnesota MN
District of Columbia DC	Mississippi MS
Florida FL	Missouri MO
Georgia GA	Montana MT
Hawaii HI	Nebraska NE
Idaho ID	Nevada NV
Illinois IL	New Hampshire NH
Indiana IN	New Jersey NJ
Iowa IA	New Mexico NM

New York NY
North Carolina NC
North Dakota ND
Ohio OH
Oklahoma OK
Oregon OR
Pennsylvania PA
Puerto Rico PR
Rhode Island RI
South Carolina SC

South Dakota SD
Tennessee TN
Texas TX
Utah UT
Vermont VT
Virginia VA
Washington WA
West Virginia WV
Wisconsin WI
Wyoming WY

GUIDELINES FOR WRITING AND REVISING LETTERS

1. Is the letter attractive? Is the form correct, with each of the parts correctly placed?
2. Does the heading give the complete address and the full date? Are commas used to separate the city from the state and the day of the month from the year?
3. Is the inside address accurate, complete, and properly spaced?
4. Is the salutation appropriate? Is it followed by a colon?
5. In the body of the letter, are sentences grammatically correct and accurately punctuated? Are all words correctly spelled? Is paragraphing used properly?
6. Is the closing appropriate? Does the first word begin with a capital letter? Do the other words begin with a small letter? Does a comma follow the closing?
7. Is there consistent use of block or semiblock style in the letter? Is block style used on the envelope? Is the address on the envelope identical with the inside address on the letter?
8. Is the address on the envelope accurate, complete, and attractively placed?
9. Has the letter been folded to fit the envelope?
10. Is the return address on the envelope?

CHAPTER 22

Effective Diction

THE MEANINGS AND USES
OF WORDS

The quality of the words you select to express your ideas is just as important in composition as the quality of your sentence structure. The words you choose constitute your diction. For years, your teachers have urged you to enlarge your vocabulary. A large vocabulary is indeed a great asset in both reading and writing. But the acquisition of a large vocabulary, acquiring control of a number of big words, is only one way to improve your diction. It is not a guarantee of effective expression, because the effectiveness of a word does not depend on the number of its syllables or its rareness. The best word to use is always the one that conveys the exact meaning you intend. This chapter will help you to explore the levels of word meanings and to select your words wisely when you write.

SEMANTICS: THE MEANINGS OF WORDS

Linguistics is the science of language. One of its most interesting branches is called *semantics*. In semantics, you study the meanings of words and the changes in word meanings.

A word is a symbol. Like any other symbol, a word has no meaning for you unless you know what it stands for. The thing or idea that a word stands for, or refers to, is known as its *referent*. You are able to understand a word only if you know what its referent is. The referent of a word should be the same for the person using the word as for the person reading or hearing it. When two persons each have in mind a different referent for the same word, the word is useless for communication between them until they recognize the problem and agree on the same referent.

If your teacher says, "Please give me the chalk," you immediately understand the request. You know what action *give* refers to, whom *me* refers to, and what the symbol *chalk* refers to. Had your teacher said, "Please give me the *glub*," however, you would have been confused. *Glub,* which looks and sounds like a word, is not customarily used to refer to anything. Since for you it has no referent, it is not, so far as you are concerned, a word at all.

Concrete Words

Words, like other areas of study, may be divided into groups. Two groups of words are *concrete* words and *abstract* words. A concrete word is one whose referent can be touched or seen: *book, cloud, car, chalk.* An abstract word is one whose referent is an idea, something which cannot be touched or seen: *peace, need, love, freedom.*

Concrete words vary in definiteness. For example, the word *vehicle,* while its referent is something which can be seen and touched, is not at all specific. You probably do not have a clear mental picture of a *vehicle.* The word *car* is more specific; the term *station wagon* is still more specific. "John was driving a dilapidated vehicle" will not convey as clear a picture as "John was driving a dilapidated station wagon." As description, the second sentence is clearer. In all your writing, whenever you are considering several different words to express a particular meaning, select the most specific one.

EXERCISE 1. Classifying Words According to Definiteness. Arrange the words in each group so that the word with the least specific referent will come first, and the word with the most specific referent will come last.

1. seat, desk chair, chair, furniture, swivel chair
2. quadruped, creature, mammal, spaniel, dog
3. fruit juice, drink, lemonade, juice, liquid

4. storm at sea, typhoon, occurrence, storm
5. laborer, carpenter, employee, human being, woman

EXERCISE 2. Classifying General and Specific Words. For each of the following general words, list three words which have a more specific referent.

1. food 　 3. elevation 　 5. educational institution
2. boat 　 4. reward 　 6. restaurant

Abstract Words

Abstract words, which usually refer to general ideas, must always be used with care. A great many misunderstandings are caused by abstract words that have not been carefully defined. Unless two persons agree on the meaning (referent) of an abstract word, communication between them may break down. An abstract word may have many referents.

The word *freedom,* for example, has only a very vague referent until you define it. To a prisoner behind bars, *freedom* means getting out of jail. To Mr. Barnes, who resents the neighbors' criticism of his noisy family, *freedom* means the right of his family to make as much noise as they wish. Franklin D. Roosevelt defined the freedoms in which America believes as freedom of speech, freedom of worship, freedom from want, and freedom from fear. Each of these definitions provides a more specific referent for the word *freedom,* and each, in turn, could be more narrowly defined.

Sometimes an example will help to clarify the meaning of an abstract word. In the following passage the meaning of *quality* in the context "a man of quality" is made clear by an example.

> Mansfield was a man of quality. Although he never pushed himself forward or tried to assert his superiority, you could tell by his bearing, his quiet sense of humor, and his manner of speaking that he was a superior person.

EXERCISE 3. Defining Abstract Words. Without using a dictionary, write a one- or two-sentence definition of each of the following words. Compare your definitions with those of your classmates. In discussion, you may find it helpful to clarify your meaning by means of an example.

1. fairness 　 3. success 　 5. skill
2. beauty 　 4. failure 　 6. happiness

Synonyms

Synonyms are words that are similar, but rarely identical, in meaning. Careful writers select the words which have the exact referents they have in mind. For example, the words *disciple, partisan,* and *satellite* are synonyms in that each refers to a person who is a *follower* of a leader. Yet each has its own meaning, somewhat different from the others. *Follower,* the most general in meaning, may be used in place of any of the other three, but for the writer who has a specific kind of follower in mind, it lacks exactness. A writer who has in mind the followers of a professor or a religious leader, for instance, would probably use the word *disciples.* If the writer wishes to refer to the blindly devoted followers of a political or military leader, the word *partisans* might be preferable. To refer to the kind of followers who continuously and obsequiously circulate about a powerful leader, perhaps in hope of favors, the word *satellites* could be used. Do not always be satisfied with the first synonym that occurs to you.

EXERCISE 4. Identifying Meanings and Referents of Synonyms.
Without using the dictionary, explain the differences in meaning of the words in each group. Describe a situation in which each word would be properly used.

1. highway, road, street, boulevard, expressway, path, trail
2. compel, coerce, force, constrain
3. reveal, divulge, tell, betray
4. repulsive, obnoxious, abhorrent, distasteful
5. laughing, giggling, snickering, guffawing

Denotation and Connotation

Compare the meaning of the following sentences:

> Nan's persistence surprised everyone.
> Nan's stubbornness surprised everyone.

Of course, the meaning of the two sentences may be the same. *Persistence* is another word for *stubbornness,* the quality of not giving up easily. This is the *denotative* meaning of the words. But the *effect* of the words on the reader or listener is very different. *Stubbornness* suggests that Nan is unreasonable, narrow-minded, unwilling to listen to others. This *suggestive* meaning of a word is its *connotation,* or *connotative* meaning. Most words have connotations. There is nothing wrong in choosing a word for its connotations, but you must be aware of the connotations lest you say or write something you did not intend.

EXERCISE 5. Evaluating Word Connotations. Write the numbers 1–10 in a column. As you read the following list, write *F* after the number if the word or phrase has favorable, pleasing connotations for you. Write *U* if it has unfavorable connotations. Write *N* if the connotations are neutral—that is, if the word or phrase does not stir any feeling in you. Compare your answers with those of your classmates.

1. liberal	5. bureaucrat	8. communism
2. propaganda	6. stars and stripes	9. police
3. mother	7. conservative	10. grand opera
4. home		

Loaded Words

A word which, through its connotations, carries strong feelings is said to be "loaded." The propagandist, the newspaper columnist, the political speaker are likely to use loaded words. They are trying to appeal to the emotions of people. When used deliberately, loaded words are a form of persuasion of which clear thinkers disapprove.

EXERCISE 6. Analyzing Word Connotations. Discuss with your classmates and teacher the connotations of the following words:

1. plump, fat, pot-bellied, stout
2. visionary, crackpot, idealist
3. crowd, gang, mob, assemblage
4. youth, teen-ager, minor, young adult
5. determined, persevering, dogged, resolute, relentless, tenacious

THE WRITER'S CHOICE OF WORDS

When you speak, you can always supplement your words with additional explanatory words or with "body language." When you write, your meaning is dependent upon your choice of words and the ways in which you use the selected words. It is important then, that as a writer you choose your words carefully. They must effectively reach your audience, fulfill your purpose in writing, and express your message clearly.

Figurative Language

Figures of speech make writing interesting and vivid. In reading literature, especially in your study of poetry, you encounter many figures of speech. Those most commonly found are metaphor, simile, and personification. In each of these, the writer draws a comparison. Two things are compared which are not really alike, but which are similar in at least one respect. By making the comparison, the writer is able to express meaning more clearly, vividly, and convincingly than he or she could by writing a literal description or explanation.

D. H. Lawrence describes a row of distant houses on a ridge at night: "The homes stood . . . black against the sky, *like wild beasts glaring curiously with yellow eyes down into the darkness.*" Lawrence knows, of course, that houses and beasts are literally quite unlike, but the houses with lighted windows suggest to his imagination beasts with yellow eyes. This figurative description makes you see the scene as he saw it and as he thought of it. It is more arresting than would be a literal statement—"The lighted houses were black against the sky."

Note the striking effect of the four figures of speech used by Pearl Buck in describing a suddenly revealed handful of precious jewels: "There were such a mass of jewels as we had never dreamed could be together, jewels *red as the inner flesh of watermelons, golden as wheat, green as young leaves in spring, clear as water trickling out of the earth.*"

Simile

A *simile* is a comparison between things essentially unlike, expressed directly through the use of a comparing word such as *like* or *as*.

EXAMPLES Her hair was **like** silk.
He was thin **as** a stick.

If the things compared are really alike, the comparison is not a figure of speech, not a simile.

NOT A SIMILE He wore a hat like mine.

SIMILE He wore a hat **like an overturned pail.**

NOT A SIMILE   Her sister was like her mother.

SIMILE   Her sister was **like an angel.**

Metaphor

A *metaphor* is a comparison between things essentially unlike, expressed without a comparing word such as *like* or *as.* The comparison is implied rather than directly stated.

EXAMPLES   The silver lace of the branches above the river. . . .
The road was a ribbon of moonlight.

ALFRED NOYES

Personification

Personification is a figure of speech in which the characteristics of a human being are attributed to an animal, a thing, or an idea.

EXAMPLES   But, look, **the morn in russet mantle clad**
Walks o'er the dew of yon high eastern hill.

SHAKESPEARE

Only through the rusty hinges and swollen sea-moistened woodwork certain airs, detached from the **body of the wind** (the house was ramshackle after all) **crept** round corners and **ventured** indoors.

VIRGINIA WOOLF

☞ NOTE   Other figures of speech that you will find more useful in literary appreciation than in composition are *antithesis, apostrophe, hyperbole, irony, paradox,* and *metonymy.* The dictionary will give you definitions of these.

EXERCISE 7. Explaining and Evaluating Figures of Speech.
Copy the figures of speech from the following passages. After each, tell whether it is simile, metaphor, or personification. Be prepared to explain the figure and to evaluate its effectiveness. You should find fifteen figures.

1. When Alma went down into the audience room, in the midst of the chattering singers, who seemed to have descended like birds, from song flights to chirps, the minister approached her.—MARY E. WILKINS FREEMAN

2. The silence is cloven by alarm as by an arrow.—JAMES JOYCE
3. Spring was a very flame of green.—D. H. LAWRENCE
4. The edge of the colossal jungle, so dark green as to be almost black, fringed with white surf, ran straight, like a ruled line, far, far away along a blue sea whose glitter was blurred by a creeping mist.—JOSEPH CONRAD
5. Are there no water-lilies, smooth as cream
   With long stems dripping crystal?—ELINOR WYLIE
6. I felt like a small bubble on the surface of a mighty thing like the sea.— ROBERT P. TRISTRAM COFFIN
7. Night's candles are burnt out, and jocund day
   Stands tiptoe on the misty mountain tops.—SHAKESPEARE
8. The exhilarating ripple of her voice was a wild tonic in the rain.— F. SCOTT FITZGERALD
9. The farm was crouched on a bleak hillside, whence its fields, fanged with flints, dropped steeply to the village of Howling a mile away.—STELLA GIBBONS
10. Maternally the great tree protected us, sighing and groaning, as she lowered her arms to shield us from the storm.

EXERCISE 8. Using Figures of Speech in Sentences. Select five of the following items that you can express more vividly by using simile, metaphor, or personification. For each, write a sentence with the figure of speech.
1. hot August scene on a city street
2. sensations while walking in a hurricane or a blizzard
3. a person's reaction to sudden fear
4. a fruit tree in bloom
5. cars in bumper-to-bumper traffic
6. emerging from a stuffy room into a cold, clear night
7. stubbornness
8. a drink of cool water after hours of thirst
9. birds sitting on a telephone wire
10. a plane taking off

Hazards of Figurative Language

The habit of thinking metaphorically, of seeing life in terms of comparisons, can help a writer—in prose as well as in poetry—to enliven style and clarify meaning.

A writer, however, must be aware of three pitfalls that lie in wait for the glib or careless user of figurative language. The first is the use of similes and metaphors which, though much used, have become so commonplace that they weaken style. Such figures are clichés: *clear as crystal, ran like the wind, silence reigned, clear as day,* etc. The second pitfall is the use of figures which are strained. They give the reader the feeling that the writer is trying too hard. They attract attention because they are inappropriate or farfetched: "Like a boiling lobster, the dawn turned from black to red." This fault is more common in verse than in prose.

The third pitfall, however, is one which you can easily avoid, provided you understand it. This is the error of mixing your figures of speech.

Mixed Figures of Speech

A mixed figure of speech—sometimes referred to as a "mixed metaphor"—is one in which the writer starts with a comparison and then shifts to another comparison that is not consistent with the first. A few examples will make clear how a careless writer mixes metaphors.

MIXED   Flailing both wings, Mr. McCall flew to the platform and barked for silence. [The first metaphors compare Mr. McCall to a bird, and the last to a dog.]

BETTER Flailing both wings, Mr. McCall **flew** to the platform and **screeched** for silence.

MIXED   Her face reddened as mountainous waves of embarrassment broke over her, all but drying up the little confidence she had. [Mountainous waves suggest water; they would hardly "dry up" anything.]

BETTER Her face reddened as mountainous **waves** of embarrassment broke over her, all but **washing away** the little confidence she had.

EXERCISE 9. Revising Sentences by Using Consistent Figures of Speech.
Seven of the following sentences contain mixed figures of speech. Revise the sentences to remove the mixed figures. If the figure is consistently maintained, write + after its number on your paper.

1. After enduring an hour of Carl's insane driving, we ordered him into the asylum of the back seat.

2. The senator told the investigators that he would lay his cards on the table, since his life was an open book with no skeletons in the closet.

3. Bionics researchers are on a small island of knowledge in the midst of a sea of ignorance, but, like corals, they are building reefs, extending their knowledge in all directions.

4. Unfortunately the speaker did not know that he was flying too high over the head of his audience until their general restlessness made him realize that he had better get out of the depths into the shallow water where they were.

5. In college, she changed course abruptly, and instead of foundering on the submerged rocks of low grades and expulsion from school, she got on the beam, which eventually led her to a safe landing.

6. Elisa dived into her studies, afraid that she would never reach the top of the heap, but determined not to give up before the final whistle blew.

7. The productive field of psychiatry, once considered a pseudoscience, has now achieved respectability and may become a most important branch of medical research.

8. Every morning a chorus of starlings in the trees outside her window awakened her, their dissonances and harsh voices jangling her nerves unbearably.

9. She spent the morning of her career groping through the dark halls of obscurity until the publication of her third novel thrust her above the surface of the black waters into the brilliant noonday sun.

10. Unless the mayor sets a new course, our city is likely to be buried beneath a mound of debt.

EXERCISE 10. Selecting an Appropriate Figure of Speech.
Each item in the following exercise contains a figure of speech and a space where a portion of the sentence has been omitted. Beneath the sentence four wordings are suggested for this space, one of which is preferable if the figure of speech is to be maintained consistently. After the proper number, write the letter of the wording which best fits the blank space.

1. Mr. Gross, who was up to his neck in debt, . . . when his company went on strike.
    a. collapsed

    b. nearly went under

    c. was caught off base

    d. suffered a setback

2. Her path was strewn with serious problems which threatened . . .

    a. to drop on her with crippling effect.

    b. to engulf her completely.

    c. to trip her up at every step.

    d. to wreck her career.

3. The book is a treasure chest of wisdom in which you will find . . .

    a. a rich supply of bonbons to sweeten your speech.

    b. a greenhouse of rare flowers to decorate your speech.

    c. new clothes to dress up your speech.

    d. a hoard of verbal gems to adorn your speech.

4. Heavy income taxes, which exert a stranglehold on the economy, have . . . sources of new investment capital.

    a. crippled

    b. choked off

    c. tied up

    d. destroyed

5. Like a person tenderly raking leaves from a new lawn, we must always be careful that in removing the old and unwanted, we do not . . . the new.

    a. uproot

    b. bury

    c. undermine

    d. drown out

6. Mr. Browne behaves in the classroom like a tough top sergeant, . . .

    a. shouting from his pulpit and frightening even the most devout worshipers.

    b. calling all plays and carrying the ball himself.

    c. shouting out orders and brutally exaggerating the details of discipline.

    d. beating his slaves with the lash of long assignments and low grades.

7. In the character of Willie Stark, fiction has been draped about the bones of fact, and in places . . .

    a. the truth emerges.

    b. one can recognize the original.

c. the skeleton shows through.

d. the model becomes clear.

8. The moon had just risen, very golden, over the hill, and like a bright, watching spirit . . . the bars of an ash tree's naked boughs.
   a. towered above
   b. rolled behind
   c. obscured
   d. peered through

9. The characters weave the pattern of the book, . . . of motives and cross-purposes, that looks like a triangle, but is really a quadrangle.
   a. an edifice
   b. a vehicle
   c. a fabric
   d. a structure

10. After bounding around the bases like a frightened kangaroo, Mills was . . . at home plate by Smith's shot from center field.
    a. winged
    b. snared
    c. pinned
    d. dropped

Trite Expressions

Trite expressions, sometimes called *clichés,* are expressions that have grown stale through too frequent use. Originally fresh and effective, they have been used so much that they have lost any freshness and originality they once had. No doubt, the first time someone described the sensation of stage fright as "butterflies in my stomach," the description was strikingly apt, but overuse has made it too commonplace to be arresting. Similarly, such basically effective comparisons as *blanket of snow, busy as a bee, on the fence,* while still generally used in conversation, are so well known that they make writing dull rather than bright. Clichés suggest laziness and a lack of originality in the writer who uses them. They come to mind so easily when you are writing that unless you consciously guard against them, they will seriously weaken your style. The simple, straightforward statement of an idea is preferable to the use of a worn-out expression.

TRITE	SIMPLE, STRAIGHTFORWARD
bury the hatchet	stop fighting, make peace
at loose ends	disorganized
on speaking terms	friendly
fair and square	completely honest
at death's door	near death

You have probably noticed that some clichés are comparisons *(busy as a bee),* while others are simply commonplace ways of stating an idea *(fair and square).* Study the following far-from-complete list of clichés. Reading it will make you sensitive to trite expressions. You and your classmates can add to the list.

TRITE EXPRESSIONS

a good time was had by all
accidents will happen
add insult to injury
after all is said and done
at death's door
at loose ends
beat a hasty retreat
beauty is skin-deep
beyond the shadow of a doubt
bite off more than you can chew
blushing bride
break the ice
brown as a berry
budding genius
bury the hatchet
busy as a bee
by the sweat of one's brow
calm before the storm
clear as crystal
depths of despair
diamond in the rough
discreet silence
doomed to disappointment
each and every
easier said than done
eternal triangle
fair sex
Father Time

few and far between
fond parents
gala occasion
green with envy
hale and hearty
in no uncertain terms
in this day and age
irony of fate
last but not least
long arm of the law
make a long story short
none the worse for wear
on speaking terms
on the fence
out of the frying pan into the fire
point with pride
quick as a flash
ripe old age
sadder but wiser
silence reigned
straight and narrow path
supreme sacrifice
to the bitter end
trials and tribulations
view with alarm
viselike grip
white as a sheet
word to the wise

EXERCISE 11. Revising Sentences by Replacing Trite Expressions. Rewrite each of the following sentences, substituting simple, straightforward language for the trite expressions.

1. After our sumptuous repast, we agreed that a good time had been had by all.
2. In this day and age, political figures who remain on the fence when burning questions are argued will be doomed to disappointment on Election Day.
3. Although warned not to bite off more than I could chew, I signed up for six courses with the result that after all was said and done I was a sadder but wiser woman.
4. To make a long story short, I failed two courses, and to add insult to injury, my parents sent me to summer school.
5. Among the novel's characters are two members of the fair sex who wander from the straight and narrow path and are eventually embraced by the long arm of the law.
6. In the depths of despair, each and every one of us maintained a discreet silence.
7. Sensing that Mr. Stern's pleasant greeting was only the calm before the storm, I tried to beat a hasty retreat, which was nipped in the bud as, with a viselike grip, he led me into his office.
8. Busy as a bee in her ripe old age, Grandmother always pointed with pride to the beautiful garden she had made by the sweat of her brow.
9. Having known the agony of defeat as well as the dizzying heights of success, Jim was determined to fight to the finish in this tennis match, which seesawed back and forth, continually swaying the balance.
10. Green with envy, Ira watched from the sidelines as Fred kicked up his heels and danced up a storm.

Jargon

Jargon has two meanings. First, it means "the technical language used by specialists in the same profession." An engineer may use engineering jargon in a report to other engineers. An educator may use educational jargon in an article in a teacher's magazine. Jargon of this kind is an expected and usually acceptable feature of the style of a specialist writing for other specialists in the same field. There is always the danger, however, that a writer may carry the use of jargon to such an extreme that it will obscure rather than clarify meaning, even for members of the same profession. When this happens, professional jargon becomes a stylistic fault. The specialist should, whenever possible, use simple, everyday language rather than professional jargon. As a high-school student you may encounter the specialist's jargon in your reading, but you will not be likely to use it in your writing.

The second meaning of jargon is "vague, puffed-up, pretentious language that tends to confuse the reader." The writer of this kind of jargon uses words so general in meaning that they mean practically nothing. Examples of words dear to the writer of jargon are *case, factor, field, aspect, matter, concept,* etc. Vague and unnecessary phrases like the following ones usually characterize jargon: *as for the fact that, under the circumstances pertaining, along the line of, in the case of, relative to the matter, as to whether, with reference to,* etc. Perhaps these examples show why jargon has been called "fuzzy language."

Writers of jargon usually overwrite. They prefer the big word to the simple word, the unusual word to the ordinary one. To them, knives are cutlery; table napkins are napery; dogs are canines; a trailer truck is a behemoth of the highways. They rarely start or begin—they initiate or commence. In short, the "jargonist," in using vague, wordy, overwritten language, not only obscures meaning but also confuses and irritates the reader.

EXAMPLE OF COMMON JARGON

In spite of the fact that government aviation agencies were not in agreement with respect to the question of the cause of the accident at Kennedy Airport, the court decided that one of the contributing factors was a propeller that had been structurally weakened.

REWRITTEN WITHOUT JARGON

Although government aviation agencies disagreed on the causes of the accident at Kennedy Airport, the court decided that one cause was a structurally weakened propeller.

EXERCISE 12. Revising a Passage Obscured by Jargon. In the following passage, the meaning is somewhat obscured by jargon. Read the passage several times until you are sure of what the writer was trying to say. Then write a jargon-free revision.

Owing to the fact that a number of social factors along the line of unemployment and dislocation follow consequentially from the automation of industry, government, as well as labor and management, must concern itself with the implementation of the processes of adjustment of affected persons.

Degrees of Informal English

As explained in Chapter 5, there are two kinds of standard English—formal and informal. We use informal English in much of our conversation and in most of our writing. Within the general category of informal English, however, there are degrees of informality. Expressions typical of the most extreme degree of informality are never "bad" English, but they are sometimes inappropriate English. Because it is light in tone and sometimes very close to slang, extremely informal English should be carefully limited in serious composition.

Slang

Slang is highly informal language that does not conform to conventional usage.

Standard informal English, but not standard formal English, may contain both slang and colloquialisms. Slang is almost always used only in highly informal situations. Very often, slang consists of new words and phrases or established words and phrases with new meanings attached to them. Many linguists believe that slang actually began as a secret means of expression—called an *argot*—among thieves and beggars to keep them from being understood by police.

Slang today is most often used by close-knit groups, such as students, military recruits, musicians, sailors, and so on, to mark members as a part of that group. For a while, the slang may remain within the group, but then may very often, thanks to radio and television, spread to a larger population. The following slang expressions, for example, were used by jazz musicians in their everyday conversations with other musicians. Notice how many of the expressions are familiar to general audiences.

EXAMPLES   the Apple—New York City
bad—good
bread—money
bug—to bother
clinker—a missed note
cut—to leave
dig—to understand or agree with

gas—as a noun, something that especially pleases
hep—in the know, as in "hip"
put down—to belittle another's playing

Even though many of the words and phrases listed above may be familiar to you, most slang is short-lived. It is for this reason that slang from your parents' generation probably seems so outdated to you. Slang is generally considered acceptable when used only in the most informal situations. Writers often use it to depict informal language exchanges.

EXERCISE 13. Understanding the Use of Slang.   Each of the following slang expressions has been used recently. Which ones are still used today? Use your dictionary to find the meanings of these slang expressions.

1. apple polisher
2. crackerjack
3. fuzz
4. bag (noun)
5. bughouse

Colloquialisms and Idioms

Colloquialisms are words and phrases that are characteristic of spoken informal English. On very informal occasions, such as in a letter to a close friend, colloquialisms may also be found in writing. Unlike slang, colloquialisms are not found in the language of a particular group; instead, they tend to be widespread. Also unlike most slang expressions, colloquialisms tend to remain in the language, often becoming after some time a part of standard English.

Colloquialisms often have an idiomatic meaning. An *idiom* is a word or phrase whose meaning cannot be taken literally. For example, "down in the mouth" is a colloquial expression that means "depressed" or "unhappy." Although the mouth may be somewhat pulled down when one is unhappy, the meaning of the phrase cannot be understood from that literal reading.

EXERCISE 14. Understanding the Use of Colloquialisms.   Each of the following phrases is a colloquial expression. If you do not know the meaning of the phrase, look it up in a dictionary. Then for each phrase, write a sentence, as you might in a letter to a friend, in which you use the expression. Then in a second sentence, as you might write in a report for school, use words that have the same meaning but that are more appropriate for a more formal occasion.

1. hang back
2. from the horse's mouth
3. look down the (someone's) nose at
4. hang around
5. A-OK
6. for keeps
7. sent (someone) up the wall
8. clue me in
9. run out on (someone)
10. slip one over on (someone)

CHAPTER 22 WRITING REVIEW

Evaluating a Writer's Choice of Language. Select two articles from your local newspaper. Take the first one from the national news section of the paper, the other from a section such as the sports, style, or entertainment section. Read each article, looking for characteristics of the writer's choice of language. Is the language appropriate to the subject matter, the purpose, and the audience for which it was written? Be prepared to discuss your evaluation in class (or to write it if your teacher so directs).

PART FIVE

MECHANICS

CHAPTER 23

Manuscript Form

STANDARDS FOR WRITTEN WORK

A *manuscript* is any typewritten or handwritten composition, as distinguished from a printed document. More and more frequently in the years of school ahead of you, you will be asked to hand in well-prepared manuscripts. Therefore, you should learn correct form for your written work now and should prepare all future written work accordingly.

23a. **Follow accepted standards in preparing manuscripts.**

Your teacher will find it easier to read and evaluate your papers if they are properly prepared. Although there is no single way to prepare a paper correctly, the following rules are widely used and accepted. Follow them unless your teacher requests you to do otherwise.

1. Use lined composition paper or, if you type, use white $8\frac{1}{2} \times 11$-inch paper.
2. Type on only one side of a sheet of paper. Follow your school's policy about writing on both sides of composition paper.
3. Write in blue, black, or blue-black ink, or typewrite. If you type, double-space the lines.
4. Leave a margin of about two inches at the top of a page and margins of about one inch at the sides and bottom. The left-hand margin must be straight; the right-hand margin should be as straight as possible.

5. Indent the first line of each paragraph about one-half inch from the left.

6. Follow your teacher's instructions for placing your name, the class, the date, and the title on the manuscript.

7. If the paper is more than one page long, number the pages after the first, placing the number on the upper right-hand corner, about one-half inch down from the top.

8. Write legibly and neatly. If you are using unlined paper, try to keep the lines straight. Form your letters carefully so that your *n*'s do not look like *u*'s, *a*'s like *o*'s, and so on. Dot the *i*'s and cross the *t*'s. If you are typing, do not strike over letters or cross out words. If you have to erase, do it neatly.

9. Before handing in your final version, proofread it carefully.

23b. Learn the rules for using abbreviations.

In most of your writing, you should spell out words rather than abbreviate them. A few abbreviations, however, are commonly used.

The following abbreviations are acceptable when they are used with a name: *Mr., Mrs., Ms., Dr., Jr.,* and *Sr.* If they do not accompany a name, spell out the words instead of using abbreviations.

EXAMPLES **Mr.** Rugelli **Dr.** Loesster
Mrs. Corning John S. Wilbur, **Sr.**
She has an appointment with the **doctor.**
The **senior** law partner was consulted.

The abbreviations A.M. (*ante meridiem*—"before noon"), P.M. (*post meridiem*—"after noon"), A.D. (*anno Domini*—"in the year of the Lord"), and B.C. (*before Christ*) are acceptable when they are used with numbers.

EXAMPLES The *Queen Elizabeth 2* is scheduled to sail at 9:00 A.M.
Octavian (63 B.C.–A.D. 14) is now known as Augustus Caesar.
[Notice that the abbreviation A.D. precedes the number, while B.C. follows it.]

Abbreviations for organizations are acceptable if they are generally known.

EXAMPLES My sister and I joined the **Y.W.C.A.** [or **YWCA**]
Thousands visit the **U.N.** headquarters. [or **UN**]

The **FBI** cooperates closely with state police agencies. [Abbreviations for government agencies are usually written without periods.]

23c. Learn the rules for writing numbers.

Numbers of more than two words should be written in numerals, not words. If, however, you are writing several numbers, some of them one word and some of them more than one word, write them all the same way.

EXAMPLES   Edith traveled **675** kilometers on her trip to Texas.
Marlene weighs **ninety-seven** pounds.
To the north we have **750** acres, to the south **340,** to the west **182,** and to the east only **47.**

A number at the beginning of a sentence should be written out.

EXAMPLE   **Thirty-five hundred** pairs of terns were counted on the shore.

Write out numbers like **eleventh, forty-third,** and so on. If they are used with a month, however, it is customary to use numerals only.

EXAMPLES   My brother came in **eleventh** [not *11th*] in the race.
School closes on **June 6.** [or **the sixth of June;** not *June 6th*]

23d. Learn the rules for dividing words at the end of a line.

Sometimes you do not have room to write all of a long word at the end of a line. It may look better to start the word on the next line; however, if doing that would leave a very uneven right-hand margin, you should divide the word, using a hyphen after the first part. Learn the rules for dividing words (see pages 741–42). Remember that you should try to avoid dividing words. A slightly irregular margin looks better than a word which is hyphenated.

23e. Learn the standard correction symbols.

In correcting your papers, your teacher may use some or all of the following symbols. What you are to do about each marked error is explained after the given meaning of the symbol. To correct your error, use the index of this book to find the section that you need to review.

All errors requiring rewriting of one or more sentences should be numbered (1, 2, etc.) in the margin where the symbol occurs. Then on a separate "correction sheet" (or on the final page of your composition, if there is room), you should rewrite the incorrect sentence, numbering it to correspond with the numbered symbol. Errors that do not require rewriting a whole sentence are to be corrected in the composition itself at the place where the error appears.

Correction Symbols with Instructions

ms   *error in manuscript form or neatness*
Rewrite the sentence or paragraph neatly on correction sheet.

cap   *error in use of capital letter*
Cross out the incorrect letter, and write the correct form above it.

p   *error in punctuation*
Insert punctuation, remove it, or change it as required.

sp   *error in spelling*
Cross out the word; write the correct spelling above it; write the word five times, correctly spelled, on your correction sheet.

frag   *sentence fragment*
Correct the fragment by changing punctuation and capital or by rewriting on correction sheet.

rs   *run-on sentence*
Correct it by inserting the necessary end mark and capital.

ss   *error in sentence structure*
Rewrite the sentence on your correction sheet.

k   *awkward sentence or passage*
Rewrite the sentence or passage on your correction sheet.

nc   *not clear*
Rewrite the sentence or sentences on your correction sheet.

ref   *unclear reference of pronoun*
Cross out the error, and write the correction above it.

gr   *error in grammar*
Cross out the error, and write the correction above it.

w   *error in word choice*
Cross out the word, and write a better one above it.

¶   *Begin a new paragraph here.*
      This cannot be corrected but should be carefully noted.

t   *error in tense*
      Cross out the error, and write the correct form above it.

∧   *You have omitted something.*
      Insert omitted words above the line.

COMPOSITION PASSAGE MARKED BY THE TEACHER

p   "All is grass, said Heraclitus." By this he meant

gr   that all animals and people depends upon green

p   plants to store up the suns energy in forms they

sp p can use. The sun shines on all equaly, but it's en-

w   ergy would be quickly dissipated (unless) the green

         leaves of plants did not take the three inorganic

         materials—water, carbon dioxide, and sunlight—

rs   and transform them into food even electricity is a

         form of energy first trapped and stored in green

mc, k leaves. Coal is burned to make steam to drive gen-

         erators is energy stored by the leaves of now petri-

         fied carboniferous plants.

COMPOSITION PASSAGE CORRECTED BY STUDENT

p   "All is grass," said Heraclitus." By this he meant

gr   that all animals and people depends upon green

p   plants to store up the sun's energy in forms they

sp p can use. The sun shines on all ~~equaly,~~ *equally* but it's en-

w   ergy would be quickly dissipated (unless) *if* the green

         leaves of plants did not take the three inorganic

         materials—water, carbon dioxide, and sunlight—

rs   and transform them into food. *E*ven electricity is a *nc, k*

①

form of energy first trapped and stored in green leaves. Coal is burned to make steam to drive generators is energy stored by the leaves of now petrified carboniferous plants.

equally, equally, equally, equally, equally

① The energy of coal, which is burned to make steam to drive generators, is energy...

CHAPTER 24

Capitalization

STANDARD USES OF CAPITALIZATION

Capital letters are used mainly to individualize what you are writing about. When you capitalize a word, you serve notice to the reader that you are referring to some *particular* person, place, or thing rather than to the general class. Custom determines the use of capital letters, and it is the wisest course to conform to customary or standard usage.

This chapter contains the basic rules for capitalization. In your reading of books, magazines, and newspapers, you may very well find examples of capitalization or cases of a lack of capitalization that do not agree with the rules stated here. This is often a matter of the style of the piece in which the word appears. Fortunately, most writers follow the basic rules that are given here; it is only occasionally that one encounters variations. Therefore, by understanding and learning the rules, by developing the habit of applying them correctly, and by taking pride in your own writing, you can avoid capitalization errors.

Take the following diagnostic test to see how much you have to review.

DIAGNOSTIC TEST

Correcting Sentences by Using Capitalization Correctly. Number your paper 1–20. Each of the following sentences contains an error in capitalization. After the proper number, write the word correctly, supplying capitals where they are needed or omitting capitals where they are unnecessary.

EXAMPLE 1. In the Fall the trees along Main Street are lovely.
      1. *fall*

1. This year my easiest classes are geometry, spanish, and American history.
2. We went to the City of Miami on vacation.
3. They bought a videotape from the Grand Video company.
4. Colorado is located West of the Great Plains.
5. Lansing, Michigan, is in Ingham county.
6. She lives at 321 Maple boulevard, which is south of here.
7. My RCA Stereo is ten years old and still works well.
8. Carla entered her St. Bernard in the Centerville Dog club's yearly show.
9. They live half a block north of Twenty-First Street.
10. Our neighbors are alumni of Drake university in Des Moines, Iowa.
11. Last year my sister Lisa joined the National Audubon society.
12. We are holding a bake sale next Saturday to raise money for the junior Prom.
13. The club members celebrated bastille day by having dinner at a French restaurant.
14. Ms. Davis wrote to the U.S. department of Agriculture for information on soybean cultivation in the Midwest.
15. Mars was the Roman God of war.
16. The Biograph theater is a well-known site in Chicago because John Dillinger, a notorious gangster, was shot there.
17. Sean McShane is planning to take a cruise on the Caribbean sea over spring vacation.
18. Would you like to be the first student to ride in a Space Shuttle that orbits the earth?
19. That novel takes place in the Middle ages and highlights the problems of the feudal system.
20. Erica wants to be Secretary of the Shutterbug Club.

24a. Capitalize the first word in every sentence.

This is one of the first rules a schoolchild learns. It is usually broken only by students who have trouble telling where one sentence ends and another begins.

INCORRECT	Roald Amundsen and Robert Scott challenged each other in a race to reach the South Pole, with careful planning Amundsen easily won.
CORRECT	Roald Amundsen and Robert Scott challenged each other in a race to reach the South Pole. With careful planning Amundsen easily won.
INCORRECT	After studying reports on new cars, Mother said, "the models with front-wheel drive have improved."
CORRECT	After studying reports on new cars, Mother said, "The models with front-wheel drive have improved."

☞ **NOTE** The first word in a line of poetry is often capitalized.

EXAMPLE Good friend, for Jesus' sake forbear
To dig the dust enclosed here;
Blest be the man that spares these stones,
And curst be he that moves my bones.

WILLIAM SHAKESPEARE

24b. Capitalize the pronoun *I* and the interjection *O*.

INCORRECT The line i translated was "Hear us, o Zeus."

CORRECT The line I translated was "Hear us, O Zeus."

The common interjection *oh* (as in *Oh, yes!*) is capitalized only when it appears at the beginning of a sentence.

24c. Capitalize proper nouns and proper adjectives.

A *proper noun* is the name of a particular person, place, or thing. How a proper noun differs from an ordinary, common noun, which is not capitalized, can be seen from the following lists:

COMMON NOUN	PROPER NOUN
county	Wayne County
author	Shirley Jackson
lake	Crater Lake
ocean	Atlantic Ocean

Do not confuse proper nouns, which are *names,* with nouns which merely state kind or type. For instance, *subcompact* is not the name of a particular automobile company (like Ford or General Motors) or of a particular automobile model (like Sentra, Thunderbird, Model T). The word *subcompact* is merely a general name for a type of automobile, one that is smaller than a compact.

INCORRECT   On her birthday, Joy received a Honda Subcompact.

CORRECT   On her birthday, Joy received a Honda subcompact.

INCORRECT   Chris's favorite snack is a box of Sun-Maid Raisins.

CORRECT   Chris's favorite snack is a box of Sun-Maid raisins.

A *proper adjective* is an adjective formed from a proper noun.

PROPER NOUN	PROPER ADJECTIVE
France	French pastry
Arabia	Arabian horses
Scotland	Scottish terrier

Compound adjectives are frequently a source of trouble. In most cases, only the part of a compound adjective that is itself a proper noun or adjective is capitalized.

EXAMPLES   Spanish-speaking Americans, northern-Italian cuisine, God-given liberty, pro-American, German-American, anti-Axis countries

Study carefully the list that follows. It classifies in seven categories the most frequently used kinds of proper nouns and adjectives.

(1) Capitalize the names of persons.

GIVEN NAMES   Matthew, Jennifer, Kathryn

SURNAMES   Bowman, Kantor, Cruz, Ryan

In some surnames, another letter besides the first should be capitalized. This practice varies; to be sure you are right, check a reference source.

EXAMPLES   McEnroe, O'Shea, MacCartney, LeCroy

The abbreviations *Jr.* and *Sr.* (*junior* and *senior*) should always be capitalized when they follow a name.

EXAMPLES   Robert W. Wilson, Jr.
Simon L. Snyder, Sr.

(2) Capitalize geographical names.

Cities and towns: Chicago, Wooster, San Diego
Counties and townships: Orange County, Franklin Township, Blue Earth
  County
States: Virginia, Minnesota, Texas
Countries: Italy, United States of America, Brazil
Continents: Australia, North America, Europe
Islands: South Bass Island, Captiva
Bodies of water: Hudson Bay, Lake Erie, Rio Grande
Mountains: Allegheny Mountains, Mt. Saint Helens, Sierra Madre
Streets: Blair Boulevard, Sunshine State Parkway, Elm Drive, Fifty-first
  Street [In a hyphenated number, the second word begins with a small letter.]
Parks: Stone Mountain Memorial State Park, Humboldt Redwood State Park,
  Gettysburg National Military Park
Sections of the country: the South, the Northeast, the Mississippi Delta

---

☞ **NOTE** Do not capitalize *east, west, north,* and *south* when they
merely indicate direction. Do capitalize them when they refer to
commonly recognized sections of the country. The modern tendency is
to write nouns and adjectives derived from capitalized *East, West, North,*
and *South* without capital letters (an *easterner, western boots*).

EXAMPLES We entered on the east ramp and headed north.
  We are looking forward to our vacation in the South.

When an adjective indicating direction is *part of the name* of a
recognized region or political unit, capitalize it. When such an adjective merely indicates some portion of a region or political unit, do *not*
capitalize it.

EXAMPLES North Dakota, South Korea, southern California, western Missouri

EXERCISE 1. Correcting Phrases by Using Capitalization Correctly. Write the following phrases, using capital letters wherever they are required. Some phrases do not need capital letters.

EXAMPLE 1. atop granite peak
    1. *atop Granite Peak*

1. zion national park
2. bering sea
3. pro-canadian
4. an irish linen handkerchief
5. at moon lake
6. a house on starve island
7. beside the ohio river
8. in lancaster county
9. the illinois oil fields
10. near baffin bay
11. southern fried chicken
12. french vanilla ice cream
13. texas cowboys
14. forty-fifth street
15. william watson, jr.
16. the west side of the river
17. the north
18. near dundee mountain
19. colombian coffee
20. japanese-american

EXERCISE 2. Correcting Sentences by Using Capitalization Correctly. Find all words requiring a capital and write them correctly. Before each word or phrase, write the number of its sentence.

EXAMPLE   1. I always wanted to travel to the fiji islands.
   1. *Fiji Islands*

1. Everyone in our class at Evans High School in warren township wrote an essay titled "My Ideal Vacation."
2. Some of my friends dreamed of american vacations in the west.
3. Linda planned to leave cleveland, on the southern shore of lake erie, travel southwest, and cross the mississippi river at st. louis, missouri.
4. Ron would pack his camera and fly to cheyenne, wyoming, to visit his uncle, ernest wayne, jr.
5. In his dream vacation ron has planned photographic excursions to yellowstone national park, the black hills, and lake solitude.
6. Pam ambitiously designed a european tour of london, paris, and rome, followed by a cruise of the mediterranean sea.
7. After studying about south america in geography class, i wanted to go to peru and brazil.
8. Australia, an island continent, attracted scott, who wanted to scuba-dive at barrier reef in the coral sea.
9. Michael's grandparents live on kalakaua avenue in honolulu, so he planned a trip to the hawaiian islands, in the pacific ocean.
10. With her eye on the northernmost state, megan looked forward to seeing mt. mckinley and glacier bay national park in alaska.

EXERCISE 3. Correcting Paragraphs by Using Capitalization Correctly.

Read the following paragraphs. List in a column all words requiring capital letters. When two or more capitalized words belong together, list them together: *Pennington Parkway, Wilshire Square, Blue Lake,* etc. Number your list according to the numbers of the sentences in the paragraph. Do not list words already capitalized.

EXAMPLES 1. We got lost when dad turned north on pennington parkway, and we never did find wilshire square.

    1. *Pennington Parkway*
     Wilshire Square

    2. We chose, instead, a restaurant on fifty-second street near Kenton boulevard.

    2. *Fifty-second Street*
     Kenton Boulevard

1. Our choir in lawrenceburg, tennessee, decided to have an international fair to raise money for a bus trip to washington, d.c. 2. Colleen O'Roark said that the fair would feature crafts and food from many european and asian countries. 3. Juana Santiago said we should include countries of central and south america, since she is particularly familiar with venezuelan cooking. 4. Julian, who recently returned from a trip to italy, planned a display of venetian glass. 5. Karen suggested that we include items from quebec, our french-speaking neighbor to the north. 6. Erin McCall, whose family moved to lexington avenue from phoenix, arizona, decided to bring rock samples from the petrified forest. 7. Since Maxine was born in tokyo, she offered to demonstrate japanese paper folding. 8. Some of us met at Paula's house at the corner of columbus street and hickory lane in the east end of town to choose the items to represent the u.s.a. 9. We chose native american artifacts from the southwest, country crafts from the appalachian mountains, and shell gifts from the southern states along the gulf of mexico. 10. When the fair is over, I hope we will have raised enough money to include a special tour of mammoth cave national park in kentucky in our bus trip to the nation's capital.

(3) Capitalize the names of organizations, business firms, institutions, and government bodies.

Organizations and clubs: Longboat Key Club, Kiwanis Club, National Organization for Women, National Honor Society

> ☞ **NOTE** Do not capitalize such words as *democratic, republican,* and *socialist* when these words refer only to types of societies rather than to specific parties. The word *party* in the name of a political party may be capitalized or not; either way is correct: *Republican party, Republican Party.*

EXAMPLES Although Marie worked for the Democratic party in college, she has now become Republican.
Many foreign students are amazed by the democratic process.
Allen read a socialist newspaper for his history report.

Business firms: Eastern Airlines, Xerox Corporation, International Business Machines, National Broadcasting Company, Motorola, Inc.
Institutions and buildings: Stanford University, Sears Tower, Good Samaritan Hospital, Fox Theater, Boone High School, Waldorf Astoria Hotel

> ☞ **NOTE** Do not capitalize such words as *hotel, theater, college, high school* unless they are part of a proper name.

EXAMPLES the Roosevelt Hotel   a hotel in New Orleans
Marietta College   a college in Ohio
Curran Theater   a theater in San Francisco
Bayside High School   a high school in Virginia

Government bodies: the Senate, Parliament, the Nuclear Regulatory Commission, Congress

(4) Capitalize the names of historical events and periods, special events, and calendar items.

Historical events and periods: the Revolutionary War, the Industrial Revolution, the Yalta Conference, the Dark Ages, World War I, the Battle of Gettysburg
Special events: the Olympics, Boston Marathon, the Super Bowl, Inaugural Ball, the Senior Prom
Calendar items: Friday, Christmas, March, St. Valentine's Day, Hanukkah

> ☞ **NOTE** Do not capitalize the names of the seasons: summer, winter, spring, fall.

(5) Capitalize the names of nationalities, races, and religions.

EXAMPLES Jewish, Italians, Lutheran, Canadian, Indian

(6) Capitalize the brand names of business products.

EXAMPLES Häagen-Dazs ice cream, Ritz crackers, a Nikon camera

> ☞ NOTE Do not capitalize the nouns which often follow a brand name.

EXAMPLES Luden's cough drops, Sharp microwave oven, Timex watch, Apple computer

(7) Capitalize the names of ships, planes, trains, monuments, awards, heavenly bodies, and any other particular places, things, or events.

EXAMPLES the *Titanic* (a ship), the *Enterprise* (a fictional spaceship), the Congressional Medal of Honor (a medal), the Pulitzer Prize (an award), the *Orient Express* (a train)

> ☞ NOTE Planets, constellations, asteroids, stars, and groups of stars are capitalized. However, do not capitalize *sun, moon,* or *earth* unless they are used in conjunction with other heavenly bodies which are all capitalized.

24d. Do *not* capitalize the names of school subjects, except names of languages and course names followed by a number.

EXAMPLES English, Latin, German, geography, mathematics, history, music, Mathematics II, Chemistry I

> ☞ NOTE Do not capitalize *senior, junior, sophomore,* and *freshman* unless these words are part of a proper noun or are used to designate a *specific* organization.

EXAMPLES Only juniors and seniors attended the Junior Prom.
The Sophomore Class held a party for the freshmen.

EXERCISE 4. Correcting Sentences by Using Capitalization Correctly. List in order all words requiring capitals. When two capitalized words belong together, list them together. Number your list according to the numbers of the items. Do not list words already capitalized.

EXAMPLE 1. The united states abounds in exciting vacation spots, from the coast of maine to the pacific shoreline.

    1. *United States*
      Maine
      Pacific

1. The state of florida, one of the most popular vacation areas in the united states, has thousands of kilometers of coastline. The state is bounded by the atlantic ocean, the gulf of mexico, and the straits of florida.
2. Whether you travel on a daily nonstop flight aboard a delta airlines jet, on a cruise ship such as the *queen elizabeth 2,* or on a train such as the *silver bullet,* the florida bureau of visitor services will be delighted to welcome you.
3. Central florida abounds in lakes, with lake okeechobee being the largest.
4. In florida history, an important role belongs to osceola, a powerful leader of the seminole indians who guided his people through a long and costly war from 1835 to 1837. One of the most important battles of the war occurred in the everglades, a huge wilderness region.
5. The everglades national park, which includes big cypress swamp, is today a major tourist attraction. Beautiful beaches, such as those at daytona, miami, and fort lauderdale, also draw many visitors.
6. The second-largest city in the state is miami, the seat of dade county and one of the most famous resort areas in the eastern united states. Miami beach is on an island between biscayne bay and the atlantic and is connected to the city of miami by four causeways.
7. Visitors to miami may be interested in biscayne boulevard, the route to miami beach, or they may be interested in the orange bowl, the home of the city's football team.
8. Thousands of students each year attend the university of florida, located in gainesville. The university offers degrees in engineering, french, english, and many other fields.

9. Many space flights, including some to the moon, have been launched from cape canaveral, the site of the john f. kennedy space center.
10. Florida has one of the fastest-growing populations in the country. Many retired persons have settled in the state, particularly in the area near st. petersburg.

EXERCISE 5. Correcting Sentences by Using Capitalization Correctly. Follow the instructions for Exercise 4.

EXAMPLE 1. They held the picnic at potter park and threw bread crumbs to the canada geese.
1. *Potter Park*
   Canada

1. Lauren plans to attend the university of virginia after she graduates from high school in may.
2. On the second monday of every month, the historical society of lakeside meets at heritage hall.
3. A large selection of mummies from ancient egypt may be viewed at the british museum.
4. The american automobile association printed a special booklet on the memorial day celebrations in New England.
5. My favorite part of sunday breakfast is a sara lee croissant.
6. The ridgewood theater, located in the northern section of the city, features special saturday morning disney cartoons.
7. The *calypso* is the boat of famous french oceanographer jacques cousteau.
8. The original owner of avon, inc., named his cosmetics company for shakespeare's birthplace, stratford-on-avon.
9. The battle of bunker hill, which began the revolutionary war, was actually fought on breed's hill.
10. On a cold day in january, Ross likes campbell's cream of mushroom soup at lunch.

REVIEW EXERCISE. Correcting Paragraphs by Using Capitalization Correctly. As you did in Exercise 3, list all words requiring capitals in the following sentences.

EXAMPLE 1. Even though I enjoy trivia games, I need to learn more about american inventors, the korean war, and ancient history.
1. *American*
   Korean War

1. Last saturday night, may 18, marks the momentous occasion when my brother Ted and I won our first trivia match against our parents.   2. This semester Ted is studying history, political science, and french, while I am taking world literature I and geography II.   3. We surged into the lead when our parents couldn't remember that the first u.s. satellite, *explorer I,* followed the u.s.s.r.'s *sputnik I* into space.   4. From geography class I remembered that mount mckinley and death valley are the highest and lowest points on the continent and that both are located in inyo county, california.

5. Our parents rallied for the lead by knowing that the name of the boy on the cracker jack box is jack and that his dog is bingo.   6. Then Ted knew that the steel framework of the statue of liberty was designed by frenchman alexandre gustave eiffel, who also designed the eiffel tower in paris.   7. None of us knew that john wilkes booth was only twenty-six years old when he shot president lincoln at ford's theatre on good friday in 1865.   8. Because Mom has always been a staunch democrat, she knew that *engine 1401*—the southern railways loco-motive that carried franklin d. roosevelt's body from warm springs, georgia, to washington, d.c.—can now be seen in the smithsonian institution.

9. Ted and I lost some points because I didn't know that kleenex tissues were first used as gas mask filters during world war I. 10. However, Ted won the game for us because he knew that the white house was originally called the executive mansion before it was painted white to cover damage inflicted by the british during the war of 1812.

24e. Capitalize titles.

(1) Capitalize the title of a person when it comes before a name.

EXAMPLES   General MacArthur, Dr. Quigley, President Kennedy

(2) Capitalize a title used alone or following a person's name only if it refers to a high official or someone to whom you wish to show special respect.

EXAMPLES   The President spent the weekend at Camp David. [When it refers to the highest official of the United States, *President* is capitalized.]
Earl Warren, Chief Justice of the United States from 1953 to 1969, may be best remembered for his work on the Warren Report. [The office of Chief Justice is a high one.]

Alice was elected president of the organization.

You will have to see your guidance counselor before you change classes.

Ms. Larsen was promoted to manager of the computer programming department of the bank.

☞ **NOTE**   When an official is directly addressed by title, it is customary to capitalize the title.

EXAMPLES   Mr. Mayor, will you please test the microphone?

Do you intend, Governor, to visit the disaster area?

(3) Capitalize words showing family relationship when used with a person's name but *not* when preceded by a possessive.

EXAMPLES   Aunt Edith, Uncle Fred, my brother Bob, Grandmother Bechtel

---

☞ **NOTE**   When family-relationship words like *uncle, cousin,* and *grand-mother* are customarily used before a name, capitalize them even after a possessive noun or pronoun.

EXAMPLES   My Grandmother Nilsson was born in Sweden.

Did you take swimming lessons from your Uncle Wayne? [You customarily call these persons *Grandmother Nilsson* and *Uncle Wayne.*]

My sister Jeri takes riding lessons. [You do not customarily call her *Sister Jeri.*]

☞ **NOTE**   Words of family relationship may be capitalized or not when used *in place of* a person's name.

EXAMPLE   "Hello, Father" *or* "Hello, father." [*Father* is used in place of the man's name.]

(4) Capitalize the first and last word and all important words in titles of books, periodicals, poems, stories, movies, television series, paintings, and other works of art.

Unimportant words in a title are *a, an,* and *the,* short prepositions (usually those under five letters long), and coordinating conjunctions.

EXAMPLES *Harper's Bazaar* (magazine), Turner's *Crossing the Brook* (painting), *Pride and Prejudice* (novel), Treaty of Versailles, the Charter of the United Nations, the Talmud, "Under the Lion's Paw" (short story), "The Tuft of Flowers" (poem)

The words *a, an,* and *the* written before a title are capitalized only when they are part of the title. In a composition they are usually not capitalized before the names of magazines and newspapers.

EXAMPLES *The Outsiders* (book), *A Day in the Life of President Kennedy* (book)
Joan buys the *Atlantic Monthly* (magazine) and the *Rocky Mountain News* (newspaper).

(5) Capitalize the word *God* except when it refers to the gods of ancient mythology.

> ☞ NOTE   Other words referring to God are usually capitalized as well.

EXAMPLES   Father   Lord God   His will

EXERCISE 6. Correcting Sentences by Using Capitalization Correctly.
List all words requiring capitals. Number your list according to the numbers of the sentences. Do not list words already capitalized.

EXAMPLE 1. The names of norse and roman gods always stump me when I do the sunday paper's crossword puzzle.
  1. *Norse*
     Roman
     Sunday

1. One of georgia o'keeffe's finest paintings, *cow's skull, red, white and blue,* hung in the hirshhorn museum in washington, d.c.
2. In *people* magazine, Kim read details of bill cosby's television series *the cosby show.*
3. Did you recite robert frost's poem "stopping by woods on a snowy evening" to grandma Stone when you visited her at Sparrow Hospital?
4. In 1908 mary baker eddy founded the *christian science monitor* newspaper.

5. My cousin Judy's favorite statue is the *indian hunter* by manship.
6. I enjoyed reading annie dillard's *pilgrim at tinker creek,* and I particularly liked the chapter "the horns of the altar."
7. For a time, general alexander haig served as deputy to henry kissinger on the National Security council.
8. The president addressed the american people in a television news broadcast after she had met with the president of France.
9. We invited not only mayor johnson but also all the county commissioners to the ground-breaking ceremony.
10. Jane White, president of our latin club, showed us a black-and-white print of the movie *julius caesar.*

WRITING APPLICATION:
Using Capitalization to Make Your Writing Easier to Understand

When you use capitalization correctly, you make your writing easier for your readers to grasp. For example, by using a capital letter, you can signal the beginning of a sentence or the particular name of a person, place, or thing. Notice that the second sentence of the following sentences is easier to understand than the first.

> i saw stuart yesterday. he told me he bought an oldsmobile cutlass.
> I saw Stuart yesterday. He told me he bought an Oldsmobile Cutlass.

Writing Assignment

Write a paragraph giving information about a particular historical society, located in a specific town and state, that is directed by a person who is planning a parade for a national holiday. Capitalize where necessary and proofread.

CHAPTER 24 REVIEW: POSTTEST 1

Correcting Sentences by Using Capitalization Correctly. Number your paper 1–25. Each of the following sentences contains an error in capitalization. After the proper number, write the word or phrase correctly, supplying capitals where they are needed or omitting capitals where they are unnecessary.

EXAMPLE 1. Mud Lake is bordered by Delta Township on the east and Kidder county on the west.
1. *County*

1. Marco Polo, an italian merchant, is famous for his travels to China and the Mongol Empire.
2. The director chose the eastern slope of Devil's mountain to film *The Aliens Strike at Dawn*.
3. I couldn't believe that the burly wrestler at the Civic Center's wrestling matches was named Carlton Applewhite, jr.
4. Aunt Jessie was promoted to regional sales manager of the Confidential Insurance company, Inc.
5. Margaret Mead became interested in studying Anthropology while she was at Barnard College.
6. For the potluck dinner I made spinach loaf, Ginny made Southern fried chicken, and Mark made fruit compote.
7. Francine proudly rides her new Schwinn Bike on her paper route for the *Detroit Free Press*.
8. Pearl S. Buck won the pulitzer prize in 1932 for her novel *The Good Earth*.
9. When the survivors of the shipwreck were rescued by the Coast Guard, they gave thanks to god.
10. One of the most distinguished guests at the reception for the U.S. Olympic athletes was the secretary of state.
11. Do you wish you could have lived during the roaring Twenties?
12. My Mother attends all the meetings of the Eastbridge Diabetes Association.
13. The Senior Prom, called "Summer Dreams," will be held at the Royal Hotel on Forty-Eighth Street.
14. Ever since Ms. O'Hara showed us the travel film, I have wanted to visit the Pacific northwest.
15. The center of activity in Washington, D.C., is the White House, the residence and office of the president of the United States.
16. Why doesn't Patrick want to take English literature II?
17. Since the Kanes moved to the East side of town in the Old Oaks Subdivision, I rarely see them at our club meetings.
18. It is hard to concentrate on this chapter about the renaissance while the World Series is on television.
19. Dad always starts his lectures with "When I was a Freshman at the University of Utah. . . ."
20. At the awards banquet last Thursday, the city's Paramedics were commended for their fine work.

21. New York city's famous Central Park was designed by Frederick Law Olmstead.
22. Military songs such as "Tenting Tonight" were popular during the American civil war.
23. In our production of *Two Gentlemen of Verona,* we decorated the set to look like the French Quarter around Jackson square in New Orleans.
24. Mrs. Lopez and Ms. Emery asked the Government if the state scholarships would be discontinued next year.
25. Which is better for a bright Summer day, Kodak film or Fuji film?

CHAPTER 24 REVIEW: POSTTEST 2

Correcting Sentences by Using Capitalization Correctly. List all words that should be capitalized. Number your list according to the numbers of the sentences.

EXAMPLE 1. Renée searched every store in santa fe, new mexico, until she found a gift at j. c. penney for her grandparents.
      1. *Santa Fe, New Mexico*
        J. C. Penney

1. Katy and Heather study ballet at the academy of dance on mills avenue.
2. "One in a million" is the title song of her new album, which was recorded at carnegie hall in new york city.
3. Both ernest hemingway and walt disney once worked for the *kansas city star.*
4. Every thanksgiving before we sit down to dinner, grandma penny sings "the battle hymn of the republic," which was written by julia ward howe.
5. The winner of the first kentucky derby, the annual race at churchill downs in louisville, was a horse named aristides.
6. Sally field won an oscar in 1979 for her stirring performance in *norma rae.*
7. The movie *gone with the wind* premiered at loew's grand theater in atlanta, georgia, on december 15, 1939.
8. I cannot name five of the original signers of the declaration of independence, but I do know that the document was first signed at independence hall in philadelphia.

9. Charles lindbergh made the first solo flight across the atlantic ocean in his plane *the spirit of st. louis* in 1927.

10. The mystery of amelia earhart's disappearance between new guinea and howland island on her round-the-world flight has never been solved.

11. I enjoyed reading *to kill a mockingbird,* a novel about life in a small town in maycomb county, alabama.

12. *The harvesters* is a painting by pieter brueghel, a sixteenth-century artist.

13. One of the cities of the incas, machu picchu, lay hidden among the peaks of the andes in peru and was never discovered by the spanish conquerors.

14. The nobel prize was established by alfred nobel, the swedish inventor of dynamite.

15. My aunt elsie, who lives in salt lake city, showed us pioneer trails state park and the mormon temple in temple square.

16. Some historians trace the origin of valentine's day to an ancient roman festival; others believe it is connected with one or more saints of the early christian church.

17. The white mountains are in the northeastern corner of new hampshire; the green mountains cover central vermont.

18. We crossed the connecticut river, which divides vermont and new hampshire.

19. Virginia's house of burgesses was the first representative legislature in america.

20. If Beth passes english and history II, her parents will let her apply for a job at the 7-eleven store on twenty-third street.

21. Our debate team argued in favor of pro-american economic policies as the best way to foster democracy in the socialist countries of africa and south america.

22. While Shirley Chisholm served in the u.s. house of representatives, she fought for help for the nation's poor and also for an end to the vietnam war.

23. The new model for a space station, which was revealed by national aeronautics and space administration officials, looks as if it were made from a Tinkertoy set.

24. Sandra and Margo helped our team, sponsored by the evans lumber company, to win the whittier township annual wheelchair basketball championship.

25. The high school adventurers' club went white-water rafting on memorial day.

SUMMARY STYLE REVIEW

Names of Persons

Mrs. Andrew D. McCall, Jr. — a family friend
Sean O'Casey — the boy next door

Geographical Names

Kansas City — a city in Missouri
Canyonlands National Park — a national park in Utah
Great Smoky Mountains — mountains in Tennessee
Arctic Ocean — a voyage on the ocean
Monongahela River — a river in Pennsylvania
a vacation in the South — the south side of town
Baltic Sea — the sea north of Poland
Marblehead Peninsula — a peninsula in Lake Erie

Organizations, Business Firms and Products, Institutions, Government Bodies

Eastman Kodak Company — a film company
Cavalier Hotel — a restored hotel
Chrysler — an automobile
Litchfield High School — a small high school
National Association of Home Builders — a national organization
the Supreme Court of Nebraska — a Nebraska court

Historical Events and Periods, Special Events, Calendar Items

World War I — a war in Europe
the Ice Age — a prehistoric age
the Chicago World's Fair — a fair in our city
Groundhog Day — a day in February
the Fall Festival — an event in the fall

Nationalities, Races, Religions, Languages

German — a nationality
Caucasian — a race
Hinduism — a religion
Spanish — a language

Ships, Planes, Trains, Monuments, Awards, Heavenly Bodies, and Particular Places, Things, or Events

the *Mary Deere*	a famous ship
the Nobel Prize	an award
the *Silver Streak*	a train in a movie
Saturn's rings	a full moon
the Lincoln Memorial	a memorial in Washington, D.C.
Discovery	a space shuttle
Academy Awards	awards for motion pictures

Titles

Mayor Taylor	Ms. Taylor, the mayor
the President, the Prime Minister (high government officials)	the president of the club, the senator's duties
Praise God for His blessings	the gods of the ancient Greeks
Aunt Margaret	her aunt
Go with Grandmother	my grandmother
Last of the Mohicans	a novel
"The City in the Sea"	a poem
"America the Beautiful"	a song

Punctuation

END MARKS AND COMMAS

The sole purpose of punctuation is to make clear the meaning of what you write. When you speak, the actual sound of your voice, the rhythmic rise and fall of your inflections, your pauses and hesitations, your stops to take breath—all supply a kind of "punctuation" that serves to group your words and to indicate to your listener precisely what you mean. Indeed, even the body takes part in this unwritten punctuation. A raised eyebrow may express interrogation more eloquently than a question mark, and a knuckle rapped on the table shows stronger feeling than an exclamation point.

In written English, however, where there are none of these hints to meaning, simple courtesy requires the writer to make up for the lack by careful punctuation. Examine the following sentences. If you heard them spoken, you might know exactly what was meant; but as they stand, with no punctuation to show where one thought ends and another begins, they are confusing.

> For breakfast Jim ordered bacon and eggs and Jill asked for half a grapefruit and whole-wheat toast.

> The marathon course ran along the beach across the highway through the tunnel and into the stadium.

> After she slammed the door and vowed never to return Helen sheepishly knocked and asked for her keys.

Don't overpunctuate. A sentence that bristles with commas, colons, dashes, and brackets within parentheses doesn't need the services of a punctuation expert. It needs to be rewritten. Use a mark of punctuation for only two reasons: (1) because the meaning demands it or (2) because conventional usage requires it. Otherwise, do not use punctuation.

DIAGNOSTIC TEST

Correcting Sentences by Using End Marks and Commas Correctly. Rewrite the following sentences, inserting end marks and commas as needed.

EXAMPLE 1. Well what do you want me to say
        1. *Well, what do you want me to say?*

1. Although scholars are not certain of the first European printer to use movable type Johann Gutenberg is usually credited
2. The students who have signed up for the field trip may leave at noon but all others must attend classes
3. Gloria did you see where I left my bowling ball
4. Willa Cather who was born in Virginia but moved to Nebraska at the age of eight wrote most of her stories about people living on the western plains
5. The Great Pyramid of Cheops in Egypt dates back to 2680 BC
6. Vendors sold T-shirts buttons caps and pennants to the sports fans outside the stadium
7. Standing in the pouring rain I waited over an hour for you
8. We munched on unsalted roasted sunflower seeds and quenched our thirst with cold refreshing orange juice
9. Their house is I think the fourth one from the corner at 1042 Cleveland Avenue
10. My cousin a mail carrier does not appreciate jokes about postal workers
11. Rita did not call me this morning nor did she call in the afternoon
12. We rushed to the airport stood in line bought our tickets and then heard that the flight would be delayed for three hours
13. Norm has had an incredible run of bad luck yet he still says that tomorrow will be a better day for he prides himself on being an optimist
14. The Ming vase wrapped carefully in cotton and packed in a crate was delivered to the museum today

15. Of course if we arrive late for practice one more time Ms. Stubbs will kick us off the team

16. Thank goodness my sister had taught me how to swim for I could have drowned when the boat tipped over

17. On the sidelines near the home fans the coach watched the downcast discouraged team trudge off the field

18. The advertisement for toothpaste was in my opinion clearly misleading

19. In 1883 Jan Matzeliger an inventor in Lynn Massachusetts revolutionized the shoe industry with his machine that mechanically joined the top of the shoe to the sole

20. The following people should report to the auditorium after lunch hour: Robert Wilcox Amalia Gibson Phil Assad and Cora Mae Diamond

---

The rules for the correct use of end punctuation and commas are listed on the following pages. Learn the rules. Do the exercises. Read over carefully once or twice whatever you have written before handing it in, each time inserting whatever punctuation is necessary to make the writing clear and taking out marks that are unnecessary. Above all, *apply what you learn about punctuation to everything you write*.

PERIODS, QUESTION MARKS, AND EXCLAMATION POINTS

25a. A statement is followed by a period.

EXAMPLES Margaret Walker has written many beautiful poems.
Underneath the waterfall floated an ivory swan.
"I'm going to stay after school," said Barb.

25b. A question is followed by a question mark.

EXAMPLES What do you want for lunch?
Who bought the pizza?
When are you leaving?

Sometimes the way in which a writer intends a sentence to be read determines whether it is a statement or a question.

STATEMENT You're angry with me. [Read with falling inflection.]

QUESTION You're angry with me? [Read with rising inflection.]

Be sure to distinguish between a declarative sentence which contains an indirect question and an interrogative sentence, which asks a direct question.

INDIRECT QUESTION   She asked me **why I left so early.** [declarative]

DIRECT QUESTION   When is the party**?** [interrogative]

25c. An exclamation is followed by an exclamation point.

EXAMPLES   Great shot**!**
Fantastic**!**
I'm freezing**!**

25d. An imperative sentence is followed by either a period or an exclamation point.

EXAMPLES   Open the door for me, please**.** [calmly]
Open the door**!** [with strong feeling]

It is not hard to use the question mark and the exclamation point correctly. The sound of your own voice as you read your sentences under your breath gives you sufficient clues to where these marks go. It is much harder to know where to put the period. You can never be certain of this until you are certain of what a sentence is and where it ends. (Chapters 1–4 and Chapter 11 of this book should help you to recognize a sentence and therefore to know where to put the period.)

Perhaps the most common cause of end-mark errors, however, is simply carelessness. Always take time to proofread your writing.

EXERCISE 1. Correcting Sentences by Using End Marks.   In this exercise all end marks have been omitted. On your paper, write the final word of the sentence with the proper end mark, followed by the first word of the next sentence, if any.

EXAMPLE   1. Miriam Colón, a native of Puerto Rico, is an accomplished actress using her own experience, she wished to acquaint Americans with the art and culture of Puerto Rico to that end she founded and directed the Puerto Rican Traveling Theatre

1. *actress. Using*
Puerto Rico. To
Theatre.

1. Gail was assigned a report on knighthood, and she undertook the assignment eagerly she knew from the stories she had read that

knights were spotless champions of God and humanity she knew also that a long apprenticeship preceded the honor of knighthood and that young boys of the nobility started this training as soon as they were able to wield a sword or draw a bow

2. When a lad completed his training as a page, he was promoted to the rank of squire in this capacity he accompanied his lord into battle, fighting at his side and caring for the knight's horse and equipment at long last the squire himself was deemed fit to become a knight he was accorded this honor, however, only after several honorable wounds and some show of gallantry on his part had impressed the sovereign with the lad's readiness to uphold the code of chivalry

3. When the sovereign considered him ready, a day was appointed for the ceremony how long had the youth waited for this glorious hour how many times had he rehearsed in his fancy every step in the stately ceremony now that it was at last at hand, he could scarcely believe his good fortune he resolved to conduct himself always as a perfect knight—to bear true and faithful allegiance to his lord, to bow his head meekly before misfortune, to help the weak, to punish the wicked, and to answer any insult to his honor with terrible, swift power

4. These things about knighthood Gail knew already as she entered the library and opened the encyclopedia what a surprise lay in store for her she found first of all that the chivalry of Europe arose from a simple economic circumstance the first chevaliers were those rich enough to afford horses *chevalier* in French and *Ritter* in German mean ''knight,'' but these words also mean ''rider'' this fact suggests that the first knights were merely those Frankish warriors who rode into battle while their humbler fellows walked behind in the dust

5. When the cavalry of Charlemagne became the foremost military force in Europe, his way of ordering the forces was adopted by all other nations the class of soldiers comprising the cavalry became, therefore, an elite class or an aristocracy with special privileges but also with special obligations they were supported in peacetime, for example, by the labor of the rest of the population however, when the state was in danger, they were obliged to rally immediately underneath the royal standard

25e. An abbreviation is usually followed by a period.

EXAMPLES Maj. Major
Minn. Minnesota
A.D. *anno Domini*
Jan. January
lb. pound
O. J. Simpson Orenthal James Simpson

☞ NOTE Abbreviations of government agencies, service organizations, and other groups are often written without periods.

NASA National Aeronautics and Space Administration
HUD Department of Housing and Urban Development
NCTE National Council of Teachers of English
AMA American Medical Association

Abbreviations in the metric system are often written without periods, especially in science books.

km kilometer
ml milliliter

Most abbreviations are capitalized only if the words they stand for are capitalized.

WRITING APPLICATION A:
Using Periods, Question Marks, and Exclamation Points Correctly in Your Writing

When you use periods, question marks, and exclamation points correctly in your writing, you make your purpose clear to your readers. As you read the following sentences, notice that the end punctuation makes the purpose of each clear.

You want me to leave the theater. [sentence making a statement]
Please leave the theater. [sentence making a request]
Do you want me to leave the theater? [sentence asking a question]
You want me to leave the theater? [sentence intended as a question]
Leave the theater! [sentence expressing strong feeling]

You should take care to use correct end punctuation. Refer to the rules on pages 677–78 whenever you are in doubt.

Writing Assignment

Write five sentences according to the following guidelines. Use correct end punctuation.

1. Write an imperative sentence that expresses a mild emotion.
2. Write an imperative sentence that expresses a strong emotion.
3. Write a sentence that is intended as a question.
4. Write a sentence that asks a direct question.
5. Write an exclamatory sentence that begins with an interjection that expresses a strong emotion.

COMMAS

Commas are necessary for clear expression of ideas.

Items in a Series

25f. Use commas to separate items in a series.

WORDS IN SERIES The counselor distributed baseballs, bats, volleyballs, tennis rackets, and bandages to the campers. [nouns]
The dog growled, snarled, and leaped at the intruder. [verbs]

PHRASES IN SERIES We have a government of the people, by the people, and for the people.

SUBORDINATE CLAUSES IN SERIES I know I will pass the test if I take good notes, if I study hard, and if I get a good night's sleep.

☞ NOTE When the last two items in a series are joined by *and,* you may omit the comma before the *and* if the comma is not necessary to make the meaning clear.

CLEAR The entertainers sang, danced and juggled. [clear with comma omitted]

UNCLEAR We elected the club's president, vice-president, secretary and treasurer. [Not clear with comma omitted. How many officers, three or four?]

CLEAR We elected the club's president, vice-president, secretary, and treasurer.

Some words appear so often paired with another that they may be set off in a series as one item.

EXAMPLES peanut butter and jelly, bacon and eggs, pen and paper

(1) If all items in a series are joined by *and* or *or* (*nor*), you should not use commas to separate them.

EXAMPLES We ran and walked and even limped to the finish line.
A volunteer addresses envelopes or answers phones or files correspondence.

(2) Independent clauses in a series are usually separated by semicolons. Short independent clauses, however, may be separated by commas.

EXAMPLES For physical fitness we swam, we jogged, and we exercised. [short clauses]
For physical fitness we swam twenty-five laps in the pool; we jogged four miles around the lake; and we exercised with workout equipment in Pam's basement.

25g. Use a comma to separate two or more adjectives preceding a noun.

EXAMPLE The accident was a frightening, horrible sight.

When the last adjective before the noun is thought of as part of the noun, the comma before the adjective is omitted.

EXAMPLE The new elementary school will be completed in 1987.

Here the adjective *elementary* is so closely associated with the word *school* that the two words are considered a unit, a single word, or what is called a *compound noun*. Therefore, the adjective *new* modifies not just *school* but *elementary*. A comma is not used.

To determine whether it is right to put commas between two adjectives in a series of adjectives modifying a noun, substitute the word *and* for the doubtful comma. If the *and* sounds wrong, then you don't need a comma.

PROBLEM I cautiously raised my broken right hand in response. [comma before *right*?]

USE <u>AND</u> I cautiously raised my broken and right hand in response. [obviously wrong!]

SOLUTION I cautiously raised my broken right hand in response. [no comma]

EXERCISE 2. Correcting Sentences by Using Commas. Number your paper 1–20. Write each word after which a comma is needed and then add the comma. Some sentences will not need commas. If a sentence is correct with the commas omitted, write *no commas needed* after the proper number.

EXAMPLE 1. The singer wore a red vest blue shoes and white jeans.
1. *vest, shoes,*

1. Rachel Patsy and Lisa swam in the state swim meet.
2. Mark won ribbons in the swimming diving and rowing events.
3. The spectators paid the entry fee bought programs and found their seats.
4. The following students were members of my committee: Alice Patterson Susie Wong Chrissy Osborne and Neil Young.
5. Many people really love flying some merely tolerate it and others avoid it completely.
6. Tim and Jan plan to arrive today or tomorrow or even Sunday.
7. We plan to spend our vacation in San Diego San Francisco or San Bernardino.
8. Tammy Rich and Patti have exciting summer jobs at an exclusive new health resort.
9. My new alarm clock didn't go off my breakfast was cold and the school bus had a flat tire.
10. For his birthday dinner, Matt chose onion soup steak and a chocolate sundae.
11. Ellen's plaid winter coat definitely needed mending.
12. The river overflowed again and filled our basement and our neighbors' basements.
13. Alligators sharks and snakes are dangerous annoying nuisances in Florida.
14. I took a flashlight sleeping bag extra tennis shoes pocket knife and rain parka on our camping trip.
15. James Garfield Harry Truman and Gerald Ford were left-handed U.S. Presidents.
16. At the gymnastics meet Les performed on the parallel bars the rings and the high bar.
17. A little blond child in faded blue jeans emerged from the shrubbery to stare at the mail carrier.

18. Catherine of Aragon Anne Boleyn Jane Seymour Anne of Cleves Catherine Howard and Catherine Parr were wives of the notorious Henry VIII.
19. Sylvia is a fan of the great women novelists: Jane Austen the Brontë sisters Virginia Woolf Willa Cather Elizabeth Bowen George Eliot and many others.
20. With a quick powerful leap to the ground, the stuntman bounded over the burning balcony.

EXERCISE 3. Writing Sentences Using Commas Correctly. Write ten sentences, illustrating each of the following uses of the comma twice.

1. Two or more adjectives preceding a noun
2. Nouns in a series requiring a comma before the *and* between the last two items
3. Phrases in a series
4. Short independent clauses in a series
5. A sentence containing a series joined by conjunctions, requiring no commas

Commas Between Independent Clauses

25h. Use a comma before *and, but, or, nor, for, so,* and *yet* when they join independent clauses.

EXAMPLES Patrick brought the hot dogs and buns, and Cindy brought the potato salad.
We were there on time, but Jeff and Maria arrived late.

☞ NOTE Independent clauses joined by *and, but, or,* or *nor* need not be separated by a comma when they are very short. If the clauses are joined by the conjunctions *yet, so,* or *for,* they must be separated by a comma.

EXAMPLES The poodle tensed and the German shepherd growled. [Clauses are too short to require commas.]
We sprayed with insecticide, yet the bugs still found us. [Clauses are short but are separated by the conjunction *yet.* Therefore, a comma is required.]

We bought Ann a lovely gift, for she is very special to us. [Comma is needed because clauses are joined by *for*.]

SIMPLE SENTENCE Bob brought the charcoal and lighter fluid but forgot matches. [one independent clause with a compound verb]

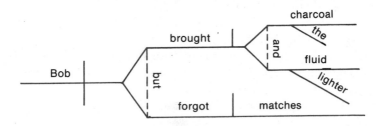

TWO CLAUSES Bob brought the charcoal and lighter fluid, but he forgot matches. [two independent clauses]

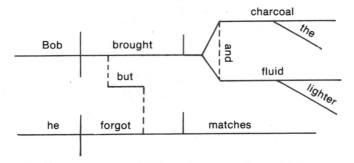

EXERCISE 4. Correcting Compound Sentences by Using Commas.

The sentences in this exercise contain independent clauses joined by the conjunctions *and, but, or, for, nor,* or *yet.* Number your paper 1–10. Decide where the commas should go, and write the word preceding each comma on your paper after the proper number. Add the comma and the conjunction following it. Do not be misled by compound verbs. If a sentence is correct without commas, write *no commas needed* after the proper number.

EXAMPLE 1. Uncle Phil carefully maneuvered the boat through the narrow channel and Lynn began baiting the hooks.
      1. *channel, and*

1. All students must arrive on time for no one will be admitted late.
2. The newspaper review complimented every performance in the movie but the leading actress received the strongest praise.
3. A few spectators tried to climb over the fence but the police ordered them back.
4. Environmentalists who try to prevent the destruction of valuable land and water areas must stay alert or their efforts may be frustrated by their opponents.
5. In general, people today work fewer hours than their grandparents did yet for some the difference is not great.
6. The cost of living is rising for consumers must pay higher prices for gasoline and other products.
7. Our guide led and we followed closely.
8. Although the manager had signaled for a bunt, Patricia hit a home run and later the manager said nothing about disobeying instructions.
9. She said she did not like the story in the science-fiction magazine nor did she enjoy the illustrations.
10. High-school graduates may go on to college or they may prefer to begin a career immediately.

EXERCISE 5. Writing Compound Sentences Using Commas Correctly. Write six compound sentences, each illustrating the use of a different one of the following six conjunctions to join independent clauses: *and, or, but, nor, for,* and *yet.* Punctuate your sentences correctly before handing them in.

Nonessential Clauses and Phrases

25i. Use commas to set off nonessential clauses and nonessential participial phrases.

A nonessential[1] clause is a subordinate clause that is not essential to the meaning of the sentence. Such clauses serve only to add some extra information or to explain something further; they could be omitted without altering the fundamental meaning of the sentence. An essential[2] clause, on the other hand, is one that cannot be omitted without changing the meaning of the sentence.

---

[1] A nonessential clause is sometimes called a nonrestrictive clause.
[2] An essential clause is sometimes called a restrictive clause.

NONESSENTIAL   Peter Lincoln, **who works with my father,** bought a new
Corvette yesterday.

Since you know without the clause who it was that bought a new
Corvette yesterday, the clause is not necessary to identify Peter Lincoln; it merely adds information about him. It is a nonessential clause
and should be set off by commas. *Most adjective clauses that modify
proper nouns are nonessential and require commas.*

ESSENTIAL   All books **that are damaged** go in these boxes.

The clause *that are damaged* is essential because it tells which
books go in these boxes. Omitting the clause would change the meaning of the sentence into something absurd. Since the clause is an
integral, or essential, part of the sentence, it is not set off by commas.
(Adjective clauses introduced by *that* are almost always essential.)

EXAMPLES   The friend **whom I invited to the beach** could not come. [essential]
Kelly, **whom I invited to the beach,** could not come. [nonessential]
The U.S. President **who enjoyed turkey hash on waffles for breakfast**
was Andrew Jackson. [essential]
Andrew Jackson, **who was a U.S. President,** enjoyed turkey hash
on waffles for breakfast. [nonessential]
The Ohio city **that was called the Rubber Capital of the World** is
near my hometown. [essential]
The meal **that I like best** is spaghetti. [essential]
Spaghetti, **which I like best,** is our meal tonight. [nonessential]

Sometimes the writer of a sentence is the only one who knows
whether the clause used is nonessential (commas) or essential (no
commas). Accordingly, in order to make the meaning clear, the writer
will either make use of commas to enclose the clause or abstain from
their use.

NONESSENTIAL   My sister, **who attends Duke University,** sent me a college
sweatshirt. [The clause is not needed to identify this sister.
Since it is nonessential, it requires commas.]

ESSENTIAL   My sister **who attends Duke University** sent me a college
sweatshirt. [I have more than one sister. The clause is
necessary to tell which sister I am talking about. It should not
be set off by commas.]

The same principles govern participial phrases. You will remember that participles are of two kinds: present participles ending in *–ing* and past participles ending usually in *–ed*. A participial phrase is a group of words in which a participle is the chief word. When such a phrase is nonessential—not necessary to the sentence—the phrase is set off by commas. When it is essential, no commas are used.

NONESSENTIAL Esther**, running at a slow, leisurely pace,** easily finished the marathon.

ESSENTIAL The woman **running at a slow, leisurely pace** easily finished the marathon.

NONESSENTIAL Vicky's silk-screen**, wrapped carefully inside a cardboard box,** arrived today.

ESSENTIAL The silk-screen **wrapped carefully inside a cardboard box** was not damaged.

EXERCISE 6. Correcting Sentences by Using Commas.

Number your paper 1–10. After the proper number, write all words in the sentence that should be followed by a comma. Write the comma after each word. Be prepared to explain your answers. Some sentences do not need commas. If a sentence does not require commas, write *no commas needed* after the proper number.

EXAMPLE 1. The idea for supermarkets which we take for granted today developed in the nineteenth century.
1. *supermarkets, today,*

1. The stores that became the world's first supermarkets were designed by Clarence Saunders.
2. Mr. Saunders who lived in Memphis, Tennessee named his stores Piggly Wiggly.
3. He got the idea for the name when he saw a fat pig wiggling under a fence.
4. The Piggly Wiggly store that Saunders developed had only one long aisle.
5. Customers who were shopping there saw all the products before they came to the exit.
6. Albert Gerrard who noticed that people had difficulty finding products opened his own grocery store.

7. All items that were for sale were arranged alphabetically.
8. The name that Gerrard selected for his store was Alpha-Beta.
9. George Hartford who founded the Great Atlantic & Pacific Tea Company in 1859 nicknamed his stores A & P.
10. The model for today's huge supermarket complexes which was developed by Michael Cullen opened in an abandoned garage in Queens, New York, on August 30, 1930.

EXERCISE 7. Writing Sentences Using Commas Correctly.
Write three sentences containing nonessential clauses, three containing essential clauses, two containing nonessential phrases, and two containing essential phrases. Label each sentence according to the kind of phrase or clause it contains.

Introductory Elements

25j. Use a comma after certain introductory elements.

(1) Use a comma after words such as *well, yes, no,* and *why* when they begin a sentence. Exclamations like *wow, good grief,* and *gee whiz,* if not followed by an exclamation point, must also be set off by commas.

EXAMPLES **No,** I haven't taken the exam yet.
Well, I'm going to the mall tomorrow.
Why, I thought you left yesterday!
Wow, look at those wheels!

(2) Use a comma after an introductory participial phrase.

EXAMPLES **Calling for a timeout,** the referee began waving her arms.
Exhausted after three hours of continuous swimming, Diana emerged from the water.

(3) Use a comma after a succession of introductory prepositional phrases.

EXAMPLE **By the light of the silvery moon in autumn,** we went on an old-fashioned hayride. [Three prepositional phrases precede the comma.]

A single introductory prepositional phrase does not usually require a comma unless the comma is necessary to make the meaning of the sentence clear.

EXAMPLES **By noon** we had hiked four miles.
In our bank, checks are sorted automatically. [The comma is needed so that the reader does not read "our bank checks."]

(4) Use a comma after an introductory adverb clause.

An introductory adverb clause is a subordinate clause preceding an independent clause.

EXAMPLES **When you have gone to this school as long as we have,** you will know your way around.
If you enter the lot from the west, you can usually find several empty parking places.
The first game of the season is Friday; **after we claim our first victory,** we'll celebrate at Darcy's Pizza parlor.

EXERCISE 8. Correcting Sentences by Using Commas. The sentences in this exercise contain introductory clauses and phrases. Decide where a comma should be used. After numbering your paper, copy the word preceding each comma, and place the comma after it. Some of the sentences may not require commas; in this case, write *no commas needed* after the proper number.

EXAMPLE 1. During the morning classes will be shortened by ten minutes.
1. *morning,*

1. For many people in the world meat is not a daily food staple.
2. Serving as a primary source of nutrition whole grains such as corn, barley, oats, wheat, and rice feed millions.
3. In Mexico a favorite nutritious meal is a corn tortilla combined with beans.
4. Because it has been a principal crop for over 5,000 years the soybean, which is high in protein, is abundantly used by people in Asian countries.
5. In an effort to economize you may want to substitute unrefined whole grains for meat occasionally in your diet.
6. As very healthful alternatives to meat whole grains contain nutrients such as vitamins, amino acids, proteins, and starches.
7. In order to make a spoilage-resistant product food manufacturers refine whole grains.
8. Refined for commercial use the grains lose most of their food value because the nutritious outer hulls are stripped away.

9. If you take time in the supermarket you should be able to find whole grains.
10. Since many cookbooks now include recipes for grains you can learn to prepare a variety of interesting snacks and meals.

REVIEW EXERCISE A. Correcting Sentences by Using Commas.
This exercise covers all uses of the comma that you have studied so far. Number your paper 1–20. Decide where commas should be used in each sentence. Write the word preceding the comma, and place the comma after the word.

EXAMPLE 1. In her lecture on cities Professor Gonzales who is an expert in her field suggested that the development of towns might have had as much to do with self-defense as with commerce.
    1. *cities, Gonzales, field,*

1. The English word *weapon* is related to the Old English *waepen* the Dutch *wapen* the German *Waffe* and some earlier common root.
2. Sticks stones and poisons were among the weapons used by primitive cultures.
3. Modern weapons which are produced by sophisticated people like ourselves are more fully developed.
4. Weapons that were produced in early times were not well developed nor were they distinct from each other in appearance function or design.
5. An object found in an archaeological dig might be an eating utensil a tool for the hearth a farming implement or a weapon of war.
6. Coming upon such an ancient object diggers might not be able to identify its function with immediate instinctive accuracy.
7. The old Assamese *dao* which was a sharp knifelike object was used to chop plants fell trees kill animals threaten enemies and carve wood.
8. The cord sling which is easily the most familiar sling was used all over the world for it was easy to put together and not too difficult to master.
9. When he slew Goliath David used a simple sling.
10. The boomerang which is a flat stick that can be thrown with accuracy was developed into a weapon by the people of Australia and the western Pacific.

11. Although they were both used as weapons the fighting boomerang and the returning boomerang are not the same.
12. Among the many kinds of weapons the stick thrown by hand became one of the most heavily specialized.
13. In many cases clubs were thrown even though they were not designed for the purpose but design played an important role in the history of most weapons.
14. The dart the arrow the spear the lance and the javelin all developed from the plain stick thrown by hand.
15. The simplest earliest development was the addition of a head to the stick transforming the stick itself into a shaft.
16. The plainest and least developed was the stick that was hardened by fire at one end and often pointed.
17. Among the more unusual weapons *bolas* consisted of weighted balls of stone wood or metal tied together with thongs.
18. The purpose of the *bola* which was somewhat different from that of most other weapons was to entangle the victim without inflicting pain injury or death.
19. Primitive undeveloped straightforward weapons like all these are somewhat easier to contemplate than the intricate devious modern weapons of our own day.
20. As anyone can see the purpose of both kinds of weapons is identical and the end results have not altered in the least.

Interrupters

25k. Use commas to set off expressions that interrupt.

There are three kinds of "interrupters" that you should be able to recognize and punctuate properly.

(1) Appositives and appositive phrases are usually set off by commas.
An appositive is a word or group of words that follows a noun or pronoun and means the same thing as the noun or pronoun. An appositive usually identifies or explains the noun or pronoun that precedes it.

EXAMPLES Nancy Landon Kassebaum, the **senator** from Kansas, was the principal speaker.
The Aegean Sea, the **highroad** of ancient Greece, is sprinkled with small islands.
I loved my gift, a pearl **ring.**

In these sentences *senator, highroad,* and *ring* are appositives.

When you set off an appositive, you include with it all the words that modify it. Together, an appositive and its modifiers constitute an appositive phrase.

EXAMPLES   Fort Sumter, **site of the opening battle of the Civil War,** stands in Charleston's harbor.
I enjoyed *At Home in India,* **a book by Cynthia Bowles.**
Neil Armstrong, **the first man to walk on the moon,** took his historic step on July 20, 1969.

Sometimes an appositive is so closely related to the word preceding it that it should not be set off by commas. Such an appositive is called a "restrictive appositive." It is usually a single word.

EXAMPLES   my brother **James**
the author **Herman Melville**
my cat **Bonkers**
your friend **Catherine**

EXERCISE 9. Correcting Sentences by Using Commas.   Rewrite the following sentences containing appositives, and insert commas where needed.

1. The *Mona Lisa* a painting by Leonardo da Vinci is a prize possession of the Louvre.
2. The painting a portrait of a young Florentine woman is slightly cracked from temperature changes.
3. In 1911 an Italian house painter Vincenzo Perugia stole the painting from its frame.
4. For two years the Paris police some of the cleverest detectives in the world were baffled by the crime.
5. Since its recovery the painting one of the most valuable portraits in the world has been carefully protected.

(2) Words used in direct address are set off by commas.

EXAMPLES   **David,** please close the door.
Did you call me, **Mother**?
Yes, **Mr. Kirk,** I gave you the paper.

(3) Parenthetical expressions are set off by commas.

These expressions are often used parenthetically: *I believe (think, suppose, hope,* etc.), *on the contrary, on the other hand, of course, in my opinion, for example, however, to tell the truth, nevertheless, in fact, on the whole, also, too, in addition, thus.*

EXAMPLES You are**,** I hope**,** planning to come.

His new poems**,** in fact**,** are as inspiring as his earlier ones.

These expressions are not *always* used as interrupters.

EXAMPLES She wore her ring **on the other hand.** [not used as an interrupter]

Who**, on the other hand,** really knows which is proper? [used as an interrupter]

I believe today is my first absence. [not used as an interrupter]

It is**, I believe,** my first absence. [used as an interrupter]

☞ **NOTE** A contrasting expression introduced by *not* or *yet* is parenthetical and must be set off by commas.

EXAMPLE Emily Brontë**, not Charlotte ,** was the author of *Wuthering Heights.*

EXERCISE 10. Correcting Sentences by Using Commas.

Number your paper 1–10. After the proper number, write the words in each sentence that should be followed by a comma, and place a comma after each word.

1. In 1984 Geraldine Ferraro a New York congresswoman became the first female vice-presidential candidate on a major party ticket.
2. However she wasn't the first woman to seek high office for Victoria Woodhull was the presidential nominee of the Equal Rights party in 1872.
3. Antonetta Ferraro Geraldine's mother worked as a crochet beader a person who fastens beads and sequins on evening dresses to send her daughter to a boarding school.
4. Geraldine was very active in school and was in fact named most likely to succeed.
5. After she graduated from college Geraldine an ambitious woman felt that a job as an elementary-school teacher was not enough.
6. Consequently she began attending Fordham Law School at night.
7. Although she married John Zaccaro in 1960 she kept her maiden name professionally.
8. When her younger daughter was seven years old Geraldine became an assistant district attorney in Queens, New York.

9. Generally speaking that experience gave her many valuable insights into the criminal justice system and helped her to form strong feelings about the rights of victims.
10. Geraldine Ferraro credits her mother for helping her become a strong yet compassionate person.

Conventional Situations

25l. Use a comma in certain conventional situations.

(1) Use a comma to separate items in dates and addresses.

In addresses the street number and the name of the street are not separated from each other by a comma. Neither are the name of the state and the ZIP code number that follows it. Similarly, in dates the day of the month and the month itself are considered one item. Commas do go between the date and the year and the city and the state.

EXAMPLES   On June 15, 1985, my best friend Cary moved to 814 Georgia Avenue, Miami Beach, Florida 33139.
Send your reservation to Juanita Miller, 314 Limestone Street, Springfield, Ohio 45503.
My cousin moved to Jackson, Mississippi, last April.
The national exam will be given on Tuesday, February 1, at the high school.
Our address is 54 Rugby Avenue, Kansas City, Missouri 64112.

(2) Use a comma after the salutation of a friendly letter and after the closing of any letter.

EXAMPLES   Dear Marcus,   Dear Aunt Meg,
Affectionately yours,   Sincerely yours,
Yours truly,

(3) Use a comma after a name followed by *Jr., Sr., Ph.D.,* etc.

EXAMPLES   Dr. Elena Moreno, Ph.D.
Russell E. Davis, Jr.
David Owens Knopp, M.D.

Unnecessary Commas

25m. Do not use unnecessary commas.

Too much punctuation can make a sentence as confusing as too little punctuation. Do not use a comma unless a rule specifically calls for it or unless the sentence would be unclear without it. When in doubt, leave it out.

EXERCISE 11. Correcting Sentences by Using Commas. Number your paper 1–10. After the proper number, write the words in each sentence that should be followed by a comma, and place a comma after each word.

EXAMPLE 1. On our way to Birmingham Alabama we stayed overnight in Chattanooga Tennessee.
1. *Birmingham, Alabama, Chattanooga,*

1. The first municipal airport opened on November 20 1919 in Tucson Arizona.
2. Send your suggestions to the U.S. Olympic Committee 1750 E. Boulder Street Colorado Springs Colorado 80909.
3. On September 1 1985 we moved from Eureka California to 220 Tuxford Place Thousand Oaks California 91360.
4. We left Tampa Florida on Monday June 15 and arrived in Albuquerque New Mexico on June 17.
5. The hotel on Gulfport Road was destroyed by fire on Tuesday March 13 1984.
6. Mother sent her recipe ideas to General Foods Corporation 250 North Street White Plains New York 10625.
7. My brother received a letter that started, "Dear John There's something I've been meaning to tell you."
8. We interviewed Franklin R. Thomas M.D. at his emergency clinic on Wilson Road.
9. Joanne did you dice the vegetables this afternoon?
10. The first cable car began operating I believe in San Francisco California in 1873.

REVIEW EXERCISE B. Correcting Sentences by Using Commas.
Rewrite the following sentences, inserting commas where necessary. Do not use unnecessary commas.

1. Last Tuesday we learned about the Pharos at Alexandria one of the wonders of the ancient world. It was I believe one of the largest lighthouses ever built.
2. The lighthouse situated on an island two hundred yards from the mainland was one of the tallest buildings of its time.
3. The rulers of Alexandria then one of the most powerful cities in the world built the lighthouse at the entrance of the city's harbor.

4. The Pharos a blocklike structure contained a military barracks at its base. Its huge lamp which was fueled by wood or oil cast a powerful beam far into the night.

5. In the fourteenth century an earthquake destroyed the lighthouse.

6. Archaeologists tell us that traces of the lighthouse remained for centuries but we could not I suppose reasonably expect to see signs of the ancient ruin today.

7. Yes Patty today there is a lighthouse at Alexandria.

8. The city itself as its name suggests was founded by Alexander the Great in 332 B.C.

9. The Heptastadium a mile-long jetty connecting the island of the Pharos to the mainland provided a way of escape for Caesar when after a furious battle he was driven out of the city by a mob.

10. Alexandria became a great and prosperous city rivaling Rome in magnificence and surpassing it as a center for learning.

REVIEW EXERCISE C. Correcting Sentences by Using Commas.

Number your paper 1–10. Select from the following sentences all words that should be followed by a comma. Write these words on your paper, placing a comma after each.

EXAMPLE 1. It was to tell the truth really my mistake.
　　　　1. *was, truth,*

1. John Adams John Quincy Adams Theodore Roosevelt Rutherford B. Hayes Franklin D. Roosevelt and John F. Kennedy were all graduates of Harvard University.

2. Many movie stars have left their footprints in cement outside Mann's Chinese Theater 6925 Hollywood Boulevard Hollywood California.

3. Yes Ms. Kim I remembered that a sonnet has fourteen lines.

4. On the other hand haiku I believe has only three lines.

5. Although Johnny Weissmuller was a champion swimmer most people remember him as Tarzan.

6. The Tony Award an annual award for theatrical excellence was named for Antoinette Perry an American theatrical producer.

7. *Steamboat Willie* Mickey Mouse's first sound cartoon debuted at the Colony Theatre in New York City on November 8 1928.

8. Sherlock Holmes a detective created by Sir Arthur Conan Doyle is I think the best-known fictional character in the world.
9. He lived at 221B Baker Street London England with Dr. John Watson.
10. Roy Rogers "King of the Cowboys" sang with the Sons of the Pioneers married Dale Evans and starred in many westerns.

REVIEW EXERCISE D. Correcting Sentences by Using Commas.
Number your paper 1–10. Write the words in each sentence that should be followed by a comma, and place a comma after each word.

EXAMPLE 1. This year our club The Pegasus Players will stage four plays.
   1. *club, Players,*

1. The word *theater* comes from the Greek word *theatron* which means I believe "a place for seeing."
2. In fact Greek tragedy was the beginning of drama as we know it today.
3. On the slope below the Acropolis in Athens Greece early plays were performed at the Theater of Dionysus.
4. The actors wore masks to show which characters they portrayed and they often appeared in several roles.
5. Yes Gary men played all the roles.
6. Although hundreds of Greek tragedies were written fewer than thirty-five survive.
7. Aeschylus the earliest Greek dramatist wrote the *Oresteia* a powerful story of murder revenge and divine mercy.
8. Aristophanes whom the ancient Greeks considered the greatest of comic dramatists wrote *The Clouds* and *The Frogs*.
9. Sophocles often regarded as the greatest dramatist of all times is credited with almost a hundred plays of which only eight have been recovered.
10. Although the play was acclaimed by the critics the public did not like it and thus refused to recommend it to their friends.

WRITING APPLICATION B:
Using Commas Correctly in Your Writing

When you use commas correctly, you are being a careful and considerate writer; you express your ideas clearly for your readers. As you read the following pairs of sentences, notice that the second sentence in each is clearer than the first because the writer has used commas correctly.

CONFUSING   In our high school students may participate in work-study programs.

CLEAR   In our high school, students may participate in work-study programs.

CONFUSING   I bought pots and pans trays and glasses for our apartment.

CLEAR   I bought pots and pans, trays, and glasses for our apartment.

Writing Assignment

Think about the sights and sounds on a street in your neighborhood or in an imagined neighborhood. Write a descriptive paragraph in which you list many of those sights and sounds. Be sure to use commas to separate the items in your sentence.

CHAPTER 25 REVIEW: POSTTEST 1

Correcting Sentences by Using End Marks and Commas. Rewrite the following sentences, inserting end marks and commas as needed. Remember to capitalize the first word of each sentence.

EXAMPLE   1. Stop the bus for I want to get off
　　　　　 1. *Stop the bus, for I want to get off!*

1. My dad works for the Parker Pen Company 1 Parker Place Janesville Wisconsin 53545
2. Water transports nutrients throughout the body aids in digestion and helps regulate body temperature
3. Why Bill I didn't know you were born in Windsor Ontario too
4. Woodrow Wilson our twenty-eighth President was born in Staunton Virginia on December 28 1856
5. Did you know that Wilson was President during World War I and was awarded the Nobel Prize for Peace in 1919
6. However the United States Senate rejected the League of Nations the project that Wilson sponsored
7. Trinidad is one of the most prosperous islands in the Caribbean but unemployment usually averages thirteen percent

8. Sugar coffee cocoa citrus fruits and bananas are Trinidad's chief crops

9. Located off the coast of Venezuela Trinidad has 1,100,000 people and 150,000 television sets

10. A group of kangaroos is called a mob but a group of geese on the other hand is a gaggle

11. We are so happy Mr. Mayor that you could join us not the other group for a victory celebration

12. If I finish my report if I do the laundry and if I promise to be home by eleven I can go to the concert

13. At the clambake on the beach George ate thirty clams four lobsters and a loaf of French bread

14. We were exhausted yet we couldn't fall asleep

15. Even though I miss Topeka I love our new home at 416 Lincoln Road Chicago Illinois 60606

16. If you could come home from your vacation a day early Janice you could come to my party on July 4

17. That wouldn't inconvenience you too much would it

18. The party which I have been planning for three months will celebrate our country's birthday my sister Megan's graduation and my parents' wedding anniversary

19. Of course I want you to come

20. When we are faced with these difficult decisions we must stop concentrate and persevere

21. Please address this letter to Phyllis M Saunders M.D.

22. Deserting the clean well-lighted supermarket they shopped every Saturday morning at the open-air farmers' market

23. He believed things would turn out all right for he always carried his lucky charm a rabbit's foot in his pocket

24. I tell you Joseph no one not even our parents will believe that we were kidnapped

25. Kuri Annie and Maggie are the three best players on our volleyball team which should win the championship this year

CHAPTER 25 REVIEW: POSTTEST 2

Correcting Sentences by Using End Marks and Commas. Rewrite the following sentences, inserting end marks and commas as needed. Remember to capitalize the first word of each sentence.

EXAMPLE   1. Although deserts cover much of the planet's surface what do we really know about them

1. *Although deserts cover much of the planet's surface, what do we really know about them?*

1. When most people think of deserts they picture camel caravans waves of sand and fertile oases   2. Of course the Sahara the world's largest desert comes to mind   3. Most people however would be surprised to learn that sand dunes make up only about 15 percent of the Sahara   4. The desert's surface is actually described as a *hammada* which is an Arabic word that means "stone plateau" or "rocky desert"   5. About 70 percent of the Sahara is covered by rocks gravel and boulder-strewn badlands

6. People also believe the desert is always hot burning under the merciless sun   7. How wrong can they be   8. Very wrong 9. Although the temperature may reach as high as 135 degrees during the day it often drops below freezing at night

10. Many people are fascinated by the romance of the desert yet few are aware of the truly serious problems of desert regions 11. Scientists environmentalists and world leaders are increasingly worried about desertification which is the process of fertile land turning into dry unproductive desert   12. From 1968 to 1974 six long tragic years the Sahel a large area south of the Sahara experienced a drought   13. Because of this devastating drought between 100,000 and 200,000 people died thousands more were forced to migrate and millions suffered from lack of food and water   14. Some people left the Sahel early enough to avoid the drought but others stayed until they were forced to migrate to other areas   15. By the middle of 1973 for example over 100,000 of the people living in the Sahel had fled to Dakar the capital of Senegal

16. Humans however were not the only ones affected by the drought   17. The United Nations Food and Agricultural Organization the FAO calculated that in one year during the drought over three million cattle died   18. On the other hand the people and animals that survived were weakened by malnutrition and their resistance to diseases like measles and smallpox was reduced to dangerous levels

19. The drought in the Sahel which also affected other areas in Africa renewed worldwide concern about desertification   20. Will the Sahara for instance continue to grow until it engulfs all of northern Africa   21. It may be possible for approximately 23,000 square miles

of land are turned into desert every year   22. If researchers can find ways to reach the vast underground water supplies under desert areas it may help to stop the process of desertification   23. One organization that is concerned about this problem the United Nations Conference on Desertification estimates that it will take about two billion dollars each year to establish new irrigation techniques and to research ways of capturing and storing water in desert areas   24. At present desertification does not pose a threat in the United States but scientists are constantly observing the nation's arid regions   25. Death Valley the Sonoran Desert the Mojave and the Black Rock Desert are among the nation's deserts that in my opinion we should watch closely

SUMMARY OF THE USES OF THE COMMA

25f.   Use commas to separate items in a series.
    (1) If all items in a series are joined by *and* or *or* (*nor*), do not use commas to separate them.
    (2) Independent clauses in a series are usually separated by semicolons. Short independent clauses may be separated by commas.

25g.   Use commas to separate two or more adjectives preceding a noun.

25h.   Use commas before *and, but, or, nor, for,* and *yet* when they join independent clauses.

25i.   Use commas to set off nonessential clauses and nonessential participial phrases.

25j.   Use commas after certain introductory elements.
    (1) Use a comma after such words as *well, yes, no,* and *why,* when they begin a sentence.
    (2) Use a comma after an introductory participial phrase.
    (3) Use a comma after a succession of introductory prepositional phrases.
    (4) Use a comma after an introductory adverb clause.

25k.   Use commas to set off expressions that interrupt the sentence.
    (1) Appositives and appositive phrases are usually set off by commas.
    (2) Words used in direct address are set off by commas.
    (3) Parenthetical expressions are set off by commas.

25l.   Use commas in certain conventional situations.
    (1) Use a comma to separate items in dates and addresses.

(2) Use a comma after the salutation of a friendly letter and after the closing of any letter.

(3) Use a comma after a name followed by *Jr., Sr., Ph.D.,* etc.

25m.   Do not use unnecessary commas.

CHAPTER 26

Punctuation

SEMICOLONS AND COLONS

DIAGNOSTIC TEST

Correcting Sentences by Using Semicolons and Colons. The following sentences contain a comma or no punctuation where there should be a semicolon or a colon. Number your paper 1–20. After the proper number, write the word that should be followed by a colon or semicolon. After the word, place the correct mark of punctuation.

EXAMPLE 1. The Arthurs are not home, they never are this time of day.
1. *home;*

1. They phrased the petition carefully and presented it at the requested time however, the governor ignored it.
2. The meeting is scheduled for 3 30 tomorrow afternoon please be prompt.
3. The following committees will report at that time budget, membership, awards, and programs.
4. As was his custom upon arising, he read a meditation for peace this morning he selected John 14 27.
5. We took some food to the stray dog it looked so forlorn standing in the doorway.
6. The modern literature class read these poems, "Incident" by Countee Cullen, "The Love Song of J. Alfred Prufrock" by T. S. Eliot, and "Ars Poetica" by Archibald MacLeish.

7. After she came to Barton Hall, Millie finished her work on time, learned her lessons, and kept her clothes mended and clean nevertheless, other girls received more attention and praise than she.

8. The social worker repeated the request, "We are in desperate need of the following items, canned food, powdered milk, and disinfectant. All contributions will be appreciated."

9. Conrad Aiken was, for a number of years, a correspondent for the *New Yorker* magazine and also wrote essays and short stories he is best known, however, for his poetry.

10. The Bering Strait links the Arctic Ocean with the Bering Sea, both the sea and the strait are named for Vitus Bering, a Danish explorer.

11. In the essay "Self Reliance," Ralph Waldo Emerson makes this statement "Whoso would be a man must be a nonconformist. He who would gather immortal palms must not be hindered by the name of goodness, but must explore if it be goodness."

12. Winners in the Douglas Fun Run last Saturday morning were Otis Williams, a sophomore, Janice Hicks, a senior, and Rodrigo Campas, a junior.

13. They opposed every motion that came before the meeting in addition, they said they would circulate petitions if any of the proposals were passed.

14. At first children were afraid, believing that they were lost only after their teacher reassured them that she knew the way did they become calm and walk along the path.

15. This design will be applied in the following types of machines commercial, manufacturing, military, and agricultural.

16. Shirley Jackson, a promising author before her untimely death in 1965, lived in Vermont most of her life as a writer she is best known for the short story "The Lottery."

17. In addition to the imaginative, eerie tales for which Shirley Jackson is known, she wrote *Life Among the Savages* and *Raising Demons* these autobiographical novels are amusing accounts of her own household.

18. In his short life Justin has lived in Tulsa, Oklahoma Tucson, Arizona Dallas, Texas and Shreveport, Louisiana.

19. The tournament was badly organized because low-handicap players were paired with partners who barely knew how to play golf

consequently, the experienced players were frustrated and the novices were confused.

20. None of the entries met the standard of quality the art museum expected for the contest therefore, no winner was named.

THE SEMICOLON

The semicolon [;] is a very useful mark of punctuation. It says to the reader, "Pause here a little longer than you do for a comma, but not as long as you do for a period."

26a. Use a semicolon between independent clauses in a sentence if they are not joined by *and, but, or, nor, for, so* or *yet*.

EXAMPLES   Everyone else in my family excels in a particular sport; I seem to be the only exception.

Mary Ellen was elected president of the Honor Society; she truly deserved that recognition.

When the thoughts of the clauses are *very closely connected*, a semicolon is better than a period.

26b. Use a semicolon between independent clauses joined by such words as *for example, for instance, that is, besides, accordingly, moreover, nevertheless, furthermore, otherwise, therefore, however, consequently, instead,* and *hence*.

EXAMPLES   Only two people registered for the calligraphy lessons; **consequently,** the class was canceled.

The dark clouds threatened rain; **nevertheless,** we were still expected at batting practice.

I am planning to go shopping tomorrow; **however,** I could wait and go with you on Saturday.

When the connectives mentioned in this rule are placed at the beginning of a clause, the use of a comma after them is frequently a matter of taste. When they are clearly parenthetical (interrupters), they are followed by a comma. The words *for example, for instance,* and *that is* are always followed by a comma. The word *however* is usually followed by a comma.

26c. A semicolon (rather than a comma) may be needed to separate independent clauses joined by a coordinating conjunction if there are commas within the clauses.

EXAMPLES My birthday gift to Margaret is a surprise, and I think she will
enjoy it. [A comma between the clauses is sufficient.]
My birthday gift to Margaret, a ticket to the rock concert next
week, is a surprise; and since she likes the group that will be
performing, I think she will enjoy it. [Additional commas make the
semicolon preferable.]

26d. Use a semicolon between items in a series if the items contain commas.

EXAMPLES There are four home stations for the Goodyear blimps: Long
Beach, California; Houston, Texas; Miami, Florida; and Rome,
Italy.
You may turn in the reports on Thursday, September 14; Friday,
September 15; or Monday, September 18.

**EXERCISE 1. Correcting Sentences by Using Commas and
Semicolons.** Write on your paper (in the order in which they appear
in the sentences below) all words you think should be followed by a
semicolon or a comma. After each word, place the mark of punctuation
you decide on. Number your list by sentences, keeping the words
from each sentence together. If a sentence is correct as written, write
no punctuation necessary after the proper number.

EXAMPLE 1. The orchestra will perform on Thursday, May 5 Friday, May 6
and Saturday, May 7 all performances begin at 8:00 P.M.
    1. *5; 6; 7;*

1. The instruments in a symphony orchestra are divided into families
many musicians can easily play different instruments within one
family.
2. One group is the woodwind family, which consists of instruments
that once were made of wood but today are made of metal or
plastic and this group includes instruments such as the flute, sax-
ophone, and clarinet.
3. When a musician blows air through the tube of a woodwind instrument, a reed vibrates this vibration produces the sound, a very
distinctive tone.
4. The oboe, bassoon, and English horn have two reeds but the
clarinet has only one.
5. Kettledrums or tympani are percussion instruments that can be
tuned to a specific pitch on the other hand the cymbals, the triangle, and the other kinds of drums cannot change pitch.

6. Brass instruments, such as the trumpet, cornet, and tuba, have valves that adjust the length of the tube to raise or lower the pitch but the trombone has a slide for this purpose.

7. There are many other musical instruments that are not regularly part of an orchestra for example the accordion, the harmonica, and the bagpipes are rarely used in concert.

8. The symphony conductor's job is to combine these diverse instruments into one harmonious sound but this responsibility is only part of the talent required for the job.

9. Conductors must study for many years furthermore they must be skilled in at least one instrument.

10. Most people see conductors in the limelight they do not realize that conductors must select the music, interpret the composer's meaning, and rehearse the orchestra.

11. The goal of every conductor is to lead a major symphony in London, England Berlin, Germany Boston, Massachusetts or Chicago, Illinois.

12. Conductors play an important role they must successfully accomplish their own jobs, as well as inspire the musicians to do their best.

13. Vocal music adds another dimension to orchestral music in fact this combination is responsible for the large repertoire of operas and oratorios.

14. An oratorio uses instruments, choruses, and soloists to tell a musical story without the aid of theatrical action or sets Handel's *Messiah* is an example of a well-known oratorio.

15. When major theatrical elements are combined with serious music, the performance is an opera, the most complex of all art forms.

16. Opera combines acting, singing, orchestral music, costumes, scenery, and ballet to tell a story furthermore the emotional power of the orchestral music makes the dramatic story more intense.

17. Opera, as we know it today, began in Italy in the 1500's and since that time it has been enjoyed in many parts of the world.

18. The best-known opera companies perform at La Scala in Milan, Italy the Paris Opera in France the Royal Opera House at Covent Garden in London, England the Festival Playhouse in Bayreuth, West Germany and the Metropolitan Opera House in New York.

19. Seeing and hearing an opera can be an exciting experience how-

ever you may want to read the libretto or a summary of the action before you attend.

20. Operas are usually sung in the original language of the composition, often Italian, French, or German consequently you will enjoy the performance more if you prepare in advance.

WRITING APPLICATION A:
Using Punctuation to Connect Ideas

For some people, hardware stores are intriguing because they stock so many handy items. For example, have you ever seen an "S hook"? It is a sturdy, rust-resistant hook that is shaped exactly like an "S." Its purpose is to connect two objects securely. In writing, one of the elements that joins ideas is the transition. Some of the most useful transitions are words such as *for example, besides, accordingly, however, therefore,* and so on. Like the "S hook," these transitional expressions connect two independent clauses that are closely related.

EXAMPLE   The math portion of the PSAT was difficult for me; **nevertheless,** I did my best.

Writing Assignment

Write ten original sentences using transitional expressions (see page 706). Use a semicolon in each sentence. Review your work carefully to make sure an independent clause follows the transitional expression.

THE COLON

The usual purpose of the colon is to call the reader's attention to what comes next. A colon means "notice the following."

26e. Use a colon to mean "note what follows."

Use a colon before a list of items, especially after expressions such as *as follows* or *the following items.*

EXAMPLES   We were allowed four articles in the examination area: pencils, compasses, rulers, and protractors.
We visited the major attractions in Washington, D.C.: the White House, the Capitol, the Washington Monument, and the Lincoln Memorial.

Over her summer vacation, Juanita read biographies of the following people: John Ross, Annie Wauneka, and Maria Martinez.

☞ **NOTE**   When a list comes immediately after a verb or preposition, do not use a colon.

INCORRECT   At the amusement park we rode: the roller coaster, the ferris wheel, the bumper cars, and the water ride.

CORRECT   At the amusement park we rode the roller coaster, the ferris wheel, the bumper cars, and the water ride. [The list follows the verb *rode*.]

CORRECT   Marching at the end of the parade were the junior high bands, the flag corps, and the mounted police.

CORRECT   The announcements of our benefit could be seen on posters, billboards, the sides of buses, and even the tops of taxis.

26f. Use a colon before a long, formal statement or quotation.

EXAMPLE   Thomas Paine's first pamphlet in the series *The American Crisis* starts with these famous words: "These are the times that try men's souls. The summer soldier and the sunshine patriot will, in this crisis, shrink from the service of their country; but he that stands it *now* deserves the love and thanks of man and woman."[1]

26g. Use a colon in certain conventional situations.

(1) Use a colon between the hour and the minute when you are writing the time.

EXAMPLES   6:15 P.M.   9:55 tomorrow morning

(2) Use a colon between chapter and verse in referring to passages from the Bible.

EXAMPLES   Psalms 8:9   Luke 10:27

(3) Use a colon after the salutation of a business letter.

---

[1] For further discussion of the use of long quotations in a composition, see pages 721–22.

EXAMPLES   Dear Ms. Weinberg:
         Dear Sir:

Use a comma after the salutation of a friendly letter.

EXAMPLE   Dear Suzanne,

EXERCISE 2. Correcting Sentences by Using Colons. Decide where colons should be used in the following sentences. Number your paper 1–10. After the proper number, write the word preceding the colon; then add the colon. If a sentence needs no colon, write *C* for correct after its number. Be able to explain your answers.

EXAMPLE   1. I began my acceptance speech as follows "Fellow students, thank you for your votes!"
         1. *follows:*

1. When we read the Sunday funnies, my family enjoys the talent of the following cartoonists Garry Trudeau, Charles Schulz, Cathy Guisewite, and Lynn Johnston.
2. Sometimes the paper comes at 6 15 A.M., but other times it doesn't hit the driveway until 9 00.
3. My little sister has several items embossed with Garfield's picture a poster, a nightgown, a notebook, and a clock.
4. It was Bruce Barton who made the perceptive comment "Many a man who pays rent all his life owns his home, and many a family has successfully saved for a home only to find itself at last with nothing but a house."
5. Sherry's favorite spy novelists are Robert Ludlum, Helen Mac-Innes, and Frederick Forsyth.
6. The story of Moses and the Pharaoh's daughter is told in Exodus 2 5–10.
7. The directions were as follows remove plastic wrap, place in oven, and bake for thirty minutes.
8. I prefer my bicycle to the car for three reasons I don't pay for gasoline, I don't pay for insurance, and it's all mine.
9. On our vacation in Florida, we visited Walt Disney World, Sea World, Cypress Gardens, Silver Springs, and the John F. Kennedy Space Center.
10. Mr. Wise asked us to bring to science class the following items a deciduous leaf, a coniferous needle or branch, an annual plant, and wax paper.

WRITING APPLICATION B:
Catching Your Audience's Interest by Using Colons

Two beachcombers, strolling along a deserted stretch of seacoast, suddenly came upon a sealed bottle partially buried in the sand at the water's edge. Carefully peeling away the waxy seal, they opened the bottle and extracted a note. It read:

> Help! I am stranded on a deserted isle.
> Please come get me and bring the
> following items: two dozen oranges, a
> pair of blue suede shoes, volumes six
> and seven of the *Oxford English
> Dictionary,* and three bagels.

Notice how the note's writer used a colon to draw the beachcombers' attention to the rescue shopping list. A colon signals to your audience to notice what follows.

Writing Assignment

Imagine that you are stranded on a deserted isle. Write two different notes to place in sealed bottles, each directed to a different audience, but each including a rescue shopping list. Be sure to use a colon to draw your audience's attention to your list.

CHAPTER 26 REVIEW: POSTTEST 1

Correcting Sentences by Using Semicolons and Colons. The following sentences contain commas or no punctuation where there should be semicolons or colons. Number your paper 1–25. After the proper number, write the word or words that should be followed by semicolons or colons. Then write the correct mark of punctuation after each word.

EXAMPLE 1. I am sending my application to four colleges, I hope I am accepted by one of them.
    1. *colleges;*

1. Included on the list of major rivers by the United States Geographical Society are the following the Missouri River, the Little Missouri River, the James River, and the Cheyenne River.

2. Centuries ago ancient Crete had three successive sets of symbols used for writing only one of them has been decoded by scholars.

3. If the earliest prehistoric people had not eaten meat, the results might have been as follows they would have had no reason to make weapons, they would have stayed where vegetables and plants were available all year, and they would not have migrated beyond a small area.

4. The band members plan to raise funds by holding a carwash on Friday, November 16, from 6 00 to 9 00 P.M. Saturday, November 17, from 10 00 A.M. to 5 30 P.M. and Sunday, November 18, from 2 00 to 6 00 P.M.

5. Ms. Bradley, our journalism teacher, always stresses accuracy, for example, she told us about the day the *Chicago Tribune* declared Thomas Dewey the winner of the presidential election when, of course, Harry Truman had won.

6. Hydroponics, the method of growing plants in water instead of soil, is a relatively new science researchers think it can increase the yield of commercial crops.

7. Takara is in charge of transportation and Martha will make reservations neither one wants to handle ticket sales.

8. Marie helps with the chores around the cabin Liz, on the other hand, tries to be the first one up and leaves before she can be assigned any work.

9. Even though I spent four hours preparing dinner, my mother, who is on a diet, couldn't eat most of the food my father, saying he had a meeting, left as we sat down and my brother, who refuses to eat anything not served on a bun, hardly touched the vegetables.

10. The recipe calls for these spices nutmeg, cinnamon, cloves, and vanilla.

11. Richard found graduate school difficult and his grades were not satisfactory nevertheless, he returned the second term, confident that he would improve.

12. Because the college offered several good programs, many out-of-state students attended in fact, some of them were from other countries.

13. Tattered curtains, shabby furniture, and stained carpets did not make her feel at ease about renting the apartment in spite of her doubts, however, she paid her deposit to the owner.

14. Kathy is so forgetful, not a day goes by that she doesn't lose some of her belongings.
15. The letter lying on the hall table is not for me, it begins, "Dear Mr. Howard We regret to inform you. . . ."
16. After questions had been raised, the chairman read this statement "The purpose of this study is to examine the environmental impact of building a new road in the river bottom lands."
17. Although he is not required to keep me informed, I wish he would after all, I am interested in the outcome, too.
18. The duties of this job are to help unload the delivery trucks, which arrive every day sweep the sidewalks and stack books on the shelves after they have been entered in inventory.
19. We found out he was the culprit I think, however, that we suspected he was guilty all along.
20. My grandmother reads the Bible daily, especially her favorite verse, Luke 9 25.
21. We will contact representatives from the following industries chemical, aerospace, and metallurgy.
22. Although she had been told that the meeting would start promptly at 2 30, she arrived at 3 00.
23. We will read the following poets in American literature class Emerson, Poe, Dickinson, and Frost.
24. Both my parents suffer from tinnitus, ringing in the ears, and have seen several doctors about it over the years therefore, I was relieved to learn about the American Tinnitus Association.
25. The proper use of safety equipment in the laboratory is important, no one wants to have a serious accident.

CHAPTER 26 REVIEW: POSTTEST 2

Correcting Sentences by Using Semicolons and Colons. Rewrite the following sentences and punctuate them correctly, using semicolons and colons where necessary.

EXAMPLE 1. Please bring the following items books, red pencils, newspapers.
　　　　 1. *Please bring the following items: books, red pencils, newspapers.*

1. If you want to send fragile items through the mail, the post office recommends that you pack them in fiberboard containers use

foam, plastic, or padding to cushion them and then seal the package carefully, reinforcing it with filament tape.

2. Mary McCleod Bethune, a forceful leader for black education in the 1930's and 1940's, founded a school for girls in Daytona Beach, Florida later she became a special adviser on minority affairs to President Franklin D. Roosevelt.

3. One of the best-known passages in the Bible comes from Psalms 23 1–6.

4. Cheryl worked hard to improve her grades last semester she wanted a record that would help her enter college.

5. If I had a million dollars, I would visit London, England Cairo, Egypt Buenos Aires, Argentina Tokyo, Japan and San Juan, Puerto Rico.

6. We have to write reports for gym class on one of the following athletes Jesse Owens, Sonja Henie, Jim Brown, Althea Gibson, or Babe Didrikson Zaharias.

7. The neighbor's cocker spaniel barked all night long if it happens again, I will have to speak to the owner.

8. Candice, who has rehearsed for the role, will take Sandra's place in tonight's performance unfortunately, Sandra sprained her ankle and cannot walk.

9. My aunt loves to play games such as backgammon and chess however, I usually win whenever we play.

10. This year the Lopez family is going on vacation in November Ana and Mariela will be excused from classes for two weeks.

11. Asia has both the highest and the lowest points on earth Mount Everest, the highest, soars 29,028 feet the Dead Sea, a salt lake, lies 1,300 feet below sea level.

12. Instructed to be prompt, we arrived at school at 7 15, but the doors were locked consequently, we waited until 8 30 before we could enter the building.

13. Indira Gandhi, who served for many years as the Prime Minister of India, was virtually raised in politics and government for her father was Jawaharlal Nehru, the first Prime Minister of India from 1947 to 1964.

14. My two friends, Ruth and Cindy, are not on speaking terms Ruth argued that people can become whatever they want, but Cindy insisted that people have no choice in their fate.

15. I really dislike writing outlines for reports nevertheless, the highest grade I ever received was for a report that I wrote from an outline.
16. Mrs. Kowalski has always regretted that she never learned to speak Polish when she was a little girl now she is taking Conversational Polish I and hopes to be able to talk with some of the older family friends.
17. The computer software industry is an enormous, growing business for instance, people can buy software for everything from balancing budgets to plotting astrological charts.
18. Every morning Esther rises at 5 00, jogs until 5 30, showers and eats breakfast by 6 15, and catches the 6 35 bus.
19. Red Cloud, leader of the Oglala Sioux, was an inspired military genius he successfully defended Sioux lands against the whites, who wanted to build a trail from Laramie, Wyoming, to Bozeman, Montana.
20. Gates of the Arctic National Park, which is located in northern Alaska, is known for the many animals that live there caribou, grizzly bears, moose, and wolves.
21. Irene is giving a party for Rick, who will turn sixteen next week and since the party is a surprise, she has made everyone promise not to say a word.
22. I have ridden bicycles, horses, and motorcycles and I have traveled in trains, buses, and planes but someday I hope to ride in a hot-air balloon.
23. Mrs. Jacobson let us choose one of the following topics for our final exam the Pacific Ring of Fire, the Crab Nebula, *Skylab,* or the San Andreas fault.
24. On our television set we can get UHF stations, VHF channels, and over twenty cable stations however, we still can watch only one program at a time.
25. Wanda has never had a hobby therefore, I taught her how to knit Joe taught her how to make pictures with wooden matchsticks and Amy taught her how to make vases out of old bottles and jars.

CHAPTER 27

Punctuation

UNDERLINING (ITALICS) AND QUOTATION MARKS

DIAGNOSTIC TEST

Correcting Sentences by Adding Italics or Quotation Marks. The following sentences contain words or phrases that should be in italics (underlined) or in quotation marks. Number your paper 1–20. After the proper number, write the words and punctuate them correctly.

EXAMPLES 1. Can you tell me the way to Logan Street? she asked.
            1. *"Can you tell me the way to Logan Street?"*
          2. We attended the production of Twelfth Night by the Shakespeare Festival Players.
            2. *Twelfth Night*

1. Tchaikovsky wrote The Nutcracker in 1892.
2. Are you going to help me, he asked, or shall I get someone else?
3. We have subscribed to the Orlando Sentinel ever since we moved here.
4. James Dickey wrote the novel Deliverance, on which the movie was based.
5. After someone told her it looked more sophisticated, she spelled her name with a y instead of an i.
6. Clarita served a delicious appetizer, called pulpo; hours later I asked her what it was, and she said it was octopus.
7. For our homework assignment we have to define ionization, electrolyte, quark, and neutrino.

8. During the Civil War, two ironclad ships became famous: the Merrimac, a Confederate ship, and the Monitor, a Union ship.
9. I never should have agreed to be chairwoman, wailed Ellie. When I asked Tina to help, she said, Not on your life. Now I'm doing all the work myself.
10. Where have you been, Ramon? asked Leroy. The bus leaves in three minutes!
11. When the principal announced the scholarship winners, she said that the following girls were, in her words, Elwood High's finest scholars: Daphne Johnson, Martha Lewis, Julia Perez, and Winsie Chung.
12. Carl Sandburg called Chicago the Hog Butcher for the World.
13. It was difficult for me to understand him because he dropped all the r's from his words.
14. Although Abraham Lincoln said it many years ago, politicians still quote his phrase, government of the people, by the people, for the people.
15. During lunch we discussed the magazine article Michael Jackson's Perfect Universe.
16. In the cartoon Home, James Thurber tells a story with a single image.
17. Susan looks cool in her new leather jacket.
18. This critic of Emily Dickinson's poems explains the term paradox, that is, a statement that seems contradictory but is true.
19. When the players came onto the field, why did the fans shout, Who cares?
20. I could study the sculpture Young Shadows, by Louise Nevelson, for hours.

UNDERLINING (ITALICS)

Italics are printed letters that lean to the right, like this:

These words are printed in italics.

When you are writing or typing, indicate italics by underlining the words you want italicized. If your composition were to be printed, the typesetter would set the underlined words in italics. For instance, if you typed

All sophomores in our school read <u>The Good Earth,</u> by Pearl Buck.

your sentence would be printed like this:

All sophomores in our school read *The Good Earth,* by Pearl Buck.

27a. Use underlining (italics) for titles of books, periodicals, works of art (pictures, musical compositions, films, television programs, statues, etc.), planes, trains, and so on.

EXAMPLES   <u>The Red Badge of Courage</u> [book]
<u>The Three Musicians</u> [work of art (painting)]
<u>National Geographic</u> [magazine]
the <u>Lusitania</u> [ship]

☞ NOTE   The words *a, an,* and *the* before a magazine or newspaper title are not underlined. Notice, however, that in titles of books these words are underlined if they are part of the title.

EXAMPLES   the <u>Runner's World</u> [magazine]
the <u>Kansas City Times</u> [newspaper]
<u>The Red Pony</u> [book]
<u>The Sound and the Fury</u> [book]

27b. Use underlining (italics) for words, letters, and figures referred to as such and for foreign words not yet adopted into English.

EXAMPLES   John, what does the <u>L</u> in your name stand for?
Write five compound sentences without using the word <u>and</u>.
There are four <u>3</u>'s in my phone number.
The red fox is of the genus <u>Vulpes</u>.

EXERCISE 1. Correcting Sentences by Adding Italics.   Number your paper 1–10. After the proper number, list all words and word groups that should be italicized. Underline each.

1. Did you know that the B in Cecil B. deMille stands for Blount?
2. The first full-length cartoon, Walt Disney's Snow White and the Seven Dwarfs, used two million drawings.
3. Among the necessities of life brought by the Pilgrims on the May-flower were apple seeds.

4. James Earle Fraser, famous for his painting End of the Trail, designed our Indian-head nickel.
5. Teddy Roosevelt, an avid reader, read Decline and Fall of the Roman Empire while on a trip in the jungles of Brazil.
6. The submarine Seaview was the ship commanded by Admiral Nelson in Voyage to the Bottom of the Sea, an old TV program.
7. Daktari is Swahili for the English word doctor.
8. Our first space shuttle was supposed to be named Constitution, but President Ford, who received 100,000 letters from Star Trek fans, changed the name to Enterprise.
9. Richard Sears met Alvah Roebuck through an ad in the Chicago Daily News.
10. The three M's in 3M Company stand for Minnesota Mining and Manufacturing.

QUOTATION MARKS

Quotation marks are used mainly to show the reader that someone's *exact words* are being reproduced. Accordingly, quotation marks come in pairs—one set marking the beginning of the quotation and the other the end.

27c. Use quotation marks to enclose a direct quotation—a person's exact words.

Do not use quotation marks to enclose an indirect quotation—not a speaker's exact words.

DIRECT QUOTATION   Joan said, "My legs are sore from the new exercise." [Joan's exact words]

INDIRECT QUOTATION   Joan said that her legs were sore from the new exercise. [not Joan's exact words]

☞ NOTE   Place quotation marks at both the beginning and the end of a quotation. Omission of quotation marks at the end of a quotation is a common error.

INCORRECT   "I'm getting my braces off tomorrow, said Reed. [second set of quotation marks left out]

CORRECT   "I'm getting my braces off tomorrow," said Reed.

27d. A direct quotation begins with a capital letter.

EXAMPLE   Bonnie asked, "When do we get our uniforms?"

> ☞ NOTE   If the quotation is only a fragment of a sentence, not intended to stand alone, do not begin it with a capital letter.

EXAMPLE   Christine promised that she would come "as soon as possible."

27e. When a quoted sentence is divided into two parts by an interrupting expression such as *he said* or *she replied,* the second part begins with a small letter.

EXAMPLES   "I hope," said Dave, "that it doesn't rain for the first part of the football game."
"Remember," Miss Jackson continued, "your science projects are due tomorrow."
"I'm not sure," replied Ann, "if I can make it to the club's rummage sale."

If the second part of a broken quotation is a new sentence, it begins with a capital.

EXAMPLE   "The date has been set," said Greg. "We can't change it now."

27f. A direct quotation is set off from the rest of the sentence by commas or by a question mark or an exclamation point.

EXAMPLES   "Where will it all end?" asked Eileen.
"Let me do that!" exclaimed Helen.
"There is no specific homework assignment for this weekend," announced Mrs. Levitt, "but remember that your term papers are due next Friday."
"Has anyone in this class," asked Mrs. Lukas, "seen a performance of *A Raisin in the Sun?*"

> ☞ NOTE   A long quotation in your composition is usually introduced by a colon and is set off by itself from the text by wider margins and by single spacing instead of double spacing (unless your teacher instructs otherwise). This practice so clearly identifies the passage as a quotation that no quotation marks are needed.

After the collapse of Europe and the tragedy of Dunkirk, the German dictator thought he had penned the British lion in its home islands and that, weakened as it was by its losses on the continent, it would easily succumb to an invasion. The British Prime Minister, voicing the grim resolve of the whole nation, warned him against such a move:

> We shall defend every village, every town
> and every city. The vast mass of London itself,
> fought street by street, could easily devour an
> entire hostile army; and we would rather see
> London laid in ruins and ashes than that
> it should be tamely and abjectly enslaved.

27g. Other marks of punctuation when used with quotation marks are placed according to the following rules.

(1) Commas and periods are always placed inside the closing quotation marks.

EXAMPLE "The concert tickets are sold out," Mary said, "and I had really hoped to go."

(2) Colons and semicolons are always placed outside the closing quotation marks.

EXAMPLES Ms. James said, "A stitch in time saves nine"; however, I'll admit I never really understood what that saying means.
The following students have been selected as, in Ms. Kovak's words, "honorary disc jockeys": Nick Paludo, Tom Weber, and Sally Ortega.

(3) Question marks and exclamation points are placed inside the closing quotation marks if the quotation is a question or an exclamation. Otherwise, they are placed outside.

EXAMPLES Maria asked, "What time is the game tomorrow?"
Why did you yell, "It doesn't matter"?
On the last lap Vicky said, "Do your best!"
Don't say "I quit"!

EXERCISE 2. Correcting Sentences by Using Capitalization and Punctuation. Rewrite the following sentences, inserting the necessary punctuation. Watch carefully for the placement of commas and end marks in relation to quotation marks and for capital letters at the beginning of direct quotations.

1. Oh, I left the bibliography for my term paper at home! exclaimed Beth.
2. Don't panic replied Natalie. Perhaps it's just lost in your notebook.
3. No, sighed Beth, I can see it now, lying on the typewriter.
4. Was it completed asked Natalie.
5. Natalie, asked Beth, did Mrs. Gwinn say that we could turn our papers in tomorrow?
6. The following students have, in the words of Coach Hatch, demonstrated leadership both academically and athletically: Steven Cline, Becky Dodge, Judith Lewis, and Fred Vine.
7. Why did Jennifer say, You ought to know?
8. Glaring at her opponent, Samantha replied, Do I look like a mind reader?
9. As I turned on the television, the reporter said, . . . ends the list of school closings; however, I didn't hear which schools were closed due to the blizzard.
10. In a crowded place, never shout fire! unless you mean it.

27h. When you write dialogue (two or more persons having a conversation), begin a new paragraph every time the speaker changes.

EXAMPLE   "And whom do we have here?" boomed Captain Jenkins.

"Actually, no one, sir," replied the young stowaway from the shadowed corner.

Captain Jenkins squinted as the anxious young man stepped forward. "I will have to turn you in to the police. Did you really think you could get away with this?" asked the captain.

"Well, sir," stammered the young man, "I just thought a kid should get a chance to fly on a space mission."

27i. When a quoted passage consists of more than one paragraph, put quotation marks at the beginning of each paragraph and at the end of the entire passage.

EXAMPLE   "Now, this car is one of the hottest sellers we've got," explained the salesman to Dad and me. "It's got bucket seats, a tape deck, and wire wheels.

"This model is also one of the safest cars on the road because of the heavy suspension and front disc brakes. All in all, it would be the perfect car for you."

27j. Use single quotation marks to enclose a quotation within a quotation.

EXAMPLES Ron said, "Dad shouted, 'A ski trip sounds great to me, too!'"
Val asked, "Did you like the new interpretation of 'America the Beautiful' that I arranged?"

27k. Use quotation marks to enclose titles of short stories, poems, songs, chapters, articles, and other parts of books and periodicals.

EXAMPLES Since we had to memorize a poem, I chose "Travel," by Edna St. Vincent Millay.
"The Unicorn in the Garden" is my favorite Thurber short story.
Begin reading Chapter 8, "Twentieth-Century Playwrights."

> ☞ NOTE The length of a written work determines whether the title should be italicized or enclosed in quotation marks. Book-length works are italicized; shorter works usually are not. However, the titles of poems long enough to be divided into books, cantos, or sections—like Longfellow's *Evangeline* and Coleridge's *The Rime of the Ancient Mariner*—are italicized.

WRITING APPLICATION A:
Using Italics and Quotation Marks as Signals

Think about the last time you wanted to select a movie to see or a record to buy. Perhaps a recommendation from a friend helped you make up your mind. You and your classmates can maintain an ongoing file of recommended books, stories, poems, plays, and songs. Just remember that when you are recommending titles to people, they want to know whether a title is for something as short as a story or as long as a novel. When you use italics and quotation marks correctly in titles, you will be sending the right signals to your audience.

Writing Assignment

Think about books, short stories, plays, poems, or songs you have enjoyed recently. In two separate paragraphs, write a recommendation for any two of these works. Be sure to use italics and quotation marks correctly.

27l. Use quotation marks to enclose slang words, technical terms, and other expressions that are unusual in standard English.

EXAMPLE We used to "hang out" at the bowling alley.

Putting slang expressions within quotation marks amounts to apologizing for them. If you are doubtful about the appropriateness of a word, do not use it.

EXERCISE 3. Correcting Sentences by Adding Italics or Quotation Marks. The following sentences contain words that should be italicized (underlined) or placed in quotation marks. Number your paper 1–10. After the proper number, write the words and punctuate them correctly.

EXAMPLE 1. He read aloud The Tell-Tale Heart from The Collected Stories of Edgar Allan Poe.
    1. "The Tell-Tale Heart" The Collected Stories of Edgar Allan Poe

1. Mr. Croce used the French word denouement as we discussed A Tale of Two Cities.
2. The counselor tried to impress the young campers by saying things like cool and right on, but they were only faintly amused by the slang from another era.
3. I read an article called El Niño, Global Weather Disaster.
4. Karen asked if there were two m's in the word accommodate.
5. Fannie Farmer, one of the first advocates of proper diets, published the Boston Cooking School Cookbook in 1891.
6. My favorite plant is the Saintpaulia ionantha, also called the African violet.
7. The next exhibit will feature many objets d'art from France; these works of art will be on display for two months.
8. At first glance, the short story Luke Baldwin's Vow is about a boy and a dog, but it also deals with conflicts in values.
9. By next Thursday I have to read the following works: A Visit of Charity, a short story by Eudora Welty; Miss Julie, a play by August Strindberg; The Climatic Effects of Nuclear War, an article in Scientific American magazine; and a newspaper article about the Nautilus, the atomic submarine.
10. She crossed the t with such a flourish that she obliterated the letters above it.

WRITING APPLICATION B:
Using Quotation Marks in Dialogue

At some time, you may see a very curious sight. The person in the car next to yours may appear to be talking to herself. That is, she is alone in the car, and her lips are moving. It may be that she is just singing along with her radio or tape player, but it still looks a little peculiar, doesn't it? Actually, you "talk to yourself" frequently. In the thinking process, you often carry on an "internal dialogue," especially if you are trying to come to a decision or think through some serious problem that has several sides.

Writing Assignment

Use an idea or significant issue of your own to write an "internal dialogue." Pretend that your thinking is divided on the issue, and that a debate is going on between two "parts" of you. Use your first initial and a raised one or two for each speaker. Be sure to use quotation marks correctly.

EXAMPLE   H^1 asked, "Are you going to go out for football or not?"

H^2 answered, "I don't think I'll have time if I'm planning to take five hard academic subjects."

"But listen," said H^1, "you have a good chance of making the varsity team this year!"

"Sure, but what good is it if I'm so buried in homework I can't move?" H^2 asked, disheartened.

CHAPTER 27 REVIEW: POSTTEST 1

Correcting Sentences by Adding Italics or Quotation Marks. The following sentences contain words or phrases that should be in italics (underlined) or in quotation marks. Number your paper 1–25. After the proper number, write the words and punctuate them correctly.

EXAMPLE 1. One of Hamlin Garland's stories in the book Main-Travelled Roads is The Return of a Private.
1. *Main-Travelled Roads*   *"The Return of a Private"*

1. The book Doctors in Petticoats consists of biographical stories about nine woman doctors who pioneered in a field of medicine.

2. This attractive, ornamental stone, an alkaline copper carbonate, is called malachite.
3. No matter how many times he reads it, my father always chuckles over Mark Twain's story Buck Fanshaw's Funeral.
4. Trying to justify all the hard work we had to do, he kept repeating, Idle hands are the devil's workshop.
5. See here, shouted the man, you will have to pay for this damage!
6. The most impressive feature of the festival is the tableau vivant, or living picture, showing famous historical scenes.
7. When their grandmother referred to her new shoes as the cat's pajamas, the children were thoroughly confused by the old slang expression.
8. Sally K. Ride, the first American woman in space, made her historical flight aboard the space shuttle Challenger in June 1983.
9. I'm not sure, but I think their address begins with two 5's and ends with a 7.
10. George Orwell was an English writer whose novels Animal Farm and 1984 portray a grim picture of totalitarian rule.
11. The fiddle-leaf fig (Ficus lyrata) requires bright, indirect sunlight and a lot of water.
12. The word maverick is said to have originated from the name of Sam A. Maverick, an early Texas cattleman who did not brand his cattle.
13. No, said Lila, that's not mine. My bracelet is silver.
14. It took me two hours to memorize the poem Remember, by Christina Rossetti! exclaimed Shirley.
15. The Queen Elizabeth, one of the most luxurious ships to sail the Atlantic, is now docked off the California coast.
16. Did you hear Marie shout, Watch out?
17. Singing the Battle Hymn of the Republic ended the concert on a patriotic note.
18. James Russell Lowell, a nineteenth-century poet, helped to edit two literary magazines, The Atlantic and the North American Review.
19. The insect we know as the praying mantis was named by the naturalist Linnaeus, who called it Mantis religiosa.

20. This morning my mother said very firmly, You can't go anywhere until your room is clean; as a result, I spent all Saturday folding, dusting, and polishing.
21. I will not tolerate any interruptions during this meeting, he said. Also, I demand that all questions be in writing.
22. During the game, all the players on our team blamed one another for every little mistake, and the coach said that we needed more esprit de corps.
23. Leonardo da Vinci's painting The Last Supper has been reproduced in many books; it is probably one of the most famous paintings in the world.
24. The following students form what Mr. Eliot calls the hottest debate team around: Michelle Knowles, Barney Poole, David McDuff, and Arlene Larsen.
25. She resented his accusation, you're never around when you're needed.

CHAPTER 27 REVIEW: POSTTEST 2

Correcting Sentences by Adding Italics or Quotation Marks. The following sentences contain words or phrases that should be in italics (underlined) or in quotation marks. Number your paper 1–25. After the proper number, write the words and punctuate them correctly. If a sentence is correct as written, write *no punctuation necessary* after the proper number.

1. He said, We should leave immediately.
2. Why did you buy another sleeping bag? she asked.
3. Mrs. Smith said that she would be at the club by 7:00 P.M.
4. Susan drove one hundred miles, he replied, to see you on your birthday.
5. Why did she say, I will not be in the play?
6. Charles Dickens' A Christmas Carol is the perfect gift for her.
7. This short poem, I Wandered Lonely as a Cloud, is by William Wordsworth.
8. How many but's did you use in the paragraph?
9. Mrs. Hoffman's favorite Latin phrase is ad infinitum.
10. There is an article in Newsweek that I would like you to read, said Joan.

11. Why do you want to read Shakespeare's play Romeo and Juliet again? asked Patricia.
12. His street address has four 4's in it, said Rose. Did you know that?
13. The dance company is performing Swan Lake, a ballet by Tchaikovsky.
14. My teacher subscribes to English Journal, a professional magazine.
15. Anita said that she could do the work.
16. Please write to me, Joyce requested. I want to keep in touch with you.
17. I'll do it! exclaimed Harriet.
18. Mr. Shore said, This nail will hold the picture in place; however, I knew that it would not.
19. While I ran, Charles said, Keep running!
20. Sally said, John just whispered, I'll be at the game tonight.
21. Our assignment for history is Chapter 14, Great Ideals in the Constitution.
22. Did you read the article The Costs of College Today?
23. You looked cool in your new glasses, said Joy.
24. The short poem The Novelist is by W. H. Auden; it is in a collection of his shorter poems.
25. You often use the French expression au revoir, said Hannah.

CHAPTER 28

Punctuation

APOSTROPHES, HYPHENS, DASHES, PARENTHESES

DIAGNOSTIC TEST

A. Correcting Sentences by Using Apostrophes and Hyphens.
Each of the following sentences contains a word that needs an apostrophe or a hyphen. Number your paper 1–10. After the proper number, write the word, adding the apostrophe or hyphen in the correct place.

EXAMPLE 1. The childrens boots were placed in a row outside the door.
      1. *children's*

1. The towns record on supporting youth projects is good.
2. We are looking forward to our three weeks vacation in the Rockies.
3. The police officer said that everyones house should be searched for the missing child.
4. Only fifty three people went to our ballet recital, and thirty of them were our relatives.
5. I bought four pairs of gloves as my two younger sisters birthday presents.
6. The team members showed their self control when the fans threw empty cups and crumpled programs on the field.
7. The womens basketball team, which is coached by an ex-Laker, has run up an impressive string of victories.
8. Were going on a field trip to the art museum to see the exhibit of post-Impressionist art.

9. Christopher's writing is hard to read because he never crosses his *t*s.

10. Sampson and Smiths Bakery, which displays its pastries in the window, is around the corner from my house.

B. Correcting Sentences by Using Dashes and Parentheses.

Number your paper 11–20. After the proper number, rewrite each of the following sentences, inserting dashes or parentheses where they are needed. (Do not add commas or colons to these sentences.)

EXAMPLE 1. The school's volunteers freshmen, sophomores, and juniors were honored during the assembly.
　　　　 1. *The school's volunteers—freshmen, sophomores, and juniors—were honored during the assembly.*

11. The flowers looked beautiful but were expensive and impractical they only lasted two days before the petals turned brown.

12. When we met my chemistry teacher at the mall, my little sister's question "Why doesn't that man have hair on his head?" embarrassed me so much I wanted to hide.

13. This report contains information about agriculture in three South American countries Brazil, Argentina, and Colombia.

14. Mr. Franklin works all day in his garden he retired last year and is always weeding, mulching, and pruning.

15. I read the wrong chapter for history class a horrible mistake!

16. Mary Ellen Jeter, a former state attorney, will speak at next Thursday's assembly I'll miss gym class then and will address the topic of student rights.

17. Our newspaper, the *Sexton High Chronicle* it used to be called the *Weekly Warrior* won the highest award in the state.

18. The new principal, Ms. Lawrence, is the best we've ever had she really cares about the students and about improving the school.

19. Rushing to catch the bus, I dropped my books in the mud I should never have overslept! and then lost the heel of my shoe.

20. Crystal's time for the fifty-yard dash the best time of anyone on the Central High School team qualified her for the regional track meet.

APOSTROPHES

The possessive case of a noun or a pronoun is used to indicate ownership or relationship.

OWNERSHIP   The **boy's** calculator
her bracelet [The bracelet is *hers*.]

RELATIONSHIP   **his** mother
one **day's** notice

In the English language the possessive case of nouns is formed by adding an apostrophe and an *s* or, with some words, merely an apostrophe, to the noun.

EXAMPLES   the dog's collar
John's jacket
two girls' cars

Making a word possessive is very easy. *Remembering* to do so, however, may be hard. When you are in doubt whether or not to use an apostrophe, try an "of" phrase in place of the word. If the "of" phrase makes good sense, then an apostrophe is called for.

EXAMPLE   yesterdays news [Should there be an apostrophe in *yesterdays*?]
news "of yesterday" [This makes good sense; therefore . . .]
yesterday's news

28a. To form the possessive case of a singular noun, add an apostrophe and an *s*.

EXAMPLES   Barbara's house
tonight's dinner
baby's stroller

☞ **NOTE**   A proper name ending in *s* may add only an apostrophe if the name consists of two or more syllables and if the addition of *'s* would make the name difficult to pronounce (*Artemis' death, Themistocles' oration*). Some singular nouns ending in *s* need the apostrophe and the *s* if the added *s* must be pronounced as a separate syllable to make the meaning clear (*waitress's uniform*). In general, adding an apostrophe and an *s* is a correct way to make any singular noun possessive.

28b. To form the possessive case of a plural noun ending in *s*, add only the apostrophe.

EXAMPLES   teachers' desks
             cities' problems

> ☞ **NOTE**   The few plural nouns that do not end in *s* form the possessive
> by adding an apostrophe and an *s*.

EXAMPLES   men's lockers
             children's stories

Take care not to use an apostrophe to form the *plural* of a noun.

INCORRECT   The four horse's performed perfectly.
  CORRECT   The four horses performed perfectly.

INCORRECT   The runner's ran all afternoon.
  CORRECT   The runners ran all afternoon.

Study the following examples of the application of these rules for
forming the singular and plural possessives of nouns. Be able to explain
how each possessive was formed.

SINGULAR	SINGULAR POSSESSIVE	PLURAL	PLURAL POSSESSIVE
coach	coach's order	coaches	coaches' orders
doctor	doctor's office	doctors	doctors' offices
ox	ox's hooves	oxen	oxen's hooves
car	car's motor	cars	cars' motors
dog	dog's tail	dogs	dogs' tails
soldier	soldier's uniform	soldiers	soldiers' uniforms
Mr. Jones	Mr. Jones's house	the Joneses	the Joneses' house
woman	woman's shoes	women	women's shoes

**EXERCISE 1. Writing the Singular, Singular Possessive, Plural,
and Plural Possessive of Nouns.**   On your paper, make a four-
column chart, and write the singular, singular possessive, plural, and
plural possessive of the following words:

1. man   3. governor   5. pencil   7. class   9. chef
2. secretary   4. deer   6. bird   8. picture 10. mouse

Pronouns in the Possessive Case

28c. Possessive personal and relative pronouns do not require an apostrophe.

The lists below show the nominative and possessive forms of personal and relative pronouns. Note that there are no apostrophes.

NOMINATIVE CASE	POSSESSIVE CASE
I	my, mine
you	your, yours
he	his
she	her, hers
it	its[1]
we	our, ours
they	their, theirs
who	whose

28d. Indefinite pronouns in the possessive case require an apostrophe and an _s_.

EXAMPLES   anyone's choice
someone's breakfast

If you need to review indefinite pronouns, see Chapter 1.

Compounds in the Possessive Case

28e. In compound words, names of organizations and business firms, and words showing joint possession, only the last word is possessive in form.

COMPOUND WORDS   sister-in-**law's** office
commander-in-**chief's** order
board of **directors'** report

BUSINESS FIRMS   Hardy and **Hudson's** Sport Shop
Billings and **Randolf's** office

JOINT POSSESSION   Bob and **Jim's** canoe
Susan and **Samantha's** house
Sean's and her car [exception: noun and possessive pronoun]

---

[1] The common form _it's_ is not possessive; it is a contraction meaning _it is_ or _it has_. See page 833.

28f. When two or more persons possess something individually, each of their names is possessive in form.

EXAMPLES **Michael's** and **Mark's** wallets
Denise's and **Lila's** hairbrushes

EXERCISE 2. Correcting Expressions by Using Apostrophes.

Some of the following expressions need apostrophes; some do not. Number your paper 1–20. After the proper number, write each expression, inserting apostrophes where needed.

EXAMPLE 1. the cameras lens
1. *the camera's lens*

1. the jets wing
2. six years of study
3. the boys gym
4. a weeks pay
5. the dishes in the sink
6. a mayors reception
7. the fishs tail
8. a months vacation
9. two pairs of tennis shoes
10. a counselors advice
11. my fathers boat
12. ducks in the pond
13. a good nights sleep
14. Demosthenes oration
15. Lynettes ring
16. the seconds ticking by
17. the two balloonists feats
18. plants in the lobby
19. a citizens rights
20. tomorrows party

EXERCISE 3. Correcting Sentences by Using Apostrophes.

List on your paper, in the order in which they appear in the numbered sentences, the words that require apostrophes. After each word with an apostrophe, write the thing possessed. Remember that plural nouns ending in *s* require an apostrophe only.

EXAMPLE 1. We drove Bettys car to last nights exciting game.
1. *Betty's car   night's game*

1. Last week I followed my parents suggestion and enrolled in an amateur photography class offered by our citys public art center.   2. I had shared my mom and dads exasperation when I spent a whole weeks allowance on poorly focused pictures.   3. I had borrowed my uncle Freds expensive camera; but even with all that cameras extra features, my photographs usually looked like childrens smudged finger paintings.

4. Everyone was really disappointed when my pictures of Bob and Ruths wedding reception, our familys social event of the year, were

destroyed when I fell into the country clubs pool with my camera.
5. Last summer I also took pictures during our months vacation in
Arizonas famous Painted Desert. 6. Unfortunately, I did not understand enough about the suns strong light at midday, and my photographs had that washed-out look.

7. My lifes most embarrassing moment occurred when I took my
class picture for the schools yearbook and discovered that I had
forgotten to put film in the camera. 8. It was also embarrassing when
I took my camera to Toms party but could not get anyones attention
long enough to pose the shots that I wanted. 9. As a result, I gave
up on people and tried to take my pets pictures; however, a dogs will
and a parakeets wings are hard to control. 10. After all these dis-
couraging experiences, I knew that I needed a professionals advice.

EXERCISE 4. Correcting Sentences by Using Apostrophes.
List on your paper, in the order in which they appear in the following
sentences, the words that require apostrophes. After each word with
an apostrophe, write the thing possessed.

1. I went to the first nights photography class with a combination
of an amateurs quest for knowledge and a cowards apprehension.
2. John Edgerton, the art centers photography instructor, immediately
relaxed everyones fears. 3. First he taught us to respect our cameras
technical abilities but not to be overwhelmed by their delicacy.
4. That night we learned photographys most important terms, *aperture*
and *shutter speed*.

5. Phil Snyder, who owns Snyders Camera Shop, was our guest
speaker for the second weeks class. 6. He presented an hours lecture
on different types of cameras and included slides that illustrated each
models features. 7. He also told us all the cameras prices and said
he would give us a special discount. 8. After his departure, John
apologized for the guests long commercial; however, he added that it
was important to be aware of a cameras accessories, as well as its
price. 9. At the end of the class period, we planned a field trip to
Craftons Lake to take some shots for our instructors evaluation.

10. The following week we all piled into Joe Joness van and looked
forward to our evenings adventure. 11. I discovered a wonderful
location for my experiments; it really looked like an artists dream.
12. The narrow trunks of two birch trees parted to frame the lakes
edge, and a rustic dock angled across the waters stillness. 13. I could

feel Johns and my other new friends eyes looking over my shoulder as I focused my shots, but I tried my best to capture the scenes perfect serenity.

14. I could hardly wait for the next class, when we would see everybodys slides.   15. Marys pictures displayed her interest in botany through close-ups of geometric shapes formed by two wildflowers petals.   16. Brian had found some fishermens shabby hats and poles and had taken some wonderful still-life shots.   17. Somehow Colleen had snapped a ducks perfect landing, and we all applauded her slides excellence.   18. As my turn approached, I could feel my throats dryness and my hands moistness.   19. Suddenly the appealing contrast of my birch trees whiteness and the old docks starkness filled the screen.   20. As I looked at the smiles on my classmates faces, I knew that I had won the groups admiration; even more important, I had restored my self-confidence.

Contractions

Contractions are shortened forms of certain words or certain word groups that commonly go together. The apostrophes in contractions are to indicate that letters have been left out.

28g. Use an apostrophe to show where letters or numbers have been omitted in a contraction.

EXAMPLES   you have   you've
            we are   we're
            it is   it's

What words or figures have been contracted, and what letters or numbers have been omitted from the following?

Rock 'n' roll is still our favorite music.
The summer Olympics of '84 were held in Los Angeles.
It's time to go.
They're almost ready for you.

EXERCISE 5. Writing Contractions.   Study the following contractions. Be able to write them when your teacher dictates to you the uncontracted expressions.

1. shouldn't   should not   4. isn't   is not
2. they've   they have   5. they'd   they would
3. o'clock   of the clock   6. haven't have not

7. we're	we are	14. they'll	they will
8. weren't	were not	15. let's	let us
9. that's	that is	16. who's	who is
10. hasn't	has not	17. she'd	she would
11. she'll	she will	18. they'd	they had
12. he's	he is	19. doesn't	does not
13. I'm	I am	20. didn't	did not

REVIEW EXERCISE A. Correcting Sentences by Using Apostrophes. Rewrite the following sentences, inserting apostrophes wherever necessary.

EXAMPLE 1. Werent you the one who didnt like eggplant?
1. *Weren't you the one who didn't like eggplant?*

1. Whos going to be at Leon and Joshs party?
2. Lets hide and see if theyll look for us.
3. I cant find them; they werent in the girls gym.
4. Is her doctors appointment at nine oclock?
5. Cleve doesnt have time to mow both his and Rays lawn.
6. Thats the best idea youve had in two days.
7. Were lucky that that dogs barking didnt awaken them.
8. Im trying to follow Pauls map to Jeans house.
9. Its hailing; therefore, I dont think you should go skiing.
10. Elise couldnt decide whether or not shed take her cat to the picnic.

Do not confuse possessive pronouns with contractions.

POSSESSIVE PRONOUNS	CONTRACTIONS
its roof	it's = it is or it has
your house	you're = you are
their house	they're = they are
whose house	who's = who is

EXERCISE 6. Using Possessive Pronouns and Contractions Correctly. This exercise is to give you practice in distinguishing between possessive pronouns and contractions. You should be able to do the exercise perfectly. Number your paper 1–10. After each number, write the correct word from each pair in parentheses.

EXAMPLE 1. (It's, Its) never too late to learn something new.
1. *It's*

1. (You're, Your) sure that (you're, your) allowed to bring (you're, your) book to the exam?
2. (Whose, Who's) ring is that on (you're, your) finger?
3. (They're, Their) trying to sell (they're, their) house.
4. (It's, Its) the best choice.
5. Do you know (who's, whose) responsible for (they're, their) leaving?
6. I hope the dog can find (it's, its) way home.
7. (It's, Its) Philip (who's, whose) always late.
8. Although (it's, its) been snowing all day, (they're, their) still planning to go.
9. (Who's, Whose) the girl at (they're, their) front door?
10. I know (you're, your) upset with the plan, but (it's, its) the only way to solve the problem.

28h. Use an apostrophe and an *s* to form the plural of letters, numbers, signs, and words referred to as words.

EXAMPLES   There are four *s*'s and four *i*'s in *Mississippi*.
The *O*'s in this directory are difficult to read.
You use too many *if*'s in your writing.
Put *X*'s by all incorrect answers.

REVIEW EXERCISE B.   List on your paper all words and symbols needing apostrophes. List them according to the sentences in which they appear. Supply the needed apostrophes.

EXAMPLE   1. You agree with the school boards decision, but I dont.
1. *school board's   don't*

1. Arent you familiar with the expression "Threes a crowd"?
2. You shouldve remembered that there are two *l*s in *llama*.
3. Tonights assignment is the first chapter of *Gullivers Travels*.
4. Check to be sure youve covered the five *W*s of a news story: *who, what, when, where,* and *why.*
5. My grandmothers favorite acting group, the Dead End Kids, broke up in 39, the year she entered high school.
6. Ive always enjoyed "Mr. Magoo," but I didnt know that I was listening to the voice of Jim Backus.
7. The fireworks were greeted with *ooh*s and *ah*s from the crowd.
8. Lewis Carrolls novel *Alices Adventures in Wonderland* was originally called *Alice's Adventures Underground.*

9. How many *n*s are in *Pennsylvania*?
10. Shes always wanted to visit Rob and Ericas home in Pine Valley.
11. Whos going to cook the babies dinner?
12. *Whats My Line?* was one of televisions classic game shows.
13. All of my friends addresses have at least three *8*s in them.
14. *Rin Tin Tin,* a popular television show of the 1950s, raised the publics opinion of German shepherds.
15. After school were going to visit Pams brother; hes in St. Marys Hospital.
16. Youre required to write a report on one of classical musics three *B*s: Bach, Beethoven, and Brahms.
17. Its been six weeks since I checked the cars oil and its tires.
18. Weve been hoping for a days vacation.
19. Your story would be better if youd remove about thirty *and*s.
20. There are two £s in the sentence, but Im not sure if theyre symbols for pounds or numbers.

WRITING APPLICATION A:
Using Apostrophes in Writing Dialect

The word *dialect* usually refers to speech used by people of a particular region. Good writers often listen carefully to the differences in speech patterns. For example, one of the distinctive characteristics of Mark Twain's writing is his ability to use dialect. In trying to write dialect, you might have to leave off letters that speakers seem to swallow. When you do this, you use an apostrophe.

EXAMPLE "Well, I should reckon! It started thirty year ago, or som'ers along there. There was trouble 'bout something, and then a lawsuit to settle it; and the suit went agin one of the men, and so he up and shot the man that won the suit—"

MARK TWAIN

Writing Assignment

Imagine that you are in a difficult situation. You may use one of the following ideas or you may think of your own. Use dialect carefully to justify or explain your problem to another person. Each time you use an apostrophe to indicate a dropped letter or syllable, underline it.

IDEAS 1. Explain to a band director or coach why you missed practice.
2. Explain to your parents why you need more money.
3. Explain to a teacher why your homework, report, or project isn't finished on time.
4. Explain to a girlfriend or boyfriend why you were seen giving a lot of attention to another person.

HYPHENS

28i. Use a hyphen to divide a word at the end of a line.

Division of words at the end of a line in order to maintain an even margin should be avoided but is sometimes necessary. A hyphen is used between parts of words divided in this way. Never divide one-syllable words. When you divide a word of more than one syllable, follow these rules:

1. Divide a word between its syllables.

INCORRECT Jenny wants to be a corporate lawyer like her father.

CORRECT Jenny wants to be a corporate lawyer like her father.

2. Words containing double consonants should be divided between the double consonants.

cor-rect, begin-ning

See Rule 3 for exceptions like *tell-ing* and *call-ing*.

3. Words with a prefix or suffix should usually be divided between the prefix and root or the root and suffix.

pro-mote, peace-ful, tell-ing, depend-able

4. Divide an already-hyphenated word only at the hyphen.

INCORRECT She raised her arm in self-defense.

CORRECT She raised her arm in self■
defense.

INCORRECT Ms. Malamud is hap-
py-go-lucky.

CORRECT Ms. Malamud is happy■
go-lucky.

5. Divide a word so that at least two of its letters are carried forward
to the next line.

INCORRECT We caught a momentar-
y glimpse of them.

CORRECT We caught a momen■
tary glimpse of them.

6. Do not hyphenate a proper name or separate a title, initials, or first
name from a surname.

INCORRECT Before signing the contract, Mrs. Davidson read the contents carefully.

CORRECT Before signing the contract,
Mrs. Davidson read the contents carefully.

EXERCISE 7. Using the Hyphen to Divide Words. Assume that
the following words come at the end of a line and have to be divided.
Write each word, indicating by the use of hyphens how it might be
divided.

EXAMPLE 1. intentional
1. *inten-tional*

1. private
2. responsible
3. message
4. merry-go-round
5. kettledrum
6. hyphen
7. anxious
8. everyone
9. difference
10. excellent

Compound Words

Hyphens are used to join the parts of some compound words. There
are three kinds of compound words in our language: solid compounds
(*stopwatch*), hyphenated compounds (*self-conscious*), and open compounds (*ginger ale*). Every year a great number of new compound
words come into the language.

In recent years the trend has been to spell compound words without hyphens, either as two words or as one word. For example, notice that *data base* and *car pool*—two new compounds—are spelled without hyphens, as two words.

Only dictionary makers can keep track of the present-day forms of compound words. Therefore, to be sure about the correct form, consult an up-to-date dictionary.

28j. Use a hyphen with compound numbers from *twenty-one* to *ninety-nine* and with fractions used as modifiers.

EXAMPLES forty-four bicycles

a two-thirds majority [*Two-thirds* is an adjective modifying *majority*.]

three fourths of the class [*Three fourths* is used as a noun.]

28k. Use a hyphen with the prefixes *ex–*, *self–*, and *all–*, with the suffix *–elect*, and with all prefixes before a proper noun or proper adjective.

EXAMPLES self-control, ex-president, all-American,

mid-December, late-Renaissance, secretary-elect,

post-Olympic, pro-Japanese

28l. Hyphenate a compound adjective when it precedes the noun it modifies. Do not use a hyphen if one of the modifiers is an adverb ending in *–ly*.

EXAMPLES a well-organized trip (But *The campaign was well planned.*)

an after-school job

a desperately rash move

EXERCISE 8. Using Hyphens in Compound Words. Number your paper 1–10. In the following sentences many compound words need hyphens. Find the words that should be hyphenated, and write them, correctly punctuated, after the proper number on your paper.

1. Ex students were not allowed at the festively decorated post prom party.
2. His self confidence faded when he forgot his well planned speech.
3. Ninety eight girls tried out for the fast paced cheerleading squad.

4. Two thirds of the class voted, but the proposal was defeated by a seven tenths majority.
5. The governor elect was once an all American football player.
6. In our debate some students were pro United Nations, but others were anti UN.
7. As an ex teacher, ex councilman, and ex representative, our new senator elect is truly a self made man.
8. We had to memorize a list of twenty five well known writers and their works.
9. You must turn in your reports by mid November.
10. Jack's achievement test scores ranked in the eighty eighth percentile.

DASHES

28m. Use a dash to indicate an abrupt break in thought.

EXAMPLES   The party——I'm sorry I forgot to tell you——was changed to next week.
When Jimbo was born——he was the last puppy——we weren't sure if he would make it.

28n. Use a dash to mean *namely, that is, in other words,* or the like before an explanation.

EXAMPLES   We think that the food here is the best in town——they serve our favorite Mexican dishes. [*that is*]
The weather was unseasonably warm——eighty-degree temperatures were a welcome change. [*in other words* or *that is*]
We need three vehicles for our family——a business car, a station wagon, and a four-wheel drive. [*namely*]

☞ **NOTE** The dash and the colon are frequently interchangeable in this type of construction.

In typewritten work you indicate a dash by striking the hyphen key twice.

PARENTHESES

28o. Use parentheses to enclose matter that is added to a sentence but is not considered of major importance.

EXAMPLES   The pyramids loomed before me (I had only seen pictures until now) and rose majestically against the purple sky.
My grandmother (she's very superstitious) hates black cats and stays inside every Friday the 13th.

Put punctuation marks within the parentheses when they belong to the parenthetical matter but outside the parentheses when they belong to the sentence as a whole.

EXAMPLES   Marsha's comment upon seeing the mummy ("Is it really dead?") embarrassed the whole class.
After we drove to Shaker Heights (it's just outside Cleveland), we met our parents for dinner.

☞ NOTE   Commas, dashes, and parentheses may all be used to enclose incidental words or phrases that interrupt the sentence and are not considered of major importance. Commas are much more commonly used in this way than dashes or parentheses.

EXAMPLES   We rehearsed for the show, a wonderful musical comedy. [a slight pause]
We rehearsed for the show—the musical event of the year! [a stronger break in the sentence]
We rehearsed (or should I say forgot our lines?) for the show. [a strong interruption]

EXERCISE 9. Correcting Sentences by Inserting Dashes and Parentheses.   Dashes and parentheses have been omitted in many of the following sentences. If a sentence is correctly punctuated as written, write *C* after the proper number. If a sentence is incorrectly punctuated, rewrite it with correct punctuation.

EXAMPLE   1. The Oak Ridge Boys and Alabama I have every one of their albums have won many awards.

   1. *The Oak Ridge Boys and Alabama (I have every one of their albums) have won many awards.*

1. Anne Murray I love her songs! has a degree in physical education.
2. "Yankee Doodle" it was the unofficial national anthem at the time was played after the signing of the Treaty of Ghent.
3. While standing at the top of Pikes Peak, Katherine Lee Bates wrote the words to "America the Beautiful."
4. There were three original members of the Sons of the Pioneers Roy Rogers his real name is Leonard Slye, Bob Nolan, and Tim Spencer.
5. A recording and a television appearance by Chubby Checker he was formerly a chicken plucker started the twist dance craze in the 1960's.
6. The Beatles used several names Foreverly Brothers, the Cavemen, the Moondogs, and the Quarrymen before they settled on *Beatles*.
7. Liberace's full name Wladziu Valentine Liberace is certainly a mouthful of words.
8. Cathy agreed to listen to Mozart's concertos what a surprise! if her parents would listen to one of David Bowie's albums.
9. Last night's concert was about average the beat was good, but the singers were uninspired.
10. Loretta Lynn remember the movie *Coal Miner's Daughter*? was married when she was fifteen years old and was a grandmother when she was twenty-nine!
11. Buying music is becoming far too complicated for me Klein's Musique Shoppe now sells albums, cassettes both eight-track and regular, videodiscs, and music videos.
12. "Making Our Dreams Come True" can you relate to that title? was the theme song of the *Laverne and Shirley* TV series.
13. Dee's taste in music is eclectic she enjoys folk music, new wave, classical music, and rock.
14. Singer and actress Liza Minnelli yes, she's Judy Garland's daughter won a Tony, an Oscar, and an Emmy in 1972.
15. Clifton Davis he starred in *That's My Mamma* wrote "Never Can Say Goodbye," which was recorded by the Jackson 5.
16. Although electronic music is common today the synthesizer was developed in 1955, some musicians still prefer the pure sound of a musical instrument.
17. Henry Mancini I used his "Pink Panther" for my dance recital sold over a million recordings of "Theme from *Peter Gunn*."

18. Frank Sinatra, whose singing career blossomed in the 1940's, has had several nicknames the Voice, the Swooner, Ole Blue Eyes, and King of the Ratpack.
19. My favorite songwriting teams are Rodgers and Hammerstein, Lerner and Loewe, and Gilbert and Sullivan.
20. The Supremes they were later known as Diana Ross and the Supremes were Motown Records' most successful singing group in the 1960's.

WRITING APPLICATION B:
Using the Dash Appropriately in Your Writing

Sometimes people use dashes ineffectively as a substitute for punctuation. On the other hand, many good writers use the dash effectively to indicate an abrupt break in thought, or to take the place of such words as *that is, in other words,* etc.

EXAMPLE   The village was stunned by the news—the plant was closing down.

Writing Assignment

Write ten sentences in which you use the dash to indicate an abrupt break in thought or to take the place of such words as *that is, in other words,* etc. Keep in mind that except for this assignment, the dash is used only occasionally.

CHAPTER 28 REVIEW: POSTTEST 1

A. Correcting Sentences by Using Apostrophes or Hyphens.
Each of the following sentences contains a word that needs an apostrophe or a hyphen. Number your paper 1–15. After the proper number, write the word, and add the apostrophe or hyphen in the correct place.

EXAMPLE   1. This stamp collection contains thirty two rare stamps.
　　　　　1. *thirty-two*

1. Because of the sudden blizzard, the armies supplies were cut off.
2. Its frustrating when the car won't start because its battery is dead.

3. After hours of discussion, the decision is that we need a two thirds majority to pass new rules in the student council.

4. I was very pleased with my grades, which were mostly Bs, but I plan to study even harder next time.

5. If you attend the game on Saturday, whos going to watch the children?

6. Miranda had the flu this week, and now she has five days worth of homework to do this weekend.

7. Rodney interviewed the treasurer elect of the Honor Society for his "Personality Plus" column in the school newspaper.

8. They were greatly disappointed in the quality of the videotape which had been produced by a well respected company.

9. One of my aunts favorite expressions is "Never let the sun set on your anger."

10. After his car ran over a nail, my brother in law had a flat tire.

11. If we return the tape recorder by five oclock, the store clerk said she would return our deposit.

12. The alarm clock hasnt worked since the day I knocked it off the nightstand.

13. The senator presented as evidence the anti American pamphlets distributed by the terrorist group.

14. You have such a lovely singing voice, I am sure youll get a part in the school musical.

15. Don't be alarmed; the red +s on your paper indicate correct answers.

B. Correcting Sentences by Using Dashes and Parentheses.

Number your paper 16–25. Rewrite the following sentences, and insert dashes or parentheses where they are needed. (Do not add commas or colons to these sentences.)

EXAMPLE 1. The books on that table they are all nonfiction are on sale today.
     1. *The books on that table—they are all nonfiction—are on sale today.*

16. The discovery of gold at Sutter's Mill brought floods of people settlers, miners, and prospectors to California in their covered wagons.

17. The old white house on Tenth Street it was once a governor's mansion is a landmark in our town.

18. My friend Josie she is crazy about animals works weekends at the Humane Society's animal shelter.
19. Five of us wrote a letter to the television networks and complained about the stereotypes we had at least sixty examples! in the new programs.
20. The Super Bowl this year was the worst football game I have ever seen the quarterback didn't throw well, and the receivers always fumbled the ball.
21. We invited Liz and Noriko they're new girls in school to our Valentine's Day party.
22. Answer the questions on this English quiz be careful, they're tricky! and then write a couplet or a limerick for extra credit.
23. The dance music if you could call it that was furnished by Swinging Eddie and the Accordionettes.
24. I am learning to develop and print my own pictures my first attempts were slightly foggy.
25. The Atacama Desert the driest region on earth receives so little rainfall that it cannot be measured.

CHAPTER 28 REVIEW: POSTTEST 2

Correcting Sentences by Using Apostrophes, Hyphens, Dashes, and Parentheses. Rewrite the following paragraphs, inserting all apostrophes, hyphens, dashes, and parentheses as needed. You may use a dictionary to check whether compound words are open, solid, or hyphenated. Be sure to use a hyphen if you must divide a word at the end of a line.

EXAMPLE 1. Margaret also called Peggy or Maggie Bourke-White photographed President elect Franklin D. Roosevelt when she was twenty nine years old.
1. *Margaret (also called Peggy or Maggie) Bourke-White photographed President-elect Franklin D. Roosevelt when she was twenty-nine years old.*

1. Margaret Bourke-White truly a pioneer in American photojournalism led a fascinating life that included travel to the worlds farthest corners. 2. Ranked as one of historys all time great photojournalists,

she depicted the stark reality and human drama of any situation she encountered.

3. Bourke-Whites career began in Cleveland, Ohio, where her first studio was in her apartment shed develop her photographs in the kitchenette. 4. Through perseverance and the conviction that industry and machines were beautiful a belief she had formed as a young girl, she made the first breakthrough in her career with her photographs they resulted from five months work of the steel pouring operations at the Otis Steel Company in Cleveland.

5. The photographs of the steel mill brought her to Henry R. Luces attention; Luce, the self made millionaire and publisher of *Time* magazine, wanted her to work for *Fortune,* his new magazine. 6. For *Fortune*s first issue, Margaret traveled to Chicago and photographed the stockyards and the Swift meat packing plant not a glamorous start! for a story about an industry at the heart of American life and its economy.

7. Margaret Bourke-White soon became a well known name, and she moved from Cleveland to a large studio in New York Citys Chrysler Building. 8. Working part time as a photographer for *Fortune,* Margaret entered the world of advertising she photographed everything from tires for the Goodyear Company to strawberry mousse for the *Ladies Home Journal.*

9. Before long, Henry his friends called him Harry Luce had another project, and he talked to Margaret about Americas new magazine that would tell the behind the scenes story of the news. 10. This new magazine at the last minute it was named *Life* expanded the young photographers horizons. 11. Since most of Margarets staff had joined *Life*s magazines staff, she moved her studio to the magazines offices the editors refused, however, to let her bring her two pet alligators.

12. When *Life*s editors sent her to the Fort Peck Dam, the worlds largest earth filled dam, they only expected brilliant photographs of the dams construction to use on the cover. 13. Margaret gave them more than that; she told the story of the people construction workers, engineers, and waitresses whose lives and work formed the story behind the dam.

14. Margarets photo essays a new idea at the time became famous, and the ex *Fortune* photographer began her world traveling days in earnest. 15. One of her trips took her to the Arctic Circle with

Canadas Governor-General, Lord Tweedsmuir; another took her to Russia, where she photographed the Russian leader, Josef Stalin he was, in Margaret's words, "the most determined, most ruthless personality I had ever encountered."

16. In the spring of 1942, when she was thirty eight years old, she became the first woman war correspondent they designed a special uniform for her accredited to the U.S. Air Force. 17. During World War II, she was on a ship that was torpedoed and sunk on its way to North Africas coast, yet she kept her self composure and even took her fellow survivors pictures while they were in the lifeboat. 18. She also went on a bombing raid a first for a woman and later photographed the horrors of Buchenwald and some little known concentration camps. 19. The soldiers regard for her was so great they let her name and christen a plane the *Flying Flitgun*.

20. After the war Margaret Bourke-Whites career took her to India during that countrys fight for independence. 21. During two years time she made several trips to India to study the peoples lives and record their hardships; she also photographed and interviewed Mahatma Gandhi her last time was only a few hours before an assassins bullet ended his life.

22. Her own last years were marked by a deep, personal struggle she had Parkinsons disease that tested her self reliance to the fullest. 23. Although shed undergone two operations and years of physical therapy, which lasted one third of her lifetime, the diseases disabling effects did not plunge her into self pity. 24. In fact, she continued to work for *Life* magazine, as well as write her autobiography its called *Portrait of Myself*. 25. The disease finally won the battle for Margarets life, but it never conquered her spirit one of her last wishes was to travel to the moon and photograph its rugged beauty.

MECHANICS
MASTERY REVIEW: Cumulative Test

A. CAPITALIZATION. The following sentences contain one or two errors in capitalization. Number your paper 1–10. After the proper number, write the incorrect words correctly, supplying capital letters where they are needed and omitting them where they are unnecessary.

EXAMPLE 1. Mary lyon established Mount Holyoke Seminary, one of the first women's Colleges.
   1. *Lyon, colleges*

1. The pilgrims, who arrived on the *Mayflower,* were religious dissenters in their homeland, england.
2. The junior Prom will be held in the Queen Victoria Room at the Continental hotel.
3. Drive east until you reach the third traffic light, and then go North for three miles.
4. Jesse and Pam went to the coronet theater to see the movie *Julia.*
5. Although I was born in the midwest, I have traveled extensively throughout our Nation.
6. On his vacation Ron visited the Steinhart aquarium in san Francisco.
7. Does the Kim family live on Forty-first street or on west Palm Boulevard?
8. My Parker Pen ran out of ink during the test in Algebra class.
9. In Hot Springs national park, Rodney took pictures of Grandpa Stone next to one of the natural springs.
10. The crowd of news Reporters gathered outside the hotel to interview one of the european ambassadors.

B. END MARKS AND COMMAS. The following sentences contain one or two errors in punctuation involving end marks or commas. Number your paper 11–20. After the proper number, write the word preceding each error and the correct punctuation mark.

EXAMPLES 1. Vickie the toaster exploded.
   1. *Vickie, exploded!*

11. Having planted the tree we made sure it received plenty of water and fertilizer.

12. Martha Benson M.D., an authority on exercise spoke at the regional conference on physical education.
13. Earl and Luis visited the Baseball Hall of Fame which is in Cooperstown New York.
14. After Lee and Po Lan had returned from Hawaii they invited us to their house for a luau.
15. All contestants who have won a prize will be contacted by Western Foods Inc. but the losers will not be notified.
16. My mother said she cannot attend the meeting for she is going on a business trip next week.
17. In many hospitals around the country scientists have been studying memory through research on amnesiacs people who have lost the power of recall.
18. Why didn't our science teacher, Mr. Leroy Washington let us choose our own topics for the final report.
19. What an absolutely marvelous exciting idea.
20. Well to be perfectly honest I thought the combination of plaids and stripes looked ridiculous.

C. SEMICOLONS AND COLONS. The following sentences contain a comma or no punctuation where there should be a semicolon or a colon. Number your paper 21–30. After the proper number, write the word preceding the error and the correct punctuation mark.

EXAMPLE 1. The child carried a battered teddy bear, it was his only reminder of home.
1. *bear;*

21. To make homemade vegetable soup, you must mix the ingredients as follows, boil the broth, add diced vegetables, and simmer.
22. For the potluck dinner at the school, Aretha brought turkey with gravy, Nona brought corn pudding, which was made from her grandmother's recipe, and Carmen brought rolls, salad, and fruit.
23. We promised to be home at 10 30, however, we didn't count on the game's going into extra innings.
24. On seeing the rampaging waters of Victoria Falls, David Livingstone wrote these words "These columns of water-smoke give the impression that the yawning gulf might describe a bottomless pit."
25. During the summer the music festival attracts many tourists to our town in fact, some of them come every year.

26. The Bible reading began with John 14 27 and ended with Psalms 39 1–6.
27. Mr. Jackson's plane arrived twenty minutes late because of the dense fog, consequently, he missed the flight to Denver.
28. I have finally narrowed my choices for a housewarming gift a self-cleaning iron, a blender, some place mats and napkins, or casserole dishes.
29. Mary and Roland, who love to go sailing, were as excited as little children they had finished first in the regatta.
30. The following clubs will have their yearbook pictures taken at 2 15, the Pep Club, the Photography Club, and the Modern Dance Club.

D. ITALICS (UNDERLINING) AND QUOTATION MARKS. In each of the following sentences are words that should be in italics (underlined) or in quotation marks. Number your paper 31–40. After the proper number, write these words and include punctuation in its correct placement.

EXAMPLES 1. The book Tales from the Plum Grove Hills includes Jesse Stuart's short story Spring Victory.
        1. <u>Tales from the Plum Grove Hills</u> "Spring Victory."
        2. Jenny asked, Won't we be late if we don't go now?
        2. "Won't we be late if we don't go now?"

31. A picture of the winning wheelchair basketball team, the Wildcats, was on the front page of the Post-Herald, our local newspaper.
32. Humming a few bars of Whistle While You Work, Roger went door to door asking people if they wanted their lawns mowed.
33. Well, Marcia, said Aunt Phoebe, have you forgotten everything I taught you?
34. The word biosphere refers to the part of the earth's atmosphere that supports life.
35. For my report on Mexico, I read an article, The Great Temple of Tenochtitlán, that appeared in Scientific American magazine.
36. Who wrote the poem that begins I never saw a purple cow?
37. The Parsley Garden is a short story by William Saroyan; he won the Pulitzer Prize for the drama The Time of Your Life.
38. Millie grows many vegetables in what she calls my backyard cornucopia: spinach, cauliflower, sweet potatoes, broccoli, and sweet corn.

39. Freda christened the new motorboat The Roaring Teacup.
40. Everyone admires Donna's joie de vivre, which is French for enjoyment of life.

E. APOSTROPHES. In each of the following sentences, two words or word groups need apostrophes. Number your paper 41–45. After the proper number, write each word or word group, and supply the correct punctuation.

EXAMPLE 1. Amalias outlook improved after she went on the Hiking Clubs wilderness survival trip.
1. *Amalia's   Hiking Club's*

41. Teds and Lucilles paintings were awarded blue ribbons.
42. Most of the city councils members favored Johnson and Halls proposal for a new shopping mall.
43. Although that dog is wagging its tail, it doesnt convince me that its friendly.
44. Whos going to speak at the luncheon at the mens club?
45. The Joneses address has four 7s.

F. HYPHENS, DASHES, AND PARENTHESES. In the following sentences, hyphens, dashes, and parentheses have been omitted. Number your paper 46–50. After the proper number, rewrite the sentences, and supply the correct punctuation as needed.

EXAMPLE 1. We compared the features of forty two cars see Table 2, and they all meet the minimum safety standards.
1. *We compared the features of forty-two cars (see Table 2), and they all meet the minimum safety standards.*

46. Before he leaves for school he always takes the early bus each morning, he exercises to the music of the well known jazz artists.
47. Carol Dodge gave the dramatic soliloquy in the last act there wasn't a dry eye in the theater, and the audience applauded wildly.
48. Approximately twenty out of every twenty five students agree that self esteem is the most important personal quality.
49. The Class of 1960 the first graduating class from Waverly High will hold an all alumni reunion this Friday.
50. We played tennis or should I say ran after wild volleys? on the recently finished tennis courts at the school.

PART SIX

AIDS TO GOOD ENGLISH

CHAPTER 29

The Library

LIBRARY ARRANGEMENT; MAIN REFERENCE BOOKS

During the Renaissance, some scholars set themselves the task of mastering all knowledge. Today no one imagines that one person can know all there is to know. There is simply too much information. As a result, modern scholars are not expected to know all the answers, but they are expected to know how to find the answers that they need.

You can find the answers to a great number of questions in a library. Books, pamphlets, and other sources of information record knowledge for you to use. To take advantage of these resources, however, you must know what your library contains and how it is arranged.

ARRANGEMENT OF BOOKS IN THE LIBRARY

29a. Learn the arrangement of books in your library.

Libraries are sufficiently alike so that when you are familiar with one library you can find your way in others.

Fiction

The fiction section contains novels and stories about imaginary people, places, and things. Here the books are arranged alphabetically according to the author's last name. Jane Austen's famous novels, for example, will come near the beginning of the section. If the library has several of her novels, they will be arranged under *Austen* alphabetically by *title*. For example, *Pride and Prejudice* will come before *Sense and Sensibility*.

Nonfiction

Since nonfiction includes so many kinds of books on so many subjects, the simple method used for arranging fiction will not do. Instead, most libraries use a system invented by an American librarian named Melvil Dewey.[1]

The Dewey decimal system classifies all nonfiction under ten major subject areas. Each of these ten classifications is assigned an identifying number which is printed on the spine of the book near the bottom.

The classifications and the numbers that stand for them are as follows:

000–099 General Works (encyclopedias, periodicals, etc.)
100–199 Philosophy (psychology, behavior, etc.)
200–299 Religion (including mythology)
300–399 Social Sciences (communication, economics, government, law, etc.)
400–499 Language (dictionaries, grammars, etc.)
500–599 Science (mathematics, chemistry, physics, etc.)
600–699 Technology (agriculture, engineering, aviation, etc.)
700–799 The Arts (sculpture, painting, music, etc.)
800–899 Literature (poetry, plays, orations, etc.)
900–999 History (geography, travel, etc.)

Within each of the ten major classifications, there are an unlimited number of subdivisions. A work of history, for example, bears a number in the 900's. Since, however, history is such a vast field and even a small library might well contain several hundred books on history, the 900's must be further broken down.

The Dewey decimal system accomplishes this by creating many subdivisions within each major class. For example, it breaks down the general class *History* in the following way:

---

[1] Many larger libraries use a somewhat different method of classification developed by the Library of Congress. This system is not described here, but if a library in your area uses this system, the librarian will tell you how it works.

900–999   History
  910–919   Geography, Travel
  920–929   Biography (arranged alphabetically according to the name of the person written about)
  930–939   Ancient History
  940–949   European History
  950–959   Asian History
  960–969   African History
  970–979   North American History
    971.0–971.99   Canadian History
    972.0–972.99   Mexican History
    973.0–973.99   United States History
     974.0–974.99   History of the Northeastern States
     975.0–975.99   History of the Southeastern States
     976.0–976.99   History of the South Central States

Therefore, a book bearing the number 972 will be generally a work of history (900), specifically a work on North American history (970), and still more specifically a work on Mexican history (972). This number, called the *call number,* may include a decimal point and additional identifying numbers to indicate a smaller division of the subject, such as a particular period of history. Large libraries find it necessary to use many numbers after the decimal point, but in smaller libraries the author's initial is usually printed under the call number to distinguish the book from other works on the same subject. For example, the call number $\frac{972}{P}$ may be used to designate William Prescott's famous history, *The Conquest of Mexico;* it will appear not only on the spine of the book itself, but also on every card in the card catalog referring to it.

Once you have learned the call number, you may either go directly to the proper shelf and pick out the book or, if the stacks are inaccessible to the public, have the librarian get the book for you.

LOCATING INFORMATION IN THE LIBRARY

The Card Catalog

29b. Learn the uses of the card catalog.

In every library there is a cabinet of small drawers containing cards. These cards list every book in the library alphabetically. In the average library there are usually three cards for each book: a *title card,* an *author card,* and at least one *subject card.*

1. **The author.** On the *author card,* as you can see on page 763, the author's name appears on the top line, last name first. If you wanted a book by a particular writer, you could look it up in the card catalog under the author's last name. All books by an author are listed on similar cards and are arranged under the author's name in alphabetical order of their *titles.* All books *about* an author (critical studies of the author's work, biographies, etc.) are listed on cards coming after the cards for the author's own books.

2. **The title.** The title of the book is printed at the top of the *title card.* Title cards are arranged alphabetically according to the first letter of the title. If this first word is an article, however—an *a, an,* or *the*— then the card is filed according to the second word of the title. Jack London's novel *The Call of the Wild* would come under the *C*'s, not the *T*'s.

3. **The subject.** The subject is printed at the top (usually in red) on the *subject card.* This kind of card is a great timesaver when you go into the library to look up information on a general topic with no particular book in mind. Subject cards direct you to whatever books in the library deal with your topic. Among the subject cards, you frequently find still other subject cards dealing with different aspects of the main topic. For example, under the subject "Languages," you may find cards labeled "Linguists," "Orthography," "Composition," as well as "see" or "see also" cards. These "see also" cards refer you to yet another part of the catalog for the information you are seeking. Under the topic "Ellis Island" you might find a card saying, "See United States—Immigrant Station, Ellis Island"; or under "Democracy," another card saying, "See also Politics."

4. **The call number.** This Dewey decimal number appears on every catalog card referring to the book.

5. **The publisher and the date of publication.** This information is important to students who wish to make sure they are consulting the latest information on any subject. A book on atomic physics published in 1980 would be vastly different from one published in 1930.

6. **The description of the book.** Claire Walter's book, for example, has 9 pages of introductory material and 731 pages of text. It is not illustrated, nor does it have maps or charts, for these would be noted here. Twenty-two centimeters is the length of the book's spine.

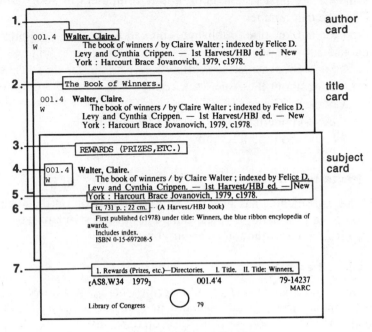

1.

001.4   Walter, Claire.
W   The book of winners / by Claire Walter ; indexed by Felice D.
          Levy and Cynthia Crippen. — 1st Harvest/HBJ ed. — New
          York : Harcourt Brace Jovanovich, 1979, c1978.

author
card

2.

          The Book of Winners.

001.4   Walter, Claire.
W   The book of winners / by Claire Walter ; indexed by Felice D.
          Levy and Cynthia Crippen. — 1st Harvest/HBJ ed. — New
          York : Harcourt Brace Jovanovich, 1979, c1978.

title
card

3.

          REWARDS (PRIZES, ETC.)

4.

001.4   Walter, Claire.
W   The book of winners / by Claire Walter ; indexed by Felice D.
          Levy and Cynthia Crippen. — 1st Harvest/HBJ ed. — New

5.

          York : Harcourt Brace Jovanovich, 1979, c1978.

6.

          ix, 731 p. ; 22 cm. — (A Harvest/HBJ book)

          First published (c1978) under title: Winners, the blue ribbon encyclopedia of
          awards.
          Includes index.
          ISBN 0-15-697208-5

subject
card

7.

          1. Rewards (Prizes, etc.)—Directories.   I. Title.   II. Title: Winners.
      [AS8.W34 1979]   001.4'4   79-14237
                                                                    MARC

          Library of Congress   79

Sample Library Cards

7. *The subject headings in the card catalog under which the book is
listed.*

EXERCISE 1. Using the Card Catalog.   Remembering that books
are catalogued by title, author, and subject, answer the following
questions by using the card catalog in your library.

1. Does the library have these books?

> *The Good Earth*   *Jane Eyre*
> *To Kill a Mockingbird*   *The Complete Adventures of*
> *The Swiss Family Robinson*   *Sherlock Holmes*

2. Does your library have any books written by Virginia Woolf,
   Thomas Mann, Marjorie Kinnan Rawlings, and John Dos Passos?
   If it does, write the title of one book by each.
3. Give the title, author, publisher, and publication date of a book
   about Martin Luther King, Jr.
4. Does your library have any books by Margaret Mead? If so, give
   the title and call number of one of them.

5. What is the most recent book about computers in your library? Give the call number.
6. Find the author, title, publisher, and call number of the following books:
   a. A book about American artists
   b. A book about the American frontier
   c. A book by George Eliot
   d. A book giving information about George Eliot
   e. A book about photography

The Parts of a Book

Once the card catalog has helped you find your book on the shelves, and you have it in hand, a quick glance at certain standard parts will tell you if it contains the information you seek.

29c. Learn the parts of a book.

Not every book has all the parts described here, but all books have some of them. They are very useful in that they enable you to get acquainted with a book with no loss of time. Every careful reader should be familiar with them.

1. *The frontispiece.* A full-page illustration usually facing the title page.

2. *The title page.* A page giving the complete title of the book, the complete name of the author (or authors), the name of the publisher, and the place of publication.

3. *The copyright page.* A page on the reverse side of the title page telling when the book was listed at the United States copyright office to protect the author's rights of ownership. The copyright page also tells by whom the book was copyrighted (sometimes the author, sometimes the publisher).

The copyright date is important when you want to know if the book's information is up-to-date. A book may be many times reprinted (each time with a new publication date) and yet be unchanged in form and content. A new copyright date, on the other hand, informs you that new material has been added. Do not confuse the copyright date with a date of reprinting. Copyrights often appear as a list of dates.

EXAMPLE Copyright © 1985, 1982, 1977, 1969

4. *The preface, foreword, or introduction.* A section at the beginning of a book in which the author speaks directly to the reader. In this place the author may comment about the writing of the book, acknowledge help received from others, indicate the purpose of the book, and generally prepare the reader for what is to come in the remainder of the book.

5. *The table of contents.* A table at the beginning giving, usually, the title of chapters, their subdivisions, and the number of the page on which each begins. The table of contents gives a general view of the book. Accordingly, it enables you to determine whether the book contains the information you want without leafing through the entire book. Works of fiction usually have no table of contents.

6. *List of illustrations.* A list telling what graphic materials (maps, diagrams, charts, etc.) are provided in the book and where they are found.

7. *The appendix.* A section containing material not included in the body of the book, which the author nevertheless considers relevant. The appendix may include charts, maps, lists, statistics, or even long quotations from other works on the same subject. A text on American history might include the *Declaration of Independence* and the *Constitution* in the appendix.

8. *The glossary.* A dictionary section, usually at the end of the book, in which technical or difficult words and expressions are explained.

9. *The bibliography.* A list of books, periodicals, films, and other sources which the author has consulted in preparing the text. Many books have bibliographies at the end of each chapter listing books which the author recommends. Others have a single bibliography at the end of the book.

10. *The index.* A guide to all information in the book. It lists alphabetically the topics treated in the book. It is much more detailed than the table of contents and gives the exact page on which a topic is discussed. For those in search of specific information, it is doubtless the most important part of the book other than the text itself.

11. *The endpapers.* Pages pasted inside the front and back covers of the book. Maps, diagrams, charts, and illustrations are sometimes printed there. For example, the endpapers of a history of California might have a map of the state.

EXERCISE 2. Understanding the Parts of a Book. Write on your paper the answers to the questions that follow.

1. List the parts of a book of nonfiction that you would probably not find in a work of fiction.
2. Explain the importance of the copyright date.
3. Why is a glossary more useful in a book about stagecraft than in a collection of modern plays?
4. What is the difference between a table of contents and an index?
5. Would a typical novel be likely to have an index?
6. By what company was this textbook published?
7. How many pages are devoted to the main index of this book?
8. What copyright dates are given for this book?
9. How many pages are devoted to the table of contents of this book?
10. Skim the preface of this book, and briefly explain its main purpose.

The *Readers' Guide*

29d. Learn to use the *Readers' Guide to Periodical Literature.*

Often in writing a report or in doing an assignment for one of your other subjects, you will have occasion to use a story, article, or poem published in a magazine. To find it conveniently, you will need to use the *Readers' Guide to Periodical Literature,* an index to the contents of more than one hundred and fifty magazines. The *Readers' Guide* is published once or twice a month—eighteen times a year—and at regular intervals these booklets are combined into a cumulative volume.

Magazine stories are listed in the *Readers' Guide* by title and author; poems and plays are listed by author and under the headings POEMS and DRAMAS. A sample excerpt from the *Readers' Guide* is reproduced on page 767. You can probably figure out the meaning of the various abbreviations. If not, all of them are explained in the front of the *Readers' Guide* itself.

EXERCISE 3. Using the *Readers' Guide.* Using the *Readers' Guide* in your school or public library, look up the answers to the following questions:

1. Choose one of the topics and look up in the *Readers' Guide* three recent articles about it. Give complete information: title and author, magazine, date, and page numbers.

France   Horses   Photography   Poetry   Football   Solar Energy

BEAR hunting — subject entry
Four-toed bear [black bear hunting] E. A. — title of article
Bauer. il Outdoor Life 165:114+ Mr '80
My 40 years with bears [ed by J. Rearden] C.
Williams. il Outdoor Life 165:82-5+ F '80
Yellowstone grizzly hunts foreseen. J. Weiss.
il Outdoor Life 165:44+ Mr '80

BEARAK, Harold
Sensuous sipping. il Essence 10:109+ F '80

BEARDS
Why men wear beards [opinions of black men]
il Ebony 35:94-6+ Mr '80 — title and issue of magazine

BEARNAISE sauce. See Sauces

BEARS
  See also
  Cooking—Game
Bear attack! [grizzlies] E. Wiseman. il por map — secondary subject heading
Outdoor Life 165:45-7+ Ja '80
  Training
Though she barely survived three close mauls,
it's still love among the bruins for Ursula
Bottcher [polar bear trainer] D. M. Clayton.
il por People 13:128-9 Ap 21 '80 — illustration reference

BEASON, S. T.
Diesel power invades the lawn. il Mech Illus
76:66+ Mr '80

BEATITUDES
Prickly pair. J. A. Tetlow. America 142:inside
back cover F 9 '80 — author entry

BEATTIE, Ann
Learning to fall [story] il Ms 8:54-5+ Ja '80

BEATTIE, Bob
Bob Beattie [interview by C. Bentsen] pors — article by author (interview)
Sports 70:24+ F '80

  about

Coaching or kibitzing on the Olympics, Bob
Beattie is America's indomitable snowman. — article about author
F. W. Martin. il pors People 13:86+ F 18 '80 *

BEATTIE, L. Elisabeth
What happens when you do stop the world and
try to get off? Glamour 78:100+ Mr '80

BEAUBOURG Center. See Paris—Georges Pom-
pidou Center

BEAUJOLAIS (wine) See Wine

BEAUPRE, Lee
Grosses gloss: breaking away at the box-office.
il Film Comment 16:69-73 Mr/Ap '80

BEAUTICIANS
  See also
  Hairstylists — cross reference

BEAUTY. See Aesthetics

BEAUTY, Personal
  See also
  Exercise
  Hair
  Hairstyling
  Make-up
  Manicuring
  Skin — list of related entries
Ask the expert. V. Sassoon and B. Sassoon. pors
Mademoiselle 86:50 F '80 — volume number
Beautiful time of life [excerpt from Newborn
beauty: a complete guide to beauty, health and
energy for the nine months of pregnancy and
the nine months after] W. D. Gates and G.
M. Meckel. il McCalls 107:96-7+ F '80 — page reference
Beauty. il N Y Times Mag p 56 Ja 20; p66 F 10; — and date of issue
82 F 24; 84 Mr 23 '80

2. Select one of the topics above, look it up in the *Readers' Guide,* and list on your paper three articles *that you could get in your library* on the subject.

3. Choose a prominent man or woman whom you admire, and in the *Readers' Guide* look up an article about the person. Give author, title, and source.

4. Suppose you are writing an essay on the President of the United States. List three articles about him that you could get in your library, and give the information from the *Readers' Guide.*

5. How many articles about motorcycles are listed in the *Readers' Guide* you are using? List three of them.

Information Files

29e. Learn the nature and proper use of the vertical file.

Useful information on current topics is often to be found in pamphlets—brief treatments of a subject, usually bound in paper covers. They are published by government agencies, industrial concerns, museums, colleges and universities, radio stations, welfare organizations, etc. The librarian files pamphlets in a special cabinet, usually referred to as the vertical file, and can help you to find material on your subject, especially if it is of contemporary interest.

In the vertical file the librarian also stores interesting pictures and important clippings from newspapers.

29f. Use microfilm and microfiche to find information.

To save space, many libraries store some publications (newspapers, magazines, and books) or documents on microfilm or microfiche. *Microfilm* is a roll or reel of film containing photographically reduced publications. You view the film through a projector that enlarges each microscopic image to a size suitable for reading. *Microfiche* is a sheet of film, rather than a roll or reel, containing photographically reduced publications. To read the microfiche, you use a machine that, like the microfilm projector, enlarges the microscopic images to a readable size. The librarian in your library can tell you which publications are stored on microfilm or microfiche, where the microfilm and microfiche are located in the library, and how to use the microfilm and microfiche projectors.

29g. Use computers to find information.

Many libraries are replacing their present book lists, catalogs, and periodical lists with a computerized system. If this is the case, you will have to use the computer to find the lists of books and periodicals in the library. Instead of looking through the card catalog or the *Readers' Guide,* you type the information you need into the computer—for example, subject: air pollution. Then the computer searches for the titles and locations of the publications on that subject and prints a list. Depending on the type of computer, you might have to read the list from the screen, or you might be able to get a printout, or printed copy, of the list of books or periodicals. The librarian will be able to tell you what kinds of computer programs your library has, where the computers are located in the library, and how to use the computers.

REFERENCE BOOKS IN THE LIBRARY

29h. Acquaint yourself with the reference books in your library.

In every library there is a section known as the reference section. Here the librarian keeps together those ready-reference volumes, which are designed to help you look up brief articles giving various kinds of information. You will find acquaintance with certain of these reference books to be very valuable.

Special Dictionaries

Various dictionaries of the English language, such as those described on pages 780–82, are in the reference sections of libraries. In addition, there are many special dictionaries written to help you with specific problems of word choice, correct usage, etc. Very often a writer has some trouble thinking of the exact word with which to express a given meaning. Often, too, a writer has used the same word so many times in a composition that it is desirable to find a synonym for it to avoid monotonous repetition. The following two books, as their titles suggest, will help you to find the right words.

Roget's Thesaurus of English Words and Phrases

The word *thesaurus* derives from a Latin word meaning "treasure," so that literally a thesaurus is a storehouse or treasury. The contents of this storehouse are synonyms and antonyms. While the thesaurus can be useful to the writer, it is also a dangerous book to use. Since the synonyms are listed without definitions or other indication of differences in meaning, it is easy to choose an inappropriate word. For example, all of the following synonyms are given for the verb *change: alter, modulate, veer, swerve,* and *deviate.* All of these synonyms have something to do with the general idea of change, but each has a specific shade of meaning that would make it unsuitable for most of the contexts in which *change* appears.

Make it a rule to use a thesaurus only as a memory aid—a reminder of words you already know. Do *not* use an unfamiliar synonym you find in a thesaurus without checking its meaning in a reliable dictionary. A strange word that you hope will sound impressive is likely to strike your reader as absurdly inappropriate.

Webster's New Dictionary of Synonyms

Much safer to use because of its detailed distinctions between synonyms, *Webster's New Dictionary of Synonyms* can be a great help to a writer in search of a word.

Encyclopedias

Any encyclopedia offers informative articles on a wide range of subjects. The articles in an encyclopedia are arranged alphabetically, but many facts and references can be found only by using the index. For example, the *Encyclopedia Americana* has a long entry on the "Olympic Games," but elsewhere in the encyclopedia, there are a number of references to this topic, which you can find only by using the index.

The *Encyclopædia Britannica* now has a different shape than most encyclopedias have. The first volume is an introduction to the rest of the encyclopedia, and can be used like an alphabetically ordered table of contents or index. The rest of the encyclopedia is divided into a "Macropædia" (*makro* is from the Greek for *big*) and a "Micropædia" (*mikro* is from the Greek for *small*). The Macropædia has long articles and the Micropædia has shorter articles. When you use the new *Britannica,* you can look up what you want in the first volume, and it will tell you where to look in the rest of the encyclopedia. When you are familiar with the rest of the encyclopedia, you will ordinarily look things up first in the Micropædia, which takes up ten of the volumes. Once you have found what you are looking for in the Micropædia, you will also find very generous cross-references to spots in the rest of the encyclopedia that deal with the same subject. This way of arranging the information in an encyclopedia is interesting; it has only been in use since 1974, but it seems to be helpful in our trying to cope with the rapidly growing, vast amounts of knowledge.

Encyclopedias are designed for quick reference. Because they give a general background on a subject, they are a good place to begin research on an unfamiliar subject. Remember, however, that encyclopedias should be the starting point, not the end, of research. Limitations of space prevent encyclopedias from treating their topics in depth. A report based entirely on encyclopedia entries is likely to be too general to be of any real merit.

Most reliable encyclopedias are kept up-to-date through frequent revisions. In addition, yearbooks are published to supply information on important developments of the preceding year.

The following general encyclopedias are well known and widely used:

General Encyclopedias

Collier's Encyclopedia
24 volumes
Bibliography and Index in Volume 24
Publishes *Collier's Yearbook*

Encyclopædia Britannica
30 volumes
Cross-referencing throughout *Micropædia*
Publishes the *Britannica Book of the Year*

Encyclopedia Americana
30 volumes
Index in Volume 30
Publishes the *Americana Annual*

World Book Encyclopedia
22 volumes
Research Guide and Index in Volume 22
Publishes an annual supplement

Biographical Reference Books

Besides the standard encyclopedias there are many reference books that give biographies of famous persons.

Webster's Biographical Dictionary

A one-volume work with very short entries giving the basic facts of the person's life.

The New Century Cyclopedia of Names

A three-volume work, the *Century Cyclopedia* contains short biographies as well as information about all sorts of proper names: people, places, things, works of art, events, literary and mythological characters.

Current Biography

Published monthly, *Current Biography* is the best source of information about prominent people in the news. A picture of the subject usually heads the biography. The monthly pamphlets are bound together into a book each year, and a cumulative index is provided. Using these indexes, the student can often follow the career of an important person from early issues of *Current Biography,* at which time the celebrity first attracted public attention, to the latest issues of the magazine, in which later achievements are reported. A separate index covers the years 1940 through 1970. The cumulative index runs from 1971 on.

Who's Who and Who's Who in America

These volumes give important data about prominent *living* persons. *Who's Who* is a British publication dealing mainly with famous English people; *Who's Who in America* provides similar information about famous Americans. In both works the biographical entries are fairly short, giving such data as parentage, date of birth, positions held and honors received, principal achievements, names of immediate family, and present address. *Who's Who* is published annually; *Who's Who in America,* every two years.

Reference Books About Authors

Some books are devoted exclusively to literary men and women. In the "author" books by Stanley Kunitz, the biographies are headed with a picture of the subject. *The Writers Directory,* which comes out every two years, lists about 18,000 writers living today.

> *British Authors of the Nineteenth Century* by Kunitz and Haycraft
> *British Authors Before 1800* by Kunitz and Haycraft
> *Twentieth Century Authors* by Kunitz and Haycraft
> *American Authors 1600–1900* by Kunitz and Haycraft
> *European Authors 1000–1900* by Kunitz and Colby
> *The Writers Directory,* St. Martin's Press, N.Y.
> *Contemporary Authors,* and *Contemporary Authors, First Revision,* Gale Research Company
> *World Authors* by Wakeman
> *Dictionary of Literary Biography,* Gale Research Company
> *American Writers* by Unger

Atlases

An atlas is chiefly a collection of maps, but it may contain, as well, a wealth of statistical material about industries, raw materials, trade routes, rainfall, air and sea currents, and many other kinds of information. Any of the following atlases are good and are likely to be found on the shelves of your library.

> *Goode's World Atlas*
> *Hammond Contemporary World Atlas*
> *New York Times Atlas of the World*
> *National Geographic Atlas of the World*

Four historical atlases of particular interest to students of world history are listed below. These atlases represent graphically historical changes from earlier times, showing the rise and fall of empires, the movement of peoples, and the spread of culture.

> Heyden's *Atlas of the Classical World*
> *The American Heritage Pictorial Atlas of United States History*
> *Rand McNally Atlas of World History*
> Shepherd's *Historical Atlas*

Almanacs and Yearbooks

For factual information on the world today, the most useful of all reference books are the almanacs. Two popular ones are the *World Almanac and Book of Facts* and the *Information Please Almanac*. All are usually published annually and are full of information and statistics about current events—sports, industry, agriculture, science, entertainment, and census information. In addition, almanacs contain articles on significant events and issues of the past year. They also contain much historical information. Indeed, in these handy volumes you can find items as diverse as the lifetime batting average of Henry Aaron and the names of the original signers of the Magna Carta.

The Statesman's Yearbook

This large volume is published annually and contains a compilation of statistical information about the world and its nations. Most of the information is in quantitative form (e.g., number of bales of cotton produced, balance of foreign payments, etc.), and can be understood without much knowledge of economics. It begins with information about international organizations, like the United Nations and the World Council of Churches, and goes on to cover individual nations and other more limited organizations.

Literature Reference Books

Bartlett's *Familiar Quotations*

Occasionally you will need to know a quotation or the author of a quotation. In such a case, the place to look is the famous Bartlett's *Familiar Quotations*.

The quotations in Bartlett's are arranged chronologically by author; that is, Emily Dickinson comes before Robert Frost. At the end of the work, there is a huge index in which every quotation is listed alphabetically by its first (and every important) word. Suppose you wished to find out who wrote

One half of the world cannot understand the pleasures of the other.

You would find this quotation by Jane Austen indexed under the words *pleasures, world,* and *half.*

Stevenson's *The Home Book of Quotations*

Used for somewhat the same purpose as Bartlett's, Stevenson's *The Home Book of Quotations* is, however, arranged differently. The quotations in this book are arranged by subjects. You can also find the author of a quotation; although, since the book is not arranged by authors, you will find the book less efficient for this purpose than Bartlett's. Stevenson's book is especially helpful if you want a quotation on a certain subject. For instance, if you want one on love or happiness or Christmas, you will find many listed under each of these topics.

Magill's *Quotations in Context*

This book of quotations includes the contexts of the quotations.

Granger's *Index to Poetry*

Granger's *Index* contains no poems. It tells you in what books you can find almost any poem or recitation (popular prose passage) you wish. If you know the title of a poem or its author, yet do not know in what books you will find the poem, look it up in Granger's. There you will find a list of books in which, for example, "The Listeners" can be found. The names of these books, however, are abbreviated, and in order to make sense of them, you must consult the list of abbreviations in the front of Granger's. Suppose, for example, that you find "The Listeners" listed as appearing in BLV. A glance at the key to abbreviations tells you that BLV means the *Book of Living Verse*. Then it is a simple matter to check the card catalog to see whether the library has the book. Granger's also indexes poems and recitations by their authors and by the first word in the line.

Stevenson's *The Home Book of Verse* and Stevenson's *The Home Book of Modern Verse*

These anthologies, containing well-known poems, are so large that you are almost certain to find the poem you wish in any one of them. They are indexed in three ways—by title, by author, and by first word. The poems themselves are collected under general headings like *Poems of Youth and Age, Poems of Nature, Familiar Verse,* and *Poems, Humorous and Satiric.* These headings are useful to students in search of a suitable poem on certain subjects. Other useful literature reference books include the following ones:

Short Story Index
Play Index
Essay and General Literature Index

EXERCISE 4. Understanding the Uses of Different Reference Books. You may be asked to give a brief description of the books in the following list with which your teacher thinks you should be familiar. Tell what sort of material the book contains, how the material is arranged, and how best to use the book.

Special Dictionaries
    Roget's Thesaurus of English Words and Phrases
    Webster's New Dictionary of Synonyms

Encyclopedias
    Collier's Encyclopedia
    Encyclopædia Britannica
    Encyclopedia Americana
    World Book Encyclopedia

Biographical Reference Books
    Webster's Biographical Dictionary
    The New Century Cyclopedia of Names
    Current Biography
    Who's Who
    Who's Who in America

Reference Books About Authors
    British Authors of the Nineteenth Century
    British Authors Before 1800
    European Authors 1000–1900
    American Authors 1600–1900
    Twentieth Century Authors
    Contemporary Authors
    Contemporary Authors, First Revision
    The Writers Directory
    World Authors
    Dictionary of Literary Biography
    American Writers

Atlases

> *Goode's World Atlas*
> *Hammond Contemporary World Atlas*
> *New York Times Atlas of the World*
> *National Geographic Atlas of the World*

Historical Atlases

> Heyden's *Atlas of the Classical World*
> *Rand McNally Atlas of World History*
> Shepherd's *Historical Atlas*
> *The American Heritage Pictorial Atlas of United States History*

Almanacs and Yearbooks

> *World Almanac and Book of Facts*
> *Information Please Almanac*
> *The Statesman's Yearbook*

Literature Reference Books

> Bartlett's *Familiar Quotations*
> Stevenson's *The Home Book of Quotations*
> Magill's *Quotations in Context*
> Granger's *Index to Poetry*
> Stevenson's *The Home Book of Verse*
> Stevenson's *The Home Book of Modern Verse*

EXERCISE 5. Selecting Reference Books. Disregarding dictionaries and encyclopedias, decide what reference book would be the best in which to look up the following items of information. Number your paper 1–10, and after the corresponding number, write the title or titles of the reference book.

1. A profile of the modern author Ursula LeGuin
2. The population of important world cities
3. A biography of someone recently in the news
4. Facts about the president of CBS News
5. The poem "Patterns"
6. Several quotations from Eleanor Roosevelt
7. A number of quotations about loneliness

8. The title of a book containing Christina Rossetti's poem "Goblin Market"
9. Results of the 1980 census
10. A map showing the first centers of civilization in the Near East

EXERCISE 6. Selecting Reference Books. Follow the directions for the preceding exercise.

1. A brief biography of Ethel Kennedy
2. A list of the Presidents of the United States
3. The gross national product of France
4. Some interesting information about the poet Edith Sitwell
5. The rest of the quotation beginning "A robin redbreast in a cage . . ."
6. The author of the poem "Abraham Lincoln Walks at Midnight"
7. A biographical sketch of the twentieth-century American poet Countee Cullen
8. The name of the present governor of the state of Oklahoma
9. A record of the last five annual games in the Rose Bowl
10. The titles of several books in which the poem beginning "All I could see from where I stood . . ." can be found

EXERCISE 7. Selecting Reference Books. Name the reference books best suited as sources for the following information. You may include the dictionary and encyclopedia. Be prepared to explain your choice.

1. A list of words meaning *knowledge*
2. An account of the construction of the Panama Canal
3. A very short biographical sketch of Coretta Scott King
4. An explanation of the difference in meaning between two common words often used interchangeably—*pretty* and *beautiful*
5. A number of pictures of San Francisco
6. The years American tennis teams won the Davis Cup
7. The site in Asia Minor of ancient Troy
8. The average annual precipitation in Ghana
9. A clear explanation of Johann Kepler's laws of planetary motion
10. The principal exports of Argentina
11. A detailed map of Israel

12. A detailed map of the Holy Roman Empire in 1500
13. The meaning of the Latin phrase *carpe diem*
14. An account of the gold rush of 1849
15. The history of the environmental movement in the United States

CHAPTER 30

The Dictionary

ARRANGEMENT AND CONTENT OF DICTIONARIES

A dictionary is a report on words and their uses. In a sense, a good dictionary is also a report on the civilization of the users of the language it deals with. "Languages," observed Dr. Samuel Johnson, "are the pedigrees of nations." A good dictionary gives a complete account of that pedigree. In addition to the present meaning and spelling of a word, dictionaries tell what a word has meant in the past, how it came to be a part of English, what other words it is related to, and other useful facts about its history. For those who know how to use it, a good dictionary contains a wealth of information about the history of English and attitudes of English-speaking people over the centuries.

In earlier years you learned how to find words in a dictionary by means of the alphabetical arrangement and the guide words at the top of each page. Being able to find a word is an essential dictionary skill, but it is not the only one. It is equally important to know how to interpret the information a dictionary gives you about a word.

KINDS OF DICTIONARIES

30a. Know the kinds of dictionaries.

Dictionaries have been prepared for many special purposes: for specialists in history, the sciences, and other special studies; for crossword puzzle enthusiasts; for poets and others with special interests. This chapter deals only with general dictionaries—those intended for the general public. There are two main kinds of general dictionaries: *unabridged* and *college* dictionaries.

The Unabridged Dictionary

An unabridged dictionary is one that is not based on a still larger dictionary. Although a large library may have several different unabridged dictionaries, the one that is best known and is most likely to be found in even the smallest library is *Webster's Third New International Dictionary,* which has been kept up-to-date through recent revisions. The newest unabridged dictionary is the *Random House Dictionary of the English Language, Unabridged Edition.*

An unabridged dictionary may contain almost a half-million words. For many words, it gives uncommon or historical, but now old-fashioned, meanings. It clarifies some of the meanings of a word by quoting examples of its use by prominent writers of the past and present. It contains fuller discussions of the distinctions in meaning between words whose meanings may seem to be very similar.

To see how unabridged and college dictionaries differ, compare the two entries reproduced on page 782.

The College Dictionary

A college dictionary is a shorter work, designed for quicker and more convenient reference. Such a dictionary may contain from 125,000 to 150,000 words, as well as some special sections giving abbreviations, biographical information of famous people, articles on spelling and punctuation, and other useful information. As the sample entries reproduced on page 782 suggest, a college dictionary does not attempt to report as fully on a word as an unabridged dictionary does. On the other hand, college dictionaries are likely to be revised more frequently and consequently are often better able to give up-to-date information on the meanings and uses of words.

Since all dictionaries must pack a great deal of information into relatively little space, they make extensive use of abbreviations, special signs and symbols, and other shortcuts. These space-saving devices are always explained in the front part of a dictionary and are usually easy enough to understand. However, each dictionary has its own system of abbreviations and symbols, and you cannot always assume that you know what one of them means because you once looked it up in a different book.

¹ten·sion \'tenchən\ n -s often attrib [MF or L; MF tension, fr. L tension-, tensio, fr. tensus (past part. of tendere to stretch) + -ion-, -io -ion — more at THIN] **1 a :** the act or action of stretching or the condition or degree of being stretched to stiffness **:** TAUTNESS ⟨to install the belt, slip it over the pulleys and adjust its ∼ —H.F.Blanchard & Ralph Ritchen⟩ **b :** STRESS ⟨arterial ∼⟩ ⟨muscular ∼⟩ **c :** a momentary state of muscular tautness in dance technique that inevitably resolves into relaxation **2 a :** either of two balancing forces causing or tending to cause extension **b :** the stress resulting from the elongation of an elastic body — contrasted with *compressive stress* **c** *archaic* **:** PRESSURE **3 a :** inner unrest, striving, or imbalance **:** a feeling of psychological stress often manifested by increased muscular tonus and by other physiological indicators of emotion ⟨went back to bed and dropped asleep suddenly with the release of ∼ —Mary Austin⟩ ⟨∼s distort personality —Bruce Bliven b. 1889⟩ **b :** a state of latent hostility or opposition between individuals or groups (as classes, races, nations) ⟨there is bitter ∼ between them —Bernard De Voto⟩ ⟨a lessening of minority-group ∼s —J.A.Morris b. 1904⟩ ⟨mob insanity explodes when ∼ reaches the flash point —*New Republic*⟩ **c :** a balance maintained in an artistic work (as a poem, painting, musical composition) between opposing forces or elements **:** a controlled dramatic or dynamic quality ⟨the ∼ which makes his sonata . . . so compelling —Stephen Spender⟩ ⟨the poetry of Dryden and Pope is characterized by the ∼ between its constituent elements —F.W.Bateson⟩ **4 :** ELECTRIC POTENTIAL **5 :** any of various devices in textile manufacturing machines or sewing machines that are used to control the tautness and movement of thread or material passing through **syn** see BALANCE, STRESS

From *Webster's Third New International Dictionary.* © 1981 by Merriam-Webster Inc., publishers of the Merriam Webster® Dictionaries. Reprinted by permission of Merriam-Webster Inc.

¹ten·sion \'ten-chən\ n [MF or L; MF, fr. L tension-, tensio, fr. tensus, pp.] **1 a :** the act or action of stretching or the condition or degree of being stretched to stiffness **:** TAUTNESS **b :** STRESS 1b **2 a :** either of two balancing forces causing or tending to cause extension **b :** the stress resulting from the elongation of an elastic body **c** *archaic* **:** PRESSURE **3 a :** inner striving, unrest, or imbalance often with physiological indication of emotion **b :** a state of latent hostility or opposition between individuals or groups **c :** a balance maintained in an artistic work between opposing forces or elements **4 :** electrical potential **5 :** a device to produce a desired tension (as in a loom) — **ten·sion·al** \'tench-nəl, -ən- l\ *adj* — **ten·sion·less** \'ten-chən-ləs\ *adj*

From *Webster's Ninth New International Dictionary.* © 1984 by Merriam-Webster Inc., publishers of the Merriam Webster® Dictionaries. Reprinted by permission of Merriam-Webster Inc.

EXERCISE 1. Using the Dictionary to Find Information.
Open to the table of contents at the front of your own dictionary. Notice where to find the introductory notes, the beginning of the definitions, and the special tables, charts, and illustrations. Then, on your paper, write down the page numbers on which each of the following items of information can be found.

1. An explanation of the way syllables are divided in the dictionary entries

2. The meaning of the abbreviation *SALT*
3. The population of Tampa
4. The capital of Uruguay
5. The dates (birth and death) of Jane Addams
6. An explanation of the metric system
7. The meaning of the abbreviations *n., adv., v.t.,* and *v.i.*
8. The meaning of the word *slalom*
9. A guide to capitalization
10. An explanation of the treatment of prefixes

KINDS OF INFORMATION IN DICTIONARIES

30b. Become familiar with the kinds of information in your dictionary and the method by which the information is presented.

As you study the following kinds of information that dictionaries contain, examine the sample column from a college dictionary on page 785.

Spelling

The boldfaced word at the beginning of a dictionary entry gives you the spelling. If there are two or more accepted spellings for a word, the various spellings are given. If one spelling is more common than another, the common one is given first. When in doubt, you will always be safe in using the first spelling given.

EXAMPLES   judgment, judgement   theater, theatre

If some grammatical change in the form of a word is likely to create a spelling problem, this form is given. For example, a dictionary gives the plural of a word if the plural is formed irregularly—*hero, heroes;* it gives the present and past participle forms of *refer,* showing that the final *r* is doubled—*referring, referred;* it gives the comparative form of *funny,* with the *y* changed to *i—funnier.*

Capital Letters

Proper nouns and proper adjectives are given with capital letters in college dictionaries. If a word is capitalized in certain meanings only, a dictionary labels these meanings *cap.*

EXAMPLE

pres·i·dent (prĕz′ə-dənt, -dĕnt′) *n. Abbr.* **p., P., pres., Pres.**
1. One appointed or elected to preside over an organized body
of people, as an assembly or meeting. **2.** *Often capital* **P.** The
chief executive of a republic, especially of the United States.
3. The chief officer of a branch of government, a corporation, a
board of trustees, a university, or any similar body. [Middle
English, from Old French, from Latin *praesidens,* present participle of *praesidēre,* PRESIDE.] **—pres′i·dent·ship′** *n.*

© 1980 by Houghton Mifflin Company. Reprinted by permission from *The American Heritage
Dictionary of the English Language.*

Division of Words into Syllables

When it is necessary to divide a word at the end of a line, the word
should be divided between syllables. Most dictionaries indicate a break
between syllables with a centered dot (el·e·va·tor). Syllable division
is indicated in the boldfaced entry word.

Pronunciation

Dictionaries indicate the pronunciation of words by means of accent
marks and respellings which show clearly how the words should
sound. The respellings are necessary because our alphabet uses more
than two hundred combinations of letters to represent the forty-two
or -three sounds of English. Each letter or special symbol used in the
respellings always stands for the same sound. The sounds represented
by the various letters and other symbols in the respellings are shown
in a key that usually appears at the front of the dictionary and at
the bottom of every pair of facing pages. Since different dictionaries
use different systems of indicating pronunciation, it is essential that
you familiarize yourself with the key and notes on pronunciation in
your own dictionary. The more detailed presentation of pronunciation
that begins on page 791 of this book shows several different systems
in wide use.

Part of Speech

After each word listed in the dictionary, an abbreviation tells what
part of speech the word is.

noun *n.*	adjective *adj.*
verb *v.*	preposition *prep.*
adverb *adv.*	conjunction *conj.*
pronoun *pron.*	interjection *interj.*

in·fec·tive (in fek′tiv) *adj.* [ME. *infectif* < OFr. < L. *infectivus*] likely to cause infection; infectious —— main entry

in·fe·cund (in fē′kənd, -fek′ənd) *adj.* [ME. *infecunde* < L. *infecundus*] not fecund; not fertile; barren —**in·fe·cun·di·ty** (in′fi kun′də tē) *n.* —— pronunciation respelling

in·fe·lic·i·tous [(in′fə lis′ə təs) *adj.* not felicitous; unfortunate or unsuitable —**in′fe·lic′i·tous·ly** *adv.* —— respelling

in·fe·lic·i·ty (-tē) [n.] [L. *infelicitas* < *infelix*, unfortunate: see IN-² & FELICITY] 1. the quality or condition of being infelicitous 2. *pl.* -**ties** something infelicitous; unsuitable or inapt remark, action, etc. —— part of speech

spelling of

in·fer (in fur′) *vt.* [-ferred′, -fer′ring] [L. *inferre*, to bring or carry in, infer < *in-*, in + *ferre*, to carry, BEAR¹] 1. orig., to bring on or about; cause; induce 2. to conclude or decide from something known or assumed; derive by reasoning; draw as a conclusion 3. *a*) to lead to as a conclusion; indicate *b*) to indicate indirectly; imply: in this sense, still sometimes regarded as a loose usage —*vi.* to draw inferences —**in·fer′a·ble** *adj.* —**in·fer′a·bly** *adv.* —**in·fer′rer** *n.* —— verb forms

numbered definitions

SYN.—**infer** suggests the arriving at a decision or opinion by reasoning from known facts or evidence [from your smile, I *infer* that you're pleased]; **deduce**, in strict discrimination, implies inference from a general principle by logical reasoning [the method was *deduced* from earlier experiments]; **conclude** strictly implies an inference that is the final logical result in a process of reasoning [I must, therefore, *conclude* that you are wrong]; **judge** stresses the careful checking and weighing of premises, etc. in arriving at a conclusion; **gather** is an informal substitute for **infer** or **conclude** [I *gather* that you don't care] —— synonyms with illustrative examples of usage and meaning

in·fer·ence (in′fər əns) *n.* [ML. *inferentia*] 1. the act or process of inferring; specif., the deriving of a conclusion in logic by either induction or deduction 2. something inferred; specif., a conclusion arrived at in logic

in·fer·en·tial (in′fə ren′shəl) *adj.* [< ML. *inferentia* + -AL] based on or having to do with inference —**in′fer·en′tial·ly** *adv.* —— etymology

in·fe·ri·or (in fir′ē ər) *adj.* [ME. < L., compar. of *inferus*, low, below < IE. *ndheros*, whence UNDER] 1. lower in space; placed lower down 2. low or lower in order, status, rank, etc.; subordinate 3. lower in quality or value than (with *to*) 4. poor in quality; below average 5. *Anat.* located below or directed downward 6. *Astron.* between the earth and the sun [Mercury and Venus are *inferior* planets] 7. *Bot.* having the sepals, petals, and stamens attached at the apex: said of the ovary of an epigynous flower 8. *Printing* placed below the type line, as 2 in NO₂ —*n.* an inferior person or thing —**in·fe′ri·or′i·ty** (-ôr′ə tē, -är′-) *n.* —— restrictive label

illustrative example

inferiority complex 1. *Psychol.* a neurotic condition resulting from various feelings of inferiority, such as derive from real or imagined physical or social inadequacy and often manifested through overcompensation in excessive aggressiveness, a domineering attitude, etc. 2. popularly, any feeling of inferiority, inadequacy, etc.: cf. SUPERIORITY COMPLEX —— cross reference

in·fer·nal (in fur′n'l) *adj.* [ME. < OFr. < LL. *infernalis* < L. *infernus*, underground, lower, infernal < *inferus*: see INFERIOR] 1. *a*) of the ancient mythological world of the dead [b] of hell 2. hellish; diabolical; fiendish; inhuman 3. [Colloq.] hateful; outrageous —**in·fer′nal·ly** *adv.* —— usage label

derived form with label

infernal machine *earlier name for* a booby trap or time bomb

in·fer·no (in fur′nō) *n., pl.* -**nos** [It. < L. *infernus*: see INFERNAL] hell or any place suggesting hell, usually characterized by great heat or flames —[I-] that section of Dante's *Divine Comedy* which describes hell and the sufferings of the damned

Since many words may be used as more than one part of speech, some entries will contain several part-of-speech labels. In the sample column on page 785, for example, the first eight definitions for *inferior* are labeled *adj.* (for *adjective*) and the last one is labeled *n.* (for *noun*). Verbs have, in addition to the label *v.*, the labels *v.i.* and *v.t.* (See the entry for *infer* on page 785.) The label *v.i.* stands for "intransitive verb," and *v.t.* stands for "transitive verb."

Meaning

Since a single word may have many different meanings, many dictionary entries contain a number of different definitions, which are distinguished from one another by means of letters and numbers. Numbers usually indicate important differences in meaning, and letters indicate differences within the numbered definitions.

In some dictionaries, these separate meanings are listed in historical order—the earliest recorded meaning first, the latest last. Other dictionaries give meanings in order of the frequency of their use—from the most common meaning to the least common. The following definitions illustrate these two methods of ordering meanings. The first is in historical order, and the second in order of use.

> **hec·tic** \'hek-tik\ *adj* [ME *etyk*, fr. MF *etique*, fr. LL *hecticus*, fr. Gk *hektikos* habitual, consumptive, fr. *echein* to have — more at SCHEME] **1** : of, relating to, or being a fluctuating but persistent fever (as in tuberculosis) **2** : having a hectic fever **3** : RED, FLUSHED **4** : filled with excitement or confusion <the ~ days before Christmas> — **hec·ti·cal·ly** \-ti-k(ə-)lē\ *adv*

From *Webster's Ninth New Collegiate Dictionary*. © 1984 by Merriam-Webster Inc., publishers of the Merriam Webster® Dictionaries. Reprinted by permission of Merriam-Webster Inc.

> **hec·tic** (hek/tik), *adj.* **1.** characterized by intense agitation, feverish excitement, confused and rapid movement, etc.: *The period preceding the trip was hectic and exhausting.* **2.** marking a particular habit or condition of body, as the fever of phthisis (**hec/tic fe/ver**) when this is attended by flushed cheeks (**hec/tic flush/**), hot skin, and emaciation. **3.** pertaining to or affected with such fever; consumptive. —*n.* **4.** a hectic fever. **5.** a hectic flush. **6.** a consumptive person. [< LL *hectic(us)* < Gk *hektikós* habitual, equiv. to *hekt-* (s. of *hézis*) state, condition + *-ikos* -IC; r. ME *etyk* < MF] —**hec/ti·cal·ly, hec/tic·ly,** *adv.* —**hec/tic·ness,** *n.*

From the unabridged *Random House Dictionary of the English Language*. Copyright © 1966, 1967, 1970, 1971 by Random House, Inc. Reprinted by permission.

Derivation

Most dictionaries indicate the history of a word. They show by means of abbreviations what language the word originally came from and what its original meaning was. English is unusual among languages for the vast number of words it has taken from other languages. The source of newly coined words is also given. Knowing the source and original meaning of a word is often a great help to you in understanding the word's present meaning and correct use.

The abbreviations used to indicate the languages from which words are derived are explained in the front of your dictionary under the heading "Abbreviations Used in This Book" or another heading of essentially the same meaning. The following derivation of *curfew* is given in *Webster's New World Dictionary:*

> **cur·few** (kur′fyōō) *n.* [ME. *curfeu* < OFr. *covrefeu*, lit., cover fire < *covrir* (see COVER) + *feu*, fire < L. *focus*, fireplace (see FOCUS)]

From *Webster's New World Dictionary of the American Language.* Second College Edition. Copyright © 1980 by Simon & Schuster. Reprinted by permission of Simon & Schuster, a Division of Gulf & Western Corporation.

The symbol < means "from" (abbreviated *fr.* in some dictionaries). If written out, this etymology would read "derived from Middle English *curfeu* from Old French *covrefeu,* literally "cover fire," from *covrir* (see COVER) + *feu,* "fire," from Latin *focus,* "fireplace" (see FOCUS).

Restrictive Labels

Most of the words defined in a dictionary belong to the general vocabulary of standard English. Some words, as well as some special meanings of otherwise standard words, require special treatment, and these usually appear with a label. There are three main kinds of labels: *subject* labels, which specify that a word has a particular meaning in a certain field: *Law, Med., Aeron.* (Aeronautics), etc.; *geographical* labels, which indicate the area in which a particular word, meaning, or pronunciation is principally used: *Brit., SW U.S.* (Southwest U.S.); and *usage* labels, which characterize a word as to its kind of usage: *informal, slang, nonstandard,* etc. As the following examples show, however, different dictionaries may not agree about giving a usage label:

> **glitch** \′glich\ *n* [prob. fr. G *glitschen* to slide, slip; akin to OHG *glitan* to glide — more at GLIDE] **1 a** : an unwanted brief surge of electrical power **b** : a false or spurious electronic signal **2** : MALFUNCTION <a – in a spacecraft's fuel cell> **3** : MISHAP *also* : a minor technical problem

From *Webster's Ninth New Collegiate Dictionary.* © 1984 by Merriam-Webster Inc., publishers of the Merriam Webster® Dictionaries. Reprinted by permission of Merriam-Webster Inc.

glitch (glich) *n.* [< G. colloq. *glitsche*, a slip < *glitschen*, to slip, slide, intens. of G. *gleiten*: see GLIDE] [Slang] a mishap, error, malfunctioning, etc.

From *Webster's New World Dictionary of the American Language*. Second College Edition. Copyright © 1980 Simon & Schuster. Reprinted by permission of Simon & Schuster, a Division of Gulf & Western Corporation.

Usage labels provide a good general guide to usage, but all writers should learn to make their own judgments. Assigning a label such as *slang* or *informal* is necessarily a subjective judgment on the part of the definer, and not all dictionaries agree about labeling the same word. (For instance, the first example has no label.)

Synonyms and Antonyms

For some entries in the dictionary, synonyms or antonyms, or both, are given. A synonym is a word having nearly the same meaning as the word being defined: *brave—courageous*. An antonym is a word having the opposite meaning: *brave—cowardly*. See the entry for *infer* on page 785.

Illustrations

If the meaning of a word can best be shown by a picture, the dictionary may give an illustration. While you, of course, cannot depend on finding a picture of the thing you may be looking up, there is a chance that you might find one, especially if the object cannot be easily described.

OTHER INFORMATION IN THE DICTIONARY

Biographical Entries

Who was Clara Barton? When did Pablo Casals die? What was Chopin's nationality? What were the dates of Queen Elizabeth I's reign? For what is Thurgood Marshall famous? What was George Eliot's real name? How do you pronounce Persephone? The answers to such simple fact questions about famous persons can probably be found in your dictionary.

Some dictionaries devote a special section called *Biographical Names* to famous persons. Others give names of persons and places in a section called *Proper Names*. Sometimes these names are included in the body of the book. You can easily discover which method your dictionary uses.

The following common pieces of biographical information are usually given in a dictionary:

1. *Name:* spelling, pronunciation, first name
2. *Dates:* of birth and death and of reign if a king or queen, or term of office if head of a government
3. *Nationality*
4. *Why famous*

The following is a typical dictionary entry for a famous name.

> **King** (kǐñg), *n.* **1. Ernest Joseph,** 1878–1956, U.S. naval officer. **2. Martin Luther,** 1929–68, U.S. Baptist minister: civil-rights leader; Nobel peace prize 1964. **3. Rufus,** 1755–1827, U.S. political leader and statesman. **4. William Lyon Mackenzie,** 1874–1950, Canadian statesman: prime minister 1921–26, 1926–30, 1935–48. **5. William Rufus De·Vane** (də vān/), 1786–1853, vice-president of the U.S. 1853.

From the unabridged *Random House Dictionary of the English Language.* Copyright © 1966, 1967, 1969, 1970, 1971 by Random House, Inc. Reprinted by permission.

Mythological and Biblical characters, as well as some literary characters, are often listed in the body of the dictionary: *Ruth, Lancelot, Naomi, Juno,* etc.

Geographical Entries

Like the biographical entries in the dictionary, the geographical entries are sometimes given in the body of the book and sometimes in a special section. This section may be called a gazetteer—a geographical dictionary.

In general the following information is given about a place:

1. *Name:* spelling, pronunciation
2. *Location*
3. *Identification:* whether a city, country, lake, mountain, river, etc.
4. *Size:* population, if a city or country (often given in thousands—225 = 225,000); area in square miles, if a country or territory or body of water; length, if a river; height, if a mountain, etc.

5. *Importance:* If a city is the capital of a state or country, this will be indicated by a star or an asterisk. The capital city of a country or state will also be given under the name of the country or state.

6. *Historical or other interesting information of importance:* Thus for Hampton Roads, Virginia,. . . . "battle of *Merrimack* and *Monitor,* March 9, 1862." For Lake Mead, formed by Hoover Dam in the Colorado River, one dictionary says "the largest artificial lake in the world."

7. *Governed or controlled by what country:* For Guam, the dictionary says "a possession of the U.S."

Miscellaneous Information

Most good dictionaries include the following kinds of information, either in separate sections or in the body of the dictionary itself.

1. *Foreign words and phrases:* spelling, pronunciation, meaning
2. *Abbreviations:* a list of abbreviations of all kinds, giving the words in full

An unabridged dictionary and some of the larger student dictionaries include

3. *Signs and symbols:* Not all dictionaries include a section of this kind, but some do, and if yours does, you should study the section to familiarize yourself with its content.
4. *Spelling rules*
5. *Punctuation rules*
6. *New words*

REVIEW EXERCISE A. Finding Information in the Dictionary.

When your teacher gives the signal, look up the answers to the following questions in the dictionary you have. Write the answers on your paper. Accuracy is more important than speed, but speed *is* important.

1. Who was Ann Lee and for what is she famous?
2. When did Sir Francis Bacon live?
3. Give the meaning of the abbreviation UNESCO.
4. Copy the pronunciation of *de facto* and *de jure,* and distinguish between the meaning of these two Latin phrases.
5. Who was Julia Howe?
6. What is the derivation of *hippopotamus*?

7. What is the height of Mont Blanc and where is it?
8. What is the area of Lake Erie?
9. What is the capital of Mali?
10. Where is the island group called the Hebrides and to what country does it belong?

REVIEW EXERCISE B. Finding Information in the Dictionary.

Look up in your dictionary the answers to the following questions:

1. Give the pronunciation and meaning of *dolce far niente*.
2. Who was Eurydice?
3. Give the more usual pronunciation of *apparatus*.
4. Of what country is Kabul the capital?
5. What is the population of Copenhagen?
6. What is the length of the Rhine River?
7. What is the derivation of *Gypsy?*
8. What country governs the Falkland Islands?
9. Who was Mrs. Malaprop? For what is she famous?
10. What is the meaning of the abbreviation CIF?

PRONUNCIATION

30c. Use your dictionary for pronunciation.

You learn the pronunciation of most words from your parents, your teachers, and the other people you talk with. Ordinarily, you consult a dictionary only for the pronunciation of words that you encounter in books but do not hear in normal conversation.

Dictionary makers try to provide a suitable pronunciation for every word, but since the same word may be pronounced quite differently in various parts of the country, this task is not always easy. The sound represented by the *a* in *water* is pronounced one way in Boston, another way in New York, and in still other ways in Richmond, Chicago, and Portland. There is not one correct way of making that sound—each different version of the vowel *a* is the right one for that area. For this reason, you may sometimes find that your dictionary tells you one thing about the sound of a word and that you hear it spoken quite differently in your part of the country. In such a case, ask your teacher about the acceptable pronunciation of the word in your area. Do not assume that the pronunciation you hear is wrong just because you cannot find it in the dictionary.

Because the actual spelling of many English words does not clearly indicate how they are pronounced, dictionaries use simplified respellings to indicate the sound of a word. Moreover, since there are more sounds in English than there are letters to represent them, special symbols called *diacritical marks* must be used to show different speech sounds represented by the same letter. The following pair of words illustrates both respelling and the use of diacritical marks.

knit (nit)   knife (nīf)

Notice that in both respellings the silent letters are dropped—both silent *k's* and the *e*. Notice also that the different sounds of the *i's* are distinguished. The *i* in *knit* is unmarked, and the *i* in *knife* is written with a straight line above it.

Indicating pronunciation is one of the dictionary maker's most difficult tasks, and it is not surprising that there is some disagreement as to how it should be done. The systems used in various dictionaries differ in a number of details. You will see some of these differences in this chapter. However, when you have need of a pronunciation, you will not need to know all the different ways of indicating it. What you will need to know is how to interpret the pronunciation given in your own dictionary. To do this, you must familiarize yourself with the explanatory notes dealing with pronunciation and with the pronunciation key. Most dictionaries explain in the introductory pages the system they use. A full key is usually given inside the front cover. Many dictionaries print a shorter key on each page or each set of facing pages. The key illustrates the function of each letter and symbol used, giving simple examples that everyone knows how to pronounce.

Consonant Sounds

The sounds that a speaker makes by squeezing or cutting off the stream of breath are called *consonants*. The last sounds in *with, this,* and *itch* are made by forcing the breath through a narrowed passage at one point or another between the throat and the lips. The last sounds in *first, wasp,* and *break* are made by cutting off the breath momentarily.

Consonants present few problems in representing pronunciation because most of them are pronounced in essentially the same way in all words. In some cases, ordinary English spelling uses one letter for two different consonant sounds. For example, the letter *c* stands for two quite different sounds in *cake* and *cell*. In giving the pronunciation of these words, the dictionary would spell the first with a *k* and the second with an *s*.

Two closely related sounds, the sound of the *th* in *thin* and its sound in *then*, are distinguished in different ways in different dictionaries. For example:

	WNC	RHC[1]
thin	thin	(thin)
then	then	(then)

Vowel Sounds

The sounds that a speaker makes when not squeezing or stopping the flow of breath are called *vowels*. Although we use five letters (*a, e, i, o, u*) and sometimes a sixth (*y*) in representing vowel sounds in writing, there are actually nine different vowels that are used by most speakers of English in America. To indicate these sounds, dictionary makers use the letters above in combination with diacritical marks.

Long Vowels

The long straight mark over a vowel is called the *macron*. When the macron appears over a vowel, the vowel is said to have the sound of its own name. Such vowels are called *long vowels*.

EXAMPLES late (lāt)
sheep (shēp)
tide (tīd)
bone (bōn)
cube (kūb)[2]

Short Vowels

The vowels in the words *hat, bed, pig, odd,* and *up* are called *short vowels*. There are two common methods of showing the sound of short vowels. One uses this symbol (˘), the breve, over the vowel; the other method leaves the short vowels unmarked.

EXAMPLES add (ăd) or (ad)
end (ĕnd) or (end)

---

[1] The abbreviations stand for *Webster's New Collegiate Dictionary* and *The Random House College Dictionary,* respectively.
[2] The long *u* sound is also represented by yo͞o or yü: kyo͞ob, kyüb.

Other Vowel Sounds

The remaining vowel sounds, which cannot be classified either as long or short, are represented by the letter and one of several other diacritical marks:

KEY WORD	WNC	RHC
order	ȯ	ô
urge	ə	û
took	u̇	o͝o
pool	ü	o͞o

In addition, a number of sounds usually considered to be a single unit are in fact combinations of two other vowel sounds. Such combinations are usually represented by two letters:

KEY WORD	WNC	RHC
oil	oi	oi
house	au̇	ou

The Schwa

Modern dictionaries use an *e* printed upside down (ə) to represent the indistinct sound of vowels in unaccented syllables. This symbol, called the *schwa* (shwa), is used in such words as:

against	(ə·genst′)
banal	(ba′nəl)
correct	(kə·rekt′)

Some dictionaries make more use of the schwa than others. Those that do, use this symbol for the same sound when it appears in accented as well as in unaccented syllables:

bun	(bən)
serpent	(sər′pənt)

EXERCISE 2. Finding the Pronunciation of Words in the Dictionary.

Look up the pronunciation of each of the following words. On your paper, copy the word after the proper number, enclosing the respelling in parentheses.

1. consummate
2. cultural
3. genuine
4. hog
5. hypothetical
6. irrevocable
7. Themistocles
8. thistle
9. those
10. Worcester

Accent

In words of more than one syllable, one syllable is pronounced louder than the others or other. The syllable stressed in this way is said to be *accented* and is marked with an *accent mark*. Dictionaries mark accents in two main ways: with a heavy accent mark (') after the accented syllable or with a mark (¢) before the syllable.

KEY WORD	WNC	RHC
compete	kəm-'pēt	kəmpēt'
pony	¢pō-nē	pō'nē

Some longer words have two accented syllables—one receiving a heavy, or primary, stress and the other receiving a light, or secondary, stress. The following example illustrates ways of showing this difference in accent.

KEY WORD	WNC	RHC
elevator	¢el-əvāt-ər	el'əvā'tər

Sometimes the same word may be accented in different ways, depending upon how the word is used. The listed words are examples of how the accent shifts when the words are used as different parts of speech.

com'pact (noun)	com·pact' (adjective)
con'duct (noun)	con·duct' (verb)
con'tent (noun)	con·tent' (adjective)
pro'test (noun)	pro·test' (verb)

EXERCISE 3. Finding the Accented Syllables and Part of Speech of Words. Rewrite each italicized word, showing the accented syllables and the part of speech as given in your dictionary.

EXAMPLE 1. I *refuse* to carry out the *refuse.*
    1. *(re fuse')* v., *(ref'use)* n.

1. One cannot *object* to the *object* of trial by jury: to allow the guilt of an accused person to be judged by peers.
2. The new track *record* was duly *recorded* in the book.
3. The Stamp Act caused the colonists to *rebel;* still, a few of them yet considered themselves *rebels* against duly constituted authority.
4. Jeeves, *conduct* this gentlemen to the door. His *conduct* has been intolerable.

5. To *console* her invalid sister, Victoria bought her a huge mahogany *console*, housing both a TV and a record player.

6. The less-developed countries have often arranged to *import* consumer products from the major powers. The *import* of these products has been undertaken to raise the standard of living in smaller nations.

7. Of all my *subjects* I dislike algebra most. My total lack of comprehension *subjects* me to much ridicule in that class.

8. Although the police did not *suspect* him, the thief sensed that to Sherlock Holmes he was already a *suspect*.

9. Intense cold caused the plastic parts to *contract*, cracking many of them. A new *contract*, therefore, had to be negotiated with the supplier for better plastic.

10. The queen's *consort* was known to *consort* openly with enemies of the crown.

EXERCISE 4. Finding the Phonetic Spelling of Words. Using the pronunciation key in the front part of your dictionary, write the vowel markings above the vowels in the following common words. Place accent marks in the words of more than one syllable. The final silent *e*, of course, should not be marked.

1. prod	11. far
2. old	12. fur nish
3. tame	13. re make
4. like	14. pro tect
5. rib	15. rob in
6. eve	16. com ment
7. lend	17. loop hole
8. boil	18. cook ing
9. us	19. un til
10. mood	20. out cast

EXERCISE 5. Writing the Phonetic Spelling of Words. Using the pronunciation key inside the front cover of your dictionary, respell the following words according to the system used by your dictionary. Make use of accent marks, diacritical markings, and divisions between

syllables. When you have finished, check your work against the word as it actually appears in the dictionary.

1. beautiful
2. Chicago
3. conduit
4. bathe
5. llama
6. unnecessary
7. apparatus
8. sough
9. sought
10. rough

CHAPTER 31

Vocabulary

LEARNING AND USING NEW WORDS

More and more these days, tests of one kind or another play an increasingly important role in our lives. They are used to measure success in school and often to decide who is accepted into a particular college or kind of job. These tests differ, but most of them place great importance upon vocabulary. To prepare for these tests, you will find it well worthwhile to take stock of your vocabulary right now and to consider ways of improving it.

The best way to increase your vocabulary is to read widely and thoughtfully. There is no other way of doing the job successfully. There are, however, ways in which to add to your vocabulary more of the new words you encounter than you may be adding now. This chapter will give you experience in using these techniques of word study.

Before you begin the chapter, take the following test to get a rough idea of how good your vocabulary is right now. Sixteen correct answers is about average for students of your age. Can you do better?

DIAGNOSTIC TEST

Selecting the Meanings of Words. Number your paper 1–25. After the proper number, write the letter of the word that is nearest in meaning to the italicized word at the left. Do not try to guess the correct answer.

1. *affluent*   a. verbose b. wealthy c. friendly
2. *assuage*   a. relieve b. rub c. make brighter
3. *brevity*   a. position b. goodness c. shortness
4. *circumvent*   a. evade b. surround c. open
5. *denizen*   a. lair b. inhabitant c. bear
6. *explicit*   a. proud b. apologetic c. definite
7. *flay*   a. arrange b. cast a rod c. strip off skin
8. *gregarious*   a. sickly b. sociable c. cheerful
9. *hierarchy*   a. system of ranks b. sound of music c. ancient manners
10. *indolent*   a. unrefined b. sorrowful c. lazy
11. *jeopardize*   a. risk b. assist c. stripe
12. *lucrative*   a. profitable b. bright c. creative
13. *miscreant*   a. sneak b. hobo c. villain
14. *nebulous*   a. indistinct b. difficult c. villainous
15. *onerous*   a. rich b. burdensome c. poor
16. *plebeian*   a. aristocratic b. common c. military
17. *preclude*   a. prevent b. preview c. prevail
18. *quaff*   a. guffaw b. drink c. tremble
19. *repugnance*   a. dislike b. insolence c. desire
20. *sinecure*   a. easy job b. hard job c. technical job
21. *subjugate*   a. sublet b. submit c. subdue
22. *turgid*   a. cloudy b. unusual c. swollen
23. *vacillate*   a. waver b. impart c. empty
24. *wreak*   a. destroy b. inflict c. stretch
25. *zenith*   a. heavenly body b. highest point c. tower

WAYS TO LEARN NEW WORDS

You have learned some of the words you know by looking them up in the dictionary, but the number of words you can learn this way is usually quite limited. Most of the words that you have in your vocabulary have come to you in other ways. You are constantly meeting new expressions in the course of your schoolwork and your conversations, but you will never be able to make them a part of your own word list unless you become *word conscious*. Keep on the alert for new words, and when you meet them, you will be able to add them to your collection.

31a. List new words with their meanings in your notebook, and use them in your speech and writing.

Set aside a special part of your notebook for new words. Write down every new word that you find, together with its meaning. Thereafter, try to use it in speech and writing as often as you can in order to make it a permanent part of your vocabulary. Begin now. Enter every word you missed on the Diagnostic Test, and to these add the new words you learn from day to day.

Context

31b. Learn new words from their contexts.

If your teacher asks you what *cumulative* or *exotic* means, or if your younger brother looks up from a book and asks if you know what *grotesque* means, you won't be able to answer their questions unless the words are already in your vocabulary. However, most of the words you encounter will not be isolated; instead, you will find them surrounded by other words and used in specific situations that will help you guess their meaning. The total situation in which a word is found is called its *context*. The *verbal context* refers to the other words in the sentence or phrase, and the *physical context* refers to the circumstances in which the word is used.

By paying careful attention to the context of a word, you can probably make an accurate guess about its meaning.

Verbal Context

The words accompanying the new word usually provide plenty of "context clues" to its meaning. For example:

> Bills relating to taxation must originate in the House of Representatives.
> The dust particles gravitated slowly to the bottom of the pool.

In the first example the verbal context clues (*relating to taxation, House of Representatives*) tell us that *bills* must certainly refer to laws or legislative acts and not some other meaning of the word, such as "part of the head of a bird" or "a statement of debt." Likewise in the second example, it is not hard for us to think of what dust particles would naturally do in a pool and arrive at a good idea of the meaning of *gravitate*—something like "to move slowly downward."

Frequently the context clues missing in the sentence are contained in the paragraph. For example, read the following two passages. Do not look up the meanings of the words in boldfaced type, but try instead to guess their meanings from the clues given in the selections.

1. Some people call them nature's thermometers.

They are rhododendrons, the **nondeciduous** broad-leaved plants that decorate thousands of suburban yards with their greenery in both the winter and summer. But when the temperature drops below freezing, their normally flat leaves become **mercurial thermal sensors,** varying their shape according to the temperature.

As a result, a veteran rhododendron watcher can peer through a frost-rimmed window and **gauge** the approximate outdoor temperature by observing how tightly curled the leaves are.

BAYARD WEBSTER

2. Somewhere in the **annals** of American folklore there is a tale about the farmer who made a scarecrow so fearsome in appearance that crows not only left his crops alone but brought back corn they had stolen years before. It is the kind of story that appeals to those who **wage** continuous battle against not only crows but other garden pests as well.

From Man's earliest efforts to protect his crops he has relied upon scarecrows. Created in his own image and more often than not dressed in his own cast-off clothing, these intimidating **minions** stand guard while he is attending to other chores. They range from simple stick figures draped with old gunny sacks to elaborate **sartorial** masterpieces, some of them fit for display in a museum.

There is evidence to show that when Columbus set foot on this continent, Indians were using scarecrows to keep vigil over their cornfields. The Colonists used them extensively as they heeded the planter's **adage** and dropped five kernels into each hill of corn, "one for the woodchuck, one for the crow, one for the cutworm and two to grow."

AVON NEAL

EXERCISE 1. Determining the Meanings of Words by Using Context Clues. Copy the italicized word in each of the following sentences. Then examine the context clues, and write down what you think the word means. Check your answers in your dictionary.

EXAMPLE   1. The scientific report was so *abstruse* that even Professor Bowen had trouble comprehending it.
     1. *abstruse—difficult to understand*

1. This word is *ambiguous;* it can have two meanings.
2. *Oblivious* of the terrible danger threatening her, she sauntered along absent-mindedly.
3. He was a very *astute* buyer, estimating values very carefully and never allowing himself to be deceived.
4. They wanted no *remuneration* in money or gifts; their only reward would be the knowledge that they had saved the child.
5. Although she profited greatly by the action, the queen could not *condone* the murder of the baron.
6. The fearful crowd watched with great *trepidation* as the rescuers inched their way along the ledge.
7. The *epitaph* on her tombstone was brief: "Here lies one who died for her country."
8. After what seemed to the impatient children an *interminable* time, the boring hour came to an end.
9. The trapped animal struggled for hours but could not *extricate* itself from the snare.
10. After a *cursory* examination of only a minute or so, the doctor said that the child probably had not been seriously hurt.

EXERCISE 2. Determining the Meanings of Words by Using Context Clues. Follow the directions for Exercise 1.

1. He was a *fastidious* dresser, always very neat and very particular about what he wore.
2. The business was an extremely *lucrative* one; in their first year their profits were five times the amount of their original investment.
3. The fire threatened to spread to the *adjacent* houses.
4. To drive home his accusation by repetition, he *reiterated* that he thought Smithers was a liar.
5. Such an ointment is likely to *mitigate* the pain of the burn.
6. Smoking is likely to have a *pernicious* effect on one's health.
7. Michael looked at the dead roach on the shelf without trying to conceal his *repugnance*.
8. Wasting no words at all and being very brief, she gave a *succinct* account of her adventures.
9. He wanted to meet the new girl, but he was too *reticent* to try to speak to her without having been introduced.

10. The overpowering odor of roses spread from room to room, *permeating* the whole house.

Kinds of Context Clues

There are a number of kinds of verbal context clues, but three in particular are extremely useful, clear, and helpful. Writers are often aware that some of their words may not be immediately clear to all of their readers, and they insure complete understanding by adding little definitions or shorter synonyms. Usually these little definitions or synonyms are preceded by *or.* A writer may put down "the person's irascibility, or "bad temper," or something similar. Sometimes wording like *that is* or *in other words* is used. A person writing about first aid may say "a tourniquet may be used to stop excessive bleeding." On reconsideration this may be changed to "a tourniquet, that is, *a tightly twisted bandage applied above the wound,* may be used to stop excessive bleeding." Sometimes these explanations are made by the use of appositives or appositive phrases (see pages 87–88). Appositives that define are often punctuated with commas, as in the sentence "The opprobrium, *the deep public disgrace,* of this treason stayed with him all the years of his life." Here the word *opprobrium* is made clear by the following appositive.

EXERCISE 3. Determining the Meanings of Words by Using Context Clues. Number your paper 1–10. Copy after each number the italicized word in the corresponding sentence. Then, after it, write the context clue that helps you to know what it means.

1. Many of the Romans were quite willing to *deify* their Caesars, to make gods of them.
2. Then the old mansion split apart and fell into the widening *abyss,* into the yawning chasm developing before it.
3. Baltimore County and the city of Baltimore are *coterminous;* that is, they have a common boundary.
4. Such preparations will *depilate* the skin; in other words, they will remove the hair.
5. She gave us the most *succinct,* or brief, answers that she possibly could.
6. The others questioned the *veracity*—the truthfulness—of these reports.

7. Ms. Jenkins was too *hypercritical,* too given to constant fault-finding, to be a very good teacher.
8. These medical students have decided to become *pediatricians;* that is, doctors specializing in the care and diseases of children.
9. The *nomenclature,* or system of naming, now used in botany is in part the work of Linnaeus.
10. The explorers were all afflicted with *nostalgia,* a yearning to return home.

Physical Context

To know the actual circumstances surrounding the use of a word, that is, its *physical* context, is often essential in distinguishing between two meanings of the same word. Take the word *foul,* for instance. If you are watching a baseball game, the word *foul* means one thing; if the game is basketball, it means something else. The word *cell* has one meaning in a biology laboratory and another in the city jail. Both kinds of context—verbal and physical—should be carefully noted, for both help you to discover the meaning of unfamiliar words.

EXERCISE 4. Determining the Meanings of Words by Using Physical Context Clues. Following are ten words. After each one are given two different physical contexts, labeled *a* and *b.* Arrange your paper with numbers 1a, 1b, 2a, 2b, etc., along the left side. After each of these numbers, write the meaning that the word in question will have in the physical context given.

EXAMPLE 1. cast a. a fishing trip
                b. a theater
      1a. *the throwing of a fishing line into the water*
      1b. *the entire group of performers in a show*

1. *delta*   a. a Greek class
             b. a geography class
2. *bench*   a. a park
             b. a court
3. *drill*   a. carpentry
             b. the army

4. *carrier*   a. a health department
              b. a naval base
5. *switch*   a. a railway yard
             b. a hairdresser's
6. *coach*   a. a railway station
             b. a gymnasium

7. *colony* a. a history class
            b. a bacteriology
               laboratory

8. *secretary* a. a business
               office
            b. a furniture
               store

9. *bridge* a. a dentist's
               office
            b. a naval vessel

10. *jacket* a. a metalworker's
               shop
            b. a book shop

Using the Dictionary

31c. Learn to find the meanings you want in the dictionary.

To build up your vocabulary systematically, do not rely entirely on context clues. Track down the word further in the dictionary.

Very few nonscientific words in English have a single meaning. Most have many meanings, often entirely different when the context is different. Therefore, the first step in finding the meaning of any new word is always to determine how it is being used when you read it or hear it for the first time in conversation.

To help you in this way, dictionaries often provide sample contexts. One dictionary, for example, lists twelve definitions of the word *bond* when it is used as a noun. The list begins with the most common use, "that which binds or holds together; a band; tie," and proceeds through more and more specialized contexts, for example, the meaning of *bond* in law, in finance, in insurance, in commerce, in building, etc., and ends with its very specialized meaning in chemistry. This arrangement of definitions allows you to find quickly the one that best suits the context of your word.

Some dictionaries enter definitions in the order of frequency or importance. In this type the first meaning given is the one considered the most common, and the one given last is considered the least common. A dictionary using historical order, for example, would give as the first definition of the word *forum* the notion of a Roman marketplace or other open public area and would list the idea of a public meeting much later. A dictionary that arranged its definitions in terms of contemporary importance would reverse this procedure.

EXERCISE 5. Finding the Meanings of Words in the Dictionary.
Number your paper 1–10. The italicized words in the following sentences all have a number of different meanings. Consult your diction-

ary to find the meaning that best fits the context of the word in the sentence. Then write the meaning after the proper number on your paper.

1. The pasture creek was fed by three tiny *affluents*.
2. Mr. Yamamoto was a teacher of high *caliber*.
3. At the bottom of the *defile,* the river appeared like a silver thread.
4. The image on the screen *dissolved* from a tube of toothpaste to a panorama of giant cacti.
5. Pails and buckets are *galvanized*.
6. The cold-induced *inertia* of grasshoppers allows anglers to catch them easily in the early morning.
7. The imprint of the huge scorpion was found in a *matrix* of Devonian sediments.
8. Joanne *executed* a series of elaborate dance steps on her skates.
9. At the bottom of the jar was a peculiar purple *precipitate*.
10. To defend her interest in the suit, Ms. Jones *retained* a young attorney.

Finding the Right Word

31d. Select the word that conveys the precise meaning and impression you want to give.

You cannot use the dictionary for very long before discovering that there are many words meaning approximately the same thing. The distinctions in meaning between synonyms, though sometimes very slight, are important and are carefully preserved by people who want their speech to be as lively and expressive as possible. Consider, for example, the multiple ways a person can *say* something:

announce	deliver	hint	plead	respond
answer	demand	insinuate	preach	retort
argue	descant	insist	probe	roar
asseverate	drawl	intimate	proclaim	state
aver	enunciate	lisp	query	threaten
comment	expatiate	observe	question	utter
coo	expostulate	opine	recite	vociferate
declare	grate	perorate	reiterate	whisper

As you can see, none of these verbs are interchangeable, but some are nearly so. Remember that a useful vocabulary is one that for every common word has a good stock of synonyms, while preserving the difference between them.

EXERCISE 6. Using Synonyms to Complete Sentences. Number your paper 1–10. For each of the following sentences, choose from the list the most appropriate synonym for the word *say*. Use a different synonym for every sentence, and change the tense of the verb to suit the context. Write the word next to the proper number on your paper.

1. Asked for the fifth time, Ted —— angrily that he had no more.
2. Endlessly, Mrs. Bronson —— the rule until the class knew it by heart.
3. Reminded of his oath, the witness —— that he had heard nothing.
4. Quick-witted Marie —— instantly to the taunt by her brother.
5. The subject was complex and difficult; accordingly, Mr. Ives —— on it slowly and methodically.
6. Told that promptly on February 2 the woodchuck comes out of its burrow to calculate the length of its shadow, Ms. Ranby, our biology teacher, removed her glasses and —— that there was more fancy than fact in that story.
7. Lucy was not bold enough to state her suspicions openly; she merely —— that our dog was guilty.
8. The President —— that henceforward the day would be dedicated to the memory of the war dead.
9. The civil authorities —— that the rioting stop.
10. Unwilling at first to announce her candidacy, Ms. Dixon —— that at a later date she would announce her intentions.

EXERCISE 7. Selecting the Synonyms of Words. Write the letter for the synonym nearest in meaning to the words in the list at the left.

1. *abut*	a. ram	b. adjoin	c. hint
2. *allay*	a. soothe	b. befriend	c. juggle
3. *anneal*	a. toughen	b. cancel	c. recover
4. *cajole*	a. heal	b. calculate	c. coax
5. *decimate*	a. operate	b. destroy	c. decide
6. *encumber*	a. burden	b. consume	c. undermine
7. *enervate*	a. soar	b. strengthen	c. weaken
8. *espouse*	a. marry	b. comb	c. respond
9. *fabricate*	a. butcher	b. make	c. descend
10. *furbish*	a. darken	b. sign	c. brighten
11. *gird*	a. plow	b. release	c. encircle
12. *imbibe*	a. bribe	b. sponsor	c. drink
13. *mollify*	a. reduce	b. soothe	c. repair

14. *ossify*   a. harden   b. classify   c. restore
15. *preclude*   a. prevent   b. pray   c. foreclose
16. *prevaricate* a. anticipate b. sicken   c. lie
17. *recant*   a. argue   b. disavow   c. republish
18. *ruminate*   a. meditate   b. enlarge   c. belittle
19. *simulate*   a. enliven   b. imitate   c. discourage
20. *vacillate*   a. anoint   b. inject   c. waver

PREFIXES AND ROOTS

Many words now part of the English language have been "borrowed" from another language. Word borrowing takes place when a foreign word comes to be used so often by speakers of another language that it becomes a part of their native language.

Many words now part of the English language have been borrowed from Latin. Latin has contributed more words to the English vocabulary than any other foreign language. Greek has also contributed a number. The different elements making up words borrowed from Latin are often quite clear at once to students of Latin, but students who have not studied Latin can, with a little study, learn some of these important word elements, for the same Latin word elements occur again and again in a multitude of English words. Once learned, they provide a key to the meaning of many unfamiliar words.

Short elements that come before the main part of a word are called *prefixes; trans–* and *circum–* are common prefixes. The main part of the word is called the *root; –port–* and *–fer–* are roots. The part which is added at the end of the main part of the word is the *suffix; –ion* and *–ence* are suffixes. *Transportation* and *circumference* are words formed from these elements.

31e. Learn some of the common Latin and Greek prefixes.

EXERCISE 8. Understanding Prefixes and Roots. Using your dictionary, give the meaning of the prefix printed in boldfaced type. Then, give the meaning of the root that follows and show how the combination gives the meaning of the word.

EXAMPLE   **ad**vent = *ad (to)* + *(come)* = *arrive*

1. **ab**erration   4. **circum**vent
2. **ad**here   5. **com**pile
3. **bi**annual

Latin Prefixes

Learn the meaning of the following prefixes:

LATIN PREFIX	MEANING	LATIN PREFIX	MEANING
contra–	against	in–	in, into, not
de–	from	inter–	between, among
dis–	away, from, not	intra–	within
ex–	out of	non–	not

EXERCISE 9. Understanding Latin Prefixes.   Show the word meanings as you did in Exercise 8.

1. **contra**band   3. **ex**cavate   5. **inter**pose
2. **dis**integrate   4. **in**carnate   6. **intra**mural

Now learn the meanings of these prefixes:

LATIN PREFIX	MEANING	LATIN PREFIX	MEANING
per–	through	retro–	back
post–	after	semi–	half
pre–	before	sub–	under
pro–	before	super–	above
re–	back, again	trans–	across

EXERCISE 10. Understanding Latin Prefixes.   Using the dictionary, write the meaning of each word in the following list. Be prepared to give the meaning of each prefix and to explain how it is related to the meaning of the word.

1. perennial   4. profane   7. semiannual   10. translucent
2. posthumous   5. revoke   8. subjugate
3. preempt   6. retroactive   9. superhuman

Greek Prefixes

The following Greek prefixes are found in many words in English as well as in other languages. Learn them for the exercise that follows.

GREEK PREFIX	MEANING
anti–	against
em–, en–	in
hemi–	half
hyper–	over, above

EXERCISE 11. Understanding Greek Prefixes. In a numbered list on your paper, write each prefix and, on the line below, each word. After each prefix, write its meaning. By referring to the dictionary, give a definition of each word.

1. antibiotic   3. embellish   5. hemisphere
2. hypercritical   4. encroach

EXERCISE 12. Understanding Greek Prefixes. By referring to the dictionary, define the following words by showing the relationship of the Greek prefix to the meaning.

1. hypo–   (under) + tension =
2. para–   (beside) + phrase =
3. peri–   (around) + meter =
4. pro–   (before) + logue =
5. syn–   (together) + thesis =

Changed Prefixes

English words sometimes use original forms of Latin and Greek prefixes, but those forms may have undergone change. The word *abbreviate,* despite its present form, does not illustrate an original *ab–* prefix but instead an original *ad–* prefix. The *d* of this prefix changed to *b* because it was much easier to say *abbreviate* than *adbreviate*. With the change in pronunciation came a change in spelling. The word now has two *b*'s in it. This kind of change is called *assimilation* and can be seen in many other prefixes besides *ad.*

ad
ad + cumulate = accumulate
ad + cord = accord
ad + peal = appeal
ad + tain = attain

dis
dis + fer = differ
dis + ficult = difficult
dis + gest = digest
dis + lute = dilute

sub
sub + ceed = succeed
sub + fix = suffix
sub + port = support
sub + pend = suspend

com
com + lect = collect
com + cord = concord
com + rupt = corrupt
com + exist = coexist

ex
ex + fect = effect
ex + fort = effort
ex + lect = elect
ex + rode = erode

in
in + legal = illegal
in + mortal = immortal
in + regular = irregular
in + reparable = irreparable

As you can see, assimilation often disguises the original prefix. Despite this change, you can easily analyze words into their original components with the aid of any dictionary. It is a great aid to vocabulary building to do so.

EXERCISE 13. Writing the Original Forms of Prefixes. Number your paper 1–10. Write opposite each number the following words in order. Then, in a second column, write the original form of the prefix. Use your dictionary to find this. In a third column, write the root or base part of the word; this will be the remaining part of it.

EXAMPLE 1. divert
        1. *divert   dis– vert*

1. access   3. annex   5. arraign   7. collide   9. corrode
2. allude   4. appose   6. collapse   8. confuse   10. efficient

EXERCISE 14. Writing the Original Forms of Prefixes. Follow the instructions for Exercise 13.

1. efface   3. elude   5. impart   7. suppose   9. symbol
2. egress   4. immerse   6. succumb   8. sustain   10. sympathy

EXERCISE 15. Identifying Words with the Original Forms of Prefixes. Number your paper 1–10. After each number, copy the words that use the italicized syllable as a *prefix*. Do not copy the other words. You may use a dictionary.

1. *ad–*   adamant, adder (snake), adjust, admire, advise
2. *bi–*   Biblical, bibliography, bilateral, bilingual, biplane
3. *com–*   coma, comedy, comet, commute, compose
4. *de–*   deacon, debtor, decimal, defect, decline
5. *dis–*   disappoint, discard, discover, disease, dislocate
6. *para–*   parachute, parade, paradise, paragraph, parasol
7. *per–*   perceive, percussion, perky, permeate, permit
8. *pre–*   preach, precious, precise, preface, pretzel
9. *re–*   rebound, recent, recite, reduce, regal
10. *sub–*   subconscious, subject, subjugate, submerge, subscribe

Latin and Greek Roots

It isn't hard to tell what beginning elements of words are prefixes. The *un–* of *unclear,* the *mis–* of *mistreat,* and the *re–* of *return* are obviously prefixes. It is somewhat more difficult, however, to identify a root.

Some roots are called *free forms*. Free forms can appear with prefixes (*untrue, distrust, misspell*), but they can also appear by themselves (*true, trust, spell*).

Bound forms, on the other hand, can appear only with prefixes or suffixes. They cannot exist alone. We can have, for example, *conclude, transgress,* and *receive,* but we cannot have *clude, gress,* and *ceive*.

Free or bound, however, roots are easy to learn; and, once learned, they allow us to understand the meanings of many different words.

31f. Learn some of the common Latin and Greek roots.

Learn the meaning of the following Latin roots in preparation for the exercise that follows.

LATIN ROOTS	MEANING	LATIN ROOTS	MEANING
–dic–, –dict–	say, speak	–spec–, –spic–	look, see
–fac–, –fact–	do, make	–tract–	draw, pull
–junct–	join	–vert–, –vers–	turn
–pon–, –pos–	place, put	–voc–	call
–scrib–, –script–	write	–volv–	roll, turn

EXERCISE 16. Writing the Meanings of Roots and Words. Copy the words in boldfaced type. Referring to the dictionary, underline the root of each word, write the meaning of each root, and give the meaning of the word as it is used in the paragraph.

The governor read the letter that the secretary handed her and began to dictate an answer in faultless **diction**. Her **facile** delivery was not marked by any hesitation for thought as she explained her **position**. "At this critical **juncture** in the affairs of our state," she said, "we place confidence in the integrity of our legislators. We do not all **subscribe** to the same party policies, but we rely on one another's **perspicuity** to see the issues clearly. These **distractions**, designed to **subvert** the public welfare, are bound to fail, and in the face of the public outrage which has been **provoked**, we will do the duty that **devolves** upon us."

EXERCISE 17. Understanding Greek Roots. Learn the following Greek roots and their meanings. While studying these words, refer to a dictionary to see how the meanings of the words in the third column are found in the meanings of their roots.

GREEK ROOT	GENERAL MEANING	WORD
1. –anthrop–	man	anthropology
2. –chron–	time	chronometer
3. –gen–	birth	genealogy
4. –geo–	earth	geology
5. –hetero–	different	heterogeneous

Study the meaning of these Greek roots.

GREEK ROOT	MEANING	GREEK ROOT	MEANING
–bio–	life	–log–	word, science
–homo–	same	–mon–, –mono–	one
–hydr–	water	–morph–	form

EXERCISE 18. Using Greek Roots to Define Words.
Using the Greek roots above, define the following words by dividing each word into its proper parts. Refer to a dictionary.

EXAMPLE 1. monogamy
      1. *mono (one) + gamy (marriage) = one marriage*

1. homogeneous
2. anthropomorphic
3. biology
4. monologue
5. metamorphosis

Now study the meanings of these Greek roots.

GREEK ROOT	MEANING	GREEK ROOT	MEANING
–neo–	new	–psych–	mind
–ortho–	straight	–scop–	seeing
–pan–	all	–tech–	skill
–phon–	sound	–tele–	far

EXERCISE 19. Writing the Meanings of Roots and Words.
Using the previous lists of Greek roots, copy the elements in boldfaced type, and write their meanings in relation to the following words. Then, by referring to the dictionary, write the meaning of the entire word.

EXAMPLE 1. live in a **demo**cracy
      1. *demo—people; democracy—rule of the people*

1. **anthrop**oid ape
2. **psych**osomatic ailment
3. a **hydr**aulic jack
4. an a**morph**ous substance

5. writing a **mono**graph
6. a **pan**demic disease
7. the science of eu**gen**ics
8. **phon**etic symbols
9. a famous **geo**physicist
10. The **ortho**pedist operated.

11. mental **tele**pathy
12. the **chron**ology of history
13. of wide **scope**
14. The words are **homo**nyms.
15. a **neo**phyte in a convent

EXERCISE 20. Selecting Vocabulary Words to Complete Sentences. Number your paper 1–10. Look up the following words in the dictionary, select the appropriate word for each blank in the sentences that follow, and write it after the proper number. Be prepared in class to identify and explain the prefixes and roots or bases.

anagram   epitome   lithograph   neolithic   philanthropist
epilogue   homophones   metabolism   orthodontist   protozoan

1. A concluding section added to a literary work is called an ——— .
2. The later Stone Age is referred to as the ——— age.
3. A dentist who specializes in straightening and adjusting teeth is called an ——— .
4. Two or more letters or groups of letters that have the same pronunciation are called ——— .
5. A microscopic, one-celled animal is called a ——— .
6. A word formed from another by transposing the letters is called an ——— .
7. A person who loves and does good for humanity is called a ——— .
8. A picture made from a stone or a plate is called a ——— .
9. The chemical process by which cells derive energy from food and get rid of wastes is called ——— .
10. A condensed account or summary is called an ——— .

EXERCISE 21. Selecting the Meanings of Vocabulary Words. Copy column A. Referring to your dictionary, write next to each word the letter of the best meaning from column B. Be prepared in class to identify prefixes and roots or bases in these words.

A	B
1. anarchy	a. the slaying of a king
2. anathema	b. a speech of praise
3. epitaph	c. a device for measuring
4. eulogy	d. a box for storing things
5. euthanasia	e. stopping and starting again

6. indictment   f. an implied comparison
7. intermittent   g. absence of a system of government
8. metaphor   h. a mass of stone
9. regicide   i. legal accusation by the grand jury
10. repository   j. painless death
    k. a person or a thing accursed
    l. a short statement on a tombstone

REVIEW EXERCISE. Using Prefixes and Roots to Define Words.

Divide each of the following words into prefixes and roots, and explain how these parts make up the meaning of the word.

EXAMPLE   1. predict
      1. *pre (before)* + *dict (say)* = *to say beforehand*

1. circumspect   11. transport
2. retrospect   12. interpose
3. repose   13. symbiosis
4. aspect   14. permeate
5. subordinate   15. induce
6. adjacent   16. recede
7. controversial   17. posthumous
8. conspicuous   18. parasite
9. bipartisan   19. homonym
10. diverge   20. periscope

WORD ETYMOLOGIES

31g. Learn the *etymologies*, or origins and histories, of words as an aid to remembering meaning.

Often, learning the etymology of a new word will help you remember it and use it well. The study of word etymologies may also provide some surprising information about words you have known for a long time.

Words with Interesting Etymologies

Many words have very interesting etymologies. Often our modern English words conceal within themselves references to romantic persons and places or to old, well-known stories. We all know the word *jersey* for instance, for a pullover upper garment, but few of us know that this word comes from the name of the island of Jersey in the channel between England and France. We all know the word *tantalize,* but few of us know that this word goes back to the Greek name *Tantalus.* Tantalus was a mythical figure who repeated the secrets told him by Zeus. He was punished by being placed in water that he could never drink because it always receded from him and by having above him branches laden with fruit that always eluded his hungry grasp. Your dictionary is likely to give you short summaries of these histories.

EXERCISE 22. Writing the Etymologies of Words. Each of the following words in italics is derived from the name of a mythological or actual person. Number your paper 1–10. Referring to your dictionary, give the etymology of the words in italics below.

EXAMPLE 1. The outraged citizens resolved to *boycott* the store of the quarrelsome merchant.
1. *boycott—refuse to do business with—from Captain Boycott, the first person so treated*

1. The *chauvinistic* politician made a warlike speech.
2. The winner said her *mentor* deserved more credit than she did.
3. The comedian kept us laughing by coming out with one *spoonerism* after another.
4. His *jovial* manner deserted him as he grew weary.
5. Rip Van Winkle's wife was a *termagant.*
6. The quiz contestant met her *nemesis.*
7. Only *herculean* strength could have accomplished the task that lay ahead.
8. It is sometimes difficult for a steady person to get along with one of *mercurial* disposition.
9. Faced by a *titanic* task, the man had the inclination to give up.
10. The quick thinking of the police officer prevented *panic.*

Recently Borrowed Words

English is filled with borrowed words. In fact, in the English language there are many more words borrowed from French, Latin, and Greek than there are from the original Anglo-Saxon or Old English phase of the language (the fifth to the eleventh centuries). Words given to illustrate Latin and Greek prefixes, bases, and roots in the preceding pages illustrate this. Many of these originally borrowed words are now so familiar to us that it comes as a surprise to think that they ever were foreign. But we have continued to borrow foreign words ever since early times, and we are still borrowing them. Sometimes we run across words borrowed rather recently, words that have been in the English language for so short a time that we still feel that they are foreign rather than English. These words may give us problems in determining their meanings (as well as their forms, spellings, and pronunciations).

EXERCISE 23. Writing the Meanings of Foreign Words or Phrases. Refer to the dictionary to find the meaning of each foreign word or phrase in column A. Copy column A. After each item write the name of the language it comes from; then write the letter of the matching item in column B.

A	B
1. nom de plume	a. a dabbler in the arts
2. junta	b. a stroke of good luck
3. dilettante	c. noninterfering
4. bonanza	d. pen name
5. laissez-faire	e. a secret council

EXERCISE 24. Writing Sentences Using Foreign Phrases. Consult your dictionary, write the meaning of the following words, and use them in a sentence.

EXAMPLE 1. à la carte
 1. *à la carte—with a stated price for each dish. Because he wanted a special combination of food, he ordered his meal à la carte.*

 1. à la mode   3. fait accompli

 2. entre nous   4. tour de force

EXERCISE 25. Writing Sentences Using Foreign Words or Phrases. Consult your dictionary, write the meaning of the following words, and use them in a sentence.

 1. bona fide   2. ex officio   3. gratis   4. ad hoc

EXERCISE 26. Selecting the Definitions for Foreign Words or Phrases. Look up each word in column A in your dictionary. Write after each number the letter of the item in Column B that expresses the meaning of the word.

	A		B
1.	alma mater	a.	sudden and decisive move
2.	con amore	b.	principal woman singer in opera
3.	blitzkrieg	c.	slip in manners
4.	denouement	d.	till we meet again
5.	hoi polloi	e.	one's school or college
6.	smörgåsbord	f.	outcome of a play or story
7.	coup d'état	g.	the masses
8.	prima donna	h.	variety of side dishes
9.	auf Wiedersehen	i.	with tenderness
10.	faux pas	j.	violent offensive in war

Word List

You will find that many of the words in the following list contain familiar prefixes and roots. Make it a regular practice to learn new words from the list. Add them to the list in your notebook, giving the pronunciation, meaning, and etymology as you find them in the dictionary. Ten words a week will be as many as you can handle efficiently. After learning the words, use them as often as you can in your writing and speaking.

abdicate	assert	casement
abound	astute	caustic
acquittal	atrocious	censure
admirably	autonomy	charisma
aesthetic	axiom	clangor
affidavit	balmy	clemency
affiliate	bayou	cliché
amiable	bedlam	clientele
amnesty	beguile	closure
analogy	besiege	coffer
annihilate	bestride	coincidental
anthropology	bias	colloquial
antiquity	botch	commence
apex	bourgeois	commendable
appease	breach	compassion
apprehensive	buffet	compatible
aptitude	callous	compliance
arbiter	canine	composure
archaic	cant	conceive
ascertain	carp	concession

condescend
condole
conducive
consolidate
constituent
contemptuous
convene
crony
curtail
debase

debut
decimate
decrepit
defunct
delectable
demure
destitute
deteriorate
detonate
devastation

diminutive
disperse
diversion
documentary
ecstatic
edifice
edify
effervescent
eject
electorate

elite
emancipate
emphatically
encompass
encumber
enjoin
ensue
episode
equilibrium
erratic

espionage
ethical
evade
evolve
excerpt
expedient
explicate
exultant
fabricate
facilitate

facsimile
farce
flagrant
fluctuate
fortitude
gloat
grimace
harass
heresy
hieroglyphic

hors d'oeuvre
immaculate
impartial
impediment
imperceptible
implacable
imposition
inaccessible
inadvertent
inalienable

inanimate
inarticulate
incendiary
incentive
inclement
inconsistent
indestructible
indict
indignant
indomitable

ineffectual
inertia
infallible
influx
inhibition
innate
innovation
insipid
insolence
intermittent

intuition
invariably
invincible
irksome
irrational
irrelevant
itinerary
jargon
jostle
judicious

juncture
lament
lapse
latitude
legacy
lexicon
livid
loathe
malignant
malleable

mandatory
mannerism
martial
meager
mediocre
melancholy
melodramatic
mentor
merge
meticulous

mettle
mien
militant
momentum
mortify
mosque
mull
mutable
mystic
naive

postulate
potency
precarious
prelude
pretext
prevalent
prolific
prophetic
protocol
protrude

sequel
simulate
sordid
sporadic
stamina
steppe
stimulant
stipulate
stratagem
stringent

negligible
notoriety
obligatory
obliterate
oblivious
odious
opportune
ornate
ossify
painstaking

proximity
purge
qualm
quantitative
quibble
rankle
ravage
reactionary
rebuke
recipient

submission
subsidiary
subsidize
substantially
succulent
succumb
synopsis
synthesis
tawny
theoretical

palatable
pallid
paradox
paraphrase
parody
pastoral
patent
paternal
patriarch
pauper

recourse
rectify
recur
redundant
rejuvenate
reminiscent
rendezvous
repress
reprieve
requiem

timorous
transcend
transition
transitory
translucent
ultimatum
unprecedented
vehement
verbatim
vigilant

perceive
perception
perseverance
personification
pertinent
pivotal
plausible
pompous
portly
posthumous

requisite
resonant
retainer
retribution
rift
rivulet
sadistic
sardonic
scenario
seethe

visage
vulnerable
wan
wane
wheedle
whimsical
wreak
zealous
zenith
zephyr

CHAPTER 32

Spelling

IMPROVING YOUR SPELLING

You must have heard the words "I never could spell" in the course of your high-school career, and you probably realize that this is just another excuse for poor spelling. Naturally-good spellers are rare people. If you belong to this group, you are indeed fortunate. If you do not and know you have difficulty, now is the time to do something about it. You can improve your spelling if you want to and if you are willing to make the effort. No one else can be of much help to you. *Learning to spell is your responsibility.*

GOOD SPELLING HABITS

There is no one way to learn to spell. What works for one person may not work for you, but careful observation and good visual memory will help, no matter what method you adopt. By using a combination of several methods, you can in time become a good speller. Some of the following ways have helped others to spell. Read them over; put them into practice.

1. *In your notebook, keep a list of the words you misspell.* Set aside a few pages in your notebook and jot down all the words you misspell in your written work for all subjects. At first, this job of entering word after word will seem wearisome and never-ending; the list itself, as it daily grows longer, may threaten to preempt your whole notebook and leave room for nothing else.

Nevertheless, you can take heart, for as the therapy takes effect, fewer and fewer words will need to be added to the list, and the day will come eventually when weeks will pass before another mistake forces you to check your notebook.

A three-column spelling sheet is best. In the first column, correctly spell the word you have missed and circle the troublesome part. In the second column, divide the word into syllables. This insures against misspelling the word by first mispronouncing it. In the third column, jot down any little counsel to yourself, warning, or trick of association that may help you to spell the word.

1. February	Feb-ru-ar-y	Pronounce correctly.
2. disapproval	dis-ap-prov-al	Study Rule 32c.
3. candidate	can-di-date	Word has three small words in it: *can, did, ate.*

2. *Get the dictionary habit.* Don't guess at the spelling of a word. There is no consistency in guessing. You may guess right today and wrong tomorrow and be no better off. Actually opening the dictionary, leafing through it, and searching down the page until you come upon your word fortifies your memory with its correct spelling and reduces the chances of misspelling it again. In addition, you can hardly fail to come across some of the cognate forms of the word you are looking for. By making the acquaintance of these "cousins" to the word in question, you deepen your knowledge of the word itself. It is much harder to misspell *denomination* after you know its kinship with such words as *nominate, nominal, denominator,* etc.

3. *Learn to spell words by syllables.* If you divide a word into small parts that can be pronounced by themselves, you divide a word into syllables. Even the hardest words look easy when they are broken down into syllables. For example, the word *pul'sate* has two syllables; the word *bul'le tin* has three syllables; the word *en vi'ron ment* has four syllables.

4. *Avoid mispronunciations that lead to spelling problems.* Careful pronunciation will help you to spell many words. The person who says *sup rise* for *surprise* will probably spell the word incorrectly, leaving out the first *r.* The person who says *mod ren* for *modern* will also probably misspell the word. You need to learn the correct pronunciation of a word in order to spell it right.

Study the pronunciation of the words in the following list. Notice how incorrect pronunciation leads to incorrect spelling.

e*s*cape	(*not* e*x*cape)
r*i*diculous	(*not* r*e*diculous)
en*t*rance	(*not* ent*e*rance)
temper*a*ment	(*not* tem*pe*rment)
equi*p*ment	(*not* equi*pt*ment)
a*th*letic	(*not* ath*a*letic)
main*te*nance	(*not* main*tai*nance)
re*c*ognize	(*not* re*c*onize)
heig*ht*	(*not* heigh*th*)
*per*spiration	(*not* *pre*spiration)

5. *Proofread your papers before handing them in. Proofreading* is the process of carefully rereading for inaccuracies whatever you have written. Proofreading is the best cure for carelessness in punctuation, capitalization, spelling, and grammar. It takes only a few minutes, yet it makes a great difference in the correctness of your work.

SPELLING RULES

Our English language owes its richness to the vast number of words it has borrowed from other languages. The cost of this richness, however, is wide variety in spelling. Words that sound alike are, all too often, not spelled alike. Nevertheless, there are strong family likenesses among many words, and the simple rules describing them are easy to learn. Learn these rules and you will be saved many trips to the dictionary.

ie and *ei*

32a. Write *ie* when the sound is long *e*, except after *c*.

EXAMPLES piece, belief, niece, deceive, receive, conceive

EXCEPTIONS either, seize, neither, weird, leisure

Write *ei* when the sound is not long *e*, especially when the sound is long *a*.

EXAMPLES neighbor, weigh, veil, freight, forfeit, height

EXCEPTIONS friend, mischief

EXERCISE 1. Spelling *ie* and *ei* Words.   Write the following words, supplying the missing letters (*e* and *i*) in the correct order. Be able to explain how the rule applies to each.

1. ach . . . ve	7. y . . . ld	13. conc . . . ve
2. rec . . . pt	8. gr . . . f	14. sl . . . gh
3. p . . . rce	9. c . . . ling	15. v . . . l
4. bes . . . ge	10. dec . . . t	16. th . . . r
5. rel . . . f	11. rec . . . ve	17. h . . . ght
6. w . . . ld	12. dec . . . ve	18. f . . . rce

–cede, –ceed, and –sede

32b. Only one English word ends in *–sede: supersede*. Only three words end in *–ceed: exceed, proceed,* and *succeed*. All other words of similar sound end in *–cede*.

EXAMPLES   recede, concede, precede

Adding Prefixes

A prefix is one or more than one letter or syllable added to the beginning of a word to change its meaning.

32c. When a prefix is added to a word, the spelling of the word itself remains the same.

il + legible = **il**legible	dis + advantage = **dis**advantage
in + sensitive = **in**sensitive	dis + similar = **dis**similar
im + partial = **im**partial	mis + lead = **mis**lead
un + usual = **un**usual	mis + spell = **mis**spell
un + necessary = **un**necessary	over + run = **over**run
re + capture = **re**capture	over + look = **over**look

Adding Suffixes

A suffix is one or more than one letter or syllable added to the end of a word to change its meaning.

32d. When the suffixes *–ness* and *–ly* are added to a word, the spelling of the word itself is not changed.

EXAMPLES   usual + ly = usually   mean + ness = meanness
EXCEPTIONS   Words ending in *y* change the *y* to *i* before *–ness* and *–ly: steady—*

steadily, sloppy—sloppiness. One-syllable adjectives ending in *y*, however, generally follow Rule 32d: *shy—shyness, dry—dryly.*

EXERCISE 2. Spelling Words with Prefixes and Suffixes. Spell correctly the words indicated.

1. *accidental* with the suffix *ly*
2. *heavy* with the suffix *ness*
3. *satisfied* with the prefix *dis*
4. *mean* with the suffix *ness*
5. *legal* with the prefix *il*
6. *spell* with the prefix *mis*
7. *understand* with the prefix *mis*
8. *sincere* with the suffix *ly*
9. *nerve* with the prefix *un*
10. *complete* with the suffix *ly*
11. *qualified* with the prefix *un*
12. *kind* with the suffix *ness*
13. *literate* with the prefix *il*
14. *ordinary* with the suffix *ly*
15. *ability* with the prefix *in*
16. *mature* with the prefix *im*
17. *consider* with the prefix *re*
18. *adequate* with the prefix *in*
19. *appoint* with the prefix *dis*
20. *sudden* with the suffix *ness*
21. *use* with the prefix *mis*
22. *stated* with the prefix *mis*
23. *noticed* with the prefix *un*
24. *special* with the suffix *ly*
25. *rate* with the prefix *over*

32e. Drop the final *e* before a suffix beginning with a vowel.

EXAMPLES   dine + ing = dining
           sense + ible = sensible
           use + able = usable

EXCEPTIONS   Keep the final *e* before a suffix beginning with *a* or *o* if necessary to retain the soft sound of *c* or *g* preceding the *e*.
               serviceable, advantageous, manageable
               dye + ing = dyeing [to prevent confusion with dying]

32f. Keep the final *e* before a suffix beginning with a consonant.

EXAMPLES   use + ful = useful
           advertise + ment = advertisement
           care + ful = careful

EXCEPTIONS   true + ly = truly
               argue + ment = argument

EXERCISE 3. Spelling Words with Suffixes. Correctly write the words formed as indicated.

1. guide + ance
2. scare + ing
3. courage + ous
4. approve + al

5. desire + able
6. separate + ing
7. nine + ty
8. taste + less
9. retire + ing
10. advance + ing
11. pronounce + able
12. compare + able

13. defense + less
14. hope + ful
15. whole + ly
16. true + ly
17. achieve + ment
18. use + ing
19. severe + ly
20. continue + ous

32g. With words ending in _y_ preceded by a consonant, change the _y_ to _i_ before any suffix not beginning with an _i_.

EXAMPLES   lively + ness = liveliness
bury + ing = burying
bury + al = burial

EXERCISE 4. Spelling Words with Suffixes.   Correctly write the words formed as indicated.

1. happy + est
2. friendly + est
3. merry + est
4. marry + ing
5. marry + ed
6. prophesy + ing
7. prophesy + ed
8. carry + er
9. beauty + ful
10. spy + ing

11. pity + ful
12. pity + ing
13. mercy + ful
14. satisfy + ed
15. try + ed
16. pretty + ness
17. busy + ly
18. busy + ing
19. gory + ness
20. glory + fied

32h. Double the final consonant before a suffix that begins with a vowel if both of the following conditions exist:

(1) The word has only one syllable or is accented on the last syllable.

(2) The word ends in a single consonant preceded by a single vowel.

EXAMPLES   win + ing = winning [one-syllable word]
omit + ed = omitted [accent on the last syllable]
begin + er = beginner [accent on the last syllable]
differ + ence = difference [accent on the first syllable]
droop + ed = drooped [single consonant ending preceded by a _double_ vowel]

EXERCISE 5. Spelling Words with Suffixes. Correctly write the words formed as indicated.

1. hit + er
2. propel +er
3. shovel + ing
4. beg + ing
5. refer + ed
6. refer + al

7. repel + ent
8. confer + ed
9. suffer + ance
10. deter + ent
11. develop + ed
12. pin + ing

13. hop + ing
14. shop + ed
15. remit + ance
16. deep + en
17. big + est
18. rebel + ion

The Plural of Nouns

32i. Observe the rules for spelling the plural of nouns.

(1) The regular way to form the plural of a noun is to add an *s*.

EXAMPLES dog, dogs   pencil, pencils

(2) The plural of some nouns is formed by adding *es*. Words ending in *s, x, z, sh,* and *ch* form the plural by adding *es*.

The *e* is necessary to make the plural form pronounceable.

EXAMPLES waltz, waltzes   trench, trenches
          bush, bushes   glass, glasses

(3) The plural of nouns ending in *y* following a consonant is formed by changing the *y* to *i* and adding *es*.

EXAMPLES city, cities   spy, spies
          enemy, enemies   penny, pennies

(4) The plural of nouns ending in *y* following a vowel is formed by adding an *s*.

EXAMPLES turkey, turkeys   essay, essays

(5) The plural of most nouns ending in *f* or *fe* is formed by adding *s*. The plural of some nouns ending in *f* or *fe* is formed by changing the *f* or *fe* to *v* and adding *es*.

EXAMPLES Add *s:*
          belief, beliefs   chief, chiefs
          roof, roofs   cliff, cliffs

Change *f* or *fe* to *v* and add *es:*

wife, wives   wolf, wolves
knife, knives   thief, thieves
leaf, leaves

(6) The plural of nouns ending in *o* preceded by a vowel is formed by adding *s*. The plural of most nouns ending in *o* preceded by a consonant is formed by adding *es*.

EXAMPLES *o* preceded by a vowel:
        patio, patios   radio, radios
      o preceded by a consonant:
        tomato, tomatoes   hero, heroes

EXCEPTIONS Words ending in *o* that refer to music form the plural by adding *s:*
        alto, altos   piano, pianos
        soprano, sopranos   solo, solos

(7) The plural of a few nouns is formed in irregular ways.

EXAMPLES child, children   woman, women   mouse, mice
         ox, oxen   tooth, teeth

(8) The plural of compound nouns consisting of a noun plus a modifier is formed by making the noun plural.

In the following examples, the phrases *in-chief* and *in-law,* and the words *on* and *up,* are all modifiers. The nouns modified by them are made plural.

EXAMPLES editor in chief, editors in chief
         son-in-law, sons-in-law
         looker-on, lookers-on
         runner-up, runners-up

(9) The plural of a few compound nouns is formed in irregular ways.

EXAMPLES drive-in, drive-ins
         lean-to, lean-tos
         two-year-old, two-year-olds

(10) Some nouns are the same in the singular and the plural.

EXAMPLES Chinese, Chinese   trout, trout   sheep, sheep
         deer, deer   salmon, salmon

(11) The plural of foreign words is sometimes formed as in the original language.

EXAMPLES   alumnus [man], alumni [men]
alumna [woman], alumnae [women]
vertebra, vertebrae
parenthesis, parentheses
datum, data
monsieur, messieurs

> ☞ NOTE The plural of other foreign words may be formed either as in the foreign language or in the regular way in English by adding *s* or *es*. Sometimes the English plural is preferred: For such words, consult the dictionary.

EXAMPLES   formula, formulae or formulas [preferred]
index, indices or indexes [preferred]
concerto, concerti or concertos [preferred]

(12) The plural of numbers, letters, signs, and words considered as words is formed by adding an apostrophe and *s*.

EXAMPLES In the equation are two *t*'s.
There are three *7*'s in my address.
Please don't use so many *and*'s.

EXERCISE 6. Spelling the Plural of Nouns. Write the plural form of each of the following nouns and the number of the rule that applies.

1. dish
2. girl
3. valley
4. oasis
5. calf
6. porch
7. sky
8. goose
9. coach
10. monkey
11. Japanese
12. ox
13. father-in-law
14. deer
15. solo
16. self
17. board of education
18. alumnus
19. loaf
20. hero

EXERCISE 7. Spelling the Plural of Nouns. Write the plural form of each of the following nouns and the number of the rule that applies.

1. alley
2. old-timer
3. justice of the peace
4. stitch

5. lieutenant governor
6. half
7. donkey
8. theory
9. handkerchief
10. bacillus
11. gallery
12. echo
13. radio
14. plateful
15. roof
16. burglary
17. mouthful
18. *b* (the letter)
19. man
20. gas

EXERCISE 8. Following Rules for Spelling Words Correctly. By referring to the rules you have learned, explain orally the spelling of each of the following words:

1. crises
2. deceive
3. writing (*e* dropped)
4. believe
5. sopranos
6. misstep
7. meanness
8. noticeable
9. relief
10. cities
11. dishonored
12. data
13. beautifully
14. weird
15. typing (*e* dropped)
16. overrun
17. overflows
18. neighbor
19. wives
20. dissimilar

WORDS FREQUENTLY CONFUSED

affect   [verb] *Affect* is usually a verb meaning *to influence.* Did that tearful movie *affect* you?

effect   [noun or verb] As a verb, *effect* means *to accomplish.* New glasses *effected* a remarkable change in his vision. As a noun, *effect* means the *result of some action.* What *effect* did the rain have on the garden?

all right   [This is the only acceptable spelling. The spelling *alright* is not acceptable.]

already   *previously* We have *already* painted the sets.

all ready   *all are ready* We were *all ready* to leave.

all together	*everyone in the same place* The teammates were *all together* in the gym.
altogether	*entirely* I am not *altogether* convinced.
brake	[noun or verb] *to slow yourself down* or the device you use to do so At the curve, Georgia *braked* the speeding car.
break	[noun or verb] *to fracture* or the fracture itself Don't *break* the speed limit.
capital	[Correct spelling for all uses except when the word means a *government building*.] What is the *capital* of Colorado? You need *capital* to start a business. Begin all sentences with *capital* letters. Do you believe in *capital* punishment?
capitol	*government building* [frequently capitalized] We could see the *capitol* from our hotel.
choose	[verb, present tense] Alicia and Katherine, *choose* partners now.
chose	[verb, past tense] When the signal was given, the girls *chose* two seniors.
coarse	*rough, crude* When he spilled the *coarse* salt, he used *coarse* language.
course	*path of action;* also used with *of* to mean *as was to be expected* *Of course,* you are always right. She skipped the first *course* at dinner. The *course* in speech helped my diction. A new golf *course* opened last week.
complement	[noun or verb] *to make whole or complete* or *that which makes whole or complete* The *complement*, or full crew, is six hundred people. The *complement* of 60° is 30°.
compliment	[noun or verb] *respect, affection,* or *esteem* Convey my *compliments* to the captain. I *complimented* her on her success.

consul	[noun] *a diplomat appointed by a government to reside in a foreign country and look after the interests of fellow citizens traveling or doing business there* The American *consul* in Rangoon arranged for my trip to the interior.
council, **councilor**	[noun] *a group meeting to discuss and take action on official matters; a member of such a group* The *councilors* on the Security *Council* voted for the Canadian resolution.
counsel, **counselor**	[noun or verb] *advice or to advise; an adviser* Sue's aunt *counseled* her to take judo lessons. Ask your guidance *counselor*.

des'ert	*a dry region* The car crossed the *desert* at night.
desert'	*to leave* The rats *deserted* the unlucky ship.
dessert	*the last part of a meal* For *dessert* we had custard.

EXERCISE 9. Completing Sentences with Words Frequently Confused. Number your paper 1–15. After the proper number, write the correct one of the words given in parentheses in the sentences that follow.

1. The illness had a strange (affect, effect) on Margie.
2. During lunch, the soccer team was (all together, altogether) at one huge table.
3. My small cousin knows the (capitol, capital) city of every state in our country.
4. The (coarse, course) material made her skin itch.
5. Of (course, coarse), you burned the (desert, dessert) again.
6. The British (council, consul) removed his pince-nez and (counciled, counseled) Marlowe to leave Stanleyville before the rains came.
7. It seemed as if we had walked miles before we reached the main door of the (capital, capitol).
8. Your answer isn't (all together, altogether) correct, but you're on the right track.

9. After all his worry, everything turned out (all right, alright).
10. The two fast guards on our basketball team are (complimented, complemented) perfectly by an exceedingly tall center.
11. A typing (coarse, course) is recommended for anyone planning to go to college.
12. We traveled for three days across the (desert, dessert).
13. The actors were (all ready, already) to audition for the play.
14. If you don't have your car's (brakes, breaks) inspected every year, you will be (braking, breaking) a state law.
15. Did you (choose, chose) a topic for your essay yet?

EXERCISE 10. Writing Sentences with Words Frequently Confused. Write sentences in which you use correctly each of the words just studied.

formally	*in a formal manner* For funerals, weddings, and christenings, one should dress *formally.*
formerly	*previously* The high ridges of the Blue Ridge Mountains were *formerly* the bed of an ancient sea.
hear	*use your ears* You will have to speak louder; I can't *hear* you.
here	*this place* You can't sit *here;* this section is only for juniors.
its	*possessive of it* The town hasn't raised *its* tax rate in three years.
it's	*it is* *It's* not time to get up.
lead	[present tense] *to go first* You *lead* because you know the way.
led	[past tense of *lead*] He *led* us five miles out of the way.
lead	[pronounced "led"] a *heavy metal;* also *graphite in a pencil* These books are as heavy as *lead.*

loose	*free, not close together* Put all the *loose* papers in the folder. His little brother has two *loose* teeth.
lose	[pronounced "looz"] *to suffer loss* Do not *lose* your tickets.

miner	[noun] *a collier* or *worker in a mine* *Miners'* canaries told them when the air grew bad in the deep shafts.
minor	*lesser* or *under legal age* In some states *minors* may not operate a vehicle after dark.

moral	*good; also a lesson of conduct* We admire a *moral* person. The *moral* of the story is to look before you leap.
morale	*mental condition, spirit* After three defeats, the team's *morale* was low.

passed	[verb, past tense of *pass*] We *passed* the papers to the front.
past	[noun or adjective or preposition] To understand the present, you must study the *past*. Adele read the minutes of the *past* meeting. The dog walked right *past* the cat and never noticed it.

EXERCISE 11. Completing Sentences with Words Frequently Confused.
Number your paper 1–15. After the proper number, write the correct one of the words given in parentheses in the sentences that follow.

1. Where did you (here, hear) that story?
2. You can (lead, led) a horse to water, but you can't make it drink.
3. If you (lose, loose) the directions, we'll never get there.
4. For the (passed, past) week she has done nothing but work on her term paper.
5. The general spoke to the troops to improve their (moral, morale).
6. While the heir was still a (minor, miner), the estate was held in trust.

7. Our horse (lead, led) all the others around the track.
8. In only a few minutes the guest speaker will be (hear, here).
9. If (it's, its) not too much trouble, would you mail this package for me?
10. After she went on a diet, her clothes were too (lose, loose).
11. (Formerly, Formally), California was part of New Spain.
12. After the house had been painted, (it's, its) appearance vastly improved.
13. In 1848, gold (minors, miners) flocked to California, hoping to strike it rich.
14. (Its, It's) not every day that her parents let her use the car.
15. After two years of struggling with French I, Barney finally (passed, past) the course.

EXERCISE 12. Writing Sentences with Words Frequently Confused. Write sentences in which you correctly use each of the words just studied.

personal	*individual* The manager gave the customer his *personal* attention.
personnel	*a group of people employed in the same place* The management added four new employees to the *personnel*.

principal	*head of a school;* also an adjective, *main* or *most important* The *principal* of our school is Mr. Grebinar. The *principal* export of Brazil is coffee.
principle	*a rule of conduct;* also *a main fact* or *law* Her *principles* are very high. On what *principle* did you base your argument?

quiet	*silent, still* To study properly, one should make sure there is complete *quiet*.
quite	*wholly* or *rather* or *very* Are you *quite* sure the studio is soundproof?

shone	[past tense of *shine*] The star *shone* in the sky.

shown   *revealed* or *demonstrated*
                The slides were *shown* after dinner.

---

stationary   *in a fixed position*
                One of the desks is movable; the other is *stationary*.

stationery   *writing paper*
                That purple and perfumed *stationery* is in bad taste.

---

than   [a conjunction, used for comparisons]
                She is smarter *than* I.

then   [an adverb or conjunction] *at that time* or *next*
                We swam for an hour; *then* we went home.
                They didn't know me *then*.

---

their   [possessive of *they*]
                Their new apartment has a view of the river.

there   *a place:* also an expletive
                I haven't been *there* in ages.
                There is too much pepper in my soup.

they're   *they are*
                They're singing off-key.

EXERCISE 13. Completing Sentences with Words Frequently Confused.
Number your paper 1–15. After the proper number, write the correct one of the words given in parentheses in the sentences that follow.

1. He doesn't understand any of the (principals, principles) of physics.
2. The sun (shone, shown) all day.
3. The rabbit suddenly stopped and remained (stationery, stationary) for a few minutes.
4. He acts much older (than, then) he really is.
5. She spoke in a (quite, quiet) voice, (quite, quiet) out of keeping with her usually raucous manner.
6. You ask too many (personnel, personal) questions.
7. A collection of his paintings was (shone, shown) to the public last week.
8. You should never bother the animals when (their, they're, there) eating.

9. In school we study the (principals, principles) on which our country was founded.
10. (Quite, Quiet) soon after the strange uproar, all became (quite, quiet) again.
11. The bookstore is having a big sale on (stationery, stationary).
12. We are going to (there, their, they're) house.
13. All the (personal, personnel) in the store received a bonus at Christmas.
14. If you see the (principle, principal) in the hall, tell him he is wanted in the main office.
15. I don't care what (their, they're, there) parents let them do; you still aren't going to come in so late at night.

EXERCISE 14. Writing Sentences Using Words Frequently Confused. Write sentences in which you correctly use each of the words just studied.

to	[preposition; also part of the infinitive form of the verb] You must return the books *to* the library. He began *to* whistle.
too	[adverb] *also, too much* Vito plays the trumpet, and Carrie plays it *too.* You are *too* young to drive.
two	*one plus one* I will graduate in *two* years.
waist	*the midsection* She wore a sash around her *waist.*
waste	[noun or verb] *to spend foolishly or a needless expense* *Waste* not; want not.
weather	*conditions outdoors* The *weather* has been perfect all week.
whether	[as in *whether or not*] They didn't know *whether* or not their parents would let them go canoeing.
who's	*who is, who has* *Who's* been using my socks? *Who's* there?
whose	[possessive of *who*] *Whose* book is that?

---

your   [possessive of *you*]
Your coat is in the closet.

you're   *you are*
You're never on time.

EXERCISE 15. Completing Sentences with Words Frequently Confused.   Number your paper 1–15. After the proper number, write the correct one of the words given in parentheses in the sentences that follow.

1. Around his (waste, waist) he wore a handmade leather belt.
2. (You're, Your) guidance counselor wants to see you today.
3. (Weather, Whether) or not you can take six subjects next term depends upon your grades this term.
4. Because there was (too, to, two) much traffic on the road, we didn't enjoy the ride.
5. (Whose, Who's) going to use her ticket now?
6. (Your, You're) going to have to work harder if you want to be a junior next year.
7. It really doesn't matter (whose, who's) fault it is.
8. You (to, two, too) can be a good speller if you really have the desire.
9. "(Whose, Who's) been leaving the lights on unnecessarily?" shouted Dad.
10. (Weather, Whether) or not it rains or snows, we will be there.
11. This is fine (whether, weather) for a softball game.
12. (Your, You're) sure that Miss Thompson wanted to see me?
13. I don't know (whose, who's) taller, Brad or you.
14. We never can have (two, too, to) many people working on the charity drive.
15. The list on the bulletin board will tell you (whose, who's) on the honor roll.

EXERCISE 16. Writing Sentences with Words Frequently Confused.   Write sentences in which you correctly use each of the words just studied.

REVIEW EXERCISE. Completing Sentences with Words Frequently Confused.   Number your paper 1–33. Select the correct one of the words in parentheses in each sentence, and write it after the proper number.

1. The dome of the (Capitol, Capital) could be seen from every part of the city.
2. If you want to win the election, you will have to plan your (coarse, course) of action now.
3. The paint has (all ready, already) begun to peel.
4. If you don't learn to (break, brake) gently, your passengers may hurt themselves.
5. If you think (its, it's) too warm, turn the heat down.
6. My (morale, moral) sank to a new low when I failed the Latin test.
7. Since I've got you (all together, altogether), I want to tell you some good news.
8. Do you remember (whether, weather) or not Mr. Allen gave us a homework assignment?
9. You must start proper nouns with a (capitol, capital) letter.
10. I had (already, all ready) finished ten problems in algebra when I realized we had to do only five.
11. Bonnie addressed us (formerly, formally): "Ladies and gentlemen of the sophomore class."
12. Whenever you (lead, led) the way, we always get lost.
13. (Their, There) hasn't been a drop of rain in months.
14. He keeps his (loose, lose) change in a cup in the china closet.
15. (Their, They're, There) are two *m*'s in *recommend*.
16. The spotlight (shone, shown) on the actress as she walked to the center of the stage.
17. Can't you write better (than, then) that, Pamela?
18. Where do you think (your, you're) going?
19. Because Chris is on a diet, he always skips (desert, dessert).
20. He has a (principal, principle) part in the play.
21. After two days at sea, he knew he wouldn't feel (alright, all right) until the boat docked.
22. The lion broke (loose, lose).
23. Slung about her (waste, waist) was a sweater.
24. (Whose, Who's) responsible for this mess?
25. If you haven't (all ready, already) bought your tickets, you should do so now.
26. Whenever (you're, your) in doubt about the spelling of a word, consult the dictionary.

27. Don't you (dessert, desert) me in my hour of need.
28. The navy was testing (it's, its) newest submarine.
29. Her coat was made from a very (course, coarse) tweed.
30. Crossing the (desert, dessert) at night, we avoided the hot rays of the sun.
31. The Town (Counsel, Council) ordered the contractor to repair the roads at once.
32. Every morning at 8:40, the (principle, principal) reads the announcements of the ·day.
33. She had a (personal, personnel) invitation from the mayor.

One Hundred Spelling Demons

ache	existence	said
again	February	says
always	forty	seems
among	friend	separate
answer	grammar	shoes
any	guess	similar
been	half	since
beginning	having	some
believe	hear	straight
blue	here	sugar
break	hoarse	sure
built	hour	tear
business	instead	their
busy	just	there
buy	knew	they
can't	know	though
choose	laid	through
color	loose	tired
coming	lose	tonight
cough	making	too
could	many	trouble
country	meant	truly
deer	minute	Tuesday
doctor	much	two
does	none	very
done	often	wear
don't	once	Wednesday
early	piece	week
easy	raise	where
enough	read	whether
every	ready	which

whole	would	writing
women	write	wrote
won't		

Three Hundred Spelling Words

absence	bankruptcy	cordially
absorption	basically	corps
abundant	beneficial	correspondence
acceptable	benefited	criticize
accidentally	bicycle	
accommodation	breathe	curiosity
accompaniment	brilliant	curriculum
accurate		definition
accustomed	calendar	delegate
achievement	category	denied
	changeable	develop
acquaintance	characteristic	difference
actuality	chemistry	disastrous
adequately	chief	disciple
administration	circumstance	dissatisfied
adolescent	civilization	
aggressive	cocoon	distinction
agriculture	commencement	distinguished
amateur		dividend
ambassador	commissioner	dominant
analysis	committed	dormitory
	comparative	earnest
analyze	comparison	easily
angel	competition	ecstasy
annual	conceivable	eighth
answered	confidential	eliminate
apparatus	confirmation	
appearance	conscientious	embroidery
appropriate	consciousness	endeavor
approximately		enemy
arousing	consequently	enormous
arrangement	considerable	equipment
	consistency	especially
ascend	continuous	essential
association	controlled	estimation
athlete	controversial	etiquette

exaggeration

examination
exceedingly
exceptional
excitable
executive
exercise
exhaustion
exhibition
expense
extension

extraordinary
fallacy
fantasies
favorably
fiery
financial
foreigner
forfeit
fragile
fulfill

fundamentally
gasoline
grammatically
grateful
guidance
gymnasium
handkerchief
happiness
heroic
hindrance

humorist
hygiene
hypocrisy
illustrate
imitation
immense
inability

incidentally
indispensable
influential

innocence
inquiry
institute
intellect
interference
interpretation
interruption
interval
irrelevant
irresistible

island
jealousy
journal
laborious
liability
lightning
likelihood
liveliest
locally
luxury

magnificence
maintenance
maneuver
mansion
martyr
maturity
medical
merchandise
merit
miniature

mischievous
missile
misspelled
monotony
mortgage

municipal
narrative
naturally
neighbor
noticeable

nuisance
obstacle
occasionally
occupy
odor
offensive
omitted
opinion
opposition
optimism

ordinary
organization
ornament
pageant
pamphlet
parachute
parallel
pastime
peaceable
peasant

peril
permanent
persistent
perspiration
pertain
phase
picnic
pigeon
playwright
pleasant

poison
politician
positively

possibility
practically
practice
precede
precisely
predominant
preferred

prejudice
preliminary
preparation
primitive
priority
prisoner
procedure
proceedings
procession
prominent

proposition
prosperous
prove
psychology
publicity
purposes
qualities
quantities
questionnaire
readily

reference
referring

regard
register
rehearsal
religious
remembrance
representative
requirement
resistance

resolution
responsibility
restaurant
ridiculous
satisfactorily
security
senator
sensibility
sheer
sheriff

significance
simile
situated
solution
sophomore
souvenir
specific
specimen
spiritual
strenuous

stretch

studying
substantial
subtle
succession
summarize
superintendent
suppress
surgeon
suspense

syllable
symbol
symphony
technique
temperature
tendency
tournament
traffic
twelfth
tying

tyranny
unanimous
undoubtedly
unforgettable
unpleasant
unusually
vacancies
varies
vengeance
villain

CHAPTER 33

Studying and Test Taking

SKILLS AND STRATEGIES

Do you sometimes feel that you spend a lot of time doing homework but don't seem to get very much done? The time you take to develop good study habits will quickly be paid back.

A STUDY ROUTINE

33a. Establish an effective study routine.

Many students waste time and effort as they clear a place for their books, hunt for the scrap of paper the assignment was scribbled on, and then blend the material they are studying into the top twenty hits blaring behind them. Others end up scrambling through a long-term project at the last minute or nodding over homework that they started too late in the evening.

Follow these rules to cut down on your homework time and make the time you do spend much more effective.

All studying has two basic purposes. You study to acquire information. You study to assimilate and apply this information in some way. This chapter explains and illustrates skills and strategies that are effective means of achieving both of these purposes.

1. *Establish a time and a place to do your homework.* Homework is part of your job as a student. You'll find you can do the job better if you have a place in your room or somewhere relatively quiet that you associate with work.

You may be reluctant to admit it, but "relatively quiet" means that you should not have your radio on. The fact is that the mind cannot process two ideas simultaneously. If you pay any attention at all to the radio—if you are aware of the lyrics or the disc jockey's remarks— you lose your focus on the material you are studying. Inevitably, you spend more time getting through the material. Particularly when the material is difficult, complete concentration is essential.

It is also important to schedule a time each day for doing your assignments. While it is reasonable to take a break right after a day of classes, do not wait until you are so tired that you cannot concentrate. In addition, make sure you plan a realistic amount of time for the amount of work you have to do.

2. *Know your assignment.* Use an assignment book or a special page in each notebook to record your assignments precisely. Instead of a general note like "English—do reading, questions," record pages, question numbers, and any special instructions. There is nothing more frustrating than discovering that you spent your time doing the wrong thing.

It is also a good idea to set up some system for signaling long-term projects that are assigned days or weeks before they are due. Work out some kind of realistic schedule for working on this kind of assignment so you don't end up cramming everything in at the last minute.

Finally, make sure you follow directions *as they are given.* Know whether you are supposed to write single words or full sentences, to label a diagram or to give definitions, to prepare questions for class discussion or to write out the answers to be turned in. Remember that it is your job to *ask* if you are not sure what your teacher means or expects in an assignment.

3. *Review the assignment as a whole before beginning intensive work.* It is much easier to do a task when you know from the outset what is expected. When you are assigned a selection to read, begin by glancing through it to get a general sense of how the material is organized. If you are reading a textbook, take advantage of the headings. Glance at the study questions as well; since they are meant to test how well you understand the material, the questions usually give some indication of what the main points are.

4. *Do study questions as a unit.* When you are actually doing the study questions, read them through as a whole before writing any answers. Very often the answer to one question serves as the basis for others that follow. Reviewing the questions will give you some sense of how much detail any particular answer should include. You are also more likely to follow the directions accurately if you read through them more than once.

Finally, when you have finished writing out an assignment, look over your answers. Be able to point to a specific place in the text that justifies each answer you wrote down.

The SQ3R Method

33b. Use the SQ3R Study Method.

An educational psychologist, Francis Robinson, developed a method of study called *SQ3R*. The name may sound a little strange, somewhat like a scientific formula, but the procedure is not at all mysterious. It has been found to be useful in many studying situations. The SQ3R Study Method is made up of the following five simple parts:

1. *S—Survey* the entire study assignment whether it is a chapter, a section, or a complete book. Look at the headings, the material in boldface and italics, the charts, outlines, and summaries. Get a general sense of the scope of the material.

2. *Q—*Make a list of *questions* to be answered after completing your reading. Sometimes the writer will have included questions; sometimes your teacher will provide them. At other times you will have to develop your own questions. The survey you completed in step one will help you to do this.

3. *R—Read* the material section by section; think of answers to your questions as you read.

4. *R—Recite* in your own words answers to each question in your list.

5. *R—Review* the material by rereading quickly, looking over the questions, recalling the answers. Bring all of the parts together.

EXERCISE 1. Applying the SQ3R Study Method to a Homework Assignment. Select an assignment in any one of your subjects. It might be a literature assignment in English or an assignment in another subject area. Follow the five steps of the SQ3R Study Method to complete the assignment.

Reading Rate

33c. Adjust your reading rate.

You probably realize that you cannot zip through your science book at the same rate that you use to read the sports page or even a short story. Learn to recognize when you should switch to each of the major reading rates.

1. *Scan* material by glancing through it very quickly to find a particular point or reference. You scan to check answers to study material or to find a name, date, or detail that you need to refer to.

2. *Skim* by looking quickly through the material, noting headnotes, italicized and boldfaced words, and other clues that help give you a general sense of what the selection is about. This is a good rate to use when reviewing just before a test. But it is also the kind of reading you do when you flip through a book or magazine you are thinking about buying or reading more thoroughly.

3. Most reading is done at a *rapid* to *average* rate. The actual speed depends on conditions such as the difficulty of the material, the interest you have in learning details, or the number of distractions there are around.

4. Expect to read carefully at a *thoughtful* rate when you are dealing with technical material, when you are reading a selection that uses a demanding vocabulary and long, complex sentences, or when you need to remember the material in detail. You should be aware of both thinking and reading when studying this kind of material. Make it a practice to stop regularly and mentally paraphrase what you have read.

Good readers not only know the different reading rates but also know how to switch from one to another in the course of reading a single selection. For example, you have just learned that it is a good idea to skim through an assigned reading before reading it more thoroughly. Similarly, it is likely that sections in a difficult work can be read at an average rate while other parts will demand very thoughtful attention.

EXERCISE 2. Analyzing Reading Rates. Use the suggestions about good study routines as you complete the following exercise.

1. Read rapidly through all the questions in this exercise before writing any answers.
2. You need to know the name of the small town a short story was set in. What reading rate do you use find it?
3. Find your thoughtful reading rate. Pick two passages you consider difficult, and pick two you find easy; record how long it takes you to read each.
4. For an extra credit project you plan to read a Harlequin romance and compare it to the nineteenth-century novel *Jane Eyre*. What rate are you likely to use for each novel?
5. Skim through the previous five pages. Copy down all the sentences that begin with "For example."
6. List two situations in which you have skimmed material recently.
7. Record the author, title, and publisher of six books, and indicate the rate which you would expect to use for each.
8. You have to find and read an article from a professional journal or advanced history textbook on economic conditions in Victorian England. What rate or rates are you likely to use for the assignment?
9. List and define the major reading rates, and give an example of when each is likely to be used.
10. Do only the even-numbered questions in this exercise, beginning with question 2. After you have completed the questions, look back over your paper to see how well you followed the directions.

Visual Aids

33d. Take advantage of visual aids.

Don't skip over the charts, graphs, maps, and diagrams in material you study. They have been carefully designed and selected to provide information that you are responsible for knowing, and they make the material clearer than a written explanation alone could. It is essential to read the information on the labels and captions of visual aids to understand exactly what is being shown.

STUDY SKILLS

In studying it is necessary to learn facts such as names, dates, places, and definitions—all categories of specific knowledge. It is just as necessary to know and remember the patterns of organization, the classification systems, and the criteria that make it possible to organize and relate these various facts.

Patterns of Organization

33e. Recognize the major patterns of organization and the kinds of information each is likely to present.

You can find random lists of facts in trivia games, but most of the time you are presented with and expected to know information that is related in some way. As you read and study, look for these four major patterns of organization; learn the kinds of information each is likely to include.

1. *Organization in terms of cause and effect.* Information that is organized to answer *How?* or *Why?* questions is usually presented in terms of cause and effect. For example, in science you read about or actually perform experiments to learn what the consequences of certain controlled actions are. English classes study the motives of characters or the events of the plot that lead to the outcome of a play or a story. So, too, you may be asked to read about the cultural influences that explain a certain sociological effect.

When you see that a selection you are reading or studying is organized in terms of cause and effect, be sure that you can identify which factors are causes and which are effects. You should know, too, that the cause must occur before the effect.

2. *Organization in terms of chronology, sequence, or placement.* Events that take place one after another or next to each other do not have to be related in terms of cause and effect. In fact, information is regularly presented in this way simply to indicate the order in which events occurred or items were placed.

When you see that the information is being presented in terms of a *When?* or a *Where?* question, be sure that you get the details in the proper sequence or placement. For example, if you are learning about the development of the American colonies, you should know that Jamestown was settled before Philadelphia. So, too, you should learn the correct order of steps in a process and be able to tell what happened when as you recount a movie or a story. When location is important, expect to have to learn how to trace a route on a map or how to identify where parts or features should be located in relation to one another.

3. *Organization in terms of description.* Many selections are organized to answer simple *What?* questions. Such selections could include such things as a description of a painting, the number or titles of the works of a certain artist, the properties of a given compound, or the requirements to run for public office.

When studying a description that answers a *What?* question, be able to tell the difference between the most important points being made about the subject and less important supporting details.

4. *Organization in terms of comparison and contrast.* Sometimes the best way to explain a certain point is to show that it is similar to or different from something else. Very often information will be presented in these terms.

Thus a geography lesson may contrast the characteristics of a coastal and an interior desert, and a chemistry lesson might compare the properties of two different hydrocarbon chains. In literature classes, you might study the similarities and differences between several characters or, for that matter, between several poems or authors. Sometimes the comparison is implied between a specific item and a general definition. For example, an article could be organized by defining "real music" and then analyzing how well hard rock meets this definition.

Whenever information is organized as a comparison that discusses "to what extent" or "in what way," look for the two parts or factors that are involved and the specific ways in which they are said to be similar or different.

Although these four patterns of organization can be distinguished, they are very often mixed. For example, a cause-and-effect discussion will be organized to some extent in terms of sequence. A description of an author's style might involve comparison or discuss how the style developed over time. A comparison may be made between events that were separated by a time period or that are related as cause and effect. Learn to look for the main way in which the selection is organized.

EXERCISE 3. Identifying Patterns of Organization. Write the main pattern of organization (cause and effect, sequence or placement, comparison/contrast, description) that you would expect to find in each of the following reading selections. Then tell something about the kind of information the selection would include.

EXAMPLE   1 How to tell an elm from an oak
            1. *Comparison/contrast; would identify main ways an elm is similar to or different from an oak tree*

1. A short biography of Martin Luther King, Jr.
2. The major characteristics of Hemingway's style
3. Why drinking and driving don't mix
4. What to do in a medical emergency
5. How a computer works
6. Nogales, Arizona—Nogales, Mexico: the two different worlds of a border town
7. Why America got out of Vietnam
8. The motives of Lady Macbeth
9. Steps in writing a research paper
10. Major tourist attractions in California

Classification Systems

33f. Identify the classification systems of the subjects you are studying.

In each subject area, experts have agreed on a specific system for classifying things in terms of characteristics that are shared. This kind of grouping is a necessary basis for describing, comparing, and relating material.

Some of these systems are part of your daily life. For example, American cash is classified as penny, nickel, dime, quarter, half dollar, and dollar; communities are identified as rural, village, town, county, suburb, city, state, etc. So, too, you should know the basic units of measure and the main parts of speech.

When you study a subject, you are responsible for learning the classification system or systems involved in that area. Learn the *category,* that is, the name of the grouping, and learn what kind of shared characteristic the name indicates. Remember that very often a category can be *subclassified,* that is, divided into smaller categories. Here are some of the major classification systems.

1. *Literary genre.* You should be able to recognize the differences between major types of writing, such as poetry, prose, drama, fiction, and nonfiction. In addition, you will often be required to identify subcategories within each form. For example, poetry can be classified as lyrics, ballads, narrative poems, or sonnets; nonfiction might be divided into expository essays, light essays, persuasive essays, etc.

2. *Scientific classification systems.* One classification system is based on the structure of units that are building blocks for the next higher category: subatomic particle, atom, compound, molecule, cell, system, organism, etc. Another gives a specific order for classifying organisms into kingdom, order, genus, species, etc.; that classification can be used further to classify living things in terms of their complexity of life form: animal, plant, invertebrate, vertebrate, mammal, etc.

3. *Social science classification systems.* Among the common systems are those that identify political organizational units: republic, monarchy, dictatorship, territory, colony, protectorate, etc. At the same time, rulers are also classified: for example, a republic may be headed by a president, prime minister, or premier; a monarchy by a king, czar, emperor, etc. Several related systems are based on geographical units, such as continent, island, ocean, sea, mountain, volcano, archipelago, strait, and peninsula.

These are just a few examples, but notice that there are many ways of classifying things—by size, by function, by structure, or by content. You will find it easier to remember the system if you remember the principle by which items are classified.

EXERCISE 4. Classifying Items. After each of the following lists, write the general classification to which the specific categories in the list belong. Choose one set, and give subclassifications for each item.

1. bank, savings and loan, money market, stocks, bonds
2. science fiction, historical fiction, fantasy, romance, myth
3. Buddhists, Hindus, Christians, Jews, Moslems
4. leaves, stems, roots, branches, flowers
5. folk, rock, classical, dance, jazz

Criteria for Evaluation

33g. Know the criteria applied in each field that you are studying.

Another aspect of learning information involves becoming aware of the standards according to which evaluations are made in a particular field.

You need to know these criteria both to be able to improve your own performance and to be able to make evaluations. Athletes, for example, often learn the standards for judging a skill at the same time that they learn how to perform the skill. When you are asked to revise a theme you have written, the teacher may expect you to recognize the ways in which you failed to meet criteria relating to grammar, usage, spelling, or clear expression of thought. To take another case, you cannot analyze a poem if you don't realize that you should look for things like how well the poet handles rhyme and meter or how concrete and vivid the images are. If you have ever taken part in a science fair, you probably were given a set of standards to keep in mind from the time you began designing your experiment.

Realize that knowing the standards or criteria for a field is not the same as being able to apply them. For example, most people watching a baseball game know that a pitched strike must cross the plate within a certain area, but many of them will be able neither to throw a strike nor to act as umpire.

EXERCISE 5. Researching Criteria. Write the answers to the following questions, or be prepared to discuss them in class.

1. Think of a sport you enjoy or of an item that you collect. List at least three criteria that are applied in judging performance in the sport or that are used to judge which particular items in your collection are more valuable than others.
2. Following your teacher's directions, find either rules for a contest of skill or directions for an assignment that include some of the criteria that will be used in deciding the winner or the grade. List those criteria.

Paraphrasing

33h. Demonstrate that you understand the material by paraphrasing it.

Memorizing is not the same as understanding. The best check as to whether or not you actually understand what you read is to see if you can *paraphrase* it, that is, express the idea in your own words.

When you are studying, make it part of your process to pause after each section and put each of the important terms or facts that you just read into your own words. If you can't seem to do anything but repeat the book word for word, go back and reread the passage until you can rephrase the meaning or can give an example that is not included in the text.

When you are reading very difficult material, you may need to paraphrase every two or three paragraphs. If you are reading a literature selection from another time period, you may need to check that you understand the vocabulary and style by paraphrasing sentences into simpler, more modern English.

At times you may decide or be asked to paraphrase in writing. Whether you are doing it orally or in writing, remember that the paraphrase should be very close to the original in terms of length and amount of detail.

A good paraphrase should meet these two criteria:

1. Although you should include important terminology (special vocabulary), try to use synonyms instead of the author's exact words. It is also a good idea to change the sentence structure somewhat.

2. Be sure that your paraphrase accurately reflects the *content* of the original. Do not confuse the content with your personal reactions or evaluations. Evaluation may accompany a paraphrase, but it is a separate step in critical thinking.

EXAMPLE   *Original:* Down through the centuries, surgery had been a desperate measure, always painful and often fatal. Only operations that could be completed in a few minutes, such as tooth extractions and limb amputations, were attempted. Patients were forcibly held down, or their senses were dulled with liquor or opium.

Paraphrase: In the past, surgery was only done when necessary. Since the patient often died and always felt pain, surgeons tended to do only quick jobs like pulling teeth or cutting off arms and legs. Patients had to be held still by force or were given drugs or liquor to make them less aware of what was happening.

EXERCISE 6. Demonstrating Understanding by Paraphrasing.
Follow the numbered directions.

1. Read through and then paraphrase the following two sentences from Jonathan Swift's "A Voyage to Lilliput."

My gentleness and good behavior had gained so far on the emperor and his court, and indeed upon the army and people in general, that I began to conceive hopes of getting my liberty in a short time.

The natives came by degrees to be less apprehensive of any danger from me.

2. Choose one paragraph that you have already read in this chapter, and paraphrase it.
3. Following your teacher's directions, copy two sentences defining an important term from another textbook. Then write a paraphrase.

Summarizing

33i. Show that you understand what is most important in a selection by summarizing it.

You have seen how to use paraphrasing to check your understanding of the content of a given sentence or paragraph. However, learning often calls for more than understanding the meaning of the individual sentences. You have to know the point of the selection as a whole. In other words, you must summarize what you learned.

You can do a mental summary as a review of the material you just read and studied. Sometimes the summary is written out as study notes or a précis. In either case, follow these steps:

1. Look quickly through the selection, including any headings and study questions, to get a general idea of how the material is focused. You will find it easier to follow what is being said if you can begin by identifying beforehand which of the four main patterns of organization is being used.

2. Read through the selection carefully, making sure you understand each part.

3. Without looking back at the text, try to identify the central idea, the main points that develop that idea, and the most important supporting details. If you have to look back at the book, go over the material again; then try the mental summary.

Sometimes you can pinpoint a topic sentence to paraphrase. However, in many selections the topic sentence is not stated directly but is implied. Critical thinking calls on your ability to distinguish what is most important about what is being said.

Again, keep in mind that a good summary focuses on what the *author* meant. You should understand that the most important point is not necessarily the one which you personally agree or disagree with most strongly or even the one you find most interesting.

Writing a Précis

33j. Be able to summarize an article or chapter in a précis.

When you are asked to summarize an article in writing or when you do so to reinforce your understanding of a selection, follow these procedures:

1. Go through the steps for summarizing under rule 33i.
2. Jot down notes about the main points of the selection. Paraphrase rather than quote. Avoid putting in too many supporting details.
3. Use your notes to write a first draft of your précis. Keep in mind that your finished summary should be about one third the length of the original.
4. Check your draft against the original. Be sure that you have included all the main points and have not put in examples, repetitions, or conversations.
5. Revise the précis, taking out all unnecessary words. Try to be as concise and as clear as possible.

As you gain practice, you will find yourself writing a précis more quickly and making fewer revisions. Remember that when you make changes, you are not correcting mistakes; you are applying the process of critical thinking and improving your understanding of exactly what the author meant to say.

Study the following example carefully. It includes the paragraph to be summarized, the summary notes, and the completed précis.

EXAMPLE   The earth is the mother of all people, and all people should have equal rights upon it. You might as well expect the rivers to run backward as that any man who was born a free man should be contented when penned up and denied liberty to go where he pleases. If you tie a horse to a stake do you expect he will go far? If you pen an Indian up on a small spot of earth and compel him to stay there, he will not be contented, nor will he grow and prosper. I have asked some of the great white chiefs where they get their authority to say to the Indian that he shall stay in one place, while he sees white men go where they please. They cannot tell me. (134 words)

CHIEF JOSEPH

Notes: Main points
1. All people have equal rights to the earth.
2. All are unhappy when they cannot move freely.
3. It's not right for Indians to be limited to one area while whites can be free.

Précis: The land belongs equally to all, and any restriction on one's right to move about freely is painful. Whites have no right to make Indians stay in one place while whites go where they like. (35 words)

EXERCISE 7. Writing a Précis.   Follow instructions to write a précis for each of the following items. In each case, list the number of words in your précis to show that you have kept it to one third of the original length. Ask your teacher if you should include the notes you took in preparing to write.

1. Write a précis of the forty-eight-word paragraph on page 854 that begins with "Down through the centuries, . . ." Your summary should not be more than sixteen words long. Be prepared to discuss the difference between the précis and the paraphrase.

2. Write a précis of the following paragraph taken from *Adventures in American Literature.*

America, toward the end of the nineteenth century, was an exciting country to live in. It was still growing, still prospering, the most powerful nation in the Western Hemisphere and about to become a major power among the nations of the world. By the 1890's the frontier was gone and with it the Old West, although the tradition of the frontier is still a powerful force in our society. The process of expansion changed from that of pushing into new territory to that of settling and developing those areas. While the United States was still predominantly an agricultural nation, industry was becoming a more and more important part of the country. New inventions—the telephone, the electric light, the Bessemer steel process—were changing the lives of Americans. The United States was still the land of opportunity to hundreds of thousands of immigrants, who had fled from poverty in their native lands. Men such as Andrew Carnegie and

John D. Rockefeller, who began with only a few dollars, built up great personal fortunes. Millions of Americans dreamed of matching their success. (187 words)

3. Write a précis of the following paragraphs, taken from *Adventures in American Literature*.

Among the forms of fiction the short story is perhaps the one to which American writers made the most significant contributions. Edgar Allan Poe, more than anyone, furthered the craft of the short story by insisting that the short story is a distinct form with special rules of composition: a short story must have "a certain unique or single *effect*. . . . In the whole composition there should be no word written, of which the tendency, direct or indirect, is not to the one preestablished design." Around the turn of the century, Henry James pursued his ideal of the "art of fiction" in creating many masterly short stories which were always unified, organic compositions, and which remain exemplars of the art.

As the United States approached the twentieth century, however, some writers felt that the short story was in danger of becoming an empty form. A fresh style seemed necessary to express the complexities and uncertainties of modern life. Sherwood Anderson, the most impressive of the early experimentalists, argued against "wrapping life up into neat little packages," and began to create stories with an "open form," in which plot development was less important than the expression of mood and character. The modern American short story can be said to begin with Anderson's "open form," which influenced several important later writers, including Ernest Hemingway and William Faulkner. (230 words)

4. Following your teacher's directions, choose two rules presented in this chapter; write a précis of the discussion of each rule.

Classifying Kinds of Statements

33k. Analyze and classify the different types of statements in a reading selection.

You have learned about the different patterns of organization. You also have seen how recognizing such patterns increases your ability to understand and think about the material. A good student is also able to analyze different kinds of statements or sections that will be included in reading and study assignments. Being able to recognize fact, opinion, assumptions, and nonliteral statements is an important skill.

Fact or Opinion

In order to understand and evaluate many statements, you need to recognize whether you are dealing with a statement of fact or a statement of opinion.

A statement of *fact* presents information that can be proved true or false. Be prepared to check whether or not a given fact is accurate; that is, whether it can be shown to be true either by direct experience or by support from a reliable source such as an encyclopedia or a textbook.

A statement of *opinion,* on the other hand, expresses what someone feels or believes. Although they cannot be established in the same way as facts, statements of opinion should be well supported; that is, they should be reasonable conclusions in view of established facts.

EXAMPLE *Statement of fact:* California is the third-largest state in the Union in terms of physical size. [This can be verified in an encyclopedia or an almanac.]

Statement of opinion: California's large, diverse population and many resources make it an important state to take into account when discussing the United States' economy and politics. [The opinion that California is an important state to consider is supported by the facts given: It has a large, diverse population and many resources. These facts can be verified by sources such as an encyclopedia, Census Bureau figures, or textbooks.]

Assumptions

Both statements of fact and statements of opinion can be based on hidden assumptions; that is, the speaker or writer takes for granted that the audience knows or agrees with something that is not expressed. For example, a description of a science project that states that "the agar culture was saturated with a glucose solution" assumes that the reader is familiar with such technical terms as *agar culture, saturated,* and *glucose solution.*

An editorial writer who declares that "Tom Jones, who openly admits he reads the newspaper comics daily, cannot expect to be considered a serious candidate for public office" makes a somewhat different kind of assumption. Here the implication is that everyone would agree that reading the comics in the newspapers daily is a sign of childishness or lack of seriousness or intelligence. The writer takes it for granted that it is not necessary to offer any evidence that there is a direct link between maturity or intelligence and reading the funnies. In evaluating this kind of statement, you must decide for yourself if you accept the reasoning or not.

It is important both to recognize when assumptions are being made and to respond to them properly. You may need to do some background work to understand material that assumes you already know about the subject area. When you encounter assumptions about what you feel or believe, analyze whether or not the unstated fact or opinion is valid.

Nonliteral Statements

Finally, it is important to recognize and understand nonliteral statements. The meaning of such statements depends on a *comparison,* a *figurative expression,* or an *allusion* that the reader is expected to understand.

For example, "The deadly poison of fear filled the small room" does not mean that fear is an actual gas or liquid that can kill but that it is *like* such a substance in the effect it had on the people in the room.

If someone says, "I saw red when I saw what Gonzo had done to my room," you are not supposed to think the speaker actually saw the color red; you should recognize the expression "seeing red" as a figurative way of saying someone was very angry.

So, too, when you call someone a "real Hercules," you are saying that the person is very strong. You expect others to know that Hercules is a mythological character known for his strength.

EXERCISE 8. Analyzing Statements.   As your teacher directs, complete the following items in writing or in group discussion.

A. For each item, first write whether the sentence is a statement of fact (*F*) or a statement of opinion (*O*). Then, for a statement of fact, list one place the fact could be checked; for a statement of opinion, write *yes* or *no* to indicate whether it is supported as presented.

1. The giant dinosaur, *Tyrannosaurus rex,* lived in the late cretaceous period.

2. Its huge size, strong jaws, and razor-sharp teeth made *Tyrannosaurus rex* one of the most fearsome creatures that ever prowled the earth.
3. Washington Irving's character Rip Van Winkle has great appeal for all people who feel that they can't keep up with changes.
4. Washington Irving published "The Legend of Sleepy Hollow" in 1819.
5. Unlike many writers, Washington Irving did not worry about being "original," because his best-known stories are based on legends and folk tales.

B. For each item, write whether the statement is based on an unstated assumption (*A*) or if it should be understood as a nonliteral statement (*NS*). Then identify each assumption and explain each comparison, figurative expression, or allusion.

1. The thousand days of John F. Kennedy's presidency have sometimes been described as a kind of American Camelot.
2. It would be easier to trap smoke in your hands than to get those kids to stay in one orderly group.
3. "Of course I did not ask him to sit with us," Lord Prowed said. "He doesn't even have a manservant."
4. According to the principles of quantum mechanics, the electron seems to have properties of both a wave and a particle.
5. The new mayor was horrified to discover how deeply the city's finances were in the red.

C. Look through textbooks, newspapers, or magazines to find one example of each of the following kinds of statements. Copy the statements, and label them as you did in parts A and B.

1. Statement of fact
2. Statement of opinion
3. A statement that assumes the reader has some expert knowledge in the subject or area
4. A statement that assumes the reader knows and accepts a belief or point of view
5. A nonliteral statement that uses a comparison

6. A nonliteral statement that depends on an allusion
7. A nonliteral statement that uses a figurative expression

TEST–TAKING SKILLS

When a test is announced, try to find out exactly what kind it will be so that you can study for it effectively. Preparing for an exam that tests how well you can recognize or express points of information is not quite the same as studying for a test that will call on your critical thinking skills to interpret, analyze, and evaluate material.

33l. Schedule your time and focus your attention when taking a test.

Knowing how to take a test can improve your grade. Learn and follow these strategies:

1. Always begin by skimming rapidly through the test as soon as you get it. Note the number and type of questions and how much each is worth. Get a sense of what sections seem manageable and which seem difficult. Then figure out how much time you should spend on each section of the test.

2. Work steadily and with concentration through the test. Read the instructions and each question carefully so that you do not lose points because of careless errors. But try to keep to your schedule. Even if all the answers you put down are correct, you will fail if the test is only half complete.

It may be easier to say than do, but don't distract yourself and weaken your performance by putting energy into worrying. Take a deep breath and concentrate on doing the best you can.

Objective Tests

33m. Identify and review specific information likely to be included in an objective test.

Multiple-choice, true-or-false, fill-in-the-blank, and short-answer tests characteristically test how well you remember and understand information you have learned. As a rule, each question will have only one right answer.

Given these characteristics, preparing for an objective test is fairly straightforward.

1. Look through your textbook, and study notes to identify the specific points on which you are likely to be tested. For the most part, do not worry about having to know every minor detail; master the important points. Many textbooks highlight key terms by putting them in boldface or italic or by including a glossary or list of important words in the chapter review materials. Some teachers will give guidelines about the material to be included.

2. Use the list of likely points of information to test yourself. Try to remember the information in different forms. For example, work from a list of terms to see if you can define each of them. Then ask someone to quiz you by reading a definition, a character from a story or play, or a historical event, and see if you can identify it.

Study and try to sketch and label any diagrams or maps that are likely to be included. Do practice problems for your math and science classes. You can redo ones you did for homework so that you can check the answers when you are done.

33n. Know the strategies that will help you take objective tests.

Do not spend too much time on any single question in an objective test. Since you are drawing on your memory, the first answer you think of is usually correct. If you are not at all sure of one item, come back to it later. In general, it is better to put down something—you cannot get any credit for an unanswered question.

Keep the following points in mind for each of the main types of objective tests.

1. *Multiple-choice questions.* As you look at the possible answers in a multiple-choice question, assume that one of the four will be quite obviously wrong and one will be less but still clearly wrong if you know the material. The two remaining choices may both seem possible, but one will be either too general, too specific, or related to another part of the subject. Only one will actually fit the question as it is asked.

EXAMPLE Which of the following is the largest of the fifty states that borders another state in the U.S.A.? a) California; b) Alaska; c) Texas; d) Minnesota [The answer is c; Alaska is the largest state, but it does not border another U.S. state.]

2. *True-or-False Questions.* Always pay careful attention to the wording of true-or-false questions. If any part of the statement is not true, mark the question false. Be especially alert when you see words like *all, never, only,* and *always* that suggest there are no exceptions to what is being said. Don't worry about wild improbabilities, but be sure that the statement can be generalized before marking it as true. However, don't assume either that statements that rule out exceptions are necessarily false.

EXAMPLES   1. There must always be someone who serves as Vice-President of the United States.
     1. *F*
     2. A sentence in standard English must always include a verb.
     2. *T*

3. *Fill-in-the-blank and short-answer identification questions.* Think of these two kinds of questions as the reverse of each other. For example, you might be given a definition and asked to fill in the word, or, alternatively, you might be given a word and told to define it.

In all cases, use the vocabulary, definitions, or facts that have been stressed in class or that are appropriate to the subject area as the basis of your answer. At the same time, be brief, but be as specific as possible. In some cases, the instructions may specify things you should take into account.

For example, if a biology test included *flower* among terms to be defined, the answer should be neither a vague "something that grows in the woods and in gardens" nor an elaborate discussion of various species. One or two sentences should indicate the special characteristics of a flower as one part of the structure of a plant.

EXAMPLES   1. Briefly identify one official who serves in each of the three main branches of the U.S. government. Include how the position is achieved, term of office, and function.
     1. *Legislative branch—senator, two elected from each state for six years to serve in U.S. Senate as a lawmaker; Executive Branch—Cabinet officer, appointed by President for an indefinite term to oversee one of the main executive branches and advise the President; Judicial Branch—Supreme Court Justice, appointed by President for life to rule on constitutionality of cases brought before the Supreme Court*
     2. The secretaries of State, Defense, and the Treasury are several members of the President's —— .
     2. *Cabinet*

EXERCISE 9. Applying Test-Taking Skills. Follow directions in writing answers to the questions.

1. Identify ten to twelve key terms or points that you might be tested on in an objective test on this chapter.
2. Using the terms and points you chose, prepare for a test on this chapter by writing sample questions. Include two of each of the following types:
   a. multiple-choice
   b. true-or-false
   c. fill-in-the-blank
   d. short-answer identification

Essay Tests

As you begin to take more advanced classes, you are likely to be asked to write longer, essay answers to questions about the material you are responsible for knowing. As a rule, you will be under pressure to use your critical thinking skills on a specific topic without consulting your notes and to plan, write, and revise your work in a specified time.

The very best preparation for this kind of test is to think of several possible questions and write out answers to them. Even if you do not come up with a question that is on the test, this kind of preparation will help you review and think about the material.

Every composition is different, so there can be no single correct answer to an essay question the way there can be to an objective test. However, keep in mind the following points about how to write an essay test.

33o. Be sure to answer the question that is asked.

The questions for an essay test are often more than one sentence long; they also are likely to include several directions. Therefore, before beginning to answer, *read the entire question carefully and thoughtfully*.

1. Look for key terms that indicate which of the four patterns of organization you are expected to use.

EXAMPLES *Cause-and-effect approach:* analyze, explain, criticize, defend, show why, give factors that led to, tell the effect of

Comparison-and-contrast approach: compare, contrast, show the differences, what do they have in common, find likenesses, in what way are they similar

Sequential or placement approach: list and discuss, trace, review, outline, give the steps, locate

Description approach: describe, identify, give examples of, tell the characteristics of

2. Note specific points that are to be included in your answer. It may be necessary to do more than one thing. For example, look at this essay question: "Show the difference between internal and external conflict. Include examples from at least three of the short stories studied in this unit." These directions specify three points that must be included for you to get full credit for your answer:

 a. Contrast internal and external conflict.
 b. Use examples.
 c. Draw the examples from three different stories.

33p. Think through and then answer essay questions.

Follow these steps in writing your answer.

1. Use the point value given for the question to estimate how detailed your answer should be and how much time you should spend on it.

2. Develop a thesis statement that will act as the basis for a very brief three- or four-point outline. Check that the outline includes points related to all the directions in the question.

3. Write out your answer using the thesis statement as an introduction. Be sure you make some reference to the test question. Allow one paragraph for each main supporting point. Be sure to include specific details, examples, and references. Teachers tend to see vague generalizations as a sign that you did not really master the material.

4. End with a conclusion that summarizes your essay.

5. Allow a few minutes to proofread your essay for missing words, unclear statements, and spelling and usage errors. If you do run out of time, try to jot down your outline so that the teacher will see that you have some grasp of the material.

 The following material is a sample of an essay test question and answer. Carefully study how the test question is developed into an answer.

TOTAL TEST TIME 40 minutes

Question 1. (60 points) allow 24 minutes

Discuss the question: Who is the great tragic hero of *Julius Caesar*—
  Brutus or Caesar?
Thesis: Brutus is the real tragic hero.

OUTLINE (1) Brutus in all five acts; Caesar dies in third.
    (2) Brutus, not Caesar, is lamented at the end—"The noblest Roman
      of them all."
    (3) Inner conflict occurs in Brutus, not in Caesar.

There is room for much honest debate as to
whether Caesar or Brutus is the real tragic hero
of Shakespeare's *Julius Caesar.* In my close reading of the play, however, I found three compelling
reasons for believing that Brutus is the protagonist.

*The first reason is that Brutus has a much
bigger role than Caesar.* Caesar dies in Act III;
Brutus is present in every act. It has been argued
that Caesar's ghost continues to make his presence and influence felt throughout the rest of the
play. Such an influence is not evident in the number of lines reserved for the ghost, who speaks
only three times, a total of sixteen words. Even a
master dramatist like Shakespeare cannot build a
successful final two acts with the hero offstage.
By the mere reason of his presence on the stage,
it is Brutus's play.

*The second reason is also concerned with this
matter of structure and presence.* When the play
ends, it is Brutus to whom Antony and Octavius
pay tribute. Antony's final speech is especially
significant here:

This was the noblest Roman of them all.
. . . Nature might stand up
And say to all the world, "This was a man."

*reference to the test
question*

statement of answer

first main point

supporting facts

second main point

specific example

The most compelling reason of all is found in Brutus's own nature. *It is he in whom the moral issue of the play is fought out.* He is the person — third main point — in the play who experiences the most intense inner conflict—and inner conflict in the tragic hero is — specific details — the essence of all great tragedy. There is little of this in Caesar; he is a man with few doubts and uncertainties, a character who undergoes no change. Brutus, on the contrary, is torn with doubt and pulled apart by the moral issue. The tragedy is the chronicle of his rise and fall.

By reason of what happens on the stage and — summary — *what takes place inside the characters, Brutus is the tragic hero of* Julius Caesar.

EXERCISE 10. Writing Answers to Essay Test Questions. Follow the numbered directions.

1. Estimate the amount of time you should plan to spend, the points that should be included, and a thesis statement for the following essay test questions:

   Question worth 25 points in a 40-minute test period. Writings are often classified as either fiction or nonfiction. Define one of these categories, giving examples from works you have read in the last six months.

2. Following your teacher's directions, compose your own essay question on a topic you are studying in one of your classes. Include its point value in a test intended to take 40 minutes. Schedule the appropriate amount of time to write a sample answer.

PART SEVEN

SPEAKING AND LISTENING

CHAPTER 34

Public Speaking

GIVING A TALK AND LISTENING

In high school you will often have to speak to groups of your fellow students. You will present your ideas in class, at club meetings, and at assemblies. If you can speak clearly, easily, and forcefully, you will gain a skill that can help you later in your career. In the first part of this chapter, you will learn how to handle some of the most common speech situations you will meet in school. You will also discover that there are many similarities between the steps in the writing process and the steps in preparing a speech. For this reason, you may find it helpful to refer to Chapter 13 as you work through the speaking section of this chapter.

The ability to speak before groups is a valuable asset, but an equally important talent is the ability to listen. By *listening* to what is said and not just *hearing* it, you can grasp the gist of a speaker's remarks without the need for repetition. You can also distinguish fact from opinion and good sense from nonsense. In the listening section of this chapter, you will learn how to listen carefully.

PREPARING A SPEECH

A good speech requires careful preparation. This section will guide you through the necessary steps in preparing and delivering a speech. Note that preparing a speech is in many ways like preparing a paragraph or composition. Be sure to refer to the detailed suggestions for selecting and limiting a subject and organizing content in Chapter 13.

34a. Choose an appropriate subject.

Sometimes your teacher will suggest your subject; other times you will have to select your own subject. In the latter case, you should be guided by two principles, each similar to a consideration affecting your choice of subjects for a paragraph or a composition.

1. *Choose a subject that you know well and that you find interesting.* Choose a subject about which you know a great deal. Doing so restricts your choice to your own background and encourages you to talk about things you have had experience with—your hobbies, special talents, jobs, and unusual experiences. It also ensures that you will speak with enthusiasm because the subject is close to you. If what you say engages your own interest powerfully, it will interest your audience as well. Enthusiasm is contagious. Choose your subject far in advance. Think about it daily—mulling over both what you will say and the way you will say it. The longer this sifting process goes on, the better the result.

2. *Choose a subject that is interesting to your audience.* When thinking about your subject, you should also think about your audience. Be sure to consider their needs, background, and interests when you choose a subject. For example, work-study programs can be interesting to students because students are concerned about combining work with study. If your audience is made up of adults, however, you might change your focus—emphasizing, for example, your school's need for support of work-study programs.

EXERCISE 1. Choosing a Subject for a Speech. List five subjects you feel able to speak about. Submit the list to your teacher for comments and suggestions. When it is returned, put it in your notebook for future use.

34b. Limit your subject so that it can be adequately treated in your speech and so that it reflects a definite purpose.

In the few minutes allotted to you, you may not be able to tell everything you know about your subject. You must therefore limit your subject so that you can cover it in the time allowed. For example:

BROAD SUBJECT   Modern aircraft

SUITABLE TOPIC   Vertical-takeoff aircraft

Refer to pages 317–19 of Chapter 13 for suggestions on limiting topics.

Another way in which you should limit your subject is by determining a definite purpose for your speech. A speaker should have a definite aim. If you have a purpose and keep it in mind, you can *calculate* the effect on your audience of the remarks or gestures you are thinking of using. You can then eliminate every feature that does not seem to advance your purpose.

Almost every subject can be developed for a specific purpose. The purpose may be to *inform,* to *entertain,* or to *persuade.*

Suppose, for example, that the subject of your talk is "Western movies." If your purpose is to *inform,* you may decide to discuss the first Westerns or the rise of the tradition from the dime novel.

If your purpose is to *entertain,* you might tell the class about famous Hollywood stars and how they began their careers in the movies.

And if your purpose is to *persuade,* you might urge the class to join in composing a letter to the moviemakers, accusing them of distorting the real traditions of the Old West.

As soon as you have determined your purpose, write it out in an explicit statement, or thesis.

TOPIC   Recycling bottles and cans

PURPOSE   To inform. I shall explain clearly what types of bottles and cans are best for recycling. I will give examples of successful neighborhood recycling projects.

EXERCISE 2. Developing Topics for Your Speech. Choose one subject from the list approved by your teacher in Exercise 1. Decide on a purpose for your talk; then limit the subject to three topics. Compose an explicit statement of purpose, and submit it to your teacher for suggestions and comments.

34c. Gather material for your speech.

Where will you find material for a speech? Start with yourself. Consider the vast number of facts and opinions you already have in your head. What do these ideas suggest for further exploration? The information gathering strategies used in the writing process will also be helpful here. For specific suggestions, see pages 319–28 of Chapter 13.

If you cannot find enough material for a speech from your own experience, go to outside sources such as your friends and acquaintances, newspaper and magazine articles, radio and television programs, and books.

As you find material for your speech, take notes on note cards.

EXERCISE 3. Gathering Material for Your Speech. Select a topic for a three-minute speech to your class. Make a list of the sources of information you intend to consult.

34d. Prepare an outline for your speech.

Avoid the temptation to write out and memorize your speech. Instead, outline the structure of your speech. If you wish, you may write out and memorize the opening and concluding sentences, but no more than that.

The outline of an anecdote is just a reminder of the sequence of events you intend to tell. An outline of an argument or explanation is more detailed. Head the outline with the topic; then write out the statement of purpose. After this comes the outline itself. Here is a typical outline for a persuasive talk.

Sample Outline

Topic: Water pollution must be stopped!
Purpose: To persuade listeners to protect our water supply

I. Current supply of fresh water
   A. Increasing demand—100 billion liters used every day
   B. Decreasing supply—as a result of water pollution
II. Causes of water pollution
   A. Garbage dumped by cities and towns
   B. Chemicals dumped by industries
   C. Detergents containing phosphates
   D. Oil spills
   E. Pesticides
III. What the average citizen can do
   A. Use laundry detergents without phosphates
   B. Conserve water whenever possible
   C. Write letters to state and federal legislators
   D. Watch for sources of water pollution; report offenders to environmental authorities

EXERCISE 4. Preparing an Outline for Your Speech. Using the topic and the sources you chose for Exercise 3, prepare an outline for your three-minute speech.

34e. Make sure that your talk has a good introduction and conclusion

In your introduction, try to arouse interest. Often you can do this with an arresting sentence or question.

EXAMPLE Pollution never seemed important to me until the day I took a canoe trip down Bushmill Creek.

For other specific suggestions about writing introductory paragraphs, see pages 455–58 in Chapter 16.

There are two disappointing ways for a talk to end: (1) to sputter to a stop like a motor out of gas and (2) to be checked in full course by the teacher's admonition, "Time's up." Do not allow your speech to end in this way. Conclude strongly by summing up what you have said or by leaving in the mind of your audience a dominant impression of your talk.

EXAMPLE Rusty cans, discarded tires, and other garbage may destroy our water in years to come. Let's join together and stop this pollution!

For other specific suggestions for concluding a speech, see pages 463–64 in Chapter 16.

EXERCISE 5. Writing an Introduction and a Conclusion for Your Speech. Write an attention-getting introduction and an emphatic conclusion for the topic you worked on in Exercise 4.

GIVING THE SPEECH

So far we have been discussing the *content* of a good speech. This section will discuss the *technique*.

Good public speakers know their audiences thoroughly. They understand the needs, background, and interests of their particular audience. They look at the audience as they talk. They have friendly manners, speak distinctly, and pitch their voices so that they are easily heard. Although they are slightly more formal when addressing large groups, they always speak as naturally as if they were conversing with friends.

If you view public speaking as conversation with a large group and take every opportunity you can to speak in public, you will notice yourself growing in self-confidence and skill.

34f. Conquer nervousness.

Do not reproach yourself if you are somewhat tense. Even veteran performers are tense before they go on. Tension is merely the body's signal that it is ready for whatever demands the next few minutes will make on it. Once you are "on stage," excess tension usually disappears.

Here are the five best antidotes for nervousness:

1. *Know your topic.* Know your topic so thoroughly that it tells itself.

2. *Know your audience.* Know the needs and interests of your particular audience.

3. *Keep your purpose in mind.* Think of what you want your listeners to believe, feel, or do. Concentrate on *why* you are speaking.

4. *Practice.* Practice imprints on your memory the sequence of your talk and makes it very hard to get "stuck."

5. *Relax.* Deep breathing helps. One well-known trick of professional orators is to sigh deeply before inhaling. By forcing all the air out of your lungs, you also relax your muscles.

34g. Develop a good speaking manner.

1. *Rehearse your presentation.* Using your outline as a guide, practice your speech aloud at home. Do not write out or memorize what you are going to say. Each rehearsal will be different, and when you finally deliver your speech, it will differ from all your rehearsals.

2. *Use descriptive language.* As you practice, search for images and accurate words and expressions that will make your talk more vivid. Look for words that have life and sparkle.

EXAMPLES   My little brother squirmed onto the chair and let his legs dangle.
She toppled track records like rows of dominoes.

3. *Enunciate clearly and accurately.* While practicing, be sure to speak distinctly. Slovenly speech is caused by laziness of the lips and

tongue. Be overprecise in practice, but when you speak before your classmates, concentrate on *what* you are saying rather than on *how* you are saying it. There will be some carryover from the practice to the presentation.

34h. Use nonverbal communication.

Your audience will certainly be watching you as you speak. How you stand, how you move about, and how you gesture can communicate nonverbal (unspoken) signals to them. Think of these unspoken signals as part of your speech.

Limit, or control, your movements for effective nonverbal communication.

1. *Watch your posture.* If you are standing, keep your weight evenly distributed on both feet. If you are sitting, place your feet squarely on the floor. Do not cross your legs. Careful posture helps you to avoid slouching, which is a distracting nonverbal signal.

2. *Establish eye contact with your listeners.* A speaker who looks at the floor or who stares at note cards easily loses an audience's attention. Good speakers move their glance around the room, focusing on the faces of listeners. This eye contact with the audience makes the talk more personal and easier to follow. It also enables you to notice how well your talk is being understood.

3. *Choose gestures with care.* Self-conscious speakers often gesture wildly, calling more attention to their hands and arms than to their words. Effective gestures are visual clues to meaning. Hands, for example, can indicate size, shape, or direction. As you rehearse your speech, think also of the gestures you will use.

EXERCISE 6. Delivering Your Speech. Deliver the three-minute speech you prepared in Exercises 4 and 5.

Here are some hints for practicing your speech before you deliver it.

1. Practice at home in front of a mirror.
2. Ask a friend or family member to listen to and critique your speech.
3. Record your speech on audio— or videotape; then critique your tape.

THREE SPEAKING SITUATIONS

Although all speeches have certain things in common, you can use different techniques depending on the kind of speech you are giving. The most common speeches you will be called upon to deliver will probably be the narrative talk, the explanatory talk, and the persuasive talk.

The Narrative Talk

In the narrative talk, you tell about a personal experience or relate an anecdote. It is not difficult to find a subject for such a talk if you keep in mind that it is the *manner* and not just the subject matter that makes such talks interesting. A quarrel with your brother or a funny experience on the bus can be just as fascinating as the description of a Caribbean cruise. Note that preparing to tell a story is similar to preparing to write a story. Be sure to refer to the detailed suggestions for planning and developing a story in Chapter 19.

34i. Make your narrative talk vivid.

1. *Begin with action.* After you have decided on your purpose, plunge right into your story without any preamble—to arouse the interest and curiosity of the audience.

EXAMPLE How many of you have been in a completely strange place and yet were unmistakably certain *that you had seen it all before—* perhaps in a dream? Eerie, isn't it? Well, it happened to me!

2. *Maintain suspense.* Lead your listeners up to the climax, giving them no inkling until the last moment of how the story will end. Then end it and take your seat. To linger after the end of the story, explaining away small, unimportant details, weakens the dramatic effect you are aiming at. See pages 547–48 in Chapter 19 for additional information on developing action and conflict.

EXERCISE 7. Relating an Unusual Personal Experience. Relate an unusual personal experience to the class. If you can, select an incident that illustrates a point. Arouse and maintain suspense. Use descriptive language. Pay attention to your posture and your enunciation. Practice at home before delivering your talk. Limit your talk to three minutes.

EXERCISE 8. Relating an Experience or Anecdote. Relate an experience or anecdote to illustrate a proverb. Remember to arouse the interest and curiosity of your audience. The following list contains suggestions.

1. A stitch in time saves nine.
2. Waste not, want not.
3. An empty barrel makes the most noise.
4. A fool and his money are soon parted.
5. A watched pot never boils.
6. Easy come, easy go.
7. Pride goes before a fall.
8. Spare the rod and spoil the child.
9. A cat may look at a king.
10. Early to bed, early to rise, makes a person healthy, wealthy, and wise.

EXERCISE 9. Relating an Unusual Incident. Relate an unusual incident in the life of a famous man or woman. Arouse the interest and curiosity of your audience. A list of suggested persons follows.

1. John F. Kennedy
2. Maria Tallchief
3. Susan B. Anthony
4. Bessie Smith
5. Martin Luther King, Jr.
6. Roberto Clemente
7. I. M. Pei
8. Abraham Lincoln
9. Margaret Thatcher
10. Babe Zaharias

The Explanatory Talk

From time to time you will be called upon to explain how to make or do something. To explain so that your listeners will understand easily, you must plan carefully and observe certain principles of organization and delivery.

34j. Make your explanatory talk clear.

1. *Limit your subject to a topic that can be adequately treated in your speech and in such a way that it reflects a definite purpose.*

Limit your subject to a topic that you know (or can get to know) thoroughly and that is suitable for your purpose. The more limited the topic, the more completely you can treat it in the time allowed.

2. *Choose a subject that is interesting to your audience.* Be sure to consider your audience's needs, background, and interests when you choose your subject.

3. *Gather material for your speech.* Start with yourself. Then go to outside sources such as friends and acquaintances, newspaper and magazine articles, radio and television programs, and books.

SUBJECT   Auto mechanics

  TOPIC   Reboring the cylinder head

SUBJECT   Archery

  TOPIC   How to fetch your own arrows

4. *Organize your explanation.* Your outline is all-important in a talk of this kind. In it you determine the arrangement of ideas in a step-by-step progression from the simple to the complex, the familiar to the unfamiliar, or whatever order is most suitable for your topic.

5. *Master all technical terms.* If you choose a topic that ordinarily uses technical terms, master this vocabulary so that you can explain technical terms as you go along.

6. *Use visual aids.* If you can bring to class the object, tool, or device you are going to explain and then demonstrate how it works, it will make your explanation clearer. If you cannot bring an object or device, illustrate your talk by drawing a diagram on the chalkboard.

While you talk, hold the object you are going to demonstrate in front of you so that everyone can see it. If you use a diagram, stand to one side and refer to it with a pointer.

EXERCISE 10. Giving an Explanatory Talk.   Give an explanatory talk to the class. Your talk should last about five minutes. Use one of the topics from the following list or choose your own.

1. A science experiment that you can do at home
2. Balanced meals for good health
3. How our local government is organized

4. How to train a dog
5. How to drive safely

The Persuasive Talk

Speakers must plan carefully, arrange arguments thoughtfully, and speak forcefully if they want to persuade others or get them to act.

34k. Make your persuasive talk effective.

1. *Choose a controversial opinion.* Facts and personal opinions are not arguable, but controversial opinions are.

2. *Arrange your arguments carefully.* Reword your outline until the speech it represents is logical, well supported, and hard-hitting.

3. *Rehearse your talk.* Rehearsing your talk in front of your parents or friends gives them the opportunity to raise questions and objections that you have overlooked. Once you are aware of these flaws, you can make changes to correct them. For further help in planning and developing a persuasive talk, see pages 422–25 of Chapter 15 and pages 496–530 of Chapter 18.

EXERCISE 11. Giving a Persuasive Talk.   Give a persuasive talk to the class on some topic you think is important. Choose one of the topics listed here or select one of your own.

1. More money should go into the space program.
2. A free college education ought to be the right of all.
3. Networks should stop showing violence on television.
4. Students should have less homework.
5. Put a woman in the White House!
6. All drivers should take a road test every five years.
7. Air bags should be mandatory in cars.
8. High-school students should not have part-time jobs.

LISTENING WITH A PURPOSE

This section will help you to become a more skillful listener. As such, you will be able to apply your full attention to any matter that warrants it—to understand what is said; to sift fact from opinion, the weighty from the trivial; and to evaluate what you hear.

34l. Listen courteously.

Good listening manners require that you listen and do nothing else. Do not let yourself be distracted. Be patient and quiet if a speaker experiences difficulty. You will be grateful for such treatment when your turn comes.

34m. Listen accurately.

The greatest enemy to accurate listening is a wandering mind. You can often force your attention to stick to the subject by giving it the following tasks:

1. *Listen to understand and recall what was said.* Of course we cannot recall everything, but memory can be trained, and by constant practice we can remember a lot more than we might suppose. Pay close attention to what is said and review it immediately afterward in your mind, rehearsing the main points and repeating them to yourself in the order given.

EXERCISE 12. Listening Accurately. Compose five questions similar to those that follow. Read them aloud, pausing for about five seconds between questions to allow your classmates time to jot down their answers. When you have finished, your classmates will check their answers to determine how accurately they have listened.

1. In the series of numbers *8—9—4—3—1,* the third number is —— ?
2. In the list of words *on—off—at—or—in,* the fourth word is —— ?
3. In the list of words *but—can—stop—then—until,* the word beginning with *c* is —— ?
4. In the announcement "Send your replies to Box 665, Los Angeles, California 90047, before March 31, together with a box top from our product," the post office box number is —— ?
5. In the statement "Fran will keep the score, Lucy will be captain of one team and Rose of the other, and Lena and Pam will pitch," what is Fran's assignment?

EXERCISE 13. Listening Accurately. Compose an announcement in which essential information is omitted. Read it aloud and test your classmates' attentiveness by asking them to point out the details you have forgotten.

EXAMPLE   Tomorrow our basketball team will play one of the strongest teams
in our county league. The game will be played at 4:00 P.M.
Admission is free to all members of our Student Organization.
Nonmembers can purchase tickets for fifty cents. This promises to
be one of the most exciting games of the season. Everyone should
attend. [Note that the announcement omits the name of the opposing
team and where the game will be played.]

2. *Listen to understand the underlying structure of a talk or a
lecture.* This exercise trains your powers of analysis so that you can
understand and recall the gist of a complicated talk by knowing what
its main arguments will probably be. It can be done from the signals
a speaker gives in the opening remarks indicating what the main ideas
are going to be.

For instance, of the following two sets of opening remarks, the
listener might ask, "What is the speaker's topic?" and then "How
will the argument proceed?" The listener might then jot down the
notes that follow each set of remarks.

There are two reasons, among others, for finishing high school; first,
to get a better job; and second, to extend your interests and thus get more
enjoyment out of life.

NOTES   Finish high school
1. Better job
2. Better person

This morning we pay tribute to Theodore Roosevelt as a conservationist, President, and advocate of the outdoor life.

NOTES   Theodore Roosevelt
1. As conservationist
2. As President
3. As outdoor enthusiast

EXERCISE 14. Analyzing the Introduction of a Talk or Lecture.
Cut out the introductory paragraph of a short magazine article. Read
it to the class, asking them what they think the main points of the
article will be. Then compare these versions with the actual article.

3. *Listen to grasp the main ideas.* As the speaker finishes the
introductory remarks and develops the subject, the listener, pencil in
hand, asks, "What arguments support the speaker's main points?"
and "What factors are offered as proof?"

A speaker's main points frequently stand out because of the emphasis given to them. Forceful speakers punctuate each main idea by tone, gesture, and expression. They restate the arguments frequently, illustrating them, citing statistics in their support, and bringing in authoritative opinions on their behalf.

The transitions from one point to the next are signaled by words like *therefore, consequently, on the other hand,* and *however* and should be carefully noted by the listener. Other clues to the development of an argument are expressions such as *for example* and *for instance,* which usually indicate that the ideas that follow illustrate a point. Still others show that the speaker is about to summarize: *in conclusion, finally, to sum up.*

EXERCISE 15. Listening to Understand the Underlying Structure of a Talk. Your teacher will read to you a brief magazine article for approximately five to ten minutes. As you listen, write an outline of the lecture or article; then compare it with the outline your teacher puts on the board.

34n. Listen critically.

A critical listener insists on evaluating what is said. Critical listening is the art of making distinctions.

1. *Weigh the evidence.* To do this, you must distinguish fact from opinion.

FACT   Abraham Lincoln was born on February 12, 1809.
OPINION   Abraham Lincoln was the greatest President this country ever had.

FACT   At sea level water freezes at 0°C.
OPINION   Warm water is better for swimming.

Distinguish between reliable and unreliable authority.

RELIABLE   The U.S. Department of Commerce reports that the rate of inflation increased last month.
UNRELIABLE   Wednesday Jones, the popular star, says that inflation statistics are never accurate.

Distinguish between generalizations based on sufficient evidence and those based on insufficient evidence.

SUFFICIENT   Decatur High's team won every game in our league; our team lost every game. Therefore, Decatur's team is better than ours this season.

INSUFFICIENT I know three students from Decatur High School. Each has red hair. Therefore, most Decatur students have red hair.

Distinguish between proper and improper comparisons or analogies.

PROPER Esme, whom I can usually beat at bowling, beats Ruth regularly. Therefore, I probably can beat Ruth too.

IMPROPER John, who lives next door, read *Sounder* and didn't like it. Therefore, I probably won't like it either.

2. *Recognize and avoid unfair argument.* Because it is always easy to let emotion rather than reason control our judgments, a critical listener must be on guard against propaganda devices that may deceive or misguide. The following are some of these propaganda devices:

Prejudice. Opinions based on prejudice are really not opinions at all, for in most cases they simply ignore the truth.

EXAMPLES Country resident: City dwellers are stuck-up, devious, and untrustworthy.
City resident: Country folks are lazy, unimaginative, and suspicious.

Bandwagon appeals. These play on the fear of being "different."

EXAMPLE All over the country people are switching to Warwick soup. It's the thing to do.

Name calling. By labeling problems with simple and emotionally charged names and slogans, the propagandist avoids rational argument. Name calling can also damage someone's reputation by repeating false charges.

EXAMPLE Of federal safety guidelines: "This is just more government red tape."

Slogans. A favorite device of propagandists, catchy slogans are easily remembered, quickly shouted, and impossible to refute. Like name calling, slogans are designed to take the place of sober reasoning.

EXAMPLES Our country right or wrong!
Be the first to own one!

Snob appeal. Most people like to think of themselves as successful and deserving. Advertisers play on these feelings by trying to make their products status symbols—visible signs of success.

EXAMPLE Move up to the Champion class in ten-speed bicycles!

Unproved assertions. Advertisers and speakers often make statements without proof. Unless a statement is supported by reasons, figures, examples, or the opinions of competent and unbiased authorities, it should be questioned. The following statements seem to prove a point but actually do not because no evidence is offered.

EXAMPLES Cigarette smoking causes cancer. It injures body tissue. It irritates the lungs, poisons the blood, and affects digestion.

Cigarette smoking does not cause cancer. Smokers are not physically impaired. There is no danger to the throat, lungs, heart, or arteries. Smoking is harmless.

EXERCISE 16. Evaluating Arguments.   In the following statements you will find examples of invalid and unfair argument. Identify each type of unfair argument, and explain briefly how each violates the standards of good reasoning.

1. The wise merchant will never employ a teen-ager. As any newspaper shows, teen-agers are undependable, dangerous, and larcenous.
2. My opponent is a demagogue whose philosophy is "soak the rich." This kind of policy will surely kill the goose that lays the golden eggs.
3. Olaf, Niels, and Karen are all excellent skiers. They are Swedish. All Swedes are excellent skiers.
4. Oneonta High won all of their games right after adopting a new cheer. For heaven's sake, let's end our losing streak by adopting a new cheer, too!
5. The math test was terribly unfair! I spent three days reviewing for it and only got a *C*.
6. The representative was against space travel for this reason: "If humans were meant to fly, they would have been given wings."
7. General Smith is certain to make a fine governor. After all, he had a brilliant military career and was decorated many times for heroism in battle.

8. Let's end foreign aid at once. Foreigners don't deserve our help. They don't believe in the American way and are so slick in diplomatic dealings that we, who have been taught always to live up to our end of a deal, are certain to lose our shirts.
9. Never vote for a Democratic candidate, for it is well known that Democrats steal from the rich to pay the poor.
10. Senator Jones failed to vote for the nuclear arms treaty. That action shows that he is a hawk on defense issues.

EXERCISE 17. Listening Critically.   From reading or television viewing, collect two examples each of the following items.

1. A statement by a reliable authority
2. A statement by an unreliable authority
3. A generalization from sufficient evidence
4. An unproved assertion
5. A bandwagon appeal
6. A slogan

EXERCISE 18. Writing and Listening Critically to Arguments. Compose a one-paragraph argument for or against some idea, in which you deliberately break the rules of fair and honest thinking. Try to make your argument somewhat subtle so that your classmates must exercise their ingenuity to discover the abuse. If you cannot compose one yourself, look through a magazine, and cut out an advertisement that makes obvious use of some propaganda device. Bring it to class for discussion.

SUMMARY OF LISTENING TECHNIQUES

1. Give the speaker your full attention.
2. Be patient, and do not interrupt the speaker.
3. Review the speaker's main points in your mind immediately after the speaker has finished speaking.
4. Pay attention to signals that the speaker may give during a talk to indicate the main points presented.
5. Weigh the evidence the speaker presents. Distinguish fact from opinion, reliable from unreliable authority, sufficient from insufficient

generalization, and proper from improper comparisons or analogies.

6. Recognize and avoid unfair arguments, such as name calling, snob appeal, and unproved assertions.

CHAPTER 35

Group Discussion

DISCUSSION, PARLIAMENTARY PROCEDURE, INTERVIEWS

Group discussion skills will help you participate effectively in college and in a career. Through discussion you will learn the meaning of freedom of speech and the responsibilities that go with it. You will discover that persons with differing views can disagree in an atmosphere of mutual respect and can work together for the common good without abandoning their beliefs.

Even when discussion does not result in a solution, the time spent is seldom wasted because the participants may perceive the extent of a problem more clearly by exchanging opinions and may become more willing to compromise.

TYPES OF GROUP DISCUSSION

There are four kinds of group discussion:

Social conversation is private and unplanned, and it touches lightly on many topics. It requires no leader, although a host or hostess may occasionally steer it. Its aim is enjoyment, persuasion, or instruction.

Informal group discussion resembles social conversation except that it is usually more purposeful and deals with a single topic or a limited number of topics decided beforehand by the participants. An informal group, such as a small committee, may or may not be guided by a discussion leader.

Formal group discussion is public and planned. It considers many aspects of a single topic. It is directed and summarized by a discussion leader. Its aim is to reach an agreement, solve a problem, or start action.

A *debate* is public and planned, like formal group discussion, but considers only two sides of a question. The supporters of one side attempt to defeat their opponents by arguments. The victor is determined by a judge or group of judges.

A debate may grow out of a group discussion. The numerous solutions developed in a discussion may be narrowed to one, which is then offered to a wider public for acceptance or rejection.

35a. Learn the characteristics of the various forms of group discussion.

The *round table* is a group discussion in which the participants exchange views around a table (not necessarily round) under the guidance of a discussion leader. The number of people usually does not exceed a dozen. The discussion is informal. There is no audience.

The most common example of a round-table discussion is the committee meeting. Most organizations conduct a large part of their business through committees. A committee considers matters referred to it and reports its findings and recommendations to the entire organization.

A *forum* is any type of speaking program that is followed by audience participation. For example, a lecture followed by questions from the audience is a forum. A forum is most successful when the audience is small; otherwise, people are reluctant to stand up and speak their minds.

A *symposium* consists of prepared talks by several speakers on different aspects of a single topic. When all the speakers have finished their presentations, the discussion leader invites the audience to ask questions, contribute additional information, or express agreement or disagreement with the speakers' views.

A *panel discussion* is like an overheard conversation. It consists of a leader and four to eight participants seated, usually in a semicircle, before an audience. The participants remain seated during the discussion. They speak in conversational style, generally not longer than one to two minutes at a time. They express opinions and disagree with and question one another. The leader acts as a moderator, stimulating, directing, and summarizing the discussion. After a while the audience joins in the conversation. The leader summarizes the discussion before bringing it to an end.

PREPARATION FOR GROUP DISCUSSION

35b. Select a topic that lends itself to a profitable group discussion.

Before selecting a topic for discussion, ask the following questions:

1. Is it sufficiently limited for the time allowed?
2. Is it worthwhile?
3. Is it timely?
4. Is it related to the needs, experience, and interests of listeners and speakers?
5. Is it stimulating?
6. Is it many-sided?

What are good sources of topics for group discussion? Your own experience may suggest some: for example, "Teen-age problems," "Trends in popular music," or "Choosing a career." Your school courses may suggest others: for instance, "Why study mathematics and science?" or "The most valuable subject in the curriculum." Books, newspapers, magazine articles, movies, and television programs can often stimulate discussion. Current events, especially controversial matters, can also capture and hold an audience's attention.

A discussion topic should be a question of policy rather than a question of fact. "Do we have a supply of gasoline?" is a question of fact, and the only appropriate reply is a direct, factual answer. "Should we stop using gasoline to power cars?" is a question of policy that stirs discussion.

Topics that are trivial or timeworn, have no audience appeal, do not evoke strong differences of opinion, or can be answered *yes* or *no* are not suitable.

Select an up-to-date controversial topic.

EXAMPLES   What's wrong with today's economy?
How can we prevent food shortages?
Who should pay for college?

₂gies for selecting and limiting subjects, see Chapter 13, page
pages 317–19.

**Prepare for a group discussion by thinking, talking, and reading
out the topic.**

Many discussions fail because of insufficient preparation by the participants.

To prepare for a discussion, everyone must think, talk, and read
about the topic before the discussion takes place. When the topic is
announced, follow these three steps:

1. *Think about it.* What is your opinion? On what evidence is it
based?

2. *Talk to others about it.* Discuss it with your friends and parents.
Discuss it with someone who is an authority on the subject. Be ready
to modify your previous opinion in the light of your new knowledge.

3. *Consult reference books, recent publications, magazine articles,
and editorials.* Inform yourself as thoroughly as you can about the
topic. Keep an open mind while you are learning.

35d. Learn the duties of the discussion leader.

In addition to thinking and learning about the topic before the discussion, a discussion leader is responsible for knowing the background
and special interests of each speaker. If possible, a preliminary meeting
of all the speakers should be arranged to go over the topic and procedure of the discussion.

When the discussion begins, the leader should make a brief introductory statement focusing on the purpose of the discussion. The
discussion leader both introduces each speaker to the audience and
mentions something about each speaker's background or interests.

While the discussion continues, the leader should ask questions of
the speakers. The leader should also try to prevent fruitless digressions
and ensure that everyone has a chance to speak.

At the close of the discussion, the leader should summarize the
major points and thank the audience and speakers.

35e. Learn the duties of speakers at a round table, forum, symposium, or panel discussion.

Speakers invited to a discussion should be able to listen carefully and courteously to others, speak so that everyone can hear, and be sure that the comments they give are directly related to the topic.

35f. Learn the duties of members of the audience.

A member of the audience should listen to the speakers with an alert mind, take notes if necessary, and join in the discussion when the leader invites questions from the spectators. Questions should, of course, relate directly to the topic under discussion and be spoken in a clear voice that everyone can hear.

EXERCISE 1. Selecting Topics for a Group Discussion. List five topics suitable for a group discussion. Test them against the criteria listed in the previous sections. The topics may be related to school, community, state, national, or international affairs.

TAKING PART IN A GROUP DISCUSSION

You can be more successful in communicating your ideas to others if you learn something about speaking and listening effectively in group discussions.

You and the Group

A group is made up of individuals who are attempting to achieve a common goal. A basketball team, for example, is a group of players who are trying to win a game. A photography club is a group of photographers who might want to organize an exhibition.

Within every group, each individual must accept and work for the group's common goal. An individual, however, might have private goals not shared by the group. Psychologists call these private goals a "hidden agenda." As you enter a group discussion, you should be aware of the difference between the goal of the discussion and the private goals of individual members. Avoid the impulse of imposing your private intentions on the whole group. Participating in a group discussion depends chiefly on individual cooperation.

35g. Learn to speak effectively in a group discussion.

1. *Think before you speak.* Know what you are going to say before you begin. Take a few seconds to organize your ideas before you start talking; clear thinking precedes clear speaking.

2. *Keep the other person in mind.* Try to understand the other person's point of view. Avoid sarcasm and ridicule; they hurt unnecessarily and are a sign that your own arguments are weak. In the midst of heated discussion, remain calm. Your calmness will show up in your tone of voice, facial expression, and rate of speaking.

3. *Be brief.* Omit long and unnecessary explanations. Know the point you want to make and go directly to it. Speak simply but naturally and enthusiastically. Listeners like an enthusiastic speaker.

35h. Learn to listen accurately and critically while taking part in a group discussion.

In a group discussion the interplay of personalities is often so interesting that your attention may wander or you may fail to recognize that a speaker's comments are not relevant to the topic.

You can focus your attention by taking notes. Jotting down the arguments will enable you to see the merits of each point. Follow these principles:

1. *Recognize and guard against your own prejudices.* Don't let emotions color your thinking. For example, your reactions to a speaker's appearance, accent, or gestures may affect your acceptance or rejection of what you hear. Think fairly, and test ideas on rational, not emotional, grounds.

2. *Recognize a speaker's bias and take it into account.* When a speaker has an ax to grind, a listener must be careful. The arguments may be valid, but they may also be one-sided and rooted in prejudice.

3. *Watch for words, phrases, and attitudes that are emotionally loaded.* Some words report a fact objectively. They have few emotional overtones, if any. Others are loaded with emotion.

Compare the following pairs of words. Notice how one member of each pair is relatively colorless, while the other arouses feelings.

house—shack   dwelling—mansion
reply—rebuke   defeat—rout

verse—doggerel	recline—sprawl
farmer—peasant	failure—fiasco
work—drudgery	dog—mongrel

Loaded words carry positive or negative charges. A positively charged word creates a favorable reaction; a negatively charged word, an unfavorable one. Propagandists make use of loaded words to influence listeners. They employ positively charged words to sway you to their way of thinking and negatively charged words to make you reject what they oppose.

EXERCISE 2. Identifying Loaded Words. Number your paper 1–10. After the proper number, indicate by a plus or a minus sign whether each of the following words affects you positively or negatively.

1. adorable
2. skinny
3. generous
4. crude
5. glamorous
6. fabulous
7. miserly
8. rebellious
9. sympathy
10. screech

4. *Don't be misled by catchy slogans and generalized introductory statements.* Advertisers and political organizations often employ slogans to popularize ideas, candidates, or products. A complex argument cannot be summarized fairly in a capsule expression.

EXAMPLES See America first. [slogan promoting travel in the United States, as opposed to foreign travel]
Put yourself in our shoes. [advertising slogan]

Generalized introductory statements often have no basis in fact, but they imply that disagreement is impossible.

EXAMPLES It is common knowledge that . . .
Everybody knows that . . .

5. *Look for and weigh evidence for every important statement.* If a speaker offers no evidence, ask for it. If the evidence is insufficient, ask for more.

EXERCISE 3. Conducting a Round-Table Discussion. Conduct a round-table discussion on a topic that concerns all the participants. Appoint a discussion leader who will end the discussion after twenty minutes, summarize, and invite class discussion. You may use one of the five suggested topics on the following page.

1. The school yearbook
2. Improving the student organization
3. Building school spirit
4. Improving the school cafeteria
5. Assembly programs

EXERCISE 4. Conducting a Symposium. Conduct a symposium on discipline. The speakers should represent the viewpoints of a student, a parent, a law-enforcement officer, an educator, and a community leader.

EXERCISE 5. Conducting a Panel Discussion. Select a discussion leader, and present a panel discussion on any of the following topics or one of your own choosing. Each panel should meet beforehand to settle matters of procedure and scope.

1. Radio and television advertising
2. Comic books
3. Youthful crime
4. Violence on the screen
5. Prejudice—and how to overcome it
6. The impact of the young voter
7. The ideal school
8. Professional versus amateur sports
9. Our foreign policy
10. Ways to prevent war

EXERCISE 6. Listening Critically. Why should you be particularly careful in listening to each of the following speakers?

1. The president of a college fraternity speaking about the advantages of fraternity life
2. A movie actress advertising a cold cream
3. A candidate of a political party speaking about the party's platform
4. A disc jockey delivering a commercial
5. A parent of a failing student criticizing a school

EVALUATION OF A GROUP DISCUSSION

35i. Evaluate a group discussion by asking key questions about it.

By considering the merits and faults of a group discussion after it is over, you can learn to improve future discussions. The following questions will help you evaluate a group discussion.

1. Was the discussion purposeful? Were the causes of the problem considered? Were various solutions proposed and analyzed? Did the discussion ramble, or did it proceed in an orderly fashion?

2. Were the outcomes worthwhile? A group discussion need not reach a solution or agreement. It may be successful if it brings areas of disagreement into the open.

3. Were the participants thoroughly familiar with the problem? Did they present facts, instances, statements of competent and unbiased authorities, and statistics to support their opinions?

4. Was the discussion lively and general? Was there a give-and-take of opinion in an atmosphere of mutual respect? Did all participate? Did anyone monopolize the meeting, or did everyone speak briefly and to the point?

5. Did the participants reach a solution justified by the evidence? Do you agree with the solution? Why?

6. Were the audience's questions thought-provoking? Did the speakers answer them directly and fully?

7. Was the discussion courteous? Did each speaker exercise self-control by refraining from interrupting when another was speaking? Were statements and objections phrased courteously?

8. Did the discussion leader's introductory remarks arouse interest? Did the discussion avoid valueless digressions? Was everyone encouraged to join in? Was there a summary?

EXERCISE 7. Evaluating a Radio or Television Discussion.
Evaluate a radio or television discussion you have heard. Consider such matters as choice of topic, the speakers' familiarity with the topic, the quality of the discussion, and audience participation. In what ways could the discussion have been improved?

PARLIAMENTARY PROCEDURE

Many organizations conduct their meetings according to a code known as *rules of order* or *parliamentary procedure.*

Parliamentary procedure protects the rights of all and enables individuals to work together efficiently. It is a means of determining the will of the majority and at the same time safeguarding the rights of the minority.

Elections

When a club is organized, the founding members draw up a constitution establishing its bylaws. This document sets forth the name and purpose of the club and the rules by which it will operate. Among these rules is one regulating the election of officers.

35j. Officers are elected and perform duties according to a constitution.

Officers may be nominated by a nominating committee, or individual members may make nominations from the floor. Elections are usually held immediately after nominations are closed.

A majority vote is usually required for election unless a bylaw states otherwise. If no one receives a majority, a new vote must be taken, limited to the two candidates who received the highest number of votes on the first ballot. Depending on the constitution of the organization, officers may be elected by either an open or a secret ballot.

Duties of Officers

The president presides over meetings, appoints committees, calls special meetings if necessary, and sees that the organization's constitution and bylaws are observed.

The vice-president acts in place of the president if the latter is absent. The vice-president may have other duties specified in the constitution.

The secretary notifies members of meetings, takes the minutes, keeps a record of attendance, and answers letters as the president directs.

The treasurer receives dues and other income, pays the club's bills, and keeps a record of all receipts and disbursements. At every meeting the treasurer gives a report on the organization's current financial status.

Club Business

35k. The regular procedure at meetings is called the order of business.

The following is a typical order of business:

EXAMPLE   1. Call to order
              2. Roll call
              3. Reading of minutes of previous meeting

4. Treasurer's report
5. Committee reports
6. Unfinished business
7. New business
8. Adjournment

35l. A motion is a proposal for discussion and action.

EXAMPLES   "I move that we purchase new uniforms for the basketball team."
"I move that we publish a monthly bulletin."
"I move that this question be referred to a committee of three appointed by the chair."
"I move that we adjourn."

An organization transacts all its business at meetings through motions.

Steps in Making a Motion

1. A member requests and receives recognition by the chair. If two or more members rise at the same time, the chair recognizes the one who addressed the chair first.

MEMBER   "Mr. (Madam) Chairman."

CHAIR   "Mr. Jones."

2. The member states a motion.

MEMBER   "I move that our club hold a skating party."

3. Another member seconds the motion. This means the member agrees with the motion. All motions must be seconded before they can be considered.

ANOTHER MEMBER   "I second the motion."

4. The chair repeats the motion, using the original words.

CHAIR   "It is moved and seconded that our club hold a skating party. Is there any discussion?"

5. The members discuss the motion.
6. When the discussion is finished, the chair repeats the motion.
7. The chair puts the motion to a vote.

CHAIR "All those in favor, say 'aye'; those opposed, 'nay.' "

8. The chair announces the result.

CHAIR "The motion is carried."

If the vote is taken by a show of hands or by ballot, the chair may announce the exact count.

CHAIR "By a vote of 25 to 8, the motion is carried."

Except for special motions, only one motion may be considered at a time.

EXERCISE 8. Practicing the Steps in Making a Motion. Practice the steps in making a motion. With one class member acting as chair, the others will offer various motions. Here are some suggested subjects for motions:

1. Abolition of homework
2. Class picnic
3. Purchase of books
4. Petition to the principal
5. Field trip
6. Publication of a class newspaper

Amending a Motion

To amend a motion means to change the wording of the motion. Not more than one amendment can be considered at a time. Another amendment may be proposed when the first has been voted on.

35m. A motion may be amended by adding, striking out, or substituting words.

EXAMPLES "I move to amend the original motion by adding the word *monthly* before *dance*."

"I move to amend the original motion by striking out the word *new*."

"I move to amend the original motion by substituting the word *semiannual* for *annual*."

EXERCISE 9. Practicing the Steps in Making and Amending a Motion. Practice making and amending motions, using the topics listed in Exercise 8 or others of your own devising.

Special Motions

Certain motions affect how a meeting is run and how decisions are made.

Motion to adjourn. The purpose of this motion is to bring the meeting to an end. It cannot be debated or amended and must be put to a vote as soon as it is seconded.

EXAMPLE "I move that this meeting be adjourned."

Motion to table. This action can postpone debate or a vote on a particular motion. If passed, the motion being considered is set aside until members agree to "take from the table." A motion to table cannot be debated or amended.

EXAMPLE "I move to table this motion."

Motion to close debate. This motion cuts off discussion and brings a question to a vote.

The motion to close debate may not be debated or amended. It requires a *two-thirds* vote for adoption. (Notice that any motion restricting freedom of speech requires a two-thirds vote in order to protect minority rights.)

EXAMPLE "I move to close debate and vote on this question at once."

Motion to refer to committee. This motion assigns a question to a committee for study and report. This motion can be debated and amended.

MOTION "I move that this question be referred to committee."

AMENDMENT "I move that the motion be amended by adding the words 'and that the committee report its findings at our next meeting.' "

Point of Order

A point of order is not a motion. It requires no second and no vote. Points of order require members to follow the rules of order. Typical points of order are absence of a quorum, irrelevant remarks by a speaker, and a motion that violates the club's constitution.

MEMBER "Mr. (Madam) Chairman, I rise to a point of order."

CHAIR "State your point of order."

MEMBER "I make the point of order that the meeting is so noisy that the speaker cannot be heard."

CHAIR "The point is well taken, and the meeting will come to order."

EXERCISE 10. Practicing Group Discussion Procedures. Practice the following procedures in class.

1. Proposing, discussing, and voting on a main motion
2. Rising to a point of order
3. Adjourning a meeting
4. Nominating and electing officers
5. Proposing a special motion

EXERCISE 11. Proposing, Discussing, and Voting Motions.
With one class member acting as chair, other members of the class will propose, discuss, and vote on motions. Here are some examples:

1. That the members purchase a birthday gift for the custodian
2. That students be allowed to use the cafeteria for cooking lessons
3. That the admission price for school dances be increased
4. That one member should attend parent-teacher meetings
5. That future meetings be held each week

EXERCISE 12. Understanding Parliamentary Procedure. Attend a meeting of a club, council, or association, and report orally on the way the meeting was conducted. What did you learn about parliamentary procedure that you did not previously know?

EXERCISE 13. Understanding Other Rules of Parliamentary Procedure. Read one of the following references and report on it. Explain a topic not taken up in this chapter so clearly that everyone understands. (Some suggested topics: duties and rights of members, the motion to reconsider)

1. Cushing's *Manual of Parliamentary Procedure*
2. Eliot's *Basic Rules of Order*
3. Robert's *Rules of Order*
4. Sturgis' *Standard Code of Parliamentary Procedure*

EXERCISE 14. Understanding Freedom of Discussion and Majority Rule. Two features of parliamentary procedure are freedom of discussion and majority rule. Which is the more important? Why?

SUMMARY OF PARLIAMENTARY PROCEDURE

1. Parliamentary procedure protects the rights of all and enables individuals to work together efficiently.
2. A club's bylaws set forth the rules regarding the election of officers.
3. Meetings are conducted according to the order of business.
4. A motion is a proposal offered to the membership for discussion and action.
5. An organization conducts all of its business at meetings through motions.
6. Motions, except for certain special motions, can be amended.
7. Points of order require members to follow the rules of order.

THE INTERVIEW

The interview is purposeful. It is concerned with one matter only. Though it is conducted in a friendly spirit, it avoids the variety of topics and the digressions that are the charm of informal conversation. In some forms of interview there is a give-and-take of opinion between the participants, and in other forms one person necessarily monopolizes the conversation; but always there is a dominating purpose that the interview tries to achieve. One common type of interview with which you should be familiar is the interview for gathering information.

The Interview for Gathering Information

While preparing a composition, you may wish to obtain information from someone who is knowledgeable about your particular topic.

Be sure to make arrangements for this interview well in advance. You may request the interview in a letter, by a telephone call, or through a personal visit. State who you are and the reason for your request. Mention in general terms what days and times are most acceptable to you for a meeting, but allow the other person to specify the exact time and place.

Preparing for the Interview

Your questions should be planned carefully in advance. Write each question on a separate card or page so that you will have enough room to jot down the replies. If you are using a tape recorder, of course, you need only write your questions in a list.

Give plenty of thought to each question you ask. Your interview will be much more successful if you can focus on important issues and avoid minor details. Ask questions that will elicit useful responses. Newspaper reporters, who conduct interviews daily, often prepare only a few broad questions. The answers they receive suggest follow-up questions.

Ask questions that require extended replies. For example, rather than asking, "Do you think students should be required to study a foreign language?" ask, "Why should students be required to study a foreign language?" The first question can be answered with a simple *yes* or *no*. The second question requires a much more detailed answer.

Be sure that the questions you ask are clear and straightforward. If the other person seems confused by a question you ask, be prepared to restate it.

Conducting the Interview

Arrive on time. Allow for traffic delays in setting out for your appointment. It is better to be early than late. Lateness for an appointment is discourteous, and it may create a bad impression.

Try not to rush through the interview, asking questions in rapid-fire order. Allow yourself and the other person enough time to consider and respond thoughtfully to each question. During the interview, remain tactful and courteous. Do not try to provoke argument, although you may disagree with some of the points being made.

Using a Tape Recorder

Before recording the interview, be sure to ask permission of the person whom you are interviewing. At the end of the interview, agree to play back the recording if you are asked to do so. Permit the person to modify any statements you have recorded.

Concluding the Interview

Before concluding the interview, ask whether you have omitted any aspect of the topic that the other person would like to discuss. When the interview has run its course, express appreciation for the privilege extended to you, and take your leave.

Whatever the purpose of the interview, it is always a good policy to send a thank-you note.

EXERCISE 15. Conducting an Interview. Conduct an interview to gather information for a composition. Get your teacher's approval of the topic of your interview, and be prepared to report on it in class.

INDEX
AND
TAB KEY INDEX

Index

Tab Key Index

Key to
English Workshop Drill

To supplement the lessons in *English Grammar and Composition, Fourth Course*, there is additional practice in grammar, usage, punctuation, capitalization, composition, vocabulary, and spelling in *English Workshop, Fourth Course*. This chart correlates the textbook rules with the lessons in *English Workshop*.

Text Rule	Workshop Lesson	Text Rule	Workshop Lesson	Text Rule	Workshop Lesson
1a	1	6l	75	15f	121
1b	1,86	6m	76	15g	123
1c	1	6n	74	15j	125–130
1d	2	6p	72		
1e	3			16a	131
1f	4	7a–d	83–84	16b–k	131–135,137
1g–h	5	7e	33–34		
1i	6	7f	85	18a–g	136
2a	58	8a–b	92	21a	138
2b–c	16	8c	92–94,96–97		
2d	16,17	8d–e	71,92	24c	9–10
2e–f	16			24d	12
2g	16,58	9a	102–103	24e	11
2h	18,19	9g–h	106–108		
2i–j	18			25f–g	44
2k	19	11a	56–58	25h	50
		11b	60–62	25i	48–49
3b–d	4			25j	51
3f–g	37,38	12a	112	25k	45–46
3h–k	39	12b	40,115		
3m	45	12c	114	26b	63
		12d–e	113	26c–d	68
4a–c	31,32	12f	40,116–118	26e	69
4d	33,34	12g	40	26f–g	68
4e	31,32				
4f	35	13g	123	28a–d	24–26
4g	20,36	13k	109	28g	27
				28h	22,27
6a–b	71	14a	120		
6c	73	14b	121	32i	14,22
6d	74	14f	122		
6g–i	74	14g	124		
6k	73				

NOTES

NOTES

NOTES

NOTES

NOTES

NOTES

NOTES

NOTES

NOTES